FINANCIAL ACCOUNTING

A.R. JENNINGS
BA(Hons), FCCA

Principle Lecturer in Accounting,
Department of Accounting and Finance,
Nottingham Polytechnic, Nottingham

DP PUBLICATIONS LTD
Aldine Place, 142/144 Uxbridge Road,
Shepherds Bush Green, London W12 8AW

1990

Acknowledgements

The author would like to express thanks to the Chartered Association of Certified Accountants (ACCA) and the Association of Accounting Technicians (AAT) for giving permission to reproduce past examination questions.

A CIP catalogue record for this book is available from the British Library.

Copyright A.R. Jennings © 1990
ISBN 1 870941 59 4

First edition 1990
Reprinted 1991

Printed and bound by
The Guernsey Press Co. Ltd.
Guernsey, Channel Islands

Preface

AIM

This book has been designed to provide complete coverage, to the requisite depth, of the ACCA paper 2.9 syllabus. At the same time it coincides with the financial accounting content of CIMA Stage 2 Financial Accounting, CIMA Stage 3 Advanced Financial Accounting and AAT Paper 9 - Financial Accounting. Additionally it provides coverage of the financial accounting content of ICSA, RSA, LCC and BTEC HND/C courses.

SCOPE AND LAYOUT

The book is divided into seven sections, the first five of which deal with the various topics:

Section I The accounts of unincorporated businesses

II Accounting practice for specialised transactions

III The accounts of companies (excluding groups)

IV Analysis of financial statements

V The accounts of groups of companies.

Each section contains chapters on items within its subject area. Two further sections follow containing supportive material to support the first five sections:

Section VI Questions without answers

VII Appendices giving statutory disclosure requirements and the Annual Report and Accounts of an actual company.

USING THE BOOK EFFECTIVELY

The sections and chapters, which need not necessarily be studied in the sequence in which they have been presented, are fairly uniform in structure. Each chapter gives the general background of the topic so that it can be understood in context. The operating arrangements which underlie the financial procedures are then outlined and explained briefly. Thirdly, the basic accounting methods and procedures are stated and supported by examples. Finally, test exercises and questions of varying difficulty are set. Examination questions set by the ACCA and AAT appear at the end of the chapters. Answers to all of these exercises and questions are given in a separate Students Solutions Manual, together with full explanations of points of especial difficulty, where appropriate.

SPECIAL NOTE FOR LECTURERS

Section VI of this book contains a selection of test exercises and examination questions, some from the past papers of professional bodies, so that lecturers who adopt the book as a course text can use them for coursework or homework or assignment purposes. Outline answers to these are available, free of charge, to lecturers on application to the publishers

A.R. Jennings
Nottingham
25 May 1990

Contents

PREFACE

SECTION I   THE ACCOUNTS OF UNINCORPORATED BUSINESSES

1	Incomplete records	3
2	Sole traders	6
3	Partnerships	12
4	Clubs and societies	68

SECTION II   ACCOUNTING PRACTICE FOR SPECIALISED TRANSACTIONS

1	Consignments	79
2	Joint ventures	85
3	Branches	93
4	Hire purchase and credit sales	123
5	Leasing	153
6	Long-term contracts	171
7	Investments	192
8	Bills of exchange	209
9	Royalties	212
10	Containers	218
11	Foreign currency transactions	221

SECTION III   THE ACCOUNTS OF COMPANIES (EXCLUDING GROUPS)

1	Share and loan capital	245
2	Distributable profits	272
3	Taxation	278
4	Final accounts	300
5	Value added statements	380
6	Amalgamations and absorptions	391
7	Reorganisations and reconstructions	413
8	Earnings per share	427
9	Changing price levels	442

SECTION IV   **ANALYSIS OF FINANCIAL STATEMENTS**

    1   Ratio analysis   477

    2   Cash flows and funds flow analysis   518

SECTION V   **THE ACCOUNTS OF GROUPS OR COMPANIES**

    1   Final accounts   549

    2   Acquisitions and mergers   653

SECTION VI   **QUESTIONS WITHOUT ANSWERS**

SECTION VII   **APPENDICES**

    I   Companies Acts 1985 and 1989 disclosure requirements   753

    II   Annual Report and Accounts BPP Holdings   777

Section I

The Accounts of Unincorporated Businesses

Chapter

1   Incomplete records

2   Sole traders

3   Partnerships

4   Clubs and societies

1 Incomplete Records

GENERAL BACKGROUND

1.0 On occasions accountants are required to produce accounting statements from basic records in varying degrees of completeness.

1.1 Many sole proprietorships, for example, are operated by those who, though highly skilled and knowledgeable in their own specialisms, lack the ability and/or time to keep any but the simplest financial records.

1.2 Under other circumstances, proper records may have been maintained but subsequently lost or destroyed as the result of a catastrophy such as a fire, or an accident or a burglary.

1.3 The reconstruction of missing figures and accounting statements using incomplete records techniques are part of the core syllabus for the Level 1 Accounting 1.1. paper.

1.4 This chapter assumes that students studying for Level 2 Paper 2.9 are fully conversant with and understand those techniques. For that reason they are not repeated here.

1.5 At Level 2, this topic can be examined in greater breadth and depth than at the earlier level, by the introduction, for example, of a greater volume of financial data and/or more complex situations.

STUDENT SELF TESTING

Test Exercises

1. After completing a training course at a technical college, Michael Faraday set up in business as a self–employed electrician on 1 January 19–5.

    He was very competent at his job but had no idea how to maintain proper accounting records. Sometime during 19–5 one of his friends asked Michael how well his business was doing. He replied "All right...I think...but I'm not quite sure".

    In the ensuing conversation his friend asked whether he had prepared accounts yet, covering his first quarter's trading, to which Michael replied that he had not. His friend then stressed that, for various reasons, it was vital for accounts of businesses to be prepared properly.

    Shortly afterwards Michael came to see you to ask for your help in preparing accounts for his first quarter's trading. He brought with him, in a cardboard box, the only records he had, mainly scribbled on scraps of paper.

    He explained that he started his business with a car worth £700, and £2,250 in cash of which £250 was his savings and £2,000 had been borrowed from a relative at an interest rate of 10% per annum. It was his practice to pay his suppliers and expenses in cash, to require his customers to settle their accounts in cash and to bank any surplus in a business bank account. He maintained lists of cash receipts and cash payments, of supplies obtained on credit and of work carried out for customers and of appliances sold, on credit.

    The list of suppliers comprised:

Date supplied 19–5	Supplier	Amount owed £	Date paid 19–5	Amount paid £	Remarks
January	Dee & Co.	337.74	March	330.00	Received discount £7.74
	AB Supplies	528.20	March	528.20	
February	Simpson	141.34	March	138.00	Received discount £3.34
	Cotton Ltd	427.40	March	130.00	Payment on account
			April	297.40	Remainder
	Dee & Co.	146.82	March	140.00	Received discount £6.82
March	AB Supplies	643.43	April	643.43	
	Simpson	95.60			Not yet paid

The purchase in January from Dee & Co. was of tools and equipment to enable him to carry out electrical repair work. All the remaining purchases were of repair materials, except for the purchase in February from Cotton Ltd. which consisted of electrical appliances for resale.

In addition to the above credit transactions, he had bought repair materials for cash, as follows:

19–5	£
January	195.29
February	161.03
March	22.06

Other cash payments comprised:

19–5		£
January	Rent of premises for January to June 19–5	400.00
	Rates of premises for January to March 19– 5	150.00
	Stationery	32.70
	Car running expenses	92.26
February	Sundries	51.54
	Car running expenses	81.42
March	Sundries	24.61
	Car running expenses	104.52
	Transfer to bank	500.000

He had also withdrawn £160.00 in cash at the end of each month for living expenses.
The list of credit customers comprised:

Date of Sale 19–5	Customer	Amount owed £	Date received 19–5	Amount received £	Remarks
January	D. Hopkins	362.80	February	357.00	Allowed discount £5.80
	P. Bolton	417.10	March	417.10	
February	G. Leivers	55.000	March	55.00	
	M. Whitehead	151.72	April	151.72	
	N. John Ltd	49.14	April	49.14	
	A. Linneker	12.53	March	12.53	
March	E. Horton	462.21	April	462.21	
	S. Ward	431.08	March	426.00	Allowed discount £5.08
	W. Scothern & Co.	319.12			Not yet received
	N. Annable	85.41			Not yet received

The above amounts relate to charges for repair work which he had carried out, except that the amounts shown in February for G. Leivers, N.John Ltd. and A. Linneker are for sales of electrical appliances.
In addition to the above credit transactions, he had cash takings, as follows:

19–5		£
January	Repair work	69.44
February	Repair work	256.86
March	Repair work	182.90
	Appliances	112.81

He estimated that, at the end of March 19–5, his stock of electrical repair materials was £691.02 and of electrical appliances for resale was £320.58, his tools and equipment were worth £300.00 and his car, £600.00.
Apart from loan interest, the only accrual was for heating and lighting, £265.00.

Required:

a. Prepare

   i. purchase daybook with analysis columns for type of purchase, and

   ii. sales daybook with analysis columns for class of business undertaken.

b. Open, post to 31 March 19–5 only, and balance a columnar cash book suitably analysed to facilitate ledger postings.

c. Open, post to 31 March 19–5 only, and balance a creditors ledger control account and a debtors ledger control account. Use the closing balances in your answer to (g) below. [NB. Individual accounts for creditors and debtors are NOT required].

d. Open, post and balance sales and cost of sales accounts, each with separate columns for "Repairs" and "Appliances".

e. Prepare M. Faraday's trading account for the quarter ended 31 March 19–5, distinguishing between gross profit on repairs and on appliance sales.

f. Prepare M. Faraday's general profit and loss account for the quarter ended 31 March 19–5.

g. Prepare M. Faraday's balance sheet as at 31 March 19–5.

2 Sole Traders

GENERAL BACKGROUND

1.0 The simplest of all business organisations is that of a sole proprietor or trader.

1.1 The feature of such a formation is that the same person is not only the owner but is often the manager and maybe the workforce as well. A freelance artist or author would fall into this category.

1.2 Where the business involves providing goods or services to members of the public, for example, a solely owned electrical repair business or veterinary surgery, the owner may need to engage employees as the workforce to operate for or with him.

1.3 Many sole traders record only the basic financial data which they then hand over periodically to their accountants for processing, reporting and appraisal.

1.4 The collection, recording and processing of this data for reporting purposes is part of the core syllabus for the Level 1 Accounting 1.1. paper.

1.5 This chapter assumes that students studying for Level 2 Paper 2.9 are fully conversant with and understand these matters, together with the associated routine work, including, for example, the detection and correction of errors, suspense accounts, bank reconciliation statements, etc. For that reason they are not repeated here.

1.6 At Level 2, this topic can be examined in greater breadth and depth then at the earlier level, by the introduction, for example, of a greater volume of financial data and/or more complex situations.

STUDENT SELF TESTING

Test Exercises

1. a. I. Wright is a professional author whose income is derived mainly from royalties, that, is payments from his publisher based on the number of his books sold. He also receives fixed rate fees for articles and features which he writes for magazines and periodicals. Two of his books have been reproduced in instalments by a weekly newspaper which pays serialisation fees to his publisher who then pays Wright a proportion of these fees. Additionally, he derives a small part of his income from publicity activities and from lecturing.

   He carries out his writing activities in a purpose–equipped study room at his home. His accounting year ended on 31 May 19–2, for which the following information is available.

	£
Royalties Received (including Advance Royalties, £900) (*see note (8)*)	23,650
Fees received for articles and features published	8,000
Serialisation fees received	5,400
Fees received for publicity activities (*see note (9)*)	2,734
Fees received for lecturing on Writers' Residential Courses	250
Expenses:	
Rates (*see notes (1) and (2)*)	440
Heating and Lighting (*see notes (1) and (3)*)	916
Postages	414
Stationery *see note (4)*)	659
Telephone charges (*see notes (1) and (5)*)	762
Secretarial expenses	6,866
Travelling expenses (*see note (9)*)	3,427
Photocopying expenses	640
Fees paid to artist (for providing illustrations for inclusion in his books)	715
Insurance (*see notes (1) and (6)*)	308
Subscriptions –to professional societies	70
– to writers' periodicals and magazines	226

Miscellaneous expenses *see note (9))*	691
Other information:	
Drawings by cheque during the year	21,547
Office equipment at 1 June 19–1 (cost	
£2,200)	1,700
Office furniture at 1 June 19–1 (cost £600)	510
Bank balance at 31 May 19–2	2,265
Cash balance at 31 May 19–2	28
Capital account at 1 June 19–1	2,150

The above items need to be adjusted, where appropriate, to reflect the following:

1. When invoices are received which include combined business and private expenses, it is Wright's practice to pay them out of business bank account and to make the necessary transfers at the end of the accounting year.

2. Rates of £480 for the six months 1 April to 30 September 19–2 have not yet been paid. One quarter of the total rates is attributable to his study room.

3. An electricity invoice for £60 in respect of the three months ended 31 May 19–2 has been received but not yet paid. One quarter of the total heating and lighting charge is attributable to his study room.

4. Items of stationery (typing and duplicating paper, typewriter ribbons and carbons, etc.) unused at 31 May 19–2 amount to £213.

5. A telephone invoice has been received, but not yet paid, as follows:

	£
Telephone rental (main installation and extensions) (three months 1 June to 31 August 19–2)	24
Telephone calls (for three months 1 February to 30 April 19–2)	270
	£294

An estimated one–third of all calls have been made for private purposes not connected with Wright's authorship.

6. Insurance premiums have been prepaid by £72. One half of the total insurance charge has been incurred for private purposes.

7. Depreciation of fixed assets is to be provided on the original cost at the following rates:

	%
Office equipment	25
Office furniture	20

There were no additions to fixed assets during year ended 31 May 19–2.

8. Advance Royalties are a fixed fee paid by publishers to authors when the contract is signed and/or when the draft manuscript is delivered to hem. If, for any reason, the author does not fulfil the terms of the contract, they must be repaid. The £900, therefore, remains repayable until publication takes place.

9. Publicity fees include a total amount of £456, being reimbursement of travelling expenses £370, and of miscellaneous expenses, £86, incurred by Wright in carrying out these activities.

Required:
Prepare the Profit and Loss account for Wright for the year ended 31 May 19–2 and his Balance Sheet at that date

(b) Wright is concerned about the efficiency with which he is operating his professional affairs and has consulted you for your opinion whether his net profit for the year expressed as a percentage of his net assets is a suitable indicator.

Required:
Advise Wright on a suitable 'operating' indicator in his particular circumstances.

2. In 19–3, Keith Maltby had bought a cafe which he re–opened under the name 'Keith's Kaff'.
In February 19–5 he rented a grocery shop which he renamed 'Keith's Larder'.
Notes on the operations of the businesses:

2 : Sole Traders

1. The annual rental of the grocery shop is £3,200 payable quarterly in advance on the last day of March, June, September and December.

2. The shop buys food in bulk both for resale to the public and for supply to the cafe. Food is transferred to the cafe at cost.

3. Each establishment is under the control of a manageress who is paid a basic salary plus a commission of 10% (calculated to the nearest £1) of the net profit of her establishment *before* charging the commission (see note (9) but after crediting the Enterprise Grant instalment (see note (11).

4. The office work for both establishments is carried out by the shop manageress who receives an annual payment of £600 for the extra responsibility. Two-thirds of this sum is charged to the cafe (see note (9)).

5. Maltby's accounting year runs from 1 April to 31 March and he accounts for the cafe and the shop as separate departments.

6. The shop manageress lives above the shop in self-contained accommodation for which she pays an inclusive rental of £60 per month, payable one month in arrears (see note (9)).

7. Depreciation of fixed assets is provided on the reducing balance method at the following rates:

	%
Premises	2
Fixtures, etc	10
Vehicles	20

8. Closing stocks at 31 March 19-7, at cost

	£
Food – cafe	3,513
– shop	1,774
Cleaning materials – cafe	30
– shop	24
Wrapping materials – cafe	10
– shop	12

9.

	£
At 31 March 19-7	
Electricity accrued –cafe	131
– shop	78
General expenses accrued – cafe	46
– shop	68
Shop manageress' office allowance due	600
Shop manageress' accommodation rent receivable	60
Commission – cafe manageress	to be calculated
– shop manageress	to be calculated
Rent payable prepaid – shop	800

10. On 31 March 19-6, Maltby obtained a Business Development Loan for the cafe, to be repaid in one lump sum in 19-1, at a concessionary rate of interest (10% per annum), payable half yearly on 30 August and 31 March.

11. Maltby has also been awarded an Enterprise Grant of £5,000 for the cafe, with effect from 1 April 19-6. He has decided to hold this sum in suspense and to credit it to the cafe profit and loss account in five equal instalments in the year ended 31 March 19-7 to 19-1 inclusive. However, at 31 March 19-7 the £5,000 had not yet been received.

12. The sales of both the shop and the cafe are for cash, except that the cafe has a contract to supply meals to a local factory which is then invoiced with the cost, for which seven days' credit is allowed.

13. The overdraft finances Maltby's operations in general but is accounted for as a liability of the shop.

At 31 March 19-7, the following balances were extracted from the ledger.

	Cafe	Shop
	£	£
Premises (at cost)	25,000	–
Fixtures, fittings (at cost)	7,500	–
Vehicles (at cost)	–	6,000

Provisions for depreciation at 1 April 19–6:

Premises	6,000	–
Fixtures, fittings	1,600	–
Vehicles	–	1,000
Rent paid (see note 1)	–	4,000
Manageresses' salaries and related charges (see notes 3 and 9)	4,200	3,900
Assistants' wages and related charges	2,100	900
Electricity charges	1,874	851
Telephone charges	209	411
Stationery (see note 4)	–	126
Turnover	36,791	27,430
Food transferred from shop to cafe (see note 2)	19,427 (Debit)	19,427 (Credit)
Stocks at 1 April 19–6:		
Food	1,272	303
Cleaning materials	44	32
Wrapping materials	27	28
Purchases:		
Food (see note 2)	–	30,432
Cleaning materials	71	68
Wrapping materials	45	53
Loan interest paid (see note 10)	700	–
Business Development loan (see note 10)	7,000	–
Bank overdraft (see note 13)	–	2,209
Bank overdraft interest (see note 13)	–	37
Creditors:		
Food	–	4,582
Other items	15	6
Rates (general and water)	2,943	1,864
General expenses	605	756
Cash	109	155
Rent receivable (see note 6)	–	660
Debtors:		
Trade (see note 12)	1,312	–

The only other balances are the personal accounts of the proprietor and are not allocated to departments:

£

K. Maltby:
Capital 9,000
Current account 1,634 (credit)

Required:

Prepare a departmental trading and profit and loss account for the year ended 31 March 19–7 and a departmental balance sheet at that date, in each case using separate columns for the cafe, the shop and the total business.

ACCA EXAMINATION QUESTIONS

3. The following Balance Sheet has been prepared by B. Swift as at 30 November 1982.

Capital Account	£	£	Fixed Assets	£	£
Balance 1.12.81	76,132		Equipment, at cost	54,000	
Add: Net Profit for year	25,000		Depreciation	9,600	
					44,400
	101,132		Motor vehicle, at cost	25,200	
Less: Drawings	10,000		Depreciation	14,400	

		91,132			10,800
Current Liabilities			*Current Assets*		
Creditors	28,000		Stock	30,000	
Accruals	2,070		Debtors 40,000		
Bank overdraft	3,664		Provision 2,400	37,600	
		33,734			67,600
			Suspense		2,066
		£124,866			£124,866

The Debtors' total of £40,000 in the Balance Sheet is the balance appearing on the Sales Ledger Control Account in the General Ledger. Individual personal accounts for debtors are kept on a memorandum basis. The accounting system used to record credit sales transactions was as follows:

Sales recording

i. Copy sales invoices are batched in date order. Each batch is add listed by a clerk who enters the batch total in a batch total register. The register is then passed to the machine operator to post the Sales Ledger Control Account in the General Ledger.

ii. Each batch of copy invoices is passed to a machine operator who makes the appropriate entry on the debtor's ledger card. A copy of the amount is accumulated and at the end of posting the individual accounts, the accumulated total is posted to the Sales Account in the Nominal ledger.

Remittance recording

iii. The cheques received from debtors are listed in the cashier's office. A memorandum with details of the total is passed to a machine operator who posts the Sales Ledger Control Account and Cash Account in the General Ledger.

iv. The detailed list is passed to a machine operator who makes the appropriate entries in the individual debtor's ledger card.

Reconciliation

i. The control account is reconciled with the list of Sales Ledger balances monthly. At 30 November 1982 the list of ledger balances totalled £41,520.

The accountant discovered the following items.

a. *Relating to the debtors*

i. On one of the add–lists of copy sales invoices, the clerk omitted to include an invoice for £2,100. It appeared to her to be an unusually large item and she intended to query it. In the event, it was omitted from the add–list but passed through with the rest of the batch for ledger posting. The accountant verified that the sale had been correctly authorised.

ii. An invoice for £250 was correctly add–listed but removed by the clerk who noticed an error in the address. The invoice was still in her pending tray at 30 November 1982 and consequently had not been passed to the machine operator.

iii. One invoice for £799 was posted to the debtor's ledger card as £979.

iv. A credit entry of £150 was made in R. Black's ledger account although no cheque had been received and no credit authorised.

v. One of the lists of cheques was correctly totalled at £4,400 but posted in the General Ledger Control Account as £4,040 and in the General Ledger Cash Account as £4,004.

b. *Other errors*

i. On 1 October 1982 Swift had paid rent of £1,200 to cover the period 1 October 1982 to 31 March 1983. In the accounts to 30 November 1982 an accrual of £400 has been raised for the rent thought to be outstanding for the period 1 October 1982 to 30 November 1982.

ii. A bank reconciliation revealed that a standing order payment of £150 for Swift's subscription to a video film club had passed through the bank statement on 25 November

1982 and bank interest of £200 had been debited on 30 November 1982 but no entries had been made in the Cash Account.

iii. Stock included a video recorder (cost £500) that had been purchased by Swift for his personal use with his own funds. The evaluation of stock items was correct but the stock sheets were overcast by £1,000.

iv. The Fixed Assets of £54,000 included an office copying machine that was being purchased on hire purchase. The agreement was dated 1 December 1981. The terms were:

	£	
Cost	20,000	
Deposit	4,000	
	16,000	
Interest	3,200	
Balance	£19,200	payable in 24 monthly instalments of £800

The Fixed Asset Account was debited with £23,200 and depreciation has been charged on this at 10% per annum.

The creditors (£28,000) include the hire purchase suppliers balance of £9,600 (being £19,200 less 12 instalments of £800).

Required:

a. Show the amended balance on the Sales Ledger Control Account and reconcile with Sales Ledger balances.

b. Show the effect of the necessary corrections to the profit for the year to 30 November 1982.

c. Draw up the amended Balance Sheet as at 30 November 1982.

d. Journalise the clearance of the Suspense.

(ACCA 2.9(2) December 1982)

3 Partnerships

GENERAL BACKGROUND

1.0 This section is concerned with certain problem areas of partnership accounting. Legal requirements governing the conduct of partnerships together with the preparation of final accounts, including appropriation and final accounts, are assumed to have been learned at an earlier stage of study and are not repeated in this section.

1.1 Specific problems considered are those which arise on:

a. formation of partnerships

b. changes in the constitution of partnerships

c. dissolution of partnerships.

FORMATION OF PARTNERSHIPS

2.0 A partnership may be formed in one of several ways, for example.

a. as a partnership at the outset of the business

b. by the amalgamation of two or more sole proprietorships, and, more rarely,

c. by conversion from a limited company.

2.1 The formation of a partnership as such at the outset presents no particular accounting problems. The values of the assets contributed to the firm by each of the partners constitute their respective capitals.

2.2 Problems may arise when sole proprietors amalgamate to form a partnership.

EXAMPLE

2.3 Two professional men, G and H, decided to amalgamate their practices and to form a partnership with effect from 1st May 19-0.

Their respective balance sheets on 30th April 19-0, disclosed the following figures.

	G	H		G	H
	£	£		£	£
Capital	15,300	23,300	Premises	7,000	12,000
Creditors	200	400	Office etc equipment	2,600	10,000
Loan from business			Stock of stationery		
associate	–	9,000	etc	500	900
			Debtors for fees	3,200	5,700
			Bank and Cash	2,200	4,100
	15,500	32,700		15,500	32,700

For the purposes of the amalgamation:

G's premises were revalued at £10,000 and were to be used as a branch office and office equipment, valued at £800, was written off as obsolete; the fee debtors included an amount of £600 which was to be regarded as irrecoverable; the creditors were paid out of the bank balance; otherwise assets were brought in at book value.

H had agreed to acquire out of his private resources additional equipment costing £3,000, to pay his creditors from his bank balance, to repay the loan from his private resources, and to bring his other assets in at book value.

Prepare the balance sheet for the partnership of GH & Co on 1st May 19-0.

SOLUTION

2.4 A balance sheet prepared immediately after the amalgamation would be based on the balance sheets in 2.3 as modified by the narrative.

GH & Co
Balance Sheet as at 1 May 19-0

	Workings G £	Workings H £	£	£
Fixed Assets				
Premises	10,000	12,000	22,000	
Office etc, Equipment	1,800	13,000	14,800	
				36,800
Current Assets				
Stock of stationery	500	900	1,400	
Debtors for fees	2,600	5,700	8,300	
Bank and cash	2,000	3,700	5,700	
				15,400
Current Liabilities				
Creditors	–	–	–	–
	16,900	35,300		52,200
Capital – G				16,900
– H				35,300
				52,200

The capitals of G and H as partners are different from what they were as sole proprietors, thus reflecting the effects of the new arrangements.

2.5 Similar considerations apply when a limited company is converted into a partnership. The winding up entries in the company's ledgers on liquidation are outside the scope of this chapter, but the entries in the ledger of the partnership follow the same pattern as those which are needed when a partnership is formed as described in 2.1 to 2.4. That is, the assets are brought into the ledgers at the values at which they are acquired from the limited company. The partners may also assume responsibility for some or all of the company's liabilities which would then appear as creditors in the partnership books. Lastly the contribution of each partner would be brought in as his capital and partnership loan (if applicable).

EXAMPLE

2.6 The balance sheet of CHJ (Warehousing) Ltd on 30 September 19-0 disclosed

	£		Cost £	Depn £	Net £
Share Capital		**Fixed Assets**			
Ordinary Shares of £1.00	300,000	Freehold premises	100,000	10,000	90,000
Reserves		Vehicles	70,000	30,000	40,000
Profit and Loss	62,000	Equipment	20,000	12,000	8,000
	362,000		190,000	52,000	138,000
Current Liabilities		**Current Assets**			
Creditors	65,000	Stocks		181,000	
		Debtors		86,000	
		Bank		22,000	
				289,000	
	427,000			427,000	

At the date, the company's assets, excluding cash, were acquired by the partnership of P, C and A, trading as Sawley Stockholders, on the following terms:

Item	Agreed takeover value £	Basis
Freehold premises	120,000	Professional valuation
Vehicles	30,000	Useful lives reassessed
Equipment	8,000	Book value
Stocks	155,000	Damaged and obsolete items eliminated
Debtors	82,000	Bad debts written off
Creditors	65,000	Book value

The purchase consideration was negotiated at £355,000 and was contributed as capital by P £150,000, by C £100,000, by A £55,000 and as a loan by P £50,000. A paid a further £30,000 into the partnership bank account as additional capital.

Prepare a balance sheet for the partnership immediately after completion of these arrangements.

SOLUTION
2.7 Sawley Stockholders Balance Sheet as at 1 October 19-0

	£	£		Cost £	Depn £	Net £
Capital			**Fixed Assets**			
– P	150,000		Freehold			
– C	100,000		premises	120,000		120,000
– A	85,000		Vehicles	30,000		30,000
[55000 + 30000]			Equipment	8,000		8,000
		335,000				
				158,000	–	158,000
Loan – P		50,000	**Goodwill**			25,000
Current Liabilities			**Current Assets**			
Creditors		65,000	Stocks		155,000	
			Debtors		82,000	
			Bank		30,000	
						267,000
		450,000				450,000

It can be seen that the value at which the partnership takes over the company's net assets is not necessarily book value but a realistic assessment of current value. The cost of fixed assets is the cost to the partnership and takes account of the present condition of the asset, consequently no depreciation is provided at this juncture. Goodwill appears in the balance sheet of the partnership although it did not appear in the company's balance sheet. In fact it represents the excess of the purchase consideration over the value of the net assets acquired, ie.

£355,000 - £(120,000 + 30,000 + 8,000 + 155,000 + 82,000 - 65,000) = £25,000

CHANGES IN THE CONSTITUTION OF PARTNERSHIPS

3.0 Various changes can occur in the constitution of an established partnership. Some involve actual physical changes in the composition of the partnership for example

a. partners may die
b. partners may retire
(in each case with or without being replaced by incoming partners)
c. additional partners may be admitted.

On the other hand, there may be a constructive change whereby the original partners remain the same but there is a change in the agreed profit and loss sharing ratios. The ultimate change is when the partnership goes out of existence altogether or is converted into a limited company, but this gives rise to other problems also and is dealt with in a separate subsection (4.0 to 4.49) Dissolution of partnerships.

Combinations of these circumstances may also occur.

3.1 Whenever there is a change of a type listed in 3.0 partnership net assets must be revalued and the net surplus or deficit must be apportioned between the partners.

3.2 In some instances the partners may decide to retain the revalued figures in the books, in other cases they may decide to write them back again. At first sight this may seem to be a pointless set of manoeuvres. However the original partners are credited (in the original profit sharing ratio) with the surplus (or debited with a deficit). If the surplus is not to be permanently retained in the books, the new partnership individuals are debited in the new profit sharing ratio.

EXAMPLE

3.3 R. S and T had been in partnership for a number of years sharing profits and losses equally.

With the prior agreement of his partners, T was to devote more time to his other business interests from the start of the new financial year on 1st August 19-0 when the balance sheet showed

	£		£
Capital – R	20,000	Premises	21,000
– S	17,000	Equipment	11,000
– T	14,000	Vehicles	9,000
Current Accounts – R	1,500		
– S	1,000	Stock	5,000
– T	500	Debtors	6,000
Creditors	2,000	Bank	4,000
	56,000		56,000

It was agreed that from this date profits and losses should be shared 3:2:1 respectively and that the following revaluations, which were not to be permanently reflected in the books, should be made

	£
Goodwill	13,000
Premises	26,000

Show the entries in the accounts to reflect these arrangements.

SOLUTION

3.4 A Revaluation Account must be opened and the revaluation deficits/surpluses debited/credited, with corresponding entries in the asset accounts concerned. In this case also, an account must be opened for Goodwill which had not hitherto been recorded.

The net deficit/net surplus is then shared between the partners on Capital Account in the old ratio of 1:1:1, that is, one third to each partner.

Goodwill

	£		£
Revaluation	13,000	Balance c/d	13,000
Balance b/d	13,000		

Premises

	£		£
Balance b/d	21,000	Balance c/d	26,000
Revaluation	5,000		
	26,000		26,000
Balance b/d	26,000		

Revaluation

	£		£
Balance c/d	18,000	Goodwill	13,000
		Premises	5,000
	18,000		18,000
Capital – R ($\frac{1}{3}$)	6,000	Balance b/d	18,000
– T ($\frac{1}{3}$)	6,000		
– T ($\frac{1}{3}$)	6,000		
	18,000		18,000

Capital

	R £	S £	T £		R £	S £	T £
Balances c/d	26,000	23,000	20,000	Balances b/d	20,000	17,000	14,000
				Revaluation	6,000	6,000	6,000
	26,000	23,000	20,000		26,000	23,000	20,000
				Balances b/d	26,000	23,000	20,000

The question stated that the revaluations were not to be permanently retained in the books. Consequently, the revaluation entries must be reversed, using the newly agreed ratio of 3:2:1 for sharing the write-back between the partners.

Goodwill

	£		£
Balance b/d	13,000	Revaluation	13,000

Premises

	£		£
Balance b/d	26,000	Revaluation	5,000
		Balance c/d	21,000
	26,000		26,000
Balance b/d	21,000		

Revaluation

	£		£
Revaluations written back			
– Goodwill	13,000	Capital – R (3/6)	9,000
– Premises	5,000	– S (2/6)	6,000
		– T (1/6)	3,000
	18,000		18,000

Capital

	R £	S £	T £		R £	S £	T £
Revaluation	9,000	6,000	3,000	Balance	26,000	23,000	20,000
Balances c/d	17,000	17,000	17,000				
	26,000	23,000	20,000		26,000	23,000	20,000
				Balances c/d	17,000	17,000	17,000

Comparing the "before" and "after" positions, there is no change in total assets and liabilities but individual partners capitals have altered viz:

	R £	S £	T £	Total £
Original capital	20,000	17,000	14,000	51,000
Revised capital	17,000	17,000	17,000	51,000
Increase/(decrease)	(3,000)	–	3,000	–

At first sight it may seem strange that T has gained £3,000 whilst R has lost a similar amount, but looking at the position from another angle,

	R	S	T	Total
Original sharing ratio (equally)	2	2	2	6
Revised sharing ratio	3	2	1	6
Shares gained/(lost)	1	–	(1)	–

It can be seen that R has gained the share of profit/loss which T has lost by voluntary surrender.

T is therefore compensated for the loss of 1/6 of the profits by receiving 1/6 of the revaluation surplus. One sixth of £18,000 is £3,000, the amount by which T's capital is increased. R, who has benefited from the revised arrangements, has in effect paid for it by giving one sixth of his revaluation surplus to T. Hence the decrease and increase of £3,000 in R's and T's respective capitals. The partners' capitals now reflect the latest asset revaluations without those revaluations remaining on the asset accounts concerned.

GOODWILL

3.5 As has already been seen, goodwill may be encountered in partnership accounts when the partners take over sole traders or a limited company (as described in 2.2 and 2.5) or, when there is a change in the constitution of a partnership (as described in 3.0).

3.6 In the former instance, goodwill is said to be purchased in that it is the excess of the purchase consideration over the value of the net assets acquired (as noted in 2.7). On the other hand, goodwill brought into account on a constitutional change is usually internally generated, that is, it does not exist as the result of a purchase transaction. The usual procedure is for internally generated goodwill to be brought into account for the purposes of inter-partner capital adjustments but not to be permanently retained in the ledger. This treatment was illustrated in 3.3 and 3.4.

3.7 Numerous theories exist as to the nature and valuation of goodwill. Many theorists are in broad agreement that goodwill is the value of the commercial advantages which a particular business enjoys over its competitors.

3.8 The very subjectiveness of goodwill gives rise to problems of valuation. Because of the many diverse factors which give rise to goodwill (for example, location of business, reputation of quality and reliability of products, customer relations, possession of patents, trademarks or a monopoly) all of which are impossible to quantify in monetary terms when taken individually and collectively, accountants have to resort to calculating an acceptable, rather than an accurate, figure for goodwill.

3.9 Methods used to value goodwill vary from the crude to the sophisticated. For example, a simple method in the case of a retail trading business might be to apply a factor to the average weekly or monthly turnover. A similar method employed by some professional businesses (solicitors, architects etc) is to apply a factor to the gross annual fees averaged over a stated number of years. An alternative might be to apply a factor to the average net profit of a stated number of years.

EXAMPLE

3.10 The net profits of a particular business for the last five years have been

Year	£
19-6	6,100
19-7	7,800
19-8	10,200
19-9	12,400
19-0	16,000

Calculate goodwill as representing two years' purchase of the average annual profit of the five years.

SOLUTION

3.11

Year	Net profit £
19-6	6,100
19-7	7,800
19-8	10,200
19-9	12,400
19-0	16,000
Total	52,500

Average annual net profit $\frac{52,500}{5}$ £10,500

Goodwill (two years' purchase) = £21,000
(2 × £10,500)

3.12 Another approach is based on evaluating the excess of actual profits over the normal return of comparable businesses. A modification of this method when a business is being sold or, say, there is a change in the constitution of a partnership, is to use forecast (as opposed to past) profits. These two approaches are termed the super-profits method. The calculation may involve a stated number of years purchase of the average super-profits (as illustrated in 3.13 but substituting super-profits for net profit) or by capitalising the average super-profits at a special risk rate which reflects the uncertainty of them arising. This is illustrated in 3.15. A further refinement (not illustrated) would be to discount the forecast super-profits back year by year to a present value.

EXAMPLE

3.13 A, B and C have been in partnership for a number of years and the senior partner A, is about to retire and a new partner, N, will be admitted.

Using the formula $\frac{P - rA}{m}$ when

P = adjusted forecast maintainable profits (before tax)
r = normal rate of return (before tax), 20%
A = net forecast tangible assets £38,150
m = risk rate of return (before tax), that is,
the capitalisation rate, 25%

calculate goodwill if the (unadjusted) forecast maintainable profits (before tax) are £40,000. The following matters, to operate from the start of the "new" partnership, are to be taken into account:-

i. A is to act as a part-time consultant to the partnership for an annual retainer of £4,000.
ii. B's partnership salary will be discontinued. The outside equivalent part-time salary for a person carrying out his duties would be £5,000 per annum.
iii. C's partnership salary will be doubled to £4,000 per annum to compensate him for taking over A's duties as senior partner, but they will still be £5,000 below the "open market" rate for similar responsibilities.
iv. additional depreciation of £6,000 per annum will be charged.

SOLUTION

3.14 One underlying factor contributing to goodwill (and not previously mentioned) is the present expectation of future profits. This aspect is recognised by the use of future, rather than past, profits for calculation purposes.

Before setting out the calculations, it is first worth considering the significance of the outside equivalent salaries quoted in notes ii. and iii. The net profits of any partnership are artificially inflated in the sense that the remuneration of the working partners is not charged in arriving at net profit but is an appropriation of it. In order to correct this distortion the net profit should be adjusted by the amount which an employee could earn if carrying out the partner's duties and such amount may well be substantially different from the nominal sum appropriated as a partnership salary.

	£	£
Unadjusted forecast maintainable profits (before tax)		40,000
Adjustments		
i. part-time consultancy fee (A)	(4,000)	
ii. outside equivalent part-time salary (B)	(5,000)	
iii. outside equivalent salary (C)	(9,000)	
iv. extra depreciation	(6,000)	
		(24,000)
Adjusted forecast maintainable profits (before tax) (ie P in the formula)		16,000

As mentioned above, partners' salaries, being appropriations and not charges, do not affect profit before tax.

It now remains to substitute figures in the formula

$$\frac{P - rA}{m}$$

and then to resolve it

Goodwill is thus: $\quad \dfrac{16,000 - 0.2(38,150)}{0.25} = \dfrac{16,000 - 7,630}{0.25}$

$$= \frac{8.370}{0.25} = £33,480$$

As P - rA = super-profits and $\frac{100}{m}$ is the number of years purchase, an alternative way of viewing the goodwill figure of £33,480 is that it represents 4 years ($\frac{100}{25}$) purchase of the super–profits (£8,370), that is

$$4 \times £8,370 = £33,480$$

DISSOLUTION OF PARTNERSHIPS

4.0 A partnership may be terminated by force of circumstances (for example, by the death of a partner or as the result of the business failing during an economic recession) or by mutual agreement when one or more partners reaches retiring age or when the business has expanded to the point where it is necessary to convert it into a limited company. Each of these different sets of circumstances is accompanied by characteristic problems which are considered in the following subsections.

CONVERSION OF PARTNERSHIPS INTO LIMITED COMPANIES

4.1 This situation is a frequent source of examination questions. When a partnership is so converted, there are two separate sets of problems - those concerned with dissolving the partnership and those concerned with constituting the limited company - both of which are dealt with below.

ENTRIES IN PARTNERSHIP LEDGER

4.2 A Realisation account is opened in the partnership books to which all the assets (excluding Bank and Cash, unless these are taken over by the company) are debited, the corresponding credit entries appearing in the respective asset accounts thus closing them down. Provision accounts (for depreciation, bad debts etc) are similarly closed down and transferred to Realisation as credits.

4.3 Partnership assets taken over personally by the partners - for example, partners sometimes retain their cars at an agreed valuation - are credited to Realisation and debited to the appropriate Capital account.

4.4 Dissolution expenses are debited to Realisation account (and credited to Bank) whilst allowances from Creditors are credited (and debited to Creditors). Net creditors taken over by the company are debited to Creditors and credited to Realisation. Current Account balances are transferred to the corresponding Capital Account. Any creditors not taken over are settled by crediting Bank and debiting Creditors.

4.5 The purchase consideration is debited to an account opened in the name of the company and credited to Realisation. The realisation surplus or deficit is transferred to Capital accounts in the profit sharing ratio.

4.6 The consideration may be discharged by an issue of shares or by payment of cash or by an issue of debentures or loan stock or by any combination of these methods.

4.7 When received, the cash element is debited to Bank, the share element to Shares in (the name of the company) the debenture element to Debentures in (the name of the company) the corresponding credit appearing in the Company's account (see 4.5)

4.8 The cash and/or debentures etc are then credited to their respective accounts and debited to partners' Capitals. Any balances on capital accounts are cleared by the partners paying in, or withdrawing, cash thus completing the dissolution.

ENTRIES IN COMPANY'S LEDGER

4.9 A Business Purchase account is opened to which the purchase consideration is credited and liabilities taken over are debited. The double entry is completed by making entries in the appropriate asset and liability accounts.

4.10 The company is not restricted to assigning the same values to the assets as did the partnership. Any excess of consideration over total values assigned constitutes Goodwill, any shortfall constitutes Capital Reserve.

4.11 When the purchase consideration passes, Business Purchase account is debited and Share Capital (Share Premium if applicable), Bank and Debentures are credited with, respectively, shares (share premium), cash, and debentures.

EXAMPLE

4.12 Immediately prior to its conversion into a limited company, the Balance Sheet of Exe and Wye, who shared profits and losses 3/5 and 2/5, disclosed

Exe, Wye and Company
Balance Sheet as at 30 June 19-0

	£	£		£	£
Capital – Exe	20,000		Fixed Assets		
– Wye	10,000		Premises (cost)		15,000
		30,000	Equipment (cost)	10,000	
			less depreciation	3,000	
Current Liabilities					7,000
Creditors	7,000				22,000
			Current Assets		
			Stocks	8,000	
			Debtors	5,000	
			Bank	2,000	
					15,000
		37,000			37,000

For the purposes of the conversion all assets (except Bank) were taken over at book values but Premises were revalued by the company at £30,000. Creditors were taken over by the company, YZ Ltd and the agreed consideration was £48,000 to be discharged by the issue of 40,000 Ordinary shares of £1.00 per share at a premium of 10% and £4,000 in cash. Exe and Wye each received 20,000 shares.

Required:

a. the Realisation, Bank, YZ Ltd, Shares in YZ Ltd and Capital accounts in the ledger of Exe, Wye and Company.

b. Journal entries of YZ Ltd to record the conversion.

SOLUTION

4.13 a. Exe, Wye and Company Ledger

Realisation

	£		£
(Assets transferred at book values)		Provision for depreciation	3,000
		Creditors	7,000
Premises	15,000	YZ Ltd	48,000
Equipment	10,000		
Stocks	8,000		
Debtors	5,000		
Surplus c/d	20,000		
	58,000		58,000
Capital – Exe (3/5)	12,000	Surplus b/d	20,000
– Wye (2/5)	8,000		
	20,000		20,000

YZ Ltd

	£		£
Realisation	48,000	Shares in YZ Ltd (40,000 × £1.10 per share)	44,000
		Bank	4,000
	48,000		48,000

Shares in YZ Ltd

	£		£
YZ Ltd	44,000	Capital – Exe	22,000
		– Wye	22,000
	44,000		44,000

Capital Accounts

	Exe	Wye		Exe	Wye
	£	£		£	£
Shares in YZ Ltd	22,000	22,000	Balances b/d	20,000	10,000
Bank	10,000	–	Realisation	12,000	8,000
			Bank	–	44,000
	32,000	22,000		32,000	22,000

Bank

	£		£
Balance b/d	2,000	Capital – Exe	10,000
YZ Ltd	4,000		
Capital Wye	4,000		
	10,000		10,000

Y's Capital account was in debit after the realisation and share entries had been posted. He then had to pay in £4,000 to clear the debit balance. There was then just sufficient cash to repay Exe's credit balance of £10,000.

b. YZ Ltd Journal

	Dr	Cr
	£	£
Premises	30,000	
Equipment	7,000	
Stocks	8,000	
Debtors	5,000	
Goodwill	5,000	
To Creditors		7,000
Business Purchase		48,000
Assets and liabilities taken over from		
Exe, Wye and Co.	55,000	55,000
Business Purchase	Dr 48,000	
To Ordinary Share Capital		40,000
Share Premiums		4,000
Bank		4,000
Discharge of purchase consideration	48,000	48,000

Note:
In the first journal entry Goodwill is the balancing figure (see 4.10)

TERMINATION AND DISSOLUTION OF PARTNERSHIP.

4.14 When a partnership is terminated and goes out of existence, the closing down entries on dissolution are similar to, but not identical with, those already encountered on a conversion into a limited company.

4.15 The partnership dissolution entries are exactly as noted in 4.2, 4.3 and 4.4, except that in 4.4 net creditors taken over by a limited company are transferred to Realisation. In a dissolution/termination situation they are not transferred because liability for them is not assumed by another entity.

4.16 Further entries are then needed to record the actual sums realised (debit Bank, credit Realisation).

4.17 External (third party) liabilities are settled when sufficient cash is available (debit Creditors etc, credit Bank). Next in order of priority are partners' loan repayment (debit Loan, credit Bank).

4.18 After these entries have been completed, the balance on Realisation representing either a surplus (credit balance) or a deficit (debit balance) is transferred to Capital accounts in the profit/(loss) sharing ratio.

4.19 The Capital accounts are then balanced. Any partner whose capital account is in debit pays into the firm's bank account a sufficient sum to clear his balance. The procedure when he is unable to do so is dealt with in 4.25 to 4.28.

4.20 There is then a balance at Bank just sufficient to repay those partners whose capitals are in credit. This done, the partnership dissolution entries are complete.

EXAMPLE

4.21 Ess, Tee and Vee who are in partnership sharing profits and losses 2 : 2 : 1, decide to dissolve the partnership on 30th September 19-0 at which date their Balance Sheet was:-

Ess Tee and Vee
Balance Sheet as at 30 September 19-0

	£	£		£	£
Capital Accounts			Fixed Assets (at wdv)		
– Ess	39,000		Freehold Property	30,000	
– Tee	13,000		Equipment	15,000	
– Vee	2,000				45,000
		54,000			
Current Accounts			Current Assets		
–Ess	700		Stock	8,000	
–Tee	(300)		Debtors	4,500	
–Vee	200		Cash at Bank	2,100	
		600			14,600
Current Liabilities					
Creditors	3,000				
Loan – Tee	2,000				
		59,600			59,600

The partners were unable to sell the business as a going concern and disposed of the assets separately for the following sums:

	£
Freehold property	31,000
Equipment	4,800
Stock	2,900

Debtors paid in full and creditors gave discounts totalling £100. Dissolution expenses totalled £800.
Required:
Prepare all the accounts of the partnership on dissolution.

SOLUTION
4.22

Freehold Property
	£		£
Balance b/d	30,000	Realisation	30,000

Equipment
	£		£
Balance b/d	15,000	Realisation	15,000

Stock
	£		£
Balance b/d	8,000	Realisation	8,000

Debtors
	£		£
Balance b/d	4,500	Realisation	4,500

Realisation

	£		£
Freehold Property	30,000	Bank (freehold property)	31,000
Equipment	15,000	(equipment)	4,800
Stock	8,000	(stock)	2,900
Debtors	4,500	Creditors(discount)	100
Bank-expenses	800	Bank (debtors)	4,500
		Balance c/d	15,000
	58,300		58,300
Balance b/d	15,000	Capital – Ess (2/5)	6,000
(loss on realisation)		– Tee (2/5)	6,000
		– Vee (1/5)	3,000
	15,000		15,000

Creditors

	£		£
Realisation (discount)	100	Balance b/d	3,000
Bank	2,900		
	3,000		3,000

Loan (from Tee)

	£		£
Bank	2,000	Balance b/d	2,000

Capital

	Ess £	Tee £	Vee £		Ess £	Tee £	Vee £
Current a/c	–	300	–	Balances b/d	39,000	13,000	2,000
Realisation (loss)	6,000	6,000	3,000	Current a/c	700	–	200
Bank (final payments)	33,700	6,700	–	Bank (payment of sum overdrawn)	–	–	800
	39,700	13,000	3,000		39,700	13,000	3,000

Current Accounts

	Ess £	Tee £	Vee £		Ess £	Tee £	Vee £
Balance b/d	–	300	–	Balances b/d	700	–	200
Capital a/c transfer	700	–	200	Capital a/c transfer	–	300	–
	700	300	200		700	300	200

Bank

	£		£
Balance/bd	2,100	Creditors	2,900
Realisation		Realisation –	
(freehold property)	31,000	expenses	800
(equipment)	4,800	Loan–Tee	2,000
(stock)	2,900	Capital – Ess (final	33,700
(debtors)	4,500	– Tee payment)	6,700
Capital – Vee	800		
	46,100		46,100

INSOLVENCY OF PARTNER ON DISSOLUTION.

4.23 In the above solution Vee's Capital account was in debit to the extent of £800 after his share of the realisation loss. Vee eliminated this deficit by paying £800 into partnership Bank account.

4.24 If, however, at this point Vee had been insolvent and therefore unable to make this contribution to eliminate his debit balance, his deficiency would, in the absence of any contrary agreement between the partners, be shared by the solvent partners (Ess and Tee) in the last capital account proportions. For this purpose Current Account balances are disregarded. This arrangement is known as the rule in Garner v. Murray who were two of the parties in a High Court case decided in 1904.

4.25 Assuming that in Example 4.21 Vee was insolvent and that the partners had not agreed to share such losses in the profit and loss ratio, the debit balance on Vee's account (£800) would be shared by Ess, £600 ($\frac{3}{4}$ × £800) and Tee, £200 ($\frac{1}{4}$ × £800). Ess and Tee had fixed capitals of £39,000 and £13,000, giving a ratio of 3 : 1 (Their profit and loss sharing ratio for all other purposes is 2 : 2)

4.26 Under the arrangements in 4.25, capital accounts would be:

Capital

	Ess £	Tee £	Vee £		Ess £	Tee £	Vee £
Current a/c	–	300	–	Balance b/d	39,000	13,000	2,000
Realisation (loss)	6,000	6,000	3,000	Current a/c	700	–	200
Transfer from				Transfer to Ess and Tee	–	–	800
Vee	600	200	–				
Bank	33,100	6,500	–				
	39,700	13,000	3,000		39,700	13,000	3,000

The total amount finally paid to Ess and Tee, £39,600 is £800 less than in 4.22, thus reflecting the fact that Vee had failed to contribute this amount.

PIECEMEAL REALISATIONS AND DISTRIBUTIONS

4.27 When a partnership is in the process of being dissolved it is unlikely that the sums realised will be received simultaneously (unless, of course, the business is being sold as a single unit).

4.28 More frequently the individual assets are received in cash over a prolonged period. For example, some debtors may pay only if pressurised, fixed assets may have to be sold by tender or auction, thus final dissolution may take longer than a year.

4.29 The partners do not usually wish to wait for all the cash to be collected in before they receive such return of capital as is due to them. It is common practice therefore for interim distributions to be made.

4.30 A great problem may be the fact that the partners have not contributed capital in the same proportions as they share profits and losses. Another problem is the uncertainty of future realisations.

4.31 Means have therefore been devised which permit interim distributions to be made in such a way that any partner who has contributed a disproportionately great amount of capital by comparison with his co–partners, receives his surplus capital back in priority. At the same time, the distribution has to be conducted so that each partner bears his share of possible losses at each distribution stage, thus avoiding the necessity of recoupment from him at a subsequent stage.

4.32 Two accepted methods of calculating the interim distributions are the "Surplus Capital" (Method A) and "Assumed loss" (Method B) methods.

METHOD A – SURPLUS CAPITAL

4.33 This is suitable when all the partners are solvent and are likely to remain so. By a series of calculations, illustrated in 4.43 the partners' capital contributions (including current account balances) are geared to the profit and loss sharing ratio and the partners whose capitals are relatively surplus are ranked according to the degree of excess.

4.34 From these calculations the Distribution Sequence can be established (also illustrated in 4.43).

4.35 Actual realisations in cash are accumulated and utilised to discharge external liabilities, and secondarily, if any, partners' loan advances (as noted in 4.17). Any remaining balances is then distributed to partners in accordance with the predetermined Distribution Sequence. The schedule showing the disposition of available cash appears as 4.44 and the actual distribution as 4.45.

METHOD B – ASSUMED LOSS.

4.36 Where a partner (or partners) is known to be insolvent (or is likely to become insolvent) and thus unable to make the payment (noted in 4.19) to clear a debit balance on his capital account, it is safer to use this alternative method which has inbuilt safeguards embracing the Garner v. Murray rule (stated in 4.24).

4.37 Under this method, illustrated in 4.46 actual realisations of cash are accumulated (as with Method A) in addition to which a cumulative total of cash and non–cash (eg discounts from creditors) realisations is maintained.

4.38 When sufficient cash is available the external liabilities are discharged, followed by partners' loan advances (if any). In this regard the two methods agree and the amount of the balance available for distribution is identical.

4.39 The difference arises in the manner of distribution. Method B requires the total distributable realisations (at each distribution date) to be offset against the total book value of the assets. The resultant figure is assumed to be irrecoverable and is apportioned between the partners in the profit and loss sharing ratio.

4.40 Any partner(s) whose apportioned loss exceeds his capital plus current account balance is assumed for this purpose to be insolvent and his debit balance is allotted to the "solvent" partners in their capital account proportions (as illustrated in 4.25 and 4.26).

4.41 This process is repeated at each distribution stage, the cumulative realisations showing an increase and the "assumed loss" diminishing. The actual payment for the second and subsequent distributions is cumulative net realisations minus distributions made to date.

EXAMPLE

4.42 The facts are as in 4.21 except that proceeds of realisations were received as follows:

	£
Oct 10	600
Oct 31	900
Nov 11	1,800
Jan 29	31,000
Feb 23	8,900

SOLUTION – METHOD A (SURPLUS CAPITAL)
4.43

		Distribution Sequence Schedule			
		Total	Ess	Tee	Vee
		£	£	£	£
	Capital Accounts	54,000	39,000	13,000	2,000
	Current Accounts	600	700	(300)	200
(1)	Total	54,600	39,700	12,700	2,200
(2)	Profit Sharing ratio	5	2	2	1
		£	£	£	£
(3)	(1) ÷ (2)	Not applicable	19,850	6,350	2,200
(4)	Using line (1) column corresponding with lowest figure in line (3), as base, capitals in profit sharing ratio	11,000	4,400	4,400	2,200
(5)	(1) – (4) = Surplus capitals	43,600	35,300	8,300	–
(6)	(5) ÷ (2)	Not applicable	17,650	4,150	–
(7)	Repeating line (4) procedure for lines (5) and (6)	16,600	8,300	8,300	
(8)	(5) – (7) = Surplus capital	27,000	27,000	–	–
	Distribution sequence				
	First £27,000 (2:0:0)	27,000	27,000	–	–
	Next £16,600 (2:2:0)	16,600	8,300	8,300	–
	Cumulative Over £43,600 (2:2:1)	43,600	35,300	8,300	–

4.44

Disposition of Cash Schedule

Date	Cash Available £	Item	Settlement of External Liabilities £	Settlement of Partner's Loan £	Distributions First (11 Nov) £	Distributions Second (29 Jan) £	Distributions Final (23 Feb) £
Oct 1	2,100	Balance					
10	600	Realisation					
31	900	Realisation					
31	3,600	Balance					
		Settlement of					
31	(2,900)	Creditors (net)	2,900				
31	(700)	Loan (Tee) (part)		700			
31	–	Balance					
Nov 11	1,800	Realisation					
11	(1,300)	Loan (Tee) (part)		1,300			
11	(500)	Distribution			500		

26

	11	–	Balance					
Jan	29	31,000	Realisation					
	29	(31,000)	Distribution				31,000	
	29	–	Balance					
Feb	23	8,900	Realisation					
	23	(800)	Costs					
	23	(8,100)	Distribution					8,100
	23	–	Balance					
			Totals	2,900	2,000	500	31,000	8,100

4.45

	Statement of actual distribution			
	Total £	Ess £	Tee £	Vee £
First £27,000 (2: 0: 0)				
1st Distribution 11th November	500	500	–	–
2nd Distribution (part)				
29th January	26,500	26,500	–	–
Total (2: 0: 0)	27,000	27,000	–	–
Next £16,600 (2 :2 :0)				
2nd Distribution (balance)				
29th January	4,500	2,250	2,250	–
Final Distribution				
23rd February	8,100	4,050	4,050	
Adjustments (see note)	–	(200)	200	–
Total	12,600	6,100	6,500	–
Cumulative	39,600	33,100	6,500	–

Notes:

In 4.33 it was stated that Method A is suitable when all the partners are solvent. If it turns out (as here) that a partner becomes insolvent, an adjustment is needed from that point onwards.

The total loss is £15,000 (see Realisation Account in 4.22) of which Vee's share is £3,000 ($\frac{1}{5} \times £15,000$) thus putting his Capital account into debit (the distribution ratio for the final distribution is 2: 2: 0), whereas in insolvency situations such a loss should be borne in capital proportions (3 : 1) by the solvent partners. An adjustment is required to give effect to this rule:–

	Total £	Ess £	Tee £
Loss in profit and loss sharing ratio (2: 2: 0)	(800)	(400)	(400)
Loss in capital contribution ratio (3: 1)	(800)	(600)	(200)
Adjustment required	–	(200)	200

At the third and final distribution, Ess would receive £3,850 and Tee £4,250.

SOLUTION – METHOD B (ASSUMED LOSS)
4.46

Total Cash Available	Total Realisa--tions		Distribution Schedule			
			Total	Ess	Tee	Vee
£	£		£	£	£	£
		Capital Accounts	54,000	39,000	13,000	2,000
		Current Accounts	600	700	(300)	200
		(1) Total	54,600	39,700	12,700	2,200
		Profit Sharing ratio	5	2	2	1
			£	£	£	£
		(2) Total Assets	59,600			
2,100	2,100	Bank balance				
600	600	Realisation Oct 10				
900	900	Oct 31				
–	100	Creditors discount				
		Settlement				
(2,900)		creditors (net)				
(700)		loan (Tee) (part)				
1,800	1,800	Realisations Nov 11				
		Settlement				
(1,300)		loan (Tee) (Balance)				
	5,500	(3) Net Realisations	5,500			
		(4) Assumed loss				
		(2) – (3)	(54,100)	(21,640)	(21,640)	(10,820)
500		(5) Total distributable				
		(1) – (4)	500	18,060	(8,940)	(8,620)
		(6) Transfer to assumed				
		solvent partners	–	(17,560)	8,940	8,620
		(7) **1st Distribution**	500	500	–	–

28

Total Cash Available	Total Realisa -tions			Distribution Schedule			
				Total	Ess	Tee	Vee
£	£			£	£	£	£
31,000	31,000		Realisation Jan 26				
	36,500	(8)	Net Realisations	36,500			
		(9)	Assumed loss				
			(2) – (8)	(23,100)	(9,240)	(9,240)	(4,620)
31,500		(10)	Total distributable				
			(1) – (9)	31,500	30,460	3,460	(2,420)
		(11)	Transfer to assumed solvent partners in capital ratio	–	(1,815)	(605)	2,420
		(12)	(10) ± (11)	31,500	28,645	2,855	–
		(13)	less previous distributions (7)	500	500	–	–
		(14)	2nd Distribution	31,000	28,145	2,855	–
(800)	(800)		Costs				
8,900	8,900	(15)	Realisations Feb 23				
	44,600	(16)	Net realisations	44,600			
		(17)	Actual loss				
			(2) – (16)	(15,000)	(6,000)	(6,000)	(3,000)
39,600		(18)	Total distributable				
			(1) – (17)	39,600	33,700	6,700	(800)
		(19)	Transfer to solvent partners in capital ratio	–	(600)	(200)	800
		(20)	(18) ± (19)	39,600	33,100	6,500	–
		(21)	less previous distributions (12)	31,500	28,645	2,855	–
		(22)	**Final distribution**	8,100	4,455	3,655	–

Note: By comparison with the distributions under Method A in 4.45, the total amount of each of the three distributions is identical, but the sums received by each of the partners in the interim are different.

STUDENT SELF TESTING
Test Exercises

1. Robert and Marjorie jointly held the entire share capital of Independent Caterers Ltd. It was resolved that the company should go into voluntary liquidation but that they should acquire the assets, take over responsibility for the liabilities, and continue the business as a partnership, to be known as Kwikfoodz, sharing profits and losses equally.

The balance sheet of the company at liquidation date was:

Independent Caterers Ltd
Balance Sheet as at 31 December 19–4

	£ Cost	£ Depreciation	£ Net
Fixed Assets			
Premises	37,000	3,000	34,000
Equipment	18,700	7,400	11,300
Vehicles	11,600	6,900	4,700
	67,300	17,300	50,000

Current Assets

Stock	8,200	
Debtors	9,100	
Bank and Cash	3,400	
	20,700	

Current Liabilities

Creditors	7,600	

Working Capital 13,100

Net Assets Employed 63,100

Financed by:

Share Capital

Ordinary shares of £1.00 per share 48,000

Reserves

Profit and loss 5,100

Shareholders' Funds 53,100
Long-term loans 10,000

14% Debentures 63,100

The following values were agreed:

£

Purchase consideration 74,600

Premises	40,000
Equipment	10,000
Stock	7,700

All other assets and liabilities were taken over at book values, except for the 14% debentures which were redeemed from the proceeds of a loan (also at 14% per annum) from Robert to the partnership. Robert's capital was agreed at £30,000 and Marjorie's at £25,000. Any sum then required was to be provided by Robert as a 5% per annum loan to the partnership.

Required:

Prepare the balance sheet of Kwikfoodz immediately after the partnership has been formed on 1 January 19-5.

2. Two sole traders, Denman and Norton, agreed to amalgamate their businesses to form a partnership, to be called Radford Suppliers, with effect from 1 January 19-5.

Their separate balance sheets disclosed:

Balance Sheets
as at 31 December 19—4

Denman			Norton	
£	£		£	£
		Fixed assets (at written down values)		
22,000		Shop premises	29,000	
6,800		Equipment	9,200	
3,600		Fittings and fixtures	4,100	
	32,400			42,300
		Current assets		
5,400		Stock	8,000	
700		Debtors	1,100	
1,300		Bank and cash	1,500	
7,400			10,600	

		less		
		Current liabilities		
2,900		Creditors	4,500	
–		Bank Overdraft	2,200	
2,900			6,700	
	4,500	**Working capital**		3,900
	36,900	**Net assets employed**		46,200
		Financed by		
	30,900	Capital		46,200
	6,000	Loan from Hartley		–
	36,900			46,200

The assets and liabilities of the two parties were revalued as part of the amalgamation procedure and the following figures were agreed:

	Denman	**Norton**
	£	£
Premises	40,000	50,000
Equipment		8,800
Fittings and fixtures	7,600	
Stock	5,100	7,600
Debtors	600	900

All other assets were taken over by Radford Suppliers at book values.

Denman agreed to pay creditors amounting to £1,200 out of his private resources. The partnership assumed responsibility for the remainder and for the loan from Hartley.

Norton settled the bank overdraft privately.

It was agreed that the capital of Radford Suppliers should be subscribed by Denman, 2/3rds and by Norton 1/3rd.

Required:

Prepare the balance sheet of Radford Suppliers immediately after the amalgamation has taken place.

3. The firm of Trafalgar Traders consisted of three partners, Birkin, Palin and Ortzen who shared profits and losses in the ratio 1/3, 1/2 and 1/6 respectively.

From 1 October 19–5 Palin acquired other business interests which left him with less time to devote to partnership matters. It was mutually agreed that there should be a general re-arrangement of duties between the partners, accompanied by a change in the sharing ratios to reflect these new arrangements. The new ratios were to be Birkin 1/2, Palin 1/4 and Ortzen 1/4.

On the occasion of the change, goodwill, which had not previously been brought into account was valued at £18,000.

Partners capital account balances had remained static since inception at

	£
Palin	15,000
Birkin	12,000
Ortzen	10,000

Required:

Post the entries necessary in the capital accounts to introduce, and then to write back, goodwill.

4. The outline balance sheet of Scanlon, Wimbourne and Guthrie trading as Bentinck Merchants on 31 March 19–5 was:

Bentinck Merchants
Balance Sheet as at 31 March 19–5

	£	£
Fixed assets (at written down values)		
Premises	39,000	
Equipment	7,200	
Fixtures and fittings	8,100	
		45,300

Current assets		
Stock	17,800	
Debtors	4,300	
Cash	1,100	
	23,200	
Less		
Current Liabilities		
Creditors	6,400	
Bank overdraft	9,700	
	16,100	
Working capital		7,100
Net assets employed		52,400
Financed by		
Capital		
Scanlon	20,000	
Wimbourne	20,000	
Guthrie	10,000	
		50,000
Current accounts		
Scanlon	3,600	
Wimbourne	(2,100)	
Guthrie	900	
		2,400
		52,400

Up to this date the partners had shared profits and losses equally. It had been agreed, however, that from 1 April 19–5 this would change to Scanlon 1/2, Wimbourne 1/3, Guthrie 1/6. At the same time the assets were revalued at the following amounts:

	£
Premises	55,000
Equipment	6,000
Fixtures & fittings	8,000
Stock	16,500
Debtors	4,100
Goodwill	12,000

Required:

Prepare the Revaluation and Capital accounts and balance sheet on the assumption that the above revaluations are to be retained in the books of Bentinck Merchants.

5. The facts are as in 4. The partners subsequently decide that goodwill is not to be retained in the books.

Required:

Prepare the Capital accounts of the partners to show the write off of goodwill.

6. Redoubt and Company is about to admit more partners to enable the firm's business to be expanded. The partners have decided that goodwill is to be raised as part of the revaluation process and are considering three different methods of calculating it:

a. On the basis of two years' purchase of the average profits over the last five consecutive years. These were

Year	£
19–1	36,000
19–2	28,000
19–3	26,000
19–4	38,000
19–5	46,000

b. On the basis of three years' purchase of the super-profits of the last five years. For this purpose the normal profits are to be taken as £30,000 per annum.

c. On the basis of the formula $\frac{P - rA}{m}$

where P = £60,000

r = 20%

A = £200,000

m = 25%

Required:

Calculate goodwill on the basis of each of the three methods (a) to (c) above.

7. On 30 April 19–5, the outline balance sheet of Lonsdale, Foster and Garfield in partnership sharing profits and losses equally, was

Balance Sheet as at 30 April 19–5

	£	£
Fixed Assets at written down values		
Premises	40,000	
Equipment	18,000	
Vehicles	15,000	
		73,000
Current assets		
Stock	19,000	
Debtors	14,000	
Bank and Cash	2,000	
	35,000	
Current liabilities		
Creditors	16,000	
Bank overdraft	15,000	
	31,000	
Working capital		4,000
Net assets employed		77,000
Financed by:		
Capital		
Lonsdale	32,000	
Foster	28,000	
Garfield	16,000	
		76,000
Current accounts		
Lonsdale	700	
Foster	1,200	
Garfield	(900)	
		1,000
		77,000

On that date the partnership was converted into a limited company, Delign Ltd. The agreed consideration was £83,000 to be discharged by a payment to the partners of £18,000 and by the issue of 50,000 ordinary shares of £1.00 per share at a premium of 30% fully paid. The shares were taken up by Lonsdale, 20,000 shares, Foster, 20,000 shares and Garfield 20,000 shares.

Required:

Prepare the Realisation, Delign Ltd and Capital accounts of the partnership to record the conversion.

8. The facts are as in 7. On conversion Delign Ltd revalued assets as follows:

	£
Premises	46,000
Equipment	16,000
Stock	17,000

The former partners then acquired additional shares for cash (at a premium of 30%) as follows:

	No.
Lonsdale	10,000
Foster	10,000
Garfield	20,000

The company then settled the outstanding liability of the overdraft.

Required:

Prepare the balance sheet of Delign Ltd immediately after the above arrangements had been effected.

9. The facts are as in 7, except that on 30 April 19–5, the partnership was dissolved and the assets sold publicly as follows:

	£
Premises	60,000
Equipment	13,000
Vehicles	5,000
Stock	14,500

Debtors realised £13,600. Creditors were settled in full and the bank overdraft was repaid.

Lonsdale personally took over a vehicle at a valuation of £7,000 and Foster a vehicle at a valuation of £3,500.

Dissolution expenses amounting to £1,000 were paid.

Required:

Prepare the Realisation, Bank and Capital accounts to record the dissolution.

10. Bridport, Chesil and Medway had been in partnership for many years as Canterbury Suppliers and shared profits and losses in the ratio of 1 : 2 : 2. Their respective capitals were:

	£
Bridport	10,000
Chesil	10,000
Medway	2,000

The partners decided to dissolve the partnership after a succession of losses following a fall off in demand.

On dissolution there was a loss of £15,000 to be shared between the partners. Medway was insolvent and unable to contribute anything towards his deficiency which had to be borne by his co–partners.

Required:

Prepare the partners' capital accounts to record the above matters.

11. On 1st January 19–8 the partners of Gee and Co and Bee & Co agreed to amalgamate their business. The new firm is to be called Beegee & Co. The initial capital of £18,000 is to be shared as to one half by the partners of Gee & Co and one half by the partners of Bee & Co.

The division of the one half share to the individual partners is to be in the ratio of their capital in the former partnerships. Any adjustments in the old partnerships are to be made personally between the partners. The balance sheets on 31st December 19–7 showed the following position:

	Gee & Co			Bee & Co	
	£	£		£	£
Capital Accounts					
Alan	4,000		Desmond	4,000	
Brian	3,000		Ernest	2,000	
Colin	2,000				
		9,000			6,000
Current Accounts					
Alan	800		Desmond	1,350	
Brian	620		Ernest	1,250	
Colin	180				
		1,600			2,600
Creditors		900			1,100
		11,500			9,700

Fixed Assets				
Goodwill	1,500		1,750	
Fixtures &fittings	1,250		1,000	
		2,750		2,750
Current Assets				
Debtors	7,000		6,000	
Work in progress	900		750	
Cash	850		200	
		8,750		6,950
		11,500		9,700

For the purposes of the amalgamation it was agreed as follows:

1. Goodwill in the new firm is to be £4,000
2. Fixtures and fittings are to be taken over from Gee & Co at a value of £600 and from Bee & Co at a value of £500
3. Debtors are to be taken over at the amounts shown in the old firms' balance sheets on 31st December 19–7 less a discount of 5%. Work in progress is to be valued at 10% of the net debtors taken over. Responsibility for the creditors of both firms is to be assumed by the new firm.
4. The balance required for the initial capital is to be provided in cash.
5. All partners in the new firm are to receive a salary at the rate of £4,000 per annum, interest on capital at 8% per annum, and share in the balance of profits/losses in proportion to their capital in the firm. No interest is to be given on current accounts.
6. The only drawings by each partner against his share of the profits were monthly payments of £300 and an additional payment equal to 5% of his capital at the end of each quarter.

On 1st October 19–8 Desmond was killed in a motor accident. A repayment of capital amounting to £1,000 was made immediately to his estate but no further payments were made in 19–8. Interest on the outstanding capital account was agreed at 10% per annum. No adjustments were made to the remaining partners' capital accounts and the profit sharing ratios between the individual partners did not change.

Profits for the year ended 31st December 19–8 amounted to £37,472.

You are required to prepare:

a. the initial balance sheet of Beegee & Co immediately after the amalgamation, and
b. partners' current accounts in columnar form for the year ended 31st December 19–8

12. Hook and Line held the entire share capital of Sinker Ltd between them, Hook holding 75,000 shares and Line 25,000 shares. They decided to cease trading as a company, but to continue as a partnership, taking over the assets and liabilities of the company at book value, and to share profits in the same ratio as they enjoyed previously, and also to continue to use the same books of account. This new arrangement was to take effect from the end of the company's accounting period, ie 30 September 19–4. A balance sheet prepared as of that date revealed the following position:

Sinker Ltd Balance Sheet as of 30 September 19–4

	Cost	Acc.Depn.	
	£	£	£
Fixed Assets			
Freehold land and buildings	50,000	–	50,000
Plant and equipment	65,000	25,000	40,000
Motor vehicles	15,000	5,000	10,000
	130,000	30,000	100,000
Current Assets			
Stock		45,000	
Debtors		35,000	
Bank		5,000	
		85,000	

Less: Current Liabilities			
Creditors		25,000	
			60,000
			160,000
Financed by:			
Share capital and reserves			
Share capital			
Authorised, issued and fully paid			
Ordinary shares of £1 each			100,000
Reserves			
Share premium		10,000	
Profit and loss account		30,000	
			40,000
			140,000
Long-term liabilities			
10% debentures (secured)			20,000
			160,000

Fisher was admitted as a partner as from 1 April 19– 5, paying in cash £30,000 in payment for a one-fifth interest in the partnership, Hook and Line continuing to participate in the remainder in the same ratio as previously. For the purpose of the admittance of Fisher as a partner, goodwill was valued at £20,000 and freehold land and buildings at £80,000 but neither of these transactions had as yet been recorded in the books.

A Trial Balance prepared as of 30 September 19–5, showed the following:

Trial Balance as of 30 September 19–5

	£	£
Freehold land and buildings at cost	50,000	
Plant and equipment at cost	95,000	
Accumulated depreciation		
– 1 October 19–4		25,000
Motor vehicles at cost	25,000	
Accumulated depreciation		
– 1 October 19–4		5,000
Stock – 1 October 19–4	45,000	
Creditors/Debtors	50,000	30,000
Share Capital		100,000
Share premium account		10,000
Profit and loss account		
– 1 October 19–4		30,000
Purchase/Sales	400,000	600,000
Administrative expense	65,000	
Selling expense	50,000	
Capital – Fisher		30,000
Distribution expense	25,000	
Financial expense	1,000	
Life assurance premiums on partners' lives	10,000	
Bank	14,000	
	830,000	830,000

Additional information

1. Stock at 30 September 19–5 was valued at £50,000
2. Depreciation rates:

Plant and equipment	10%	on cost
Motor vehicles	20%	

3. Salaries were allotted to the partners as follows:

Hook	£10,000 per annum
Line	5,000 per annum
Fisher	5,000 per annum

4. The life assurance policies at 30 September 19–5 had a surrender value of £11,000
5. The partnership was to trade under the same Sinker
6. Assume that revenue and expenditure accrues evenly throughout the year.

Required:

a. Prepare the trading and profit and loss account for the partnership for the year ended 30 September 19–5; and

b. prepare a balance sheet as at that date.

(ACCA)

13. Reg, Sam and Ted are in partnership, sharing profits and losses equally. Interest on capital and partnership salaries is not provided. The position of the business at the end of its financial year is:

Balance Sheet 30 June 19–6

	£	£		£	£
CapitalAccounts:			Buildings		17,000
Reg	9,000		Equipment		3,300
Sam	8,000		Stock		900
Ted	8,000		Debtors		2,020
		25,000	Bank		2,840
Current Accounts:					
Reg	140				
Sam	200				
	340				
Ted (debit)	100				
		240			
Creditors		820			
		26,060			26,060

Reg died suddenly on 31 October 19–6.

The partnership agreement provides that in the event of the death of a partner the sum to be paid to his estate will be the amount of his capital and current account balances at the last financial year-end adjusted by his share of profit or loss since that date together with his share of goodwill. A formula for calculation of goodwill is given, and its application produced a figure of £7,500. No goodwill account is to remain in the books after any change of the partnership constitution.

The stock value at 31 October has been calculated and all other accounts balanced off, including provisions for depreciation, accrued expenses and prepaid expenses. This results in the following position at 31 October.

	£
Buildings	17,000
Equipment (including additions of £400)	3,480
Stock	1,100
Debtors	2,230
Bank balance	3,370
Creditors	980

There were no additions to, or reductions of, the capital accounts during the four months, but the following drawings have been made:

Reg	£2,000
Sam	£1,600
Ted	£1,800

It has also been agreed that the share of a deceased partner should be repaid in three equal instalments, the first payment being made as on the day after the day of death.

The surviving partners agree that Abe (son of Reg) should be admitted as a new partner with effect from 1 November, and it is agreed that he will bring into the business £4,000 as his capital together with a premium for his share of the goodwill (using the existing valuation). The new profit-sharing agreement is: Sam, two-fifths; Ted, two-fifths; and Abe one-fifth.

Required:

a. Show the partnership Balance Sheet as at 1 November 19–6, on the assumption that the above transactions have been completed by that date.

b. Abe has proposed that the new agreement should allow for payment of life assurance premiums for a survivorship policy so that a depletion of funds available to the firm does not occur. Briefly outline how you would deal with this in the accounts.

(ACCA)

14. Jim and Ken have been trading in partnership for several years, sharing profits or losses equally after allowing for interest on their capitals at 8% p.a. At 1 September 19–7 their manager, Len, was admitted as a partner and was to have a one-fifth share of the profits after interest on capital. Jim and Ken shared the balance equally but guaranteed that Len's share would not fall below £6,000 p.a. Len was not required to introduce any capital at the date of admission but agreed to retain £1,500 of his profit share at the end of each year to be credited to his capital account until the balance reached £7,500. Until that time no interest was to be allowed on his capital. Goodwill, calculated as a percentage of the profits of the last five years was agreed at £15,000 at 1 September 19–7, and Len paid into the business sufficient cash for his share. No goodwill account was to be left in the books. Land and buildings were professionally valued at the same date at £28,400 and this figure was to be brought into the books, whilst the book value of the equipment and vehicles was, by mutual agreement, to be reduced to £15,000 at that date. Len had previously been entitled to a bonus of 5% of the gross profit payable half-yearly: the bonus together with his manager's salary were to cease when he became a partner. It was agreed to take out a survivorship policy and the first premium of £1,000 was paid on 1 September 19–7.

The trial balance at the end of the 19–7 financial year is given below. No adjustments had yet been made in respect of Len's admission, and the amount he introduced for goodwill had been put into his current account. The drawings of all the partners have been charged to their current accounts.

It can be assumed that the gross profit and trading expenses accrued evenly throughout the year. Depreciation on the equipment and vehicles is to be charged at 20% p.a. on the book value.

	£	£
Capital accounts Jim		30,000
Ken		15,000
Current accounts Jim	7,800	
Ken	7,100	
Len		1,800
Land and buildings	18,000	
Equipment and vehicles	21,000	
Stock	9,200	
Gross profit		42,000
Trading expenses	15,000	
Manager's salary	4,000	
Manager's bonus	1,050	
Debtors and creditors	4,850	3,100
Premium and survivorship policy	1,000	
Bank Balance	2,900	
	91,900	91,900

Required:

a. Prepare the Profit and Loss account and the partners' capital and current accounts for the year ended 31 December 19–7, and a Balance Sheet at that date.

b. Briefly explain why the goodwill payment was made and comment on the method of valuation.

c. Justify your treatment of the insurance premium and contrast it with an alternative method which might have been used.

(ACCA)

15. Pigg and Boar have been in partnership for several years, and for the last 10 years Lamb has successfully managed the manufacturing side of the business for them. On 1 January 19–6, the partners decide to admit Lamb to the partnership, with Lamb receiving a one-fifth share of the profits and Pigg and Boar sharing the remainder equally. For the purpose of the admission of Lamb into the firm, it is agreed that the book value of the net tangible assets is a reasonable representation of their value, but it is agreed that a valuation be made of goodwill and that this be recorded in the books, and shared equally between Pigg and Boar.

For the purposes of the valuation, it is agreed that past profits will not be a satisfactory basis on which to value goodwill and that projected future profits will give better results.

A balance sheet prepared as of 31 December 19–5, revealed the following position:

Pigg and Boar
Balance Sheet as at 31 December 19–5

	£ Copt	£ Acc.Depn.	£
Fixed Assets			
Land and buildings	50,000	–	50,000
Plant and equipment	75,000	25,000	50,000
Fixtures and fittings	15,000	5,000	10,000
Motor vehicles	25,000	12,500	12,500
	165,000	42,500	122,500
Current Assets			
Stock in trade		35,000	
Debtors		27,000	
Prepayment		1,000	
Bank		15,500	
		78,500	
Less: Current Liabilities			
Creditors – Trade	21,000		
– Expense	2,000		
		23,000	
			55,500
			178,000

	£	£
Financed by:		
Capital Accounts:		
Pigg		50,000
Boar		50,000
		100,000
Current Accounts:		
Pigg		48,000
Boar		30,000
		78,000
		178,000

Additional information.

1. Forecast profits for the next five years average £85,000 per annum.

2. Partners' salaries per annum for the next five years are expected to be: Pigg £10,000; Boar £10,000, and Lamb £5,000.

3. The expected rate of return before taxation for each of the five years is estimated to be 16%.

4. The risk factor is assessed at 4%.

Required:

a. Compute the valuation of goodwill under two methods; and

b. Comment on the problem of the valuation of goodwill, with particular reference to the methods used in a. and the answers obtained.

(ACCA)

16. Yew, May and Holly have been in partnership for a number of years sharing profits in the ratio 6:5:3. Work in progress was not brought into the accounts.

The balance sheet of the partnership as on 31st March 19–6 showed the following position:

	£		£	£
Capital accounts:		Fixed assets		22,400
Yew	25,000	Goodwill		12,950
May	18,000	Current assets		
Holly	8,700	Debtors	73,500	
		Balance at bank	10,450	
Sundry creditors	67,600			83,950
	119,300			119,300

On 31st March 19–6 Yew retired from the partnership and it was agreed to admit Oak as a partner on the following terms:

1. Goodwill in the old partnership was to be revalued to two years purchase of the average profits over the last three years. The profits of the last three years have been £12,400, £13,600 and £14,005. Goodwill was to be written off in the new partnership.

2. Yew to take his car out of the partnership assets at an agreed value of £1,000. The car had been included in the accounts as on 31st March 19–6 at a written down value of £594.

3. Although work in progress had not been and will not be included in the partnership accounts the new partners were to credit Yew with his share based on an estimate that work in progress was equivalent to 20% of the debtors.

4. The new partnership of May, Holly and Oak were to share profits in the ratio 5 : 3 : 2. The initial capital to be £25,000 subscribed in the profit sharing ratios.

5. May, Holly and Oak were each to pay to Yew the sum of £5,000 out of their personal resources in part repayment of his share of the partnership.

6. Yew to lend to Oak any amount required to make up his capital in the firm from the monies due to him, and any further balance due to Yew was to be left in the new partnership as a loan, bearing interest at 9% per annum. Any adjustments required to the capital accounts of May and Holly were to be paid into or withdrawn from the partnership bank account.

You are required to prepare:

a. the capital accounts, in columnar form, of the partners reflecting the adjustments required on the change in partnership, and

b. a balance sheet on completion

17. Prince, Senior and Clarke have been trading in partnership for several years, sharing profits and losses in the ratio of 4 : 3 : 1 respectively.

They have decided to convert the business into a limited company (Priorark Ltd) as from 1 December 19– 7. The balance sheet immediately prior to this is shown below:

Balance sheet 30 November 19–7

	Prince	Senior	Clarke	Total
	£	£	£	£
Capital account	12,00	8,000	6,000	26,000
Current account	520	640	280	1,440
Loan	2,000	–	–	2,000
				29,440

	£
Freehold buildings	12,000
Vehicles (cost £6,000 less depreciation)	4,800
Equipment (cost £4,000 less depreciation)	2,500
Stock	6,125
Debtors (£5,015 less provision)	4,815
Bank Balance	2,200
	32,440
Less Creditors	3,000
	29,440

All of the assets except for the cash and one vehicle are to be transferred to the company and, by agreement with the creditors, the company will become liable to settle their accounts. One of the two cars is to be taken over by Clarke personally at a valuation of £2,000. The purchase consideration as follows:

		£
Freehold buildings		23,000
Vehicle		2,400
Equipment		1,600
Stock		4,000
Debtors		4,600
Goodwill		8,000
		43,600
Less Creditors		3,000
		40,600

The company is to issue fully paid 20p ordinary shares at a premium of 5p per share to meet the whole of the purchase consideration, and will be issuing further shares for cash.

Required:

a. Make all the relevant entries to close off the books of the partnership on the assumption that transactions are completed on 1 December 19–7. Ignore realisation expenses. Make your own assumptions about how the shares would be distributed. The original asset and liability accounts (except for Bank) do not need to be shown. Indicate how many shares each partner will receive.

b. Briefly justify your allocation of the shares.

(ACCA)

18. Abe and Bob have been trading in partnership for several years, sharing profits and losses three–fifths and two–fifths respectively after allowing for 5% p.a. interest on capital. A summary of the balance sheet at 31 December 19–7 shows:

	£	£
Land and buildings (at cost)	24,800	
Less: Outstanding mortgage with building society	9,110	
		15,690
Equipment		14,200
Net current assets		12,110
Capital (Abe £30,000; Bob £12,000)		42,000

They decide to convert the business into a limited company with effect from 1 January 19–8, and to raise finance from friends and relatives, partly to release some of their own capital and also to ensure a continuity as they get older. The company, Abob & Co Ltd, is to have an issued share capital of 40,000 £1 ordinary shares. Of these, 15,000 are issued at par to Abe, and 6,000 to Bob, and the partners are also to receive cash from the company totalling £36,000 in settlement of the purchase consideration. The balance of the shares are issued at par for cash on 1 January 19–8 and the company also issues £20,000 10% debenture stock fully paid for cash on the same date.

The purchase consideration is for all of the assets and liabilities of the partnership and was calculated after estimating that the land and buildings should be revalued at £32,000, and that a general provision of £200 should be made for doubtful debts. Abe and Bob are to get salaries of £6,000 and £4,000 respectively, and directors' fees of £500 each.

At 31 December 19–8 the accounts had not yet been adjusted for the change of proprietorship, nor for the revaluations but the cash of £36,000 had been paid to the partners. A trial balance showed:

	£	£
Gross profit for year		48,400
Stock	16,310	
Selling and administration expenses	24,760	
Directors' salaries	10,000	
Formation expenses	600	
Capital accounts: Abe and Bob		6,000
Debtors and creditors	9,480	6,630
Payments to building society (including £300 interest)	910	
Cash from other shareholders and debenture holders		39,000
Land and buildings	15,690	
Equipment (net of depreciation)	11,360	

41

Depreciation			2,840
Bank			8,080
		100,030	100,030

(Of the debts receivable at 1 January, all had paid in full except for one of £80 which is now regarded as irrecoverable).

Required:

a. prepare the company's Profit and Loss Account for the year ended 31 December 19–8, and a Balance Sheet at that date, making adjustments and provisions as you think necessary. (Ignore taxation).

b. If the company had been formed to take over the partnership from 1 January 19–8 but had not been incorporated until 1 March 19–8, how would this have affected your answer to a.?

c. Calculate the amount of cash which Abe and Bob should have received respectively from the total of £36,000.

d. Briefly comment on the allocation of shares to Abe and Bob.

(ACCA)

19. On 31st December 19–7 Fairway Ltd was incorporated with an authorised share capital of £100,000 in shares of £1 each to take over the business carried on at that date by the partnership of Par, Green and Bogey.

The balance sheet of the partnership on 31st December 19–7, showed the following position:

	Par £	Green £	Bogey £	£
Capital accounts	24,000	18,000	15,000	57,000
Current accounts:				
Balances as on 31st December 19–6	11,940	8,480	6,000	
Add: Interest on capital accounts	720	540	450	
Share of profit for year	6,126	6,126	4,084	
	18,786	15,146	10,534	
Less: Drawings	8,926	8,726	4,064	
	9,860	6,420	6,470	22,750
				79,750

Represented by:

	Cost £	Depreciation £	£
Fixed Assets			
Freehold land and buildings	26,000	–	26,000
Plant and machinery	42,000	22,000	20,000
Motor vehicles	19,700	4,700	15,000
	87,700	26,700	61,000
Current Assets			
Stocks		22,400	
Debtors		12,200	
Balance at Bank		19,750	
		54,350	
Less: Creditors		35,600	
			18,750
			79,750

You are also given the following information:

1. Freehold land and buildings are to be transferred to the limited company at a valuation of £30,000 and plant and machinery at £15,000. Stocks, debtors and creditors are to be transferred to the company at book value as on 31st December 19–7.

2. The motor vehicles are to be withdrawn from the business by the partners at the following valuations: Par £4,900, Green £3,500 and Bogey £3,600.

3. It is estimated that the company will require an opening balance at bank of £15,000.

4. Sufficient 9% Unsecured loan stock is to be issued by the company to the partners so that they will receive the same interest as they received on capital in the partnership for the year ended 31st December 19–7.

5. Ordinary shares are to be issued at par to each partner in proportion to their share in the partnership profits.

6. Any surplus or deficiency on partners' accounts on realisation after taking into account loan stock and shares issued is to be withdrawn or paid in, whichever the case may be.

You are required to prepare:

a. Your computation of the shares and loan stock in Fairway Ltd to be issued to each partner,

b. partners' accounts in columnar form, showing all the necessary entries to dissolve the partnership, and

c. a Balance Sheet of the company upon completion

20. Earl, Baron and Knight have been partners for 15 years sharing profits and losses in a 2 : 2 : 1 ratio. Accounts have been prepared on an annual basis to 31st December of each year. Earl, the only active partner, died on 31st October, 19–4, and the remaining partners decided to cease business from that date. The assets are to be realised, outstanding debts paid and the remainder is to be shared by the partners (including the executor for Earl's estate) in an equitable manner, distributions of cash being made as soon as possible.

A balance sheet prepared as of 31st October 19–4, revealed the following position.

Earl, Baron and Knight
Balance Sheet as of 31st October 19–4

	£ Cost	£ Acc.Depn.	£
Fixed Assets			
Goodwill	50,000	–	50,000
Freehold Land and Buildings	75,000	–	75,000
Plant and Machinery	66,500	27,900	38,600
Fixtures and Fittings	15,000	6,500	8,500
Motor Vehicles	16,000	12,000	4,000
	222,500	46,400	176,100
Current Assets			
Stock		32,000	
Debtors	32,500		
Less: Provision for doubtful debts	3,000		
		29,500	
Cash		80	
		61,580	
Less: **Current Liabilities**			
Creditors	28,500		
Bank Overdraft	64,180		
		92,680	
		(31,100)	
		145,000	
Financed by:			
Capital Accounts			
Earl		50,000	
Baron		30,000	
Knight		20,000	
		100,000	
Current Accounts			
Earl		20,000	
Baron		15,000	

		35,000
		135,000

Long-term Liabilities

Loan – Earl · 10,000

145,000

Additional information

1. Premiums have been paid on life assurance policies for each partner to provide the firm with cash funds on death. The premiums have been charged to insurance expense, and the cash sum payable on the death of any partner is £20,000.

2. The assets were duly sold and monies received as follows:

19–4		£
November 14	Life policy on Earl's life	20,000
	Life policies on the lives of Baron and Knight surrendered for	10,000
December 16	Freehold land and buildings	100,000
	Debtors (part)	15,000
	Stock (part)	10,000
19–5		
January 20	Plant and Machinery	25,500
	Fixtures and Fittings	6,000
	Motor Vehicles	2,500
March 15	Stock (remainder)	18,000
	Debtors (remainder)	21,000

3. Provision was made for dissolution expenses of £1,200.

4. As soon as sufficient money was available to pay all outstanding creditors, this was done, discounts being received amounting to £500.

5. Dissolution expenses amounted to £1,000 and these were paid on 31st March 19–5.

Required: From information given, prepare;

a. Statements showing how the proceeds of the dissolution would be shared between the partners; and

b. The realisation account, and capital account.
(ACCA)

21. Penn, Fyle and Roole have been in partnership for a number of years, sharing profits/losses in the ratio 5 : 3 : 2, as wholesale stationers trading under the name of Foolscap & Company.

They decided to convert their partnership into a limited company (with effect from 1st January 19–1) to be known as Afour Ltd.

Immediately prior to this conversion, the balance sheet of the partnership as at 31st December 19–0 disclosed the following figures.

	£	£	£
Fixed Assets (at written down values)			
Premises		40,000	
Equipment		25,000	
Vehicles		15,000	
			80,000
Current Assets			
Stocks		70,000	
Debtors		25,000	
Bank (No.1 Account)		6,000	
		101,000	
Less Current Liabilities			
Creditors	21,000		
Bank (No.2 Account)	16,000		
		37,000	
			64,000
Net Assets			144,000

	Capital Account £	Current Account £	
Capital and Current Accounts			
Penn	80,000	5,000	
Fyle	30,000	2,000	
Roole	10,000	3,000	
	120,000		120,000
		10,000	10,000
Long Term Liabilities			
Loan – Penn	4,000		
Loan – Small Businesses (Financings) Ltd	10,000		
		14,000	
		144,000	

The terms of the conversion are that Afour Ltd is to take over the assets and liabilities of Foolscap and Company as follows:

	Valuation for Takeover £
Premises	90,000
Equipment	20,000
Vehicles	8,000
Stocks	70,000
Debtors	24,000
Bank (No.2 Account)	(see below)
Creditors	21,000
Goodwill	7,000

The closing balance on Bank (No.1 Account) is to be transferred to Bank (No.2 Account) before all the other dissolution entries are effected in the partnership ledgers.

Fyle took over one of the partnership cars at an agreed figure of £1,500. All other liabilities were paid from the Bank (No.2 Account).

The purchase consideration is discharged by an issue at par of £48,000 11% Debentures (fully paid) to the partners in their capital account proportions as shown in the above balance sheet, plus 432,000 ordinary shares in Afour Ltd of £0.25 per share (fully paid) to make up the balance due to each partner.

Required:

i. Prepare the closing entries in the ledger of Foolscap & Company for the following accounts only:

> Realisation
> Capital
> Afour Ltd.
> Bank (No.1 Account)
> Bank (No.2 Account)

ii. Prepare the Business Purchase and Foolscap & Company's accounts in Afour Ltd's ledger.

22. In 19–9 Kristle and Borle founded a business consultancy partnership, registered as Askham & Co. Within a few years the practice grew to the point where it was necessary to appoint a member of staff at senior level.

Forsyte was appointed in 19–3 with special responsibility for developing the taxation planning services offered by the partnership and was told at the interview that he would be admitted as a partner after five years if he succeeded in doing this.

As time went by, the partners became highly satisfied with the manner in which Forsyte performed his duties and decided to admit him as a partner from the beginning of the financial year 1st October 19–8.

Up to that point the partners had shared profits and losses equally but Borle wanted to devote more time to other business interests and so it was decided that the new ratios would be:– Kristle 1/2, Borle 1/3, Forsyte 1/6.

On 30th September, 19–8, the summarised Balance Sheet disclosed:–

Askham & Co Balance Sheet (Summarised)
as at 30th September 19-8

	£	£
Fixed Assets (at written down values)		
Premises	25,000	
Cars	4,100	
Office Furniture and equipment	4,260	
		33,360
Net Current Assets		2,420
		35,780
Financed by		
Capital – Kristle	17,000	
– Borle	17,000	
		34,000
Current Accounts		
– Kristle	950	
– Borle	830	
		1,780
		35,780

The following matters were agreed for the purposes of the change in constitution on 1st October, 19-8:

1. Premises to be revalued at £40,000 but Premises Account to remain undisturbed.

2. Goodwill to be valued on the basis of three years purchase of the average annual super profits forecast for the next five years.

	Estimated net profit (before appropriations)
Year	£000
19-9	30
19-0	34
19-1	36
19-2	39
19-3	41

Average annual profits for the same period for a business of that type have been estimated at £28,000. An account for goodwill is not to be opened.

3. Kristle is to take over one of the partnership cars, to give to his wife, at its written down value of £1,500. The partnership is then to acquire two new cars, costing £3,800 each, on the same day, 1st October, 19-8.

4. Forsyte's capital contribution has been fixed at £10,000 but he is able to pay only £8,000 on admission.

5. To finance the expansion of the business, Kristle is to lend the new firm £7,000 at the interest rate prescribed by section 24, Partnership Act, 1890.

6. Kristle is to receive a partnership salary of £2,520 per annum and all partners are to receive interest on capital at 6% per annum.

7. In the first year after Forsyte's admission, all partners are to restrict their drawings to the partnership salary (if any) plus 60% of the residual profits, except that Forsyte is not to make any drawings until he has built up the agreed balance on his capital account by transfer from his current account.
Taxation is to be ignored.

Required:

On the basis of the information supplied, prepare:–

a. a balance sheet for the new firm, immediately after Forsyte's admission on 1st October, 19-8.

b. estimated appropriation and partners' current accounts for year ended 30th September, 19-9.

23. Richards, Gower and Border were in partnership under the name of Bab & Co., sharing profits and losses in the proportions Richards 3: Gower 2: Border 1.

The following credit balances appeared in the firm's Balance Sheet as at 30th June 19–5:–

	Richards	Gower	Border
	£	£	£
Capitals	108,000	72,000	36,000
Current Accounts	7,200	7,500	4,800

Interest at the rate of 5% p.a. on capital was credited to partners' current accounts. No interest was charged on drawings.

Gower was paid a salary of £600 per month.

The partnership agreement provided that, on the death of a partner, his personal representative should be entitled to receive, in addition to the sums standing to his credit as shown in the last balance sheet preceding his death as reduced by any subsequent drawings:–

a. Any salary and interest from the date of the last balance sheet to the date of his death;

b. A further 10% p.a. on his capital for the same period in lieu of his share of profits;
   and

c. His share of the total partnership goodwill calculated at 2 years purchase of the average profits (before charging partners' salaries and interest on capital) for the three years ended on the date of the last balance sheet preceding his death.

The balance due to a deceased partner's estate was to be paid in four equal instalments. The first instalment was to be paid one month after death, the other three at six–monthly intervals from that date together with interest at 8% p.a. from the date when the first instalment fell due.

Gower died on 30th November 19–4 and the first two instalments due to his estate were paid on the due dates.

The partnership profits (before charging interest on capital and partners' salaries) were:–

Year to 30th June 19–2 £13,800
Year to 30th June 19–3 £21,000
Year to 30th June 19–4 £30,000
Year to 30th June 19–5 £33,000

Gower's drawings for the five months preceding his death amounted to £3,400. Richards and Border continued to share profits in the same ratio as before.

Required

a. The profit and loss appropriation account for the year ended 30th June 19–5.

b. The account of Gower in the firm's books from 30th June 19–4 to 30th June 19–5.

24. Sam, James and Hester have been in partnership for a number of years. Profits and losses were shared in the ratio of 3 : 4 : 3

On 30 April 19–5 it was decided to dissolve the partnership. The balance sheet at that date showed:

	£
Partners Capital Accounts	
Sam	10,000
James	40,000
Hester	50,000
	100,000
Trade Creditors	25,000
	£125,000
Fixed assets	12,000
Debtors	20,000
Stocks	75,000
Cash	18,000
	£125,000

During the dissolution, the following cash and other transactions arose:

19–5

3 May	Sam agreed to settle a hire purchase debt outstanding on a motor car. The amount was £1,500 and is to be adjusted in his capital account.
3 May	Debtors were assigned to Hester for the agreed sum of £17,500.
3 May	Hester settled one creditor for £750 by giving him one of her private paintings.
3 May	The fixed assets, apart from the car, which had a book value of £2,250 were sold at auction for £8,500. This car is to be taken at book value by Hester. Again adjustment is to be made in her capital account.
1 June	Realisation expenses of £1,750 were paid.
10 June	Cash transfers among partners were completed.
16 June	The remaining creditors were paid.

On 1 May 19–5, James and Hester formed a new partnership by merging with another firm. The partners in the other firm, Jack and Jill, shared profits and losses equally. The new amalgamated firm will be called James & Co and will take over the stocks of both firms.

All parties have agreed the following values for assets which will be taken over:

	James and Hester	Jack and Jill
	£	£
Stocks	42,000	54,000
Furniture	–	6,000
Motor Vehicles	–	10,000
Goodwill	10,500	30,000

The parties also agreed that profits and losses would be shared:

James	–	20%
Hester	–	15%
Jack	–	30%
Jill	–	35%

Capital is to be contributed in the same proportions after allowing £8,000 for working capital. Goodwill is not to appear in any set of books.

Required:

1. Show the accounts closing the books of the Sam, James and Hester partnership.
2. Prepare a Balance Sheet for James & Co as at 1 May 19–5.

ACCA EXAMINATION QUESTIONS

25. Peek, Poke and Basic are three systems analysts who started up in partnership on 1 July 1980 to sell accounting packages to small companies. Poke and Basic introduced capital of £23,000 and £17,000 respectively. Peek was unable to introduce capital. It was agreed that:

a. Profits/Losses should be shared equally.

b. The business would be run for 2 years and if by 30 June 1982 the turnover had not reached £200,000 per annum the partnership would be dissolved.

c. If the turnover reached £200,000 per annum then from 1 July 1983 interest would be allowed on capital at the rate of $12\frac{1}{2}\%$.

In the first year of trading, all three partners were busy generating business and they did not prepare detailed accounts. However, they maintained the customary VAT record and at 30 June 1981 made a brief note of their financial position. This showed:

a. There were shopfittings which had cost £5,000 when installed on 1 July 1980 into their shop premises. These premises were leased for 4 years at a rental of £1,000 per annum. No premium had been paid for the lease. It was decided to write off the fixtures over the term of the lease.

b. There was a stock of accounting packages that had cost £10,375.

c. Customers owed £21,475 (including £2,800 VAT) for packages that had been supplied and were working satisfactorily.

d. Suppliers and freelance programmers were owed £11,250 (including £1,200 VAT).

e. There was a bank overdraft of £1,200 and cash in hand of £450.

f. Each of the partners had withdrawn £4,000 for their living expenses during the year.

Each partner felt slightly depressed that they were running into overdraft and there was a general reluctance to finalise the accounts at 30 June 1981. Consequently they agreed that they would continue with the basic records kept by Mr Peek and have final accounts prepared at 30 June 1982 when hopefully the position would be improved.

At 30 June 1982 Mr Peek took the following records to their accountant:

a. *Cash and Bank Analysis–period 1.7.81– 30.6.82*

Cash Receipts:	£
Cash received from customers (including £22,376 VAT)	171,551
Cash drawn from Bank	64,375
Additional capital from Basic on 1 April 1982	5,000

Cash payments		:
		£
(i)	Suppliers of packages (including £10,500 VAT)	97,575
(ii)	Peek for drawings	8,000
(iii)	Basic for drawings	7,000
(iv)	Selling expenses (including £900 VAT)	10,900
(v)	Office expenses (including £500 VAT)	15,500
(vi)	Shop salaries	25,875
(vii)	Into bank	75,150

Cheque Payments:		
(i)	Selling expenses (including £400 VAT)	14,600
(ii)	Office expenses (including £250 VAT)	10,250
(iii)	VAT	9,000
Cash in hand		700

b. Closing debtors, creditors and stock were:

(i)	Debtors	£22,475	(including £2,900 VAT)
(ii)	Creditors	£5,175	(including £450 VAT)
(iii)	VAT Payable	3,276	
(iv)	Bank	£24,425	
(v)	Stock of packages	£13,725	

The accountant obtained the following additional information at his interview with Mr Peek:

a. *Debtors*

One customer was dissatisfied with the package supplied and is refusing to pay £4,025 (including £525 VAT). The work had been done by a freelance programmer, Mr Bug, who had since given up programming and it was not possible to rectify the errors.

b. *Creditors*

i. The freelance programmer, Mr Bug, was owed £1,179 (including £154 VAT) for work done on the defective package.

ii. Bank charges of £150 appeared in the bank statements but were not included in the cash analysis.

iii. A private account of £500 had been paid for Basic but had been included as an office expense.

It was clear to each of the partners that the business had failed to reach its sales target of £200,000 for 1982. They decided, therefore, to carry out their original intention to dissolve the partnership on 30 June 1982.

The dissolution arrangements were that:

a. An agreement should be concluded immediately with a competitor who had made an offer to acquire the lease, stock of accounting packages and debtors for £34,000. The purchase price was to be paid in two instalments of £30,000 on 1 August 1982 and £4,000 on 1 December 1982.

b. The dissolution expenses of £1,425 were to be paid by the partnership.

c. Mr Peek should pay £5,125, the proceeds of surrendering an endowment policy, into the partnership on 31 July 1982. He has no more private assets and will not be able to make any further contribution.

Required:

a. Prepare a Trading Account and Profit and Loss Account for the year ended 30 June 1982 and a Balance Sheet as at 30 June 1982.

b. Prepare a statement showing clearly the cash distribution to the partners on 1 August and 1 December following the dissolution of the partnership.
(ACCA 2.9(2) June 1982)

26. John Smith and Richard Smith carry on business as the partnership 'Smith Brothers' sharing profits and losses equally. They have prepared draft accounts for the year ended 30 April 1983 and the Balance Sheet is shown.

Balance Sheet of Smith Brothers as at 30 April 1983
Balance Sheet of Smith Brothers as at 30 April 1983

	£	£		£	£
Capital Accounts			Fixed Accounts		
John Smith	10,000		Fixtures &		
Richard Smith	12,000	22,000	Fittings		4,000
			Motor Vehicles		12,000
Current Accounts					
John Smith	17,125				
Richard Smith	10,110	27,235			
Current Liabilities			Current Assets		
Trade Creditors	26,000		Stock	25,000	
Accrued			Debtors	15,000	
Expenses	3,000		Bank	23,735	
Hire Purchase	2,000		Cash	500	
		31,000			64,235
		£80,235			£80,235

They have noticed that the cashier has recently acquired a new car and are suspicious that there may have been a misappropriation of funds from the partnership.

Consequently they have obtained the Bank Statements for the period up to 30 April 1983. These show:

a. a credit balance of £23,385 at 30 April 1983:

b. on comparing the bank statements with the cash book they find that the following items have not been recorded in the cash book:

i. Bank charges at 30 April 1983 of £400

ii. A standing order to the Hire Purchase creditor of £450 (which includes interest of £150). The hire purchase creditor is shown in the Balance Sheet at the invoice cash price of the vehicle.

iii. A cheque for £100 from a debtor had been returned by the bank as the debtor had insufficient funds to meet the cheque. Enquiries indicate that the debtor has left the country and there is little prospect of recovery.

iv. A cheque for £300 had been paid into the bank direct by a firm that was paying rent as a subtenant. This was a new agreement and no formal lease or invoice had yet been raised for the period 1 March–31 May 1983.

v. Private expenses had been paid by cheques drawn on the business account for John Smith (£1,100) and Richard Smith (£400).

vi. Cheques drawn in favour of suppliers but not yet debited totalled £5,000.

vii. Funds received from customers but not yet credited totalled £3,200 made up of £1,250 and £1,950.

They have also obtained the Cash Received Book and Bank Paying In Book for April. These show:

APRIL	Cash Received Book £	Bank Paying In Book £
18 Monday	1,150	1,150
19 Tuesday	1,200	1,200
20 Wednesday	1,500	
21 Thursday	1,020	1,500
22 Friday	1,600	1,020
25 Monday	1,700	1,600
26 Tuesday	900	
27 Wednesday	1,050	1,700
28 Thursday	1,250	900
29 Friday	1,950	1,050
	£13,320	£10,120

An examination of the bank statements for the period after 30 April 1983 showed a payment into bank of £1,250 on 2 May and £1,950 on 4 May 1983.

A cash count at 30 April 1983 showed a balance of £650 although the cash book recorded a balance of £500 as shown in the Balance Sheet.

Required:

a. Prepare a Bank Reconciliation Statement at 30 April 1983.

b. Prepare a Revised Balance Sheet incorporating any necessary amendments.

c. Discuss, with illustrations from the data given, whether the preparation of the bank reconciliation statement and subsequent checking of outstanding credits with the Bank Statement is conclusive evidence that the cashier has not misappropriated funds.

(ACCA 2.9(2) June 1983)

27. Ahmed and Bennet are in partnership trading as booksellers. Bennett receives a salary of £15,000 per annum and after that the profits are divided in the ratio of 3:2

The partnership Balance sheet as at 30 June 1984 showed the following:

Fixed assets	£	£	£
Premises		230,000	
Fixtures		54,000	
			284,000
Current assets			
Stock	215,000		
Debtors	26,000		
		241,000	
Current liabilities			
Creditors	127,000		
Bank overdraft	126,000		
		253,000	
Working capital			(12,000)
			£272,000

Financed by
Capital accounts

Ahmed	154,000		
Bennett	102,000		
		256,000	

Current accounts

Ahmed	26,000		
Bennett	(10,000)		
		16,000	
		£272,000	

The annual profit of the partnership before the salary deduction for Bennett has fluctuated between £65,000 and £90,000 over the past five years. It is expected that the average annual profit over the next five years will be £80,000.

The partners have received a proposal from R. Gandhi that he should be admitted as a partner to open up a new shop in a neighbouring town to sell books and computer games. Gandhi has obtained details of suitable premises that could be purchased for £160,000 and estimates that £100,000 will be required to purchase the initial stock for the shop. The premises will become available on 1 January 1985. Gandhi estimates that the new business would produce a profit of £50,000 per annum with profits accruing evenly throughout the year.

The detailed proposal is that Gandhi should be admitted as a partner on the following terms.

  i. He would introduce £325,000 as capital.
 ii. Stock should be revalued.
iii. Interest of 10% per annum to be allowed on partners' capital accounts in the year 1984/85 and 12% per annum in subsequent years.
 iv. Profits and losses to be shared equally between Ahmed, Bennett and Gandhi.
  v. No goodwill implications are to be assumed or recorded.

The existing partners considered that all tangible assets should be revalued and this was agreed. The revaluation showed Premises to have a value of £364,000, Stock £200,000 and Fixtures £45,000.

Bennett discussed the proposal with his accountant who suggested that, as an alternative to taking Gandhi into partnership, the existing partnership should consider borrowing £260,000 and undertake the venture alone. The accountant could introduce them to a client prepared to lend at a fixed nominal interest of 10% per annum over 5 years, repayable in equal monthly instalments. If the partners chose the option of proceeding without Gandhi and borrowing the £260,000 it would be necessary to appoint a manager to operate the new shop at an annual salary of £12,000.

Required:

  a. Prepare a forecast profit and loss appropriation account for the year ended 30 June 1985 on the assumption that Gandhi is admitted into the partnership on 1 January 1985.

  b. Prepare a statement to calculate the income that Ahmed and Bennett would receive in the years ended 30 June 1985 and 30 June 1986 under each of the two new alternatives.

  c. Briefly advise Bennett as to his best course of action.

(ACCA 2.9(2) December 1984)

28. **Required:**

Calculate and show clearly the cash and/or shares which the partners will receive on 1 January, 1 February and 1 March 1983 consequent upon the sale of the Partnership to Health Sales Ltd.

(ACCA 2.9(1) June 1984)

Appendix 1

Information about group structure

Black Root Ltd is a company that imports liquorice into the United Kingdom and sells to pharmaceutical companies and confectionery manufacturers. After a period of falling sales the company decided to acquire shares in a confectionery manufacturer and to acquire retail outlets in the health food market.

Accordingly on 1 January 1983 it paid £3,205,000 in cash to acquire 1,209,600 shares in Confectioners Ltd. On 31 December 1983 Confectioners Ltd made a Rights Issue for cash of 1 Ordinary £1 share for every 6 shares held at 250p per share, payable immediately. Black Root Ltd took up its full entitlement.

Also on 1 January 1983 Black Root Ltd subscribed for 1,190,000 Ordinary shares of £1 each, at par, in a newly formed company, Health Sales Ltd.

Health Sales Ltd entered into an agreement on 1 January 1983 to acquire the retail business carried on by the partnership of Pharar, Khadir and Benson. The purchase consideration was 510,000 Ordinary shares of £1 each issued at a premium of 50p per share and a cash payment of £714,000. Health Sales Ltd acquired all of the assets of the partnership and all of the liabilities, with the exception of the bank account. The freehold land was revalued at £1,020,000 otherwise the closing balance sheet values were accepted as those shown in Appendix 3.

Appendix 3
Draft Balance Sheet of Pharar, Khadir and Benson as at 31 December 1982

Capital Accounts	£	£	£	£
Pharar		368,000		
Khadir		552,000		
Benson		100,000	1,020,000	
Current Accounts				
Pharar		(120,800)		
Khadir		(56,000)		
Benson		(170,000)	(346,800)	673,200
				£673,200

Fixed Assets	Cost	Depreciation	Net Book Value	£
	£	£	£	
Freehold	617,000	–	617,000	
Shop Fittings	602,000	301,000	301,000	
Total Fixed Assets				918,000
current Assets				
Stock		212,400		
Debtors		265,200	477,600	
Current Liabilities				
Creditors		112,200		
Bank		610,200	722,400	
				(244,800)
				£673,200

Appendix 5
Additional information relating to the partnership

1. Pharar, Khadir and Benson share profits and losses in the proportion 3:2:1 respectively.
2. The Partnership agreement allowed 15% interest on their capital accounts.
3. The draft profit for the year ended 31 December 1982 was £346,800.
4. Before finalising the Balance Sheet as at 31 December 1982 the following errors were discovered:

   a. Interest had been calculated at 10% on the partners' capital accounts.

   b. Stock valued at £5,100 withdrawn by Khadir had been recorded in Benson's Current Account.

   c. The depreciation on the shop fittings for the year had been calculated at 10% of the original cost instead of 15% of the net book value.

   d. No record had been made of the stopping of a cheque for £2,550. The cheque, payable to a creditor for goods, had been duplicated by mistake.

5. The agreement entered into with Health Sales Ltd. provided that the purchase consideration should be paid in three instalments as follows:

1 January 1983 – Cash Payment of £707,650
1 February 1983 – Issue of shares
1 March 1983 – Balance of Cash.

6. Benson was adjudicated bankrupt on 31 December 1982 and will be unable to make any contribution to the partnership.

29. Len Auck and Brian Land trade as partners in Auckland Manufacturing Company making components for mini-computers. To cope with increasing demand the partners intend to extend their manufacturing capacity but are concerned about the effect of the expansion on their cash resources during the build up period from January to April 1986.

The following information is available:

a. The balance sheet of Auckland Manufacturing Company at 31 December 1985 is expected to be:

	£	£
Fixed assets		
Plant and machinery at cost		65,000
Less depreciation		28,000
		37,000
Current assets		
Stocks – raw materials	10,500	
– finished goods	18,500	
Debtors	36,000	
Cash at bank	4,550	
	69,550	
Current liabilities		
Creditors	27,550	
		42,000
		£79,000
Partners' capital accounts –		
Len Auck		40,000
Brian Land		39,000
		£79,000

b. Creditors at 31 December 1985 are made up of:
Creditors for materials supplied in November and

	£
December at £13,000 per month	26,000
Creditors for overheads	1,550
	£27,550

c. New plant costing £25,000 will be delivered and paid for in January 1986.

d. Raw material stocks are to be increased to £12,000 by the end of January 1986, thereafter raw material stocks will be maintained at that level. Payment for raw materials is made two months after the month of delivery. Finished goods stocks will be maintained at £18,500 throughout the period. There is no work in progress.

e. Sales for the four months are expected to be:

	£
January	18,000
February	22,000
March	22,000
April	24,000

Sales for several months prior to 31 December had been running at the rate of £18,000 per month. It is anticipated that all sales will continue to be paid for two months following the month of delivery.

f. The cost structure of the product is expected to be:

	%
Raw materials	50
Direct wages	20
Overheads, including depreciation	$17\frac{1}{2}$
Profit	$12\frac{1}{2}$
Selling price	100

g. Indirect wages and salaries included in overheads amount to £900 for the month of January and £1,000 per month thereafter.

h. Depreciation of plant and machinery (including the new plant) is to be provided at £700 per month and is included in the total overheads.

i. Wages and salaries are to be paid in the month to which they relate, all other expenses are to be paid for in the month following the month to which they relate.

j. The partners share profits equally and drawings are £400 per month each.

k. During the period to April an overdraft facility is being requested.

Required:

a. A forecast profit and loss account for the four months January to April 1986 and a balance sheet as at 30 April 1986.

b. A month by month cash forecast for the four months showing the maximum amount of finance required during the period.

For the purposes of this question taxation and bank interest may be ignored.

(ACCA 2.9(2) December 1985)

30.

Required:

a. Draft a revised balance sheet for Leisure Supplies as at 31 December 1983 as it would be if on that date Mr Anthony retired from Leisure Supplies and was paid out in full, and Mr Christopher introduced £202,500 cash to become a new partner with Mr Bernard, sharing profits and losses 75% to Mr Bernard and 25% to Mr Christopher.

    i. on the basis that the book value of the assets is revised to reflect market values; and

    ii. on the basis that the book value remains unchanged and that any necessary adjustments are made in the partners' capital accounts.

b. Draft the opening balance sheet of Leisure Supplies Ltd as at 1 January 1984 on the alternative assumption that the company was formed to acquire all of the assets and liabilities (including Mr Anthony's loan) of the partnership of Anthony and Bernard at current market values in return for the issue of 135,750 ordinary shares of £1 each.

c. Show the shareholding in Leisure Supplies Ltd on the assumption that Mr Christopher acquires £202,500 worth of shares at their net asset value from Mr Anthony.

    If the transaction would lead to the division of a share, Mr Anthony keeps the share that would be divided and makes a private payment to Mr Bernard, for the fraction of the share that he keeps.

(ACCA 2.9(1) December 1985)

Appendix 1 Introduction to Mr Anthony's business interests

Mr Anthony commenced business in 1950 as a travel agent in London using the business name of "Self Reliant Tours" and this has remained his major business activity.

In 1972 he also entered into partnership with a local electrician, Mr Bernard, to supply and install sauna cabins. The partnership traded under the business name of "Leisure Supplies" from premises in London and the partners shared profits and losses equally.

In 1978 the partnership opened a branch shop in Manchester to sell swimming pool products.

In 1983 Mr Anthony suffered a serious illness and he has been considering whether to dispose of his interests in Self Reliant Tours and Leisure Supplies.

He and Mr Bernard have accordingly approached a local firm of certified accountants, Messrs Wellinformed, for assistance and advice.

They informed Messrs Wellinformed that they have been approached by a Mr Christopher concerning Leisure Supplies. Mr Christopher was interested in entering into a partnership with Mr Bernard or alternatively forming a company, Leisure Supplies Ltd, to acquire the partnership business.

Appendix 2 Leisure Supplies:draft balance sheet as at 31 December 1983

Capital accounts	£	£
Anthony	236,250	
Bernard	231,750	
		468,000
Loan account		
Anthony		78,750
Capital employed		546,750
Represented by:		
Fixed assets		
Goodwill	18,000	
Shop freeholds	146,250	
Vehicles	30,375	
		194,625
Current assets		
Stock	257,500	
Debtors	109,000	
Bank	85,625	
	452,125	
Current liabilities		
Creditors	100,000	
Working capital		352,125
		546,750

Note: Current market values were estimated as follows:

	£
Goodwill	45,000
Shop freeholds	191,250
Vehicles	27,000
Stock	265,000
Debtors	107,875

31. Maria Smidt and Rhavindar Dillon are equal partners in a business making and selling plastic jewellery. The regular financial year end for the business was 31 December. They decided to convert their business into a limited company on 1 April 1984. Their accountant accordingly formed a company, The Sparkling Jewel Ltd, which took over the partnership as at 1 April 1984. No entries were made in respect of the conversion in the books of the business. The trial balance taken out at 31 December 1984 showed the following:

Trial balance as at 31 December 1984

	£	£
Sales		770,250
Purchases	570,000	
Discount allowed	16,000	
Bad debts	8,000	
Rent	18,000	
Salaries	54,000	
Marketing expenses	6,000	
Formation expenses	2,400	
Sundry expenses	9,500	
Capital accounts:		
Maria Smidt		180,000
Rhavindar Dillon		130,000
Creditors		93,000
Furniture and fittings	24,000	
Motor vehicles	28,000	
Stock	250,000	
Debtors	81,000	
Bank	56,350	
Drawings: Maria Smidt	27,000	
Rhavindar Dillon	23,000	
	£1,173,250	£1,173,250

The following information is also available:

i. The partners continued to use the books of the business without a break and no entries have been made consequent upon the company formation.

ii. The trade is seasonal with the average monthly sales in the last quarter of the year being twice the average monthly sales of the first three quarters of the year.

iii. Discounts allowed are to be apportioned in accordance with monthly sales.

iv. The bad debts arose from the following sales.

  a. £3,500 on a sale made in September 1983. The debt was written off on 1 September 1984.

  b. £4,000 on a sale made in January 1984. The debt was written off on 1 April 1984.

  c. £500 on a sale made in May 1984. The debt was written off on 31 December 1984.

v. A new motor vehicle was acquired for £7,000 in February 1984.

vi. Depreciation is to be provided using the reducing balance method. The rate of depreciation used by the partnership was 10% per annum for furniture and fittings and 20% per annum on vans.
The company has decided to use the same method but use the rate of 12% for furniture and fittings and 18% for motor vehicles.

vii. Except where mentioned, expenses occur on a time basis.

viii. The rate of gross profit has remained constant during the year.

ix. Stock at 31 December 1984 was valued by the company directors at £280,825.

x. In the quarter to 31 March 1984 the partners drew:-

Smidt   £6,000
Dillon £13,000

xi. Smidt and Dillon are executive directors of the company. Their remuneration has been agreed at £18,000 per annum for each of them.

xii. The company issued 250,000 £1 ordinary shares in settlement of the purchase of the assets and liabilities from Smidt and Dillon at 1 April 1984.

Required:
Prepare the Profit and Loss Account for The Sparkling Jewel Ltd for the period ended 31 December 1984 and a Balance Sheet as at that date for internal use.
(ACCA 2.9(2) June 1984)
32. **Required:**

a. Prepare the opening balance sheet of Specialist Limited after the acquisition of the partnership on the terms stated in Appendix 2.

b. Prepare the closing capital and current accounts of the partnership on the acquisition by Specialist Limited.

c. Prepare an alternative proposal for the issue of shares, at par, to the three partners which maintains their respective rights to capital and profits as required by Mr Preston in Appendix 5. Your proposal should (i) include a calculation of the number of shares of each class that you propose to issue to each of the partners and (ii) show the distribution of profit before extraordinary items under both the initial and alternative proposals.
(ACCA 2.9(1) December 1986)

Appendix 1: Introduction to the partnership business known as Special Books

Forth, Preston and Weeks have been partners in a book selling business for a number of years. The partnership agreement provides that:

i. Weeks is to receive an annual salary of £6,000.

ii. Interest is to be allowed on capital accounts at 10% per annum based on the balance at the end of the year.

iii. No interest is to be allowed or charged on current accounts

iv. Interest is to be allowed on the partnership development loans at 10% per annum

v. Profits and losses are to be shared as follows:

Forth	50%
Preston	30%
Weeks	20%

Appendix 2: Proposed acquisition of Special Books by Specialist Limited

The partners are considering transferring the partnership assets and liabilities to a new company, Specialist Limited, with effect from 1 January 1985. They are considering the following terms for the takeover:

i. Goodwill is to be calculated by the super profits method using 18% as the required return on the net tangible assets at 31 December 1984 as shown in Appendix 3 and $33\frac{1}{3}$% as the capitalisation ratio for super profits based on the profit before extraordinary items as shown in Appendix 4.

ii. Assets are to be transferred at book values except for stock and debtors (whose fair values are estimated to be £110,000 and £22,126 respectively) and cash in hand. The current accounts are to be cleared in cash and the cash in hand balance adjusted accordingly.

iii. Specialist Limited is to issue 20,000 £1 10% preference shares and 40,000 £1 ordinary shares. The partners propose to allocate the preference shares to satisfy the partners' development loans and to allocate the ordinary shares in profit sharing ratios.

Appendix 3: Special Books - draft balance sheet as at 31 December 1984 (after the preparation of the profit and loss account but before preparation of the profit and loss appropriation account)

Fixed assets	Notes	£	£
Tangible assets	1		55,742
Current assets			
Stock		129,368	
Debtors		25,490	
Prepayments		2,166	
Cash at bank and in hand		4,137	
		161,161	

Creditors (due within 1 year)

Trade creditors	72,700
Accruals	11,832
Bank overdraft	20,546
Bank development loan	3,500
	108,578

Net current assets	52,583
Total assets less current liabilities	108,325

Creditors (due after 1 year)

Bank development loan	27,708
Total assets less current liabilities less external finance	80,617

Partners' capital accounts	59,842
Partners current accounts	(9,780)
Partners' development loan accounts	20,000
Profit and loss account for year ending 31 December 1984	10,555
Capital employed	80,617

Note 1

Tangible fixed assets	Leasehold premises £	Fixtures £	Cars £	Total £
Cost at 1 January 1984	84,763	524	5,182	90,469
Additions	–	–	–	–
Disposals	(22,253)	–	(170)	(22,423)
Reclassification	(2,199)	2,199	–	–
	60,311	2,723	5,012	68,046
Depreciation				
At 1 January 1984	–	26	698	724
Provision for year	10,311	301	1,138	11,750
Disposal	–	–	(170)	(170)
At 31 December 1984	10,311	327	1,666	12,304
Net book value				
At 1 January 1984	84,763	498	4,484	89,745
At 31 December 1984	50,000	2,396	3,346	55,742

Note 2	Forth £	Preston £	Weeks £	Total £
Capital accounts				
At 1 January 1984	30,000	19,500	10,342	59,842
Current accounts				
At 31 December 1984	(5,000)	(2,179)	(2,601)	(9,780)
Development loan accounts				
At 31 December 1984	10,000	10,000	–	20,000

Appendix 4: Special Books-draft profit and loss account for the year ended 31 December 1984

	£	£
Sales		610,085
Cost of Sales:		
Stock at 1 January 1984	69,500	
Purchases	520,815	
	590,315	
Stock at 31 December 1984	129,368	
		460,947
Gross profit		149,138
Salaries	55,096	
Rent and rates	14,773	
Light and heat	1,529	
Repairs	319	
Printing and stationery	10,268	
Postage and carriage	3,994	
Telephone	2,765	
Travel and motor expenses	3,353	
Insurance	2,078	
Cleaning and shop expenses	1,079	
Computer rental	6,000	
Computer maintenance	1,227	
Security installation rental	752	
Advertising	1,081	
Trade subscriptions	750	
Fees (accountancy, surveyor)	989	
Bank charges	10,632	
Sundry expenses	555	
Depreciation: lease	1,903	
fixtures	301	
cars	1,138	
		120,582
Profit before extraordinary items		28,556
Loss on sale of fixed assets	9,593	
Amortisation of lease	8,408	
		18,001
		10,555

Note: No entries have been made for partners' loan interest or other appropriations.

Appendix 5: Mr Preston's reservations about the allocation of shares to the partners

Preston is dissatisfied with the terms proposed in Appendix 2 for the allocation of shares to the partners. He consequently approached the accountant and made the following observations:

i. The profit for 1984 was much lower than normal because of the extraordinary losses arising from the transfer of their partnership business from its previous address to new shop premises. Surely this should be taken into account when deciding on the share allocation.

ii. The partners had not contributed capital in proportion to profit sharing ratios.

iii. The correct approach was surely to allocate the shares so that the partners in a normal year would receive the same amount from both the partnership and the new company.

iv. He was uncertain how to decide on the number of preference shares and ordinary shares to issue but his objective was that the accountant should prepare an alternative proposal for the issue of shares, at par, to the three partners in such a way that the partners' rights to capital and profits were maintained.

33. The accountant of Hook, Line and Sinker, a partnership of seven people has asked your advice in dealing with the following items in the partnership accounts for the year to 31 May 1987.

a.   i.   Included in invoices prepared and dated in June 1987 were £60,000 of goods despatched during the second half of May 1987.

ii. Stocks of components at 31 May 1987 include parts no longer used in production. These components originally cost £50,000 but have been written down for purposes of the accounts to £25,000. Scrap value of these items is estimated to be £1,000. Another user has expressed interest in buying these parts for £40,000.

b.   After May 1987 a customer who accounts for 50% of Hook, Line and Sinker sales suffered a serious fire which has disrupted his organisation. Payments for supplies are becoming slow and Hook, Line and Sinker sales for the current year are likely to be substantially lower than previously. This customer owed £80,000 to Hook, Line and Sinker at 31 May 1987.

c.   During the year to 31 May 1987 Hook, Line and Sinker commenced a new advertising campaign using television and expensive magazine advertising for the first time. Sales during the year were not much higher than previous years as the partners consider that the effects of advertising will be seen in future years.

Expenditure on advertising during the year is made up of:

	£
Television	50,000
Advertisement in magazines	60,000
Advertisement in local papers	25,000

All the expenditure has been treated as expense in the accounts but the partners wish to carry forward three quarters of the television and magazine costs as it is expected that this cost will benefit future years' profits and because this year's profits will compare unfavourably with previous years if all the expenditure is charged in the accounts.

d.   Three projects for the construction of sinkers have the following cost and revenue characteristics:

	Project A	Project B	Project C
Degree of completion	75%	50%	15%
	£	£	£
Direct costs to date	30,000	25,000	6,000
Sales price of complete project	55,000	50,000	57,500
Overheads allocated to date	4,000	2,000	500
Costs to complete – Direct	10,000	25,000	40,000
– Overheads	2,000	2,000	3,000

No profits or losses have been included in the accounts.

e.   After considerable discussion with management, the sales of a newly developed special purpose hook have been given the following probabilities:

First year of production

Sales	Probability
£	
15,000	0.2
30,000	0.5
40,000	0.3

Second year of production

Increase over first year	Probability
£	
10,000	0.1
20,000	0.5
30,000	0.4

Second year sales may be assumed independent of first year levels.

Cost–volume–profit analysis shows that the break even point is £50,000.

Production of the special purpose hook started prior to the end of the accounting year and stocks of the finished product are included at cost amounting to £20,000. It has been decided that if there is less than 0.7 probability of break even being reached in the second year then stocks should be written down by 25%.

f. During the year it was discovered that some stock sheets had been omitted from the calculations at the previous year end. The effect is that opening stock for the current year, shown as £35,000 should be £42,000. No adjustment has yet been made.

Required:

Discuss the treatment of each item with reference to relevant Statements of Standard Accounting Practice, and accounting concepts and conventions. Recommend appropriate treatment for each item showing the profit effect of each recommendation made.

(ACCA 2.9(2) June 1987)

34. Lock, Stock and Barrel have been in partnership as builders and contractors for many years. Owing to adverse trading conditions it has been decided to dissolve the partnership. Profits are shared Lock 40% Stock 30% Barrel 30%. The partnership deed also provides that in the event of a partner being unable to pay off a debit balance the remaining partners will treat this as a trading loss.

The latest partnership balance sheet was as follows:

Fixed tangible assets	Cost	Depreciation	
	£	£	£
Freehold yard and buildings	20,000	3,000	17,000
Plant and equipment	150,000	82,000	68,000
Motor vehicles	36,000	23,000	13,000
	206,000	108,000	98,000
Current assets			
Stock of land for buildings		75,000	
Houses in course of construction		115,000	
Stocks of material		23,000	
Debtors for completed houses		62,000	
		275,000	
Current liabilities			
Trade creditors	77,000		
Deposits and progress payments	82,000		
Bank overdraft	132,500		
		291,500	
Excess of current liabilities over current assets			(16,500)
			81,500
Partners' capital accounts			
Lock		52,000	
Stock		26,000	
Barrel		3,500	
			81,500

During the six months from the date of the latest balance sheet to the date of dissolution the following transactions have taken place:

	£
Purchase of materials	20,250
Materials used for houses in course of construction	35,750
Payments for wages and subcontractors on building sites	78,000
Payments to trade creditors for materials	45,000
Sales of completed houses	280,000
Cash received from customers for houses	225,000
Payments for various general expenses	12,500
Payments for administration salaries	17,250
Cash withdrawn by partners: Lock	6,000
Stock	5,000
Barrel	4,000

All deposits and progress payments have been used for completed transactions.

Depreciation is normally provided each year at £600 on the freehold yard and buildings, at 10% on cost for plant and equipment and 25% on cost for motor vehicles.

The partners decide to dissolve the partnership on 1 February 1987 and wish to take out the maximum cash possible, as items are sold. At this date there are no houses in course of construction and one third of the stock of land had been used for buildings.

It is agreed that Barrel is insolvent and cannot bring any money into the partnership. The partners take over the partnership cars at an agreed figure of £2,000 each. All other vehicles were sold on 28 February 1987 for £6,200. At the same date stocks of materials were sold for £7,000, and the stock of land realised £72,500. On 30 April 1987 the debtors paid in full and all the plant and equipment was sold for £50,000.

The freehold yard and buildings realised £100,000 on 1 June 1987, on which date all remaining cash was distributed.

There are no costs of realisation or distribution.

Required:

a. Prepare a partnership profit and loss account for the six months to 1 February 1987, partners' capital accounts for the same period and a balance sheet at 1 February 1987.

b. Show calculations of the amounts distributable to the partners.

c. Prepare a realisation account and the capital accounts of the partners to the final distribution.
   (ACCA 2.9(2) June 1987)

AAT EXAMINATION QUESTIONS

35. The following information for the year to 31 March 19–9 relates to Back and Pack who are in partnership as general dealers:

	£
Net profit for the year to 31 March 19–9 (before any partnership appropriations)	78,000
Capital account balances as at 1 April 19–8:	
Back	100,000
Pack	20,000
Current account balances as at 1 April 19–8:	
Back	3,000
Pack	2,000 (debit)
Drawings during the year to 31 March 19–9:	
Back (on 30 June 19–8)	24,000
Pack (on 30 September 19–8)	16,000

Additional information:

1) Back and Pack share profits and losses in the ratio 2 to 1.

2) Pack is entitled to a salary of £11,200 per annum: Pack had not received any of his salary for the year to 31 March 19–9.

3) Interest is allowed on the capital account balances as at 1 April at a rate of interest of 10% per annum.

4) Interest is charged on drawings at a rate of interest of 20% per annum.

Required:

Prepare the following ledger accounts for the year to 31 March 19–9:

   i. profit and loss appropriation account (in vertical format);

  ii. the partners' current accounts (in columnar format);
      and

  iii. the partners' capital accounts (in columnar format).

(AAT)

36. Lukin and Vale are in partnership. The following balances were extracted from their books of account as at 30 June 19–9:

	Dr. £	Cr. £
Accruals		9,000
Capital accounts: (at 1 July 19–8): Lukin		4,000
Vale		1,000
Cars: at cost	55,000	
accumulated depreciation (at 30 June 19–9)		25,000
Cash at bank and in hand	21,000	
Drawings: Lukin (all on 31 December 19–8)	15,000	
Vale (all on 31 March 19–9)	10,000	
Furniture: at cost	20,000	
accumulated depreciation (at 30 June 19–9)		8,000
Net profit (for the year to 30 June 19–9)		149,000
Prepayments	3,000	
Salary: Vale	20,000	
Stocks at cost (at 30 June 19–9)	70,000	
Trade creditors		118,000
Trade debtors	100,000	
	£314,000	£314,000

Additional information:

1. The partnership agreement includes the following arrangements between the partners;

   a. profits and losses are to be shared in the ratio 3 to 2;

   b. interest of 15% per annum is to be paid on the partners' capital account balances as at the beginning of each year;

   c. current accounts are not to be kept;

   d. interest at a rate of 10% per annum is to be charged on the partners' drawings;

   e. Vale is to be paid a salary of £20,000 per annum.

2. On 1 July 19–9 a company called Posket Limited was formed in order to make an offer for the purchase of the partnership. The arrangements were as follows:

   a. Vale was to purchase one of the cars at an agreed valuation of £5,000;

   b. other assets and liabilities (apart from cash) were taken over by the company at the following values:

	£
Cars	18,000
Furniture	10,000
Stocks	74,000
Trade debtors	80,000
Prepayments	Nil
Trade creditors	116,000
Accruals	10,000

   c. goodwill is to be valued at one year's purchase of the weighted average net profit of the preceding three years, viz.

	Weighting	Amount
		£
Year to 30 June 19–7	1	73,000
Year to 30 June 19–8	2	130,000
Year to 30 June 19–9	3	149,000

   d. additional costs incurred by the partnership in arranging the sale of the business to Posket Limited amounted to £3,000;

   e. the company agreed to issue 150,000 ordinary shares of £1 each at a premium of 24%, the shares to be divided equally between the partners.

   f. any remaining balance on the partners' capital accounts was settled between them in cash.

Required:

   a. Prepare the partners' profit and loss appropriation account for the year to 30 June 19–9;

   b. prepare the partners' realisation account as on 1 July 19–9;

   c. write up Lukin and Vale's capital accounts for the year to 30 June 19–9, and enter any transactions that took place as a result of the partnership being wound up on 1 July 19–9; and

   d. prepare Posket Ltd's balance sheet as at 1 July 19–9.

(AAT)

37. Amis, Lodge and Pym were in partnership sharing profits and losses in the ratio 5:3:2. The following trial balance has been extracted from their books of account as at 31 March 19–8:

	£	£
Bank interest received		750
Capital accounts (as at 1 April 19–7):		
Amis		80,000
Lodge		15,000
Pym		5,000
Carriage inwards	4,000	
Carriage outwards	12,000	
Cash at bank	4,900	
Current accounts:		
Amis	1,000	
Lodge	500	
Pym	400	
Discounts allowed	10,000	
Discounts received		4,530
Drawings:		
Amis	25,000	
Lodge	22,000	
Pym	15,000	
Motor vehicles:		
at cost	80,000	
accumulated depreciation (at 1 April 19–7)		20,000
Office expenses	30,400	
Plant and machinery:		
at cost	100,000	
accumulated depreciation (at 1 April 19–7)		36,600
Provision for bad and doubtful debts		
(at 1 April 19–7)		420
Purchases	225,000	
Rent, rates, heat and light	8,800	
Sales		404,500
Stock (at 1 April 19–7)	30,000	
Trade creditors		16,500
Trade debtors	14,300	
	£583,300	£583,300

Additional Information:

1. Stock at 31 March 19–8 was valued at £35,000.
2. Depreciation on the fixed assets is to be charged as follows:
   Motor vehicles – 25% on the reduced balance
   Plant and machinery – 20% on the original cost.
   There were no purchases or sales of fixed assets during the year to 31 March 19–8.
3. The provision for bad and doubtful debts is to be maintained at a level equivalent to 5% of the total trade debtors as at 31 March 19–8.
4. An office expense of £405 was owing at 31 March 19–8, and some rent amounting to £1,500 had been paid in advance as at that date. These items had not been included in the list of balances shown in the trial balance.
5. Interest on drawings and on the debit balance on each partner's current account is to be charged as follows:

	£
Amis	1,000
Lodge	900
Pym	720

6. According to the partnership agreement, Pym is allowed a salary of £13,000 per annum. This amount was owing to Pym for the year to 31 March 19–8, and needs to be accounted for.

7. The partnership agreement also allows each partner interest on his capital account at a rate of 10% per annum. There were no movements on the respective partners' capital accounts during the year to 31 March 19–8, and the interest had not been credited to them as at that date.

Note: The information given above is sufficient to answer part a) i) and ii) of the question, and notes 8) and 9) below are pertinent to requirements b) i), ii) and iii) of the question.

8. On 1 April 19–8, Fowles Limited agreed to purchase the business on the following terms:

   a. Amis to purchase one of the partnership's motor vehicles at an agreed value of £5,000, the remaining vehicles being taken over by the company at an agreed value of £30,000;

   b. the company agreed to purchase the plant and machinery at a value of £35,000 and the stock at a value of £38,500;

   c. the partners to settle the trade creditors: the total amount agreed with the creditcrs being £16,000;

   d. the trade debtors were not to be taken over by the company, the partners receiving cheques on 1 April 19–8 amounting to £12,985 in total from the trade debtors in settlement of the outstanding debts;

   e. the partners paid the outstanding office expense on 1 April 19–8, and the landlord returned the rent paid in advance by cheque on the same day;

   f. as consideration for the sale of the partnership, the partners were to be paid £63,500 in cash by Fowles Limited, and to receive 75,000 in £1 ordinary shares in the company, the shares to be apportioned equally amongst the partners.

9. Assume that all the matters relating to the dissolution of the partnership and its sale to the company took place on 1 April 19–8.

Required:

a. Prepare:

   i. Amis', Lodge's and Pym's trading, profit and loss and profit and loss appropriation account for the year to 31 March 19–8;
   and

   ii. Amis', Lodge's and Pym's current accounts (in columnar format) for the year to 31 March 19–8 (the final balance on each account is to be then transferred to each partner's respective capital account);
   and

b. Compile the following accounts:

   i. the partnership realization account for the period up to and including 1 April 19–8;

   ii. the partners' bank account for the period up to and including 1 April 19–8;
   and

   iii. the partners' capital accounts (in columnar format) for the period up to and including 1 April 19–8.

   Note: Detailed workings should be submitted with your answer.

(AAT)

4 Clubs and Societies

GENERAL BACKGROUND

1.0 In contrast to those formations encountered so far – sole traders, partnerships and limited companies – which exist primarily to make a profit for their respective owners – individuals, partners and shareholding members – other formations exist whose main aim is to provide a service to their members.

1.1 Included in this latter category are amateur sports, football and athletic clubs and literary and musical appreciation societies, amateur dramatic and operatic societies and the like.

1.2 Organisations such as these provide their members with facilities which enable them to pursue their sports, hobbies, and pastimes or to socialise.

1.3 In so doing, the organisations aim to provide the facilities at or near cost. Too many variable factors are involved for the club or society to break even, consequently, in any accounting period, a small profit or small loss usually arises. In the long–term, however, profits are accumulated only to the extent that they are needed, for example, to enable self-financing expansion to take place.

1.4 The (usually) voluntary officials of these undertakings are elected more for their commitment than for their financial knowledge. Usually, therefore, only the simplest records are maintained, including a cash book.

1.5 Periodically the records are passed to the undertakings' accountants who may prepare a Receipts and Payment account, if one does not already exist, followed by an Income and Expenditure account.

1.6 The preparation of Receipts and Payments accounts and of Income and Expenditure accounts are part of the core syllabus for the Level 1 Accounting 1.1 paper.

1.7 This chapter assumes that students studying for Level 2 Paper 2.9 are fully conversant with and understand the preparation of those accounts. For that reason they are not repeated here.

1.8 At Level 2, this topic can be examined in greater breadth and depth than at the earlier level, by the introduction, for example, of a greater volume of financial data and/or more complex situations.

STUDENT SELF TESTING

TEST EXERCISES

1. On 2 November 19–3, the Treasurer of the Olympiad Athletics Club died. The financial year of the club, which had been formed to provide training facilities for both field and track event athletes, had ended two days previously on 31 October 19–3. An extraordinary general meeting was convened for the purpose of appointing a new treasurer whose task it would be to prepare the annual accounts for that financial year.

   An enthusiastic club member, Guy Rowppe, was duly appointed but, having only an elementary knowledge of book–keeping, soon found himself in difficulty.

   He sought your assistance which you agreed to give. During your conversation he said, 'The previous treasurer maintained a Cash and Bank account. I have summarised the detailed entries into what I think you call a Receipts and Payments Accounts, and have rounded the figures to the nearest £1'.

   At this point he supplied you with a copy of the following document:

Olympiad Athletics Club

Receipts and payments Account for 12 months ended 31 October 19-3

Note N.	Receipts	Cash £	Bank £	Note No.	Payments	Cash £	Bank £
	Balance b/d	73	–		Balance b/d	–	105
	Membership fees:			(4)	Insurance premiums		
(1)	entrance	80	170		paid to brokers		580
(1)	annual subscriptions	215	4,465	(7)	Payments to suppliers		
(2)	life membership		530		of sporting requisites		5,270
(3)	Training ground fees	454	7,206	(5)	Wages of groundsman		3,600

	Insurance:			(8)	Postages and telephones	692
(4)	premiums		638	(9)	Stationery	629
(4)	commissions		53		World–wide	
(11)	Interest received				Athletics Club	
	from investments		626		affiliation fee	50
(12)	Sale of office			(10)	Rates of training	
	furniture		370		ground	846
(6)	Sale of sporting				Upkeep of training	
	requisites		8,774		ground	1,200
	Advertising revenue		603		Transfers to bank	700
	Transfers from cash		700	(11)	Purchase of	
					investments	5,600
				(11)	Short term deposits	3,000
					Balances c/d	122 2,563
		£822	£24,135			£822 £24,135

Balances b/d	122	2,563

After you had perused the above account, Guy Rowppe explained the numbered items, as follows:

1. On admittance to membership of the club, new members pay an initial entrance fee together with their annual subscription. At 31 October 19–2, annual subscriptions of £70 had been paid in advance and £180 was owing but unpaid; of this latter amount, £40 related to members who left during the current year and is now no longer recoverable. The figures at 31 October 19–3 are £100 subscriptions in advance and £230 subscriptions in arrear. The policy of the club is to take credit for subscriptions when due and to write off irrecoverable amounts as they arise.

2. As an alternative to paying annual subscriptions, members can at any time opt to pay a lump sum which gives them membership for life without further payment.
   Amounts so received are held in suspense in a Life Membership Fund account and then credited to Income and Expenditure Account in equal instalments over 10 years; the first such transfer takes place in the year in which the lump sum is received. On 31 October 19–2 the credit balance on the Life Membership Fund Account was £4,720, of which £850 was credited as income for year ended 31 October 19–3.

3. The club has a permanent training ground. Non–members can use the facilities on payment of a fee. In order to guarantee a particular facility, advance booking is allowed. Advance booking fees received before 31 October 19–3 in respect of 19–4 total £470. The corresponding amount paid up to 31 October 19–2 in advance of 19–3 was £325. Members can use the facilities free of charge.

4. Club members can take out insurances through the club at advantageous rates. Initially, premiums are paid by members to the club. Subsequently, the club pays the premiums to an insurance broker and receives commision. At 31 October premiums received but not yet paid over to the broker amounted to £102 and commissions due but not yet received were £11. The corresponding amounts at 31 October 19–3 are £160 and £13 respectively.

5. The groundsman is employed for the six months April to September only. He is then paid a retaining fee to secure his services for the following year. At 31 October 19–2 the groundsman had been paid a retainer (£250) for 19–3. Included in the Wages figure (£3,600) is the retainer (£300) for 19–4.

6. Sporting requisites are sold only on cash terms. There are therefore no debtors for these items.

7. On 31 October 19–2 sums owed to suppliers of sporting requisites totalled £163; the corresponding figure on 31 October 19–3 was £202.
   Stock of unsold sporting requisites on 31 October 19–2 was £811 and on 31 October 19–3, was £927. In arriving at this latter figure, the sum of £137, representing damaged and unsaleable stock at cost price, had been excluded.

8. Postage stamps unused at 31 October 19–3, totalled £4.

9. Stock of stationery on 31 October 19–2 and 19–3 was £55 and £36 respectively.

10. Rates are payable to the District Council in two instalments (in advance) each year. £360 had been paid on 1 October 19–2, £390 on 1 April 19–3 and £456 on 1 October 19–3.

11. The club receives interest on investments bought a number of years ago at a cost of £7,400 (current valuation £7,550). At the end of October 19–3, the club had acquired further investments which cost £5,600 (current valuation £5,600) and at the same time placed £3,000 in a short–term deposit account.

12. The written down value of the furniture which had been sold during the year was £350; it had

originally cost £800.

Other Matters:

Initially, the training ground had been acquired freehold from a farmer at an inclusive cost of £4,000. Subsequently, the club had some timber buildings erected to provide various facilities for members. The total cost of these buildings was £35,000; depreciation is calculated at the rate of 10% per annum on a straight line basis. At 31 October 19–2, the provision for depreciation account had a balance of £9,400.

At 31 October 19–2, the furniture and equipment etc. was recorded in the club's books as £7,900 (cost) against which there was a provision for depreciation of 4,150 (calculated on the same basis as for buildings). Apart from the disposal referred to in note (12) (above) there had been no other disposals or acquisitions during the year.

Required:

Prepare the club's Income and Expenditure Account for year ended 31 October 19–3 and the Balance Sheet at that date.

All workings must be shown.

2. The Dohray Amateur Musical Society has a treasurer who is responsible for receipts and payments which he records in cash and bank books. Periodically, these books are handed over to the firm of certified accountants which employs you.

One of your tasks is to prepare the final accounts of the Society. As a preliminary step, you have prepared the receipts and payments account (rounded to the nearest £1) for the year ended 31 May 19–5. This is shown below, together with the explanatory notes which the treasurer has supplied to enable you to understand the nature of some of the items.

Dohray Amateur Musical Society
Receipts and Payments Account
for year ended 31 May 19–5

Receipts	Cash £	Bank £	Payments	Cash £	Bank £
Opening balances b/d	31	309	Creditors:trade		
Debtors: members			fixed assets (note 4)		
joining fees (note 1)	190	160	musical instruments		522
annual subscriptions			trophies		83
(note 2)	285	70	Creditors: trade		
Annual concert (note 3)			purchases for resale		
takings	1,791		(note 4)		
Sales of goods (note 4)			sheet music		118
sheet music	140		musical instruments		336
musical instruments	287		Annual concert (note 3)		
Prize money (note 7)	190		hall booking fees		490
Sponsorship grant			printing of publicity		
(note 5)		300	posters		112
Refreshment sales	113		hire of professional		
Raffle profits	64		soloists		236
PAC grants (note 6)			musicians		174
revenue		100	adjudication fees		50
capital		400	Musical Festivals (note 7)		
Transfers from cash a/c		2,910	entrance fees		250
			hire of buses		281
			Honoraria (note 8)		
			secretary		150
			treasurer		100
			R.M.F.C affiliation fee		
			(note 9)		72
			Rent of society's premises		
			(note 10)		510
			Refreshment purchases	72	
			Bank charges		42

Sundry expenses	60	
Transfers to bank a.c.	2,910	
Closing balances c/d	49	723

3,091	4,249	3,091	4,249

Explanatory notes supplied by the treasurer

1. On joining the Society, members pay a non–returnable fee of £10 (before 1 June 19–2, the fee had been £5). It has been found from experience that, on average members remain in the Society for five years. On this basis, one fifth of each joining fee is credited to Income and Expenditure account each year.

New members' statistics are

During year ended 31 May	Number of new members No.	Joining fees in suspense at 31 May 19-4 £
19–1	20	20
19–2	24	48
19–3	32	192
19–4	27	216
19–5	35	Nil
		£476

2. Annual subscriptions are due on 1 June each year. It is the Society's policy to credit these to income and expenditure account on an actual receipts basis, not an accruals basis. However, if subscriptions are received in advance, the amounts are credited to income and expenditure account for the year in respect of which they are paid.

3. The Society's major money raising event is its annual public concert. This is given in a large hall which the Society hires. The Society also hires professional musicians and soloists and has to pay the fees of the adjudicators (judges).

4. The Society buys trophies (silver bowls and shields) to present to the winners of the individual musical items at the annual concert. It also buys musical instruments some of which are for use by the members and others for resale to the members. Musical scores and sheets are also bought for resale to the members.

5. A local building company has given a grant to the Society for a period of three years in return for publicity. The sponsorship grant was received in full on 1 June 19–4 and is being credited to income and expenditure account in equal instalments in each of the three years to 31 May 19–7.

6. The Performing Arts Council (PAC) has awarded the Society an annual grant towards the running costs. In addition the PAC makes capital grants. The Society's policy is to hold capital grants in suspense and to release each year's grant to income and expenditure account over a period of five years from the year of grant onwards. At 31 May 19–4 capital grants held in suspense were analysed as follows:

In respect of year ended 31 May	Capital grants suspense £
19–1	30
19–2	70
19–3	120
19–4	120
	£340

7. Throughout the year, the Society competes at various musical festivals. Cash prizes won by individual members are retained by the Society and credited to income and expenditure account in order to reduce the cost of attending the festivals.

8. The offices of secretary and treasurer are unpaid but the Society gives each of them an ex–gratia (honorary) cash award, termed an honorarium.

9. In order to participate in the musical festivals, the Society has to be affiliated to the Regional Musical

Festival Committee (RMFC). The annual fee, which has remained the same for a number of years, is paid on 1 March in each year.

10. The Society pays rent for its premises. The rental, which is inclusive of rates, heating, lighting, cleaning etc. is reviewed annually on 31 March. The payment shown in the receipts and payments account represents quarterly payments in advance, as follows:

	Payment
19–4	**£**
30 June	120
30 September	120
31 December	120
19–5	
31 March	150
	£510

Further information was supplied by the treasurer as follows:

	19–4	19–5
(1) Creditors at 31 May	£	£
Fixed assets		
musical instruments	79	119
trophies	23	13
Purchases for resale		
sheet music	14	20
musical instruments	45	39
(2) Subscriptions		
Payments in advance included in the		
actual receipts for the year	30	40
(3) Stocks at 31 May		
Goods for resale		
sheet music	31	52
musical instruments	70	94
Refreshments	not brought into account on the grounds that it is not material in amount	
(4) Fixed assets (at cost) at 31 May		
Musical instruments	1,378	to be
Trophies	247	derived

There were no fixed asset disposals during the year

(5) Provision for depreciation at 31 May		
Musical instruments	704	to be
Trophies	96	derived

Depreciation is calculated on the cost of these assets at the end of financial year. The straight line method is employed using the following assumed asset lives.

Musical instruments	5 years
Trophies	10 years

The Society had been formed on 1 June 19–0.

Required:

Prepare for the Dohray Amateur Musical Society.

a.   the Income and Expenditure account for year ended 31 May 19–5, showing the surplus or deficit on each of the activities:

> Annual concert,
> Musical festivals,
> Sales of goods;

and

b. the Balance Sheet at that date.

Note: WORKINGS are an integral part of the answer and must be shown.

ACCA EXAMINATION QUESTION

3. The staff of Plasm Ltd were entitled to join the Plasm Staff Social Club on payment of a monthly subscription of £1 or a single life membership payment of £150. The company supported the Club with an annual cash grant of £3,000.

On 30 November 1982, the Social Club had the following assets and liabilities.

	£
Games equipment (cost £12,500)	6,600
Subscriptions paid in advance	180
Creditors for supply of food	2,250
Bank overdraft	4,210
Stock of food	5,125
Life membership fund (28 staff)	1,400

During the year ended 30 November 1983, the bank withdrawals and deposits were:

	£
Payment of food suppliers	17,100
Overhead expenses	6,150
Repairs and additions to games equipment	900
Social function expenses	1,120
Grant from company	3,000
Subscriptions	3,300
Social function takings	2,650
Sale of meals	19,250
Sale of games equipment	125

The following information refers to items appearing in the bank withdrawals and deposits:

i. The £900 spent on games equipment was estimated to be 75% for additions and 25% for repairs.

ii. The subscriptions included £80 relating to December 1983 and £150 from a new life membership. The life membership is brought into income over a period of 10 years. There was £62 outstanding at 30 November 19-3.

iii. The cash received from the sale of meals was banked after paying out £750 for cash purchase of food and £1,150 for the cleaner's wages.

iv. The games equipment that was sold had cost £500 four years ago. Equipment is depreciated by 25% of the reducing balance each year.

The following additional information is available for year end adjustments:

i. Stock of food at 30 November 1983 was £4,100.

ii. Creditors for food at 30 November 1983 were £2,480.

The Social Club committee received a proposal in January 1983 that the Club should enter into a Joint Venture with Prestige Bicycles Ltd. Prestige Bicycles Ltd proposed that they would supply bicycles to the Social Club for sale to the club members. The committee approved the Joint Venture on 1 June 1983 on the following terms:

i. The Social Club would be entitled to 2% commission on all cash received from sales arranged through the Club (excluding cash collected by Bicycle Factors).

ii. Profit on the Venture would be apportioned one-third to the Club and two-thirds to Prestige Bicycles Ltd.

iii. Prestige Bicycles Ltd would supply bicycles to the Club at a cost of £50 to cover material and labour plus a further amount to cover Prestige Bicycle Ltd's overheads.

Prestige Bicycles Ltd supplied a budget statement of the costs expected to be incurred in the

Assembly and Spraying departments which were the two involved in the bicycle production. The overhead charge was to be calculated on the basis that each bicycle would require 3 hours direct labour in the Assembly department and 2 hours direct labour in the Spraying department.

Budget Overhead Cost Statement for Six Months 1 June 19–3–30 November 19–3

	Production Departments		Service Departments		
	Assembly	Spraying	Maintenance	Stores	Administration
Direct Wages	£40,000	£33,000			
Operating Hours	24,000 hrs.	18,000 hrs.			
Overheads:	£	£	£	£	£
Wages	3,750	1,000	5,037	3,625	7,800
Salaries					9,250
Consumables	730	628	1,390	–	696
Repairs	1,265	983	768	919	367
Fuel	960	1,825	365	197	175
Rent, Rates	2,400	1,600	285	495	365
Depreciation	1,190	1,762	214	98	61
	£10,295	£7,798	£8,059	£5,334	£18,714
Apportionment:					
By work done	5,717	2,342	(8,059)		
By work done	4,134	1,200		(5,334)	
By direct wages	10,254	8,460			(18,714)

iv. The Social Club would open a special bank account for Joint Venture receipts and payments. The following transactions occurred in the period 1 June 1983–30 November 1983:

i. Prestige Bicycles Ltd supplied 900 bicycles to the Club.

ii. The Club sold 780 bicycles on payment terms of a £40 deposit and three monthly payments of £10 per bicycle.

iii. The Club made the following payments out of the special Bank Account:

	£
Delivery charges	1,560
Telephone	130
Packaging	390
Insurance	156
Casual Labour	700

iv. Prestige Bicycles Ltd made a payment out of its own bank account of £780 for delivery and £63 for insurance.

v. The cash received during the period was:

	by the Social Club (banked in Special Account)	by Prestige Bicycles Ltd (banked in Prestige Bicycle Ltd Account)
Deposits	£28,800	£2,400
Instalments	£16,200	£1,350

vi. At 30 November 1983 the following information was available:

a. Creditors for services supplied for the Joint Venture incurred in the name of the Social Club for

Packaging £112
Telephone £ 18

and incurred in the name of Prestige Bicycles Ltd for

Packaging £75
Insurance £37

b. £250 was irrecoverable from customers.

c. 30 of the bicycles were defective and were sold for cash to a dealer for £40 each.

d. The stock of bicycles on hand was to be divided equally between the Social Club and Prestige Bicycles Ltd. Prestige Bicycles Ltd would take their share of the bicycles back at direct cost plus overheads, the Social club would retain the bicycles at direct cost plus overheads plus a further $12\frac{1}{2}\%$ of total cost.

e. Unpaid instalments, excluding the irrecoverable items, were to be collected by Bicycle Factors. Bicycle Factors retained an introductory fee of £150 plus 1% of the total amount being factored, and paid the balance to the Social Club on 30 November 1983.

f. Plasm's commission on sales amounted to £975 for the year and the share of joint venture profit was £1,768. There was a balance of £38 on joint venture bank account and bicycles in stock were valued at £2,835.

Required:

Prepare an Income and Expenditure Account for the Plasm Staff Social Club for the year ended 30 November 1983.

Prepare a Balance Sheet for the Plasm Staff Social Club as at 30 November 1983.

(ACCA 2.9(2) June 1984).

Section II

Accounting Practice for Specialised Transactions

Chapter

1   Consignments

2   Joint Ventures

3   Branches

4   Hire purchase and credit sales

5   Leasing

6   Long-term contracts

7   Investments

8   Bills of Exchange

9   Royalties

10   Containers

11   Foreign currency transactions

1 Consignments

GENERAL BACKGROUND

1.0 It is not always possible, or commercially desirable, for a business to sell its goods directly to its customers.

1.1 If, for example, a business wishes to sell goods abroad, establishing a sales showroom and/or office in each country may not be a viable proposition unless the volume of sales justifies such a course.

1.2 One way by which these difficulties can be overcome is for the business to appoint a selling agent in the country concerned. This agent is then responsible to organising all aspects of marketing the goods and for the collection of cash from the customers. For his services, he is remunerated on a commission basis.

OPERATING ARRANGEMENTS

2.0 Goods sent to an agent are usually despatched in bulk and are termed a consignment.

2.1 The party sending the goods is the consignor and the agent is the consignee.

2.2 Both parties incur expenses in connection with the consignment.

2.3 Periodically, the consignee sends an Account Sales to the consignor. This is a document which shows the sales made by the consignee, along with his expenses and commission. A banker's draft for the net balance may accompany the Account Sales.

2.4 Sometimes, the consignee guarantees that all the trade debts will be collected and, should any prove to be bad, that he will bear the loss. He receives an extra commission (known as del credere) on all sales for the additional undertaking.

ACCOUNTING ARRANGEMENTS

3.0 The act of consigning goods to an agent does not constitute a sale by the consignor but merely a transfer of location of the goods concerned.

3.1 Ownership of such goods remains vested in the consignor although they are in possession of the consignee.

3.2 The sale arises when the goods are sold by the consignee to third parties.

3.3 The accounting arrangements reflect this situation and are different from each of the two parties.

CONSIGNOR'S ACCOUNTING ARRANGEMENTS

3.4 Transfers of goods are recorded by debiting a Consignment to (name of agent) account and by crediting a Goods on Consignment account.

3.5 This procedure is analogous to that of certain branch accounting transactions (see Chapter 3, 4.0) whereby the movement of goods from head office to branch is recorded as a transfer, not as a sale. The closing balance of Goods on Consignment is debited at the end of the period and is credited to Trading Account to prevent distortion of the gross profit figure on non-consigned goods, which appears in that account.

3.6 The consignor debits the expenses which he incurs in connection with the consignment to the Consignment to Agent account, the opposite entries appearing in Bank, Cash, Creditors etc, as appropriate.

3.7 On receipt of the Account Sales (see 2.3) the consignee's expenses and commission are debited to the Consignment to Agent account and the sales are credited. The opposite entries are posted to a personal account opened in the name of the agent. The balance on this account is settled in cash or by bill of exchange or is carried forward to the next accounting period.

3.8 At the end of the period unsold stock in the agent's possession is valued and credited in the Consignment to Agent account to be carried down as a debit at the start of the next accounting period. Valuation of stock on consignment gives rise to special problems considered in 3.11, 3.12 and 3.15 to 3.23.

3.9 After the closing stock figure has been posted, the difference between the two sides of the Consignment to Agent account constitutes either a profit or a loss.

3.10 Despite its name the Consignment to Agent account is effectively a trading and profit and loss account for the consignor. In this regard it fulfils a similar purpose to the Branch Stock account in Chapter 3, Section 4.0.

VALUATION OF STOCK ON CONSIGNMENT

3.11 In arriving at the closing stock valuation, only amounts relating to unsold stock are included; thus the agent's expenses incurred on the incoming consignment are included but certain items of a marketing nature (delivery to customers, for example) are excluded from the calculation on the grounds that they relate to the goods which have been sold and not to those remaining unsold.

3.12 Closing stock value thus comprises the aggregate of the initial cost of the goods plus the attributable costs of both the consignor and consignee, but a further refinement is required when stock losses occur. This situation is dealt with in 3.15 to 3.23. An example of the preparation of consignment accounts now follows:

EXAMPLE

3.13 Wheeler consigned 4 crates, each containing 30 identical cycles, valued at £1,500 to his agent Sellars on 1st April 19-1.

Insurance and transport costs paid by Wheeler amounted to £150 and £250 respectively.
Sellars paid insurance of £200, storage charges of £300 and delivery charges £50.
By the end of that quarter, Sellars had sold 90 of the cycles for £7,200. He sent a cheque for the amount due after deducting his agreed sales commission of 10%.

Required:
Prepare the appropriate accounts for the June Quarter 19-1 in Wheeler's ledger.

SOLUTION

3.14 Wheeler's ledger

Goods on Consignment

	£		£
Trading	6,000	Consignt to Sellars	6,000

Consignment to Sellars (part)

	£		£
Goods on consignt	6,000	Balance c/d	6,400
Bank – insurance	150		
– transport	250		
	6,400		6,400

At this stage these are the only entries which Wheeler is able to post. Subsequently to receiving details from Sellars on the Account Sales (see 2.3) he is able to proceed as follows:

Consignment to Sellars (continuation)

	£		£	
Balance b/d	6,400	Sellars – sales		7,200
Sellars – insurance	200	Stock c/d		1,725
– delivery	50		£	
– storage	300	(goods	6,000	
– commission	720	ince	150	
(10% × £7,200)		transpt	250	
		ince	200	
		storage	300	
Profit and Loss	1,255		6,900	× $\frac{30}{120}$)
	8,925			8,925
Stock b/d	1,725			

Sellars

	£		£
Consign to Sellars – sales	7,200	Consgnt to Sellars	
		–insce	200
		–storage	300
		–dely	50
		–comm.	720
		Bank – settlement	5,930
	7,200		7,200

STOCK LOSSES

3.15 When goods on consignment are lost or stolen or damaged in transit further accounting problems arise.

3.16 Firstly, Consignment to Agent account is credited with the cost of the loss (calculated as shown in 3.20) and a suitable account is debited; usually this is insured losses or uninsured losses, as appropriate.

3.17 Secondly, the stock in agent's hands has to be calculated in two stages, the results of which are then added together to give the stock value.

3.18 Initially, a calculation has to be made of

$$\frac{\text{stock quantity}}{\text{total consignment quantity}} \times \text{consignor's attributable costs (to point of loss)}$$

3.19 A further calculation is then made of

$$\frac{\text{stock quantity}}{(\text{total consignment quantity - quantity lost})} \times \text{consignee's attributable costs (to point of loss)}$$

3.20 The stock loss noted in 3.16 is calculated as quantity of units lost x consignor's attributable costs to the point of loss.

3.21 If the loss of goods occurs after their receipt by the consignee, suitable modifications must be made to the above calculations.

EXAMPLE

3.22 A consignor despatched 25 identical articles at a total cost (including expenses) of £1,000.

En route to the consignee 5 articles were stolen. This loss was covered by insurance.

The consignee incurred further expenses (other than marketing expenses) of £400 and at the end of the period there are 10 unsold.

Required:

Show the value of the

i. stock loss

ii. closing stock.

SOLUTION
3.23

i. **Stock loss**

	£
$\frac{5}{25} \times £1,000$ (to point of loss)	200

that is, it excludes a proportion of the consignee's expenses since these were incurred after the theft had taken place and related solely to the 20 still remaining.

ii. **Closing stock**

	£
$\frac{10}{25} \times £1,000$ (consignor's expenses to point of loss)	400

plus

	£
$\frac{10}{(25-5)} \times 400$ (consignee's expenses to point of loss)	200
Total	600

The consignor incurred expenses on the whole consignment whereas the consignee incurred expenses only on the 20 which he received.

BILLS OF EXCHANGE

3.24 When the consignee signs his acceptance on a bill of exchange originated by the consignor for the balance due (see 3.7) and the consignor subsequently discounts the bill with the bank, the discounting charge (see Chapter 8, 2.4 and 2.5) may not be regarded as an expense of the consignment but may instead be charged against profit and loss account.

CONSIGNEE'S ACCOUNTING ARRANGEMENTS

3.25 On receipt of the consignment, the consignee makes a memorandum record of quantities etc, but does not record their value in his ledger.

3.26 However, he opens an account in the name of the consignor to which he debits all the expenses which he incurs in connection with the consignment, together with his commission on sales. Sales are credited to this account. Opposite entries for all these transactions are made in the consignee's Bank, Commissions Received, Debtors etc accounts as appropriate.

3.27 At the end of the period, the consignee does not bring the closing stock balance into account because the value of the consignment was not originally recorded in the accounts (see 3.25).

3.28 The balance on the Consignor's account at the end of the period represents the net sum due from the consignee to the consignor, and may be settled by payment or carried forward to the next accounting period, depending on the agreement between the parties. It should agree in amount with the balance on the agent's account in the consignor's ledger. (see 3.7).

EXAMPLE.

3.29 The facts are the same as in 3.13.

Required:

Prepare the appropriate account for the June Quarter 19-1 in Sellars' ledger.

SOLUTION

3.30 **Sellars' ledger**

Wheeler

	£		£
Bank – insurance	200	Debtors – sales	7,200
– delivery	50		
– storage	300		
Commissions received	720		
Bank – settlement	5,930		
	7,200		7,200

OTHER POINTS TO NOTE.

4.0 Questions on consignment accounts in the form of the examples set out in this section are relatively rare at professional level, and for that reason no examination questions are appended.

4.1 The tendency is for examiners to examine this area of knowledge in a more oblique manner which nevertheless still requires a knowledge of the basic principles contained in this section. For this reason, a number of test exercises are given below.

4.2 When consignments are sent to a non-sterling country, the consignor must maintain a memorandum currency column in his accounts and the consignee a memorandum sterling column. Any balance on the sterling coluumns not matched by a figure in the currency column represents a gain or a loss on exchange. A fuller treatment of foreign currency transactions is given in Chapter 11.

STUDENT SELF TESTING

Test Exercises

1. During February 1905, X of Exbury consigned 40 boxes of toys, costing £20 per box, to his selling agent, Y of Wyeville.

   X paid (by cheque) transport charges £51 and sundry expenses, £13. After receipt of the boxes, Y paid (by cheque) advertising charges, £58, sundry expenses, £14 and delivery charges to customers, £8.

   By the end of March 19-5, Y had sold the whole consignment for £50 per box, on which he was entitled to a commission of 10%, and had paid to X the balance due.

   Required:

Open, post and balance the Goods on consignment, Consignment to Y and the Agent Y accounts recording the above transactions in X's ledger.

2. The facts are precisely the same as in 1 (above).
   Required:
   Open, post and balance the Consignor X account recording the above transactions in Y's ledger.

3. The facts are precisely the same as in 1 (above), except that, by 31 March 19-5 Y had sold only 30 of the boxes, and had paid delivery charges of £6.
   Required:
   Calculate the cost of stock held by the consignee at 31 March 19-5.

4. The facts are precisely the same as in 3 (above).
   Required:
   Open, post and balance the appropriate accounts in the consignor's ledger recording the stated transactions to 31 March 19-5.

5. The facts are precisely the same as in 3 (above), except that, on arrival at Y's premises, the contents of 5 boxes were found to be damaged and unsaleable. They had not been insured. Sundry expenses paid by Y were £12.
   Required:
   Calculate

   a. the cost of the stock loss, and

   b. the cost of stock held by the consignee at 31 March 19-5.

6. The facts are precisely the same as in 5 (above).
   Required:
   Open, post and balance the appropriate accounts in the consignor's ledger recording the stated transactions to 31 March 19-5.

AAT EXAMINATION QUESTION

7. Fleet is a London merchant. During the financial year to 31 March 19-8, he sent a consignment of goods to Sing. his agent in Balli. The details of the transaction were as follows:

   1. On 1 April 19-7, 1,000 boxes were sent to Sing. These boxes had originally cost Fleet £20 each.
   2. Fleet's carriage, freight and insurance costs of the consignment paid on 30 April 19-7 amounted to £2,000.
   3. During the voyage to Balli, ten boxes were lost. On 30 September 19-7, Fleet received a cheque for £220 as compensation from his insurance company for the loss of the boxes.
   4. On 1 March 19-8, Fleet received £20,000 from Sing.
   5. Both Fleet and Sing's accounting year end is 31 March.
   6. On 15 April 19-8, Fleet received the following Interim Account Sales from Sing:

Interim Account Sales

The Water Front
Gama
Balli

31 March 19-8

Consignment of goods sold on behalf of Fleet, London: 950 boxes of mechandise.

	£	£	£
Sales:			
950 boxes at £30 each			28,500
Charges:			
Distribution expenses (at £2 per box)		1,900	
Landing charges and import duty (at £1 per box)		990	
Commission (5% × £28,500)		1,425	
			4,315
NET PROCEEDS PER DRAFT ENCLOSED			£24,185

31 March 19-8
Sing (signed)
Balli

Required

Prepare the following ledger accounts for the year to 31 March 19-8:

a. in Fleet's books of account:

   i.   Goods sent on consignment account;

   ii. Consignment to Sing's account;

   iii. Sing (consignee) account;

   and

b. in Sing's books of account;

   i.   Fleet (London) account;

   ii. Commission account.

(AAT)

2 Joint Ventures

GENERAL BACKGROUND

1.0 On occasions, businessmen pool their physical, financial and entrepreneurial resources. This pooling may be a permanent arrangement which they formalise by entering into a partnership agreement.

1.1 By contrast, the arrangement may be for a limited period or for a limited objective.

1.2 The impermanence of their association makes the establishment of a partnership inappropriate and unnecessary.

1.3 Instead, the parties combine informally in what is known as a joint venture.

1.4 A joint venture is an arrangement similar to a partnership but without the formalities attendant upon this form of enterprise and is usually formed with specific limited objectives.

OPERATING ARRANGEMENTS

2.0 Each co-venturer, as the parties are termed, contributes specialist resources. One party may provide manufacturing facilities; others may provide technical expertise, finance, business contacts, marketing skills etc.

2.1 Joint ventures can be found in almost any business sphere. In agriculture, for example, one party may grow the crops, another may market them, a third co-venturer may supply the transport from grower to market and a fourth may finance the whole operation.

2.2 Profits or losses made by the venture are shared in pre-arranged proportions.

ACCOUNTING ARRANGEMENTS

3.0 Sometimes a separate set of books is maintained for the venture. If this is the case, there are no special accounting problems. All the transactions of the joint venture are passed through in the normal way.

3.1 More frequently this is not the case. Each venturer records in his own ledger the transactions undertaken by him on behalf of the venture.

3.2 This is effected by each venturer opening an account in the name of his co-venturer(s).

3.3 Debited to this Joint Venture account would be the value of resources acquired for or appropriated to the venture, including such items as purchases, expenses, transfers out of cash and cost of facilities used.

3.4 Credits to the Joint Venture account would include sales and transfers in of cash.

3.5 Each venturer is thus cognisant of only those transactions in which he is personally involved.

3.6 At some stage of the venture, either at the end or, if sooner, at the financial year-end of one of the venturers, an overall picture is needed.

3.7 The method employed is for each venturer to send his co-venturers a summarised statement of all the transactions passed through his Joint Venture account, including, if appropriate, a valuation of any stock held at that date.

3.8 Each party then builds up a composite Joint Venture account in memorandum, that is outside the double entry system, which shows the total position from which the total profit or loss can be calculated and its division between the respective parties.

3.9 Assuming that none of the parties makes an error, they should all arrive at the same result. Each venturer then debits his share of the profit (or credits his share of the loss) to the Joint Venture account in his ledger; the opposite entry appears in profit and loss account.

3.10 The Joint Venture accounts are then balanced. Final balances on Joint Venture accounts for all the parties should in total be equal and opposite.

3.11 Balances are then carried down to the next accounting period or settled by transfer of cash or other assets as mutually agreed.

EXAMPLE

3.12 Trann and Sista entered into a joint venture, effective from 1st January 19-1, to repair television sets and audio equipment.

It was agreed that Trann should secure the orders, collect the items from the customers, transport them to Sista (who would then carry out the repair work), deliver them back to the customers and collect the cash.

85

Each party was to charge his expenses against the joint venture and profits and losses were to be shared. Trann 2/5 Sista 3/5, settlement to be made quarterly. In arriving at profit and loss, work-in- progress was to be disregarded.

During the first quarter of 19-1, the following transactions arose:

Trann assisted in financing Sista by sending him a cheque for £600.

Sista bought a stock of spares, components and other materials for £700 of which £400 worth were still in stock at 31 March 19-1.

Trann placed advertisements in local papers at a cost of £100, and collected cash from customers amounting to £4,900.

Wages paid to part-time staff by Sista totalled £1,950 and by Trann, £550. An allowance of £500 was made to Trann for vehicle running expenses and £200 to each party for use of their general services.

Required:

Prepare a joint venture accounts in the books of each venturer, together with the (memorandum) joint venture account, for the March quarter 19-1.

SOLUTION.

3.13 The first step is to post the transactions in the joint venture accounts opened in the books of each party.

Trann's ledger

Joint Venture with Sista

	£		£
Bank		Bank – cash collected	4,900
– cheque to Sista	600		
– advertisements	100		
– wages	550		
Vehicle running expenses	500		
General services	200		
Balance c/d	2,950		
	4,900		4,900
		Balance b/d	2,950

Sista's ledger

Joint Venture with Trann

	£		£
Bank		Bank – cheque from	
– purchases	700	Trann	600
– wages	1,950	Stock c/d	400
General services	200	Balance c/d	1,850
	2,850		2,850
Balance b/d	1,850		
Stock b/d	400		

At this juncture each party sends his co-venturer a schedule of the transactions on joint venture account recorded in his ledger.

From the total information now available each party is able to construct a memorandum joint venture account, combining their individual transactions and disclosing the profit or loss on the venture for the period. The bank entry, being a contra, is ignored.

Memorandum Joint Venture account

	£		£
Purchases	700	Sales	4,900
Advertisements	100	Stock of unused	
Wages (1950 + 550)	2,500	materials c/d	400
Vehicle running expenses	500		
General services (200 + 200)	400		
Profit c/d	1,100		
	5,300		5,300
Trann 2/5	440	Profit b/d	1,100
Sista 3/5	660		
	1,100		1,100
Stock b/d	400		

Now that the profit has been ascertained, each party posts his share to the joint venture account in his ledger and balances his ledger again, thus:

Trann's ledger

Joint Venture with Sista

	£		£
Profit and Loss	440	Balance b/d	2,950
Balance c/d	2,510		
	2,950		2,950
Bank – cheque to Sista	2,510	Balance b/d	2,510

Sista's ledger

Joint Venture with Trann

	£		£
Balance b/d	1,850	Stock c/d	400
Stock b/d	400	Balance c/d	2,510
Profit and Loss	660		
	2,910		2,910
Balance b/d	2,510	Bank – cheque from	
Stock b/d	400	Trann	2,510
		Stock c/d	400
	2,910		2,910
Stock b/d	400		

After the final balancing stage there is a credit balance of £2,510 in Trann's ledger and this is matched by a debit balance of the same amount in Sista's ledger. Settlement is effected by Trann sending a cheque for this amount to Sista.

Stock b/d in Sista's ledger is the first entry of the second quarter's transactions.

STUDENT SELF TESTING
Test Exercises

1. Tee and Vee entered into a joint venture to acquire surplus and reject crockery from manufacturers and to sell it at a series of one-day markets. They agreed to share joint venture profits and losses, Tee 3/5, Vee 2/5.

   At the outset, Tee sent Vee a cheque for £2,000 to provide him with funds for his participation in the venture.

They managed to sell all the goods they had brought by 31 January 19-4 by which date their cash transactions had been

	Tee £	Vee £
Sales	3,200	2,100
Travelling expenses	327	463
Advertising	103	91
Stall rents/market tolls	85	70
Wages of casual helpers	48	–
Sundry expenses	59	29
Purchases	1,600	1,100

Settlement between the co-venturers then took place by cheque.

Required:

Open, post and balance

a. memorandum joint venture account b. joint venture with Vee account in Tee's ledger c. joint venture with Tee account in Vee's ledger.

2. The facts are the same as in 1 (above) except that by 31 January 19-4, Tee's sales were £1,700 and Vee's £1,000 and stocks in hand (at cost) were, Tee £750 Vee £600.

Unfortunately, on the way back from a market that day, Vee's van was involved in a collision with another vehicle and overturned totally destroying all Vee's stock.

Tee personally took over (from his joint venture stock) goods which had cost £36 to give as a wedding present to a relative. Settlement between the co-venturers to date then took place by cheque.

Required:

Open, post and balance

a. memorandum joint venture account b. joint venture with Vee account in Tee's ledger c. joint venture with Tee account in Vee's ledger.

3. Digit and Thumb entered into a joint venture to trade in electronic machines. It was agreed that Digit would be entitled to a commission of 5% on all gross sales of machines exported, and the profit and losses of the venture be shared as to Digit four–sevenths and Thumb three–sevenths.

The following transfers took place:

1st May	Digit purchased machines at a cost of £19,460 paying £15,420 in cash and accepting a bill of exchange for the balance.
3rd May	Digit sent to Thumb machines which had cost £8,420. Thumb paid the carriage charges on the machines amounting to £126 and paid £2,055 to Digit.
10th May	Thumb purchased machines at a cost of £7,671.
3rd June	Thumb paid the bill which had been accepted by Digit.
15th June	Thumb paid shipping and insurance costs of export sales amounting to £426 and inland carriage charges of £304.
30th June	It was agreed to close down the joint venture by which time sales by Digit were £16,490, including exports of £12,400, and those of Thumb £17,250, including exports of £4,260. Digit agreed to take over the remaining stock at cost for £540.

On 28th June Digit had been notified by a customer in France that a machine he had sold for £400 was being returned as faulty and who claimed a refund of the full price together with costs and damages of £110. It was agreed that Digit would forgo his commission on the sale but that the loss would be borne by the venture. Thumb agreed to pay £510 into a special bank account to enable Digit to settle the claim, and that this amount should be provided in the joint venture account as on 30th June.

The final settlement between Digit and Thumb was deferred until such time as the French claim had been settled.

On 30th September Digit settled the claim for £429 and paid the money out of the special bank account. The returned machine was sold by Digit as scrap for £10 and the proceeds retained by him. The special bank account was closed by payment out to Digit and Thumb of the amounts due to them.

You are required to prepare:

a. the joint Venture Account in the books of both Digit and Thumb and

b. the Memorandum Joint Venture Account, showing the position both at 30th June and 30th September.

4. On 1st July 19-1 Antony and Crespel entered a joint venture to trade in second hand textile machinery. Crespel receives a commission of five per cent on sales satisfactorily completed. All remaining profits and losses are to be shared as to Antony three quarters and Crespel one quarter.
    The following transactions took place:

1st July	Antony purchased a machine for £14,500, paid in full. He incurred expenditure totalling £525 refurbishing the machine during July.
1st August	Antony purchased a second machine for £920. There were carriage costs of £22 met by Crespel whose van was used to transport the machine.
12th August	Crespel purchased a machine for £1,500 for which he received £2,500 from a customer on 15th September. The machine was returned by the customer on 18th September as defective and an allowance of £2,300 was paid by Crespel to the customer. The machine was unsold at 30th September and it was agreed that Crespel would take it at valuation of £1,000.
20th August	The machine purchased in July was sold by Antony for £17,500. Delivery costs of £1,525 were paid and borne by the customer.
21st August	The machine purchased by Antony for £920 was sold by Crespel for £1,200.
3rd September	The purchaser of the machine sold on 21st August informed Crespel that it was faulty and would be returned to Crespel who refunded the cost of £1,200 to the customer. A claim for damages was agreed at £150 to cover return carriage and associated costs. Crespel sold the machine for scrap and it realised £100 which was paid to the customer in part settlment of his damages claim. The balance of the damages claim, £50, was paid by Antony direct to the customer when he visited him on business.
30th September	The venture came to an end and final settlement was effected.

You are required to prepare:

a. the joint venture accounts in the books of Antony and Crespel, and

b. a memorandum joint venture account.

(ICAEW)

ACCA EXAMINATION QUESTIONS

5. Required:

a. Prepare a Memorandum Account in $ only of the Joint Venture with Ideas Ltd as at 31 December 1982.

b. Prepare the Joint Venture Account in the books of the Brighton Metal Company in $'s and £.

c. Calculate the exchange rate for the period October-December 1982 that would result in the Brighton Metal Company recovering only its costs of £720,000.

(ACCA 2.9(1) December 1982)
Appendix 5
Proposal for Joint Venture with Ideas Limited.
The Brighton Metal Company has been approached by an American direct selling organisation, Ideas Limited, with a proposal that the Brighton Metal Company should enter into a Joint Venture with

Ideas Limited. The terms of the proposal were that:

a.   Brighton Metal Company should manufacture 6,000 television trolleys in 1982, the trolleys to be shipped from England to America at the rate of 1,000 trolleys per month.

b.   The trolleys were to be invoiced to Ideas Ltd at a fixed rate of $240 per trolley.

c.   Brighton Metal Company estimate that their production cost will be £120 per trolley.

d.   Ideas Ltd were to pay the customs and warehouse charge of $1.5 per trolley.

e.   Ideas Ltd were to sell the trolleys for $400 each. They estimated that they would need to grant 1 month's credit and that there would be a 4% bad debt rate on sales.

   They estimated that they would sell 750 trolleys per month in the period July to December 1982, and they undertook to remit $ 250,000 per month to the Brighton Metal Company starting on 1 August 1982.

f.   Commission of 10% of invoiced sales less bad debt provision would be payable to Ideas Ltd. Profits and losses on sale would be calculated in $ (dollars) and shared 1/5th to Ideas Ltd and 4/5ths to the Brighton Metal Company. Profits and losses on exchange on remittances were to be borne by the Brighton Metal Company.

g.   It was estimated that 20% of the stock on hand at 31 December 1982 would be defective and Ideas Ltd had arranged for the sale of defective trolleys at a fixed price of $80 per trolley.

h.   The Brighton Metal Company accountant estimated that the exchange rates would be:

   1 July-30 September $2 = £1
   1 October-31 December $1.5 = £1

i.   Ideas Limited agreed to acquire all remaining stock at 31 December 1982 at the invoice price of $240 per trolley.

6. The staff of Plasm Ltd were entitled to join the Plasm Staff Social Club on payment of a monthly subscription of £1 or a single life membership payment of £150. The company supported the Club with an annual cash grant of £3,000.

   On 30th November 1982, the Social Club had the following assets and liabilities:

	£
Games equipment (cost £12,500)	6,600
Subscriptions paid in advance	180
Creditors for supply of food	2,250
Bank overdraft	4,210
Stock of food	5,125
Life membership fund (28 staff)	1,400

During the year ended 30 November 1983, the bank withdrawals and deposits were:

	£
Payment of food suppliers	17,100
Overhead expenses	6,150
Repairs and additions to games equipment	900
Social function expenses	1,120
Grant from company	3,000
Subscriptions	3,300
Social function takings	2,650
Sale of meals	19,250
Sale of games equipment	125

The following information refers to items appearing in the bank withdrawals and deposits:

i.   The £900 spent on games equipment was estimated to be 75% for additions and 25% for repairs.

ii. The subscription included £80 relating to December 1983 and £150 from a new life membership. The life membership is brought into income over a period of 10 years. There was £62 outstanding at 30 November 1983.

iii. The cash received from the sale of meals was banked after paying out £750 for cash purchase of food and £1,150 for the cleaner's wages.

iv. The games equipment that was sold had cost £500 four years ago. Equipment is depreciated by 25% of the reducing balance each year.

The following additional information is available for the year end adjustments:

i. Stock of food at 30 November 1983 was £4,100.

ii. Creditors for food at 30 November 1983 were £2,480.

The Social Club committee received a proposal in January 1983 that the Club should enter into a Joint Venture with Prestige Bicycles Ltd. Prestige Bicycles Ltd proposed that they would supply bicycles to the Social Club for sale to the club members. The committee approved the Joint Venture on 1 June 1983 on the following terms:

i. The Social Club would be entitled to 2% commission on all cash received from sales arranged through the Club (excluding cash collected by Bicycle Factors).

ii. Profit on the Venture would be apportioned one-third to the Club and two-thirds to Prestige Bicycles Ltd.

iii. Prestige Bicycles Ltd would supply bicycles to the Club at a cost of £50 to cover material and labour plus a further amount to cover Prestige Bicycle Ltd's overheads.

Prestige Bicycles Ltd supplied a budget statement of the costs expected to be incurred in the Assembly and Spraying departments which were the two involved in the bicycle production.

The overhead charge was to be calculated on the basis that each bicycle would require 3 hours direct labour in the Assembly department and 2 hours direct labour in the Spraying department.

Budget Overhead Cost Statement for Six Months 1 June 1983-30 November 1983

| | Production Departments | | Service Departments | | |
	Assembly	Spraying	Maintenance	Stores	Administration
Direct Wages	£40,000	£33,000			
Operating Hours	24,000 hrs	18,000 hrs			
Overheads:	£	£	£	£	£
Wages	3,750	1,000	5,037	3,625	7,800
Salaries					9,250
Consumables	730	628	1,390	–	696
Repairs	1,265	983	768	919	367
Fuel	960	1,825	365	197	175
Rent, Rates	2,400	1,600	285	495	365
Depreciation	1,190	1,762	214	98	61
	£10,295	£7,798	£8,059	£5,334	£18,714
Apportionment:					
By work done	5,717	2,342	(8,059)		
By work done	4,134	1,200		(5,334)	
By direct wages	10,254	8,460			(18,714)

iv. The Social Club would open a special bank account for Joint Venture receipts and payments. The following transactions occurred in the period 1 June 1983-30 November 1983:

i. Prestige Bicycles Ltd supplied 900 bicycles to the Club.

ii. The Club sold 780 bicycles on payment terms of a £40 deposit and three monthly payments of £10 per bicycle.

iii. The Club made the following payments out of the Special Bank Account:

	£
Delivery Charges	1,560
Telephone	130
Packaging	390
Insurance	156
Casual Labour	700

iv. Prestige Bicycles Ltd made a payment out of its own bank account of £780 for delivery and £63 for insurance.

v. The cash received during the period was:

	by the Social Club Account) (banked in Special Account)	by Prestige Bicycle Ltd (banked in Prestige Bicycle Ltd Account)
Deposits	£28,800	£2,400
Instalments	£16,200	£1,350

vi. At 30 November 1983 the following information was available:

a. Creditors for services supplied for the Joint Venture incurred in the name of the Social Club for

Packaging	£112
Telephone	£18

and incurred in the name of Prestige Bicycles Ltd for

Packaging	£75
Insurance	£37

b. £250 was irrecoverable from customers.

c. 30 of the bicycles were defective and were sold for cash to a dealer for £40 each.

d. The stock of bicycles on hand was to be divided equally between the Social Club and Prestige Bicycles Ltd. Prestige Bicycles Ltd would take their share of the bicycles back at direct cost plus overheads, the Social club would retain the bicycles at direct cost plus overheads plus a further 12 1/2% of total cost.

e. Unpaid instalments, excluding the irrecoverable items, were to be collected by Bicycle Factors. Bicycle Factors retained an introductory fee of £150 plus 1% of the total amount being factored and paid the balance to the Social Club on 30 November, 1983.

Required:

a. Prepare the Memorandum Joint Venture Account for the period 1 June 1983 to 30 November 1983.

b. Prepare the Joint Venture with Prestige Bicycles Ltd in the books of the Social Club.

(ACCA 2.9(2) June 1984)

3 Branches

GENERAL BACKGROUND

1.0 Many businesses operate through branches. A building society or a firm of estate agents may operate principally from a large town or city but also open subsidiary branch offices, perhaps staffed for only a few days each week, in the surrounding areas.

1.1 At the other end of the scale, very large organisations may set up retail outlets throughout the country. Well-known examples of merchandising businesses which operate along these lines are Boots, Marks and Spencer and Woolworths.

1.2 Examination questions involving branch accounting are almost exclusively concerned with this latter type of situation and the remainder of this section is concerned solely with this aspect. In the event of an examiner setting a question about branches of a different nature, say, a professional practice such as that of a solicitor or an accountant or a veterinary surgeon, it should not be too difficult to adapt the financial procedures, which follow, to the particular circumstances.

OPERATING ARRANGEMENTS

2.0 All businesses of the type described in 1.1 have a main or head office (HO) which controls, to varying degrees, the operations of its branches.

2.1 In the first instance, HO procures the premises and other physical resources which each branch needs before it can become operational.

2.2 When the branch has been established and is operating normally, various arrangements may apply. Many HOs buy in bulk for all their branches. The goods are then delivered to each branch either direct from the supplier or from HO central warehouse. This arrangement enables the advantages of centralised buying and storage to be obtained. However, to allow the branches some degree of flexibility, a certain amount of local buying is usually permitted.

2.3 Payment by customers for goods supplied by branches may be made to the branch itself in the case of cash sales and certain credit sales, or, in the latter instance, to HO direct. Such cash as the branch collects should be banked in HO Bank Account intact each working day. Sums of money which the branch requires for everyday running purposes eg petty cash, staff wages, etc should be supplied separately by HO.

2.4 These arrangements can be illustrated in diagram form thus:

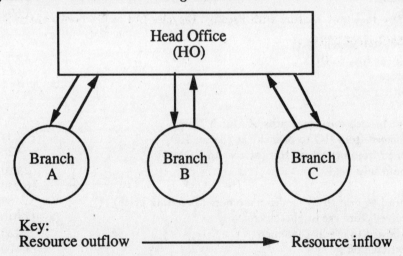

Key:
Resource outflow ⟶ Resource inflow

2.5 Resource outflows from HO/inflows to branches represent the transfer values of fixed assets (eg premises, fixtures, vehicles etc) and of current assets (eg stock, cash); those in the reverse direction comprise such items as stock returns and remittances of cash collected from cash and credit customers.

ACCOUNTING ARRANGEMENTS

3.0 There are two main ways of accounting for branch transactions:
   either
   i. HO maintains the financial accounts of all its branches along with those of its own operations
   or

ii. branches individually maintain their own financial accounts and periodically submit certain information from them to HO to enable the accounts for the business as a whole to be prepared.

3.1 Three different bases are recognised on which HO may transfer goods to its branches as noted in 2.2. either

a. at cost price (to HO)

or

b. at selling price (by branch)

or

c. at cost price plus a predetermined percentage.

These bases are illustrated in 4.0 to 4.8.

BRANCH ACCOUNTS MAINTAINED IN HO LEDGERS

4.0 Typical accounting arrangements for the first alternative given in 3.0 would be that HO opens the following accounts separately for each branch:-

> Branch Stock (despite its name, it serves the purpose of a Branch Trading Account)
> Branch Debtors (if the branch sells goods on credit)
> Branch Bank and cash
> Branch Expense Accounts for each expense
> Other accounts as necessary

In addition, a Goods sent to Branches Account is opened. At a later stage when the HO Trading Account is being prepared, the goods thus sent can be deducted from total HO Purchases. If this were not done, the figure for Purchases in the HO Trading Account would consist of purchases for resale for both HO itself and the branch. As a consequence, this inflated figure would then form part of the Cost of Sales figure set against HO Sales resulting in the understatement of HO Gross Profit.

EXAMPLE

4.1 Let us take a simple set of transactions and see how their recording would vary under each of these three bases.

	£
Opening balances (1st March 19-1)	
Branch stock (at cost to HO)	6,300
Branch debtors	2,710
Branch bank	1,820
Closing balances (31 March 19-1)	
Branch stock (at cost to HO)	4,800
Branch debtors	} to be derived
Branch bank	
Transactions at branch during months of March 19-1	
Goods transferred from HO to branch (at cost to HO)	12,900
Goods returned from branch to HO (at cost to HO)	240
Cash sales paid into bank	2,520
Credit sales	16,240
Goods returned to branch by credit customers (at selling price)	60
Cheques received from credit customers	17,010
Discounts Allowed to credit customers	150
Bad Debts written off	30
Cash transferred from branch bank to HO Bank Account	17,390
Rent and Rates	220
Wages	80
General expenses	70

Transactions at HO on behalf of branch during month of March 19-1

Goods transferred to branch (at cost to HO)	as above
Goods returned from branch (at cost to HO)	as above
Cash received from branch	as above
Salaries of branch staff	750

Post the respective accounts.

SOLUTIONS
4.2 Basis A-Goods are transferred from HO to branch at cost price to HO

Branch Stock

Mar		£	Mar		£
1	Opening balance b/d	6,300	31	Goods sent to branch	240
31	Goods sent to branch	12,900		(returns to HO)	
31	Branch Debtors		31	Branch Bank (Sales)	2,520
	(returns from customers)	60	31	Branch Debtors (Sales)	16,240
31	Branch Profit and Loss	4,540	31	Closing balance c/d	4,800
	(gross profit) (derived)				
		23,800			23,800
Apr					
1	Opening b/d	4,800			

Goods sent to branch

Mar		£	Mar		£
31	Branch Stock	240	31	Branch Stock	12,900
31	HO Trading	12,660			
		12,900			12,900

Branch Debtors

Mar		£	Mar		£
1	Opening balance b/d	2,710	31	Branch Stock	60
31	Branch Stock	16,240	31	Branch Discount	
	(credit sales)			Allowed	150
			31	Branch Bad Debts	30
			31	Branch Bank	17,010
			31	Closing balance c/d	1,700
				(derived)	
		18,950			18,950
Apr					
1	Opening balance b/d	1,700			

Branch Discounts Allowed

Mar		£	Mar		£
31	Branch Debtors	150	31	Branch Profit & Loss	150

Branch Bad Debts

Mar		£	Mar		£
31	Branch Debtors	30	31	Branch Profit & Loss	30

Branch bank

Mar		£	Mar		£
1	Opening balance b/d	1,820	31	Branch Rent & Rates	220
3i	Branch Stock	2,520	31	Branch Wages	80
31	Branch Debtors	17,010	31	Branch General	
				Expenses	70
			31	HO Bank	17,390
			31	Closing balance c/d	3,590
				(derived)	
		21,350			21,350

Apr					
1	Opening balance b/d	3,590			

Branch Rent and Rates

Mar		£	Mar		£
31	Branch Bank	220	31	Branch Profit & Loss	220

Branch Wages

Mar		£	Mar		£
31	Branch Bank	80	31	Branch Profit & Loss	80

Branch General Expenses

Mar		£	Mar		£
31	Branch Bank	70	31	Branch Profit & Loss	70

Branch Salaries

Mar		£	Mar		£
31	HO Bank	750	31	Branch Profit & Loss	750

Head Office Bank

Mar		£	Mar		£
1	Opening balance b/d	not stated	31	Branch Salaries	750
31	Branch Bank	17,390			

As is typical in questions of this nature, some figures are not supplied and have to be derived.

4.3 Basis B - Goods are transferred from HO to branch at selling price.

For the purpose of this example, selling price is assumed to be cost price plus $33\frac{1}{3}\%$.

There are two possible methods of recording the stock transactions.

4.4 i. Memorandum column method

The Branch Stock Account contains, on each side of the account an extra (memorandum) column which does not form part of the double entry system. The normal double entry columns contain figures at cost price for stocks and for transfers to and from HO and the memorandum columns contain figures at the corresponding selling price.

Branch Stock

		£ (Memo selling price)	£				£ (Memo selling price)	£
Mar				Mar				
1	Balance b/d	8,400	6,300	31	Goods sent to branch		320	240
31	Goods sent to branch	17,200	12,900	31	Branch Bank		2,520	2,520
31	Branch Debtors	60	60	31	Branch Debtors		16,240	16,240
31	Branch Profit & Loss		4,540	31	Balance c/d		6,400	4,800
				31	Stock discrepancy			180
		25,660	23,800				25,660	23,800
Apr								
1	Balance b/d	6,400	4,800					

The stock discrepancy is a derived figure representing the excess of debits over credits, thereby indicating a stock loss. Conversely, a figure appearing on the debit side would represent a stock gain.

One advantage of this method of recording is that the branch manager is not able to calculate the amount of profit the branch is making hence HO is able to preserve the secrecy of certain key information. Another advantage is that it highlights stock discrepancies (as noted above). Separate adjustment is not required in the double entry columns for these discrepancies as they are automatically included in the gross profit figure viz.

	£	£
Sales – cash	2,520	
– credit	16,240	
	18,760	
Less Returns from customers	60	
		18,700
Opening stock	6,300	
Add Transfers in from HO	12,900	
	19,200	
Less Returns to HO	240	
	18,960	
Less Closing Stock	4,800	
Cost of Sales		14,160
Gross Profit per Branch Stock Account		4,540
Cost of Sales (as above)		14,160
Gross Profit ($33\frac{1}{3}\% \times 14,160$)		4,720
Less Stock loss (per memorandum column)		180
Gross Profit per Branch Stock Account		4,540

The other accounts for Goods sent to Branches, Branch Debtors, Branch Bank etc would be prepared in exactly the same manner as under basis A.

4.5 ii. Adjustment account method

The Goods to Branch and Branch Stock accounts are maintained at selling price for Stocks and for transfers to and from HO and the profit element contained in these figures is "siphoned off" into a Branch Stock Adjustment Account. Under this method, gross profit is disclosed by the Branch Stock Adjustment Account, the closing balance of which, representing unrealised profit, is deducted from Stock in the balance sheet.

Branch Stock

Mar		£	Mar		£
1	Balance b/d	8,400	31	Goods sent to branch	320
31	Goods sent to branch	17,200	31	Branch Bank	2,520
31	Branch Debtors	60	31	Branch Debtors	16,240
			31	Balance c/d	6,400
			31	Branch Stock Adjustment (Stock Loss)	180
		25,660			25,660

Apr			
1	Balance b/d	6,400	

Goods sent to Branch

Mar		£	Mar		£
31	Branch Stock (returns)	320	31	Branch Stock	17,200
31	Branch Stock Adjustment (25% × 17,200)	4,300	31	Branch Stock Adjustment (25% × 320)	80
31	HO Trading	12,660			
		17,280			17,280

Branch Stock Adjustment

Mar		£	Mar		£
31	Goods sent to branch	80	1	Balance b/d (25% × 8,400)	2,100
31	Branch Stock (stock loss)	180			
31	Balance c/d (25% × 6,400)	1,600	31	Goods sent to branch	4,300
31	Branch Profit & Loss	4,540			
		6,400			6,400
			Apr		
			1	Balance b/d	1,600

Note: The question states (in 4.3) that profit is $33\frac{1}{3}$% of cost. When using selling prices this becomes 25% of selling price and this latter figure has been used in the calculations in the above accounts.

Proof of this is quite simple as the following example shows for an imaginary article:

		£
	Cost Price	9
Add	Gross Profit ($33\frac{1}{3}$% × 9)	3
	Selling Price (Cost plus $33\frac{1}{3}$%)	12
	Selling Price	12
Less	Gross Profit (25% × 12)	3
	Cost price	9

(Selling price minus 25%)

The other accounts for Branch Debtors, Branch Bank etc would be prepared in exactly the same manner as under Basis A in 4.2.

In the Balance Sheet at 31st March, Branch Stock would be shown.

	£	£
Stock at branch	6,400	
Less Branch Stock Adjustment	1,600	
		4,800

4.6 Basis C - Goods are transferred from HO to branch at cost plus a predetermined percentage.

For the purpose of this example, transfer price is assumed to be cost price plus 20%.

This basis may be used, for example, when the actual mark-up rate is for any reason subject to fluctuation or to act as a target.

Either the Memorandum column or the Adjustment account method can be used.

4.7 i. Memorandum column method

Branch Stock

		£ (memo transfer price)	£			£ (memo transfer price)	£
Mar				Mar			
1	Balance b/d	7,560	6,300	31	Goods sent to branch	288	240
31	Goods sent to branch	15,480	12,900	31	Branch Bank	2,520	2,520
31	Branch Debtors	60	60	31	Branch Debtors	16,240	16,240
31	Branch Profit and Loss	1,708	4,540	31	Balance c/d	5,760	4,800
		24,808	23,800			24,808	23,800
Apr							
1	Balance b/d	5,760	4,800				

The balancing figure of £1,708 appearing as gross profit in the memorandum column is the difference between the actual and the predetermined profit, viz:

	£
Cost of sales (see 4.4 workings)	14,160
Predetermined profit (20% × £14,160)	2,832
Add "surplus" profit per memorandum column	1,708
Actual gross profit per Branch Stock Account	4,540

It can be seen that stock discrepancies are not now highlighted, as they were under Basis B in 4.4, but have lost their identity by merger into the "surplus" profit figure.

The other accounts would be prepared in exactly the same manner as under Basis A in 4.2.

4.8 ii. Adjustment account method

Branch Stock

Mar		£	Mar		£
1	Balance b/d	7,560	31	Goods sent to branch	288
31	Goods sent to branch	15,480	31	Branch Bank	2,520
31	Branch Debtors	60	31	Branch Debtors	16,240
31	Branch Stock Adjustment (balancing figure)	1,708	31	Balance c/d	5,760
		24,808			24,808
Apr					
1	Balance b/d	5,760			

Goods sent to Branch

Mar		£	Mar		£
31	Branch Stock Adjustment ($\frac{1}{6} \times 15,480$)	2,580	31	Branch Stock	15,480
31	Branch Stock	288	31	Branch Stock Adjustment ($\frac{1}{6} \times 288$)	48
31	HO Trading	12,660			
		15,528			15,528

Branch Stock Adjustment

Mar		£	Mar		£
31	Goods sent to branch	48	1	Balance b/d ($\frac{1}{6} \times 7,560$)	1,260
31	Balance c/d ($\frac{1}{6} \times 5,760$)	960	31	Goods sent to branch ($\frac{1}{6} \times 15,480$)	2,580
31	Branch Profit & Loss	4,540	31	Branch stock	1,708
		5,548			5,548
			Apr		
			1	Balance b/d	960

The other accounts would appear as for Basis A in 4.2. Note that a gross profit of 20% on cost price is equal to $\frac{1}{6}$th of transfer price.

4.9 In the Balance Sheet as at 31st March, Branch Stock would be included thus:

	£	£
Stock at branch at transfer price	5,760	
Less Branch Stock Adjustment	960	
		4,800

4.10 When the accounts have been posted, it is a relatively simple matter to prepare the profit and loss account:

**Branch Profit and Loss Account
for month ended 31 March 19-1**

	£	£
Gross Profit		4,540
Less		
Salaries	750	
Wages	80	
Rent and Rates	220	
Discount Allowed	150	
Bad Debts	30	
General Expenses	70	
		1,300
Net Profit		3,240

OTHER POINTS TO NOTE.

4.11 For examination purposes, it is unlikely that you will be required to deal with more than three branches. In the example, for simplicity, only one branch was illustrated but remember that when more than one branch is involved, separate accounts must be opened for each branch.

BRANCH ACCOUNTS MAINTAINED IN BRANCH LEDGERS

5.0 In 3.0 it was stated that there are two basic methods of accounting for branch transactions. The second of these alternatives is for each branch to maintain the financial accounts relating to its own operations. Such arrangements apply in, say, large branches where the scale of operations justifies the cost of operating an independent accounting system.

5.1 Under this sort of system, the branch sends suitable records of its transactions, assets and liabilities etc to HO for amalgamation with those of other branches and of HO so that combined results for the business as a whole can be prepared.

5.2 Initially, HO transfers out of its own ledger the values of the resources supplied to each branch. For simplicity, the illustration which follows assumes that HO has only one branch.

EXAMPLE

5.3 The balances on certain accounts of a business on 31st August were:

	£
Land and Buildings	120,000 Dr
Fixtures	43,000 Dr
Provision for depreciation	
– land and buildings	9,000 Cr
– fixtures	13,000 Cr
Bank	51,000 Dr

On that date the business accorded branch status to one of its outstations. The branch was given a set of ledgers to be maintained independently of HO and the following transfers were made to it from the HO ledger.

	£
Land and Buildings	40,000
Fixtures	13,000
Provision for depreciation	
– land and buildings	4,000
– fixtures	4,500
Bank	7,000

Post and balance the requisite accounts in the ledgers of

a. HO, and

b. the branch

SOLUTION.

5.4 Head Office opens an account, called a current account, to which it posts the resources transferred (Where there is more than one branch, a separate current account is opened for each). After the postings had been made the accounts, when balanced, would appear thus

Land and Buildings

	£		£
Balance b/d	120,000	Branch C/A	40,000
		Balance c/d	80,000
	120,000		120,000
Balance b/d	80,000		

Fixtures

	£		£
Balance b/d	43,000	Branch C/A	13,000
		Balance c/d	30,000
	43,000		43,000
Balance b/d	30,000		

Provision for depreciation
(Land and Buildings)

	£		£
Branch C/A	4,000	Balance b/d	9,000
Balance c/d	5,000		
	9,000		9,000
		Balance b/d	5,000

Provision for depreciation
(Fixtures)

	£		£
Branch C/A	4,500	Balance b/d	13,000
Balance c/d	8,500		
	13,000		13,000
		Balance b/d	8,500

Bank

	£		£
Balance b/d	51,000	Branch C/A	7,000
		Balance c/d	44,000
	51,000		51,000
Balance b/d	44,000		

Branch Current Account

	£		£
Land and Buildings	40,000	Provision for depreciation	
Fixtures	13,000	– land and buildings	4,000
Bank	7,000	– fixtures	4,500
		Balance c/d	51,500
	60,000		60,000
Balance b/d	51,500		

The branch now opens accounts for all the items it receives from head office. The double entry is completed by Head Office Current Account.

Land and Buildings

	£		£
Head Office C/A	40,000		

Fixtures

	£		£
Head Office C/A	13,000		

Bank

	£		£
Head Office C/A	7,000		

Provision for depreciation
(Land and Buildings)

	£		£
		Head Office C/A	4,000

Provision for depreciation
(Fixtures)

£		£
	Head Office C/A	4,500

Head Office Current Account

	£			£
Provision for depreciation		Land and Buildings		40,000
– land and buildings	4,000	Fixtures		13,000
– fixtures	4,500	Bank		7,000
Balance c/d	51,500			
	60,000			60,000
		Balance b/d		51,500

It will be noted that in the HO ledger the balance on Branch Current Account is £51,500 debit whilst in the Branch ledger the balance on HO Current Account is £51,500 credit.

The Current Accounts serve as a link between the two accounting units and the balances at any particular time represent the amount of capital employed by HO in the branch.

INTER–BRANCH CURRENT ACCOUNTS.
5.5 When the branch is fully operational it will open further accounts, as required, to record its assets, liabilities, expenses and revenues. If other branches are opened it will also open and maintain a Current Account with each of them. Likewise, they will open and maintain Current Accounts with all other branches.

GOODS TRANSFERRED.
5.6 It was noted in 2.3 that HO may supply branches with goods which have been centrally bought. These may be supplied to branch at cost or at a transfer price above cost eg at selling price or at cost plus a fixed percentage. In the branch ledger the amount involved, irrespective of the charging basis used, is debited to a Goods from HO Account (as being the cost to the branch) and credited to HO Current Account. Conversely, in the HO ledger, Goods to Branch Account is credited and Branch Current Account is debited.

EFFECT OF TRANSER PRICING ON HO, BRANCH AND TOTAL BUSINESS RESULTS
5.7 If the goods are transferred at a transfer price in excess of cost a complication arises when the final accounts are being prepared. The Trading Account of HO can correctly take credit for the goods supplied to branch so that the transfer profit element of gross profit offsets the extra administration etc expenses of maintaining the branch which appear in the Profit and Loss Account. Similarly branch Trading Account is correctly debited with the cost to the branch of the goods supplied. (Note that when a transfer price is used, cost to the branch exceeds cost to HO and to the business as a whole). From the total business viewpoint, however, profit can only arise from external sales and not from internal transfers. Consequently when a combined business Trading and Profit and Loss Account is prepared, the figures shown for Cost of Sales and Gross Profit will not be the arithmetical addition of the individual HO and branch figures. The difference is the movement in the Provision for Unrealised Profit which HO raises to suspend the transfer profit on goods supplied to branch but not yet realised by sale to third parties.

REMITTANCES
5.8 The cash, cheques etc received by branch for cash sales and receipts from credit customers should be banked daily as noted in 2.4 either by the branch physically taking the money to HO or, as is more usual, by the branch banking it locally for the credit of HO Bank Account. In the branch ledger the sums involved are debited to a Remittances to HO Account (and credited to Branch Cash Account and/or Branch Bank Account). The entries in HO ledger are a debit to Bank and a credit to Remittances from Branch. The remittance accounts in the two sets of ledgers are simply a device to relieve the Current Accounts of a lot of unnecessary detail, bearing in mind that entries arise during each working day. Periodically, the remittance accounts are closed off by transfer to their respective current accounts.

ITEMS IN TRANSIT.
5.9 A minor source of difficulty at a period end is the treatment of items in transit from HO to branch and vice-versa. HO posts its ledger accounts when the Goods are despatched/invoiced, but the branch

can post its ledger accounts only when the documentation is received. Similarly, branch posts its ledger accounts when the money for HO is banked whereas HO can make the coresponding entry only when the copy lodgement slip is received. Thus at the period end there is usually a discrepancy between the Goods to Branch Accounts in the HO ledger and the Goods from HO Account in the branch ledger and between Remittances from Branch Account in the HO ledger and Remittances to HO Account in the branch ledger. There are two recognised ways of accounting for such items. Either the ledger of the recipient accounting unit is adjusted (ie branch ledger for goods in transit and HO ledger for remittances in transit) or the adjustments are all made in HO ledger; the latter alternative is the more usual. Whichever alternative is used the adjustments must be posted before the periodic accounts of the combined business are prepared.

5.10 The matters dealt with in 5.6 to 5.9 are illustrated in the following example.

EXAMPLE.

A trading business with a head office in Hull operates a branch shop in Grimsby. The trial balances as at 31st March 19-1 were:

	HO (Hull) £	Branch (Grimsby) £
Debits		
Fixed Assets (at written down values)	38,000	15,400
Stocks at 1st April 19-0		
– HO (at cost)	28,000	
– Branch (at transfer price)		17,000
Debtors	17,448	3,904
Bank and Cash	30,614	5,768
Purchases	195,900	
Remittances to Hull		112,860
Goods from Hull (at transfer price)		69,940
General expenses	34,000	20,000
Grimsby branch current account	126,532	
	470,494	244,872
Credits		
Goods to Grimsby (at transfer price)	71,540	
Remittances from Grimsby	112,380	
Sales	194,020	119,400
Creditors	16,234	540
Hull Current Account		124,932
Capital at 1st April 19-0	74,620	
Provision for unrealised profit on stocks on 1st April 19-0	1,700	
	470,494	244,872

Notes:

a. Hull invoices goods supplied to Grimsby branch at cost plus one ninth.

b. At 31st March 19-1

	£
Stocks at HO (at cost)	25,400
Stocks at Branch (at transfer price)	9,600
Stocks in transit (at transfer price)	1,600
Cash in transit to HO	480

c. Provide for depreciation on fixed assets at 20% per annum on the reducing balance.

Required:

a. Prepare a Trading and Profit and Loss Account for year ended 31st March 19-1 and a Balance sheet at that date, separately for

104

i. HO

ii. Branch

iii. The business as a whole

b. Post and balance both Current Accounts.

SOLUTION

5.11 The Trading and Profit and Loss accounts can conveniently be prepared in columnar form with separate columns for HO and for branch. An adjustment column is used to convert the sum of the HO and branch columns into a total business figure where appropriate. The Goods from HO in the branch trading account plus the Goods in transit are a contra item to the Goods to branch in the HO trading account.

Trading and Profit and Loss Accounts
for year ended 31st March 19-1

	Hull (HO) £	£	£	Grimsby (Branch) £	Adjustments by HO £	Total Business £	£
Sales	194,020			119,400			313,420
Goods to Branch	71,540 ¢				(71,540)		
		265,560			(71,540)		
Less							
Opening Stock	28,000		17,000		(1,700)	43,300	
Purchases	195,900				Provn for	195,900	
Goods from HO			69,940 ¢		U/P (69,940)		
	223,900		86,940		(71,640)	239,200	
Less					Provn for		
Closing stock	25,400		9,600		U/P (1,120) *	35,480	
					Stock in transit 1,600 ¢		
Cost of Sales		198,500		77,340	(72,120)		203,720
Gross Profit		67,060		42,060	580		109,700
Less							
General Expenses	34,000		20,000			54,000	
Depreciation	7,600		3,080			10,680	
		41,600		23,080			64,680
Net Profit		25,460		18,980	580		45,020

* (Transfer profit, one ninth of cost, is equal to 10% of transfer price)

	Stocks at transfer price £	Provision for unrealised profit (10%) £
Branch – opening	17,000	1,700
Branch – closing	9,600	960
Stock in transit	1,600	160
	11,200	1,120
Increase/(decrease)	(5,800)	(580)

The effect of maintaining the Provision for unrealised profit is that total business stocks are reduced to cost to the business thus leaving a credit of only the realised portion of transfer profit.

Gross profit for the total business comprises:

	£
HO	67,060
Branch	42,060
Decrease in provision for unrealised profit	580
	109,700

The Balance Sheet can be prepared in a similar format to the Trading and Profit and Loss Accounts. An adjustment column is used to convert the sum of the HO and branch columns into a total business figure where appropriate.

Balance Sheets
as at 31st March 19-1

	Hull (HO) £	£	Grimsby (Branch) £	£	Adjustments by HO £	Total Business £	£
Fixed Assets(at wdv) (£38,000–£7,600) (£15,400–£3,080)		30,400		12,320			42,720
Current Assets					Provn for		
Stocks	25,400		9,600		U/P (1,120) 1,600 Stock in transit	35,480	
Debtors	17,448		3,904		Cash in transit 480	21,352	
Bank and Cash	30,614		5,768			36,862	
	73,462		19,272		960	93,694	
Less **Current Liabilities**							
Creditors	16,234		540			16,774	
	16,234		540			16,774	
Working Capital		57,228		18,732			76,920
Net Assets Employed		87,628		31,052	960		119,640

Financed by:
Capital 1st April 19-0   74,620
Add Net Profit for year   45,020

                                                   119,640

The completed Current Accounts would appear thus:-
Hull (HO) ledger

Grimsby Current Account

	£		£
Balance b/d	126,532	Remittances from branch	112,380
Profit and Loss	18,980	Cash in transit c/d	480
		Stock in transit c/d	1,600
		Balance c/d	31,052
	145,512		145,512
Balance b/d	31,052		
Cash in transit b/d	480		
Stock in transit b/d	1,600		

Grimsby (branch) ledger

Hull Current Account

	£		£
Remittances HO	112,860	Balance b/d	124,932
Balance c/d	31,052	Profit and Loss	18,980
	143,912		143,912
		Balance b/d	31,052

The profit (or loss) made by the branch is transmitted to HO via the Current Account.
On completion of the Current Accounts, not only are the closing balances equal and opposite:

                                          £

HO ledger – Grimsby Current Account   31,052   Debit
Grimsby ledger - Hull Current Account   31,052   Credit

but they also agree with the Net Assets Employed at the Grimsby branch as disclosed by the Balance Sheet £31,052.

STUDENT SELF TESTING
Test Exercises

1. A retail business in Aytown had a branch shop in Beetown for which it maintained ledger accounts. The main shop supplied the branch shop with goods for resale when required.
The following balances related to the branch for the year ended 31 December 19-4

	£
Stock of goods for resale, 1 January 19-4	28,000
Goods transferred from Aytown	120,000
Goods returned to Aytown	2,000
Goods returned to Beetown from customers (at selling prices)	2,500
Cash sales	133,000
Credit sales	7,000
Stock of goods for resale, 31 December 19-4	36,000

Required:
Open, post and balance the following accounts in the Aytown ledger, on the assumption that all goods are supplied to the branch at cost:

     Goods sent to Beetown
     Beetown branch stock

2. The facts are precisely the same as in 1 above, except that Aytown invoices goods to Beetown at selling price which is cost price plus 25%.
   Required:
   Prepare the same accounts as in 1 above, using the "memorandum column" method for the branch stock account.

3. The facts are precisely the same as in 2 above.
   Required:
   Prepare the same accounts as in 1 above, together with a branch stock adjustment account to record the profit element.

4. The facts are precisely the same as in 1 above, except that Aytown invoices goods to Beetown at a transfer price which is cost plus 20%.
   Required:

   a. Prepare the same accounts as in 2 above.

   b. State what the balancing figure in the memorandum column of the branch stock account represents.

5. The facts are precisely the same as in 4 above.
   Required:

   a. Prepare the same accounts as in 3 above.

   b. State what the balancing figure in the branch stock account represents.

6. The balances on the current accounts of a head office and its branch were £34,900 before the transaction listed below were posted:

	£
Goods sent to branch by head office	86,350
Goods received from head office by branch	81,000
Remittances sent to head office by branch	47,200
Remittances received by head office from branch	44,600
Branch profit for the period	29,700
Goods in transit to branch from head office	5,350
Cash in transit to head office from branch	2,600

   Required:
   Open, post and balance the current accounts in the ledgers of head office and the branch.

7. A head office in Seaville had one branch in Wytown and another in Zedham. At the beginning of the period in the Seaville ledger the current account balances were Wytown £56,000, Zedham £78,000. These balances agreed with the corresponding Seaville balances in the branch books.
   The following transactions arose during the period

			£
At Seaville	:	goods sent to Wytown	24,000
	:	goods sent to Zedham	18,000
At Wytown	:	goods returned to Seaville	600
	:	remittances sent to Seaville	27,000
	:	goods sent to Zedham	2,600
	:	profit for period	9,000
	:	goods returned to Zedham	200
At Zedham	:	goods returned to Seaville	100
	:	remittances sent to Seaville	15,000
	:	goods sent to Wytown	1,300
	:	loss for period	2,000

   Required:
   Open, post and balance the columnar current accounts in the ledgers of head office and branches.

8. Trent Traders Ltd. has a head office in Thurgarton and a branch in Gainsborough.
   The following transactions arose during the year ended 31 December 19–5:

	£
At Thurgarton	
Sales	242,000
Transfers to Gainsborough (at transfer prices)	74,000
Stocks: on 1 January 19–5 (at cost prices)	73,000
: on 31 December 19–5 (at cost prices)	81,000
Purchases	217,000
At Gainsborough	
Sales	108,000
Transfers from Thurgarton (at transfer prices)	68,000
Stocks : on 1 January 19–5 (at transfer prices)	21,000
: on 31 December 19–5 (at transfer prices)	14,000

Transfer profit is 20% of transfer price.

Required:

Prepare, in columnar form, a trading account for year ended 31 December 19–5 for

  i. Thurgarton head office

  ii. Gainsborough branch

  iii. Trent Traders Ltd.

Adjustments made to the sum of (a) plus (b) in arriving at (c) should be shown in a separate column.

9. The facts are precisely the same as in 8 above and the following additional information is available; at 31 December 19–5.

	£
Ordinary shares of £1.00 per share in issue	180,000
Profit and loss account balance carried forward	76,500

	Thurgarton	Gainsborough
	£	£
Fixed assets (at written down values)		
– premises	54,000	48,500
– fixtures etc.	18,200	17,900
Current assets (other than stocks)		
– debtors	52,000	27,000
– bank/cash	10,700	1,500
Current liabilities		
– creditors	49,800	22,600

At 31 December 19–5 there was cash in transit   2,100

Required:

Prepare, in columnar form, a balance sheet as at 31 December 19–5 for

  a. Thurgarton head office

  b. Gainsborough branch

  c. Trent Traders Ltd.

Adjustments made to the sum of (a) plus (b) in arriving at (c) should be shown in a separate column.

10. Henry established a retail business in Ayville several years ago and has since opened branch shops at Beetoun, Seathorpe and Deeford. Each branch has a manager and one or more part-time assistants. All the purchasing and administration is done at Ayville. Branches sell both for cash and on credit terms but all invoices for credit sales are despatched from Ayville and payments from credit customers received there. The average gross profit that managers are expected to achieve is 50% on cost price. The following information relates to the Beetoun branch for the first six months of 19–6.

	£
Opening stock of goods at branch (cost price)	2,800
Opening Debtors	900
Goods sent to branch (selling price)	18,000
Credit sales	6,000
Cash sales	10,200
Transfers from other branches (to B) (selling price)	1,200
Transfers to other branches (from B) (selling price)	2,100
Goods returned to Ayville (selling price)	600
Cash from debtors received at Ayville	5,300
Bad debts written off	200
Goods returned by credit customers to the branch	240
Goods returned by credit customers to Ayville	120
Closing stock of goods at branch (selling price)	4,500

Required:

a. Briefly outline the main objective of an accounting system in the type of situation described in the first paragraph.

b. From the information given prepare the appropriate accounts for the Beetoun branch for the first six months of 19–6.

(ACCA)

11. Mutt and Jeff, retailers of ladies' fashion goods, having traded for many years from their only premises in Euston, opened two small boutiques one in Waterloo and the other in Victoria during their financial year ended 30th June 19–4.

The arrangements were that all stock for resale was to be obtained from Euston and taken into the branch books at cost plus $33\frac{1}{3}\%$ mark up, all sales were to be for cash, no credit being allowed, and all takings after deducting any small petty cash payments were to be banked each evening. All the other expenses of the branch were to be paid by Euston and each branch was to have a float of £100 for change.

Owing to a misunderstanding proper branch accounts were not kept in the head office books. From the head office books you obtain the following:

	Waterloo £	Victoria £
Cost of fixtures and fittings	3,500	4,200
Cash floats at branches	100	100
Branch wages and overheads	6,200	7,300
Goods to branches at cost	27,000	36,000
Goods returned by branches at cost	300	150
Cash received from branches	31,450	43,000

and from the branch books:

	Waterloo £	Victoria £
Sales	32,350	43,340
Float at 30th June 19–4	100	100
Goods purchased and paid for locally at cost	500	—
Sundry expenses	400	340
Banked for head office account	31,450	43,000
Goods to head office at selling price	400	200
Goods to other branch at selling price	700	200
Stock at 30th June 19–4 at selling price	3,300	4,740
Damaged stock scrapped at selling price	20	15

You ascertain that:

a. The goods purchased locally were sold at a mark up of 50% on cost in the Waterloo branch and that its closing stock included £60 in respect of these goods, all other sales being at a mark up of 33 1/3% on cost.

b. During "sales" week all prices were reduced by 10% and the takings during this week were Waterloo £900, Victoria £1,080.

c. Each branch is to be charged £500 in respect of services by head office not directly chargeable.

d. Each branch is to bear a depreciation charge of 10% of the cost of its fixtures and fittings.

e. There was no stock or cash in transit at 30th June 19–4.

You are required to prepare in columnar form the following accounts as they would appear in the head office books for the year ended 30th June 19–4:

a. Branch Stock

b. Branch Adjustment,

c. Goods Sent to Branch, and

d. Branch Profit and Loss

12. Blunt and Sharp Ltd. operate retail stores in Edinburgh, which is the head office, and Glasgow. A trial balance prepared as of 31st May 19–5, revealed the following position:

Blunt and Sharp Ltd.

Trial Balance as of 31st May, 19–5

	Head Office		Branch	
	Debit £	Credit £	Debit £	Credit £
Share Capital – Authorised, Issued and fully paid in ordinary shares of £1 each		260,000		
Share Premium Account		40,000		
General Reserve		30,000		
Profit and Loss Account		55,000		
Debtors/Creditors	47,500	35,000	14,700	7,200
Head Office Current Account				51,500
Goodwill at cost	75,000			
Land and Buildings at cost	175,000		50,000	
Fixtures and fittings at cost	50,000		20,000	
Motor Vehicles at cost	45,000			
Accumulated depreciation				
– Fixtures		10,100		6,400
– Motors		3,600		
Stock at cost or mark up				
– 31st May 19–4	48,500		15,400	
Bank	14,900		2,600	
Cash	1,000		500	
Purchases/Sales	255,000	229,700	148,500	199,700
Administration Expenses	31,000		10,500	
Selling and Distribution expenses	10,500		2,100	
Provision for unrealised profit on stocks		1,400		
Branch current account	60,000			
Financial, legal and professional expenses	5,400		500	
Goods sent to branch		154,000		
	818,800	818,800	264,800	264,800

Additional information

a. All goods sold by the branch are supplied from head office at cost plus 10 per cent. At 31st May, 19–5, goods to the value of £5,500 were in transit to the branch.

b. The branch deposited £3,000 on behalf of head office in the local branch of the company's bankers on 31st May, 19–5. No record of this transaction had been made in Head Office books.

c. Stock at 31st May 19–5, excluding the goods in transit, were valued as follows:-

$$£$$

Head Office at cost   54,500

Branch at mark-up   17,600

Required:

From the information given, prepare, in columnar form to show the results for

   i.   Head Office

  ii.   Branch and

iii.   combined

   a.   Trading and Profit and loss accounts for the year ended 31st May 19–5; and

   b.   A balance sheet as at that date.

(ACCA)

13. After the end of the financial year (31st December, 19–8), the head office of a trading concern in Nottingham received a copy of the trial balance from each of its three branches.

The balances on the various Current Accounts were as listed below:

	Dr	Cr.
	£	£
Newark branch ledger Current Accounts:-		
Head Office		4,570
Worksop branch		2,410
Retford branch	1,420	
Retford branch ledger Current Accounts:-		
Head Office		3,550
Newark branch		2,570
Worksop branch		1,780
Worksop branch ledger Current Accounts:-		
Head Office		4,780
Newark branch	4,560	
Retford branch	3,020	

The following matters need to be adjusted before the final accounts can be prepared.

1. Retford branch had informed Newark branch that the invoice received for goods supplied by Newark branch had been under added by £1,150. The correct figure had been posted in the Retford ledger but no further entry had yet been made in the Newark ledger.

2. Worksop branch had returned faulty goods (originally invoiced at £1,045) to Newark branch. This entry had not yet been made in the Newark ledger.

3. South Yorkshire Factors had made a contra entry of the £1,105 which it owed to Newark branch against a debt due to South Yorkshire Factors by Worksop branch. The necessary entry had been made only in the Newark ledger.

4. Retford branch had not recorded goods valued at £1,240 received from Worksop during the year.

5. A credit customer of the Newark branch had paid £1,084 directly to Head Office. This had been recorded in the Head Office ledger but not in the Newark ledger.

6. A remittance of £1,330 from Worksop branch on the last working day of the financial year was not received by Head Office until early 19–9.

7. The net profit of each branch for the year was Newark, £3,500, Retford £1,600, Worksop £4,695.

Required:

Post the inter-branch Current Accounts in the Head Office and branch ledgers, as appropriate, for the items listed above and for the transfer to Head Office of the adjusted closing balances.

ACCA EXAMINATION QUESTIONS

14. Johnson started up in business on 1 April 1981 in a shop that he acquired in Croydon on an 8 year lease. He also rented premises in Manchester that were managed by a salaried branch manager. (Manchester is 200 miles from Croydon.)

He acquired jobs lots of plastic toys and packaged them to customers' order. The packaging was a feature of his marketing and so he spent 10% of the cost price of the toys on the packaging and sold them at a profit of 12% of selling price.

Packaged toys were sent to Manchester at selling price less 6%.

The Trial Balance at 31 March 1982 showed:

	Head Office		Branch	
	£	£	£	£
Capital		50,000		
Fixtures in Croydon	8,000			
Purchase of toys	200,000			
Purchase of packaging	22,000			
Sales		140,000		75,000
Goods sent to branch		79,900	78,452	
Expenses	20,000		2,000	
Debtors	14,000		7,500	
Creditors		20,000		2,000
Current Account:				
Head Office				14,052
Branch	18,000			
Bank Balance	7,900		3,100	
	£289,900	£289,900	£91,052	£91,052

The following information is also given:

a. Packaged goods despatched by Croydon to Manchester on 29 March were not received in Manchester until 5 April 1982. The selling price of the goods to the public was to be £1,540.

b. Manchester had sent £2,500 to Croydon on 30 March 1982. The cash was not received in Croydon until 6 April 1982.

c. The annual stocktake on 31 March 1982 revealed:

   i. Toys costing Croydon £500 were considered obsolete.

   ii. Packaging material at Croydon costing £250 was unusable because of damp.

   iii. The Manchester stocktake revealed a stock shortage of £650 at invoice price from Croydon to the branch.

d. Provision is to be made for a bonus to the Manchester manager of 10% of net profit after commission.

e. Provision is to be made for depreciation on fixtures over the term of the lease.

Required:

Prepare an operating statement for the year ended 31 March 1982 and Balance Sheets for the Head Office, the Branch, and the whole business as at 31 March 1982:

(ACCA 2.9(2) June 1982)

15. Required:

Prepare a columnar Trading and Profit and Loss Account for the year ended 30 November 1983 for internal use which will show separately the results of:

   i. the Head Office,

   ii. the Manchester Branch, and

   iii. the whole business.

(ACCA 2.9(1) December 1983)

Appendix 1A – according to legislation of Gt. Britain.

Brief note on Prism PLC together with the Trial Balance as at 30 November 1983

Prism PLC is a public company that has its head office in London. It sells a range of educational toys through its own retail shops in the London area and through a branch shop in Manchester which is 200 miles from London.

The authorised share capital of the company consists of 8,000,000 ordinary shares of 25p each.

The following balances have been taken from the ledger and branch ledger of Prism PLC as at 30 November 1983:

Debits	Head Office £	Manchester Branch £
Fixed assets at cost at 1 December 1982:		
Freehold properties	500,000	45,000
Fixtures & fittings	1,032,000	18,000
Vehicles	86,000	25,000
Stocks at 1 December 1982	1,885,482	
Stocks at 1 December 1982 at transfer price		89,375
Debtors	500,165	18,170
Development expenditure	104,000	
Cash	29,618	13,532
Freehold property revalued on 1 January 1983 by	94,000	
Vehicles purchased during year	72,000	16,000
Quoted investments at cost at 1 December 1982	750,000	
Purchases	6,132,685	
Goods from Head Office to branch at transfer price		350,000
Administration expense	1,020,800	111,900
Distribution expense	932,120	83,460
Interim dividend paid June 1983	35,000	
ACT paid on interim dividend	15,000	
Branch current account	360,615	
Remittances to head office		306,000
Bank overdraft interest paid	11,700	
	£13,561,185	£1,076,437

Credits	£	£
Ordinary share capital	2,000,000	–
Share premium	50,000	–
Revaluation reserve	94,000	–
Retained profits	124,000	–
Valued added tax	19,000	3,200
Bank overdraft	75,000	
Goods to Manchester Branch	360,615	
Remittances from Manchester Branch	300,000	
Sales (excluding VAT)	9,182,537	689,745
Creditors	388,133	3,697
Head Office current account		350,000
12% loan (repayable 1987)	100,000	
Income from investments (net of ACT)	92,155	
Proceeds from sale of vehicles	7,745	6,295
Corporation tax payable	64,000	
Deferred tax	150,000	
Provision for depreciation at 1 December 1982:		
Freehold properties	20,000	3,000
Fixtures and fittings	492,000	6,500
Vehicles	42,000	14,000
	£13,561,185	£1,076,437

Appendix 2
Information concerning Head Office and Branch transactions
The following information is relevant to the preparation of the Head Office, Branch and whole business Trading and Profit and Loss Accounts for the year ended 30 November 1983.

1. Head Office invoiced goods out to the Manchester branch at cost plus ten per cent.

2. The Retained Profits of £124,000 included in the Trial Balance given in Appendix 1 includes the provision for unrealised profits on the opening stock held at the Manchester branch.

3. There was stock in transit from Head Office to branch at 30 November 1983 at an invoiced price to the branch of £10,615.

4. There was cash in transit from the branch to Head Office at 30 November 1983 of £6,000.

5. Stocks at 30 November 1983 were as follows:

	Head Office £	Branch £
At cost	1,250,000	
At transfer price		66,990

6. Depreciation is to be charged at the following rates:

Freehold properties	2% of revalued amount
Fixtures and fittings	10% on original cost of assets held at 30 November 1983.
Vehicles	25% of written down value of assets held at 30 November 1983.

7. The company disposed of vehicles during the year. The details were as follows:

	Cost £	Cumulative Depreciation £
Head Office	28,000	14,500
Branch	12,000	8,000

Appendix 3
Further year end information on expenses and balance sheet items.
The following information may be relevant for the preparation of the published profit and loss account for the year ended 30 November 1983 and the balance sheet as at 30 November 1983.

1. The quoted investments are included in the trial balance at 30 November 1983 at cost. The details concerning the respective cost of each holding were not available at the date the draft accounts were being prepared. The Finance Director instructed that they should be treated as trade investments pending clarification and entered in the Balance Sheet at cost.

2. The 12% loan was raised on 1 June 1983 and is due for repayment on 31 May 1987. No loan interest has been paid or provided for.

3. The Administration Expenses included the following:

	£
Audit fee	56,000
Charitable donations	8,000
Salaries:	
Chairman	7,500
Managing Director	37,500
Finance Director	23,200

4. The Distribution Expenses included the following:

	£
Marketing Director's salary	28,000
Hire of vehicles	15,000

5. Corporation Tax for 1982-83 has been agreed at £67,000. The estimate for the current year on ordinary activities is £230,000. A transfer of £15,000 is to be made to the Deferred Taxation Account.

6. A final dividend of 1.5p per share has been proposed. It will be paid in March 1984.

7. The development expenditure has been incurred in a programme undertaken by the company to prepare an assembled prism toy that would, by rotating the prism, make pictures of footballers appear to move. The Finance Director has instructed that the expenditure of £104,000 should be

treated as an asset in the Balance Sheet.

8. Notification of redundancy has been given to a number of staff to take effect from 31 December 1983. The cost to the company of redundancy payments will be £265,000. There will be an estimated reduction in tax payable by the company of £130,000 arising from this item.

9. The freehold of the Head Office premises in London was valued at current open market valuation on an existing use basis at £394,000. The original cost was £300,000. No adjustment is to be made to the accumulated depreciation provision to 1 December 1982 consequential upon this revaluation.

10. Dividends received during the year were as follows:

Shares	Date	Amount received
		£
AJAX	May 1983	78,655
SCRUBBER	July 1983	3,500
SCRAPER	August 1983	10,000
Total		£92,155

16. On 1 March 1983, the Overseas Toy Company Ltd resolved to open a branch in Paris to sell its new range of bi-lingual dolls. The manager was authorised to purchase local French toys for resale but it was expected that the major proportion of the sales would be of the bi-lingual dolls supplied by the Head Office in London. The manager was to be allowed a commission of 1% on the sales of the dolls supplied by Head Office. No commission was to be allowed on locally purchased products.

On 29 February 1984, the trial balances were as follows:

	LONDON HEAD OFFICE		PARIS BRANCH OFFICE	
	£	£	Francs	Francs
Share capital		400,000		
Reserves		50,000		
Profit and Loss Account		35,800		
Creditors		44,250		123,312
Premises at cost	225,000			
Fixtures and Fittings, at cost	147,000		840,000	
Provision for depreciation of Fixtures		58,800		
Stock at 1 March 1983	143,786			
Debtors	125,941		351,024	
Bank Balance	101,938		270,792	
Cash in hand	9,821		86,004	
Sales		1,010,786		2,661,345
Purchases	586,535		2,065,005	
Goods sent to branch		135,200		
Goods sent to branch	169,000			1,565,000
Branch Stock Adjustment Account		33,800		
Remittances from branch		110,000	1,293,500	
Advance to branch	100,000			1,040,000
Administration expenses	187,128		285,173	
Distribution expenses	82,487		198,159	
	1,878,636	1,878,636	5,389,657	5,389,657

You have the following additional information:

1. Stock on hand at 29 February 1984 was

London	£141,600	
Paris—ex London	263,000	Francs
Local purchase	82,000	Francs

2. Goods were invoiced by London to Paris at cost plus 25%. Paris sold the goods at invoiced price plus 50%. The value of goods sent to Paris was based on a fixed conversion rate of 10 Francs to the £.

3. There were goods in transit that had been recorded in the London books at £12,500 but had not been received or recorded by Paris at 29 February 1984.

4. Paris had sent a remittance of 58,000 Francs on 28 February 1984. It was received in London on 5 March 1984 and converted to £4,375.

5. The advance of £100,000 was remitted to Paris when the exchange rate was 10.4 Francs to the £. The fixtures and fittings were acquired when the exchange rate was 10.5 Francs to the £, on 1 June 1983.

6. Depreciation of the London and Paris fixtures and fittings is to be provided at the rate of 10% per annum of cost.

7. Rates of exchange at other dates were:

As at 1 March 1983	10 Francs to the £
As at 29 February 1984	12 Francs to the £
Average for financial year	11 Francs to the £

8. The company policy on the translation of the branch balances at 29 February 1984 was to use the following exchange rates:

> Fixed assets-rates of exchange at date of acquisition.
> Current assets-rate of exchange at 29 February 1984.
> Current liabilities-rate of exchange at 29 February 1984.
> Sales, local purchases and expenses-average rate for the year.
> Goods sent from London-fixed rate of 10 Francs to the £.

Required:

a. Prepare a trading and Profit and Loss Account in Columnar Form for the Head Office, the Paris Branch and the Whole Business for the year ended 29 February 1984.

b. Prepare a Balance Sheet as at 29 February 1984 for the Whole Business.
Show all relevant workings.

(ACCA 2.9(2) June 1984)

17. **Required:**

a. Calculate the profit made by the Manchester branch of Leisure Supplies for the year ended 31 December 1983.

b. Comment critically on the statement produced by Mr Anthony in Appendix 3(e) to support the decision to discontinue the branch.

(ACCA 2.9(1) December 1984)

Appendix 3 Leisure Supplies: information relating to the Manchester branch

a. Included in the accounts of Leisure Supplies at 31 December 1982 were the following balances arising from cash outlays made by the Manchester branch:

	£
Freehold shop	25,000
Stock at cost price	20,750
Creditors	4,025
Vehicles	17,500
Expense accrued	325
Bank balance (overdrawn)	3,500

b. During 1983 the following cash transactions occurred:

		£
Receipts –	cash sales	215,050
	sale of all vehicles on 1 Jan 1983	16,250
Payments –	creditors	145,000
	purchase of vehicles on 1 Jan 1983	15,000
	manager's salary	12,000
	other staff salaries	5,250
	rates	1,500
	motor expenses	1,850
	general expenses including bank interest	1,650

purchase of job lot stock from
Leisure Supplies on 1 Jan 1983 at
cost plus 25%   65,535

All of the job lot was sold by 31 December 1983 at a profit of 15% on sales.

Before banking the receipts from cash sales, the manager paid wages of £425 per week.

c. At 31 December 1983 there was the following information:

   i. Freehold shop

     A valuation had been carried out at 31 December 1983 and the following information is available:

Cost price	£25,000
Existing use value	£36,000
Alternative use value	£26,000
Gross replacement cost	£86,000
Net replacement cost	£43,000
Forced sale value	£32,000

   ii. Stock

Cost price was	£27,750
Realisable value was	£34,687.5
Net realisable value was	£31,000

   iii. Vehicles

     The insurance value was £9,750

   iv. Creditors

     The creditors listing totalled £9,035

   v. Accrued expenses An analysis of expense items showed £875 to be outstanding.

   vi. Staff bonus. A staff bonus was payable at the end of each year. For 1983 this is estimated to be £6,250. If there is any stock loss, the bonus will be reduced by one-third of the value of the lost stock.

   vii. There was a gross profit on the standard line of stock calculated as 25% of the cost price of the stock sold.

   viii. Depreciation of vehicles was to be provided at the rate of 25% of the reducing balance.

d. During the year Mr Anthony had been analysing the effect on costs if the branch was closed. The indications were that:

   i. Motor vehicles would be retained by Leisure Supplies but the running costs would be reduced by £750.

   ii. The manager would be employed in the London office at a reduced salary of £9,000 per annum.

   iii. Other staff salaries and wages would be reduced by £12,250 and the bonus agreement would be terminated.

   iv. General expenses would be reduced by £1,200.

   v. Rates would cease to be payable.

e. Mr Anthony prepared the following statement based on his analysis which indicated that there would be savings of £15,573 per year. He discounted these savings over a period of 5 years at 10% to arrive at a present value of £59,037 for closing the branch.

Expenses	Reduction if branch closed £	Present value of annuity at 10%	Present value
(i) Motor expenses	750		
(ii) Manager's salary	3,000		
(iii) Other staff wages	12,250		

(iv)	General expenses	1,200		
(v)	Rates	1,500		
		18,700		
	Less Profit on job lot	(13,107)		
		5,593		
	Add Stock loss	9,980		
		£15,573	3.791	£59,037

18. The Fairly Free Company Ltd has four branches in England, Scotland, Wales and Northern Ireland at each of which it manufactures plastic bottles.

Each of the branches has been controlled by a manager with full responsibility for all aspects of the branch affairs including the purchase locally of fixed assets.

During 1984 there have been problems in that, although in total the company has had cash funds, because the branches operate separate bank accounts, there have been simultaneously debit and credit bank balances.

The directors have, therefore, decided to centralise the purchase of fixed assets, the raising of loans, and the payment of tax and dividends.

You are provided with (a) the Balance sheet of Fairly Free Company Ltd as at 31 December 1984, (b) the forecast Profit and Loss Accounts from each of the branches for the year ended 31 December 1985 and (c) additional information on proposed capital expenditure, movements in working capital and proposed raising of loans.

(a) Balance sheet of Fairly Free Company Ltd as at 31 December 1984

	£	£	£
Fixed assets at cost		750,000	
Less depreciation		125,000	
			625,000
Current assets			
Stock of materials	100,000		
Work in progress	10,875		
Stock of finished products	178,125		
Debtors	57,250		
Cash at bank	12,500		
		358,750	
Less Current liabilities			
Creditors	18,750		
Taxation	23,750		
Proposed dividends	20,000		
		62,500	
Working capital			296,250
Capital employed			£921,250
Share capital			
Ordinary shares of 50p each, fully paid up		500,000	
5% preference shares of £1 each, fully paid up		50,000	
		550,000	
Retained earnings		371,250	
Shareholders' funds			£921,250

(b) Forecast profit & Loss Accounts for the year ended 31 December 1985

	England		Scotland		Wales		N.Ireland	
	£	£	£	£	£	£	£	£
Sales		275,000		150,000		50,000		25,000
Materials used	137,500		30,000		15,000		10,000	
Wages	27,500		7,500		7,500		2,500	
Overheads	12,250		23,000		7,375		4,625	
Depreciation	50,000		17,500		6,250		1,250	
Change in work in progress	(1,000)		(500)		(250)		125	
Cost of Production	226,250		77,500		35,875		18,500	
Change in Finished Goods stock	(6,250)		(2,500)		(875)		250	
Cost of sales		220,000		75,000		35,000		18,750
Gross profit		55,000		75,000		15,000		6,250
Less:								
Administration expense	10,000		12,500		1,250		1,000	
Salaries	11,250		5,000		3,125		1,125	
Selling expense	6,250		5,000		1,250		750	
Salaries, commission	13,750		7,500		1,875		875	
		41,250		30,000		7,500		3,750
Operating profit		£13,750		£45,000		£7,500		£2,500

(c)

i. The proposed capital expenditure for 1985 is:

England	£100,000
Scotland	£6,250
Wales	£12,500
N.Ireland	£25,000

There were no proposed sales of fixed assets.

ii. Branch working capital at 31 December 1984 was:

	Stock of materials	Work in progress	Finished goods	Debtors	Creditors
	£	£	£	£	£
England	62,500	6,250	125,000	30,000	12,250
Scotland	25,000	2,125	43,750	16,250	5,000
Wales	8,750	1,625	6,250	7,500	1,000
N.Ireland	3,750	875	3,125	3,500	500

iii. Branch working capital at 31 December 1985 is estimated to be:

	Stock of materials	Work in progress	Finished goods	Debtors	Creditors
	£	£	£	£	£
England	71,250	7,250	131,250	40,000	16,000
Scotland	27,375	2,635	46,250	22,500	6,250
Wales	10,000	1,875	7,125	7,875	1,750
N.Ireland	3,875	750	2,875	4,625	1,000

iv. The company proposes to raise £62,500 by the issue of 8% debentures on 1 January 1985. Interest on overdraft is estimated to be £1,250.

v. The opening balances at bank on 1 January 1985 were England £6,000, Scotland £2,500. Wales £3,000, N.Ireland £1,000.

vi. **The fixed assets at 31 December 1984 were:**

	Cost	Depreciation	Net book value
	£	£	£
England	500,000	80,000	420,000
Scotland	175,000	17,500	157,500
Wales	62,500	18,750	43,750
Ireland	12,500	8,750	3,750

vii. The company pays the preference dividend for the year on 30 December of each year. It is proposed to pay a dividend for 1985 of 5% on the ordinary shares.

viii. The Corporation tax charge for 1985 has been agreed at £31,250. Ignore ACT.

Required:

a. Prepare a statement to show how much cash each branch will be able to transfer to Head Office and still maintain a credit balance of £3,000 at each branch as at 31 December 1985.

b. Prepare a forecast Balance Sheet for internal use for Fairly Free Company Limited as at 31 December 1985.

(ACCA 2.9(2) June 1985)

AAT EXAMINATION QUESTION

19. Mapp Ltd's head office is in London, and it has a branch in Brighton. The following trial balances have been extracted from the respective books of account of both the head office and the branch as at 30 June 19–8.

	Head office Dr. £	Head office Cr. £	Branch Dr. £	Branch Cr. £
Administrative expenses	135,000		9,000	
Branch current account	46,000			
Called up share capital (ordinary shares of £1 each)		300,000		
Cash at bank and in hand	19,000		2,000	
Creditors		22,500		5,000
Debtors	15,000		20,000	
Distribution costs	30,000		12,000	
Goods sent to branch		166,000		
Head office current account				24,000
Plant and machinery (net book value)	383,000		38,000	
Profit and loss account (at 1 July 19–7)		28,000		
Provision for unrealised profit on stock held by the branch		1,500		
Purchases	225,000		154,000	
Sales		350,000		215,000
Stock at cost or cost to branch at 1 July 19–7	15,000		9,000	
	£868,000	£868,000	£244,000	£244,000

Additional information:

1. Stock at 30 June 19–8 was valued as follows:

	£
Head office at cost	20,000
Branch at cost to branch	24,000
Goods in transit to branch at cost to branch	12,000

2. Goods purchased by the head office and sold to the branch are transferred at cost plus 20%.

3. At 30 June 19–8 the branch had transferred £10,000 to the head office's bank account but as at that date, no record had been made in the head office's books of account.

   Required:

   Prepare in adjacent columns the following:

   a. the head office, the branch, and the combined trading, and profit and loss accounts for the year to 30 June 19–8;

   and

   b. the head office, the branch, and the combined balance sheets as at that date.

(AAT)

4 Hire Purchase and Credit Sales

GENERAL BACKGROUND

1.0 When a supplier allows a customer to receive goods for other than an immediate cash payment, various financial arrangements may be made.

1.1 For example, the transaction may be financed by the normal terms of trade which require settlement within an agreed period or by the acceptance of a bill of exchange (see Chapter 8).

1.2 Alternatively, the transaction may be under a credit sale agreement whereby, the goods become the property of the buyer immediately but payment for them takes place over a stipulated period.

1.3 A fourth alternative is for the transaction to be subject to a hire purchase agreement. The goods remain the property of the supplier and the customer pays hire charges over a stipulated period at the end of which he pays a further amount, termed an option to purchase, which then gives him ownership.

1.4 A variation of this procedure is that the supplier sells the goods outright to a finance company which then follows the procedure in 1.3 and enters into a hire purchase contract with the customer.

1.5 Of the methods mentioned in 1.1. accounting entries for transactions on credit are well known and do not need to be repeated here; those for bills of exchange are dealt with in Chapter 8. The remainder of this Chapter is thus concerned with accounting for credit sale and hire purchase transactions (1.2 to 1.4) from the point of view of both the supplier (or finance company) and of the customer.

GENERAL ARRANGEMENTS

2.0 In 1.3 it was stated that under a hire purchase agreement the customer obtains possession of the goods at the outset, but that the ownership remains with the supplier (or finance company) until the end of the hiring period.

2.1 On a strict legal interpretation of the facts, the supplier (or finance company) should not take credit for any profit and the customer should not debit the cost of the items until the hiring period has ended.

2.2 Accounting, however, looks at the substance of the transaction rather than at its legal form. Consequently the supplier (or finance company) recognises profit as arising over the period of hire instead of at the end. Similarly the customer makes the necessary entry in Purchases or Fixed Assets at the beginning of the period and not after the option fee has been paid.

2.3 With both credit sale and hire purchase agreements the accounting arrangements are identical and from this subsection onwards, references to hire purchase transactions would apply equally to credit sale transactions.

2.4 Under a hire purchase transaction, the selling price consists of cost price plus gross profit (thus giving cash selling price) plus a further sum of hire purchase interest by way of compensation to the supplier for the delay in receiving full payment and for the attendant risks. This is a reasonable imposition because the supplier may have had to borrow money (and thus pay interest) to finance the deal, alternatively the money tied up in the deal might have been earning a return by being invested inside or outside the business.

2.5 Different accounting considerations apply to the suppliers and to the customers of goods on hire purchase. The problems of each of these parties and the manner in which they can be resolved will now be considered separately.

2.6 The accounting arrangements for hire purchase transactions are dealt with in Statement of Standard Accounting Practice 21 previously ED29 (Accounting for leases and hire purchase contracts).

OPERATING ARRANGEMENTS

GOODS BOUGHT ON HIRE PURCHASE

3.0 Items of this nature dealt with in the accounts of businesses are invariably fixed assets because it is illegal to dispose of the items during the hiring period and to acquire trading stock on hire purchase would require so short a hiring period as to nullify the advantages of this arrangement.

3.1 From the point of view of the buyer under a hire purchase contract, the purchase price consists of two elements – the "cash" cost price and the hire purchase interest – which together make up the hire purchase price but which must be accounted for separately.

ACCOUNTING METHODS.

3.2 There are two recognised ways of accounting for items bought on hire purchase. The main features are:

Method A   The asset account is debited with the "cash" cost of the item and the finance company is credited with the same amount.

Interest is debited to HP Interest and credited to the finance company when each instalment is due.

Deposit and instalments paid are debited to the finance company's account, the balance of which is included in creditors in the balance sheet.

The balance carried down each year on the finance company's account is the unpaid portion of the cash cost.

Method B   The asset account is debited with the "cash" cost of the item but the finance company is credited with the full hire purchase price, the interest element of which is debited to HP Interest Suspense.

When each instalment is due, the appropriate amount of interest is released from the HP Interest Suspense to HP Interest.

Deposit and instalments paid are debited to the finance company's account, the balance of which, minus the balance on the HP Interest Suspense, is included in creditors in the balance sheet.

3.3 For reasons stated in 2.2 and 3.0 the buyer treats his acquisitions as fixed assets when he obtains possession after becoming party to the contract, despite the fact that he is not the legal owner at that stage.

3.4 Depreciation on fixed assets bought on hire purchase must be charged from the date of acquisition of possession (not from date of legal ownership) and calculated on the cash cost price.

3.5 Under Method A and B an account is maintained for the finance company and, under Method B, for the suspended interest. The amount shown as the balance on the finance company's account is not due for payment within the immediate future or in one lump sum but as a series of payments, possibly over a number of years. Similarly, the balance on HP Interest Suspense represents interest due to be paid at various future times but not immediately due.

EXAMPLE

3.6 An example illustrating the points mentioned so far now follows and is solved using each of the methods A and B in turn, so that their effects can be compared and contrasted.

Langdale Transport Co Ltd acquired two new 30 ton articulated units on 1st January 19–0 for £129,150. The cash price of these units was £90,000.

The deal was financed by TSPT (Financings) Ltd and the terms of the hire purchase contract required a deposit of £30,000 on delivery, followed by three instalments on 31st December 19–0, 19–1 and 19–2 of £33,000, £33,000 and £33,150 respectively. The true rate of interest was 30% per annum.

The depreciation policy of Langdale Transport Ltd was to write off 20% per annum on a straight line basis assuming a residual value of nil.

Required:

Prepare the appropriate accounts in the books of Langdale Transport Ltd to record the above transactions. You should ignore the fact that this company has an opening balance on its Vehicles and Provision for depreciation on vehicles accounts. Accounts after the end of 19–2 need not be prepared.

Show the relevant balance sheet entries at the end of 19–0.

SOLUTION

3.7 A separate answer for each of the two methods outline in 3.2 now follows:

Method A

Langdale Transport Co.Ltd ledger

Vehicles

19–0		£	19–0		£
Jan 1	TSPT (Financings) Ltd	90,000	Dec 31	Balance c/d	90,000
191			19–1		
Jan 1	Balance b/d	90,000	Dec 31	Balance c/d	90,000
19–2			19–2		
Jan 1	Balance b/d	90,000	Dec 31	Balance c/d	90,000

TSPT (Financings) Ltd

19–0		£	19–0		£
Jan 1	Bank – deposit	30,000	Jan 1	Vehicles	90,000
Dec 31	Bank – 1st Instalment	33,000	Dec 31	HP Interest	18,000
				$(30\% \times (90,000 - 30,000))$	
Dec 31	Balance c/d	45,000			
		108,000			108,000
19–1			19–1		
Dec 31	Bank – 2nd Instalment	33,000	Jan 1	Balance b/d	45,000
Dec 31	Balance c/d	25,500	Dec 31	HP Interest	13,500
				$(30\% \times 45,000)$	
		58,500			58,500
19–2			19–2		
Dec 31	Bank – Final Instalment	33,150	Jan	Balance b/d	25,500
			Dec 31	HP Interest	7,650
				$(30\% \times 25,500)$	
		33,150			33,150

HP Interest

19–0		£	19–0		£
Dec 31	TSPT (Financings) Ltd	18,000	Dec 31	Profit and Loss	18,000
19–1			19–1		
Dec 31	TSPT (Financings) Ltd	13,500	Dec 31	Profit and Loss	13,500
19–2			19–2		
Dec 31	TSPT (Financings) Ltd	7,650	Dec 31	Profit and Loss	7,650

Provision for depreciation on vehicles

19–0		£	19–0		£
Dec 31	Balance c/d	18,000	Dec 31	Profit and Loss	18,000
19–1			19–1		
Dec 31	Balance c/d	36,000	Jan 1	Balance b/d	18,000
			Dec 31	Profit and Loss	18,000
		36,000			36,000
19–2			19–2		
Dec 31	Balance c/d	54,000	Jan 1	Balance b/d	36,000
			Dec 31	Profit and Loss	18,000
		54,000			54,000

Method B

The Vehicles, Hire Purchase Interest and Provision for depreciation accounts are exactly as for Method A and are not repeated.

TSPT (Financings) Ltd

19–0		£	19–0		£
Jan 1	Bank – deposit	30,000	Jan 1	Sundries	129,150
Dec 31	Bank – 1st Instalment	33,000			
Dec 31	Balance c/d	66,150			
		129,150			129,150
19–1			19–1		
Dec 31	Bank – 2nd Instalment	33,000	Jan 1	Balance b/d	66,150
Dec 31	Balance c/d	33,150			
		66,160			66,150
19–2			19–2		
Dec 31	Bank – Final Instalment	33,150	Jan 1	Balance b/d	33,150

Hire Purchase Interest Suspense

19–0		£	19–0		£
Jan 1	TSPT (Financings) Ld	39,150	Dec 31	Hire Purchase Interest	18,000
			Dec 31	Balance c/d	21,150
		39,150			39,150
19–1			19–1		
Jan 1	Balance b/d	21,150	Dec 31	Hire Purchase Interest	13,500
			Dec 31	Balance c/d	7,650
		21,150			21,150
19–2			19–2		
			Dec 31	Hire Purchase Interest	7,650
Jan 1	Balance b/d	7,650			

The calculation of the amount of interest transferred out each year is the same as under Method A and the workings are not repeated here.

The amounts which would be disclosed in the balance sheet at the end of each year would be identical for methods A and B, but different in composition. Thus, at the end of the first year (19–0) the following would appear. (The distinction between creditors is a Companies Act 1985 disclosure requirement)

		£	£
Method A	(Fixed assets)		
	Vehicles (at cost)	90,000	
	less provision for depreciation	18,000	
			72,000
	(Creditors: amounts falling due within one year)		
	Other creditors: hire purchase		
	[33,000 − 13,500]		
	[or 45,000 − 25,500]		19,500
	(Creditors: amounts falling due after one year)		
	Other creditors: hire purchase [33,150 − 7,650]		25,500
Method B	(Fixed assets)	£	£
	Vehicles (at cost)	90,000	
	less provision for depreciation	18,000	
			72,000
	(Creditors: amounts falling due within one year)		
	Other creditors: hire purchase		
	[66,150 − (33,150 + 13,500)]		19,500
	(Creditors: amounts falling due after one year)		
	Other creditors: hire purchase		
	[33,150 − 7,650]		25,500

In each case, the net effect of fixed assets (72,000) less combined creditors (£45,000, that is £19,500 plus £25,500)) is £27,000.

This figure is equivalent to:

	£	£
Deposit paid		30,000
1st Instalment paid	33,000	
less interest element	18,000	
		15,000
		45,000
less depreciation		18,000
		27,000

In other words, it represents the written down value of the accumulated deposit plus interest exclusive element of instalments paid.

Additionally, a note should be appended showing the hire purchase payments to which Langdale Transport Co. Ltd. is committed separately for the next year, for the second to fifth years and in total after that. In fact in this question there are only two further years involved.

The note required could be worded:

Hire Purchase payments

The payments to which the company is committed under hire purchase contracts are:

	£
Payable in next year	33,000
Payable in two to five years	33,150
	66,150

less finance charges allocated
to future periods [13, 500 + 7, 650]   21,150

45,000

It can be seen that this figure is equal to the aggregate of the two creditors figures included in the balance sheet extract at 31 December 19–0. [£19,500 + £25,500 = £45,000].

Another note should disclose the gross amounts of assets held under hire purchase contracts together with the related aggregate depreciation and the depreciation charge for the period should be disclosed for each major class of asset.

The note could be worded

Assets held under hire purchase contracts

		Depreciation	
	Cost	Accumulated	Current year
	£	£	£
Vehicles	90,000	18,000	18,000

HIRE PURCHASE INTEREST

3.8 As has been noted in 3.1 and following hire purchase interest is an element of the hire purchase price which must be written off as an expense over the life of the contract.

3.9 Ideally, hire purchase interest should be written off during the contract period in such a way as to produce a constant periodic rate of return on the remaining balance of the interest exclusive liability for each period.

ACTUARIAL METHOD

3.10 Of the write–off methods in use, only one, the actuarial method satisfies the criterion stated in 3.9. This is the method used in Example 3.6 and Solution 3.7. Usually, the interest percentage rate has to be obtained from actuarial tables, or by using a mathematical model or simply by trial and error. Here, however, the rate (30%) was given and this will ordinarily be the case in an examination question. If it is not given and it is not easy to calculate, an alternative method must be selected.

Actuarial methods are illustrated in detail in Chapter 5 of this Section in paragraphs 5.0 and following.

OTHER METHODS

3.11 The two common feasible alternative methods are the sum of the digits methods (sometimes termed the Rule of 78 method) and the equal instalment (or straight line) method. This latter method, although quite commonly used, fails to satisfy the 3.9 criterion.

SUM OF THE DIGITS METHODS

3.12 Under this method, interest is written off over accounting periods on a reducing method based on digits, as illustrated in 3.13 to 3.15. In order to arrive at the total digits, for each period end the remaining number of individual periods over which the contract is then outstanding, are added together. The interest written off in any period is that period's proportion of the total. It is important to ascertain whether instalments are paid at the start or end of a period because in the latter case there will be one more period to account for than in the former.

EXAMPLE

3.13 A company bought an asset under a hire purchase agreement. Instalments were due each quarter for 3 years. Hire purchase interest included in the hire purchase price was £78,000.

Required: Calculate the amount of interest to be written off in each quarterly period, assuming

a. instalments were paid at the end of the quarter

and

b. instalments were paid at the beginning of the quarter.

SOLUTION
3.14

Quarter Number	a. Instalments paid at the end of quarter			Instalments paid at beginning of quarter		
	No.of periods outstanding (digits)	Fraction	H.P. interest written off £	No. of periods outstanding (digits)	Fraction	H.P. interest written off £
1	12	12/78	12,000	11	11/66	13,000
2	11	11/78	11,000	10	10/66	11,818
3	10	10/78	10,000	9	9/66	10,636
4	9	9/78	9,000	8	8/66	9,455
5	8	8/78	8,000	7	7/66	8,273
6	7	7/78	7,000	6	6/66	7,091
7	6	6/78	6,000	5	5/66	5,909
8	5	5/78	5,000	4	4/66	4,727
9	4	4/78	4,000	3	3/66	3,545
10	3	3/78	3,000	2	2/66	2,364
11	2	2/78	2,000	1	1/66	1,182
12	1	1/78	1,000	0	–	–
Total	78		78,000	66		78,000

3.15 If the sum of the digits had been applied in Example 3.6 above, interest allocated to years would have been:

Year	No. of years outstanding	Fraction	H.P. Interest written off £
19–0	3	3/6	19,575
19–1	2	2/6	13,050
19–2	1	1/6	6,525
	6		39,150

COMPARISON OF METHODS
3.16 The effects of the different amounts written off which the three methods produce can be seen from the following table. In each case column (1) shows the interest exclusive outstanding liability, column (2) the amount of hire purchase interest written off and in column (3) the rate of return, that is, column (2) expressed as a percentage of column (1).

Year	Actuarial method			Sum of the digits method			Straight line method		
	Out-standing liability (1) £	H.P. interest written off (2) £	Rate of return (3) %	Out-standing liability (1) £	H.P. Interest written off (2) £	Rate of return (3) %	Out-standing liability (1) £	H.P. interest written off (2) £	Rate of return (3) %
19–0	60,000	18,000	30.0	60,000	19,575	32.6	60,000	13,050	21.8
19–1	45,000	13,500	30.0	46,575	13,050	28.0	40,050	13,050	32.6
19–2	25,500	7,650	30.0	26,625	6,525	24.5	20,100	13,050	65.0

From the above table it can be clearly seen that the straight line method fails completely to satisfy the criterion noted in 3.9 and for that reason, one of the other two methods is to be preferred.

CHOICE OF ACCOUNTING METHOD
3.17 Two methods of accounting for hire purchase items in the buyer books have been described in 3.2 and following and have been illustrated in 3.6 and following. In the absence of explicit or implicit directions in an examination question the method selected should be the one most appropriate under the circumstances.

OPERATING ARRANGEMENTS.

GOODS SOLD ON HIRE PURCHASE

4.0 Goods which are sold on hire purchase terms tend to fall into one of two broad categories:

1. large items which business buyers treat as fixed assets, or
2. small items most of which are retailed to members of the general public and for which therefore, the corresponding "buying" entries are not raised in the books of any business.

4.1 From the point of view of the seller under a hire purchase contract, the selling price consists of three elements – the cost price and gross profit, which together give the "cash" selling price, and hire purchase interest which mades the latter up to the hire purchase selling price.

ACCOUNTING METHODS

4.2 The accounting method employed depends upon the category of item in 4.0. There are different approaches for category 1. from those employed for category 2. and these will now be considered separately.

CATEGORY 1. ITEMS

4.3 For category 1. items (large items) the amounts involved are substantial and/or relatively infrequent and the supplier or finance company is able to identify the transactions surrounding each hire purchase contract with ease.

4.4 Consequently the supplier can spread the gross profit and hire purchase interest over the contract period without much difficulty. Where a supplier sells goods to a customer via a finance company, the seller can take full credit for gross profit at point of sale, but the finance company should take credit for hire purchase interest over the contract period on some suitable basis, for example, the sum of the digits or actuarial methods illustrated in 3.10 to 3.15. The objective is to produce a constant rate of return on the net investment in the contract in each period. Net investment is hire purchase instalments less finance charges allocated to future periods.

4.5 There are two common methods of accounting for category 1. items sold on hire purchase. The main features are:

Method A The customer's account is debited with the "cash" sale price of the items and HP Sales account is credited.

Interest is debited to the customer's account (when each instalment is due) and is credited to HP Interest Received.

Deposits and instalments received are credited to the customer's account. At the end of the period the balance on this account represents that part of the cash sale price not yet due or received. In the balance sheet it is included under current assets as HP Debtors not yet due.

At the end of each period the balances on HP Sales and on HP Interest Received are transferred to HP Trading as credits. This latter account is then debited with the cost of the hire purchase goods sold.

A provision for unrealised profit is raised to suspend the appropriate portion of gross profit included in selling price. Movements in this provision are reflected in HP Trading and in Provision for unrealised profit account.

The balance on HP Trading is called gross profit but is really a combined figure of pure gross profit and of hire purchase interest earned during the period and is transferred to the general trading account if different classes of business are transacted, or to profit and loss account if they are not.

Method B This is the same as Method A except for the following variations.

The customer's account is debited with the hire purchase sale price of the item, HP Sales account is credited with the cash price and HP

130

Interest Suspense with the full amount of interest on the contract. Deposits and instalments received are credited to the customer's account, as under Method A, but the balance on this account at the end of the period represents that part of the hire purchase sale price not yet due or received. In the balance sheet it is included under current assets, minus the balance on HP Interest Suspense, as HP Debtors not yet due.

The appropriate amount of interest, calculated on the outstanding balance of the cash price, as under Method A, is transferred at the due date by debiting HP Interest Suspense and crediting HP Interest Received. This latter account is then disposed of as under Method A.

4.6 For reasons stated in 2.2 and 3.0, the seller treats his disposals of goods as sales on parting with possession of them after becoming party to the contract, despite the fact that he is still the legal owner at that stage.

4.7 The amount shown as the balance on the customer's account is not due for collection within the immediate future or in one lump sum but as a series of receipts, possibly over a number of years. Similarly, the balance on HP Interest Suspense represents interest receivable at various future times but not immediately due.

4.8 The provision for unrealised profit required under both methods is calculated using the formula.

$$\frac{\text{Balance of cash selling price not yet due}}{\text{Total cash selling price}} \times \frac{\text{Gross profit}}{1}$$

or more simply,

$$\text{Gross profit } \% \times \text{ Balance of cash selling price not yet due.}$$

EXAMPLE

4.9 An example using each of the methods A and B so that their effects can be compared and contrasted now follows.

The facts are similar to those in 3.6.

Langdale Transport Co. Ltd acquired two new 30 ton articulated units on 1st January 19–0 for £129,150.

The vehicles were supplied and financed by P.A.G. Jay (New Sawley) Ltd and the terms of the hire purchase contract required a deposit of £30,000 on delivery, followed by three instalments on 31st December 19–0, 19–1, and 19–2 of £33,000, £33,000 and £33,150 respectively. The true rate of interest was 30% per annum.

The cost of the vehicles to the suppliers was £60,000 and their cash selling price was £90,000.

Required:

Prepare the appropriate accounts in the books of P.A.G. Jay (New Sawley) Ltd to record the above transactions for each of the three years.

Show the relevant balance sheet entries at the end of 19–0.

SOLUTION

4.10 A separate answer for each of the two methods outlined in 4.5, now follows.

Method A

P.A.G. Jay (New Sawley) Ltd Ledger

Langdale Transport Co. Ltd

19–0		£	19–0		£
Jan 1	HP Sales	90,000	Jan 1	Bank – deposit	30,000
Dec 31	HP Interest Rec.	18,000	Dec 31	Bank – 1st	
	(30% × (90,000 − 30,000))			instalment	33,000
				Balance c/d	45,000
		108,000			108,000
19–1			19–1		
Jan 1	Balance b/d	45,000	Dec 31	Bank – 2nd	
Dec 31	HP Interest Rec.	13,500		instalment	33,000
	(30% × 45,000)		Dec 31	Balance c/d	25,500
		58,500			58,500
19–2			19–2		
Jan 1	Balance b/d	25,500	Dec 31	Bank – Final	
Dec 31	HP Interest Rec.	7,650		instalment	33,150
	(30% × 25,500)				
		33,150			33,150

HP Interest Received

19–0		£	19–0		£
			Dec 31	Langdale Transport	
Dec 31	HP Trading	18,000		Co. Ltd	18,000
19–1			19–1		
			Dec 31	Langdale Transport	
Dec 31	HP Trading	13,500		Co Ltd	13,500
19–2			19–2		
			Dec 31	Langdale Transport	
Dec 31	HP Trading	7,650		Co. Ltd	7,650

HP Sales

19–0		£	19–0		£
			Jan 1	Langdale Transport	
Dec 31	HP Trading	90,000		Co Ltd	90,000

HP Trading
for year ended 31/12/19–0

	£		£
HP Cost of Sales	60,000	HP Sales	90,000
Provn. for unrealised profit	15,000	HP Interest Received	18,000
Gross profit	33,000		
	108,000		108,000

for year ended 31/12/19–1

	£			£
Gross profit	20,000	HP Interest Received		13,500
		Provn. for unrealised profit (released)		6,500
	20,000			20,000

for year ended 31/12/19–2

	£			£
Gross Profit	16,150	HP Interest Received		7,650
		Prov. for unrealised profit (released)		8,500
	16,150			16,150

Provision for unrealised profit

19–0			£	19–0			£
Dec 31	Balance c/d ($33\frac{1}{3}\% \times 45,000$)		15,000	Dec 31	HP Trading		15,000
19–1				19–1			
Dec 31	Balance c/d ($33\frac{1}{3}\% \times 25,500$)		8,500	Jan 1	Balance b/d		15,000
Dec 31	HP Trading		6,500				
			15,000				15,000
19–2				19–2			
Dec 31	HP Trading		8,500	Jan 1	Balance b/d		8,500

Method B.

The HP Sales, HP Trading and Provision for unrealised profit accounts are the same as under Method A and are not repeated.

Langdale Transport Co. Ltd

19–0			£	19–0			£
Jan 1	Sundries		129,150	Jan 1	Bank – deposit		30,000
				Dec 31	Bank – 1st instalment		33,000
				Dec 31	Balance c/d		66,150
			129,150				129,150
19–1				19–1			
Jan 1	Balance b/d		66,150	Dec 31	Bank – 2nd instalment		33,000
				Dec 31	Balance c/d		33,150
			66,150				66,150
19–2				19–2			
				Dec 31	Bank – Final instalment		33,150
Jan 1	Balance b/d		33,150				33,150

133

HP Interest Suspense

19–0		£	19–0		£
Dec 31	HP Interest Received	18,000	Jan 1	Langdale Transport	
Dec 31	Balance c/d	21,150		Co. Ltd	39,150
		39,150			39,150
19–1			19–1		
Dec 31	HP Interest Received	13,500	Jan 1	Balance b/d	21,150
Dec 31	Balance c/d	7,650			
		21,150			21,150
19–2			19–2		
Dec 31	HP Interest Received	7,650	Jan 1	Balance b/d	7,650

HP Interest Received

19–0		£	19–0		£
Dec 31	HP Trading	18,000	Dec 31	HP Interest Suspense	18,000
19–1			19–1		
Dec 31	HP Trading	13,500	Dec 31	HP Interest Suspense	13,500
19–2			19–2		
Dec 31	HP Trading	7,650	Dec 31	HP Interest Suspense	7,650

The amounts which would be disclosed in the balance sheet at the end of each year would be identical for Methods A and B but different in composition. Thus at the end of the first year (19–0) the following would appear. (The distinction between debtors is a Companies Act 1985 disclosure requirement).

Method A   £

  (Current Assets)

   Debtors: amounts due within one year

   Net investment in hire purchase contracts
    [33,000 − 13,500] [or, 45,000 − 25,500] 19,500

   Debtors: amounts due in more than one year

   Net investment in hire purchase contracts
    [33,150 − 7,650] 25,500

  (Provisions for liabilities and charges)

   Other provisions
   :Provision for unrealised profit on hire purchase
    contracts 15,000

Method B   £

  (Current Assets)

   Debtors: amounts due within one year

   Net investment in hire purchase contracts
    [66,150 − (33,150 + 13,500)] 19,500

   Debtors: amounts due in more than one year

Net investment in hire purchase contracts [33, 150 − 7, 650]	25,500

(Provisions for liabilities and charges)

Other provisions	
Provision for unrealised profit on hire purchase contracts	15,000

Under both methods it is essential to append a note to the balance sheet, as follows:

	£
Cost of assets acquired for hiring under hire purchase contracts	60,000
Net investment in hire purchase contracts	45,000

This latter figure, £45,000, equals the aggregate of the two individual amounts shown as debtors [19, 500 + 25, 500]

The gross investment represents the interest exclusive outstanding instalments.

CATEGORY 2.ITEMS

4.11 For items which are categorised under 4.0.2. (small items), the amounts involved (per item) are relatively small but the volume of such items is likely to be large.

4.12 It would be impractical for the supplier to employ the methods outlined in 4.5 as it would require an amount of clerical effort disproportionately greater than the resultant advantages.

4.13 An acceptable expedient is employed in that no attempt is made to calculate the amounts of gross profit and hire purchase interest received for separate crediting to HP Trading account nor are calculations made for each individual contract.

4.14 Instead, calculations, are based on the total of all transactions in a particular accounting period of a particular class of items under hire purchase contracts and for the purposes of the calculations, "pure" gross profit and hire purchase interest are combined into one figure. It is this combined figure which is apportioned over the hire purchase period.

4.15 There are two common methods of accounting for category 2. items sold on hire purchase, these are termed

    a. Stock on hire method, and

    b. Provision for unrealised profit method.

Both of these methods produce identical figures for profit and for current assets but differently composed.

STOCK ON HIRE METHOD

4.16 This method is so called because goods on hire purchase in customers' hands are regarded as stock out on hire at cost.

ACCOUNTING ENTRIES

4.17 Goods sold on hire purchase are debited to HP Debtors and credited to HP Sales at hire purchase selling price.

4.18 Deposits and instalments received are debited to Bank and credited to HP Debtors. The balance of this latter account represents sums owing on hire purchase contracts but not yet due.

4.19 An amount equivalent to the deposits and instalments received in a particular period is debited to HP Sales and credited to HP Trading. The balance on HP Sales account is then equal and opposite to that on HP Debtors and the two therefore cancel out and do not appear in the balance sheet.

4.20 The cost price of goods sold on hire purchase is debited to HP Trading and credited to the (general) Trading account.

4.21 At the end of each period stock on hire is calculated, using the formula.

$$\frac{\text{HP Debtors owing not yet due(4.18)}}{\text{Total HP Sales (4.17)}} \times \frac{\text{Cost of HP goods (4.20)}}{1}$$

This figure is credited to the HP Trading Account and carried down as a debit to the next period. In the balance sheet, net investment in hire purchase contracts is shown, split between current and non-current amounts, together with a note of the gross investment and of interest allocated to future periods, as illustrated in 4.10.

4.22 The balancing figure on HP Trading then represents "pure" gross profit plus hire purchase interest earned during the period and is carried to (general) Trading account. The hire purchase interest component is calculated as shown in 3.8 to 3.16.

EXAMPLE

4.23 The following figures are a summary of the sales on hire purchase made by a retailer of electrical goods during his first year of trading.

	£
Goods sold on hire purchase	
– at cost price	45,000
– at hire purchase selling price	75,000
Deposits received	25,000
Instalments received	30,000

The terms of the standard contract require a deposit of one third of the hire purchase price of the goods followed by 12 equal monthly instalments.

Required:

Prepare the appropriate accounts for the year using the Stock on hire method.

SOLUTION

4.24 Stock on hire method

Hire Purchase Debtors

	£		£
HP Sales	75,000	Bank – deposits	25,000
		– instalments	30,000
		Balance c/d	20,000
	75,000		75,000
Balance b/d	20,000		

Hire Purchase Sales

	£		£
HP Trading	55,000	HP Debtors	75,000
(25,000 + 30,000)			
Balance c/d	20,000		
	75,000		75,000
		Balance b/d	20,000

Hire Purchase Trading

	£		£
Trading (cost of hp sales)	45,000	HP Sales	55,000
Gross Profit	22,000	Stock on hire c/d	
		$\left(\dfrac{20,000}{75,000} \times \dfrac{45,000}{1} \right)$	12,000
	67,000		67,000
Stock on hire b/d	12,000		

PROVISION FOR UNREALISED PROFIT METHOD

4.25 This method receives its name from the fact that a provision is raised against the profit included in hire purchase debtors not yet due, to reduce them to cost.

ACCOUNTING ENTRIES

4.26 Goods sold on hire purchase are debited to HP Debtors and credited to HP Sales at hire purchase selling price, as in 4.17.

4.27 Deposits and instalments received are debited to Bank and credited to HP Debtors, as in 4.18. The balance of HP Debtors also represents sums owing on hire purchase contracts but not yet due.

4.28 The balance on HP Sales is debited (to close off that account) and credited to HP Trading.

4.29 The cost of goods sold on hire purchase is debited to HP Trading and credited to the (general) Trading Account, as in 4.20.

4.30 A provision for unrealised profit ("pure" gross profit plus hire purchase interest) is raised by debiting HP Trading and crediting Provision for unrealised profit using the formula

$$\frac{\text{HP Debtors not yet due (4.27)}}{\text{Total HP Sales (4.26)}} \times \frac{\text{Total profit (4.26 minus 4.29)}}{1}$$

This provision is recalculated each period. The difference between the opening and closing balances is transferred to HP Trading account.

4.31 The balancing figure on HP Trading then represents "pure" gross profit plus hire purchase interest earned during the period and is carried to (general) Trading account. The hire purchase interest component is calculated as shown in 3.8 to 3.16.

4.32 In the balance sheet net investment in hire purchase contracts is shown split between current and non–current amounts, together with a note of the gross investment and of interest allocated to future periods, as illustrated in 4.10.

EXAMPLE

4.33 Using the same facts as in 4.23, prepare the appropriate accounts for the year using the Provision for unrealised profit method.

SOLUTION

4.34 This is the alternative method of preparing the accounts.

Obviously, in a practical situation, the retailer would opt for one method or the other, but not for both.

Provision for unrealised profit method

Hire Purchase Debtors

	£		£
HP Sales	75,000	Bank – deposits	25,000
		– instalments	30,000
		Balance c/d	20,000
	75,000		75,000
Balance b/d	20,000		

Hire Purchase Sales

	£		£
HP Trading	75,000	HP Debtors	75,000

Hire Purchase Trading

	£		£
Trading (cost of hp sales)	45,000	HP Sales	75,000
Provision for unrealised profit	8,000		
$\left(\dfrac{20,000}{75,000} \times \dfrac{75,000 - 45,000}{1} \right)$			
Gross Profit	22,000		
	75,000		75,000

Provision for unrealised profit

	£		£
Balance c/d	8,000	HP Trading	8,000
		Balance b/d	8,000

REPOSSESSIONS

4.35 Sometimes, the buyer of goods on hire purchase refuses to continue paying the instalments. The Hire Purchase Acts permit the seller (after complying with certain legal requirements designed to protect genuine buyers who have merely fallen behind with their payments) to repossess the goods.

4.36 Goods repossessed in this manner may be sold. Firstly, however, they may need to be repaired or reconditioned. Deposits and instalments received are retained by the seller.

4.37 Repossessed goods can be accounted for within the Hire Purchase Trading account under both of the methods – Stock on hire and Provision for unrealised profit – already mentioned.

4.38 Preferably, however, the figures relating to repossessed items should be segregated from those which continue under hire purchase contracts in the normal way. Repossessions are then accounted for in a separate account of that name.

4.39 One advantage of this approach is that the gross profit (from which the gross profit percentage is then calculated) appearing in Hire Purchase Trading, is not distorted by the (abnormal) profit or loss on repossessed goods.

ACCOUNTING ENTRIES

4.40 Irrespective of the accounting method used, the entries in respect of repossessed goods are identical.

4.41 HP Debtors is credited and HP Sales is debited with the hire purchase selling price of the repossessed goods. Under the Provision for unrealised profit method the effect of this is to reduce the amount subsequently transferred to HP Trading.

4.42 HP Debtors is debited and Repossessions account is credited with the deposits and instalments already received on the repossessed goods. Under the Stock on hire method, the effect of this is to reduce the amount of deposits plus instalments equivalent subsequently transferred to HP Trading.

4.43 The cost of goods sold on hire purchase is split. That relating to repossessed goods is debited to Repossessions and the rest, relating to goods still under hire purchase in the normal way, is debited to HP Trading. In each case the corresponding credit is in (general) Trading.

4.44 The valuation figure of repossessed stock is credited to Repossessions and then carried down on that account as a debit balance.

4.45 The balance on Repossessions is profit or loss and is transferred to (general) Trading account.

EXAMPLE

4.46 Using the same facts as in 4.23 and 4.33, goods costing £900 and sold on hire purchase for £1,500 were repossessed after deposits of £500 and instalments of £200 had been received.

These goods were then valued at £300, subject to reconditioning estimated at £50.

Required:

Prepare the appropriate accounts to record these matters.

Compare and contrast the solution with those given in 4.24 and 4.34.

SOLUTION

4.47 This solution shows the accounts as they would appear under each of the two methods.

Stock on hire method

Hire Purchase Debtors

	£		£
HP Sales	75,000	Bank – deposits	25,000
Repossessions	700	– instalments	30,000
		HP Sales	1,500
		Balance c/d	19,200
	75,700		75,700
Balance b/d	19,200		

Hire Purchase Sales

	£		£
HP Debtors	1,500	HP Debtors	75,000
HP Trading	54,300		
(25,000 + 30,000 − 700)			
Balance c/d	19,200		
	75,000		75,000
		Balance b/d	19,200

Hire Purchase Trading

	£		£
Trading (cost of hp sales)	44,100	HP Sales	54,300
(45,000 − 900)		Stock on hire c/d	11,520
Gross profit	21,720	$\left(\dfrac{19,200}{73,500} \times \dfrac{44,100}{1} \right)$	
	65,820		65,820
Stock on hire b/d	11,520		

Repossessions

	£		£
Trading (cost of sales)	900	HP Debtors	700
Gross Profit	50	Stock (at valuation) c/d	250
		(300 − 50)	
	950		950
Stock (at valuation) b/d	250		

(Repossessed stock has been valued at net realisable value, this being lower than cost).

Provision for unrealised profit method

Hire Purchase Debtors

	£		£
HP Sales	75,000	Bank – deposits	25,000
Repossessions	700	– instalments	30,000
		HP Sales	1,500
		Balance c/d	19,200
	75,700		75,700
Balance b/d	19,200		

Hire Purchase Sales

	£		£
HP Debtors	1,500	HP Debtors	75,000
HP Trading	73,500		
	75,000		75,000

Hire Purchase Trading

	£		£
Trading (cost of hp sales)	44,100	HP Sales	73,500
Provn. for unrealised profit	7,680		
$\left(\dfrac{19,200}{73,500} \times \dfrac{73,500 - 44,100}{1} \right)$			
Gross Profit	21,720		
	73,500		73,500

Provision for unrealised profit

	£		£
Balance c/d	7,680	HP Trading	7,680
		Balance b/d	7,680

Repossessions

	£		£
Trading (cost of sales	900	HP Debtors	700
Gross Profit	50	Stock (at valuation)	250
		(300 − 50)	
	950		950
Stock at valuation b/d	250		

CHOICE OF ACCOUNTING METHOD.

4.48 In this section various methods of accounting for hire purchase transactions in the books of the seller, have been illlustrated.

4.49 The problem remains to be resolved as to which method shopuld be employed when answering examination questions.

4.50 Sometimes the question is explicit and specifies the method to be used.

4.51 At other times the method is implicit in the question. For example, a trial balance or narrative instructions in a hire purchase selling question might refer to deposits and instalments and/or stock on hire and this would indicate the method which the examiner is looking for.

4.52 Where the question does not indicate or imply a particular method, the one most suitable under the circumstances should be selected.

STUDENT SELF TESTING

Test Exercises

1. On 1 January 19–1 Contractors Ltd bought a hydraulic crane from Hi–lift Ltd. on hire purchase. The terms of the hire purchase contract were that an initial deposit of £40,000 was payable, followed by three instalments of £37,978 on 31 December in each of the next three years from 19– 1 onwards. The cost of the crane for cash purchase would have been £120,000. Interest is charged on the balance outstanding at 31 December at the rate of 20% per annum.

   The financial year of both companies ends on 31 December.

   Required:

   Answer the following questions:

   a. what was the amount of hire purchase interest included in the hire purchase price?

   b. what amounts of interest would be allocated to each of the three years if the sum of the digits methods were used?

   c. post the Hi–lift Ltd. account in Contractors Ltd's ledger for 19–1 using the 20% per annum interest rate.

   d. show an extract from Contractors Ltd's balance sheet relevant to the contract as at 31 December 19– 1 and using the facts in (c). Depreciation on cranes is at 25% per annum straight line on cost.

   e. show an extract from Hi–lift Ltd's balance sheet relevant to the contract as at 31 December 19–1. The company includes in its instalments receivable interest at 20% per annum on the outstanding balance. The manufacturing cost of the hydraulic crane was £90,000.

2. A business commenced selling retail goods on hire purchase on 1 January 19–1. During the first year, goods which had cost £15,300 were sold on hire purchase for £26,500. Deposits and instalments received totalled £13,060.

   Required:

   Post the relevant ledger accounts using

   a. provision for unrealised profit method

   and

   b. stock on hire method.

3. GH Limited acquired three excavators from MN Limited under hire purchase agreements which provided for a deposit of 10% with the balance to be paid in three annual instalments, the first of which was due one year after the signing of the agreement and the payment of the deposit. The date of purchase, capital cost and annual repayments are as under:

Excavator	Date of acquisition	Capital cost £	Annual repayment £
A	31 December, 19–5	15,000	5,428
B	31 December, 19–5	15,000	5,428
C	31 December, 19–7	25,000	8,042

   All instalments were paid on the due dates except that when the excavator C was purchased the vendor agreed to take back excavator A on the basis that GH Limited was to be credited with £5,000 in lieu of a deposit on excavator C and that no further payment was to be made in respect of excavator A after the instalment paid on 31st December 19–7.

   The practice of GH Limited was to capitalise the cash value of each excavator immediately on purchase crediting it to the vendor. Each yearly instalment included interest at the rate of 10% per annum calculated on the outstanding balance at the beginning of the year.

   GH Limited makes up its accounts to 31st December of each year and provides depreciation on excavators at the rate of 20% on reducing balance.

   You are required to:

   a. write up in the books of GH Limited in columnar form for the three years ended 31st December 19–8:

   i. asset account for each excavator;

   ii. vendors account for excavator;

    iii. asset disposals account;

    iv. depreciation provision account for each excavator;

  b. show how the figures relating to the excavators should appear in the balance sheet of GH Limited at 31st December 19–8.

    Taxation is to be ignored.

    (ICMA)

4. a. What is the basic principle involved in accounting for Hire Purchase Transactions? Describe how that principle is accommodated by two of the accounting methods commonly used to account for Hire Purchase Transactions.

  b. Neilson Electronics commenced business on 1st April, 19–3, selling television sets both on a cash basis and by instalments. Instalment sales required a deposit of one third of the cash selling price with the balance payable in 18 equal monthly instalments. No additional charge is made for this service. At the end of each financial year, the firm takes credit for the profit on instalment sales only in respect of the proportion represented by deposits and instalments actually received.

The following transactions took place during the two years ended 31st March, 19–5:

	19–4	19–5
	£	£
Cash Sales	32,022	43,770
Instalments Sales	282,978	397,980
New TV sets purchased	231,000	250,379
Cash collections on instalment contracts:		
Initial deposit	94,326	132,660
Monthly instalments – 19–4 Sales	64,413	92,079
– 19–5 Sales		83,940
Stocks at 31st March:		
New sets at cost	54,600	72,015

Required:

  i. Prepare trading accounts in respect of cash sales for each of the years ended 31st March, 19–4 and 31st March 19–5.

  ii. Show the gross profit on instalment sales for each of the years ending 31st March, 19–4, and 31st March 19–5.

    (ACCA)

5. Syncopating Sounds Ltd, whose accounting period ends on 31 December of each year, made a hire purchase sale to Jeremy Kunz of a Mazurka organ on 1 September 19–5. The cost of the organ was £3,000 and the terms of the sale were: initial payment of £1,000 and the payment of £160 on the 1st of each month for the next 24 months, commencing 1 October 19–5.

Kunz defaults on the March 19–6 payment and informs the company that he is unable to make any further payments. A court order is obtained and the organ is repossessed on 1 June 19–6, at which date it has a trade–in value of £2,200 and a second–hand sales value of £3,800.

Required:

  a. Give the differing amounts which can be reported as the profit on this transaction in the year ended 31 December 19–5, and indicate the conditions under which each of the differing amounts might be considered to conform with generally accepted accounting principles. (Make any further assumptions you wish).

  b. Ignoring taxation considerations, explain the support each amount has in relation to generally accepted accounting principles.

  c. Show the entries necessary under each of the methods shown in your answer in respect of the repossession.

    (ACCA)

6. Tom Potter set up in business on 1 January 19–7 to sell snooker tables of a standard size and quality designed for home use. He leased a store room and needed no fixed assets. His opening capital was £8,000, represented initially by the bank balance. The tables are purchased for £72 each and sold for cash or monthly credit terms for £100 each. Towards the end of the first year Tom decided to try hire purchase trading, financing it himself. He required a deposit of £30 followed by 18 monthly instalments of £5 each, the first one payable one month after purchase.

During the year he bought a total of 300 tables and sold 210 of them for cash or on monthly credit terms. His hire purchase sales were 12 in October, 20 in November and 30 in December, but two of those sold in October had to be repossessed in December – the deposit and one instalment had been paid in each case. One of the repossessed tables was badly damaged and would need repairs estimated at £24 after which it would probably be offered for sale at half the normal cash price. The other one had hardly been used and could be treated as new stock.

It can be assumed that all the hire purchase sales were made on the first day of the month and that the instalments were paid promptly on the last day of each month (eg for the October sales, three instalments would have been received by 31 December). Not being too sure about the accounting implications of hire purchase trading, Tom Potter credited all sales to the Sales account, including the total H.P. price for hire purchase sales and debited either Debtors or Bank. At the end of the year he had the following balances:

Trial Balances 31 December 19–7

	Dr £	Cr £
Capital		8,000
Purchases	21,600	
Sales		28,440
Debtors	6,270	
Creditors		576
Expenses	1,800	
Drawings	6,400	
Bank balance	946	
	£37,016	£37,016

Required:
Calculate the net profit for the year and prepare the Balance Sheet at 31 December 19–7.
(ACCA)

7. On 1 April 19–6 John Sharpe opened a business dealing in a new type of power tool of which there was one model only.

The cost price of each tool is £40 and he deals with them in the following ways:

a. sells for cash from the shop for £56 each.

b. sends to an agent on a sale–or–return basis, the agent charging £56 each but deducting his commission of $12\frac{1}{2}\%$;

c. sells on hire purchase, the HP selling price is £64 comprising a deposit of £16 and 8 quarterly instalments of £6 each;

d. hires out at the rate of £2 per day: this rate has been calculated by assuming that after allowing for repairs, maintenance, and othe costs, he will want to recover £80 per tool and the probable number of days of working life is 40. A deposit of £20 is charged and an adjustment made when the tool is returned.

During the first year he bought 500 tools and these can be accounted for as follows:

Sold for cash from shop	188
Sold by agent	80
Held for the purposes of hire (of which all have been out at least once, and 18 are still out at year–end)	50
Sold on HP terms, the agreements still continuing	100
Repossessed from HP customers	2

143

In agent's hands at year–end	20	
In stock at the shop at year–end	60	

500

A summary of the cash receipt during the year shows:

	£	£
Cash sales from shop		10,528
Sales by agent, *less* commission	3,920	
less amount owing	392	
		3,528
Hire charges, where accounts have been settled		
(400 days)		800
Deposits for tools out on hire		360
Hire purchase sales:		
40 – deposit only	640	
60 – deposit and 2 instalments due	1,680	
	2,320	
Less: Instalments outstanding	30	
		2,290
Hire purchase repossessions:		
2 – deposit and 1 instalment received before		
repossession		44
		£17,550

The two tools which have been repossessed are in quite reasonable condition and John Sharpe has decided to add them to the 50 available for hire.

When the business was started, Sharpe brought in £10,000 cash as his capital. He has paid for all the 500 tools and also £3,000 for working expenses. There are no assets or liabilities other than those arising from the above.

Required:

a. Calculate the amount of profit which you would bring into this first year's accounts, explaining any assumptions you make.

b. Show the Balance Sheet at the end of the first year.
(ACCA)

8. N Limited and R Limited, both engaged in hire–purchase trading, have agreed to amalgamate. However, the basis used for calculating the profits and the value of stock in customers' hands by N Limited is different from that used by R Limited.

The policy of N Limited has been not to take credit for profit on any sale until the original cost has been received from the customers, after which all receipts are treated as profits.

The policy of R Limited has been to take profit in the proportion which customers' payments received bear to the total hire–purchase price.

Using the information given below concerning N Limited, you are required to calculate for that company:

a. the profits for each of the four years 19–4, 19–5, 19–6, and 19–7 on the basis used by R Limited, as stated above;

b. the value of stocks in customers' hands as at 31st December, 19–7 as calculated on:

  i. the existing basis;

  ii. the basis used by R Limited.

1. N Limited commenced trading on 1st January, 19– 4.
2. Hire–purchase prices are fixed by the addition of 43% to cost of goods.

3. The terms of sale require the customer to pay a deposit of 25% of the hire-purchase price at time of delivery and three equal annual instalments payable on the anniversary of the sale.
The accounts of N Limited on the existing basis show the following results:

| | 19–4 | 19–5 | 19–6 | 19–7 | 19–8 | 19–9 |
	£	£	£	£	£	£
Hire-purchase profit	Nil	Nil	1,305	7,392	6,256	8,681
less Other expenses	1,400	1,200	1,100	1,400	1,500	1,300
Profit	–	–	205	5,992	4,756	7,381
Loss	1,400	1,200	–	–	–	–

9. Frost and Keen commenced trading in partnership on 1st July 19–5, retailing frozen foods and deep freeze cabinets. Frost agreed to manage the department selling the freezers and Keen the department selling frozen foods. Each partner is to receive 10% of the net profit of his department, after charging such commission and the balance of profit is to be shared equally.

The partners acquired premises at a rental of £2,100 per annum. It is agreed that two-thirds of the premises will be occupied by the frozen food department and expenses are to be allocated accordingly. The freezers are all of a standard type which costs £84 and retails at £126. Sales of freezers on credit terms and on hire purchase terms are made with a deposit of £30 followed by 12 and 24 equal monthly payments respectively. Finance charges are calculated on the balance of the cash price at 12.5% for credit sales and 25% for hire purchase sales. Some freezers are also leased to customers at £3 per month for five years.

Freezers have an estimated life of five years after which they have no scrap value.

Of the initial purchase of freezers it was agreed that 20 should be transferred to equipment and used in the frozen food department for storage purposes.

Proper accounting records have not been kept, but you obtain the following information for the year ended 30th June 19–6:

1. The number of freezers sent out to customers during the year fell into the following categories:

Cash sales	96
Credit sales	62
Hire purchase sales	80
On lease	32

2. Full gross profit is to be taken on cash and credit sales.

3. At the year end amounts outstanding to suppliers for freezers totalled £2,940, and for frozen foods £1,016. Expenses accrued were rates £245 and electricity £51.

4. Stock of frozen foods, at cost, on 30th June 19–6 amounted to £4,171.

5. A summary of the bank transactions for the year showed the following:

	£		£
Capital introduced by Frost		Purchases:	
and Keen equally	10,000	Freezers	22,764
Freezers:		Frozen food	28,167
cash sales	12,096	Rent	1,575
deposits on credit and hire		Rates	685
purchase sales	4,260	Electricity	240
credit sales – instalments	1,890	General expenses	193
hire purchase sales –		Balance as on 30th June	
instalments	2,000	19–6	7,910
lease rentals	1,080		
Frozen foods – balance of sale	30,208		
	61,534		61,534

6. Cash payments deducted from frozen foods sales each week before paying into the bank were: wages – freezer department £27; wages – frozen food department £46; general expenses £2; drawings – Frost £39; and drawings – Keen £44.

You are required to prepare departmental Trading and Profit and Loss Accounts for the year ended 30th June 19–6, in accordance with recognised accounting principles and a Balance Sheet as on that date.

10. Tee Vee Services has existed for a number of years, selling television sets for cash and on hire purchase. The following figures were extracted from the books as at 31st December 19–7.

	No. of sets	Amount £
Available for sale (at cost)	20	3,240
Awaiting repair (at valuation)	4	360
Showroom display/demonstration models – at cost	8	780
– at written down value		180

	Date of Agreement			
	19–5	19–6	19–7	Total
	£	£	£	£
HP Debtors (at h.p. selling prices)	2,460	7,080	15,150	24,690
Less Provision for unrealised profit	1,010	2,920	6,240	10,170
HP Debtors (at cost)	1,450	4,160	8,910	14,520

During the year 19–8, Tee Vee Services

a. entered into a leasing agreement with Fairview Properties Ltd., the owners of a block of luxury flats, for the installation and maintenance of 60 colour television sets at an annual rental of £5,400 (including a maintenance element of £300), payable in advance. This arrangement operated from 1st July 19–8.

   The latest model sets were bought specifically for this contract in June, 19–8 at a cost of £9,120 and are expected to be valueless at the end of three years.

   Up to 31st December, 19–8, £40 had been expended by Tee Vee Services in carrying out repairs under the agreement.

b. bought 300 sets (additional to those referred to in note a. above) at a cost of £51,000.

c. sold 92 sets, costing £15,460, for £19,330 cash.

d. sold 186 sets, costing £31,480, on hire purchase for £53,520.

e. received hire purchase deposits and instalments as follows:–

	Date of Agreement				
	19–5	19–6	19–7	19–8	Total
	£	£	£	£	£
HP deposit/instalments	2,460	4,320	8,220	28,380	43,380

f. The display and demonstration sets were replaced by new models in stock at £1,320 on 1st May 19–8. Depreciation was to be based on a two year life assuming no residual value.

   The 8 original sets were reconditioned, at a cost of £170, and together with the 4 sets on which repair work of £50 had been carried out, were sold to a dealer for £900 cash.

g. Other expenses, incurred for the business as a whole, amounted to £10,590 for the year.

NB. Value Added Tax, which has been ignored above, should be disregarded for the purposes of your answer.

Required:

a. Prepare a statement of profit for the year 31st December, 19–8, showing separately the profit/loss arising under each of the headings:

Cash sales	–to the public
	–to dealers
H.P. Sales	–19–5 agreements
	–19–6 agreements
	–19–7 agreements
	–19–8 agreements
Leasing	–to Fairview Properties Ltd.
Net Profit	

b. Prepare a statement of quantities and values of stocks and of hire purchase debtors as at 31st December 19–8, in a form comparable with that given (as at 31st December, 19–7) as the introductory data preceding note a. at the beginning of this question.

c. Post the Provision for Maintenance (Leased Sets) Account up to 31st December 19–8:

ACCA EXAMINATION QUESTIONS

11. James and Giles Porter started up in business on 1 January 1980 as Porter Brothers sharing profits James 7/10 and Giles 3/10. They marketed a single product under the trade name 'Automated Office'. Each 'Automated Office' consisted of a microcomputer, disc drive, printer and database software. The firm had decided to sell the complete system only under the 'Automated Office' trade name. Their Balance Sheet at the end of their first year is set out below:

Balance Sheet of Porter Brothers as at 31 December 19–0

Fixed Assets	Cost	Dep'n	NBV	
	£	£	£	£
Leasehold premises	6,000	1,000	5,000	
Fixtures	4,800	800	4,000	
Motor vehicles	10,000	2,000	8,000	
Total Fixed Assets				17,000
Current Assets				
Stock of 'Automated Offices'		49,920		
Debtors		16,000		
Cash		2,000	67,920	
Current Liabilities				
Trade creditors		15,000		
Working capital				52,920
Net Capital Employed				£69,920
Represented by:				
Capital accounts:				
James Porter			35,000	
Giles Porter			35,000	70,000
Current accounts:				
James – Profit		8,344		
– Drawings		(6,000)	2,344	
Giles – Profit		3,576		
– Drawings		(6,000)	(2,424)	(80)
				£69,920

For 1981, they decided to extend their marketing to include rental, cash sales, hire purchase, leasing and credit sales. The terms of trading in 1981 were to be:

a. *Purchases*

The firm would continue to acquire the product at a price of £2,496 for each 'Automated Office'. Credit of two months was allowed to the firm (November purchases were paid for in January).

b. *Supplies to customers*

i. Rental terms would be £1,040 per annum with agreements for a standard period of one year, payments to be made quarterly commencing in the month of sale.

ii. Cash sales would be made at the retail price of £3,120. A cash discount of 5% would be allowed on all cash sales.

iii. Hire Purchase terms were that there should a deposit of £1,037 and 24 monthly payments of £100, the first monthly payment being made in the month of sale.

iv. Lease agreements were for a period of 5 years at £800 per annum, payable quarterly in advance.

v. Credit sale agreements were for a period of 6 months with six monthly payments of £555, the first monthly payment being made in the month of sale.

The number of 'Automated Offices' purchased and supplied during 1981 are given below:

4 : Hire Purchase and Credit Sales

		Jan.	Feb.	Mar.	Apr.	May	June	July	Aug.	Sept.	Oct.	Nov.	Dec.
(a)	*Purchased*	4	4	4	8	8	8	8	12	8	8	8	8
(b)	*Supplied*												
	Rental				3			4			2		
	Cash Sales				2	1						1	1
	Hire Purchase	2	3	1	5	5	5	4	6	4	3	4	5
	Lease	4			3			8					
Credit	Sales					5					8		

The partners supplied the following information:

i. Each 'Automated Office' was estimated to have an effective life of 5 years.

ii. The lease of the premises was for a term of 6 years from 1 January 1980.

iii. The fixtures were to be written off over the term of the lease.

iv. The vehicles were to be depreciated at 20% of reducing balance.

v. The Establishment, Administration, Selling and Distribution expenses totalled £22,000 for 1981.

vi. Drawings during 1981 totalled £5,000 for James and £7,000 for Giles Porter.

vii. The acounting treatment for Hire Purchase contracts was to record them as stock and to take credit for profit and interest in proportion to cash received.

viii. The Accounting treatment for the lease agreements was to record them as a sale and to take credit for the whole of the profit on the cash sales price in the year in which the agreement was signed. Credit is taken for interest in proportion to cash received.

ix. The Accounting Treatment for credit sale agreements is to take credit for the interest in proportion to the instalments received.

Required:

a. Prepare a COLUMNAR INTERNAL TRADING ACCOUNT for the year ended 31 December 1981, to show the result of each method of marketing.

b. Prepare a Profit & Loss Account for the year ended 31 December 1981 and a Balance Sheet as at 31 December 1981.

(ACCA 2.9(2) (June 1983)

12. B Hassocks commenced business on 1 January 1984 selling television sets direct to the public for cash and on hire purchase.

He started with capital of £45,000 and acquired leasehold premises with a ten year life for a premium of £24,000, fixtures and fittings for £15,000 and a motor van. The motor van was acquired under a hire purchase contract. The terms were:

Cash price	£12,000
Deposit	£3,000 payable on 1 January 1984
Interest rate	10% per annum

Three equal instalments on 31 December in 1984, 1985 and 1986.

The lease and fixtures are to be depreciated over the life of the lease and the motor van is to be depreciated at the rate of twenty five per cent per annum on the reducing balance:

During the period 1 January to 30 April 1984 the number of sets sold were:

	January	February	March	April
Cash sales	20	60	90	120
Hire purchase sales	–	30	60	90

The prices and terms of purchase and sale were:

Cost price	£300
Cash price	£420
Hire purchase price	£500
Hire purchase terms	Deposit of £170 payable on the day of sale followed by eleven monthly instalments of £30 starting in the month following the sale.

During the period 1 January to 30 April 1984 the following payments were made:

Wages to Sales assistant	£6,840
Rent, rates and other expenses	£10,000
Suppliers	£112,500

On 30 April 1984 the firm repossessed three television sets that had been sold on hire purchase on 1 February 1984 and on which only one instalment has been paid. Hassocks valued the three repossessed sets at £70 each. Hassocks decided to take credit for gross profit in proportion to cash received in the accounting period and to spread interest evenly over the life of the agreeement, except for repossessed sets when it was proposed to deal with them separately and to include a Profit or Loss on Repossession as a separate item in the Profit and Loss Account.

There were 40 television sets on hand at 30 April 1984 excluding the sets that had been repossessed.

Required:

Prepare a trading and Profit and loss account for the period 1 January to 30 April 1984 which shows clearly the separate contributions from cash and hire purchase sales and a balance sheet as at 30 April 1984.

(ACCA 2.9(2) December 1984)

13. Smith and Jones are partners in Western Co. which has a high street shop dealing in domestic electrical goods both for outright sale and under hire–purchase agreements. Whilst Smith was working on the partnership records at home there was a fire which destroyed some of the records.

Smith and Jones have provided you with:

a. a draft profit and loss account for the first year's trading to 31 March 1985 and a draft balance sheet at that date.

b. a list of debtor balances.

The first year's accounts had been produced by an accountant who was not a member of the Association.

The draft accounts for the first year's trading are as follows:

Profit and Loss account for the year ended 31 March 1985

	£	£
Sales		95,000
Purchases	58,379	
Less: Closing stock	10,500	
		47,879
		47,121
Rent and rates	7,500	
Wages	10,250	
Printing, stationery and miscellaneous expenses	746	
Suspense	3,250	
		21,746
		25,375
Share of profit – Smith	12,688	
Jones	12,687	
		25,375

Balance sheet at 31 March 1985

	£	£
Shop fixtures, fittings and equipment		15,500
Stock	10,500	
Debtors	43,692	
Cash at bank	933	
	55,125	
Creditors	6,250	
		48,875
		64,375

Partners' capital accounts

Smith – capital introduced		25,000	
profit		12,688	
		37,688	
drawings		3,500	
			34,188
Jones – capital introduced		22,000	
profit		12,687	
		34,687	
drawings		4,500	
			30,187
			64,375

On investigating the first year's draft accounts it is discovered that:

i. All hire–purchase sales are for a two year period and 16% of the cash price is added for interest. On signing a hire–purchase contract the customer pays 20% of the cash price as deposit and thereafter 24 equal instalments are paid at monthly intervals.

ii. Sales in the draft accounts include the full amount of the hire–purchase sales including the interest charged for the full two year period. The partners consider that hire–purchase interest should be spread over the 24 month period on a 'rule of 78' basis, and they have been told that the factor for a two year contract is 300. Credit should be taken for the cash sales price in the month of sale. The calculations of interest using the 'rule of 78' are shown in the schedule of hire–purchase sales (note viii).

iii. A sum of £2,300 in outright sales not paid for in the year were not recorded as debtors although the figure is included in sales.

iv. A payment of £950 for fittings for the shop was made in the year. This amount is in the cash book but has not been posted to any nominal ledger account.

v. No depreciation has been provided on the shop fixtures, fittings and equipment 15% on the reducing balance is agreed to be appropriate.

vi. Closing stock has been understated by £500.

vii. All hire–purchase instalments due have been paid.

viii. The records for the year to 31 March 1985 show the hire–purchase sales to be:

Hire Purchase Sales

	Total including HPinterest	Interest included	Amount relating to year to 31 March 1985	
1984	£	£	Factor	£
April	1,160	160	209	111
May	2,320	320	195	208
June	1,740	240	180	144
July	6,380	880	164	481
August	5,220	720	147	353
September	2,900	400	129	172
October	6,960	960	110	352
November	8,700	1,200	90	360
December	9,280	1,280	69	294
1985				
January	7,830	1,080	47	169
February	4,176	576	24	46
March	7,540	1,040	–	–

An analysis of the debtors list reveals the following information at 31 March 1986:
Ordinary debtors for sales £2,450

Hire–purchase debtors		Balance	No. of instalments paid	Interest included Factor	£
1984/85 Sales		40	23	1	1
		160	22	3	3
		180	21	6	5
		880	20	10	29
		900	19	15	36
		600	18	21	28
		1,680	17	28	90
		2,400	16	36	144
		2,880	15	45	192
		2,700	14	55	198
		1,584	13	66	127
	17,124	3,120	12	78	270
1985/86 Sales		3,640	11	91	340
		4,480	10	105	448
		6,000	9	120	640
		5,120	8	136	580
		4,760	7	153	571
		6,480	6	171	821
		7,600	5	190	1,013
		9,600	4	210	1,344
		12,600	3	231	1,848
		14,080	2	253	2,159
		7,360	1	276	1,178
	88,440	6,720	0	300	1,120

Included in the balance for which 15 instalments have been paid is a debtor for £360 who has defaulted, his goods had been repossessed and sold for £25. There are no other bad debts or defaults.

The following information is relevant to the second year's trading:

i. The margin on sales has remained constant throughout the year at 45% of sales price (before adding hire–purchase interest). One month's credit is taken on purchases. Purchases in March 1986 were £8,000.

ii. Rent and rates remained at the same level as in 1984/85, wages amounted to £12,000 in the year.

iii. Printing, stationery and miscellaneous expenses were £1,550 for the year.

iv. Amounts paid into the bank in respect of non hire–purchase sales were £15,250.

v. Smith has withdrawn £80 per week from the business during the year and Jones has withdrawn £100 per week.

vi. Closing stocks of goods for resale had the same value as at 31 March 1985.

vii. All sales moneys were banked intact and all expenses and withdrawals were made by cheque payments.

Required:

a. A revised profit and loss account for the year ended 31 March 1985 and a balance sheet as at that date.

b. A profit and loss account for the year ended 31 March 1986 and a balance sheet as at that date.
(ACCA 2.9(2) June 1986

AAT EXAMINATION QUESTION

13. On 1 January 19–7, Carver bought a machine costing £20,000 on hire purchase. He paid a deposit of £6,000 on 1 January 19–7 and he also agreed to pay two annual instalments of £5,828 on 31 December in each year, and a final instalment of £5,831 on 31 December 19–9.

The implied rate of interest in the agreement was 12%. This rate of interest is to be applied to the amount outstanding in the hire purchase loan account as at the beginning of the year.

The machine is to be depreciated on a straight line basis over five years on the assumption that the machine will have no residual value at the end of that time.

Required:

a. Write up the following accounts for each of the three years to 31 December 19–7, 19–8 and 19–9 respectively:

    i.   machine account;

    ii. accumulated depreciation on machine account; and

    iii. hire purchase loan account; and

b. show the balance sheet extracts for the year as at 31 December 19–7, 19–8 and 19–9 respectively for the following items;

    i.   machine at cost;

    ii. accumulated depreciation on the machine;

    iii. long term liabilities: obligations under hire purchase contract; and

    iv. current liabilities: obligations under hire purchase contract.

(AAT)

5 Leasing

GENERAL

1.0 Figures published by the Equipment Leasing Association, the representative body of the major leasing companies in the UK, reveal that there has been a phenomenal increase in the leasing of assets during the last two decades. From a figure of £130m in 1971 the value of leased assets had soared to £2,674m by 1981 (in each case, the figures represent new business during the years concerned). Currently it is a multi–billion pound industry. During 1990 the value of leased assets (new business) is expected to exceed £8,000m and the outstanding value to exceed £30,000m.

1.1 Acquisition of assets under hire purchase contracts was a well established practice prior to 1970. Accounting for hire purchase and credit sale transactions is the subject of Chapter 4.

1.2 The introduction of 100% first year capital allowances and of stock relief in the 1970s put many industrial concerns in the position of being unable to utilise those sizeable allowances and reliefs due to insufficient taxable profits.

1.3 Such companies found an alternative in leasing their assets from other companies established for that purpose and able to avail themselves of capital grants and taxation allowances which they were able to pass on to their lessees in the form of lower leasing rental charges.

1.4 Considerable mutual advantages derived from an arrangement of this sort. The lessor is usually a subsidiary company of a major UK bank. Capital allowances from the assets acquired for leasing can be fully utilised to "shelter" the profits of other companies within the group. The lessee, too, benefitted substantially because the leasing rentals are allowable expenses for tax purposes and are spread over the leasing life of the items concerned instead of being concentrated as capital allowances into the first year if those same items were acquired by outright purchase or on hire purchase. (But see 1.6 (below).

1.5 Cash flow, too is benefitted for the lessee in that regular, fixed sums, of lower amount than the comparable hire purchase repayments, flow out of the business instead of a large single sum in the case of outright purchase.

1.6 The Finance Act 1984 had an impact on leasing business in that the progressive reduction of first year allowances (100%) between 1984 and 1986 to the level of writing down allowances (25%) has inevitably had an adverse effect in that the taxation advantages, passed on to the lessees in the form of lower rentals, has been reduced.

DIFFERENCE BETWEEN LEASING AND HIRE PURCHASE TRANSACTIONS.

2.0 When one business acquires an asset from another business on lease, the legal title to the asset remains vested in the lessor business. If that same asset is acquired under a hire purchase contract, the legal title would remain vested in the supplying or financing business for the duration of the contract and is then acquired by the hire purchaser on payment of the option fee.

ACCOUNTING TREATMENT OF LEASING AND HIRE PURCHASE TRANSACTIONS

3.0 In the accounting records of the hire purchaser it has been a long established principle that substance takes precedence over form in that the cost of the asset (excluding the hire purchase interest element) is capitalised (and depreciated) whilst the future liability for instalments not yet due is shown under appropriate creditor headings.

3.1 Directly contrasting with this treatment, leased items had not in the past usually been brought into the body of the balance sheet of the lessee but instead been mentioned in a note. Reasons advanced for this treatment were that the items concerned were not owned by the lessee and that future rentals did not constitute a current (or long–term) liability.

3.2 This treatment came under closer scrutiny by the accounting profession after the collapse in 1974 of a major UK company. It was subsequently discovered that the company had entered into substantial (non–cancellable) leasing contracts and that the lessors ranked as creditors for future rentals. The phrase "off balance sheet finance" has since been coined to describe the situation where known future liabilities are excluded from the balance sheet. Against this background ED 29 was published in 1981. This was then converted into SSAP 21 in 1984.

SSAP 21 – ACCOUNTING FOR LEASES AND HIRE PURCHASE CONTRACTS (issued August 1984)

3.3 The SSAP defines a lease as a contract for the hire of a specific asset, (the lessor retaining ownership

153

but granting the lessee the right to use the asset for a specified length of time at an agreed rental) refers to finance leases and operating leases, distinguished thus:

    a. **finance lease** – over the life of the contract, the lessee pays to the lessor, in the form of rentals,

        i. the full cost of the asset, and

        ii. a return on the finance provided.

    under a contract which cannot normally be cancelled. Effectively, the lessee is the owner (though not in law) and enjoys the benefits of ownership whilst at the same time bearing the risks and responsibilities of ownership, for example, by bearing the maintenance and insurance costs of the asset.

    b. **operating lease** – is a lease other than a finance lease. In practice the lessee hires the asset for less than the life of the asset. The lessor retains the risks and responsibilities of ownership and bears the cost of maintenance and insurance etc.

3.4 There is little to distinguish the substance of a finance lease from that of a hire purchase contract, except that under the former, the lessor retains the legal title throughout and is thus able to claim the Regional Development Grant under suitable circumstances and also the taxation capital allowances.

3.5 An asset held under a hire purchase agreement is accorded by SSAP 21 almost the same accounting treatment as an asset held under a finance lease if it is of a financing nature; otherwise it is accounted for in the same way as an operating lease.

ACCOUNTING TREATMENT BY LESSORS

3.6 A finance lease should be shown in the lessor's balance sheet as a debtor at its net investment amount defined as

      the aggregate of the minimum lease payments
      plus
      any unguaranteed residual value accruing to the lessor
      less
      grants (from government or other sources) for the use or purchase of the asset
      and less also
      gross earnings allocated to future periods (including in the lease payments).

    If necessary, a provision for bad and doubtful rentals receivable should be raised against this net investment figure. Amounts due under hire purchase contracts to a finance company should be accounted for on a similar basis to finance leases, subject to 3.5 (above).

3.7 Where a hire purchase contract is treated as a finance lease, the gross earnings are to be allocated to the accounting periods during the life of the contract in such a way as to produce a constant periodic rate of return on the net investment. (In practice this means using either an actuarial method or the sum of the digits method). Gross earnings appear under Turnover in the profit and loss account.

3.8 Under a finance lease proper, however, allocation of the gross earnings to the accounting periods during the life of the lease should be in such a way as to produce a constant periodic rate of return on the net cash investment.

3.9 SSAP 21 defines net cash investment as the amount of funds invested in a lease by a lessor taking into account, as appropriate:

      government or other grants receivable for the purchase or use of the asset
      the fair value of the asset at the outset of the lease
      rentals received
      taxation payments and receipts (including the effect of capital allowances)
      residual values
      interest payments and receipts
      profit taken out of the lease

3.10 Alternatively, gross earnings may be allocated at an amount equal to the lessor's estimated cost of finance included in the calculation of net cash investment and the remainder on a systematic basis.

3.11 Any tax–free grants received (see 1.3 and 3.4) in respect of the purchase price of the assets acquired for leasing should be credited in the profit and loss account at either the actual amount received, or, this sum grossed–up by the notional amount of tax.

3.12 Commission, legal fees etc incurred by a lessor in arranging a lease should be apportioned over the life of the lease on a rational basis.

3.13 Assets held for use in operating leases should be treated as fixed assets and depreciated accordingly. Rentals (exclusive of charges for services) should be recognised on a straight line basis over the period of the lease unless a preferable alternative basis exists.

3.14 Selling profit should not be recognised by a manufacturer under an operating lease but may be so under a finance lease, to the extent of the excess of fair value over cost but reduced by grants receivable.

FINAL ACCOUNTS' DISCLOSURES BY LESSORS

3.15 Separate disclosure is required:

  a. in the profit and loss account of

        rentals receivable from finance leases
        rentals receivable from operating leases
        notional amounts by which profit before tax and the taxation charge have been increased, if applicable, (see 3.11 above)

  b. in the balance sheet, of

        cost of acquisition of finance lease assets
        net investment (see 3.6) separately for finance leases and hire purchase contracts.
        gross assets held for operating leases, analysed by major class of asset, together with the related accumulated depreciation.

  c. any other information of significance to users of financial statements, including statement of accounting policies for finance and operating leases.

ACCOUNTING TREATMENT OF LESSEES

3.16 A finance lease should be shown in the lessee's balance sheet both as an asset and as a liability (for future rentals), initially at the fair value (the purchase cost of the asset adjusted by grants receivable) or at the present value of the minimum lease payments calculated using a commercial rate of interest. If the fair value is more than the minimum lease payments, the amounts to be capitalised (and therefore depreciated) should be the minimum lease payments. Depreciation should be over the shorter of the lease term or the useful life of the asset.

3.17 Rentals payable should be apportioned between the finance charge and the outstanding obligation payable over future periods. Allocation of the finance charge should be on the basis of producing a constant periodic rate of return on the remaining balance of the obligation for each accounting period. (An actuarial method or the sum of the digits method can be used for the purpose of this calculation). The finance charge should appear under the heading Interest payable and other charges in the profit and loss account.

3.18 Operating lease rentals should be charged to profit and loss account over the life of the lease on a straight line basis, unless a preferable alternative basis exists.

3.19 A similar basis to that outlined above in 3.16 and 3.17 should be applied by a hirer to an asset held under a hire purchase contract, except that a hire purchase asset should be depreciated over its useful life.

FINAL ACCOUNTS' DISCLOSURES BY LESSEES

3.20 Separate disclosure is required:

  a. in the profit and loss account of

        total finance charges for the period
        total operating lease rentals charged as an expense, analysed between hire of plant and machinery and other
        depreciation for each major class of asset for finance leases and hire purchase contracts (combined)

  b. in the balance sheet of

        gross amounts of assets held, analysed by major class of asset, together with the related accumulated depreciation for finance leases and hire purchase contracts (combined). Alternatively, these figures may be combined with those for owned assets and only the net amount of assets held under finance leases and hire purchase contracts (combined) be disclosed, together with their depreciation for the period.

        either, gross obligations, that is, total minimum lease and hire purchase payments outstanding (combined) ,or, net obligations, exclusive of finance charges, should be disclosed as payable in the next year, in the second to fifth years and then thereafter in total. If gross obligations are disclosed, finance charges are deducted in total. The same information must be shown for operating leases, analysed between land and buildings (combined) and other items.

operating lease payment commitments, separately for land and buildings and for other, payable in the next year, expiring in that year, in two to five years, and in more than five years.

statement of finance lease commitments entered into but not yet operative.

c. any other information of significance to users of financial statements, including a statement of accounting policies for finance and operating leases.

SALE AND LEASEBACK TRANSACTIONS

3.21 In order to obtain the benefits of leasing, some businesses which own, say, plant sell that plant to a leasing company and then lease it back again. This is simply a financial manoeuvre as the plant concerned never actually leaves the premises of the original business which, however, benefits immediately from the net cash inflow. This arrangement is commonly applied to land and buildings as well as to plant.

3.22 An apparent profit or loss, being the difference between the sale price of the asset and its carrying value, should, if the arrangement results in

a. a finance lease, be deferred and amortised over the shorter of the term of the lease or the useful life of the asset in the financial statements of the seller–lessee

b. an operating lease, for a transaction.

    i.   at fair value, profit or loss is recognised immediately.

    ii. at below fair value, profit or loss is recognised immediately unless the loss is matched by future rentals at below commercial rate. That amount should be amortised over the remainder of the lease term.

    iii. at above fair value, the excess of sale price over fair value should be deferred and amortised over the remainder of the lease term or until the next rent review, if sooner.

REACTIONS TO ED 29.

3.23 Lease accounting is a notoriously controversial subject, as is evident by the length of time, six years, it took to produce the exposure draft.

3.24 The controversy showed no signs of abating because, after publication of ED 29, the Equipment Leasing Association, whose members transact about 80% of all the leasing business in the UK, issued an official statement opposing certain of the proposals. The main opposition was to the treatment of Regional Development Grants and to the inclusion in the body of the balance sheet (of lessees) of their obligations under finance leases together with the capitalised leases.

REGIONAL DEVELOPMENT GRANTS

3.25 Regional Development Grants are tax–free grants from the government under the Industry Act 1972. Many leasing companies are eligible for capital based grants on their purchases of assets for leasing. SSAP 4 (Accounting for government grants) prescribes that such grants should be held in suspense and credited to revenue over the lives of the assets concerned. The usual way that this is done is by crediting profit and loss account each period with an appropriate amount and debiting the suspense account.

3.26 Because leasing rentals charged to lessees have been abated not only by the capital allowances on the items concerned but also by the regional development grants (if applicable) some leasing companies bolster up the credits to profit and loss account by grossing up the regional development grant by a notional amount of tax (which is then included under the taxation heading).

3.27 The effect of this manoeuvre is to show an improved profit before tax figure or, as is frequently the case, to convert what would otherwise be a loss before tax into a profit before tax. Whether the grant is grossed up or not, profit after tax is unaffected. It is, therefore, in the nature of a window dressing device which members of the Equipment Leasing Association were strongly in favour of preserving. The reaction of the Accounting Standards Committee was that this is more a matter of accounting for tax–free grants than for leasing. However, this practice is now permitted under SSAP 21.

INCLUSION OF CAPITALISED LEASES
AND LEASING OBLIGATIONS ON THE BALANCE SHEET.

3.28 The capitalisation of leases and their inclusion on the balance sheet together with the liability for future rentals was strenuously opposed by the leasing industry on four main grounds.

3.29 Firstly, there was the fear that at some future time the Revenue authorities would withdraw capital allowances from lessors and grant them to lessees who were unlikely to have sufficient profits to be able to utilise the allowances properly.

3.30 Secondly, the inclusion on the balance sheet of the liabilities for future rentals might have placed some lessee companies in breach of their borrowing powers.

3.31 Thirdly, the inclusion noted in the previous paragraph might have deterred some companies from becoming lessees out of fear of their disclosable liabilities being increased. Advocates of this viewpoint asserted that this would lead to a reduction in leasing buisness which would be bad for both lessor and lessee companies and for the economy as a whole. The Equipment Leasing Association's alternative to these two points was that leasing arrangements should be disclosed by way of footnotes. The Accounting Standards Committee did not accept this as an acceptable alternative; footnotes are no substitute for proper inclusion – omission understates both assets and liabilities and distorts financial relationships (ratio calculations).

3.32 Fourthly, it was claimed that the calculations needed were too elaborate and complicated for small companies.

3.33 ED 29 was accorded standard status and has been designated SSAP 21.

APPLICATION OF ACCOUNTING TREATMENT
AND DISCLOSURE REQUIREMENTS

LESSORS

EXAMPLE–FINANCE LEASE

4.0 YZ (Leasing) PLC is the lessor of plant which had an initial fair value of £250,000. The plant was leased on a five year non–cancellable lease at an annual rental of £60,000, payable in advance, from 1 January 19–5.

Required:

a. Calculate the total gross earnings over the life of the lease.

b. State how YZ would show this transaction (including notes) in a balance sheet prepared on 1 January 19–5, assuming that the first rental received included the gross earnings allocation of £28,000.

c. Calculate the fractions to be used in allocating the gross earnings to accounting years over the life of the lease, using the sum of the digits methods.

d. Calculate the gross earnings allocated to accounting years on the basis of your answer to c. above.

e. Show extracts from YZ (Leasing) PLC's balance sheet (including notes) at 31 December 19–5, relating to the leasing arrangements.

SOLUTION

4.1

a.

	£
Total rentals over life of lease [5 × £60,000]	300,000
less Initial fair value	250,000
Gross earnings	50,000

b. **Extract from balance sheet as at 1 January 19–5**

	£
Current Assets	
Debtors: amounts due in more than one year	
Net investment in finance leases	
[(4 × 60,000) − (50,000 − 28,000)]	218,000

157

Notes £
Cost of assets acquired for letting under finance leases 250,000
Net investment in finance leases 218,000

c.	At 1 January: (after rental received)	No. of years outstanding	Fraction
	19–5	4	4/10
	19–6	3	3/10
	19–7	2	2/10
	19–8	1	1/10
	19–9	0	–
		10	

d.	Year	Fraction	Gross earnings allocation £
	19–5	4/10	20,000
	19–6	3/10	15,000
	19–7	2/10	10,000
	19–8	1/10	5,000
	19–9	–	Nil
			£50,000

These sums would appear as gross earnings (turnover) in the profit and loss accounts for their respective years.

e. **Extract from balance sheet as at 31 December 19–5**
Current Assets £
Debtors: amounts due in less than one year
Net investment in finance leases
[60,000 − 15,000] 45,000

Debtors: amounts due in more than one year
Net investment in finance leases
[3 × £60,000) − (10,000 + 5,000)] 165,000

Notes £
Cost of assets acquired for letting under finance leases 250,000
Net investment in finance leases
[equivalent to 45,000 + 165,000 above] 210,000

EXAMPLE–OPERATING LEASE

4.2 VW (Leasing) PLC is the lessor of plant which it acquired at a cost of £400,000 on 1 January 19–5. This plant, which has an estimated life of 10 years with no residual value, was leased on that same day for an initial period of four years, under operating lease arrangements, at an annual rental of £60,000.

Required:

Show how VW would treat this transaction (including notes) in a profit and loss account for the year 19–7 and in a balance sheet at 31 December 19–7.

SOLUTION

4.3 **Extract from profit and loss account for year ended 31 December 19–7**

£000
Turnover (leasing rental) 60

Cost of sales (depreciation based on
useful life–10% × £400,000) 40

Notes	£000
Aggregate operating lease rentals receivable in the period	60

Extract from balance sheet as at 31 December 19–7

	£000
Fixed assets	
Tangible assets	
Plant and machinery (included in)	280

Notes	£000
Plant held for leasing: gross	400
aggregate depreciation	
[3 × 40]	120
	280

LESSEES

EXAMPLE–FINANCE LEASE

4.4 WX PLC entered into a five–year non–cancellable finance lease on plant from 1 January 19–5 at an annual rental of £40,000 payable in advance. The plant could have been bought outright on 1 January 19–5 for £150,000.

Required:

a. Calculate the total finance charge over the life of the lease.

b. State how WX would show this transaction (including notes) in a balance sheet prepared on 1 January 19–5, assuming that the first rental payment included the finance charge allocation of £16,000.

c. Calculate the fractions to be used in allocating the finance charge to accounting years over the life of the lease, using the sum of the digits method.

d. Calculate the finance charges allocated to accounting years on the basis of your answer to c. above.

e. Show extracts from WX's balance sheet (including notes) as at 31 December 19–5, relating to the leasing arrangements. WX normally charges depreciation on plant at 10% per annum at cost.

f. Recalculate the fractions to be used in allocating the finance charge to accounting years over the life of the lease using the sum of the digits method, if the lease rentals were payable annually from 31 December 19–5.

g. Calculate the finance charges allocated to financial years on the basis of your answer to f. above.

SOLUTION
4.5

		£
a.	Total rentals payable over the life of the lease [5 × £40,000]	200,000
	less	
	Cash price	150,000
	Finance charge	**£50,000**

b.	**Extract from balance sheet as at 1 January 19–5**	
	Fixed assets	£
	Plant held on finance lease (at cost)	150,000
	Creditors: amounts due in more than one year	
	Obligations under finance leases	
	[(4 × 40,000) − (50,000 − 16,000)]	126,000

Notes:
Obligations under non–cancellable finance leases

159

	£
Payable in next year	40,000
Payable in two to five years	120,000
	160,000

less

Finance charges allocated to future periods
[50,000 − 16,000]   (34,000)

126,000

c.

At 1 January (after rental paid)	No of years outstanding	Fraction
19–5	4	4/10
19–6	3	3/10
19–7	2	2/10
19–8	1	1/10
19–9	0	–
	10	

d.

Year	Fraction	Finance charge allocation £
19–5	4/10	20,000
19–6	3/10	15,000
19–7	2/10	10,000
19–8	1/10	5,000
19–9	–	Nil
		£50,000

These sums would appear under the heading Interest payable, as finance charges on finance leases, in the profit and loss accounts for their respective years. The depreciation charge would be included in the Cost of Sales figure. Both finance charges and depreciation on finance lease assets would be separately identified in notes to the accounts.

e. **Extract from balance sheet as at 31 December 19–5**

	£
Fixed assets	
Plant held on finance leases (at cost)	150,000
less Depreciation	(30,000)
	120,000

NB. Depreciation has been charged at the rate of 20% per annum, that is, over the life of the lease, this being shorter than the normal life of the asset.

	£
Creditors: amounts due in less than one year	
Obligations under finance leases	25,000
(see workings)	
Creditors: amounts due in more than one year	
Obligations under finance leases	105,000
(see workings)	

Notes:

Obligations under non–cancellable finance leases.

	£
Payable in next year	40,000
Payable in two to five years	120,000
	160,000

less
Finance charges allocated to future periods
[see workings]   (30,000)
Total [equivalent to 25,000 + 105,000 above]   130,000

Workings:
Obligations under finance leases as at 31 December 19-5

Year	Rental	Element Finance charge	Principal
	£	£	£
19-6	40,000	15,000	25,000
19-7	40,000	10,000	30,000
19-8	40,000	5,000	35,000
19-9	40,000	Nil	40,000
	120,000		105,000
	£160,000	£30,000	£130,000

f.

At 1 January	No of years outstanding	Fraction
19-5	5	5/15
19-6	4	4/15
19-7	3	3/15
19-8	2	2/15
19-9	1	1/15
	15	

g.

Year	Fraction	Finance charge allocation
		£
19-5	5/15	16,667
19-6	4/15	13,333
19-7	3/15	10,000
19-8	2/15	6,667
19-9	1/15	3,333
		£50,000

EXAMPLE – OPERATING LEASE

4.6 RS Ltd. entered into a non–cancellable operating lease contract on plant from 1 January 19–5 at an annual rental of £60,000 for a period of four years.

Required:

Show how RS would treat this transaction (including notes) in a profit and loss account for the year 19–7 and in a balance sheet at 31 December 19–7.

SOLUTION

4.7 **Extract from profit and loss account for year ended 31 December 19–7**

	£000
Cost of sales	60

Notes	£000
Profit before tax is after charging operating lease rentals in respect of: plant and machinery	60
other	Nil

Extract from balance sheet as at 31 December 19–7
Notes
Annual commitments under non–cancellable operating leases

161

	Land and buildings £000	Other £000
Expiring within one year	Nil	60
Expiring in two to five years	Not applicable because the	
Expiring in more than five years	contract ends in 19– 8)	

ACTUARIAL METHODS OF ALLOCATION

5.0 It has been seen from 3.7, 3.8, 3.17 and from SSAP 21 that the gross earnings of the lessor (and hire purchase seller) and the finance charges of the lessee (and hire purchase buyer) have to be allocated over accounting periods.

5.1 There are three recognised methods of doing this. The sum of the digits and straightline methods have been explained and illustrated in this Section in Chapter 4 paragraphs 3.11 to 3.16 and need no further comment. The more sophisticated approach to the allocation problems is to adopt an actuarial method.

5.2 This method involves applying a constant percentage to the outstanding obligation of the lessee and to the net investment or net cash investment of the lessor. Each of these circumstances are illustrated in the paragraphs below.

5.3 The percentage to be applied is obtained from actuarial tables or by mathematical calculation or in complex situations, by computer program. For examination purposes, however, the appropriate percentage will ordinarily be part of the given information.

LESSEES

5.4 Each rental payable (or, instalment payable in the case of hire purchase buyers) consists of two elements – the finance charge and part of the outstanding obligation on the principal sum payable over future periods.

5.5 The obligation at the outset is either the present value of the minimum lease payments or the fair value. For illustration purposes, the fair value will be used throughout this chapter from this point.

5.6 At any time, the outstanding obligation will be the fair value minus the finance charge exclusive element of the rentals received to date. Aggregate rentals outstanding minus finance charges allocated to future periods also produce this same figure of outstanding obligation.

EXAMPLE

5.7 A lessee acquired an asset under a 5 year non– cancellable finance lease from 1 January 19–7, at a rental of £26,000, payable annually in advance. The fair value of the asset at the outset was £100,000 but residual value was assumed to be nil. The constant periodic rate of return on the outstanding obligation has been ascertained as 15.15% per annum.

Required:

Calculate the balance of outstanding obligation and the finance charge for each of the years of the lease.

SOLUTION
5.8

Year	Opening obligation	Rentals paid	Period obligation	Finance Charge (15.15%)	Closing obligation
	£	£	£	£	£
19–7	100,000	26,000	74,000	11,211	85,211
19–8	85,211	26,000	59,211	8,970	68,181
19–9	68,181	26,000	42,181	6,390	48,571
19–0	48,571	26,000	22,571	3,429 Ø	26,000
19–1	26,000	26,000	–	–	–
		130,000		30,000	

Ø includes rounding adjustment (£10)

The difference between the aggregate rentals (£130,000) and the initial fair value (£100,000) constitutes the total finance charge for the five years (£30,000).

An alternative way of viewing the outstanding obligation is given in 5.6 above. Applying that to the closing obligation for 19–8, we get:

	£	£
Initial fair value		100,000
less Rentals to date	52,000	
less Finance charges included [11,211 + 8,970]	20,181	
		31,819
Closing obligation 19–8		68,181

In the final accounts for 19–8, the profit and loss account would disclose £8,970 as Interest payable whilst the balance sheet would include £60,000 in fixed assets (£100,000 less accumulated depreciation, assuming straight line method employed) and £68,181 as leasing obligations, disclosed as in 4.5 above. this is also equal to rentals outstanding (£78,000) minus finance charges allocated to future periods [6,390 + 3,429].

LESSORS

5.9 Each rental receivable (or, instalment receivable in the case of hire purchase sellers) consists of two elements – gross earnings and reduction in net investment.

5.10 The gross earnings element may be either before or after tax, according to the method used. In this context before tax means that the taxation implications are ignored. The converse applies in the "after tax" methods.

EXAMPLE

5.11 The facts are the same as in 5.7 except that they relate to a transaction from a hire purchase seller's viewpoint. Thus, the supplier finances an asset under a 5 year hire purchase contract from 1 January 19–7 at an instalment of £26,000 payable annually in advance. The cost of the asset was £100,000. The constant periodic rate of return on the net investment has been ascertained as 15.15% per annum.

Required:

Calculate the net investment and gross earnings for each of the years of the contract, ignoring the taxation implications.

SOLUTION

5.12 The calculations are identical with those in 5.8 but the description heads are, of course, different, thus,

Year	Opening net investment	Instalments received	Period net investment	Gross earnings (15.15%)		Closing net investment
	£	£		£		£
19–7	100,000	26,000	74,000	11,211		85,211
19–8	85,211	26,000	59,211	8,970		68,181
19–9	68,181	26,000	42,181	6,390		48,571
19–0	48,571	26,000	22,571	3,429	Ø	26,000
19–1	26,000	26,000	–	–		–
		130,000		30,000		

Ø includes rounding adjustment (£10)

Total gross earnings are £30,000, being the difference between cost (£100,000) and instalments received (£130,000).

In the final accounts for 19–8, the profit and loss account would include £8,970 as Gross earnings under hire purchase contracts (or as Turnover), whilst the balance sheet would disclose Net investment in hire purchase contracts (£68,181) under Debtors, together with the other detail as in 4.1 above.

An alternative way of viewing net investment has already been stated in 3.6 above. Applying that to the closing net investment for 19–8, we get:

	£
Minimum contract payments [3 × £26,000]	78,000
less Gross earnings allocated to future periods [6,390 + 3,429]	(9,819)
Closing net investment 19–8	68,181

163

5.13 In the Example 5.11 and its solution the gross earnings were allocated to periods on the basis of net investment. As has been noted in 3.7, this is an acceptable practice to apply to those hire purchase contracts which are akin to finance leases. For finance leases proper, however, allocation should be on the basis of net cash investment, as explained and defined in 3.8 and 3.9.

EXAMPLE

5.14 A lessor leased an asset on a 5 year non– cancellable finance lease from 1 January 19–7, at a rental of £26,000, payable annually in advance. The cost of the asset was £100,000.

The lessor's corporation tax rate is 35% and payment (or recovery) of corporation tax takes place nine months after the year end on 31 December. The leased asset is eligible for writing down allowances at the rate of 25%.

The constant periodic rate of return (after tax) on the net cash investment is assumed to be 10.25% per annum.

Required:

Calculate the net cash investment and the gross earnings for each of the years of the lease, together with the net investment at the end of 19–8.

SOLUTION

5.15 The information supplied clearly indicates that an "after tax" method must be employed. As the calculations are based on net cash investment, the taxation figures appear in the years in which they are paid or recovered and not in the years in which they arise.

Year	Net Cash investment (opening)	Cash inflows/ (outflows)		Net Cash investment average	Profit after tax (10.25%)	Net Cash investment (closing)
	£	£	£	£	£	£
19–7	–	(100,000)	26,000	(74,000)	(7,585)	(81,585)
19–8	(81,585)	(350)	26,000	(55,935)	(5,733)	(61,668)
19–9	(61,668)	(2,540)	26,000	(38,208)	(3,916)	(42,124)
19–0	(42,124)	(4,180)	26,000	(20,304)	(2,081)	(22,385)
19–1	(22,385)	(5,410)	26,000	(1,795)	(185)	(1,980)
19–2	(1,980)	1,980	–	–	–	–
		130,000			(19,500)	

The cash flows attributable to taxation included above are calculated thus:

	19–8	19–9	19–0	19–1	19–2
	£	£	£	£	£
(Previous year's) Rental received	26,000	26,000	26,000	26,000	26,000
Writing down allowance [25% × 100,000]	(25,000)	(18,750)	(14,063)	(10,547)	(7,910)
Unrelieved expenditure					(23,730)
Taxable	1,000	7,250	11,937	15,453	(5,640)
Corporation tax at 35% (paid)/recovered	(350)	(2,540)	(4,180)	(5,410)	1,980

The figure for gross earnings for each year is arrived at by taking the profit after tax figures and grossing them up on the basis of the corporation tax rate, that, is the post–tax figures are 65% of the pre–tax figures. Thus the aggregate profit after tax (£19,500) becomes £30,000 on a pre–tax basis [19,500/(1.00 – 0.35)] and constitutes total gross earnings which is also the difference between the fair value of the asset (£100,000) and the aggregate rentals received (£130,000).

	Years					
	19–7	19–8	19–9	19–0	19–1	Total
	£	£	£	£	£	£
Gross earnings/ profit before tax [1/0.65× profit after tax]	11,669	8,820	6,025	3,201	285	30,000
Corporation tax liability	(350)	(2,540)	(4,180)	(5,410)	1,980	(10,500)
Deferred tax	(3,734)	(547)	2,071	4,290	(2,080)	–
Profit after tax	7,585	5,733	3,916	2,081	185	19,500

Corporation tax has been shown in its year of incidence, unlike in the previous table where it was shown in its year of cash flow. The difference between that figure and the corporation tax based on gross earnings is disclosed as deferred taxation. For example, in 19–7, Corporation tax at 35% on gross earnings of £11,669 is £4,084. Of this figure £350 appears as corporation tax for 19–7 and the balance (£3,734) as deferred tax.

Net investment at the end of year 19–8 would be:

	£
Minimum lease payments [3 × £26,000]	78,000
less Gross earnings allocated to future periods [6,025 + 3,201 + 285]	(9,511)
Closing net investment 19–8	68,489

This figure would appear in the balance sheet as Net investment in finance leases and disclosed as in 4.1

5.16 Sometimes a lessor borrows funds to finance the leases. The interest charges on the borrowings affect the net cash investment and lead to a more refined treatment to that shown in 5.14 and 5.15.

EXAMPLE

5.17 The facts are the same as in 5.14, except that interest of 10% per annum is calculated on the net cash investment in each period and the periodic rate of return (after tax) is 3.75%.

Required:

Calculate the net cash investment and the gross earnings for each of the years of the lease, together with the net investment at the end of 19– 7.

SOLUTION

5.18

Year	Net Cash investment (opening)	Cash inflows/ (outflows)		Net cash investment (average)	Interest (10%)	Profit after tax (3.75%)	Net cash investment (closing)
	£	£	£	£	£	£	£
19–7	–	(100,000)	26,000	(74,000)	(7,400)	(2,775)	(84,175)
19–8	(84,175)	2,240	26,000	(55,935)	(5,594)	(2,098)	(63,627)
19–9	(63,627)	(580)	26,000	(38,207)	(3,821)	(1,433)	(43,461)
19–0	(43,461)	(2,841)	26,000	(20,302)	(2,030)	(761)	(23,093)
19–1	(23,093)	(4,698)	26,000	(1,791)	(179)	(67)	(2,037)
19–2	(2,037)	2,037	–	–	–	–	–
			130,000		(19,024)	(7,134)	

The cash flows attributable to taxation included above are calculated thus:

	19–8 £	19–9 £	19–0 £	19–1 £	19–2 £
(Previous year's)					
Rental received	26,000	26,000	26,000	26,000	26,000
Writing down allowance	(25,000)	(18,750)	(14,063)	(10,547)	(7,910)
Unrelieved expenditure					(23,730)
Interest	(7,400)	(5,594)	(3,821)	(2,030)	(179)
Taxable	(6,400)	1,656	8,116	13,423	(5,819)
Corporation tax at 35% (paid)/recovered	2,240	(580)	(2,841)	(4,698)	2,037

The figure for gross earnings for each year is arrived at by taking the profit after tax figures and grossing them up on the basis of the Corporation tax rate, that is, the post–tax figures are 65% of the pre–tax figures. Thus the aggregate profit after tax (£7,134) becomes £10,976 on a pre–tax basis [7,134/(1.00–0.35). To this figure of pre–tax profit is added the interest of £19,024 to give an aggregate gross earnings figure of £30,000 being the difference between the fair value of the asset (£100,000) and the aggregate rentals received.

	Years					
	19–7 £	19–8 £	19–9 £	19–0 £	19–1 £	Total £
Gross earnings	11,669	8,822	6,026	3,201	282	30,000
Interest	(7,400)	(5,594)	(3,821)	(2,030)	(179)	(19,024)
Profit before tax [1/0.65× profit after tax]	4,269	3,228	2,205	1,171	103	10,976
Corporation tax liability	2,240	(580)	(2,841)	(4,698)	2,037	(3,842)
Deferred tax	(3,734)	(550)	2,069	4,288	(2,073)	–
Profit after tax	2,775	2,098	1,433	761	67	7,134

As in 5.15, corporation tax has been shown in its year of incidence, the effect on cash flow and net cash investment being time–lagged by one year, as can be seen in the first two tables in this paragraph. The difference between the corporation tax shown and that calculated on profit before tax is disclosed as deferred taxation. Thus, in 19–0 corporation tax at 35% on profit before tax of £1,171 is £410, of which £4,698 appears as corporation tax and £4,288 as a release of deferred taxation.

Net investment at the end of year 19–7 would be:

	£
Minimum lease payments [4 × £26,000]	104,000
less Gross earnings allocated to future periods [30,000 – 11,669]	(18,331)
Closing net investment 19–7	85,669

This figure would appear in the balance sheet as Net investment in finance leases and disclosed as in 4.1

STUDENT SELF TESTING
Test exercises

1. AB PLC entered into a five year non– cancellable finance lease on a machine from 1 January 19–5 at an annual rental of £24,000 payable in advance. The machine could been bought outright on 1 January 19–5 for £100,000.

   Required:

   a. Calculate the total finance charge over the life of the lease.

b. State how AB would show this transaction (including notes) in a balance sheet prepared on 1 January 19–5 assuming that the first rental payment included a finance charge allocation of £8,000.

c. Calculate the fractions to be used in allocating the finance charge to accounting years over the life of the lease, using the sum of the digits method.

d. Calculate the finance charges allocated to accounting years on the basis of your answer to c. above.

e. Show extracts from AB's balance sheet (including notes) as at 31 December 19–5 relating to the leasing arrangements. The company charges depreciation on machinery at 10% per annum on cost.

f. Recalculate the fractions to be used in allocating the finance charge to accounting years over the life of the lease, using the sum of the digits method, if the rentals were payable annually from 31 December 19–5.

g. Calculate the finance charges allocated to financial years on the basis of your answer to f. above.

2. CD (Leasing) PLC is the lessor of plant which had an initial fair value of £100,000. The equipment was leased on a five year non–cancellable lease at an annual rental of £26,000, payable in advance from 1 January 19–5.

Required:

a. Calculate the total gross earnings over the life of the lease.

b. State how CD would show this transaction (including notes) in a balance sheet prepared on 1 January 19–5, assuming that the first rental received included a gross earnings allocation of £12,000.

c. Calculate the fraction to be used in allocating the gross earnings to accounting years using the sum of the digits method.

d. Calculate the gross earnings allocated to accounting years on the basis of your answer to c. above.

e. Show extracts from CD's balance sheet (including notes) as at 31 December 19–5 relating to the leasing arrangements.

ACCA EXAMINATION QUESTIONS

3. The Finance Director of the Small Machine Parts Ltd company is considering the acquisition of a lease of a small workshop in a warehouse complex that is being redeveloped by City Redevelopers Ltd at a steady rate over a number of years. City Redevelopers are granting such leases for five years on payment of a premium of £20,000.

The Accountant has obtained estimates of the likely maintenance costs and disposal value of the lease during its five year life. He has produced the following table and suggested to the Finance Director that the annual average cost should be used in the financial accounts to represent the depreciation charge in the Profit and Loss Account.

Table prepared to calculate the annual average cost

Years of Life	1	2	3	4	5
	£	£	£	£	£
Purchase Price	20,000	20,000	20,000	20,000	20,000
Maintenance/Repairs					
Year 2		1,000	1,000	1,000	1,000
3			1,500	1,500	1,500
4				1,850	1,850
5					2,000
	20,000	21,000	22,500	24,350	26,350
Resale Value	11,500	10,000	8,010	5,350	350
Net cost	8,500	11,000	14,490	19,000	26,000
Annual average cost	8,500	5,500	4,830	4,750	5,200

The Finance Director, however, was considering whether to calculate the depreciation chargeable using the Annuity method with interest at 15%.

Required:

a. Calculate the entries that would appear in the Profit and Loss Account of Small Machine Parts Ltd for each of the five years of the life of the lease for the amortisation charge, the interest element in the depreciation charge and the income from secondary assets using the ANNUITY METHOD.

Calculate the Net Profit for each of the five years assuming that the operating cash flow is estimated to be £25,000 per year.

b. Discuss briefly which of the two methods you would recommend.

The present value at 15% of £1 per annum for 5 years is £3.35214.

The present value at 15% of £1 received at the end of year 5 is £0.49717.

Ignore Taxation.

(ACCA 2.9(2) June 1984)

4. **Required:**

a. Summarise the effect on the profit and loss accounts and the balance sheets of Specialist Limited for each of the years ending 31 December 1985 to December 1988 if the company decides to treat the computer transaction of Appendix 6 as a financial lease.

b. Calculate the effect on the draft profit and loss account of Special Books for the year ended 31 December 1984 and the draft balance sheet as at 31 December 1984 if it is decided to amend the 1984 accounts to show the computer transaction as a financial lease.

(ACCA 2.9(1) December 1986)

Appendix 3: Special Books – draft balance sheet as at 31 December 1984
(after preparation of the profit and loss account but *before* preparation of the profit and loss appropriation account)

	Notes	£	£
Fixed Assets			
Tangible assets	1		55,742
Current assets			
Stock		129,368	
Debtors		25,490	
Prepayments		2,166	
Cash at bank and in hand		4,137	
		161,161	
Creditors (due within 1 year)			
Trade creditors		72,700	
Accruals		11,832	
Bank overdraft		20,546	
Bank development loan		3,500	
		108,578	
Net current assets			52,583
Total assets less current liabilities			108,325
Creditors (due after 1 year)			
Bank development loan			27,708
Total assets less current liabilities			
less external finance			80,617

168

Partners' capital accounts	59,842
Partners' current accounts	(9,780)
Partners' development loan accounts	20,000
Profit and loss account for year ending 31 December 1984	10,555
	———
Capital employed	80,617

Appendix 4: Special Books–draft profit and loss account for the year ended 31 December 1984

	£	£
Sales		610,085
Cost of sales:		
Stock at 1 January 1984	69,500	
Purchases	520,815	
	———	
	590,315	
Stock at 31 December 1984	129,368	
	———	
		460,947
		———
Gross profit		149,138
Salaries	55,096	
Rent and rates	14,773	
Light and heat	1,529	
Repairs	319	
Printing and stationery	10,268	
Postage and carriage	3,994	
Telephone	2,765	
Travel and motor expenses	3,353	
Insurance	2,078	
Cleaning and shop expenses	1,079	
Computer rental	6,000	
Computer maintenance	1,227	
Security installation rental	752	
Advertising	1,081	
Trade subscriptions	750	
Fees (accountancy, surveyor)	989	
Bank charges	10,632	
Sundry expenses	555	
Depreciation: lease	1,903	
fixtures	301	
cars	1,138	
		120,582
		———
Profit before extraordinary items		28,556
Loss on sale of fixed assets	9,593	
Amortisation of lease	8,408	
	———	
		18,001
		———
		10,555

Note: No entries have been made for partners' loan interest or other appropriations.

Appendix 6: Further details on the computer rental
The following information was obtained about the computer equipment shown in the draft profit and loss account of Special Books in Appendix 4.

Yearly rental payable in advance	£6,000
Term of lease	5 years
Data agreement was signed	1 January 1984
Anticipated residual value on disposal at the end of the lease term	£2,500
Lessees interest in the residual proceeds	95%
Anticipated life of the equipment	7 years

A trainee accountant has produced the following notes:

i. Because the lessor has less than 10% interest in the residual value, the lease should be classified as a financial lease.

ii. The typical implicit interest rate for a lease of this type of computer equipment is 10%.

iii. The practice of charging the rental of £6,000 to the profit and loss account is incorrect and should not be followed in the accounts for future years.

Note: Discount factors are set out below:

Year	8%	10%	12%
1	.9259	.9090	.8930
2	.8573	.8264	.7972
3	.7938	.7513	.7118
4	.7350	.6830	.6355
5	.6806	.6209	.5674
6	.6302	.5645	.5066

6 Long–term Contracts

GENERAL BACKGROUND

1.0 There are special problems associated with accounting for businesses which carry out long term building and civil engineering projects. (Long term in this context means that the period from starting until completion is usually in excess of one year). Many businesses within the construction industry fall into this category.

1.1 One problem is that these projects usually involve application of very substantial amounts of physical and financial resources (which, of course, have to be accounted for) and the contract price is commensurately high.

1.2 Another problem is that the production cycle can be very long by comparison with, say, general manufacturing businesses. For example, a motorway construction contract could extend over a number of years.

1.3 Stemming from the foregoing is the problem of how much (if any) profit or loss to recognise and at what point(s) in time to recognise it and, as a corollary, how to evaluate work in progress.

OPERATING ARRANGEMENTS

2.0 A business engaged on this sort of work usually controls its resources on a contract by contract basis.

2.1 Each job or contract is given a separate identifying code number and the costs of all resources supplied to that contract are charged to it. At the end of each accounting period unused resources are credited to the contract.

2.2 At intervals throughout the life of each contract, engineers and/or architects, as appropriate, make an approximation of the degree of completion of each contact (in terms of the contract price) and issue certificates to this effect to the contractor.

2.3 The certificates enable an estimate to be made of the profit earned (or loss sustained) on the contract to date and also of the value of the work in progress and are the basis of the claim by the contractor against the customer for interim payments (known as progress payments) on account of the final contract price for work completed to date.

2.4 The contractor therefore does not necessarily have to wait until the end of the contract either to recognise profit or to receive payment.

2.5 It is usual, however, for the customer to deduct an agreed percentage (frequently 10%) from each progress payment by way of retention.

2.6 The purpose of a retention is to safeguard the customer in the event of substandard workmanship etc latent at the time the certificates are issued. If the contractor defaults in rectifying the work the customer can withhold the retention money and pay another contractor to carry out the remedial work. The customer waits for a suitable interval to elapse after the contract has been completed before paying over the balance of retentions.

ACCOUNTING ARRANGEMENTS.

3.0 A separate account is opened for each contract. There are the two methods of proceeding.

ARCHITECTS'/ENGINEERS' CERTIFICATES METHOD

3.1 Each contract account is debited with the cost of materials supplied wages, contract overheads, payments to subcontractors, general expenses etc and the cost of any fixed assets required specifically for that contract.

3.2 At the end of the period, the contract account is credited with the architects' or engineers' certificates (the debit for which is made in the customer's account), with the value of work done but not yet certified and with the value of unused resources. These latter may comprise unused materials and the value of fixed assets. Any difference between the cost of fixed assets debited (per 3.1) and the value credited in this subparagraph represents depreciation.

3.3 A credit balance on the contract account indicates an apparent profit at that stage. Unless the end of the contract had been reached, part of this profit would be placed in suspense by debiting the contract account and by crediting a Profit Suspense account. The calculation of the profit taken on the contract is dealt with in 4.0 to 4.15. When calculated, it is debited to contract account and credited to profit and loss.

3.4 If the balance remaining after the 3.1 and 3.2 entries have been made indicates a loss, the whole of it must be written off to profit and loss account in the period. Furthermore, if the contract is at an intermediate stage, an appraisal must be carried out to see whether provision for further losses is needed. The provision for future losses would involve a debit to contract account and a credit to the provision account. The actual loss on contract account is credited to contract account and debited to profit and loss.

3.5 The customer's account is debited with the value of the architects' certificates (see 3.2) and credited with progress payments received and with retentions (the opposite entires are Bank and Retentions, respectively). The balance of the account then represents progress payments receivable.

EXAMPLE

3.6 The following figures have been extracted from the records of Prefabricated Constructions for the year ended 31st December 19–0, in respect of an office block commissioned by the Inner City Development Corporation.

	£
Office block contract	
Expenditure during year 19–0	
Plant	150,000
Wages etc	260,000
Materials	330,000
Subcontract work	200,000
Sundries	30,000
Contract overheads	240,000
Balances at 31st December 19–0	
Plant	100,000
Materials	50,000
Work certified during year 19–0	1,500,000
Work awaiting certification at 31st December 19– 0	20,000
Retentions at 1st January 19–0	100,000
Progress payments received during year 19– 0	1,100,000
Progress payments receivable at 31st December 19– 0	250,000
Retentions during year 19–0	150,000
Profit on contract to be taken for year 19– 0	180,000

(At this stage this is an assumed figure.
The method of calculation is dealt with in
4.0 to 4.15).

Required:

For the year 19–0 prepare the following accounts in the book of Prefabricated Constructions.

Office block contract
Inner City Development Corporation
Architects' Certificates
Retentions

SOLUTION
3.7 Prefabricated Constructions ledger.

Office block contract

	£		£
Plant	150,000	Balances c/d	
Wages etc	260,000	Plant	100,000
Materials	330,000	Materials	50,000
Subcontract Work	200,000	Work not certified	20,000
Sundries	30,000	(at cost)	
Contract Overheads	240,000	Work Certified (at cost)	1,040,000
		(balance)	
	__1,210,000__		__1,210,000__
Work certified (at cost) b/d	1,040,000	Architects' certificates	1,500,000
Profit and loss (given)	180,000	(at contract price	
Profit Suspense (balance)	280,000	including profit	
		element)	
	__1,500,000__		__1,500,000__
Plant b/d	100,000		
Materials b/d	50,000		
Work not certified b/d	20,000		

Inner City Development Corporation

	£		£
Architects' Certificates	1,500,000	Bank	1,100,000
		Retentions	150,000
		Balance c/d (progress	
		payments receivable)	250,000
	__1,500,000__		__1,500,000__
Balance b/d	250,000		

Architects' Certificates

	£		£
Office block contract	__1,500,000__	Inner City Devel.Corpn.	__1,500,000__

Retentions

	£		£
Balance b/d	100,000	Balance c/d	250,000
Innter City Devel.Corpn.	150,000		
	__250,000__		__250,000__
Balance b/d	250,000		

WORK IN PROGRESS METHOD.

3.8 A variation of the preceding method is the "work in progress" method.

3.9 The contract account is debited with all the items mentioned in 3.1 and is credited with the value of unused resources noted in 3.2, but not with the value of work awaiting certification or with architects' certificates.

3.10 Profit to be taken on the contract is calculated as noted in 4.0 to 4.15 and is debited to the contract account.

3.11 The balance on the contract account at that stage represents work in progress valued at cost plus attributable profit and is carried down to the start of the next period.

3.12 In the event of a loss, the treatment is as in 3.4.

3.13 The customer's architects' certificates and retentions accounts are prepared as in 3.5, but the value of the architects' certificates is not debited in that account or credited to contract account until the end of the contract.

EXAMPLE

3.14 The facts are the same as in 3.6 except that the company prepares the contract account on the work in progress method. Work in progress on 1st January 19-0 was £1,760,000.

SOLUTION
3.15

Office block contract

	£		£
Work in progress b/d	1,760,000	Balances c/d	
Plant	150,000	Plant	100,000
Wages etc	260,000	Materials	50,000
Materials	330,000	Work in progress (balance)	
Subcontract work	200,000	(see below)	3,000,000
Sundries	30,000		
Contract overheads	240,000		
Profit and loss (given)	180,000		
	3,150,000		3,150,000
Balances b/d			
Plant	100,000		
Materials	50,000		
Work in progress	3,000,000		

Reconciliation of work in progress

	£	£
Work in progress 1st January 19-0		1,760,000
Cost of (per 3.7)		
Work certified	1,040,000	
Work not certified	20,000	
Profit recognised during year 19-0	180,000	
Work in progress increase during year 19- 0		1,240,000
Work in progress 31st December 19-0 (as above)		3,000,000

CALCULATION OF INTERIM PROFIT ON CONTRACTS.

4.0 The method of calculation of profit recognised at intermediate stages during the life of a contract may be different for those businesses which are subject to Statement of Standard Accounting Practice 9 (Stocks and Work in Progress) and (Stocks and Long-term contracts)(revised).

CALCULATIONS FOR BUSINESSES NOT SUBJECT TO SSAP 9.

4.1 Prior to the introduction of SSAP 9 in January 1976 and for those few businesses not subject to it, the traditional method of arriving at an interim contract profit figure was to calculate the profit for the period, as being

	£
Value of work certified for period	
(at contract price, that is, inclusive of the profit element)	x
Less	
Cost of work certified for period	x
Profit on contract for period	x

4.2 This profit figure was then scaled down by the fraction

$$\frac{\text{Progress payments received (that is, excluding retentions)}}{\text{Value of work certified}}$$

A further (arbitrary) fraction of $\frac{2}{3}$ was then applied as a matter of prudence. The whole formula then becomes

$$\frac{2}{3} \times \frac{\text{Progress payments received}}{\text{Value of work certified}} \times \frac{\text{Profit on contract}}{1}$$

The resultant figure was the amount of profit recognised in the period.

4.3 The difference between total profit in 4.1 and the profit recognised in 4.2 was credited to Profit Suspense (see 3.3) if the "architects' certificates" method of recording was being operated.

EXAMPLE

4.4 The builder of a small housing development has the following information available for the year 19–5.

	£
Value of work certified	306,000
Cost of work certified	232,000
Progress payments received	254,000
Progress payments receivable	21,400

Required:

Calculate the profit accounted for in the housing development contract account for the year 19–5.

SOLUTION

4.5 Using the formula in 4.2 and substituting figures for narrative, we get

			£
$\frac{2}{3} \times \dfrac{254,000}{306,000} \times \dfrac{(306,000 - 232,000)}{1}$	=		40,950

	£
Total profit in 19–5 was (306,000 – 232,000)	74,000
Less Profit recognised (above)	40,950
Profit transferred to Suspense	33,050

CALCULATIONS FOR BUSINESSES SUBJECT TO SSAP 9 (up to 30 June 1988)

4.6 SSAP 9 became effective for accounting periods starting on or after 1st January 1976, and applies to all except the smallest of construction businesses. It has now been replaced by a revised version, the contents of which are given in 6.0 and following.

4.7 The standard states that, as an overriding principle, no profit can be attributed to a contract until the outcome of that contract can be reasonably foreseen. Furthermore, a business is bound to take into account any known inequalities of profitability at various stages of a contract and to regard as earned only that part of the attributable profit which prudently reflects the amount of work performed to date.

4.8 One implication of this is that the fact that some of the work has been certified does not necessarily mean that some profit can be recognised.

4.9 Another is that profit should be calculated on a cumulative basis and that the profit recognised in any period is simply the difference between the present and previous cumulatives.

4.10 At each stage at which it is proposed to calculate profit, the following computation should be made.

	£	£
Total contract price		x
Less		
Costs to date	x	
Estimated costs to completion (including future cost increases, rectification and guarantee work)	x	
Estimated contract costs		x
Estimated contract profit		x

4.11 The estimated profit figure is then incorporated into the following formula for calculating profit to be recognised.

$$\frac{\text{Progress payments received}}{\text{Value of work certified}} \times \frac{\text{Value of work certified}}{\text{Total contract price}} \times \frac{\text{Estimated contract profit}}{1}$$

In the event of abnormal circumstances, a further reduction factor may be applied. The resultant figure is the cumulative figure of profit to be recognised.

An alternative formula is

$$\frac{\text{Cost of work completed}}{\text{Total contract cost}} \times \frac{\text{Estimated contract profit}}{1}$$

4.12 The amount of profit to be recognised during the period in question is then obtained thus

	£
Cumulative profit to be recognised	x
Less	
Profit recognised to end of previous period	x
Profit recognised during current period	x̲

4.13 If the workings in 4.10 disclose an estimated loss on the contract, it must be provided in full in that period's accounts.

EXAMPLE

4.14 The facts are as stated in 3.6 but this further information is available for the office block under construction by Prefabricated Constructions for year ended 31st December 19–1.

	£
Contract price	4,000,000
Cumulative figures	
– to 31st December 19–0 – profit recognised	230,000
– to 31st December 19–1 – total costs	2,600,000
– work certified	2,500,000
– progress payments received	2,000,000
– progress payments receivable	150,000
– retentions	350,000
Estimated further costs to completion	600,000

Required:

Calculate the amount of profit which can prudently be recognised in the year ended 31st December 19–1. There are no abnormal circumstances which affect the calculation.

SOLUTION
4.15

	£	£
Total contract price		4,000,000
less		
Costs to date	2,600,000	
Estimated further costs to completion	600,000	
Estimated total contract cost		3,200,000
Estimated profit on contract		800,000
Profit to be recognised to 31st December 19–1		400,000

$$\left(\frac{2,000,000}{2,500,000} \times \frac{2,500,000}{4,000,000} \times \frac{800,000}{1} \right)$$

	£
Less profit recognised to 31st December 19–0	230,000
Profit recognised during year ended 31st December 19–1	170,000

VALUATION OF LONG TERM CONTRACT WORK IN PROGRESS (up to 30 June 1988)

5.0 SSAP 9 stipulates that the inclusion of long term contract work in progress in periodic financial statements should be on the basis of cost plus attributable profit but minus foreseeable losses, progress payments received and progress payments receivable (including retentions), with separate disclosure of the two main elements.

a. work in progress (at cost) plus attributable profit, less foreseeable losses and

b. progress payments received and receivable to date.

EXAMPLE.

5.1 The facts are as in 3.6, 4.14 and 4.15.

Required:

Calculate the figure which would appear as long term contract work in progress in the Balance Sheet of the company as at 31st December 19–1.

SOLUTION

5.2

	£	£
Costs to 31st December 19–1		2,600,000
Attributable profit		400,000
		3,000,000
Less		
Progress payments – received	2,000,000	
– receivable	150,000	
Retentions (see note)	350,000	
		2,500,000
Work in progress per balance sheet as at 31st December 19–1		500,000

Note:

Retentions are deducted because effectively they are progress payments receivable in the longer term.

In the examples given so far it has been assumed that progress payments are due on the basis of the whole of the work certified (subject, of course, to retentions). The terms of some contracts may stipulate other arrangements.

SSAP 9 (REVISED SEPTEMBER 1988)

STOCKS AND LONG–TERM CONTRACTS

6.0 The original SSAP 9 (Stocks and work–in–progress) was reissued in a revised form and with a new title and became operative for accounting periods starting on or after 1 July 1988.

6.1 The main changes affecting long–term contracts are that the profit and loss account should disclose, on a contract by contract assessed basis contract turnover and related costs, and the previous methods of calculating and disclosing work–in–progress have been completely changed.

PROFIT AND LOSS ACCOUNT

6.2 The principles by which profit is calculated remain the same as in 4.7, that is, no profit can be attributed until the outcome can be assessed with reasonable certainty and its amount must be calculated to take account both of the work completed to date and any known inequalities of profitability.

6.3 Contract costs incurred in reaching that stage are matched with turnover which, in effect, includes the profit element on a cumulative basis.

6.4 Up to the stage where profit can be recognised, turnover and costs will appear in the profit and loss account at the same figure, the effect of which is to produce a nil profit figure.

6.5 As previously, the whole of any loss must be recognised as soon as foreseen.

BALANCE SHEET

6.6 There has been a fundamental change in long term contract disclosure. The previous procedure is described in 5.0 to 5.2. The new procedure recognises a number of situations.

6.7 An excess of turnover over payments on account should be classed as amounts recoverable on contracts and included within debtors as a separate item. (The term payments on account is a misnomer because it includes amounts receivable – progress payments invoiced but not yet settled, and retentions – as well as sums actually received).

6.8 Payments on account should first be matched against turnover and then offset against long–term contract balances; any balance remaining should be disclosed as a separately identifiable amount – payments on account – within creditors.

6.9 The amount disclosed as long–term contracts under the heading of stocks in the balance sheet consists of the excess of costs incurred on contracts over the amount transferred to cost of sales reduced not only by foreseeable losses but also by the excess of payments on account - over turnover. Separate disclosure by way of note is required of the net cost less foreseeable losses and of the excess payments on account.

6.10 Where the provision or accrual for losses is greater than the balance of costs incurred after transfers to cost of sales, the excess should be included within provisions for liabilities and charges or within creditors, as appropriate.

EXAMPLE

6.11 The following data relates to an engineering contract in a contractor's books:

		£000
Cumulative	: costs incurred	130
	: costs transferred to cost of sales	130
	: attributable profit	40
	: value of work certified	120
	: progress payments received	80
	: progress payments invoiced, not yet received	30
	: retentions by contractee	10
	: turnover	170

Required:
In the contractor's books, in accordance with SSAP 9 (revised),

prepare the relevant profit and loss account and balance sheet extracts.

SOLUTION

6.12

Profit and loss account extract

	£000
Turnover	170
Cost of sales	130
Gross profit	40

Balance sheet extract

	£000
Current assets	
Debtors	
Amounts recoverable on contracts	50
Retentions on contracts	10
Progress payments receivable	30

EXAMPLE

6.13 The following data relates to an engineering contract in a contractor's books:

		£000
Cumulative	: costs incurred	145
	: costs transferred to cost of sales	130
	: attributable profit	40
	: value of work certified	200
	: progress payments received	130
	: progress payments invoiced, not yet received	50
	: retentions by contractee	20
	: turnover	170

Required:
As for 6.11.

SOLUTION

6.14

<u>Profit and loss account extract</u>

	£000
Turnover	170
Cost of sales	130
Gross profit	<u>40</u>

<u>Balance sheet extract</u>

	£000
Current assets	
Debtors	
Retentions on contracts	20
Progress payments receivable	50
Creditors	
Payments on account on contracts	15

$$[((130 + 50 + 20) - 170) - (145 - 130)]$$

EXAMPLE

6.15 The following data relates to an engineering contract in a contractor's books:

		£000
Cumulative	: costs incurred	145
	: costs transferred to cost of sales	70
	: value of work certified	105
	: progress payments received	80
	: progress payments invoiced, not yet received	10
	: retentions by contractee	15
	: turnover	65
	: provision required for estimated loss	25

Required:
As for 6.11.

SOLUTION
6.16

<u>Profit and loss account extract</u>

	£000
Turnover	65
Cost of sales [70 + 25]	95
Gross loss	(30)

<u>Balance sheet extract</u>

	£000
Current assets	
Stocks	
Long-term contracts	10
[75 − (40 + 25)]	
Debtors	
Retentions on contracts	15
Progress payments receivable	10

<u>Note to balance sheet</u>

	£000
Long-term contracts	
Net cost	75
less foreseeable losses	25
	50
less applicable payments on account	40
[(80 + 10 + 15) − 65]	
	10

EXAMPLE

6.17 The following data relates to an engineering contract in a contractor's books:

		£000
Cumulative	: costs incurred	145
	: costs transferred to cost of sales	130
	: value of work certified	100
	: progress payments received	70
	: progress payments invoiced,	
	not yet received	20
	: retentions by contractee	10
	: turnover	120
	: provision required for estimated loss	60

Required:
As for 6.11.

SOLUTION
6.18

Profit and loss account extract

	£000
Turnover	120
Cost of sales [130 + 60]	190
Gross loss	(70)

Balance sheet extract

	£000
Current assets	
Debtors	
Amounts recoverable on contracts	20
[120 − (70 + 20 + 10)]	
Retentions on contracts	10
Progress payments receivable	20
Provisions for liabilities and charges	
Provisions for losses on contracts	45
[(130 + 60) − 145]	

EXAMPLE

6.19 The facts are as in 3.6. Turnover has been calculated at a figure of £1,220,000.

   Required:

 a. Rewrite the solution given in 3.7 in the ledger of Prefabricated Constructions in a manner consistent with SSAP 9 (Revised), on the assumption that the contract started on 1 January 19–0 (that is, ignoring retentions etc., at that date).

 b. Prepare the relevant profit and loss account and balance sheet extracts.

SOLUTION

6.20

   (a) Prefabricated Constructions ledger.

Turnover

	£		£
Profit and loss	1,220,000	Engineers' certificates	1,220,000

Architects' certificates

	£		£
Turnover	1,220,000	Inner City Development	
Payments on account	280,000	Corporation	1,500,000
	1,500,000		1,500,000

Payments on account

	£		£
Balance c/d	280,000	Architects' certificates	280,000

Inner City Development Corporation

	£		£
Architects' certificates	1,500,000	Bank	1,100,000
		Retentions	150,000
		Balance c/d	250,000
	1,500,000		1,500,000
Balance b/d	250,000		

Office block contract

	£		£
Sundries	1,210,000	Cost of sales	1,040,000
		Balances c/d	
		: plant	100,000
		: materials	50,000
		: work not certified	20,000
	1,210,000		1,210,000
Balances b/d			
: plant	100,000		
: materials	50,000		
: work not certified	20,000		

Cost of sales

	£		£
Office block contract	1,040,000	Profit and loss account	1,040,000

Retentions

	£		£
Inner City Development Corporation	150,000	Balance c/d	150,000
Balance b/d	150,000		

(b)

Profit and loss account extract

	£
Turnover	1,220,000
Cost of sales	1,040,000
Gross profit	180,000

<u>Balance sheet extract</u>

		£
Fixed assets		
Plant		100,000
Current assets		
Stock		
Materials		50,000
Debtors		
Retentions on contracts		150,000
Progress payments receivable		250,000
Creditors		
Payments on account		
on contracts		260,000
[280,000 − 20,000]		

STUDENT SELF TESTING
Test Exercises

1. J Fitzalan PLC has been engaged during 19–4 in the construction of a water treatment plant for the Leen Water Authority at an agreed price of £250,000.

   Plant valued at £110,000 was assigned exclusively to the site and materials costing £64,700 were delivered during 19–4.

   Expenditure on the contract during the year 19–4 included

	£
Wages	27,600
Sub–contract work	19,500
Sundries	4,100
Overheads	34,800

   At 31 December 19–4 site plant was revalued at £97,000 and unused materials amounted to £39,700. Other balances at that date included

	£
Work certified by civil engineers	150,000
Work awaiting certification	20,000
Contract profit suspended	27,300

   Required:
   Prepare the Water Treatment Plant contract account in Fitzalan's ledger under each of the following methods.

   a. engineers' certificates

   b. work–in–progress

2. The facts are precisely the same as in 1 above, but the following further information is available.

	£
Progress payments received	117,000
Retentions	13,000

There were no further progress payments invoiced awaiting receipt.

Required:

Prepare, on the basis of the engineers' certificates method, each of the following accounts in Fitzalan's ledger.

    a. Leen Water Authority

    b. Engineers' certificates

    c. Retentions

3. The facts and answers are as in 1 and 2 above, and the further estimated costs to the completion of the contract amount to £86,000, the outcome of which can be reasonably foreseen.

        Required:

        On the basis of SSAP 9 (original),

        a. calculate the amount of profit which should be recognised on the contract in 19–4.

        b. show the compilation of the work–in– progress figure for inclusion in the balance sheet at 31 December 19–4.

4. The following figures relate to a civil engineering contract:

	£
Contract price	5,000,000
Cumulative to 30 June 19–5:	
Costs: work certified	3,000,000
work not certified	600,000
Progress payments: received	2,200,000
: invoiced, not yet received	200,000
Retentions	300,000
Profit recognised (to 30 June 19–4)	240,000
Estimated further costs to completion	600,000

Required:

On the basis of SSAP 9 (original),

    a. calculate the profit to be recognised for the year ended 30 June 19–5

    b. calculate the work–in–progress figure for inclusion in the balance sheet as at 30 June 19–5.

5. During its financial year ended 30 June 19–7, E. Beavers ltd, an engineering company has worked on several contracts. Information relating to one of them is given below.

    Contract X201

    Date commenced: 1 July 19–6

    Original estimate of completion date: 30 September 19–7.

    Contract price: £240,000

Proportion of work certified as satisfactorily completed up to 30 June 19–7: £180,000.

Amounts received from contractee: £150,000

Costs up to 30th June 19–7:

Wages	£91,000
Materials sent to site	£36,000
Other contract costs	£18,000
Proportion of head office costs	£6,000

Plant and equipment is expected to have a book value of about £1,000 when the contract is completed.

Stock of materials at site, 30 June 19–7: £3,000

Expected additional costs to complete the contract:

Wages	£10,000	
Materials	£12,000	(including stock at 30 June 19–7)
Other	£8,000	

At 30 June 19–7 it is estimated that work to a cost value of £19,000 has been completed but not included in the certifications. If the contract is completed one month earlier than originally scheduled, an extra £10,000 will be paid to the contractors. At the end of June 19–7 there seemed to be a good

chance that this would happen.

Required:

a. Show the account for the contract in the books of E. Beavers Ltd up to 30 June 19–7 including any transfer to the profit and loss account which you think is appropriate. Show also the personal account of the contractee.

b. Briefly justify your calculation of the profit (or loss) to be recognised in the 19–6/7 accounts

(ACCA)

6. Wellbuild Ltd commenced business on the 1 June 19–5 as building contractors. The following details relate to the three uncompleted contracts in the company's books on 31 May 19–6.

	Rosebank £	Millfield £	St.George £
Cost of work to 31 May 19–6, all certified (see note)	30,470	27,280	13,640
Value of work to 31 May 19–6 as certified by contractees' architects	38,500	22,000	14,300
Progress payments invoiced to 31 May 19–6	33,000	17,600	11,000
Progress payments received by 31 May 19–6	27,500	17,600	11,000
Estimate of:			
Final cost including future costs of rectification and guarantee work	33,000	38,500	66,000
Final contract price	41,800	30,800	88,000

Note: The cost of work to 31 May 19–6 has been determined after crediting unused materials and the written down value of Plant in use.

You are required:

a. to prepare a statement for the Board of Directors showing your calculation for each contract of the valuation of Work in Progress at 31 May 19–6, and of the profit (loss) included therein.

b. To show as an extract therefrom, the information which should appear in the Balance Sheet for Work in Progress.

The statement a. should include any notes and recommendations that you consider necesary to assist the deliberations of the Board and should take into account the requirements of Statement of Standard Accounting Practice number 9 (original).

(ACCA)

7. C Ltd, whose year ends on 30th June, had contracted to develop an industrial estate for R Ltd at a contract price of £2.5 million. Work began on 1st June 19–5 and was finished by 31st March 19–8, the date agreed for completion.

From the following you are required to prepare for C Ltd for each year of the contract.

a. the contract account

b. the account of R Ltd

c. the relevant entries in the balance sheet of C Ltd.

	Year ended 30th June				
	19–5 £000	19–6 £000	19–7 £000	19–8 £000	19–9 £000
Plant purchased (see note 1.)	400	–	–	–	–
Plant sold	–	–	–	29	–
Wages charges	12	248	200	152	–
Direct expenses incurred	2	10	–	–	–
Materials purchased	200	300	200	100	–
Materials used	7	343	250	180	–
Value of architects' certificates received during the year	–	900	800	600	200

Cash received during the year	–	810	720	540	430
Cost of work done not certified	–	30	62	150	–

The following notes are given:

1. At the commencement of the contract the plant was estimated to have a residual value of £26,000 at the completion of the contract.
2. Materials not used are taken into stock at the end of the contract at cost less 10%.
3. A central administration charge is made to each contract of 25% on the wages.
4. Credit for profit is taken on the basis of cash received to work certified.
(ICMA)

8. William Derr Ltd is a civil engineering contractor currently engaged on three major contracts, as follows:-

Contract	Commissioning Authority	Description	Date of Starting	Completion
201	Loamshire County Council	Trunk Road Construction	19–7	19–1
204	Upper Leen Water Authority	Reservoir Construction	19–9	19–2
205	Radford Area Health Authority	Hospital Complex	19–0	19–5

At the end of the company's financial year, 31st December 19–0, the following data is available.

	Contract No.		
	201	204	205
	£000	£000	£000
Expenditure during year ended 31st December 19–0			
Materials – issued direct	270	220	200
– ex stores	28	5	10
Wages and related charges	430	265	125
Salaries and related charges	152	54	35
Payment to sub–contractors	110	–	–
Plant hire	30	26	–
Contract overheads	140	45	26
Other information			
Contract price	6,000	3,000	10,000
Plant bought for contracts			
Written down value–1st January 19–0	800	75	–
– 31st December 19–0	650	45	–
Stock of unused materials – 1st January 19–0	54	12	–
– 31st December 19–0	110	30	36
Total costs from start of contract to 31st December 19–0	4,560	1,080	360
Estimated further costs from 31st December 19–0 to completion	960	1,470	7,000
Work completed			
– Not certified (at cost) 1st January 19–0	4	2	–
31st December, 19–0	3	310	–
– Certified by Architects' certificates			
(at contract price) 1st January, 19–0	3,600	800	–
31st December 19–0	5,000	1,300	–
Progress Payments – received to 31st December,			
19–9	2,400	5,300	–
during 19–0	600	470	–
– receivable at 31st December 19–9	300	37	–
at 31st December 19–0	920	10	–

Retentions at 31st December 19–9	270	63	–
at 31st December 19–0	450	120	–
Profit recognised to 31st December 19–9	130	Nil	–

Notes:

i. All these contracts have standard variation clauses whereby increases in material prices, wages etc. awards can be added to contract price.

ii. There are no abnormal circumstances affecting the incidence of profit.

Required:

In the books of William Derr Ltd,

a. Post the contract accounts in columnar form for the year ended 31st December 19–0. Show your workings for the amount of profit or loss recognised on each contract for that year.

b. Post separate personal accounts for each commissioning authority for the year ended 31st December 19–0.

c. Prepare a statement showing the composition of the item long term contract work in progress which would be included in the balance sheet as at 31st December 19–0.

d. Write explanatory notes justifying:

   i. The amount in a. of profit or loss which you have recognised on each contract.
   ii. The amount in c. of long term contract work in progress.

9. The Mitchell Construction Co. is engaged in an engineering project for Nottingham County Council. The contract has a value of £950,000.

On 1 April 19–6 plant and equipment were assigned to the contract having a value of £175,000. Costs for the year were as follows:

	£
Direct Wages	84,500
Direct Materials	399,000
Overheads	121,600
Miscellaneous expenses	15,000
Payments to subcontractors	54,200

On the 31st March 19–7 the following balances were extracted from the books:–

	£
Plant and Equipment	124,000
Direct materials	53,000
Work certified by civil engineers	620,000
Work not certified at cost	122,300
Profit for year recognised	53,777
Work certified at cost	550,000
Progress payments received	413,000
Progress payments invoiced	100,000
Retentions	40,000

The estimated costs to completion are £154,000.

Required

a. Prepare a Contract Account using the Work in Progress Method.

b. Using SSAP 9 (original) calculate the amount of profit to be recognised from the contract.

c. Calculate the amount of Work in Progress to be shown in the Balance Sheet at 31 March 19–7.

10. The following cumulative data relates to a building contract in a building company's books:

	£000
Costs incurred	390
Costs transferred to cost of sales	330
Turnover	520
Value of work certified	440

The value of work certified has been invoiced and/or received.

Required:

Prepare, so far as the information given permits, on the basis of SSAP 9 (revised), the relevant extracts from the profit and loss account and balance sheet of the company.

11. The facts are the same as in 10, except that,

	£000
Value of work certified	560

Required:
As for 10.

12. The facts are the same as in 10, except that,

	£000
Turnover	320
Value of work certified	370
Provision required for foreseeable loss	75

Required:
As for 10.

13. The facts are the same as in 10, except that,

	£000
Turnover	325
Value of work certified	365
Provision required for foreseeable loss	35

Required:
As for 10.

ACCA EXAMINATION QUESTIONS

14. Custom Boatbuilders are an old established firm carrying on business as manufacturers of sailing dinghies with a trade price in the range of £2,000–£5,000 and also as builders of individually designed yachts under contract.

The following data has been supplied by the firm's accountant for the year ended 30 November 1982.

	Total for Year	Dinghies at 30.11.82		Contract Yachts at 30.11.82		
		Work in Progress	Finished Stock	Yacht X	Yacht Y	Yacht Z
	£	£	£	£	£	£
Direct Material	500,000	20,000	40,000	20,000	32,000	5,000
Direct Labour	400,000	10,000	35,000	25,000	38,000	1,000
	£900,000	£30,000	£75,000	£45,000	£70,000	£6,000

Overheads:	£
Production	800,000
Selling	100,000
Administration	200,000
	£2,000,000

The following data has been provided by the management to assist in valuing the stock for inclusion in the Balance Sheet:

a. The Finished Stock (£75,000) includes the cost of three dinghies that fail to satisfy class specifications and it is proposed to offer the three for sale at £2,000 each. The records show that the cost incurred in building the three dinghies was £9,000 (being Material £5,000 and Labour £4,000).

The Marketing Manager estimates that the remaining dinghies in Finished Stock will realise £200,000.

b. The data in respect of the Yachts (X, Y, Z) being built under contract is as follows:

	Yacht X £	Yacht Y £	Yacht Z £
Estimate of Final Cost:			
Direct Material	24,000	36,000	40,000
Direct Labour	30,000	42,000	25,000
	54,000	78,000	65,000

	Yacht X £	Yacht Y £	Yacht Z £
Value of work certified at 30.11.82	110,000	160,000	6,000
Progress Payments received by 30.11.82	85,000	90,000	4,000
Progress Payments invoiced but not received at 30.11.82	5,000	10,000	–
Final Contract Price	130,000	175,000	110,000

Required:

a. Calculate the valuation of Finished Stock, Work in Progress and Long Term Contracts for inclusion in the Balance Sheet as at 30 November 1982 and show an appropriate Balance Sheet extract.

b. Briefly discuss the relevant provisions of the Statement of Standard Accounting Practice on Stock and Work in Progress and state any assumption you have made in calculating your valuation.

(ACCA 2.9(2) December 1982)

15. **Required:**

a. Calculate the profit for the year ending 31 December 1983 and the estimated profit for the year ending 31 December 1984 arising from the sale of sauna cabins on a basis that the accounting policy is to calculate profit when the installation is completed.

b. Show the entries in the balance sheets as at 31 December 1983 and 1984 in respect of the installation and sale of sauna cabins on the alternative basis that:

   i. the work in progress is valued on the basis of work done; and

   ii. the work done is regarded as a long term contract for a single customer.
    (ACCA 2.9(1) December 1985)

Appendix 4 Leisure Supplies: information on the installation of sauna cabins

Leisure Supplies provides and installs sauna cabins. The cabins are purchased by the firm from Swedish Saunacraft Ltd, the plumbing is then subcontracted to Sauna Plumbing and the electrical work is carried out by Leisure Supplies' own workforce.

The firm advice that during 1983 sauna cabins were sold for £8,500 each, and that their direct cost was £6,580 made up of £3,500 for the cost of the cabin, £1,400 for the plumbing and £1,680 for the electrical work. The indirect cost absorption rate is found to be 25% of the direct plumbing and electrical costs.

The terms of sale were £2,500 deposit on receipt of the order, £1,000 on delivery of the sauna cabin to the customer's site, £2,000 on completion and the balance after one calendar month. The final price is to be the one ruling at the date that the final statement is submitted to the customer.

During 1983 orders were received for 36 sauna cabins. Completion of cabins was as follows:

Date	Number completed
January–September	21
October	1
November	3
December	6

At 31 December 1983 there were 5 sauna cabin installations in progress. Of these, 2 were complete (but the final statements were not submitted to the customers until January 1984), 1 was supplied to the customer's site with the plumbing 100% and the electrical work 25% complete and 2 were supplied to site and the plumbing was 100% complete.

189

It is estimated that during 1984 there will be 50 new orders for sauna cabins. Due to inflation it is expected that the selling price and costs will increase from 1 January 1984, as follows:

	Increased by
Selling price	8%
Sauna cabin cost	8%
Plumbing cost	$12\frac{1}{2}$%
Electrical cost	5%
Indirect cost absorption rate	20%

It is estimated that at 31 December 1984 there will be 9 sauna cabin installations in progress. Of these, 5 will be supplied on site but with no plumbing or electrical work, 3 will be supplied with plumbing work 100% complete, and 1 will be supplied with the plumbing work 100% complete and the electrical work 40% complete.

It is estimated that on 1 January 1985 costs will increase as follows:

	Increased by
Sauna cabin cost	10%
Plumbing cost	8%
Electrical cost	5%

The indirect cost absorption rate will rise to 32% of the direct plumbing and electrical costs.

7 Investments

GENERAL BACKGROUND

1.0 It is fairly common practice for a business to invest in stocks and/or shares and/or debentures of other companies. There are numerous and varied reasons for this practice.

1.1 For some companies (investment companies) it is the sole reason for their existence; the investment income is their main, or only, revenue.

1.2 Investments may be acquired by any business as a temporary but profitable refuge for surplus funds.

1.3 Alternatively, funds may be set aside and invested to provide finance for a specific future objective. This might be a major expansion programme or the redemption of the company's debentures (see 5.7). In both these instances the investments would be sold, as required, to provide cash to enable the objective to be achieved.

1.4 An investing company may acquire a controlling interest in another company by obtaining a majority holding, that is, in excess of 50% of that company's voting shares. The company thus controlled is then termed a subsidiary of the investing company, which is then referred to as a holding company.

1.5 In lieu of gaining outright control, as in 1.4 the investing company may secure a substantial, but not a controlling, interest in another company, in order to influence that company's policy decisions. Where the investment comprises 20% to 50% of the other company's voting shares, the latter may be termed an associated company. The Companies Act 1985 uses the term related company.

1.6 A company may also place money on short term deposit to take advantage of high interest rates but this practice is not further considered in this Section.

OPERATING ARRANGEMENTS

2.0 There are two basic categories of trade investments.

a. those which carry a fluctuating rate of return on nominal value – ordinary shares (equities), and

b. those which carry a fixed rate of return on nominal value – preference shares and debentures etc.

2.1 A distinction can also be made between those investments which are

a. listed, that is, quoted on a recognised Stock Exchange, and

b. unlisted, that is, unquoted on a recognised Stock Exchange

2.2 On the acquisition of trade investments the capital cost includes brokerage and other charges associated with the purchase. On disposal the capital proceeds are the net amount after deduction of all expenses associated with selling. In each case, also, further adjustment may need to be made in the light of accrued fixed interest or fixed dividend (see 2.3 to 2.10 and 3.0 to 3.14).

2.3 Fixed rate securities (type 2.0b) are ordinarily bought cum dividend (if fixed rate shares) or cum interest (if fixed rate debentures etc). that, is inclusive of accrued dividend or interest. The quotation is given per £100 nominal.

2.4 These terms are shortened to cum div (or simply, cd) and to cum int (or simply ci). The implication of a cum div/cum int quotation is that the buyer receives the whole of the next payment of dividend or interest without having held the investment for the whole of the period to which that payment relates. Payments may be on a quarterly, half yearly or annual basis. Quotations are always cum div/cum int unless specifically stated to be ex div/ex int.

2.5 The institutions paying the dividend or interest do so to the registered owners of the shares etc. Each time the shares change hands the institution has to amend the appropriate statutory records, for example, the Register of Shareholders.

2.6 On payment date, the dividend or interest is paid to the latest registered holder.

2.7 About one month before payment date, each institution closes its transfer lists and ceases to record changes of ownership of its shares etc. This is done for administrative convenience. If it were not done, the institution would be placed in a position of great difficulty and would be unable to prepare the payment documents until after payment date in order to make those documents out to shareholders who had acquired their holdings at or near payment date.

2.8 The effect of suspending the recording of transfers until after payment date means that, where securities have changed hands during this period, payment of dividend or interest will be made to the original, not to the current, holder.

2.9 On suspension of recording of transfers, the quotation changes from cum div or cum int to ex dividend or ex interest, shortened to ex div (or simply xd) and to ex int (or simply xi).

2.10 The implication of this is that the next payment of dividend or interest is paid in its entirety to the original holder despite the fact that he is no longer the holder at that time. However, in an ex div or ex int quotation that part of the dividend or interest which the new holder will not receive from the paying institution reduces the buying price. (Conversely, in 2.4 the cum div or cum int quotation means that the accrued dividend or interest, applicable to the period from the last payment date to the change of ownership date, receivable by the buyer (and therefore foregone by the original holder) is added in arriving at the buying price).

2.11 These arrangements are inapplicable to type 2.0a securities.

2.12 An investing company may receive additional shares of a class which it already holds by means of a bonus issue (see 4.0 to 4.9) and/or a rights issue (see 5.0 to 5.3).

ACCOUNTING ARRANGEMENTS

3.0 In the books of the investing business a separate account is opened for each security.

3.1 Each investment account has three columns on each side of the account:-

Column 1 –   a memorandum column in which is recorded the nominal value of each transaction in either value or quantitative terms.

Column 2 –   a (double entry) income column to record the investment income transactions.

Column 3 –   a (double entry) capital column to record the investment capital transactions.

and is ruled thus:

Ordinary/Preference Shares/Debentures in.............

Nom No/£	Inc £	Cap £		Nom No/£	Inc £	Cap £

CUM DIV/INT PURCHASES

3.2 When securities are acquired cum div or cum int. the accrued dividend/interest element (see 2.10) is debited to income column and the balance, being the capital cost (see 2.2) is debited to the capital column.

3.3 In practice the accrued interest would be debited less income tax, but the taxation aspect is ignored in this section and dealt with in Section III Chapter 3.

EXAMPLE.

3.4 A company bought £100,000 12% Marlshire County Council Loan Stock on 1st September 19–0 at 94 cum int. Interest is payable half yearly on 30th June and 31st December.

Required:

Show the entries in the investing company's ledger for its financial year ended 30th June 19–1. Ignore transfer etc charges and income tax.

SOLUTION

3.5 In diagrammatic form, the position is:

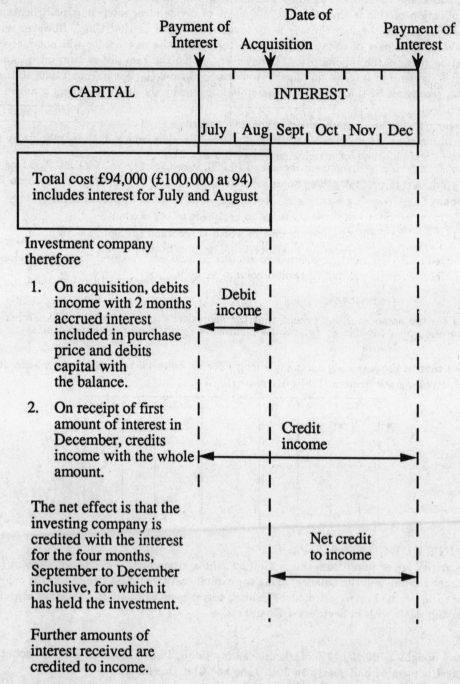

In account form therefore, the transactions would be recorded as follows in the investing company's ledger:

12% Marlshire County Council Loan Stock

		Nom £	Inc £	Cap £			Nom £	Inc £	Cap £
19–0					19–0				
Sept 1	Bank	100,000	2,000	92,000	Dec 31	Bank Int.		6,000	
[(inc) 2/12 × (12%					[6/12 × (12%				
×100,000)					×100,000]				
(Cap) (100,000 at									
94 = 94,000) – 2000]									
19–1					19–1				
June 30	Investment				June 30	Bank int.		6,000	
	Income		10,000		June 30	Balance			
						c/d	100,000		92,000
		100,000	12,000	92,000			100,000	12,000	92,000
July 1	Balance								
	b/d	100,000		92,000					

The amount transferred to investment income, £10,000, is equivalent to 12% of £100,000 for 10 months, that is, for the number of months in the financial year during which the investment has been held by the investing company.

EX DIV/INT PURCHASES

3.6 When securities are acquired ex div or ex int, the amount of dividend or interest by which the buying price has been reduced (see 2.10), is debited to capital column and credited to income column and the whole of the purchase cost is debited to capital column as well.

EXAMPLE

3.7 The facts are the same as in 3.4 except that the acquisition took place on 1st December 19–0 when the price was 91 ex int.

Required:

Show the entries in the investing company's ledger for its financial year ended 30th June 19–1. Ignore transfer etc charges and income tax.

SOLUTION

3.8 In diagrammatic form, the position is:

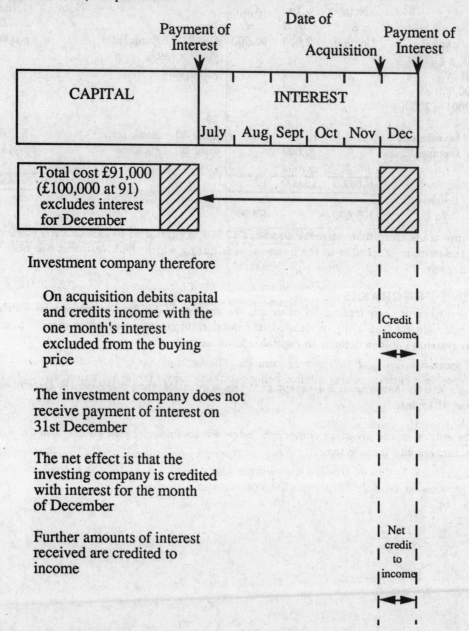

Investment company therefore

On acquisition debits capital
and credits income with the
one month's interest
excluded from the buying
price

The investment company does not
receive payment of interest on
31st December

The net effect is that the
investing company is credited
with interest for the month
of December

Further amounts of interest
received are credited to
income

In account form, therefore, the transactions would be recorded as follows in the investing company's ledger:

12% Marlshire County Council Loan Stock

	Nom £	Inc £	Cap £			Nom £	Inc £	Cap £
19–0				19–0				
Dec 1 Bank	100,000		92,000	Dec 1 Transfer		1,000		
[(inc) 1/12 × (12%				[1/12 × (12%				
×100,000)				×100,000) = 1000]				
= 1,000 plus								
(100,000 @ 91								
= 91,000]								
19–1				19–1				
June 30 Investment				June 30 Bank int.			6,000	
Income		7,000		[6/12 × 12%×				
				100,000)				
				June 30 Balance				
				c/d		100,000		92,000
	100,000	7,000	92,000			100,000	7,000	92,000
July 1 Balance								
b/d	100,000		92,000					

The amount transferred to investment income, £7,000 is equivalent to 12% of £100,000 for 7 months, that is, for the number of months in the financial year during which the investment has been held by the investing company.

CUM DIV/INT SALES
3.9 When securities are sold cum div or cum int, the accrued dividend/interest element (see 2.10) is credited to income column and the balance being capital proceeds (see 2.2), is credited to capital column.

EXAMPLE
3.10 The facts are the same as in 3.4.

Required:

Show the entries in the ledger of the seller (ie the previous investing company) for the financial year ended 30th June 19–1. Ignore transfer etc charges and income tax and assume that the balance on the loan stock account on 1st July 19–0 was £100,000 nominal at a cost of £90,000.

SOLUTION
3.11 In diagrammatic form the position is:

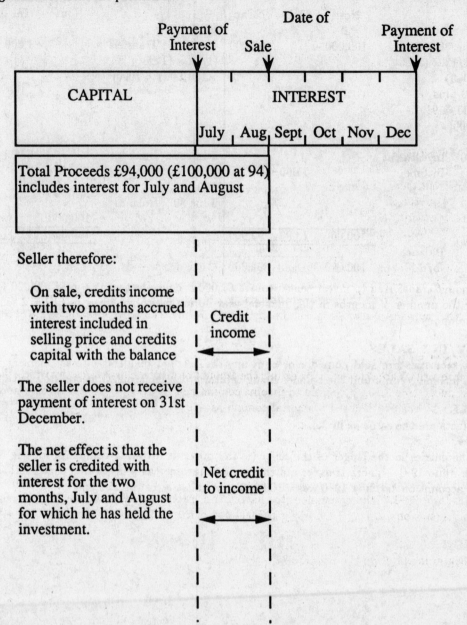

In account form, therefore, the transactions would be recorded as follows in the ledger of the seller (the previous investing company):

12% Marlshire County Council Loan Stock

		Nom £	Inc £	Cap £			Nom £	Inc £	Cap £
19–0 July 1	Balance b/d	100,000		90,000	19–0 Sept 1	Bank – sale	100,000	2,000	92,000
						[(Inc) 2/12 × (12% × 100,000)			
						(Cap) (100,000 at 94 = 94,000) – 2,000]			
19–1 June 30	Investment Income		2,000						
June 30	Profit on disposal of investments (92,000 – 90,000)			2,000					
		100,000	2,000	92,000			100,000	2,000	92,000

The whole of the holding was sold and there is no balance left to carry down. Profit on disposals is dealt with more fully in 3.17 to 3.26.

The amount transferred to investment income, £2,000, is equivalent to 12% of £100,000 for 2 months, that is, for the number of months in the financial year during which the investment has been held by the seller.

EX DIV/INT SALES

3.12 When securities are sold ex div or ex int, the amount of dividend or interest by which the selling price has been reduced (see 2.10) is debited to income column and credited to capital column and the whole of the net sale proceeds are credited to capital column as well.

EXAMPLE.

3.13 The facts are the same as in 3.7.

Required:

Show the entries in the ledger of the seller (ie the previous investing company) for the financial year ended 30th June 19–1. Ignore transfer etc charges and income tax and assume that the balance on the loan stock account on 1st July 19–0 was £100,000 nominal at a cost of £90,000.

SOLUTION

3.14 In diagrammatic form the position is:

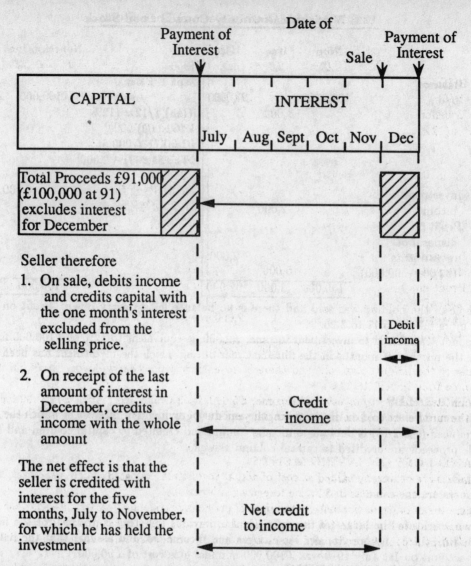

Seller therefore
1. On sale, debits income and credits capital with the one month's interest excluded from the selling price.

2. On receipt of the last amount of interest in December, credits income with the whole amount

The net effect is that the seller is credited with interest for the five months, July to November, for which he has held the investment

In account form, therefore, the transactions would be recorded as follows in the ledger of the seller (the previous investing company).

12% Marlshire County Council Loan Stock

19–0		Nom £	Inc £	Cap £	19–0		Nom £	Inc £	Cap £
July 1	Balance b/d	100,000		90,000	Dec 1	Bank – sale	100,000		92,000
Dec 1	Transfer [(Inc) 1/12 × (12% ×100,000]		1,000			[(Cap) 1/12× (12% × 100,000)] = 1,000 plus (100,000 at 91 = 91,000)]			
					Dec 31	Bank int [6/12 × (12%× 100,000)]		6,000	
19–1									
June 30	Investment Income		5,000						
June 30	Profit on sale of investments (92,000 – 90,000)			2,000					
		100,000	6,000	92,000			100,000	6,000	92,000

The whole of the holding was sold and there is no balance left to carry down. Profit on disposals is dealt with more fully in 3.17 to 3.26.

The amount transferred to investment income, £5,000, is equivalent to 12% of £100,000 for 5 months, that is, for the number of months in the financial year during which the investment has been held by the seller.

PROFIT AND LOSS ON INVESTMENTS

3.15 Investments are ordinarily valued at cost of actual acquisition, adjusted, where necessary, for the cum or ex div/int quotation as illustrated in the foregoing subsections.

3.16 Over time the quotations fluctuate in the light of prevailing economic, marketing and other conditions. Subject to what is stated in 6.0 to 6.5, it is not usual to record these market profits/losses.

3.17 In investment accounts, profits and losses are normally recognised only when actually realised.

PARTIAL DISPOSAL OF HOLDING.

3.18 In the examples given so far, the sale has been of a complete holding. Minor complications arise when there is a sale of only part of a holding.

3.19 The question arises how to value the cost of the investment sold (for comparison with the sale proceeds to see whether a profit or loss results).

3.20 Where, as in the examples up to this point, the holding was acquired at a single point in time, it is simply a matter of taking that proportion of the original cost which the nominal disposals bear to the total original nominal holding.

EXAMPLE.

3.21 The facts are as in 3.13 except that on 1st December 19–0, only £25,000 nominal stock was sold.
   Required:
Show the investment account in the seller's ledger for the year ended 30th June 19–1.

SOLUTION
3.22

12% Marlshire County Council Loan Stock

		Nom £	Inc £	Cap £			Nom £	Inc £	Cap £
19–0					19–0				
July 1	Balance b/d	100,000		90,000	Dec 1	Bank – sale	25,000		23,000
Dec 1	Transfer		250		[1/12 × (12% ×25,000) = 250				
[1/12 × (12% 25,000)]					plus (25,000 at 91) = 22,750]				
					Dec 31 Bank int			6,000	
					[6/12 × (12% ×100,000)]				
19–1					19–1				
June 30	Investment Income		10,250		June 30 Bank int.			4,500	
June 30	Profit on sale of investments			500	[6/12 × 12% ×75,000]				
[23,000 – (25/100 × 90,000)]					June 30 Balance c/d		75,000		67,500
					[(Cap) 75/100× 90,000]				
		100,000	10,500	90,500			100,000	10,500	90,500
July 1	Balance b/d	75,000		67,500					

3.23 Where the holding has been built up by successive acquisitions at different times and prices, a difficulty may be encountered when attempting to arrive at a "cost of sales" figure for working out the profit or loss on sale.

3.24 One method is to evaluate the cost of the disposal on a weighted average cost basis; an alternative is to use a FIFO basis. The former method is more commonly used than the latter.

EXAMPLE

3.25 An investing company originally acquired £40,000 9% Debentures in Zed PLC at a capital cost of £36,000 and subsequently increased its holding by a further £80,000 (nominal) at a capital cost of £76,000.
Eventually the company sold £60,000 (nominal) of its holding.

Required:

Calculate the cost of investments sold for the purposes of arriving at a profit or loss on sale using

a. the weighted average cost method, and

b. the FIFO method.

SOLUTION
3.26

a. Weighted average cost method

	Nominal £	Capital cost £
1st acquisition	40,000	36,000
2nd acquisition	80,000	76,000
	120,000	112,000

Weighted average cost of disposals =

$$\frac{60,000}{120,000} \times \frac{112,000}{1} = £56,000$$

b. FIFO method

	Nominal	Capital cost	
	£	£	
from 1st acquisition	40,000	36,000	
from 2nd acquisition			
(balance)	20,000	19,000	$\left(\dfrac{20,000}{80,000} \times \dfrac{76,000}{1} \right)$
Cost of disposals	$\underline{60,000}$	$\underline{55,000}$	

SPECIAL NOTE

3.27 In practical situations, for a variety of reasons, apportionments of interest and fixed dividends are usually ignored but in examination questions the previously described procedures should be operated unless contrary instructions are given.

RIGHTS ISSUES.

4.0 A relatively easy and inexpensive way for any well known company, whose shares are listed on the Stock Exchange, to raise additional capital, is to make a rights issue of ordinary shares.

4.1 The company allots rights certificates (to the amount of the required additional capital) on a pro rata basis to its existing shareholders. These certificates entitle the holder to subscribe for extra shares in the company at very advantageous rates.

4.2 The recipients have three concurrent courses of action open to them, either

  a. to take up the rights (and subscribe for the shares), and/or
  b. to sell the rights to third parties (who then subscribe for the shares), and/or
  c. to renounce the rights (in which case the directors can then dispose of the shares to third parties as described in Section 1 Chapter 1)

ACCOUNTING ARRANGEMENTS (OF INVESTOR)

4.3 In the books of the investing company, the accounting entries in the Investment account will vary according to the course of action chosen in 4.2.

4.4 The declaration of a rights issue by a company and the issue of rights certificates does not necessitate any entries in the investment account.

4.5 If any of the rights are taken up (4.2a) the nominal value of the shares acquired is added to the nominal column and their cost is debited to capital column.

4.6 A sale of rights to third parties (4.2b) does not affect the nominal column at all but the proceeds from the sale of rights are credited to the capital column, since the proceeds are regarded as a capital receipt.

4.7 Renunciation of rights does not affect the investment account at all, except that excess proceeds (see Section 3 Chapter 1) would be credited to the capital column.

EXAMPLE

4.8 One of the trade investments of a company is a holding of 50,000 Ordinary Shares of £1.00 per share in ZXY PLC which originally cost £130,000.

ZXY PLC have now declared a 1 for 5 rights issue at price of £1.20 per share. The investing company took up 60% of its entitlement and sold the remaining 40% at £0.50 per share on 30th April 19-0.

Required:
Record these transactions in the investing company's ledger for the year ended 31st December 19-0.

SOLUTION
4.9

Ordinary Shares in ZXY PLC

		Nom £	Inc £	Cap £			Nom £	Inc £	Cap £
19–0					19–0				
Jan 1	Balance b/d	50,000		130,000					
Apr 30	Rights issue (taken up)	6,000		7,200	Apr 30	Bank (sale of rights)			2,000
	[(60% × (1/5× 50,000)) × £1.20]					[40% × (1/5× 50,000)) ×£0.50]			
					Dec 31	Balance c/d	56,000		135,200
		56,000		137,200			56,000		137,200
19–1									
Jan 1	Balance b/d	56,000		135,200					

Note:

The buyer of the rights will be able to acquire 4,000 Ordinary Shares in ZXY PLC [40%×(1/5×50,000)] at a cost of £1.70 per share, that is, for £0.50 to acquire the rights to subscribe plus £1.20 for the shares themselves.

BONUS ISSUES.

5.0 Sometimes a company declares a bonus (or scrip) issue of ordinary shares. This is because the company has considerable reserves which it cannot distribute either by law or as a matter of financial prudence or because they are represented by fixed assets and stocks and/or debtors.

5.1 The declaration of the bonus issue gives de facto recognition to the conditions noted in 5.0 and inter alia also has the effect of bringing down the price of the shares thus making them more marketable.

ACCOUNTING ARRANGEMENTS (OF INVESTOR).

5.2 In the books of the investing company, the accounting entries appear only in the nominal column. The capital and income columns are unaffected.

EXAMPLE.

5.3 The facts are the same as in 4.8 except that instead of declaring a rights issue, ZXY PLC declared a 2 for 5 bonus issue on 30th April 19–0.

Required:

Record these transactions in the investing company's ledger for the year ended 31st December 19–0.

Ordinary Shares in ZXY PLC

		Nom £	Inc £	Cap £			Nom £	Inc £	Cap £
19–0					19–0				
Jan 1	Balance b/d	50,000		130,000	Dec 31	Balance c/d	70,000		130,000
Apr 30	Bonus issue	20,000							
	[1/5 × 50,000]								
		70,000		130,000			70,000		130,000
19–1									
Jan 1	Balance b/d	70,000		130,000					

Note:

The investing company has received these shares free of charge.

VALUATION OF INVESTMENTS FOR BALANCE SHEET PURPOSES.

6.0 The value value placed on investment in shares or stock or debentures is dependent upon the purpose for which the investment was acquired. Some of the purposes for which businesses acquire investments were set out in 1.1 to 1.6.

6.1 Short term investments (1.2) are usually included in the balance sheet at cost (including the accompanying buying costs). Market fluctuations may be reflected in the valuation, if significant. The market valuation in this instance is based on the middle market price, that is, the average of the buying and selling prices as obtained from the Stock Exchange list for that day but, of couse, can only be calculated in this manner for listed securities. Unlisted securities have to be valued by the directors. It will be seen in Appendix 1 that the valuations of investments have to be disclosed in the published accounts of public limited companies.

6.2 For a long term investment (1.3) the usual practice is to value at cost (including the accompanying buying costs) for balance sheet purposes. Market fluctuations are normally ignored unless there is a substantial, permanent fall in value in which case a provision should be raised for the loss. Market values are arrived at as in 6.1 and disclosed in the published accounts.

6.3 Financial institutions such as investment trusts 1.1 are in a special position. For these companies, investments are effectively their operating assets and are revalued according to their market valuation. Unrealised revaluation surpluses less unrealised loses are held in a special reserve.

6.4 A holding company (1.4) values its investment in subsidiary companies in its own balance sheet at original cost less, (if any), sums written off and dividends received from pre acquisition profits. This investment does not appear as such in the group balance sheet.

6.5 The valuation of an investment in an associated (related) company (1.5) in the balance sheet of an investing company is either at a special valuation or at cost less sums written off and dividends received from pre-acquisition profits and in the group balance sheet at this same figure plus the group's share of post acquisition reserves.

STUDENT SELF TESTING

Test Exercises

1. Fremount Ltd., whose accounting year ends on 31 December, decided to invest some surplus liquid funds in marketable securities.

   Required:

   In respect of each of the following occurrences,

   i. post and balance, for the year concerned, the investment account in Fremount Ltd's ledger, assuming that the appropriate amount of interest is received on the due date(s)

   and

   ii. as a separate calculation, justify the figure of investment income for the year

   Taxation should be ignored along with brokerage etc. charges.

   a. Initial investment on 1 April 19–1 in £200,000 (nominal) 12% Beech Borough Council Loan Stock at 93 c.i. Interest is payable half yearly on 30 June and 31 December.

   b. The facts are as in (a). The holding was sold on 1 May 19–2 at 96 c.i.

   c. The facts are as in (a). The holding was sold on 1 June 19–2 at 88 x.i.

   d. The facts are as in (a). A further £50,000 (nominal) was acquired on 1 June 19–1 at 90 x.i.

   e. The facts are as in (a). A further £50,000 (nominal) was acquired on 1 May 19–1 at 92 c.i.

   f. The facts are as in (e). £100,000 (nominal) was sold on 1 August 19–2 at 96 c.i. The company applies the FIFO method of calculating cost of disposals.

   g. The facts are as in (f) except that the company employs the averaging method of calculating costs of disposals.

   h. On 4 March 19–5, Fremount Ltd acquired 400,000 ordinary shares of £0.25 per share in Qwiksnax PLC at a cost of £132,000. Qwiksnax paid a dividend (on the 19–4 profits) of 5% on 26 June 19–5.

   On 2 September 19–5 Qwiksnax declared a 1 for 4 bonus issue.

   i. The facts are as in (h), except that on 2 September 19–5, Qwiksnax declared a 1 for 4 rights issue at £0.20 per share.

   Fremount Ltd took up half the rights on 24 September and sold the other half for £0.24 per share.

2. James Porterfield carried out the following transactions in connection with his investment holdings during the year ended 31st March 19–5, at which date he closed his accounts.

19–4

April 15	Purchased £100,000 12% convertible debentures in Bloodstock PLC at 125 1/2. Interest is paid on 15th September and 15th March. The debentures are convertible into ordinary shares of £1 each at the rate of £2 debentures for each ordinary share.
June 1	Purchased £250,000 12% debenture in Gainsboro PLC for £275,000. Interest is paid on 1st October and 1st April.
June 15	Converted the debentures in Bloodstock PLC into ordinary shares. The market price of the shares was £2. The accrued interest to date was paid.
Aug.25	Received dividend of 20% on the ordinary shares in Bloodstock PLC.
Dec.15	Bloodstock PLC made a rights issue of one ordinary share for every 20 shares held at £1.60 per share. The market value of the shares was £2.

19–5

Jan 10	Porterfield sold the rights for £0.30 per share.
March 15	Sold 10,000 ordinary shares in Bloodstock PLC at £2.50 per share.

Required:

Record the above transactions in Porterfield's ledger. (Ignore Income Tax and broker's charges).
(ACCA)

3. Myreton Ltd raised additional capital to carry out its budgeted expansion plan. The economic situation, however, has made it advisable for the company to postpone its plans until a more favourable time, and, in consequence, the company has surplus funds for temporary investments. The following transactions took place during the year ended 30 September 19–6.

19–5

October 1	Purchased £100,000 9% treasury stock, 19–2–19–6, at 68. Interest payable 1 January and 1 July.
October 1	Purchased £100,000 10% City of London stock, 19–7 at 98, ex div. Interest payable 31 March and 30 September.
October 1	Purchased 50,000 Midland Bank £1 ordinary shares at 280.
December 31	Sold £50,000 10% City of London stock, 19–7 at 97.
	Purchased £50,000 9% treasury stock, 19– 2–19–6 at 70, ex div.

19–6

January1	Received interest on 9% treasury stock.
March 31	Received interest on 10% City of London stock.
	Received interim dividend on Midland Bank shares at 4p per share.
July 1	Received interest on 9% treasury stock, 19–2– 19–6.
September 15	Received final dividend of 6p per share on Midland Bank shares.
September 30	Received interest on 10% City of London stock, 19–9.

At 30 September 19–6, the market values of the securities were:

9% treasury stock 19-2-19-6	66
10% City of London stock, 19-7	99
Midland Bank Shares	270

Ignore taxation brokerage and other fees.

Required:

a. Prepare the investment accounts of Myreton Ltd in respect of the year ended 30 September 19-6.

b. Indicate, and briefly comment on, the information to be given in the company's balance sheet at 30 September 19-6 with regard to these investments.

(ACCA)

4. Surfundz PLC whose account year ends on 31 December, invested in marketable securities:

Required:

In respect of each of the following occurrences.

a. post and balance for the year concerned, the investment account in Surfundz PLC's ledger, assuming that the appropriate amount of interest is received on the due dates.

b. as a separate calculation, justify the figure of investment income for the year.

i. Initial investment on 1 September 19-4 in £500,000 (nominal) 12% Daleford Borough Council Loan Stock at 92 c.i. Interest is payable half-yearly on 30 June and 31 December.

ii. The facts are the same as in i. A further £100,000 (nominal) was acquired on 1 December 19-5 at 95 x.i.

iii. The facts are the same as in i. A further £100,000 (nominal) was acquired on 1 October 19-5 at 94 c.i.

iv. The facts are the same as in iii. Loan stock of £300,000 (nominal) was sold on 1 December 19-5 at 95 x.i. The company applies the FIFO method of calculating cost of disposals.

v. The facts are the same as in iii. Loan stock of £300,000 (nominal) was sold on 1 February 19-6 at 93 c.i. The company applies the averaging method of calculating cost of disposals.

(ACCA)

5. T and W entered into a joint venture for the purpose of buying and selling shares. They agreed that:

i. dividends were to be shared equally, credit was to be taken only when they were actually received.

ii. Costs of buying and selling were to be borne by T;

iii. other profits and losses were to be shared 3/5 T and 2/5 W.

Their transactions were as follows:

1st January	W paid into T's bank account £3,000.
2nd January	T bought 2,000 ordinary £0.25 shares of Z Limited quoted at £0.625/£0.650; buying costs were £40.
9 February	T bought 3,000 ordinary £0.10 shares of X Limited quoted at £0.475/£0.500; buying costs were £39.
5th March	T sold, 1,500 ordinary £0.25 shares of Z Limited quoted at £0.700/£0.725; selling costs were £12.
29th March	W bought 4,000 ordinary £0.50 shares of P Limited quoted at £0.750/£0.800; buying costs were £78.
26th April	T received a dividend of 15% from Z Limited followed by a bonus issue of one share for every two shares held.
2nd May	A rights issue of one share for every four shares held was made by P Limited, at £0.5 per share. Half of the rights were sold personally to W in nil paid form at £0.35 per share; the remainder were paid for by W on behalf of the venture on 4th June.
7th June	T received a dividend of 30% from X Limited.

25th June	T sold the remaining shares in Z Limited quoted £0.450/£0.475; selling costs were £4.
2nd July	T sold half of the shares in X Limited quoted £0.400/£0.425; selling costs were £8.
15th July	A dividend of 2.5% was received by W from P Limited in respect of shares held on joint venture account.
19th July	W took over personally 2,000 shares in P Limited for £2,000.

In each case the two prices quoted are for selling and buying respectively. The agreed valuation of the shares held on joint venture account at 31st July was:

	£
P Limited	2,500
X Limited	600

Assuming that each wished to close his books as at 31st July, you are required to prepare:

a. the accounts kept by T and W to record the venture.

b. the entries in the separate balance sheets of T and W as at that date, relating to this venture.

Taxation is to be ignored. Calculation to be to nearest £.

(ICMA)

ACCA EXAMINATION QUESTION

6. **Required:**

Write up the Investment Account for Plastics PLC in the books of The Easiglide Company.

(ACCA 2.9(1) June 1983)

Appendix 2

Transactions in the shares of Plastic PLC during the year ended
31 December 1982

15 January	Purchased 20,000 ordinary £1 shares for £40,000.
31 January	Sold 5,000 ordinary shares for £12,000 cum div.
31 March	Received an interim dividend of £.05 per share.
30 April	Plastics PLC resolved to:
	(a) Make a Bonus Issue of 1 share for every 5 held on 31 May, 1982.
	(b) Give members the right to apply for a Rights Issue of 4 shares for every 10 held at 31 March payable in full on 30 June 1982. The issue price was £1.50 per share. Rights could be sold for £0.25 per share.
31 May	Plastics PLC made Bonus Issue.,
30 June	Company applied for three quarters of its Rights Issue and sold the rights to the remaining quarter.
30 September	Company sold 5,000 shares for £1.90 per share, ex div.
31 October	Company received a final dividend of £.10 per share.
30 November	Plastics PLC converted the £1 shares to 25p Nominal Value.
31 December	The market price per share was £0.55.

8 Bills of Exchange

GENERAL BACKGROUND

1.0 Under normal trading arrangements, the period of time which elapses between goods and services being supplied and being paid for can vary from two weeks to six months or even longer.

1.1 The supplier may not wish to wait so long for payment because he may need the cash to finance his current operations. One way in which the supplier can obtain payment at an early stage whilst at the same time allowing the purchaser the benefit of the full credit period is for the parties to agree to the use of a bill of exchange to finance the transaction.

OPERATING ARRANGEMENTS.

2.0 In the Bills of Exchange Act 1882, a bill of exchange is defined as: "An unconditional order in writing addressed by one person to another, signed by the person giving it, requiring the person to whom it is addressed to pay on demand, or at a fixed or determinable future time, a sum certain in money to, or to the order of, a specified person or to bearer".

   (A cheque is a specialised form of bill of exchange, drawn on a banker and payable on demand).

2.1 The main parties to a bill are the supplier who is the drawer, the customer who is the drawee and the party to whom the money is payable, the payee. The drawer and payee may be the same, or different, parties.

2.2 After drawing up the bill, the drawer sends it to the drawee who signs it to signify that he accepts the liability, writes the word "Accepted" on the face of it and returns it to the drawer. The drawee is then said to be the acceptor.

2.3 The accepted bill is a Bill Receivable from the drawer's point of view and a Bill Payable from the point of view of the drawee.

2.4 In order to achieve the purpose in 1.1 for which the bill was drawn up in the first place, the drawer can discount the bill with his bank.

2.5 Under this arrangement, the bank pays the drawer the amount due on the bill, less interest (at the current discount rate) from the date of discounting to the date of maturity.

2.6 When the bill matures, the drawer's bank, being the new holder, collects the full proceeds from the drawee's banker.

2.7 As an alternative to 2.4 the drawer may transfer the bill to one of his creditors in settlement of his account. The creditor then collects the full proceeds from the drawee's banker on maturity.

2.8 Should the drawee's bank refuse or be unable to pay on maturity, the bill is said to be dishonoured and the drawer's bank (under 2.4) or creditor (under 2.7) will seek full reimbursement from the drawer who then acquires a legal right of action against the drawee.

ACCOUNTING ARRANGEMENTS

3.0 The accounting arrangements do not become effective until acceptance has taken place.

3.1 The drawer credits the drawee's account and debits Bills Receivable.

3.2 Conversely, the drawee debits the drawer's account and credits Bills Payable.

3.3 When the drawer discounts the bill with the bank, Bank is debited and Bills Receivable credited with the full value of the bill. At the same time Bank is credited and Discount on Bills is debited with the discount. The discount is ultimately charged to Profit and Loss.

3.4 Discounting does not give rise to any entries in the drawee's ledger.

3.5 At maturity, the collection of the proceeds of the discounted bill is the concern of the drawer's bank but does not give rise to any entries in the drawer's ledger. In the drawee's ledger, however, Bills Payable is debited and Bank credited.

EXAMPLE

3.6 DE sold goods on credit to ST for £20,000 on 1st February 9-0. The deal was financed by a bill of exchange drawn for seven months after date and accepted on 7th February.

   On 1st March DE discounted the bill with his bank at a discount of £800. The bill was met at maturity.

   Prepare the relevant accounts in the ledgers of both DE and ST.

SOLUTION
3.7 DE's ledger

ST

19-0		£	19-0		£
Feb 1	Sales	20,000	Feb 7	Bills Receivable	20,000

Bills Receivable

19-0		£	19-0		£
Feb 7	ST	20,000	Mar 1	Bank	20,000

Bank (extract)

19-0		£	19-0		£
Mar 1	Bills Receivable	20,000	Mar 1	Discount on B/R	800

Discount on Bills Receivable

19-0		£	19-0		£
Mar 1	Bank	800			

As noted in 3.5, the collection of the bill at maturity is not reflected in DE's ledger when the bill has been previously discounted.

At the financial year-end, any bills receivable not discounted or transferred, would be shown as a Current Asset. Discounted or transferred bills would not be included in the Balance Sheet but a footnote should be appended stating that there is a contingent liability (that is, to reimburse the bank - see 2.8) of £x for Bills Receivable discounted.

ST's ledger

DE

19-0		£	19-0		£
Feb 7	Bills Payable	20,000	Feb 1	Purchases	20,000

Bills Payable

19-0		£	19-0		£
Aug 4	Bank	20,000	Feb 7	DE	20,000

At the financial year end, any bills payable not yet matured would be shown as a Current Liability.

3.8 In the event of the bill being dishonoured (see 2.8) the entries in the drawer's ledger are a debit to the drawee's account and a credit to bank of the full amount of the bill plus the associated bank charges.

OTHER POINTS TO NOTE.

4.0 It is very unlikely that the detailed book- keeping entries will be examined. For this reason I have omitted mention of a number of the more elaborate and obscure entries which can arise with bills of exchange and I have not appended any examination questions at the end of this section.

4.1 Professional level students need an appreciation of bills of exchange accounting to enable them to cope with the sometimes oblique references to bills of exchange which can occur in questions which primarily test other areas of knowledge such as Consignments, Joint Ventures, final accounts of limited companies etc. For this reason, some test exercises are given below.

STUDENT SELF TESTING
Test Exercises

1. During the year ended 31 December 19-4, Faraday Manufacturing Co. Ltd accepted bills of exchange totalling £78,932. Of these, the drawers discounted £51,300 with their various banks for discounts totalling £4,070.

    By the end of the year the company had met, on maturity, bills amounting to £46,500.

    Required:

    State to what extent, if any, the above matters would directly appear in the company's balance sheet at 31 December 19-4.

2. During the year ended 31 December 19-4, Faraday Manufacturing co. Ltd. drew bills of exchange totalling £132,600. Of these, the company discounted £97,700 with their bank at a discount of £3,560.

By the end of the year, bills totalling £91,230 (including discounted bills £72,640) had been met on maturity.

Required.

State to, what extent, if any, the above matters would directly appear in the company's balance sheet at 31 December 19-4.

9 Royalties

GENERAL BACKGROUND

1.0 The owner of a certain legal right may, as a business arrangement allow another party to exercise that right.

1.1 In an accounting context, the rights commonly encountered are

   a. to copy the work of an author or artist (copyright)
   b. to use a device or process patented by its originator or inventor (patent rights)
   c. to extract minerals from ground belonging to someone else (mineral rights).

1.2 The consideration paid by the party exercising the right to the party owning it, is termed a royalty.

OPERATING ARRANGEMENTS.

2.0 As royalties are calculated on the basis of the extent to which rights are exercised, payment can only be made after the extent has been ascertained, that, is in arrear.

2.1 In the early stages, rights may not be exercised to any great degree and as a consequence royalty payments would therefore be low. To overcome this, the contract made between the respective parties may stipulate a guaranteed minimum payment.

2.2 The difference between the actual royalties, calculated on a utilisation basis, and the minimum payment, is termed shortworkings. Shortworkings thus represent the amount of make–up.

2.3 Contracts often allow shortworkings to be recouped out of future royalties which exceed the guaranteed minimum but there is usually a time limit within which the concession may be exercised.

ACCOUNTING ARRANGEMENTS FOR ROYALTIES PAYABLE.

3.0 The party exercising the right (the grantee) opens an expense account – Royalties Payable – and a liability account in the name of the owning party (the grantor). If shortworkings are involved, an asset account – Shortworkings Recoverable – is also opened.

3.1 When ascertained, the royalties are then debited to Royalties Payable and credited to the grantor's account. If applicable, the make–up is debited to Shortworkings Recoverable with the corresponding credit in the grantor's account.

3.2 At the end of the period, the debit balance on Royalties Payable is closed by transfer to Operating Account or Manufacturing Account or Profit and Loss Account, as appropriate. The credit balance on the grantor's account is usually carried down (and paid in the next period) and treated as a Current Liability. The debit balance on the Shortworkings Recoverable is also carried down and being a debtor (effectively), is included in Current Assets.

3.3 If, in a future period, royalties payable exceed the guaranteed minimum and the period concerned is within the stipulated time limit, recoupment is effected by crediting Shortworkings Recoverable and by debiting the grantor's account after the royalty entries (described in 3.1) have been posted. The effect of this is that the amount which would otherwise have been paid to the grantor is reduced by the amount of the clawback.

3.4 When the recoupment period has elapsed, any irrecoverable amount is debited to Profit and Loss Acccount and credited to Shortworkings Recoverable.

EXAMPLE

3.5 Gravel Extractors Ltd. acquired the rights to remove gravel deposits from land owned by A Farmer. The agreement provided for:

   a. the payment of a royalty of £0.40 per tonne of gravel removed
   b. a minimum payment of £2,000 per annum
   c. recoupment rights (for shortworkings) to be extinguished at the end of year 3.

   During the first four years of the contract the following quantities of gravel were removed:

	tonnes
Year 1	4,000
Year 2	4,800
Year 3	5,400
Year 4	5,600

The company's accounting year ends on 31st December and payment to A. Farmer is made on 1st February following.

Prepare the appropriate accounts in the Company's ledger for each of the four years.

SOLUTION

3.6 Preliminary workings are necessary to provide the basic figures for posting the accounts:—

Year	Extraction (tonnes)	Royalties Payable (£0.40 per (tonne)	Minimum Payment	Short- Workings	Amount Payable	Short-Workings Re- couped	Short-Workings Written off
		£	£	£	£	£	£
1	4,000	1,600	2,000	400	2,000	–	–
2	4,800	1,920	2,000	80	2,000	–	–
3	5,400	2,160	2,000	–	2,000	160	320
4	5,600	2,240	2,000	–	2,240	–	–

Royalties Payable

		£			£
Year 1			Year 1		
Dec 31	A.Farmer	1,600	Dec 31	Operating A/C	1,600
Year 2			Year 2		
Dec 31	A. Farmer	1,920	Dec 31	Operating A/C	1,920
Year 3			Year 3		
Dec 31	A.Farmer	2,160	Dec 31	Operating A/C	2,160
Year 4			Year 4		
Dec 31	A. Farmer	2,240	Dec 31	Operating A/C	2,240

A. Farmer

		£			£
Year 1			Year 1		
Dec 31	Balance c/d	2,000	Dec 31	Royalties Payable	1,600
			Dec 31	Shortworkings Recov.	400
		2,000			2,000
Year 2			Year 2		
Feb 1	Bank	2,000	Jan 1	Balance b/d	2,000
Dec 31	Balance c/d	2,000	Dec 31	Royalties Payable	1,920
			Dec 31	Shortworkings Recov	80
		4,000			4,000
Year 3			Year 3		
Feb 2	Bank	2,000	Jan 1	Balance b/d	2,000
Dec 31	Shortworkings Recov.	160	Dec 31	Royalties Payable	2,160
Dec 31	Balance c/d	2,000			
		4,160			4,160
Year 4			Year 4		
Feb 1	Bank	2,000	Jan 1	Balance b/d	2,000
Dec 31	Balance c/d	2,240	Dec 31	Royalties Payable	2,240
		4,240			4,240
			Year 5		
			Jan 1	Balance b/d	2,240

Shortworkings Recoverable

Year 1		£	Year 1		£
Dec 31	A. Farmer	400	Dec 31	Balance c/d	400
		400			**400**
Year 2			Year 2		
Jan 1	Balance b/d	400	Dec 31	Balance c/d	480
Dec 31	A.Farmer	80			
		480			**480**
Year 3			Year 3		
Jan 1	Balance b/d	480	Dec 31	A Farmer	160
			Dec 31	Profit and Loss	320
		480			**480**

As noted in 3.2 the closing balances would appear in the Balance Sheet. For example, at the end of Year 2, the £2,000 credit balance on A. Farmer's account would be included in Creditors whilst the debit balance of £480 on Shortworkings Recoverable would be included as a Current Asset.

ACCOUNTING ARRANGEMENTS FOR ROYALTIES RECEIVABLE

4.0 The party owning the right (the grantor) opens a revenue account – Royalties Receivable – and an asset account in the name of the grantee. If shortworkings are involved, a liability account – Shortworkings Allowable – is also opened.

4.1 When ascertained, the royalties are credited to Royalties Receivable and debited to the grantee's account. If applicable, the make–up to the agreed minimum sum is debited to the grantee's account and credited to Shortworkings Allowable.

4.2 At the end of the period the credit balance on Royalties Receivable is closed by transfer to Profit and Loss Account. The debit balance on the grantee's account is carried down (and received in the next period) and treated as a Current Asset (debtor). The credit balance on Shortworkings Allowable is also carried down and is included in Current Liabilities.

4.3 If, in a future period, royalties receivable exceed the guaranteed minimum and the period concerned is within the stipulated time limit, the rebate is effected by debiting Shortworkings Allowable and by crediting the grantee's account after the royalty entries (described in 4.1) have been posted. The effect of this is that the amount which would otherwise have been received from the grantee is reduced by the amount of the rebate.

4.4 When the rebate period has elapsed any sum not refunded is debited to Shortworkings Allowable and credited to Profit and Loss.

EXAMPLE

4.5 Using the same facts in 3.5 and assuming that A. Farmer's accounting year also ends on 31st December, prepare the appropriate accounts in his ledger for each of the four years.

SOLUTION

4.6 Similar preliminary workings to those shown in 3.6 would be prepared (with suitably adapted headings) but it is not necessary to repeat those workings at this point.

Royalties Receivable

Year 1		£	Year 1		£
			Dec 31	Gravel Extractors	
Dec 31	Profit and Loss	1,600		Ltd	1,600
Year 2			Year 2		
			Dec 31	Gravel Extractors	
Dec 31	Profit and Loss	1,920		Ltd	1,920
Year 3			Year 3		
			Dec 31	Gravel Extractors	
Dec 31	Profit and Loss	2,160		Ltd	2,160
Year 4			Year 4		
			Dec 31	Gravel Extractors	
Dec 31	Profit and Loss	2,240		Ltd.	2,240

Gravel Extractors Ltd

Year 1		£	Year 1		£
Dec 31	Royalties Receivable	1,600	Dec 31	Balance c/d	2,000
Dec 31	Shortworkings				
	Allowable	400			
		2,000			2,000
Year 2			Year 2		
Jan 1	Balance b/d	2,000	Feb 1	Bank	2,000
Dec 31	Royalties Receivable	1,920	Dec 31	Balance c/d	2,000
Dec 31	Shortworkings				
	Allowable	80			
		4,000			4,000
Year 3			Year 3		
Jan 1	Balance b/d	2,000	Feb 1	Bank	2,000
Dec 31	Royalties Receivable	2,160	Dec 31	Shortworkings	
				Allowable	160
			Dec 31	Balance c/d	2,000
		4,160			4,160
Year 4			Year 4		
Jan 1	Balance b/d	2,000	Feb 1	Bank	2,000
Dec 31	Royalties Receivable	2,240	Dec 31	Balance c/d	2,240
		4,240			4,240
Year 5					
Jan 1	Balance b/d	2,240			

Shortworkings Allowable

		£			£
Year 1			Year 1		
Dec 31	Balance c/d	400	Dec 31	Gravel Extractors Ltd	400
Year 2			Year 2		
Dec 31	Balance c/d	480	Jan 1	Balance b/d	400
			Dec 31	Gravel Extractors Ltd	80
		480			480
Year 3			Year 3		
Dec 31	Gravel Extractors Ltd	160	Jan 1	Balance b/d	480
Dec 31	Profit and Loss	320			
		480			480

STUDENT SELF TESTING

Test Exercises

1. Sand Quarries (Midlands) Ltd. acquired the right to extract sand from land owned by A. Freeholder.

   a. the payment of royalties at the rate of £0.60 per tonne extracted

   and

   b. a minimum payment of £1,200 per annum.

   and

   c. a right to recoup shortworkings up to the end of year 2 after which the right was to be extinguished.

   During the first three years of the contract, the following quantities of sand were extracted:

Year	tonnes
1	500
2	2,400
3	4,000

   The accounting years of both the company and of the landowner end on 31 December. The landowner receives payment of 1 February following the year end.

   Required:

   Prepare a schedule of workings for these transactions to enable the company's accounts to be prepared for each of the three years.

2. The facts are as in 1 above.

   Required

   a. Open, post and balance the appropriate accounts in the books of Sand Quarries (Midlands) Ltd. for each of the three years.

   b. Show an extract from the company's balance sheet as at the end of year 1. Taxation implications should be ignored.

3. The facts are the same as in 1 above, except that

   i. shortworkings recoupment rights can be exercised up to the end of year 3, after which they are extinguished.

   and

   ii. during the first three years of the contract, the following quantities of sand were extracted:

Year	tonnes
1	500
2	2,400
3	3,000

Required:

Prepare a schedule of workings for these transactions to enable the land–owner's accounts to be prepared for each of the three years.

4. The facts are as in 3 above.
   Required:

   a. Open, post and balance the appropriate accounts in the books of A. Freeholder for each of the three years.

   b. Show an extract from the landowner's balance sheet as at the end of year 2.

   Taxation implications should be ignored.

5. White has negotiated with Black for a licence to manufacture and sell paintsprayers for which Black is the patentee. The agreement provides for a royalty to be paid to Black of £2 for each unit sold in a year, subject to a minimum sum of £20,000 per annum. The shortfall in any year can be recouped from any excess of royalties over the minimum sum in the following year only.
   White sold 8,000 sprayers in 19–5 and 11,000 in 19–6.
   From the beginning of 19–7 White issued a sub– licence to Grey for the manufacture and sale of the same units, on the terms of a royalty of £2.50 each, a minimum sum of £12,000 per annum and the right to recover any shortfall for a year from an excess in the following year.
   The sales volumes for the two following years were:

	White	Grey
19–7	12,000	3,000
19–8	14,000	4,000

   Required:
   Show the accounts in White's books for each of the four years, indicating the amounts to be transferred to the Profit and Loss account each year and the amounts being carried forward at the end of each year. Assume that all the sums due were received or paid in the appropriate year.
   (ACCA)

AAT EXAMINATION QUESTION

6. Lugg Limited received the rights to manufacture and market a commemoration plate from Wyke public limited company.
   Lugg agreed to pay Wyke £2 per plate sold, subject to a minimum annual payment of £100,000. Any shortfall in the minimum annual payment is to be recovered within two years following the year in which it arises.
   During the first five years of the agreement, Lugg's sales were as follows:

Year to 31 December	Number sold
19–4	30,000
19–5	40,000
19–6	60,000
19–7	70,000
19–8	45,000

   The amount due to be paid to Wyke in respect of amounts owing as at 31 December was to be paid on 31 January in the following year.
   Required:
   Record the above transactions in Lugg's books of account using the following ledger accounts:

   i. royalties payable;

   ii. Wyke plc (patent holder);
      and

   iii. short workings recoverable account.

   (Note: Be careful to balance each account at the end of the respective financial year, and to bring down the appropriate balance.)

   (AAT)

10 Containers

GENERAL BACKGROUND

1.0 For many products some sort of packaging is essential. Items of food are usually put into bags or wrappers or tins, as appropriate. Cigarettes are put into packets, paint and motor oil are sold in metal or plastic cans.

1.1 Certain other products require much stronger containers. Acid is stored and transported in a non-corrosive (usually glass) carboy, radio–active materials in special casks.

OPERATING ARRANGEMENTS

2.0 Containers of the types mentioned above may or may not be re–usable.

2.1 The packaging of those items mentioned in 1.0 cannot be re–used and is thrown away by the consumer when the product which it is protecting is used up.

2.2 The more substantial and expensively produced containers of the type referred to in 1.1. can usually be re–used and are returnable to the manufacturers or suppliers, when empty.

ACCOUNTING ARRANGEMENTS

3.0 The accounting treatment of containers regarded as expendable is different from the treatment of those which are not.

3.1 Primary packaging which is in effect an integral part of the product, as in 1.0, and which is discarded when the product is used up, constitutes part of the manufacturing cost of that product and forms part of the Cost of Sales figure of the manufacturer.

3.2 Re–usable secondary packaging, for example, crates and primary packaging instanced in 1.1 are treated as a distribution cost if not returned to the manufacturer or supplier.

3.3 In those instances where the manufacturer or supplier is eager for the container to be returned, a deposit is invariably imposed on the customer. This is refundable in full or in part, according to the condition of the container, if returned.

3.4 From 3.3 it is apparent that the manufacturer or supplier must keep records showing containers bought, lost, damaged, scrapped and in stock and records showing deposits receivable, refunded and refundable.

3.5 The necessary accounting entries could all be made within a single Containers account. Preferably, however, for greater clarity, two accounts should be opened as follows, each with separate columns for quantities, unit values and total amounts.

3.6 Containers Stock to record containers bought, scrapped, retained by customers and in stock. Containers in customers' hands but capable of being returned are regarded as stock but distinguished from stock available for despatch to customers. Sums written off the value of containers are also passed through this account.

3.7 Containers Suspense to record opening and closing refundable deposits, deposits receivable, refunded and forfeited (through non–return), sums written off the value of containers, and expenses such as repair costs.

3.8 When period end accounts are prepared, the derived figure of profit or loss on containers is transferred to Profit and Loss account, whilst the closing balance, representing refundable deposits appears partly or wholly, as appropriate, as a deduction from Debtors or as Creditors. The closing balance on Containers Stock is included in Stock.

EXAMPLE

3.9 RC Ltd despatched its products to customers in bulk in wooden crates. The crates are bought from the manufacturers at £15 each but are valued for stock purposes at £10 each. Customers are charged a deposit of £25 per crate, £20 of which is refunded when the crate is returned.

At the beginning of 19–1, RC Ltd was holding 1,750 crates on its premises, whilst 1,460 were held by customers. The corresponding figures at the end of the year were 3,021 and 1,983 crates respectively.

During the year 19–1, the company bought 2,000 crates charged out 5,663 crates to customers and made refunds on 5,104. Of the remainder, 170 crates were scrapped and 36 were retained by customers.

The company incurred £257 in making damaged crates re–usable.

Required: Prepare the Crates Stock and Crates Suspense accounts for the year 19–1.

SOLUTION
3.10

Crates Stock

19–1	Quantity No	Rate £	Amount £	19–1		Quantity No	Rate £	Amount £
Balances b/d								
: on premises	1,750	10	17,500	Crates Suspense				
: with customers	1,460	10	14,600	: scrapped		170	10	1,700
				: retained		36	10	360
Purchases	2,000	15	30,000	: depreciation		–		10,000
				$[2,000 \times (15-10)]$				
				Balances c/d				
				: on premises		3,021	10	30,210
				: with customers		1,983	10	19,830
	5,210		62,100			5,210		62,100

Crates Suspense

19–1	Quantity No	Rate £	Amount £	19–1	Quantity No	Rate £	Amount £
Debtors (refunds)	5,104	20	102,080	Balance b/d	1,460	20	29,200
Crates Suspense							
: scrapped	–		1,700	Debtors (charges)	5,663	25	141,575
: retained	36	10	360				
: depreciation	–		10,000				
Repairs	–		257				
Balance c/d	1,983	20	39,660				
Profit and Loss			16,718				
(profit) (derived)							
	7,123		170,775		7,123		170,775

The profit can be reconciled as follows:

	£
Profit on hire $[5,663 \times (25-20)]$	28,315
Profit on retained crates $[36 \times (20-10)]$	360
Expenses $[1,700 + 257 + 10,000]$	(11,957)
Profit as above	16,718

STUDENT SELF TESTING
Test Exercises

1. A components manufacturer despatches his items to wholesalers in reinforced cartons which are returnable.

    At the beginning of 19–5 he held 912 cartons at his factory whilst a further 871 were with his customers.

    During 19–5 he bought a further 1,000 cartons and scrapped 39 which were irreparable. Customers were charged for 3,064 cartons, retained 53 and were refunded for 2,855. An amount of £142 was spent on repairs to damaged cartons.

    At the end of 19–5 there were 1,664 cartons in stock in the manufacturer's factory and another 1,027 with his customers.

    Cartons were bought in at £10 each but valued for stock at £6. The charge to customers was £15 per carton, £13 of which was refunded on their return.

    Required:
    Prepare the Cartons Stock and Cartons Suspense accounts for the year 19–5.

ACCA EXAMINATION QUESTIONS (with answers)

2. The manager of Garden Products delivers goods to customers in crates which are invoiced to them

at £5 each and credited in full if returned within two months of delivery.

The crates are purchased by Garden Products at a cost of £4 each. Until 30 September 1983 all crates purchased were made of wood; from 1 October 1983 all new crates are made of plastic.

On 1 October 1983 there were 2,500 crates in the warehouse, 8,500 crates with customers and 120 crates in transit. At that date the supplier of the crates to Garden Products was owed £760.

During the year to 30 September 1984 the following transactions took place:

i. 9,200 wooden crates and 1,000 plastic crates were invoiced to customers.

ii. 11,000 wooden crates and 500 plastic crates were returned and credited at the full invoice price.

iii. 110 wooden crates were returned late by customers. Of these 50 crates were credited in full and the balance were credited at £2.25 each.

iv. Garden Products paid £6,960 to the supplier of the crates.

v. The supplier was owed £600 at 30 September 1984.

vi. Repairs were made to wooden crates at a cost of £260.

vii. 30 Wooden crates and 10 plastic crates were damaged and discarded.

On 30 September 1984 a stock take at the warehouse showed a count of 4,300 wooden crates and 950 plastic crates. It was estimated that there were 6,550 wooden crates and 180 plastic crates in the hands of customers which could be returned within the period allowed for full credit. There were 100 wooden crates and 60 plastic crates in transit.

Crates in stock (both plastic and wood) are always valued at £3.50 each to allow for wear and tear. There is an insurance policy in operation under which the company recoups fifty per cent of the cost of crates that are lost provided that they do not exceed ten per cent of the number in stock or with customers at the beginning of the accounting year together with additions during the year. Losses exceeding this mean that no costs are recouped for *any* lost crates. The insurance company have indicated that they propose in future to treat claims for plastic crates separately from wooden crates.

Required:

a. Prepare appropriate accounting records for all crate transactions in the books of Garden Products for the year ended 30 September 1984.

b. Calculate the effect on the profit for the year if the lost crates are treated in accordance with the proposed insurance treatment.

(ACCA 2.9 (2) December 1984)

11 Foreign Currency Transactions

GENERAL

1.0 It is quite common for a business in one country to conduct operations in other countries whose currencies are different from the currency of the country of the "parent" business. For example, a UK company may have branches in France, Germany and Italy whose currencies are francs, deutschmarks and lire, respectively and subsidiary companies in the USA and Sweden, whose respective currencies are dollars and kroner.

1.1 The books of the overseas branches and/or subsidiaries are maintained in the local currency. Before the financial results of the business can be ascertained the local currency figures must be translated into sterling. The two main methods of translation are the temporal and closing rate methods which are dealt with in 2.0 to 3.4 below. There are several variations of these methods which are used in practice.

BASIC TEMPORAL METHOD.

2.0 This method has been extensively used in the past in the UK and in the United States, following the issue in 1975 by the Financial Accounting Standards Board (FASB) or FAS 8 – Accounting for the translation of foreign currency transactions and foreign currency financial statements. Translation is based on the rates ruling at the point of transaction as shown in the following table.

2.1

Item	Translation rate
Fixed assets	At the date each asset was acquired.
Depreciation	The same as the fixed asset to which it relates.
Capital	At the date of issue
Long–term liabilities	At trial balance date or contract rate, if applicable.
Stocks	At the average for the period in which the stocks were acquired.
Current assets (excluding stocks) and current liabilities	At the trial balance date, that is opening current assets/liabilities at the previous closing trial balance rate and closing current assets/liabilities at the present closing trial balance rate.
Remittances of cash and stock.	At the actual date of each remittance.
Retained profits brought forward	The actual sterling amount carried forward at the end of the previous period.
Retained profits carried forward	The residual sterling amount carried forward at the end of the current period.
All revenues and expenses which result in cash flows (that is, excluding depreciation)	At the average for the period.

2.2 It is usual to prepare a translation trial balance, whereby the translated sterling amounts are arrayed alongside their corresponding currency amounts. The balancing difference on the sterling columns, representing either a profit or a loss on translation, is passed through the profit and loss account for the period.

221

BASIC CLOSING RATE METHOD

3.0 This is simpler than the temporal method in that, as its name implies, currency items, as a general rule, are translated at the closing rate for the period.

3.1 Exceptions to this rule are remittances and stock acquired in sterling (as opposed to in local currency). Translation of these items is at the actual rate of each remittance or acquisition. Similarly, capital is translated at the actual rate at the date it was issued.

3.2 Further exceptions are revenues and expenses resulting in a cash flow (that is, business transactions) which are translated at the average rate for the period.

3.3 Exchange differences resulting from the use of the closing rate are regarded as adjustments to reserves to the extent that they arise from the restatement, at the closing rate, of fixed assets and net borrowings used to finance those fixed assets. Other differences are passed through the profit and loss account.

3.4 Modifications of the basic temporal and closing rate methods are now used in the UK when accounting for foreign currency transactions and operations, following the adoption of SSAP 20 which is summarised below.

SSAP 20 – FOREIGN CURRENCY TRANSLATION
(issued April 1983)

4.0 Foreign currency translation is the subject of SSAP 20 which recognises two types of situation.

   i. a company may engage in transactions which are denominated in a foreign currency. For example, the business may consign goods to an overseas consignee.

   ii. a company may conduct operations via a subsidiary in a foreign country which has a currency different from that of the parent company's country.

4.1 As regards 4.0 above, there is separate consideration of

   a. the preparation of the individual financial statements of each company concerned.

   b. the preparation of consolidated financial statements.

   each of which are now considered below.

PREPARATION OF INDIVIDUAL COMPANY FINANCIAL STATEMENTS

4.2 A modified temporal method is used in that each asset, liability, cost and revenue is translated at the rate ruling at the date of the transaction or at a period average rate, or at a contracted rate when a company undertakes transactions which are denominated in a foreign currency.

4.3 For balance sheet purposes monetary assets and liabilities in currency should be retranslated at the closing rate or at the rate at which the transaction is contracted to be settled in the future. Non–monetary assets should be carried at the amounts translated according to 4.2 (above).

4.4 Exchange differences from extraordinary items should be included as part of the extraordinary items.

4.5 Other exchange differences should be reported as part of the pre–tax profit for the year because they already have, or soon will, affect the company's cash flows.

4.6 Where a company has borrowed in foreign currency to finance (or hedge against) foreign equity investments, these latter should be translated at closing rate, subject to certain conditions, and any exchange differences should be taken to reserves to be offset against exchange differences arising on borrowings which would otherwise be taken to profit and loss account. Only the excess of differences on borrowings over those on the investments are then dealt with in arriving at the pre–tax profit figure.

PREPARATION OF CONSOLIDATED FINANCIAL STATEMENTS

4.7 The temporal method should be used when certain specified circumstances obtain. These are where the affairs of the foreign enterprise are in essence an extension of the affairs of the investing company (as opposed to it being a separate business). This state of affairs arises, for example when the assets of the subsidiary company are funded by the parent company.

4.8 Examples of the circumstances generalised in 4.7 are when the subsidiary company

   a. acts as a selling agent for the parent company or

   b. produces raw materials or products which are sent to the UK for the parent company to incorporate into its own products or

   c. is located overseas for tax or other reasons to act as a finance raising medium for other companies within the group.

4.9 Apart from in the special circumstances noted in 4.7 and 4.8 above, the modified version of the closing rate method, known as the closing rate/net investment method should be used at all times, except for translation of the profit and loss account which, alternatively, may be effected at the period average rate.

NET INVESTMENT CONCEPT

4.10 This is based on the realities of the operating arrangements in that, after a subsidiary company has been acquired which is self–financing and semi– independent, the involvement of the holding company is with the net investment, that is, with its proportion of the share capital and reserves of the subsidiary rather than with the individual assets and liabilities. It is this net investment which is at risk from fluctuating exchange rates when the closing rate method is employed. (No risks would arise from the use of the (historically fixed) temporal translation rates for individual assets if the net assets employed approach were adopted instead).

4.11 The accounts of the foreign business in local currency are considered to be the best indication of its performance in the group context; therefore a single exchange rate is considered desirable to translate the financial statements of the subsidiary. One advantage in adopting this principle is that financial relationships expressed in the form of ratios remain undisturbed because the relativities between items are preserved.

CLOSING RATE/NET INVESTMENT METHOD.

4.12 All balance sheet items of each foreign subsidiary company are translated into the currency of the holding company at the accounting period end rate, that is, at the closing rate, this being the only feasible rate to apply from the net investment viewpoint.

4.13 The closing rate should be similarly used for incorporating the results of associated companies into those of an investing company.

4.14 Exchange differences resulting from retranslating the opening net investment in a subsidiary or an associated company, together with the difference between the average rate and closing rate translation of the profit and loss account, are recorded as movements on group reserves.

4.15 The consoldiated profit and loss account thus includes the group's share of the foreign subsidiaries' translated post–acquisition profit or loss without adjustment (other than for normal consolidation adjustment, for example, for unrealised intra group unrealised profit) together with exchange differences arising from transactions (see 3.2 and 3.3) which give rise to changes in cash flows to the holding company, if, for example, it has foreign branches or subsidiaries which are regarded as extensions of the parent company for which the temporal method of translation would be employed.

EQUITY INVESTMENT FINANCED BY FOREIGN CURRENCY LOANS

COVER CONCEPT

4.16 A loan in foreign currency taken up by a holding company or by a subsidiary company would constitute a transaction (because this event would give rise to cash flows); any translation differences would ordinarily form part of the profit from operations of the company concerned (see 4.5) and would be consolidated into group profit (or loss) before tax. The acquisition by the holding company of shares in the subsidiary would also constitute a transaction but as the investment is a non–monetary asset no retranslation is necessary, consequently there will be no exchange differences on this item in the separate (as opposed to the group) accounts of the holding company.

4.17 If the proceeds of that loan were then utilised to finance an equity investment in a foreign subsidiary company, any translation differences on the net investment concerned would normally be reported as a movement on group reserves in the consolidated balance sheet (see 4.14).

4.18 However, under circumstances such as these, an exchange difference on the loan would be matched by an exchange difference in the opposite direction.

4.19 SSAP 20 specifies a cover arrangement when translation gains and losses from foreign currency borrowings and the net investment which they finance, are capable of being matched.

4.20 This can be allowed to apply only

    i.   if the foreign currency borrowings are less than the cash which the net investment can generate.

    ii. to the extent of the exchange difference on the foreign equity investment

    iii. where the circumstances require the use of the closing rate method for consolidation.

    iv. provided that the treatment is applied consistently.

DISCLOSURE

4.21 The methods used in translation and the treatment of exchange differences must be specified in financial statements.

4.22 Companies (including holding companies) must declare the net amount of exchange differences on net foreign currency borrowings with separate statement of the amount offset in reserves and the net amount passed through profit and loss account. The net movement on reserves attributable to exchange differences must also be declared.

FOREIGN OPERATIONS

5.0 Where a business conducts part of its operations through a foreign enterprise (subsidiary or related company or branch) which operates as an independent entity, the closing rate method is appropriate for translation purposes.

5.1 Where, however, the foreign enterprise is effectively an extension of the home business under circumstances outlined in 4.8, it is more appropriate to apply the temporal method.

EXAMPLE – TEMPORAL METHOD

5.2 A business in the United Kingdom has a branch in the State of Euphoria, where the local currency is Lodars (Ls). The following trial balance was received by head office:

Euphoria Branch
Trial Balance as at 31/12/19–1

	Dr Ls	Cr Ls
Fixed Assets (at cost) (see note 3)	316,000	
Provision for depreciation (see note 3)		81,800
Stock at 1/1/19–1	145,600	
Debtors	76,000	
Creditors		36,000
Goods from HO	538,000	
Sales		774,000
Expenses (various)	133,200	
Bank	30,000	
HO Current Account		347,000
	1,238,800	1,238,800

Notes:

1. Stock at 31/12/19–1   170,000 Ls
2. Exchange Rates   Ls = £1
   - 1st January 19–1   16
   - 31st December 19–1   20
3. Fixed Assets were acquired thus:

	Fixed Asset Ls	Total Depreciation Ls	Exchange Rate Ls = £1
On 1st January 19–1	96,000	4,800	16
Prior to 1st January 19–1	220,000	77,000	10
Total per Trial Balance	316,000	81,800	

4. At 31st December 19–1, the following items were in transit:

From HO to Euphoria	–	Goods	£2,000
From Euphoria to HO	–	Remittance	6,000 Ls

5. In the HO ledger, the following balances appeared at 31/12/19–1:

	£
Goods to Euphoria	31,000
Euphoria Current Account	26,150

Required:

a. Translate the Euphoria Trial Balance into £s sterling using the temporal method.

b. Prepare the Trading and Profit and Loss Accounts for the Euphoria branch for the year ended 31st December 19–1 and a Balance sheet at that date, in each case in sterling.

c. Complete the HO Current Account in sterling.

SOLUTION
5.3

Euphoria Branch Trial Balance Translation

	Local Currency Dr Ls	Cr Ls	Rate of Exchange Ls = £1	Sterling Dr £	Cr £
Fixed Assets (at cost)					
– acquired 1/1/19–1	96,000		16	6,000	
– acquired before 1/1/19–1	220,000		10	22,000	
Provision for depreciation					
on assets acquired 1/1/19–1		4,800	16		300
on assets acquired before					
1/1/19–1		77,000	10		7,700
Stock at 1/1/19–1	145,600		16	9,100	
Debtors	76,000		20	3,800	
Creditors		36,000	20		1,800
Goods from HO	538,000		Actual	29,000	
				(see note (a))	
Sales		774,000	18		43,000
Expenses	133,200		18	7,400	
Bank	30,000		20	1,500	
Head Office Current Account		347,000	Actual		25,850
					(see note (b))
	1,238,800	1,238,800		78,800	78,650
Difference on exchange (gain) (Balancing figure) (see note (c))					150
				78,800	78,800
Stock at 31/12/19–1	170,000		20	8,500	

Notes:

£

(a) Goods to Euphoria per HO — 31,000 *
Less Goods in transit not yet debited by
Euphoria branch — 2,000

Actual figure comparable with Goods from
HO per Euphoria Branch — 29,000

(b) Euphoria Current Account per HO — 26,150 Ø
Less Remittance in transit from Euphoria
6,000 Ls converted at 20 Ls = £1 — 300

Actual figure comparable with HO Current
Account per Euphoria Branch — 25,850

(c) After the currency columns have been translated the amount required to balance the sterling column represents either a loss on exchange, if it appears in the debit column, or, as here, a gain on exchange since it is needed to balance the credit column. Exchange translation differences are accounted for in the profit and loss account of the total business.

The translated figures are then used for the remainder of the answer.

Euphoria Branch Trading and Profit and Loss Account
for year ended 31st December 19–1

	£	£
Sales		43,000
Less		
Opening Stock	9,100	
Goods from HO	29,000	
	38,100	
Less Closing Stock	8,500	
Cost of Sales		29,600
Gross Profit		13,400
Less		
Expenses		7,400
Net Profit		6,000

Euphoria Branch Balance Sheet
as at 31st December 19–1

	£	£
Fixed Assets (at cost)	28,000	
Less Provision for depreciation	8,000	
		20,000
Current Assets		
Stock	8,500	
Debtors	3,800	
Bank	1,500	
	13,800	
Less Current Liabilities		
Creditors	1,800	
Working Capital		12,000
Net Assets Employed		32,000

Head Office Current Account

	£		£
		Balance b/d	25,850
		Profit and Loss: branch profit for year	6,000
Balance c/d	32,000	Exchange translation gain	150
	32,000		32,000
		Balance b/d	32,000

This closing balance agrees with the Net Assets Employed shown in the Balance Sheet (above).
Note (a) £31,000*
This amount includes goods in transit to Euphoria (£2,000)
Note (b) £26,150 Ø
This account has already been debited with the £2,000 which is then carried down as stock in transit.
Thus, £26,150 (debit) is the net of £28,150 (debit) and £2,000 (credit).

EXAMPLE – CLOSING RATE/NET INVESTMENT METHOD
5.4 The final accounts of Magnum PLC, a holding company, and Micron its wholly owned foreign subsidiary were

Summarised balance sheets as at 31 December 19–6

	Magnum PLC £ 000	Magnum PLC £ 000	Micron Drach 000	Micron Drach 000
Tangible fixed assets		740		2,900
Investment in Micron		450		
Stock	220		500	
Net Monetary Assets	250		600	
		470		1,100
		1,660		4,000
Share capital		1,000		3,200
Reserves – pre–acquisition			80	
– post–acquisition			720	
		660		800
		1,660		4,000

Summarised profit and loss accounts
for year ended 31 December 19–6

	Magnum PLC £ 000	Micron Drach 000
Profit before tax	410	900
Taxation	(90)	(180)
Profit after tax	320	720
Proposed dividends	(80)	–
Retained profit	240	720

Magnum has acquired its holding on 1 January 19–6
Exchange rates were

	Drach = £1
1 January 19–6	8
31 December 19–6	5
Average for 19–6	6

Required:

a. Translate the Micron profit and loss account and balance sheet into £s sterling using the closing rate/net investment method.

b. Prepare for the Magnum group, the consolidated profit and loss account for year ended 31 December 19–6 and consolidated balance sheet at that date.

c. Show the composition of group reserves at 31 December 19–6.

SOLUTION

5.5 Under the closing rate/net investment method, the profit and loss account can be translated at either the closing rate or, the average rate. For this answer, the latter has been selected.

(a)

Micron
Summarised profit and loss account
for year ended 31 December 19–6

	Drach 000	Rate Drach = £1	£ 000
Profit before tax	900	6	150
Taxation	(180)	6	(30)
Profit after tax	720	6	120
Proposed dividends	–		
Retained profit	720	6	120

Micron
Summarised balance sheet as at 31 December 19–6

	Drach 000	Drach 000	Rate Drach = £1	£ 000	£ 000
Tangible fixed assets		2,900	5		580
Stock	500		5	100	
Net monetary assets	600		5	120	
		1,100			220
		4,000			800
Share capital		3,200	8		400
Reserves – pre–acquisition	80		8	10	
—post acquisition	720		Balancing	390	
		800	figure		400
		4,000			800

(b)

Magnum Group
Consolidated profit and loss account
for year ended 31 December 19–6

	£000
Profit before tax [410 + 150]	560
Tax [90 + 30]	(120)
Profit after tax	440
Proposed dividends	(80)
Retained profit for year	360

Magnum Group
Consolidated balance sheet as at 31 December 19–6

	£000	£000
Goodwill [450 – (400 + 10)]		40
Tangible fixed assets [740 + 580]		1,320
Stock [220 + 100]	320	
Net monetary assets [250 + 120]	370	
		690
		2,050
Share capital		1,000
Reserves [660 + 390]		1,050
		2,050

(c)

Composition of group reserves	£000
Balance 1 January 19–6 [660 – 240]	420
Retained profit for 19–6	360

Re translation differences

– net investment [3,280/5]	656	
[less 3,280/8]	410	
		246
–profit at closing rate [720/5]	144	
–less profit at average rate [720/6]	120	
		24
Balance 31 December 19–6 per balance sheet		1,050

Note

The balancing figure of Micron's post acquisition reserves in (a) above can be reconciled as follows:

	£000
Retained profit for year	120
Retranslation differences	
– net investment	246
– profit	24
Per summarised balance sheet as at 31 December 19–6	390

COMPREHENSIVE EXAMPLE

5.6 On 1 January 19–2 Global PLC in the UK had acquired 80% holding in the equity shares of a company, Peeques Inc, in an overseas country whose local currency is Troffs (Ts).

Global had at the same time, as a financing operation, obtained a loan from the Bank of Shangrila whose currency is Eaks (Es).

The separate summarised, draft final accounts of these two companies for 19–6, before incorporating the effects of foreign currency translations, were:

Profit and Loss Accounts
for year ended 31 December 19–6

	Global PLC	Peeques Inc.
	£000	Ts000
Profit before tax	1,400	1,200
Tax	(300)	(200)
Profit after tax	1,100	1,000
Proposed dividends	(560)	(400)
Retained profit for year	540	600

Balance Sheets
as at 31 December 19–6

	Global PLC		Peeques Inc.	
	£000	£000	Ts000	Ts000
Fixed assets (at written down values)				
Tangible assets		5,200		12,000
Investments				
Shares in group company		1,000		
(cost Ts 8,000,000, £800,000)				
(restated at 31/12/19–5)				
Net current assets		540		5,000
		6,740		17,000
Creditors due in more than one year				
Bank loan		(960)		
(amount Es 9,600,000, £800,000)				
(restated at 31/12/19–5)				
Other loans				(2,000)
		5,780		15,000

Financed by

Called up share capital	4,160	10,000
Profit and loss account	1,620	5,000
	5,780	15,000

The profit and loss account of Peeques Inc. comprised:

	Ts000	Ts000
Pre–acquisition		
At 1 January 19–2		2,000
Post acquisition		
Years 19–2 to 19–5	2,400	
Year 19–6	600	
		3,000
		5,000

Rates of exchange have been:

	Ts = £1	Es = £1
At: 1 January 19–2	10	12
31 December 19–5	8	10
31 Decembr 19–6	5	6
Average for year 19–6	6	5

Required:

Prepare the final accounts, incorporating the effects of the foreign currency translations, for 19–6 for
a. Global PLC (the company)
b. Global Group (the group consolidation)

SOLUTION
5.7

a. Global PLC

When preparing the final accounts of Global PLC, as an individual company, the modified version of the temporal method, described in 4.2 to 4.6, is employed.

Thus, the investment in Peeques Inc., being a non– monetary asset, would ordinarily have been maintained at historical rate and would not have given rise to any exchange differences. On the other hand, however, the Shangrilanian loan, being a long–term monetary liability, would have been translated at closing rate. The resultant exchange retranslation difference would then have appeared in the profit and loss account as part of the profit or loss before tax figure. In this example, however, the equity investment in foreign company is stated to have been financed by the parallel borrowing of a different foreign currency. The provisions of 4.6 apply whereby the retranslation difference on the borrowing can be offset in reserves to the extent of the difference on the equity investment. Only the excess difference on the borrowing is then taken in arriving at pre–tax profit.

Thus:

	Ts000	Rate Ts = £1	£000
Equity investment in Peeques Inc.			
at 31 December			
: 19–5	8,000	8	1,000
: 19–6	8,000	5	1,600
Retranslation gain			600

	Es000	Rate Es = £1	£000
Financing loan			
at 31 December			
: 19–5	9,600	10	960
: 19–6	9,600	6	1,600
Retranslation loss			640
Excess loss, debited to Global PLC's profit before tax			40

In deciding the precise heading within the profit and loss account under which the above should be included, the nature of the transaction giving rise to the difference must first be established. If the transaction is of a trading nature, the difference should be classed as Other operating income (or expense). A difference which has arisen from a financing transaction should be classed as Interest payable and similar charges, as in the instance above, or as Other Interest receivable and similar income, if an excess gain had resulted.

A difference which has arisen as the result of a transaction regarded as extraordinary, should be classed as extraordinary also.

On the basis of the preceding paragraphs, the summarised final accounts of Global would appear as shown below.

Global PLC
Profit and Loss Account
for year ended 31 December

	£000
Profit before tax [1,400–40]	1,360
Tax	(300)
Profit after tax	1,060
Proposed dividends	(560)
Retained profit for year	500

Global PLC
Balance Sheet
as at 31 December 19–6

	£000
Fixed Assets (at written down values)	
Tangible assets	5,200
Investments	
Shares in group company	1,600
Net current assets	540
	7,340
Creditors due in more than one year	
Bank loan	(1,600)
	5,740
Financed by:	
Called up share capital	4,160
Profit and loss account	1,580
(1,620–40)	
	5,740

b. **Global Group**

The circumstances of the example coincidence with the net investment concept outlined in 4.10 and 4.11 In preparing the final accounts, the closing rate/net investment method, outlined in 4.12 to 4.15 has therefore been adopted.

It has been assumed that Global has opted to use the average rate, in preference to the closing rate, for translating the profit and loss account of Peeques Inc.

Thus:

Peeques Inc
Translation of profit and loss account
for year ended 31 December 19–6

	Ts000	Rate	£000
		Ts = £1	
Profit before tax	1,200	6	200.0
Tax	(200)	6	(33.3)

Profit after tax	1,000	6	166.7
Proposed dividends	(400)	6	(66.7)
Retained profit for year	600	6	100.0

In the balance sheet, the closing rate has been used, this being the only rate available under this method. The exception to this is that the fair value of the original net tangible assets are translated at historical rate. The reason behind this is that, in order to arrive at group goodwill (or capital reserve), it must be matched against the original cost to Global of that investment at its original sterling equivalent (£800,000). The fair value of the net tangible assets underlying the original net investment are represented by the share capital and pre–acquisition reserves and it is these figures which are translated at historical rate in the balance sheet of Peeques.

Peeques Inc.
Translation of balance sheet
as at 31 December 19–6

	Ts000	Rate Ts = £1	£000
Fixed assets (at written down values)			
Tangible assets	12,000	5	2,400
Net current assets	5,000	5	1,000
	17,000		3,400
Creditors due in more than one year			
Loans	(2,000)	5	(400)
	15,000		3,000
Financed by:			
Called up share capital	10,000	10	1,000
Profit and loss account			
Pre–acquisition at 1 January 19–2	2,000	10	200
Post–acquisition:			
to 31 December 19–5	2,400	(Balance)	600
	14,400	8	1,800
year 19–6	600	6	100
Translation gain	–	(Balance)	1,100
	15,000		3,000

The nature of the translation gain is apparent from its composition. It represents the retranslation uplift of the opening net investment together with the difference in rates used in translating the retained profit for the year. Thus,

	Ts000	Rate Ts = £1	£000
Opening net investment			
at 19–6 closing rate	14,400	5	2,880
at 19–5 closing rate	14,400	8	1,800
			1,080
Retained profit for year 19–6			
at 19–6 closing rate	600	5	120
at 19–6 average rate	600	6	100
			20
Total retranslation gain (above)			1,100

It would be wrong in principle to pass this gain through the profit and loss account for the year 19– 6 because it has arisen not from any trading, operating or financing activities of the business but due solely to the movement in exchange rates.

The group's proportion of this gain (80%) is therefore credited directly to reserves, in substitution for the gains on the investment, (which, of course, does not appear in the group balance sheet), to offset the loss on the financing loan which is also taken direct to reserves at the consolidation stage.

In view of the previous paragraph, the excess (£40,000) of the loss on the financing loan over the gain on the investment in Peeques Inc. must now be ignored in arriving at group profit.

If, however, the loss on the financing loan had, unlike in this example, exceeded the translation gain, the group's proportion of the excess loss, would have been charged against group profit before tax.

Global Group
Consolidated Profit and Loss Account
for year ended 31 December 19–6

	£000
Profit before tax [1,400 + 200] (see note above)	1,600.0
Tax	(333.3)
Profit after tax	1,266.7
Minority interest [20% × 166.7]	33.3
Profit for year attributable to Global PLC shareholders	1,233.4
Proposed dividends	(560.0)
Retained profit for year	673.4

Global Group
Consolidated Balance Sheet
as at 31 December 19–6

	£000
Fixed assets (at written down values)	
Tangible assets [5,200 + 2,400]	7,600.0
Net current assets [540 + 1,000 + 53.4] (see note below)	1,593.4
	9,193.4
Creditors due in more than one year	
Loans [1,600 + 400]	(2,000.0)
	7,193.4
Financed by	
Called up share capital	4,160.0
Capital reserve on consolidation (see workings below)	160.0
Profit and loss (see workings below)	2,273.4
	6,593.4
Minority interest [20% × 3,000]	600.0
	7,193.4

Note:

The net current assets of Peeques Inc. include an amount of £66,700 proposed dividends in current liabilities. These have not been accounted for by Global as dividends receivable and must therefore be regarded as retained within the group, as far as the amount attributable to Global is concerned. Thus £53,400(80% × £66,700) has been added back.

Workings	£000
Global PLC	
Cost of investment in Peeques Inc	800
less proportion of fair value of net tangible assets	
of Peeques Inc. at date of Global's investment,	
equivalent to:	
Share capital [80% × 1,000]	800
Profit and loss [80% × 200]	160
	960
Capital reserve on consolidation	160

233

Profit and loss	£000	£000
Retained profit for 19–6 (above)		673.4
Add		
Retained profits at 31 December 19–5:		
Global PLC [1,620 − 540]	1,080	
Peeques Inc [80% × 600) (post acquisition profit)	480	
Gain on retranslating investment in Peeques Inc. at 31 December 19–6 [1,600 − 1,000]	600 ¢	
		2,160.0
		2,833.4
Less		
Cumulative gains on translating investment in Peeques Inc. now eliminated:		
to 31 December 19–5 [1,000 − 800]	200	
year 19–6 [1,600 − 1,000] (above)	600 ¢	
		800.0
		2,033.4
Add		
Group share of retranslation gains on opening net investment in substitution for previous item [80% × 1,080]		864.0
Group share of retranslation gain on retained profit [80% × 20]		16.0
		2,913.4
Less		
Loss on retranslation of financing loan at 31 December 19–6		640.0
Profit and loss per balance sheet at 31 December 19–6		2,273.4

The reasons for the substitution of the retranslation gain for the eliminated retranslation gains on the investment have been explained in the paragraphs immediately preceding the group profit and loss account. The retranslation gain on the investment to 31 December 19–5 (£200,000) is included in the retained profit of Global at 31 December 19–5 (£1,080,000).

In the statutory note showing reserve movements in the published accounts the various retranslation gains/losses would be combined into a single net figure described as currency adjustments. Thus

Reserves. (Global Group)	£000
Profit and loss	
: at 31 December 19–5	1,360.0
[(1,080 − 200) + 480]	
: retained profit for year 19–6	673.4
	2,033.4
Currency adjustments [864 + 16 − 640]	240.0
: at 31 December 19–6	2,273.4

STUDENT SELF TESTING
Test exercises

1. The final accounts of Aitch PLC, a holding company, and its wholly owned foreign subsidiary, FS Inc. were

Summarised balance sheets as at 31 December 19–6

	Aitch PLC		FS Inc.	
	£000	£000	£000	£000
Tangible fixed assets		730		250
Investment in FS Inc.		40		–
Stocks	180		110	
Net monetary assets	150		100	
		330		210
		1,100		460
Share capital		1,000		300
Reserves – pre–acquisition			100	
–post acquisition			60	
		100		160
		1,100		460

Summarised profit and loss accounts
for year ended 31 December 19–6

	Aitch PLC	FS Inc.
	£000	£000
Profit before tax	280	96
Taxation	(120)	(36)
Profit after tax	160	60
Proposed dividends	(100)	–
Retained profit	60	60

Aitch had acquired its holding on 1 January 19–6
Exchange rates were:

	$ = £1
1 January 19–6	16
31 December 19–6	10
Average for year 19–6	12

Required:
Translate the FS Inc. profit and loss account and balance sheet into £s sterling using the closing rate/net investment method.

2. The facts are exactly the same as in 1.
   Required:

   a. Prepare for the Aitch Group, the consolidated profit and loss account for year ended 31 December 19–6 and consolidated balance sheet at that date.

   b. Show the composition of group reserves at 31 December 19–6.

3. The trial balance of the Neareast branch of Home PLC at 31 December 19–6 was

	Dr	Cr
	$	$
Tangible fixed assets (at cost)	282,000	
Provision for depreciaiton		53,400
Debtors	165,000	
Stock at 1 January 19–6	140,000	
Creditors		130,000
Goods from head office	470,000	
Sales		720,000
Expenses	66,000	
Bank and cash	90,000	
Head office current account		309,600
	1,213,000	1,213,000

Stock at 31 December 19-6 $ 50,000

Fixed assets had been acquired thus:

	Cost	Accumulated Depreciation	Exchange rate
	$	$	
	84,000	8,400	7
	198,000	45,000	9
Totals per trial balance	282,000	53,400	

Exchange rates were:

$ = £1

1 January 19-6	7
31 December 19-6	5
Average for 19-6	6

In the head office ledger, balances at 31 December 19- 6 included

£

Goods to branch	80,000
Neareast current account	62,500

Required:

Translate the Neareast branch trial balance at 31 December 19-6 into £s sterling using the temporal method.

4. The facts are exactly the same as in 3.

Required:

Prepare in £s sterling the Neareast trading and profit and loss account for the year ended 31 December 19-6 and a balance sheet at that date.

SSAP 20 – FOREIGN CURRENCY TRANSLATION

5. In accounting for individual companies.

   a. on what basis should assets, liabilities, revenues and costs be translated?

   b. at balance sheet date, on what basis should monetary assets and liabilities be translated?

   c. how should exchange gains or losses on settled transactions and unsettled short–term monetary items be reported?

   d. how should exchange gains and losses on long term monetary items be reported?

   e. where a company has borrowed in foreign currency to finance foreign equity investments or to hedge against them, what accounting treatment should be accorded?

   f. what conditions are attached to this cover procedure?

6. In preparing consolidated financial statements,

   a. which method of translation should normally be employed?

   b. how should exchange retranslation differences on the opening net investment be reported?

   c. when the closing rate/net investment method is used which rate should be used for translating the profit and loss account?

   d. if the average rate is used in translating the profit and loss account, how should the difference in amount between profit or loss at the average rate and at the closing rate be reported?

   e. under what circumstances should the temporal method of translation be employed?

   f. where foreign borrowings have been used to finance group foreign investments or to hedge against them, what accounting treatment should be accorded?

   g. what conditions are attached to this cover procedure?

7. In the financial statements of companies investing in foreign enterprises, what information should be disclosed?

8. a. In respect of the translation of foreign currency balances for accounting purposes, you are required to distinguish between:

 i. the closing rate method and

 ii. the temporal method (also referred to as the historic temporal method).

 b. The following are the summary accounts of Overseas Ltd, in foreign currency (Limas):

Balance Sheet as at 31 December 19–9.

	Limas
Ordinary share capital	630,000
Retained profits	80,000
	710,000
Plant and machinery, at cost	700,000
Less: Depreciation	70,000
	630,000
Stocks, at cost	210,000
Net monetary current assets	40,000
	880,000
Less: Long–term loan	170,000
	710,000

Profit and loss account, year to 31 December 19–9

		Limas
Sales		900,000
Less: Depreciation	70,000	
Other operating expenses	750,000	
		820,000
Net profit before taxation and appropriation		80,000

During the year, relevant exchange rates were:

	Limas to the £1
1 January 19–9	14
Average for the year	12
Average at the acquisition of closing stock	11
31 December 19–9	10

Your UK company, Sterling Ltd, had acquired Overseas Ltd, on 1 January 19–9 by subscribing £45,000 share capital in cash when the exchange rate was 14 Limas to the £1. The long term loan had been raised locally on the same date. On that day, Overseas Ltd, had purchased the plant and equipment for 700,000 Limas. It is being depreciated by the straight line method over 10 years.

You are required to show the balance sheet and profit and loss account of Overseas Ltd, in columnar form, in £s sterling, using:

 i. the closing rate method, and

 ii. the temporal method, and

to analyse the make up of the net gain on exchange arising under the *closing rate method* and say how it would be dealt with in the consolidated accounts.
(ACCA)

9. Home and Overseas Ltd registered a wholly owned subsidiary in a Caribbean island on 1st April 19–6 and subscribed the share capital at that date, when the rate of exchange was $ 1.60 to £1 sterling. When preparing the consolidated accounts as of 30th June 19–8 the rate was $ 1.86 to £1 and the balance sheet of the subsidiary showed:

	$		$
Share capital	10,000	Fixed assets (cost $ 120,000 less depreciation $ 40,000)	80,000
Loan repayable	100,000	Current assets (no stock)	30,000
	$110,000		$110,000

At 30th June 19–9 the rate was $ 2.10 to £1 and the balance sheet of the subsidiary showed:

	$		$
Share capital	10,000	Fixed assets (cost $ 120,000 less depreciation $ 70,000)	50,000
Loan repayable 19–0	100,000	Net current assets (no stock)	60,000
	$110,000		$110,000

Profit for the year ended 30th June 19–9 after depreciation of $ 30,000 was $ 50,000 which had been paid to Home and Overseas Ltd on 30th June 19–9.

Accounting policy is to translate all items at the closing rate.

You are required to:

a. prepare the adjusting entries necessary for the consolidation of the subsidiary in the 19–9 consolidated accounts and

b. show precisely how the subsidiary's financial transactions would be incorporated in the consolidated accounts for the year ended 30th June 19–9.

10. The following Trial Balance has been extracted from the books of Phoebus Ltd. in respect of its transactions in the United Kingdom and its branches in Ruritania, where the local currency is duks.

Phoebus Ltd
Trial Balance at 30th September 19–5

	United Kingdom		Ruritania	
	£	£	Duks	Duks
Land and buildings at cost	520,000		400,000	
Plant and machinery at cost	250,000		320,000	
Accumulated depreciation – Plant and machinery		90,000		120,000
Motor vehicles at cost	85,000		65,000	
Accumulated depreciation – motor vehicles		35,000		25,000
Fixtures and fittings at cost	40,000		60,000	
Accumulated depreciation – fixtures and fittings		10,000		6,000
Stock – 1 October 19–4	50,000		40,000	
Debtors/Creditors	40,000	40,000	40,000	20,000
Provision for doubtful debts		3,000		2,000
Bank	60,000		20,000	
Prepayments	500		500	
Sales		1,200,000		1,200,000
Purchases	500,000		300,000	
Administration expense	150,000		100,000	
Selling expense	50,000		50,000	
Distribution expense	10,000		10,000	
Depreciation expense	44,000		48,000	
Current account	40,500			40,500

238

Share capital – authorised, issued and fully paid in ordinary shares of £1 each	400,000
General reserve	50,000
Profit and loss account – 1 October 19–4	12,000

1,840,000	1,840,000	1,433,500	1,433,500

Additional information

1. Stock on hand at 30 September 19–5, was valued as follows:

United Kingdom   £45,000

Ruritania   Duks 30,000 (Acquired at average exchange rate
of last quarter of year)

2. Included in Ruritania's stock at 30 September 19–5, were goods supplied by head office at cost plus 25 per cent, amounting to Duks 10,000.

3. The stock held at the Ruritanian branch on 1 October 19–4, was acquired during the last quarter of the year ended 30 September 19–4.

4. The company operates the FIFO method of stock valuation.

5. The Board of Directors decide to transfer £150,000 of the profits to general reserve, and propose that a 20 per cent dividend be paid on the share capital.

6. Exchange rates in operation were as follows:

	£= 1 Duk
On purchase of fixed assets	0.90
Average for last quarter of year ended 30 September 19–4	0.92
On 1 October 19–4	0.95
Average for year ended 30 September 19–5	0.98
Average for last quarter of year ended 30 September 19–5	1.00
On 30 September 19–5	1.10

Required:

From the information given, prepare

a. Trading and profit and loss account for the year ended 30 September 19–5;
and

b. Balance Sheet as at that date.

In each case, showing the information for (1) United Kingdom, (2) Ruritania, and (3) Combined. Taxation to be ignored.
(ACCA)

11. On 1st January, 19–8 Z Limited, which had an authorised and issued share capital of £80,000 in 320,000 ordinary shares of 25 pence fully paid, decided to open a branch in Ruritania.
From the information given below you are required to prepare in sterling:

a. separate trading and profit and loss accounts in columnar form for the head office and branch for the year ended 31st December, 19–8;

b. a balance sheet as at 31st December, 19–8.

1. On 31st December 19–8, the trial balances were as follows:

	Head Office £	Head Office £	Branch Bravos	Branch Bravos
Share capital		80,000		
Fixtures and fittings, at cost	58,300		162,000	
Stock, 1st January 19–8	12,600			
Debtors	23,786		45,000	
Creditors		9,880		27,400
Cash and bank balances	25,234		65,304	
Sales		152,000		355,980

Purchases	128,620		273,396	
Goods sent to branch		29,800		
Current accounts:				
Goods	29,800			232,800
Remittances		22,660	194,300	
Capital	20,000			162,000
General expenses	23,240		38,180	
Depreciation, 1st				
January, 19–8		27,240		
	£321,580	£321,580	Bs778,180	Bs778,180

2. The local unit of currency is the Bravo (B) and the relevant rates of exchange are given below:

Average for year ended 31st December 19–8	Bs8.5	to £1
At 31st December, 19–8	Bs 10.0	to £1
Fixed rate used by branch for converting the value of goods received from head office	Bs8.0	to £1

3. Goods are invoiced to the branch at cost.

4. On 31st December, 19–8, stocks on hand, at cost, consisted of:

Head Office		£18,750
Branch		
Ex head office	Bs 25,600	
Purchased locally	Bs 5,950	
	Bs31,550	

5. A remittance of Bs 6,500 from the branch, sent on 30th December, 19–8, which subsequently realised £640 did not reach head office until 5th January 19–9.

6. On 31 December, 19–8 goods costing £700 were in transit to the branch in whose books they had not been recorded.

7. The branch fixtures and fittings had been acquired with the capital sum of £20,000 remitted for this purpose on 1st January, 19–8.

8. Fixtures and fittings at both the branch and head office are to be depreciated at 10% on cost.

ACCA EXAMINATION QUESTION

12. Rose Limited is a company that imports fertiliser in boxes of 40kg which it repackages into 1 kg cartons for sale to retail shops.

The company specialises in three types of fertiliser–the three types are Lawn, Rose and Vegetable fertiliser.

The Lawn fertiliser is imported from America at $ 259 per box and sold for £4 per carton (1 kg).

The Rose fertiliser is imported from France at 1475 francs per box and sold for £3.50 per carton.

The Vegetable fertiliser is imported from Australia at A$ 210.6 per box and sold for £3 per carton.

On 14 February 1983 there was a storm which damaged the stock held in boxes in the stockroom. The company managed to save 2 boxes of Lawn, 3 boxes of Rose and 4 boxes of Vegetable fertiliser but the remainder was rendered unsaleable.

Negotiations with the suppliers resulted in:

i. The American supplier agreed to take back the damaged boxes of Lawn fertiliser and allow $ 100 per box less a $ 20 per box handling charge.

ii. The French supplier agreed to reduce their charge to their cost price of 775 francs per box.

iii. The Australian supplier insisted on payment in full on the basis that the company should have fully insured for such a loss.

The last balance sheet produced by the company had been made up as at 31 July 1982. The following information is available.

	Lawn	Rose	Vegetable
	£	£	£
Stock in boxes on 31 July 1982	1,400	2,250	1,755
Creditors at 31 July 1982	420	625	468
Creditors at 14 February 1983	560	875	234
Amounts invoiced to retailers			
1 August to 14 February 1983	56,000	10,500	36,000

Amounts in transit from Rose Ltd to customers at selling price but awaiting invoicing at 14 February 1983	4,000	700	1,800
Payments made to suppliers from 1 August 1982 to 14 February 1983	US $ 95,830	120,850 fr	A$65,286

The rate of exchange for goods invoiced to Rose Ltd was:

American dollars US$1.85 = £1

French francs 11.8 francs = £1

Australian dollars A$ 1.80 = £1

The rate of exchange for remitting was unchanged for American and Australian dollars, but the rate for French francs moved to 12.5 francs = £1 between invoicing and payment dates. Exchange gains and losses were borne by Rose ltd.

Information on expenses for the period 1 August 1982 to 14 February 1983 showed:

	£
Creditors at 1 August 1982	300
Payment during period 1 August 1982 to 14 February 1983	2,000
Creditors at 14 February 1983	500

An examination of the insurance cover revealed that the company was inadvertently underinsured and as a result would only be able to recover 75% of any stock loss at invoice price after taking credit for any allowances granted by the suppliers.

Required:

a. Calculate the cost price of the stock that was rendered unsaleable.

b. Prepare a Profit and Loss Account for the period 1 August 1982 to 4 February 1983, which disclosed the effect of the stock loss.

c. Discuss how the company should deal with the stock loss and profit or loss on foreign exchange in its published accounts.

(ACCA 2.9(2) December 1983)

Section III

The Accounts of Limited Companies

Chapter

1   Share and loan capital

2   Distributable profits

3   Taxation

4   Final accounts

5   Value added statements

6   Amalgamations and absorptions

7   Reorganisations and reconstructions

8   Earnings per share

9   Changing price levels

1 Share and Loan Capital

GENERAL BACKGROUND

1.0 Certain matters concerning limited companies will have been met at a much earlier stage of study. For the purposes of this manual, some previous knowledge is assumed concerning:-

> types of limited company (limited by shares etc)
>
> the distinctions between public and private limited companies
>
> methods of formation of limited companies
>
> contents of Memorandum of Association
>
> contents of Articles of Association
>
> nature and types of share capital (including stock)
>
> nature and types of debentures

1.1 This chapter is concerned solely with the accounting entries in the ledger and the balance sheet when shares and debentures are issued, redeemed, purchased on the open market and when shares are forfeited.

ISSUE OF SHARES

2.0 Shares may be issued by a new company as part of the post-incorporation flotation proceedings or by an existing company increasing its issued share capital. It is a criminal offence under Section 81 Companies Act 1985 for a private limited company to issue its shares to the public.

2.1 The consideration is usually, but not necessarily in cash.

2.2 The price at which shares are issued may be identical with the nominal value of the share (an issue at par) or above it (an issue at a premium) or, prior to the passing of the Companies Act, 1980, below it (an issue at a discount). This prohibition on the issue of shares at a discount has been perpetuated in Section 100 Companies Act 1985.

ISSUE OF SHARES AT A PREMIUM

2.3 If a company issues shares at a price above par, the excess, termed share premium, must be held in a separate account in accordance with the requirements of Sections 130, 159, 160 and 162 Companies Act 1985.

2.4 The balance on Share Premium account is effectively part of the permanent capital of the company. The balance may be used for the following purposes only.

> to pay up unissued shares for distribution to members as bonus shares
>
> to write off the preliminary expenses of forming the company
>
> to write off expenses of issuing shares and debentures
>
> to write off commissions paid and discounts allowed on shares and debentures
>
> to provide the premium payable on redemption of redeemable debentures, and, under limited circumstances, of redeemable shares.

ISSUE OF SHARES AT A DISCOUNT

2.5 In very rare cases, a company may in the past have issued shares at discount. Sect. 57 Companies Act 1948 imposed the following conditions on such issues:-

> the shares must be of a class already in issue
>
> the discount issue must be sanctioned by the High Court having previously been authorised by a resolution passed in general meeting
>
> at least one year must have elapsed since the date on which the company was entitled to commence business
>
> the shares must normally be issued within one month after permission has been granted by the High Court.

Further discount issues have now been prohibited by Section 100 Companies Act 1985

ISSUE OF SHARES PAYABLE IN INSTALMENTS

2.6 When shares are issued the purchase price may be payable in full on application or in a series of instalments named in sequence, application, allotment, 1st call, 2nd call etc. The premium, if any, is frequently included with the allotment monies. The amount and time interval between instalments is governed by the company's Articles of Association and by Companies Act 1985, Section 101.

ACCOUNTING ENTRIES ON ISSUE OF SHARES BY INSTALMENTS.

2.7 The accounting entries are:

Account

	Event	Debited	Credited
1	Receipt of application monies	Bank	Share Application
2	Return of rejected application monies	Share Application	Bank
3	Retention of surplus application monies	Share Application	Share Allotment
4	Allotment of Shares	Share Application	Share Capital (called up)
		Share Allotment	Share Premium (if applicable)
5	Receipt of allotment monies	Bank	Share Allotment
6	Further Calls	1st (etc)Call	Share Capital (called up)
7	Receipt of call monies	Bank	1st (etc)Call

2.8 If a share issue is oversubscribed the excess applications may be returned with Letters of Regret (Event 2 above) or the shares allotted may be scaled down pro-rata and the surplus application monies held over on account of allotment (Event 3 above) or a combination of these methods may be used.

2.9 In 2.7 separate Application and Allotment accounts are suggested but a combined account is often met in practice, in which case Event 3 does not require an accounting entry.

2.10 When shares of different classes are being issued, a separate set of application, allotment and call accounts is required for each class. The formal contract between the company and the shareholder comes into being when the allotment letters are posted.

2.11 In the balance sheet share capital authorised, allotted, called up and paid up must be separately distinguished.

2.12 Some shareholders prefer to pay their instalment before they have been called. These are termed Calls in Advance. Bank is debited and a Calls in Advance account credited. This latter account is then debited when the Call is made and the appropriate call account credited. In the balance sheet, calls in advance are treated as called up share capital.

2.13 Conversely, some shareholders may fail to pay their calls when due. This is disclosed as a debit balance on the Call Account(s). These are termed Calls in Arrear. In the balance sheet, calls in arrear appear as Called up Share capital not paid, either as a heading in their own right, or, if insignificant in amount, as a sub-heading of debtors.

FORFEITURE AND REISSUE OF SHARES.

2.14 After the due formalities have been observed, the directors may declare as forfeit any shares on which the calls are in arrear.

2.15 These shares may subsequently be reissued at any price provided that, in combination with the payments already made, the total receipts on these shares does not fall below par value.

ACCOUNTING ENTRIES ON FORFEITURE AND REISSUE OF SHARES

2.16 The accounting entries for forfeiture and reissue which automatically produce figures in a form which complies with the requirements of the Companies Act 1985 are:

Account

	Event	Debited	Credited
8	Transfer of unpaid calls at time of forfeiture	Investments – own shares	1st(etc) Call
9	Receipt of cash on reissue of forfeited shares	Bank	Investments – own shares(with previously unpaid calls)
			Shares premium (if applicable)

EXAMPLE.

2.17 This is a comprehensive example incorporating all the points mentioned in 2.6 to 2.16.

ASJ PLC has an authorised capital of 2,600,000 ordinary shares of £1.00 per share, of which 2,000,000 have been issued at par and are fully paid.

In order to finance an expansion programme ASJ PLC issued the remainder of its share capital at a price of £2.00 per share payable.

		Per Share £
On	Application	0.25
	Allotment (including premium)	1.25
	1st Call	0.30
	Final Call	0.20
		2.00

Applications were received for 900,000 shares. Of these 200,000 were rejected and the money repaid to the applicants; the remainder were allotted pro rata on a 6 for 7 basis and the surplus application money was carried forward to allotment on account.

The calls were duly made and the sums received except that a holder of 2,000 shares paid the final call money along with the 1st Call and a holder of 4,000 shares failed to pay either call.

After the formalities had been concluded, these shares were declared forfeit but were subsequently reissued to another applicant on payment of £0.75 per share.

Required:

1. Post the relevant accounts (excluding Bank) in ASJ PLC's ledger to record the above transactions.
2. Show an extract of entries which would appear in the Balance Sheet of ASJ PLC at each of the following stages.

a. after receipt of 1st Call money
b. after receipt of Final Call money
c. after forfeiture
d. after reissue of forfeited shares.

SOLUTION

2.18 1. Postings in ASJ PLC's ledger. The reference numbers in brackets () are to the events listed in 2.7 and 2.16.

Ordinary Share Application

	£		£
Bank (2) (200,000 × £0.25)	50,000	Bank (1) (900,000 × £0.25)	225,000
Ord.Shr.Allotment (3)	25,000		
(100,000 × £0.25)			
Ord.Shr.Capital (4)	150,000		
(600,000 × £0.25)			
	225,000		225,000

Ordinary Share Allotment

	£		£
Ord.Shr.Capital(4)	150,000	Ord.Shr.Applicn.(3)	25,000
(600,000 × £0.25)		Bank(5)	725,000
Share Premium (4)	600,000	(750,000 − 25,000)	
(600,000 × £1.00)			
	750,000		750,000

Ordinary Share 1st Call

	£		£
Ord.Shr.Capital (6)	180,000	Bank (7) (596,000 × £0.30)	178,800
(600,000 × £0.30)		Investments - own shares (8)	1,200
		(4,000 × £0.30)	
	180,000		180,000

Calls in Advance

	£		£
Final Call (see 2.12)	400	Bank (see 2.12)	400
		(2,000 × £0.20)	

Ordinary Share Final Call

	£		£
Ord.Shr.Capital(6)	120,000	Calls in Advance	400
(600,000 × £0.20)		(see 2.12)	
		Bank	118,800
		[(596,000 × £0.20)	
		—400]	
		Investments − own shares (8)	800
		(4,000 × £0.20)	
	120,000		120,000

Ordinary Share Capital (Called up)

	£		£
		Balance b/d	2,000,000
		Ord.Shr.Appln.(4)	150,000
		Ord.Shr.Allotmt(4)	150,000
		Ord.Shr.1st Call (6)	180,000
		Ord.Shr.Final Call (6)	120,000
Balance c/d	2,600,000		
	2,600,000		2,600,000

Investments - own Shares

	£		£
Ord.Shr.1st Call	1,200	Balance c/d	2,000
Ord.Shr.Final Call	800		
	2,000		2,000
Balance b/d	2,000	Bank (9) (4,000 × £0.50)	2,000
	2,000		2,000

(Note: The sum credited to Share Premium account is the excess of the reissue price over the unpaid calls).

Share Premium

	£		£
		Ord.Shr.Allotmt.(4)	600,000
Balance c/d	601,000	Bank (9)	1,000
	601,000		601,000

2. Extract from ASJ PLC's balance sheets

a. after receipt of 1st call money
[Liabilities]

	£	£
Capital and Reserves		
Called up share capital		
2,600,000 ordinary shares of £1.00 per share		
Allotted		2,600,000
Called up		2,480,400
[ie. including calls in advance]		
Paid up	2,479,200	
[i.e. excluding calls in arrear]		
Share premium account		600,000

[Assets]

Current Assets

Debtors
Called up share capital not paid 1,200

249

b. **after receipt of final call money**
   [Liabilities]

	£	£
Capital and Reserves		
Called up share capital		
2,600,000 ordinary shares of £1.00 per share		
Allotted	2,600,000	
Called up		2,600,000
Paid up	2,598,000	
Share premium account		600,000

   [Assets]
   Current Assets
   Debtors
   Called up share capital not paid — 2,000

c. **after forfeiture**
   [Liabilities]

	£	£
Capital and Reserves		
Called up share capital		
2,600,000 ordinary shares of £1.00 per share		
Allotted	2,600,000	
Called up		2,600,000
Paid up	2,598,000	
Share premium account		600,000

   [Assets]

   Current Assets
   Investments
   Own shares [ie. unpaid calls on forfeited shares] — 2,000

d. **after reissue**
   [Liabilities]

	£	£
Capital and Reserves		
Called up share capital		
2,600,000 ordinary shares of £1.00 per share		
Allotted, called and fully paid		2,600,000
Share premium account		601,000

   [Assets]

   No entries needed

BONUS ISSUES

2.19 Companies sometimes capitalise part of their reserves by making a bonus issue to their existing shareholders. Share Premium account may be utilised for this purpose (see 2.4).

2.20 Bonus (or scrip) issues are made when there are large accumulated reserves which cannot, either by law (for example Share Premium (above) and Capital Redemption Reserve (see 4.15)) or as a matter of financial prudence, be distributed in cash to the shareholders as dividend.

2.21 The accounting entries are that the reserve(s) concerned are debited and Bonus Dividend account is credited; this latter account is then debited and Ordinary Share Capital is credited.

2.22 Except as noted in 2.24, no cash is paid to acquire bonus shares. The company declares, say, a 1 for 4 bonus issue. This means that for every four ordinary shares held, a shareholder will receive one free share.

2.23 If a company has 800,000 Ordinary Shares of £1.00 per share, fully paid, in issue, the market price of which is £2.00 per share (£1,600,000 in total), the effect of the bonus issue is that there will be an extra 200,000 shares issued making 1,000,000 in total. The value will remain approximately the same, consequently the listed price will drop to around £1.60 per share (£1,600,000 ÷ 1,000,000) thus making the shares more marketable. The listed price need not be exactly £1.60 per share as such prices are arrived at by market forces and not as a matter of arithmetical calculation.

2.24 Where a bonus issue would result in an awkward fractional amount to shareholders, only whole shares are allotted and the excess is disposed of for cash by the company and the shareholders concerned participate in the share-out of the proceeds.

RIGHTS ISSUES

2.25 Another device used by companies whose shares are listed on the Stock Exchange is to make a rights issue to its existing shareholders.

2.26 Existing ordinary shareholders are given rights certificates which entitle them to take up a specified number of shares at a specified price.

2.27 As with a bonus issue, a rights issue is proportionate to the existing holding, say, one new share for every five existing shares held (1 for 5).

2.28 The rights issue price is sufficiently below listed price to make the offer attractive.

2.29 Shareholders who do not wish to exercise any or all of their rights may sell them to third parties who then apply for the shares at the rights price.

2.30 Alternatively, shareholders may renounce their rights in favour of the company which may then sell the shares (to which those rights are attached) at the open market price and distribute the excess proceeds to the shareholders concerned.

2.31 After a rights issue has taken place a dilution in the listed price of the shares involved occurs in a similar manner to that noted in 2.23 in respect of a scrip issue.

ISSUE OF DEBENTURES

3.0 A company usually has powers to borrow money by way of loan capital evidenced by an issue of debentures. It is a criminal offence under Section 81 Companies Act 1985 for a private limited company to issue its debentures to the public.

3.1 Debenture holders are almost invariably secured creditors ranking above ordinary creditors in priority of repayment.

3.2 Debentures, like shares, may be payable in full on application or payable in instalments. Apart from the title of the ledger accounts - Debenture Application etc - there is nothing to distinguish the ledger posting entries from those of a share issue. Accordingly, these principles are not illustrated here.

3.3 A debenture issue may be at par or at a discount or, theoretically, although these are a rarity, at a premium. There are no legal constraints on a debenture discount or debenture premium issue comparable with those on share discount and share premium issues noted in 2.5 and 2.4. Debenture Discount is usually amortised over the life of the issue, the unamortised balance being regarded as an intangible asset.

CONVERTIBLE LOAN STOCK.

3.4 A company may also issue debenture stock which is capable of being converted into a specified number of shares over an interval of time on terms of conversion which become progressively less favourable to the holders.

3.5 The holder of convertible loan stock receives a fixed rate of interest but, if he exercises his option to convert into ordinary shares, then participates in dividend distributions as an ordinary shareholder.

REDEMPTION AND PURCHASE BY COMPANIES OF OWN SHARES

4.0 Section 58 Companies Act 1948 permitted companies to issue preference shares which could subsequently be redeemed, that is, bought back from their holders direct, on a specified date or range of dates.

4.1 An issue of 8% redeemable preference shares 1990/1995 means that the shareholders will receive a dividend of 8% per annum, subject to availability of distributable profits until the shares are redeemed and that redemption may take place at any time between 1990 and 1995.

4.2 Redeemable shares, like redeemable debentures, provide a company with medium-term to long-term finance until it is no longer needed in this form as, for instance, internally generated funds accumulate to provide an alternative source of finance.

4.3 Section 45 Companies Act 1981 (now Section 159 Companies Act 1985) drastically altered Section 58 Companies Act 1948 by extending it to cover shares of all classes, specifically including equity shares, providing, inter alia, that there are non-redeemable shares in issue as well.

4.4 Furthermore, by Section 162 Companies Act 1985, companies are now empowered to purchase their own shares on a stock exchange, subject to the observance of certain conditions.

4.5 The conditions and constraints surrounding the redemption of redeemable shares and the purchase of a company's own shares are in general more a matter of law than of accounting.

4.6 However, there are four aspects which are of particular concern to accountants, namely

    a. where a premium is paid on redemption or purchase;

    b. where redemption or purchase involves a transfer to capital redemption reserve;

    c. where a private limited company redeems or purchases its own shares out of capital;

    d. distributable profits out of which purchase or redemption can be effected.

a, b and c are considered in later sub-sections of this chapter and d is dealt with in Chapter 2.

4.7 The company, not the shareholder, takes the initiative in instituting redemption procedures. The timing is entirely at the company's discretion and it will choose a time when conditions are most favourable, for example, when the listed price of the shares is relatively low and/or the company is in a strong liquid position.

4.8 The redemption and purchase of shares may be effected either out of distributable profits or out of the proceeds of a fresh issue of shares made for this specific purpose, or by a combination of these two methods.

PREMIUM PAID ON REDEMPTION OR PURCHASE OF OWN SHARES

4.9 If shares are redeemed or purchased at a price in excess of nominal value, the premium (which is the term given to the excess) must, under Sections 160 and 162 Companies Act 1985, ordinarily be appropriated from distributable profits.

4.10 The (now repealed) Section 58 Companies Act 1948 allowed the unrestricted use of share premium account to meet the premium payable when a redemption took place.

4.11 Share premium account may now be utilised only if the shares, which are the subject of the redemption or purchase, were themselves issued at a premium, and if a fresh issue of shares is made for the purpose.

4.12 Under these exceptional circumstances only, share premium account may be utilised to meet the premium payable, but only to the extent of the lesser of

    a. its balance, after crediting any premium received on any new (that is, replacement) issue of shares

        and

    b. the premiums received on the original issue of the shares which are being redeemed.

EXAMPLE

4.13 Texcon PLC had 400,000 9% redeemable preference shares of £1.00 per share in issue, originally issued at a premium of £0.40 per share.

The company now proposes to redeem 100,000 of these shares at £1.60 per share, financed partially by the issue of 80,000 ordinary shares of £1.00 per share at £1.20.

Prior to the issue of replacement shares, the share premium account had a credit balance of £121,000.

Required:

Show the amount of premium payable on redemption to be appropriated from

    a. share premium account and

    b. distributable profits.

SOLUTION

4.14 Share premium account

	£	
- balance before issue of replacement shares	121,000	
- premium on replacement shares [80,000 × £0.20]	16,000	
- balance after issue of replacement shares	137,000	A.
Premium on issue of shares being redeemed [100,000 × £0.40]	40,000	B.
Premium payable on redemption [100,000 × £0.60]	60,000	
deduct		
- appropriation from share premium account (lesser of (A.) and (B.)	40,000	a.
Appropriation from distributable profits (balance)	20,000	b.

TRANSFERS TO CAPITAL REDEMPTION RESERVE

4.15 Section 58 Companies Act 1948 stipulated that where a redemption of preference shares took place other than out of the proceeds of a fresh issue of shares made for the purpose, an amount, equivalent to the nominal value of the shares so redeemed must be transferred, from reserves otherwise available for distribution, to the credit of Capital Redemption Reserve Fund. The balance of that account could be applied in paying up unissued shares of the company as fully paid bonus shares (see paragraph 2.20).

4.16 Section 53 Companies Act 1981 (now Section 170 Companies Act 1985) repealed Section 58 Companies Act 1948 and introduced a number of changes to the principles involved. Firstly the word "Fund" was omitted to correct the previous misnomer. Secondly, the amount to be transferred to Capital Redemption Reserve was more closely defined as the shortfall between the aggregate proceeds of a fresh issue of shares and the aggregate nominal value of shares redeemed or purchased. Thirdly, the arrangement is applicable to purchase of own share situations as well as to redemptions. Modified arrangements, however, apply in the case of private companies. These are dealt with in 4.20 and following.

4.17 The effect of these transfer requirements is that part of the distributable reserves are permanently capitalised and by thus reducing these distributable reserves, the amount which could theoretically be distributed as cash dividends, is curtailed and in so doing prevents a further outflow of cash which could cause a deterioration in a company's liquidity.

EXAMPLE

4.18 The facts are the same as in 4.13

Required:

Show the amount, if any, to be transferred to Capital Redemption Reserve as the result of the redemption.

SOLUTION
4.19

	£
Nominal value of shares redeemed	100,000
[100,000 × £1.00 per share]	
less	
Proceeds of fresh issue of shares made in partial financing of the redemption	96,000
[80,000 × £1.20 per share]	
Shortfall transferred from distributable profits to capital redemption reserve	4,000

PRIVATE LIMITED COMPANIES

4.20 New powers were contained in Section 54 Companies Act 1981 (now Section 171 Companies Act 1985) which permit private companies (only) to redeem or purchase their own shares out of capital. A number of conditions are imposed under these circumstances, the most notable of which, for accounting purposes, is that the payment out of capital must not exceed what the Act terms the "permissible capital payment".

4.21 Permissible capital payment is defined in the Act to mean the total paid on redemption or purchase of own shares minus the aggregate of distributable profits and the proceeds of any fresh issue of new shares made for the purpose of the redemption or purchase. The effect of this restriction is that payment out of capital is allowed only as a last resort after all other means have been exhausted.

EXAMPLE

4.22 Privco Ltd. is proposing to purchase 200,000 of its 10% preference shares of £1.00 per share for £1.50 per share, but at the same time to finance this operation partly out of the issue of 100,000 ordinary shares of £1.00 per share at £1.20 per share. Distributable profits amount to £110,000.

Required:
Show the amount, if any, which the company could regard as the permissible capital payment.

SOLUTION
4.23

	£
Amount required for purchase of own shares	300,000
[200,000 × £1.50]	
less	
Proceeds of new share issue made for the purpose of the purchase	120,000
[100,000 × £1.20]	
Distributable profits	110,000
Aggregate	230,000
Shortfall, constituting permissible capital payment	70,000

4.24 In the circumstances outlined above in 4.20 to 4.23 the permissible capital payment is taken into account, together with the proceeds of a new issue of shares (see 4.16 above) for the purpose of calculating the transfer to Capital Redemption Reserve. Where there is no new issue of shares, the transfer to Capital Redemption Reserve is the difference between the nominal value of the shares redeemed or purchased and the permissible capital payment.

EXAMPLE

4.25 The facts are the same as in 4.22

Required:
Show the amount, if any, which the company should transfer to Capital Redemption Reserve.

SOLUTION
4.26

	£
Nominal value of own shares purchased	200,000
[200,000 × £1.00]	
less	
Proceeds of fresh issue of shares made in partial financing of the purchase	120,000
[100,000 × £1.20]	
Permissible capital payment (per 4.23)	70,000
Aggregate	190,000
Shortfall, transferred from distributable profits to capital redemption reserve	10,000

EXAMPLE

4.27 The facts are the same as in 4.22 except that there was no fresh issue of ordinary shares.
Required:
Show the amount of

a.   permissible capital payment and

b.   transfer to capital redemption reserve

SOLUTION
4.28

		£
a.	Amount required for purchase of own shares	300,000
	[200,000 × £1.50]	
	less	
	Distributable profits	110,000
	Shortfall, constituting permissible capital payment	190,000

		£
b.	Nominal value of own shares purchased	200,000
	[200,000 × £1.00]	
	less	
	Permissible capital payment ((a) above)	190,000
	Shortfall transferred from distributable profits to capital redemption reserve	10,000

It can be seen that this gives an identical result to that in 4.26.

4.29 If, in the instance of a private company redeeming or purchasing its own shares out of capital the proceeds of a fresh share issue (if any) when aggregated with the permissible capital payment exceed the nominal value of the shares redeemed or purchased, the company can, under Section 171 Companies Act 1985, utilise an amount up to the excess to reduce any of the following accounts:

> capital redemption reserve
>
> share premium
>
> fully paid share capital
>
> revaluation reserve

EXAMPLE

4.30 The facts are the same as in 4.22, except that distributable profits are only £40,000.
Required:
Show the amount of

a. permissible capital payment and

b. amount utilisable under Section 171 Companies Act 1985.

SOLUTION
4.31

		£
a.	Amount required for purchase of own shares [200,000 × £1.50]	300,000
	less	
	Proceeds of new share issue made for the purpose of the purchase [100,000 × £1.20]	120,000
	Distributable profits	40,000
	Aggregate	160,000
	Shortfall, constituting permissible capital payment	140,000

		£
b.	Nominal value of own shares purchased [200,000 × £1.00]	200,000
	less	
	Proceeds of fresh issue of shares made in partial financing of the purchase [100,000 × £1.20]	120,000
	Permissible capital payment (above)	140,000
	Aggregate	260,000
	Excess, utilisable under Section 171 Companies Act 1985	60,000

ACCOUNTING ENTRIES ON REDEMPTION OR PURCHASE OF OWN SHARES
4.32 The accounting entries are:

	Account	
Event	**Debited**	**Credited**
1 Declaration of redemption or purchase	Share Capital	Share Redemption(Purchase)
2 Transfer of premium payable on redemption or purchase	Share Premium and/or Profit and Loss Appropriation	Share Redemption (Purchase)
3 Redemption or purchase of shares	Share Redemption (Purchase)	Bank
4 Transfer required by 170 CA 1985 (See 4.16)	Profit and Loss Appropriation	Capital Redemption Reserve

4.33 The redemption or purchase could be recorded without opening a Share Redemption (Purchase) account. However, it serves as a useful focal point for the entries and, if these transactions take place gradually, it saves the Share Capital account from being encumbered with a lot of otherwise confusing entries.

4.34 The entries required to record the issue of fresh shares would be as described in 2.6 and 2.7.

EXAMPLE
4.35 Part of the share capital of ZS PLC consisted of 600,000 8% Redeemable Preference Shares

of £1.00 per share, fully paid, originally issued at £1.10 per share. The company decided to exercise its rights and redeemed 200,000 of these shares at a premium of £0.40 per share.

To assist in financing the redemption, ZS PLC issued a further 120,000 Ordinary Shares of £1.00 per share at a premium of £0.20 per share.

Prior to the above events, the balances standing to the credit of the company's Ordinary Share Capital, Share Premium and Unappropriated profits accounts were £900,000, £26,000 and £400,000 respectively.

Required:

Post the relevant accounts (excluding Bank) in ZS PLC's ledger to record these transactions.

SOLUTION

4.36 The reference numbers in () are to the events listed in 4.32.

Ordinary Share Application and Allotment

	£		£
Ord.Shr.Capital	120,000	Bank	144,000
(120,000 × £1.00)			
Share Premium	24,000		
(120,000 × £0.20)			
	144,000		144,000

Ordinary Share Capital

	£		£
		Balance b/d	900,000
Balance c/d	1,020,000	Ord.Shr.Appln.and	
		Allotmt.	120,000
	1,020,000		1,020,000
		Balance b/d	1,020,000

Share Premium

	£		£
Preference Redemption (2)	20,000	Balance b/d	26,000
(maximum available -		Ord.Shr.Appln.and	
see 4.12 and below)		Alltmt	24,000
Balance c/d	30,000		
	50,000		50,000
		Balance b/d	30,000

8% Redeemable Preference Share Capital

	£		£
Preference Redemption (1)	200,000	Balance b/d	600,000
(200,000 × £1.00)		(600,000 × £1.00)	
Balance c/d	400,000		
	600,000		600,000
		Balance b/d	400,000

Preference Redemption

	£		£
Bank (3)	280,000	8% Redmble.Pref.Shr.Cap.	200,000
(200,000 × £1.40)		(1)(nominal value of shares)	
		Share Premium (2)	20,000
		Profit and Loss Appn. (2)	60,000
	__280,000__		__280,000__

Profit and Loss Appropriation

	£		£
Preference redemption (2)	60,000	Balance b/d	400,000
(amount needed to make up			
total premium payable)			
Capital Redemption			
Reserve (4)	56,000		
Balance c/d	284,000		
	__400,000__		__400,000__
		Balance b/d	284,000

Capital Redemption Reserve

	£		£
Balance c/d	56,000	Profit and Loss Apprpn.(4)	56,000
		(see below)	
		Balance b/d	56,000

	£
Nominal value of preference shares redeemed (200,000 × £1.00)	200,000
Proceeds from ordinary replacement shares (120,000 × £1.20)	144,000
Redemption not backed by new issue - §170 CA 1985 transfer	__56,000__

The maximum amount of share premium which can be utilised for the redemption, is the lesser of the balance on share premium account following the new issue (£50,000) and the premium raised on the original issue of the shares now being redeemed (£20,000, i.e. 200,000 × £0.10).

REDEMPTION OF REDEEMABLE DEBENTURES

5.0 Companies may finance their operations by means of debentures (a specialised form of loan) which may be either of a permanent (ie perpetual) nature or redeemable.

5.1 Where debentures are redeemable, the terms of their redemption will be stated in the Debenture Trust Deed. A company may redeem its debentures over a period of time by regular drawings of a fixed amount or spasmodically when conditions are most favourable to the company; alternatively it may redeem the whole issue at a single point in time.

5.2 Debentures when redeemed are usually cancelled but a company may invest in its own redeemed debentures and any debentures not cancelled may be reissued.

5.3 There are no legal constraints on a company, similar to those noted in 4.15 and 4.16 in relation to the redemption and purchase of shares, when debentures are redeemed out of profits.

5.4 In the absence of a compensatory cash inflow from a new issue of debentures on different terms or from a share issue, the cash outflow on redemption of debentures could place a severe strain on a company's working capital and liquidity position and on its financial stability in general.

5.5 To counteract the effects noted in 5.4, a company may as a matter of financial prudence (and not of legal necessity) take remedial measures by syphoning off profits which would otherwise be available for distribution. This is achieved by creating a capital reserve, called Debenture Redemption Reserve.

5.6 There are two ways in which Debenture Redemption Reserve operates. Under its simplest circumstances, an amount equal to the nominal value of the debentures redeemed by annual drawings is debited to Appropriation and credited to Debenture Reserve, the balance of which is transferred to Capital Reserve when the debentures have been completely redeemed.

5.7 Where, however, redemption is effected spasmodically or in one lump sum, the reserve is treated as a reserve fund, that is, it is represented by an equivalent amount of investments. Annuity tables are used to calculate the annual appropriation which the company needs to invest annually which, together with re-invested interest, will produce an amount on maturity of sufficient amount to redeem the debentures.

5.8 The amount thus calculated is each year debited to Appropriation and credited to a Sinking Fund which is the term used to describe the reserve fund under these circumstances. Debenture Redemption (Reserve) Fund is an alternative description.

5.9 On the occasion of the first appropriation, an equivalent amount of cash is invested. A Sinking Fund Investments account is debited and Bank credited. The term Debenture Redemption Fund Investments is also used. It serves as a control account for the various investment accounts in which the individual investments are recorded.

5.10 On subsequent occasions, the sum invested is adjusted by interest received on the investments and by profits and losses on the realisation of investments needed to finance spasmodic redemptions and by the differences between the redemption price and the nominal price of the debentures so redeemed. In this latter regard, Share Premium account can be utilised, if it exists, to meet any premium payable on redemption.

5.11 To provide the cash inflow for the redemption, the sinking fund investments are sold, profits and losses on sale being transferred to the sinking fund.

5.12 After all the debentures have been redeemed, the Sinking Fund account balance remains but is no longer backed by investments. In similar fashion to Debenture Redemption Reserve in 5.6, the balance on Sinking Fund is transferred to Capital Reserve for reasons given in 5.4 and 5.5.

ACCOUNTING ENTRIES WHEN A REDEMPTION RESERVE IS MAINTAINED

5.13 The accounting entries are

	Event	Account Debited	Credited
1	Annual appropriation of nominal value of debentures redeemed	Profit and Loss Appropriation	Debenture Redemption Reserve
2	Directors' approval of redemption	Redeemable Debentures	Debenture Redemption
3	Transfer of premium payable on redemption	Share Premium and/or Profit and Loss	Debenture Redemption
4	Redemption of debentures	Debenture Redemption	Bank
5	Transfer of profit on redemption	Debenture Redemption	Profit and Loss
6	Transfer after Debentures have been redeemed	Debenture Redemption Reserve	Capital Reserve

EXAMPLE

5.14 In 19-0 Exe Co PLC had issued £200,000 8% Redeemable Debentures.

Under the terms of issue, redemption was to be effected by equal annual drawings over 10 years on 31 December each year, starting in 19-6.

Eight years after that, on 1st January 19-4, the balances on 8% Redeemable Debentures and on Debenture Redemption Reserve accounts were £40,000 and £160,000, respectively.

A further redemption took place in 19-4 at 96 and the final redemption in 19-5 at par.

Required:

Post and balance the appropriate accounts for the year 19-4 and 19-5.

SOLUTION.

5.15 The reference numbers in brackets () refer to the events listed in 5.13.

8% Redeemable Debentures

19-4		£	19-4		£
Dec 31	Debenture Redemption (2)	20,000	Jan 1	Balance	40,000
Dec 31	Balance c/d	20,000			
		40,000			40,000
19-5			19-5		
Dec 31	Debenture Redemption (2)	20,000	Jan 1	Balance b/d	20,000

Debenture Redemption

19-4		£	19-4		£
Dec 31	Bank (20,000 @ 96) (4)	19,200	Dec 31	8% Red.Debs.(2)	20,000
Dec 31	Profit and Loss (5)	800			
		20,000			20,000
19-5			19-5		
Dec 31	Bank (20,000 @ par) (4)	20,000	Dec 31	8% Red.Debs.(2)	20,000

Debenture Redemption Reserve

19-4		£	19-4		£
Dec 31	Balance c/d	180,000	Jan 1	Balance b/d	160,000
			Dec 31	P & L Appropn	20,000
		180,000			180,000
19-5			19-5		
Dec 31	Capital Reserve (6)	200,000	Jan 1	Balance b/d	180,000
			Dec 31	P & L Appropn	20,000
		200,000			200,000

ACCOUNTING ENTRIES WHEN A SINKING FUND IS MAINTAINED.

5.16 The accounting entries are:

	Event	Account	
		Debited	Credited
1	Annual appropriation	Profit and Loss Appropriation	Sinking Fund
2	Sinking fund investment income	Bank	Sinking Fund
3	Investment of sums in (1) and (2) adjusted by (5), (6) and 10)	Sinking Fund Investments	Bank
4	Realisation of Investments	Bank	Sinking Fund Investments
5	Profit on realisation	Sinking Fund Investments	Sinking Fund

260

6	Loss on realisation	Sinking Fund	Sinking Fund Investments
7	Directors' approval of redemption	Redeemable Debentures	Debenture Redemption
8	Transfer of premium payable on redemption	Share Premium and/or Sinking Fund	Debenture Redemption
9	Redemption of debentures	Debenture Redemption	Bank
10	Transfer of profit on redemption	Debenture Redemption	Sinking Fund
11	Transfer after debentures have been redeemed	Sinking Fund	Capital Reserve

N.B.

1. The entries needed to record the taxation aspects of the sinking fund investment income have been ignored. This subject is dealt with in Section 1 Chapter 3.

2. The Sinking Fund and Sinking Fund Investment accounts balances are equal as well as opposite after all the entries have been made.

EXAMPLE

5.17 Several years ago, Wye Co PLC issued 5,000 6% Redeemable Debentures of £100 each at 98, payable in full on issue.

A Debenture Redemption Fund has been established by annual appropriations of £40,000 and has been invested in gilt-edged securities.

At 31 December 19-0 the account balances were:

	£
6% Redeemable Debentures	500,000
Debenture Redemption Fund	245,000
Debenture Redemption Fund Investments	205,000

During 19-1, transactions took place as follows:

19-1		£
Jan 20	Investments purchased (at cost)	42,000
July 14	Interest for first-half year received	10,000
July 26	Investments (cost £120,000) sold	165,000
Aug 1	Debentures redeemed (nominal £200,000)	170,000
Sept 30	Investments (cost £50,000) sold	45,000
Sept 30	Investments purchased (at cost)	53,000
Dec 31	Interest for second half year received	7,000
Dec 31	Annual appropriation	40,000
Dec 31	Paid interest on 6% Red.Debs.	18,000

Required:

Post the appropriate accounts for the year 19-1

SOLUTION.

5.18 The Sinking Fund is more specifically termed Debenture Redemption Fund. The reference numbers in brackets () are to the events listed in 5.16.

Debenture Interest

19-1		£	19-1		£
Aug 1	Debenture Redemption	7,000	Dec 31	Profit and Loss	25,000
Dec 31	Bank (£300,000 × 6%)	18,000			
		25,000			25,000

6% Redeemable Debentures

19-1		£	19-1		£
Aug 1	Debenture Redemption (7)	200,000	Jan 1	Balance b/d	500,000
Dec 31	Balance c/d	300,000			
		500,000			500,000
			19-2		
			Jan 1	Balance b/d	300,000

Debenture Redemption

19-1		£	19-1		£
Aug 1	Bank (9)	170,000	Aug 1	6% Red.Debs.(7)	200,000
Aug 1	Deb.Redemption Fund (10)	37,000	Aug 1	Debenture Interest (7/12 × 6% × £200,000)	7,000
		207,000			207,000

N.B. The redemption price of the debentures includes interest accumulated since the previous payment date. The amount involved is debited to Debenture Interest account.

Debenture Redemption Fund

19-1		£	19-1		£
Sept 30	Deb.Redemption Fund Inv (6)	5,000	Jan 1	Balance b/d	245,000
Dec 31	Capital Reserve (11)	200,000	July 14	Bank (2)	10,000
Dec 31	Balance c/d	179,000	July 26	Deb.Redemption Fund Inv.(5)	45,000
			Aug 1	Deb.Redn.(10)	37,000
			Dec 31	Bank (2)	7,000
			Dec 31	P & L Appropn(1)	40,000
		384,000			384,000
			19-2		
			Jan 1	Balance b/d	179,000

Debenture Redemption Fund Investments

19-1		£	19-1		£
Jan 1	Balance b/d	205,000	July 26	Bank (4)	165,000
Jan 20	Bank (3)	42,000	Sept 30	Bank (4)	45,000
July 26	Deb. Redemption Fund (5)	45,000	Sept 30	Deb. Redemption Fund (6)	5,000
Sept 30	Bank (3)	53,000	Dec 31	Bank c/d	130,000
		345,000			345,000
19-2					
Jan 1	Balance b/d	130,000			

N.B. Further investments of £49,000 (£179,000 - £130,000) would be bought in January 19-2. Individual accounts would also be maintained for each investment.

PURCHASE OF OWN DEBENTURES IN THE OPEN MARKET

5.19 As an alternative to the redemption of debentures by systematic annual drawings or in a single operation, a company may (as noted in 5.2) buy its own debentures in the open market.

5.20 This practice must be permitted by the terms of issue and only makes financial sense if the market price is below the present value (on the basis of the company's cost of capital) of the further interest payments plus the sum payable on redemption. Because of the spasmodic nature of the operation, it is frequently financed by means of a sinking fund.

5.21 After purchase, the debentures may either be cancelled or held for possible future reissue. The accounting treatment for each of these possibilities is different and is summarised in 5.25.

5.22 Debentures bought for cancellation are initially regarded as an asset - Investment in own Debentures. This account is then closed by transferring the nominal value of the cancelled debentures and the profit on redemption (after allowing for the accrued interest included in the purchase price).

5.23 When debentures are bought and retained for possible future reissue, their cost is regarded as a Sinking Fund investment. Pre-acquisition interest included in the purchase price is transferred to Debenture Interest account but post-acquisition interest "receivable" is treated as any other investment income and credited to Debenture Redemption Fund for reinvestment.

5.24 The reissue of the bought-back debentures is treated in the normal way as a Sinking Fund investment realisation.

ACCOUNTING ENTRIES WHEN OWN DEBENTURES ARE BOUGHT IN THE OPEN MARKET.

5.25 The accounting entries here are additional to those given in 5.16. This is because a sinking fund is often used to finance the operation.

	Event	Account Debited	Credited
12	Purchase of own Debentures for cancellation	Investment in own Debentures	Bank
13	Transfer of pre-acquisition interest included in purchase price	Debenture Interest	Investment in own Debentures
14	Cancellation of debentures (nominal value)	Redeemable Debentures	Investment in own Debentures
15	Transfer of profit on cancellation	Investment in own Debentures	Sinking Fund
16	Transfer after debentures have been cancelled	Sinking Fund	Capital Reserve
17	Purchase of own debentures for retention and possible future reissue	Sinking Fund Investments	Bank
18	Transfer of pre-acquisition interest included in purchase price	Debenture Interest	Sinking Fund Investments
19	Post-acquisition interest on own debentures	Debenture Interest	Sinking Fund
20	Reissue of purchased debentures	Bank	Sinking Fund Investments
21	Profit on reissue of purchased debentures	Sinking Fund Investments	Sinking Fund

As noted in 5.18, the descriptions Debenture Redemption Fund and Debenture Redemption Fund Investments are the specific titles for the Sinking Fund and Sinking Fund Investments accounts.

EXAMPLE.

5.26 O.N. PLC had £100,000 12% Redeemable Debentures 19-8/-5 in issue on 1 January 19-1. Interest is paid half yearly on 30 June and 31 December.

The company has a Debenture Redemption Fund and Debenture Redemption Fund Investment account the balances of which were £67,000 on 1 January 19-1.

Investments costing £9,500 were sold on 26 February 19-1, for £9,200 to finance the forthcoming purchase by the company of its own debentures.

£10,000 of these debentures were bought on the open market at 92 cum int on 2 March 19-1.

Required:

Prepare the appropriate accounts for the half year to 30th June 19-1 in the ledger of O.N. PLC on the assumption that:

i. the debentures were cancelled immediately, and

ii. the debentures were held for possible reissue in the future.

SOLUTION.

5.27 The reference numbers in brackets () are to the events listed in 5.16 and 5.25.

i. Immediate cancellation of debentures.

Debenture Interest

19-1		£			£
Mar 2	Investment in own debentures (13) (2/12 × 12% × £10,000)	200			
June 30	Bank (6/12 × 12% × £90,000)	5,400	June 30	Balance c/d	5,600
		5,600			5,600
July 1	Balance b/d	5,600			

12% Redeemable Debentures 19-8/-5

19-1		£	19-1		£
Mar 2	Investment in own debentures (14)	10,000	Jan 1	Balance b/d	100,000
June 30	Balance c/d	90,000			
		100,000			100,000
			July 1	Balance b/d	90,000

Investment in Own Debentures

19-1		£	19-1		£
Mar 2	Bank (12)	9,200	Mar 2	Debenture Interest (13)	200
Mar 2	Debenture Redemption Fund (15)	1,000	Mar 2	12% Redeemable Debentures (14)	10,000
		10,200			10,200

Debenture Redemption Fund (Sinking Fund)

19-1		£	19-1		£
Feb 26	Deb. Redn.Fund Investments (6)	300	Jan 1	Balance b/d	67,000
Mar 2	Capital Reserve (16)	10,000	Mar 2	Investment in own debentures (15)	1,000
June 30	Balance c/d	57,700			
		68,000			68,000
			July 1	Balance b/d	57,700

Debenture Redemption Fund Investments

19-1		£	19-1		£
Jan 1	Balance b/d	67,000	Feb 26	Bank (4)	9,200
			Feb 26	Debenture Redemption Fund (6)	300
			June 30	Balance c/d	57,500
		67,000			67,000
July 1	Balance b/d	57,500			

N.B. The slight difference between the debit balance on this account and the credit balance on the fund account will be automatically adjusted when the next purchase of investments is made.

Individual accounts would also be maintained for each investment.

ii. Debentures held for possible reissue.

Debenture Interest

19-1		£	19-1		£
Mar 2	Deb.Redm.Fund Investments (18) (2/12 × 12% × £10,000)	200			
June 30	Bank (12% × £90,000 × 6/12)	5,400			
June 30	Debenture Redemption Fund (19) (12% × £10,000 × 4/12)	400	June 30	Balance c/d	6,000
		6,000			6,000
July 1	Balance b/d	6,000			

12% Redeemable Debentures 19-8/-5

19-1		£	19-1		£
June 30	Balance c/d	100,000	Jan 1	Balance b/d	100,000
			July 1	Balance b/d	100,000

Debenture Redemption Fund (Sinking Fund)

19-1		£	19-1		£
Feb 26	Deb.Redn.Fund Investments(6)	300	Jan 1	Balance b/d	67,000
June 30	Balance c/d	67,100	June 30	Debenture Interest (19)	400
		67,400			67,400
			July 1	Balance b/d	67,100

Debenture Redemption Fund Investments

19-1		£	19-1		£
Jan 1	Balance b/d	67,000	Feb 26	Bank (4)	9,200
Mar 2	Bank (17)	9,200	Feb 26	Deb.Redn.Fund (6)	300
			Mar 2	Debenture Interest (18)	200
			June 30	Balance c/d	66,500
		76,200			76,200
July 1	Balance b/d	66,500			

N.B. The slight difference between the debit balance on this account and the credit balance on the fund account will be automatically adjusted when the next purchase of investments is made.

Individual accounts would also be maintained for each investment.

STUDENT SELF TESTING
Test Exercises

1. Independent PLC has an authorised capital of 5,000,000 ordinary shares of £1.00 per share, of which 2,000,000 have been issued at par and are fully paid.

The directors have resolved to issue a further 1,000,000 shares at £1.40 per share payable as follows

	Per share £
On	
application	0.25
allotment (including premium)	0.65
1st call	0.30
final call	0.20
	1.40

Applications were received for 1,300,000 shares, of these 100,000 were rejected and the money repaid to the applicants. The remainder were allotted pro rata on a 5 for 6 basis and the surplus application money was carried forward to allotment on account.

The calls were made and the appropriate sums received except that a holder of 20,000 shares failed to pay either call.

After the formalities had been carried out, these shares were declared forfeit, but were subsequently reissued to another applicant on payment of £0.70 per share.

Required:

a. Open, post and balance the relevant accounts (except Bank) in Independent PLC's ledger to record the above transactions.

b. show an extract from the Balance Sheet of Independent PLC at the conclusion of each of the following stages:

i. forfeiture

ii. reissue of forfeited shares.

2. Lasro PLC purchased 200,000 of the 900,000 of its own ordinary shares of £0.50 per share, which had originally been issued at £0.70 per share, for £0.80 per share.

The company issued 60,000 5% preference shares of £1.00 per share at a price of £1.20 per share as partial financing for the purchase. Prior to this new issue share premium account had a balance of £90,000. There are adequate distributable profits.

Required:

a. Calculate the amount of

i. share premium (if any) which can be utilised for meeting the premium payable on purchase of the company's own shares; and

ii. transfer (if any) to capital redemption reserve.

b. State what difference it would make to your calculations in (a) (i) and (ii), if the shares had

i. been redeemed instead of purchased; and

ii. been preference shares instead of ordinary shares.

3. The facts are the same as in 2, except that Lasro PLC is a private company, Lasro Ltd and distributable profits are £65,000.
Required:
Calculate.

a. permissible capital payment and

b. transfer (if any) to capital redemption reserve.

4. The facts are the same as in 3, except that distributable profits are £45,000.
Required:
Calculate

a. permissible capital payment and

b. transfer to capital redemption reserve or, as appropriate, the amount which could be utilised for Section 171 Companies Act 1985 purposes.

5. The facts are as in 2 a. Prior to the purchase, the balance on profit and loss appropriation account was £157,000.

Required:

Open, post and balance the necessary accounts to record the above transactions. Bank account need not be shown.

6. Connaught PLC had issued £500,000 12% redeemable debentures in 19-0, on which interest was paid half-yearly on 30 June and 31 December.

Under the terms of the issue they were to be redeemed by equal annual drawings over 10 years on 31 December from 19-6 onwards

Eight years later, on 1 January 19-4 the balances on debenture redemption reserve and 12% redeemable debentures were £400,000 and £100,000 respectively.

A further redemption was effected in 19-4 at 95 xi and the final redemption in 19-5 at par xi.

Required:

Open, post and balance the appropriate accounts to record the above transactions for each of the years 19-4 and 19-5.

7. Eight years ago, Trafalgar PLC had issued £300,000 12% redeemable debentures. Interest was payable on 30 June and 31 December.

Under the terms of the Trust Deed, the debentures could be redeemed, or bought back on the open market, at any time after 1 January 19-4.

A sinking fund had been established for this purpose. On 1 January 19-4 the balance on debenture redemption fund was £246,250 and on debenture redemption fund investments £203,500.

The following transactions occurred during 19-4:

			£
Jan 12	Sinking fund investments bought		42,600
May 25	Sinking fund investment income received		9,230
June 30	Debenture interest paid		18,000
Aug 14	Sinking fund investments sold (cost £71,200)		79,600
31	£100,000 debentures bought back on open market at 96 c.i. and cancelled		96,000
Oct 24	Sinking fund investment income received		8,720
Dec 19	Sinking fund investments sold (cost £82,500)		81,000
31	Debenture interest paid		12,000
31	£100,000 debentures redeemed at 97 xi and cancelled		97,000
31	Annual appropriation		44,000

Required:

Open, post and balance the appropriate accounts to record the above transactions.

8. The facts are the same as in 7. except that the debentures bought on Aug.31 were not cancelled but held pending possible future reissue.

Required:

Open, post and balance the appropriate accounts to record the above transactions.

9. In 19-5 G Rowth PLC had issued 3,000 6% Debentures of £100 each at 94, redeemable in 19-4/-0. A Sinking Fund has been established and annual appropriations of £16,000 made.

Debenture Interest is payable half yearly on 30 June and 31 December. At 1 January, 19-4 the following balances appeared in the ledger:-

	£
6% Debentures 19-4/-0	300,000
Sinking Fund	146,700
Sinking Fund Investments	129,300

The following transactions occurred in 19-4:-

Jan 19	Sinking Fund Investments costing £17,400 were acquired
June 29	Debenture Interest for half year paid.
July 2	Investment income received for first half year, £1,900.
Aug 29	Sold investments costing £18,800 for £19,750

Sept 1	Bought on the open market 200 of its debentures for £19,600 cum interest for immediate cancellation.
Dec 28	Debenture Interest for second half year paid.
Dec 31	Annual Sinking Fund appropriation made.
Dec 31	Investment income received for second half year £1,200.

Required:

Prepare the appropriate accounts to record the above transactions but ignore the income tax aspects of debenture interest.

10. The summarised balance sheet of Alpha PLC as at 31 December 19-5 was:-

	£000 Authorised	£000 Issued
Share Capital		
8% redeemable preference shares of £1.00 per share, fully paid	1,000	500
Ordinary shares of £1.00 share, fully paid	5,000	2,500
	6,000	3,000
Reserves		
Share premium	185	
General reserve	2,430	
Profit and Loss	1,695	
		4,310
Shareholders' funds		7,310
Loan Capital		
10% convertible loan stock	1,600	
6% redeemable debentures	1,400	
		3,000
		10,310
Represented by:-		
Net assets (excluding Bank and Cash)		9,880
Bank and Cash		430
		10,310

The following transactions took place during the year ended 31 December 19-6:-

1 Half of the preference shares were redeemed at a premium of 30%; they had originally been issued at a premium of 20%. In order to avoid a drain on the liquid assets of the company, sufficient ordinary shares were issued at par to provide all the cash needed for the redemption.

2 The market price of debentures fluctuated between 40 and 60 during the year and on 31 March 19-6 the company took the opportunity to redeem £400,000 (nominal) 6% redeemable debentures on the open market at 48ci for immediate cancellation.

Interest on the debentures was payable on 30 June and 31 December.

3 On 30 June 19-6, the company issued 1,000,000 ordinary shares of £1.00 per share for £1.80 per share. £1.00 per share (including the premium) was payable on application and the balance three months later.

The whole issue was allotted. Amounts due on the final call were subsequently received with the exception of those due on 10,000 shares. These were forfeited in November 19-6 and immediately resold for £1.50 per share.

4 The terms of the 10% convertible loan stock state that in each of the years 19-6 to 19-8 inclusive, 25% of the stock is convertible into 70 ordinary shares per £100 or, at the shareholders' option, is redeemable

at a premium of 30%. All eligible holders opted to convert on 31 December 19-6 when the market price of the ordinary shares was £2.20 per share.

5 Net profit for the year (before tax) was £948,000. Corporation tax has been estimated at £335,000.

6 The board of directors proposed the following dividends:-

a. 8% redeemable preference shares dividend

b. 10% ordinary share dividend.

Required:

a. Prepare the journal entries to record the above transactions 1 to 4 (only)

b. Prepare a summarised balance sheet as at 31 December 19-6.

c. Calculate, on the basis of ordinary shares in issue on 31 December 19-6, the amount of profit after tax needed for the year 19-6, in order to maintain the same figure of basic earnings per share as in 19-5, when profit after tax was £540,000.

11. The shareholders' funds section of the balance sheet of Kay PLC as at 31 December 19-6 disclosed

£000

Ordinary shares of £1 per share   2,000

Reserves
Share premium   300
Profit and Loss account   700

Shareholders' funds   3,000

It should be assumed that the whole of the balance on profit and loss account is distributable.
The directors have resolved to redeem 400,000 of the ordinary shares on 1 January 19-7.

Required:

Rewrite the balance sheet extract on the basis of each of the following independent assumptions:

a. the shares were originally issued at £1.20 per share and are to be redeemed at par.

b. the shares were originally issued at £1.20 per share and are to be redeemed at £1.05 per share.

c. the shares were originally issued at £1.20 per share and are to be redeemed at £1.45 per share.

d. as for (c). The redemption is to be accompanied by a simultaneous issue of 200,000 6% preference shares of £1.00 per share at a premium of £0.30 per share.

ACCA EXAMINATION QUESTIONS

12. **Required:**

Prepare Ledger Accounts, balanced at 31 December 1983, showing all transactions necessary to comply with the debenture trust deed and to record the redemption of the debentures on 31 March 1983 on the basis that these debentures will be held by Provincial Motor Spares Ltd. for re-issue

(ACCA 2.9(1) December 1984).

Appendix 1(a)
The Trial Balance of Provincial Motor Spares Ltd. as at 31 December 1983

	Dr £000's	Cr £000's
Ordinary shares of £1 each		3,600
10% cumulative preference shares of £1 each		1,000
General reserve		1,820
Profit & Loss Account at 1 January 1983		2,250
8% debentures		500
Profit for 1983		3,780
Debenture redemption reserve		290
Creditors		4,130
Tax payable on 1 January 1984		700
Deferred taxation on 1 January 1983		1,655
Investment income (net)		14
Premises	7,200	

269

Equipment	3,800	
Investments	251	
Stock	6,580	
Debtors	1,480	
Bank	428	
	19,739	19,739

a. Profits accrue evenly throughout the year.

b. Provision is to be made for:

   i. Tax of £1,900,000 on the profits of the current year

   ii. The preference dividend

   iii. The proposed ordinary dividend of ten per cent.

c. A transfer of £170,000 is to be made to the General Reserve.

d. Sales for the year totalled £21,000,000 of which £1,000,000 consisted of sales to United Motor Spares Ltd. The sales are stated exclusive of Value Added Tax.

e. The Investment Income has suffered the deduction of Income Tax at the rate of thirty per cent.

Appendix 2
Further information relating to the debentures issued by Provincial Motor Spares Ltd.

a. The accountant has obtained a copy of the trust deed of the debentures which provides that:

   i. A debenture redemption reserve was to be created by the appropriation of £100,000 each year from otherwise distributable profits.

   ii. An amount equal to the appropriation, together with any income arising from previously invested appropriations, was to be invested on 31 December each year, commencing on 31 December 1980.

   iii. Investments in the redemption fund could be realised if the market price of the debentures was to fall below par and thus, under the terms of the trust deed, become eligible for purchase.

   iv. Debentures purchased in the open market may be held for possible re-issue.

b. In addition, the accountant has obtained information about the reserve fund and the related investments:

   i. The balance on the redemption reserve account was £290,000 on 1 January 1983.

   ii. Debenture fund investments which had cost £36,000 were realised on 31 March 1983 for £39,000 which was used to purchase some of the company's own debentures having a nominal value of £40,000.

   iii. Cash received from the debenture redemption fund investments amounted to £14,000 during 19-3.

   iv. The bank figure of £428,000 in the trial balance contains the balances of both the General Bank Account and the Debenture Reserve Fund Bank Account.

AAT EXAMINATION QUESTIONS

13. During the year to 30 September 19-9, Popham public limited company issued 100,000 £1 ordinary shares. The terms of the offer were as follows:

19-9		£	
31 March	on application	0.30	(including the premium)
30 April	on allotment	0.70	
30 June	first and final call	0.20	

Applications were received for 200,000 shares. The directors decided to allot the shares on the basis of 1 for every 2 shares applied for, and apply the excess application money received against the amount due on allotment.

All amounts due on application and allotment were received on the due dates, with the exception of one shareholder who had been allotted 10,000 shares, and who defaulted on the first and final call. These shares were forfeited on 31 July 19–9, and re-issued on 31 August 19–9 at a price of £1.10 per share.

Required:

Write up the above details in the books of account of Popham plc using the following ledger accounts:

i.   application and allotment;

ii. first and final call;
     and

iii. investment – own shares.

(AAT)

14. The following information relates to Grigg plc:

1. On 1 April 19–8 the company had £100,000 10% debentures in issue. The interest on these debentures is paid on 30 September and 31 March.

2. The debenture redemption fund balance (relating to the redemption of these debentures) at 1 April 19–8 was £20,000. This fund is being built up by annual appropriations of £2,000. The annual appropriation (along with any dividends or interest on the investments) is invested on 31 March.

3. Debenture redemption fund investments can be realised at any time in order to purchase debentures in the open market either at or below par value. Such debentures are then cancelled.

4. On 31 December 19–8, £10,000 of investments were sold for £11,400, and the proceeds were used to purchase debentures with a par value of £12,000.

5. Dividends and interest on redemption fund investments during the year to 31 March 19–9 amounted to £1,600.

6. The cost of dealing with the above matters and any taxation effects may be ignored.

Required:

Write up the following ledger accounts for the year to 31 March 19–9:

i.   10% debentures;

ii. debenture redemption fund;

iii. debenture redemption fund investments;

iv. debenture redemption;
     and

v.   debenture interest.

[Note: the debenture redemption fund is sometimes known as a SINKING FUND.]

(AAT)

2 Distributable Profits

GENERAL BACKGROUND

1.0 Under Sections 160 and 162 Companies Act 1985, redemption or purchase of own shares is permitted only out of

a. the proceeds of a fresh issue of shares made for that purpose
   or
b. distributable profits

DEFINITION

2.0 The definition of distributable profits is contained within Section 263 Companies Act 1985 and comprises accumulated realised profits, so far as not distributed or capitalised, minus accumulated realised losses, so far as not previously written off in a reduction or reorganisation of capital. For the purposes of this definition it is important to know the classification of certain items (explained in 2.1 to 2.4). Special provisions apply to investment companies and to insurance companies.

2.1 Realised losses include:

> losses on revaluation of individual assets
> capitalised development costs (except in special circumstances)
> provisions, other than those specifically in respect of a diminution in value of fixed assets included in 2.2.

2.2 Unrealised losses include:

> provisions in respect of losses on revaluation of all the fixed assets, but for this purpose goodwill is disregarded.

2.3 Realised profits means such profits of a company as fall to be treated as realised in accordance with generally accepted accounting principles, but specifically includes an amount equivalent to the excess of the depreciation charge calculated on revalued amounts over that calculated on cost. They comprise both revenue and capital items.

2.4 Unrealised profits include

> profits arising from holding any fixed asset at an amount in excess of cost. (For this purpose all assets which are not current are regarded as fixed).

EXAMPLE

3.0 Included in the books of Zeta Ltd. are the following balances at 31 December 19-3.

	£000
General reserve	150
Profit and loss account	450
Fixed asset revaluation reserve	580
Capital reserve (arising from profits on sale of fixed assets	100

Adjustments have not yet been made for the following items

	£000
Provision for uninsured fire losses	130
Exchange retranslation losses (in value of foreign branch assets)	40
Additional depreciation as the result of calculating charge on revalued amount of fixed assets instead of on cost	60

Required:

Classify the above figures into realised and unrealised profits and losses and derive a figure of distributable profit.

SOLUTION
3.1

	Realised		Unrealised	
	Profits	Losses	Profits	Losses
	£000	£000	£000	£000
General reserve	150			
Profit and loss account	450			
Fixed asset revaluation reserve			580	
Capital reserve	100			
Uninsured fire losses		130		
Exchange retranslation losses				40
Additional depreciation adjustment	60			
Realised profits	760			
Realised losses	130			
Distributable profits	630			

3.2 Where a public company is concerned there is a further restriction in that distributable profit is restricted to such an amount that any distribution does not reduce the amount of net assets below the aggregate of its called up share capital and undistributable reserves (Section 264 Companies Act 1985).

3.3 For this section of the Act, undistributable reserves comprise

> share premium account
> capital redemption reserve
> excess of accumulated unrealised profits (not previously capitalised) over accumulated unrealised losses (not previously written off) (for the purposes of this sub–section, transfers to capital redemption reserve do not constitute capitalisation)
> any other reserve that the company is prohibited from distributing.

EXAMPLE
3.4 The facts are as in 3.0 except that Zeta Ltd is a public company Zeta PLC and this further information is available.

Other balances at 31 December 19-3

	£000
Share Capital	3,000
Share premium	140
Capital redemption reserve	70

Net assets at this date amounted to 4,380

Required:
Calculate the distributable profits of Zeta PLC at 31 December 19-3.

SOLUTION
3.5 Zeta PLC's status as a public company requires that the restrictions noted in 3.2 and 3.3 are superimposed on those outlined in 2.0 to 2.4.

	£000	£000	
Net assets		4,380	(A)
Share capital		3,000	
Undistributable reserves			
Share premium		140	
Capital redemption reserve		70	
Unrealised profits	580		
Unrealised losses	(40)		
Excess unrealised profits		540	
Total		3,750	(B)
Distributable profits (A) minus (B)		630	

In this instance the answer is the same as for the private company in 3.1

EXAMPLE

3.6 The facts are the same as in 3.4 except that unrealised losses amount to £640,000 and net assets to £3,780,000.

Required:
Calculate the distributable profits of Zeta PLC at 31 December 19-3.

SOLUTION
3.7

	£000	£000	
Net assets		3,780	(A)
Share capital		3,000	
Undistributable reserves			
Share premium		140	
Capital redemption reserve		70	
Unrealised profits	580		
Unrealised losses	(640)		
Excess unrealised profits		Nil	
Total		3,210	(B)
Distributable profits (A) minus (B)		570	

This illustrates the effect on public companies of the restriction in 3.2 and 3.3 whereby net unrealised losses have to be made good out of distributable profits. In other words, the distributable profits shown above are equivalent to:

	£	£
Distributable profits per 3.5		630
less		
Unrealised profits	580	
Unrealised losses	(640)	
Net unrealised losses		(60)
Distributable profits (as above)		570

STUDENT SELF TESTING

Test Exercises

1. The balances in the books of two companies at 31 December 19-3 included the following:

	Alpha PLC £000	Beta PLC £000
Net assets	5,250	3,950
Share capital	3,000	3,000
Share premium account	250	250
Capital redemption reserve	400	400
Profits		
– realised	1,400	1,400
– unrealised	800	150
Losses – realised	(450)	(450)
– unrealised	(150)	(800)

Required:

a. Calculate the distributable profits of each company at 31 December 19-3.

b. State what differences, if any, there would be if each of these companies was a private company.

ACCA EXAMINATION QUESTIONS
Required:
2.

a. Define distributable profits in a public and private company.

b. Calculate the distributable profits for Scraper Ltd as at 30 November 1983:

i. on the basis that Scraper Ltd is a private company, and
ii. on the basis that Scraper Ltd is a public company.
   (ACCA 2.9(1) December 1983)

Appendix 5

The Profit and Loss Account of Scraper Ltd. for the year ended 30 November 1983 and Balance Sheet as at 30 November 1983.

	£	£
Sales		3,066,000
Cost of sales		2,055,000
Gross profit		1,011,000
Administration expense *(Note 2)*	220,000	
Distribution expense *(Note 1)*	200,000	420,000
Operating profit		591,000
Tax		182,000
Profit after tax		409,000
Dividend 10p per share		40,000
		369,000
Balance brought forward		(113,000)
		£256,000

Note 1 Depreciation on the freehold property was £3,888 calculated at 2% of valuation. One of the properties was revalued from £30,000 to £124,000 on 1 December 1982.

Note 2 Includes debenture interest paid.

Scraper Ltd - Balance Sheet as at 30 November 1983

Fixed Assets	Cost Valuation £	Depn £	NBV £	£
Freehold property	194,400	14,400	180,000	
Vehicles	300,000	60,000	240,000	
Fixtures and fittings	28,000	12,000	16,000	436,000
Current Assets				
Stock		395,000		
Debtors		176,000		
Cash		232,000	803,000	
Creditors-amounts due less than 1 year				
Trade creditors		112,000		
HP creditors		89,100		
Bank overdraft		17,043	218,143	
Net current assets				584,857
Total assets less current liabilities				1,020,857
creditors-amounts due more than 1 year				
10% debentures (convertible 1986)		100,000		
Other creditors including tax		174,857		274,857
Net assets				£ 746,000

Capital Reserves	£
Share capital	400,000
Share premium	50,000
Capital redemption reserve	100,000
Revaluation deficit	(130,000)
General reserve	70,000
Profit and loss account	256,000
	£ 746,000

Note:

The revaluation deficit results from a reappraisal on 1 December 1982 of the fixed asset register of fixtures and fittings within one of the London properties. There was no general programme of revaluation. The gain on the freehold of £94,400 has been netted off against the loss on revaluation of fixtures.

3. An extract from the draft accounts of Either Ltd at 30 November 1985, shows the following figures before allowing for any dividend which might be proposed:

	£000s
Ordinary shares of £1 each	400
6% preference shares of £1 each	150
Capital redemption reserve	300
Revaluation reserve	125
General reserve	80
Profit and loss account	13
	1,068
Operating profit before taxation for the year	302
Taxation	145
	157

Additional information includes:

a. the revaluation reserve consists of an increase in the value of freehold property following a valuation in 1983. The property concerned was one of three freehold properties owned by the company and was subsequently sold at the revalued amount.

b. It has been found that a number of stock items have been included at cost price, but were being sold after the balance sheet date at prices well below cost. To allow for this, stock at 30 November 1985 would need to be reduced by £35,000.

c. Provision for directors' remuneration should be made in the sum of £43,000.

d. Included on the balance sheet is £250,000 of research and development expenditure carried forward.

e. No dividends have yet been paid on either ordinary or preference shares for the year to 30 November 1985, but the directors wish to pay the maximum permissible dividends for the year.

f. Since the draft accounts were produced it has been reported that a major customer of Either Ltd has gone into liquidation and is unlikely to be able to pay more than 50p in the £ to its creditors. At 30 November 1985 this customer owed £60,000 and this has since risen to £180,000.

g. It has been decided that the depreciation rates for plant and machinery are too low but the effect of the new rates has not been taken into account constructing the draft accounts. The following information is available.

Plant and machinery	£
Purchased at the commencement of the business on 1 December 1981 cost	100,000
Later purchases were 1 June 1983	25,000
29 February 1984	28,000
31 May 1984	45,000
1 December 1984	50,000

In the draft accounts depreciation has been charged at the rate of 25% using the reducing balance method and charging a full year's depreciation in the year of purchase. It has been decided to change to the straight line method using the same percentage but charging only an appropriate portion of the depreciation in the year of purchase. There have been no sales of plant and machinery during the year.

Required:

a. Calculate the maximum amount which the directors of Either Ltd may propose as a dividend to be paid to the ordinary shareholders whilst observing the requirements of the Companies Acts from 1948 to 1981 (now incorporated into the Companies Act 1985). Show all workings and state any assumptions made.

b. Outline and discuss any differences which might have been made to your answer to (a) if the company were a public limited company.

For the purpose of this question you may take it that corporation tax is levied at the rate of 50%.

(ACCA 2.9(2) December 1985)

3 Taxation

GENERAL BACKGROUND

1.0 This chapter is concerned with those taxes to which businesses are subject and which are commonly examinable material.

1.1 The bases of assessment to tax liability, the calculation of tax liability etc are more aptly considered within the subject of Taxation, and are outside the scope of this chapter which is concerned solely with accounting for taxation, that is with the recording of taxation and its presentation in financial statements.

1.2 Examiners set questions which are exclusively concerned with accounting for taxation and also where this topic is examined along with other matter, for example, the preparation of the final accounts of a limited company. Questions of the former type are appended to this chapter whilst those of the latter type are given at the end of Chapter 4.

1.3 Within this chapter of the manual the accounting aspects of the following taxes are considered:

Valued Added Tax
Income Tax
Corporation Tax (including Advance Corporation Tax and the Imputation System)
Deferred Taxation
Miscellaneous

VALUED ADDED TAX.

2.0 Value Added Tax (VAT) was introduced in the UK in 1973 and is a tax on supplies, that is, on goods and services, and is administered by HM Customs and Excise.

2.1 VAT is levied at each stage at which supplies change hands. In the case of manufactured items, this would be at the primary producer, manufacturer, wholesaler and retailer stages. It is ultimately borne by the consumer who, not being registered for VAT purposes is unable to reclaim it.

2.2 The VAT which is charged on sales of supplies is termed output tax whilst that on purchase of goods for resale, of consumables and of fixed assets is termed input tax. From June 1979 standard rate of VAT was 15%, but was increased to 17.5% in 1991.

2.3 At each stage noted in 2.1, the business concerned acts as a collector of VAT. In the ledger a VAT account is opened, is debited with input tax and credited with output tax. Subsequently it is also debited/credited with the net amount paid/refunded.

2.4 This settlement takes place on a staggered quarterly basis. At the end of a business' financial year VAT payable to/refundable by HM Customs and Excise is shown in the balance sheet as a currently liability – Creditors falling due within one year or as a current asset, Debtors.

2.5 Except as noted below, VAT does not form part either of the cost of goods and services bought by a business or of the revenue earned. For example, if goods were bought for £235 (including VAT) on credit, Purchases would be debited with £200, VAT account with £35 and the supplier's account credited with £200. Similarly VAT inclusive sales of £470 would be credited to sales as £400 and to VAT account as £70, the full amount of £400 being debited to the customer's account.

EXCEPTIONS.

2.6 Some businesses are exempt from collecting VAT either because the supplies in which they deal are exempt (eg insurance, finance) or because the annual turnover is below a certain limit (currently £35,000 Finance Act 1991). Such businesses bear VAT on their inputs but cannot charge it on their outputs or obtain a refund of their input tax. In these instances VAT input tax forms an integral part of the cost of their bought in goods and services.

2.7 As a matter of government policy, the VAT on certain inputs of all businesses is non–deductible. The inputs concerned are motor cars (unless bought for resale) and most business entertaining expenses. The accounting treatment is the same as in 2.6, that is, the VAT element constitutes part of the cost.

2.8 Other businesses deal in zero–rated supplies. Technically they charge VAT on their outputs but at a rate of 0%. Unlike exempt businesses in 2.6 businesses dealing in zero rated suplies can reclaim VAT on their inputs. Consequently, except for the non–deductible input tax in 2.7, for businesses dealing in zero rated supplies, VAT does not constitute part of the cost of bought in supplies. Examples of zero rated supplies are building construction work, books and newspapers and most food, except food supplied in the course of catering.

2.9 Partial exemption status is accorded to those businesses which deal in both exempt and taxable (zero rated and standard) supplies. The usual procedure is for the input tax to be apportioned over the exempt, zero rated and standard supplies categories on a proportionate basis. Only that attributable to the taxable supplies can then be reclaimed but there are exceptions where the proportions or amounts are below certain limits.

2.10 Accounting for VAT is the subject of SSAP 5.

EXAMPLE

2.11 In the first quarter of 19–4, the VAT exclusive turnover of a business was £1,000,000, analysed for VAT purposes as follows:–

Type of Supply		Amount £
Non taxable	Exempt	100,000
Taxable	Zero rated	200,000
	Standard	700,000
Total		1,000,000

Input tax for the same quarter was £30,000

Required:
Assuming a VAT standard rate of 15%, prepare an extract of the entries which would appear in the VAT account of the business. Support your entries with workings.

SOLUTION
2.12 Workings

		Exempt Supplies £	Taxable supplies Zero rated £	Taxable supplies Standard £	Total Supplies £
(a)	Sales	100,000	200,000	700,000	1,000,000
(b)	VAT (output tax) at 15%	– (see 2.6)	– (see 2.8)	105,000	105,000
(c)	Amount charged to customers[(a) plus (b)]	100,000	200,000	805,000	1,105,000
(d)	VAT (input tax) [apportioned pro–rata (a) – see 2.9]	3,000	6,000	21,000	30,000
(e)	Amount paid to/(claimed from) Customs and Excise [(b) minus (d) except for exempt supplies]	– (see 2.6)	(6,000) (see 2.8)	84,000	78,000

Extract from
Value Added Tax

	£		£
Purchase (input tax (6,000 + 21,000)	27,000	Sales (output tax)	105,000
Balance c/d (per workings)	78,000		
	105,000		105,000
		Balance b/d	78,000

Notes:

a. Only the input tax on the taxable supplies is reclaimed. That relating to the exempt supplies (£3,000) is dealt with as in 1.6.

b. The balance of £78,000 would be classed as a creditor until paid in the following quarter.

INCOME TAX.

INCOME TAX – SOLE TRADERS AND PARTNERSHIPS.

3.0 The profits of businesses owned by sole traders and by partnerships are subject to income tax. As will be seen in 4.0 limited companies' profits are liable to corporation tax but, as illustrated in 3.3 to 3.15 certain of a limited company's transactions are affected by income tax.

3.1 Income tax (and corporation tax) is regarded as an appropriation of profits. The actual amount of income tax which a sole trader or partner pays depends on his personal circumstances; in the case of a partner it is not simply the total liability of the partnership apportioned in the profit sharing ratio. Consideration of the calculation of tax liabilities is outside the scope of this section and if brought into an accounting examination paper, will be part of the information supplied.

3.2 In the books of a sole trader and of a partnership, income tax is debited to drawings when paid or alternatively to Current Account when raised and then credited as Income Tax (a Current Liability) and as provision for Future Income Tax (a Deferred Liability) depending on the dates it becomes payable.

INCOME TAX – LIMITED COMPANIES.

3.3 Certain payments made by limited companies are subject to the deduction of income tax. Payments of patent royalties and of mineral royalties (but not of copyright royalties (see 4.7) and interest payments (other than of bank interest) are the main items concerned and are paid net of income tax at basic rate of tax.

3.4 In these instances the company is, as a matter of administrative convenience for the Inland Revenue, acting as a collecting agent. The income tax thus deducted at source by the company is paid over to the Collector of Taxes quarterly. The recipient of the interest or royalty may not be liable to income tax at all or he may be a high income individual liable to tax at one of the higher rates. Neither of these facts is of concern to the company. In the first instance, the Inland Revenue would refund the tax and in the second instance would send a demand for the extra amount of tax.

3.5 Conversely, interest received and royalties received by a company are net of income tax at basic rate when received. Such income tax suffered by a company is capable of being recouped against the income tax deducted in 3.4 under the quarterly accounting arrangements.

3.6 Any income tax suffered which remains unrecouped at the end of the company's financial year is not carried over to the following year but is deducted in arriving at the corporation tax liability for that year.

3.7 The net sums paid and received by way of interest and royalties are grossed up for expense and revenue purposes by the amount of income tax withheld at basic rate.

3.8 For the eight fiscal years to 1985/86 the basic rate of income tax was 30%.
 In 1986/87 it was reduced to 29% and further reduced to 27% in 1987/88 and to 25% in 1988/89.

3.9 Income tax on interest paid and on royalties paid is debited to the expense account and credited to Income Tax account.

3.10 By the same rule, income tax on interest received and on royalties received is credited to the revenue account and debited to Income Tax account.

3.11 Under normal procedures, income tax on these transactions is payable to the Inland Revenue by the 14th day of the month following the recognised quarter end.

3.12 At the end of a company's financial year, a credit balance on Income Tax account, representing a sum to be paid over within 14 days of the quarter end, is carried down as a credit balance and included in the Balance Sheet as a Current Liability – Creditors: amounts falling due within one year.

3.13 One the other hand a debit balance on Income Tax account represents an amount due from the Inland Revenue either which cannot be set–off under the quarterly payment system but is debited to the provision account for Corporation Tax on the same year's profits, the corresponding credit thus closing the Income Tax accounts, or, not exceeding the income tax deducted at source by the company during that year and already paid over to the Inland Revenue, can be reclaimed, and is carried down as a debit balance and included in the balance sheet as Debtors.

EXAMPLE

3.14 A company paid and received the following net amounts during year ended 31 March 19–4.

Date 19–3	Item £	Net Receipts £	Net Payments £
Apr 30	Investment interest	2,800	–
Sept 30	Royalties Received	1,330	–
Sept 30	Debenture Interest	–	14,000
Oct 31	Investment Interest	2,800	–
19–4			
March 31	Royalties Received	1,680	–
Mar 31	Debenture Interest	–	14,000

Basic rate of income tax was 30%

Required:

1. Post and balance the appropriate accounts for the year ended 31st March 19–4 assuming that none of the accounts involved had an opening balance.

2. Show the relevant Profit and Loss account and Balance Sheet extracts after 1. above has been completed.

3. Show the effect on the Income Tax account only, if on 31 March 19–4 a further net amount of £25,200 investment interest was received.

SOLUTION

3.15 Before attempting the postings, certain essential workings must be prepared using the 19–3/–4 basic rate of 30%.

Date	Item	Net Payment (70% of gross) £	Gross (100/70 × net) £	Income Tax (30% × Gross) £
19–3				
Sept 30	Debenture Interest	14,000	20,000	6,000
19–4				
Mar 31	Debenture Interest	14,000	20,000	6,000
19–3				
Apr 30	Investment Interest	2,800	4,000	1,200
Oct 31	Investment Interest	2,800	4,000	1,200
Sept 30	Royalties Received	1,330	1,900	570
19–4				
Mar 31	Royalties Received	1,680	2,400	720

1.

Debenture Interest

19–3		£			£
Sept 30	Bank	14,000			
Sept 30	Income Tax	6,000			
19–4			**19–4**		
Mar 31	Bank	14,000	Mar 31	Profit and loss	40,000
Mar 31	Income Tax	6,000			
		40,000			40,000

Interest Received

19-3		£			£
			Apr 30	Bank	2,800
			Apr 30	Income Tax	1,200
			Oct 31	Bank	2,800
			Oct 31	Income Tax	1,200
19-4					
Mar 31	Profit and Loss	8,000			
		8,000			8,000

Royalties Received

19-4		£	19-3		£
			Sept 30	Bank	1,330
			Sept 30	Income Tax	570
19-4			19-4		
Mar 31	Profit and Loss	4,300	Mar 31	Bank	1,680
			Mar 31	Income Tax	720
		4,300			4,300

Income Tax

19-3		£	19-3		£
Apr 30	Interest Received	1,200	Sept 30	Debenture Interest	6,000
Sept 30	Royalties Received	570			
Oct 14	Bank (see 3.11)	4,230			
[6,000−(1200 + 570)]					
Oct 31	Interest Received	1,200			
19-4			19-4		
Mar 31	Royalties Received	720	Mar 31	Debenture Interest	6,000
Mar 31	Balance c/d (see 3.12)	4,080			
[6,000−(1,200 + 720)]					
		12,000			12,000
			Apr 1	Balance b/d	4,080

2.

Profit and Loss Account (extract)
for year ended 31 March 19-4

	£
Other operating Income [Royalties received]	4,300
Income from other fixed asset investments [Interest received]	8,000
Interest payable [Debenture interest]	40,000

N.B. The gross amounts are used – see 3.7.

Balance Sheet (extract)
as at 31 March 19-4

	£	£
Creditors: amounts falling due within one year		
Other creditors – Income Tax	4,080	

3.

Income Tax

19–4		£	19–4		£
Mar 31	Interest Received	10,800	Mar 31	Balance b/d per 1.	4,080
	$(30\% \times 100/70 \times 25,200)$		Mar 31	Provision for	
				Corporation Tax	2,490
				(see 3.6)	
			Mar 31	Balance c/d	4,230
				(see 3.6)	
		10,800			10,800
Apr.1	Balance b/d (income	4,230			
	tax recoupable)				

Note: Income tax borne by the company (£14,490, i.e. £(1,200 + 1,200 + 10,800 + 570 + 720)), by deduction at source from investment and royalty income, exceeds income tax withheld (£12,000, ie £(6,000 + 6,000)) by deduction from debenture interest payments.

The company can now reclaim income tax already paid to the Inland Revenue, £4,230, but £2,490 (£14,490 – £12,000) can only be recovered by reducing the provision for corporation tax for that year.

CORPORATION TAX AND THE IMPUTATION SYSTEM.
CORPORATION TAX – BACKGROUND.

4.0 From the fiscal year 1973/74 to 1982/83, company profits had been chargeable to Corporation Tax at 52% (less for small companies). Profits for this purpose have excluded Franked Investment Income (gross dividends from UK Companies) but have included chargeable gains, but these latter were reduced by a fraction so that the effective rate of corporation tax on them was 30%. The small company limits have been raised by successive Finance Acts but the latest figures are a rate of 25% for profits up to £250,000 with marginal relief for profits between £250,000 and £1,250,000. The full rate was progressively reduced from 52% to 35% by 1986/87. It is 33% for 1991/92 and chargeable gains are now taxed at the appropriate Corporation Tax rate.

4.1 For a number of years prior to the fiscal year 1964/65, profits of companies were subject to both income tax (41.25% in 1964/65) and profits tax (15% in 1964/65) but on taxable profits below £12,000 a reduced rate of profits tax was charged. Net profit remaining could be distributed without further deduction of tax thus dividends were shown net in the Appropriation Account.

4.2 This system was altered from 1965/66 onwards and up to 1972/73 Corporation tax was payable on taxable profits at rates varying from 40% to 45% and Capital Gains Tax was payable on chargeable gains. In addition, Income Tax at standard rate was deducted from distributions to the shareholders. This could be reclaimed by those shareholders not subject to Income Tax but a further amount was payable by Surtax payers. This system encouraged profit retention. In the Appropriation account dividends were shown gross. As loan interest payable was tax deductible, the majority of new issues of long–term finance in this period were in the form of loan stock and debentures.

4.3 Now that the corporation tax system has been put into its historical context, the remainder of this section will deal only with the present system outlined in 4.0.

CORPORATION TAX SYSTEM

4.4 When brought into acccount, corporation tax must of necessity be a provision. The definition of a provision, as a sum charged against profits to meet a liability which is known to exist but which cannot be quantified precisely, is an exact fit for classifying corporation tax.

4.5 At the outset, corporation tax is an estimated figure based on a combination of unknown factors. Firstly, the taxable profit to which the rate is applied can be calculated approximately but until the actual assessment has been agreed with the Inland Revenue, it is capable of being altered. The actual rate (see 4.0) is set in the Finance Act but is retrospective, thus the rates of corporation tax for normal and for small companies and small company limits and marginal reliefs included in the Finance Act 1991 relate to the year ended 31st March 1991.

4.6 The date of payment of corporation tax depended upon the date of incorporation of the company concerned. The Finance Act 1965 introduced corporation tax for the first time for companies which had previously been subject to income tax and profits tax (see 4.1 and 4.2). Companies which had been taxed under the old system were allowed to retain their previous payment dates but new companies had to abide by new rules. These matters are more fully explained in 4.7 to 4.13.

PRE 1965 FINANCE ACT COMPANIES

4.7 Companies which had been taxed under the old income tax rules were allowed to retain their payment date of 1st January in the year of assessment. The taxable profits on which corporation tax was calculated were those of the company's accounting year ending in the preceding fiscal year. This is illustrated diagrammatically in 4.8 for a company which has a financial year ended 30th April. The diagram is then explained in 4.9 and 4.10.

4.8

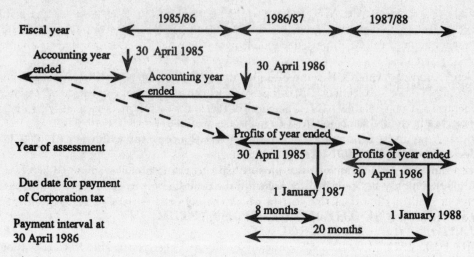

4.9 At any balance sheet date, companies in this category have two provisions for corporation tax, one in respect of the current year's profits and payable up to 21 months ahead, the other in respect of the previous year's profits and payable up to 9 months ahead. However, this system has now been progressively phased out.

4.10 In the published accounts both of these provisions may be classed as Current Taxation under Creditors: amounts falling due within one year, and the payment dates stated but it is preferable that the provision in respect of the current year's profits is regarded as a provision for future taxation and classed as a deferred liability Creditors: amounts falling due in more than one year. It follows that the Provision for Future Taxation at the end of one year becomes the Provision for Current Taxation at the end of the following year.

POST 1965 FINANCE ACT COMPANIES

4.11 For companies in this category, the payment date had been the later of one month after issue of the assessment statement or nine months after the end of the company's financial year, but this system now applies to all companies.

4.12 Payment, for a company with a financial year end on 30th April, would be at the end of the following January, or one month after assessment, if later.

4.13 At balance sheet date there is only one provision for corporation tax and this is classified as Current Taxation under Creditors: amounts falling due within one year.

GENERAL

4.14 The actual amount of Corporation tax paid may be reduced by recoupable income tax (see 3.13) and by advance corporation tax recoverable. This latter is dealt with in detail in 4.31 to 4.40.

ADVANCE CORPORATION TAX AND THE IMPUTATION SYSTEM

4.15 The broad background of the corporation tax system has been given in 4.0 and 4.2. Corporation Tax was introduced in 1965/66 and became payable on taxable profits together with income tax on dividend distributions to shareholders.

4.16 This system was substantially altered from 1973/74 onwards by what is known as the imputation system.

4.17 As previously, company taxable profits are subject to corporation tax. Unless a dividend is paid, the whole of the corporation tax is payable as a single sum from 9 to 21 months after the end of the accounting period to which it relates, as described in 4.6 to 4.13.

ACT ON QUALIFYING DISTRIBUTIONS.

4.18 When a company makes a "qualifying distribution" which includes dividend distributions, the company does not deduct income tax from the payment as it did in the period from 1965/66 to 1972/73.

4.19 Instead, the company pays to the Inland Revenue, within 14 days of the end of the quarter in which the dividend is paid, an amount of advance corporation tax (ACT) equivalent in amount to tax at basic rate on the notional gross dividend.

4.20 The basic rate applied is that in force when the dividend is actually paid (which may be different from that in force when the dividend was proposed).

TAX CREDITS

4.21 In the hands of a recipient, the ACT relative to the actual dividend received is termed a tax credit. Individuals are charged to tax on the (gross) sum of dividend received plus imputed tax credit. This credit may be reclaimable in full or in part depending upon the personal circumstances of the individual concerned.

4.22 The dividend received (from a UK company) plus imputed tax credit constitutes franked investment income (F.I.I) in the hands of a recipient UK company. F.I.I can be offset against franked payments, that is, against dividends paid plus related ACT. The effect of this is that ACT paid on qualifying distributions is reduced by tax credits on dividends received from UK companies.

MAINSTREAM CORPORATION TAX

4.23 As its name implies, ACT is an advance payment of corporation tax. It follows, therefore, that at a later stage, the amount already paid will be taken into account. In fact, ACT paid is recouped out of the corporation tax paid in respect of the year in which the dividend is paid. The resultant net sum of corporation tax is termed mainstream corporation tax (MCT).

IRRECOVERABLE ACT

4.24 When taxable profits are insufficiently high for ACT to be recouped, the unrelieved ACT can be carried back for up to six years or carried forward indefinitely. Unless, however, a company has prospects of making sufficient taxable profits out of which the ACT can be recovered, it should be written off as irrecoverable in the Taxation section of the profit and loss account.

ACT FRACTIONS

4.25 ACT is equivalent to basic rate of tax on the notional gross dividend as stated in 4.19. However, it is the net, not the notional gross, dividend which is paid and ACT is calculated by applying a fraction to this net dividend.

4.26 The fraction can be calculated thus:

$$\frac{\text{Basic rate of income tax}}{100 - \text{Basic rate of income tax.}}$$

On a basic rate of 30% this would be

$$\frac{30}{100 - 30} = \frac{3}{7}$$

and for basic rate of 29%, 27% and 25% the fraction would be 29/71, 27/73 and 25/75 respectively.

4.27 To calculate ACT, the fraction appropriate to the basic rate (operative at the date the dividend is paid) is applied to the actual dividend payment. For example, the ACT payable on an actual dividend payment of £140,000 when basic rate is 30% would be £60,000(3/7 × £140,000). The notional gross dividend (net dividend plus related ACT) would thus be £200,000 (£140,000 plus £60,000). Therefore as stated in 4.19 and 4.25 the ACT is equivalent to 30% of £200,000.

4.28 A problem of interpretation arose in connection with preference shares in issue at the date the imputation system was introduced. Para. 18, Sched. 23. Finance Act 1972 reduced existing dividend rights on preference shares to seven tenths of their former amount. Thus 10% Preference Shares became 7% Preference Shares.

4.29 The intention of the Act was that it should be a once and for all netting down arrangement. An alternative interpretation, which received support in a High Court judgement known as the Sime Darby case (Sime Darby (London) Ltd v Sime Darby Holdings 1975) was that the rate of dividend on such shares should fluctuate with basic rate.

4.30 Eventually the matter was finally resolved by para. 46 Finance Act 1976 which stated that the rate in question was the rate in force on 6th April 1973 and that......" this subsection shall be deemed always to have had effect".

ACCOUNTING ARRANGEMENTS

4.31 When a company proposes a dividend, entries for ACT are raised simultaneously by debiting an ACT Recoverable account and crediting an ACT Payable account. The dividend itself is included in the appropriation section of the profit and loss account at the net amount actually payable, that is, excluding the attributable ACT.

4.32 When a company receives a dividend from another UK company it accounts for the associated tax credit by debiting Tax Credits account and crediting Dividends Received thus bringing this latter account up to the gross figure to be transferred at the end of the accounting period to Profit and Loss – Investment Income. The Tax Credits account balance is also transferred (by crediting) and by debiting to the Taxation section of Profit and Loss account.

4.33 As noted in 4.22, tax credits reduce the ACT liability. A further entry is thus required debiting ACT Payable and crediting ACT Recoverable with the amount of the tax credit.

4.34 ACT is recoverable against the corporation tax on the taxable profits of the period in which the dividend is paid (see 4.23). When the Provision for Corporation Tax for a particular financial year is raised by debiting the Taxation section of Profit and Loss Account, and by crediting Provision for Corporation Tax, any ACT Recoverable applicable to it is transferred by debiting Provision for Corporation Tax and by crediting ACT Recoverable.

4.35 Payment of ACT involves a debit to ACT Payable and a credit to Bank. Corresponding entries are needed when MCT is paid.

4.36 At the end of a financial year, the balances on the above accounts would be classed as follows for balance sheet purposes.

Account	Balance sheet classification
ACT payable (Current liability)	Creditors: amounts falling due within one year Other creditors: ACT payable
ACT recoverable (Deferred asset)	Debtors: (due after more than one year) Other debtors: ACT recoverable (alternatively, it would be deducted from the provision for deferred taxation, if such exists)
Provision for corporation tax (current) (Current liability)	Creditors: amounts falling due within one year Other Creditors: Corporation tax
Provision for corporation tax (future) (Deferred liability)	Creditors: amounts falling due after more than one year Other creditors: Corporation tax.

4.37 The account entries can be summarised thus:–

		Account	
	Event	Debited	Credited
1	Provision for ACT raised on declaration of proposed dividend payable	ACT (Recoverable)	ACT (Payable)
2	Receipt of dividend and associated tax credit		
	– actual net receipt	Bank	Dividends Received
	– tax credit	Tax Credits	Dividends Received
3	Tax credit offset against ACT liability	ACT (Payable)	ACT (Recoverable)
4	Transfer of tax credit to profit and loss	Profit and Loss (Taxation Section)	Tax Credits

5	Transfer of Dividend received (notional gross amount)	Dividends Received	Profit and Loss – Investment Income
6	Payment of ACT on dividends paid (less tax credits, if applicable)	ACT (Payable)	Bank
7	Provision for corporation tax raised	Profit and Loss (Taxation section)	Provision for Corporation Tax (Current or Future)
8	Transfer of ACT recoverable to provision for corporation tax of relative year	Provision for Corporation Tax (Current or Future)	ACT (Recoverable)
9	Proposal of dividend payable (actual ACT exclusive amount)	Profit and Loss Appropriation	Proposed Dividend
10	Payment of proposed dividend (interim dividend)	Proposed Dividend/ (Interim Dividend)	Bank
11	Reclassification of corporation tax at end of financial year	Provision for Corporation Tax (Future)	Provision for Corporation Tax (Current)
12	Adjustment of Provision for Corporation Tax on receipt of assessment		
	– underprovision	Profit and Loss (Taxation Section)	Provision for Corporation Tax (Current or Future)
	–overprovision	Provision for Corporation Tax (Current or Future)	Profit and Loss (Taxation Section)
13	Payment of Mainstream Corporation Tax	Provision for Corporation Tax (Current)	Bank
14	Write off of irrecoverable ACT	Profit and Loss (Taxation Section)	ACT (Recoverable)

4.38 The treatment in the accounts of companies of taxation under the imputation system is the subject of SSAP 8 dealt with in 3.42 to 3.47.

EXAMPLE

4.39 At 1st January 19–5, the following balances appeared in the books of Namtax PLC.

£

Provisions for Corporation Tax
- Current (on 19–3 profits) 88,075
- Future (on 19–4 profits) 100,000

ACT payable	27,000	(credit)
ACT Recoverable	27,000	(debit)
Proposed Dividends	63,000	

The MCT on the 19–3 profits was paid on 2nd January, the proposed dividend on 27th June and the related ACT on 14th July.

A cheque for £14,000 was received on 11th August, being a dividend from a UK trade investment.

An interim dividend of £35,000 on the first half year's profits was paid on 22nd August and its related ACT on 13th October.

The assessment of the 19–4 profits was agreed at £92,500 on 3rd October.

At 31st December 19–5, a final dividend of £70,000 was proposed. Trading profits (before tax) were £400,000 on which corporation tax was estimated at £140,000.

Assume a corporation tax rate of 35% and an ACT fraction of 3/7.

Required:

1. Prepare the appropriate ledger accounts to record the above transactions.

2. Show extracts from the profit and loss account for the year 19–5 and from the balances sheet at 31st December 19–5.

SOLUTION

4.40 References numbers in brackets () are to events listed in 4.37.

1.

Provision for Corporation Tax (Current)

19–5		£	19–5		£
Jan 2	Bank (13)	88,075	Jan 1	Balance b/d	88,075
Dec 31	Balance c/d	92,500	Dec 31	Provn for Corpn Tax (Fut) (11)	92,500
		180,575			180,575
			19–6		
			Jan 1	Balance b/d	92,500

Provision for Corporation Tax (Future)

19–5		£	19–5		£
Dec 31	Profit and Loss (12) (Taxation Section)	7,500	Jan 1	Balance b/d	100,000
Dec 31	Prov for Corpn Tax (Current)(11)	92,500	Dec 31	Profit and Loss (7) (Taxation Section)	140,000
Dec 31	ACT (Recoverable) (8)	36,000			
Dec 31	Balance c/d (MCT on 19–5 profit)	104,000			
		240,000			240,000
			19–6		
			Jan 1	Balance b/d	104,000

288

Note: At the end of 19–5, the adjusted provision for corporation tax (£92,500) on the 19–4 profits, hitherto regarded as future taxation, is reclassified as current taxation as it is payable on 1st Jan 19–6. The provision for corporation tax on the 19–5 profits, being payable on 1st January 19–7, is now regarded as future taxation.

ACT (Recoverable)

19–5		£	19–5		£
Jan 1	Balance b/d	27,000	Aug 11	ACT (Payable) (3)	6,000
June 30	ACT (Payable) (1)	15,000		(3/7 × 14,000)	
	(3/7 × 35,000)		Dec 31	Provn for Corpn	
Dec 31	ACT (Payable)(1)	30,000		Tax (Fut)(8)	36,000
	(3/7 × 70,000)		Dec 31	Balance c/d	30,000
		72,000			72,000
19–6					
Jan 1	Balance b/d	30,000			

ACT recoverable is held in this account until it can be transferred against the corporation tax provided for the accounting year in which the related dividend is paid (not for the year in respect of which it is paid). (See 4.23 and 4.34).

For the year ended 31st December 19–5 the position is thus:

Dividend Payments			Payment	Related
Type		Amount	Date 19–5	ACT
		£		£
Final proposed for 19–4		63,000	June 27	27,000
Interim 19–5		35,000	Aug 22	15,000
				42,000
				Related Tax Credit
Less				
Dividends Received 19–5		14,000	Aug 11	6,000
Net ACT paid in 19–5 and recoverable against provision for corporation tax on 19–5 profits by transfer (8) above				36,000

The remaining ACT recoverable relates to dividends which will not be paid until 19–6. There is therefore no provision for corporation tax at the end of 19–5 against which it can be matched. Consequently, it is held in ACT (Recoverable) account until the end of 19–6 when the corporation tax provision for that year is raised. When this happens it is transferred out of ACT (Recoverable) to the Provision for Corporation Tax account per Event (8). At the end of 19–5 the debit balance on ACT (Recoverable) is shown in the Balance Sheet as a deduction from the credit balance on Deferred Taxation account (if one exists) or as Debtors (due in more than one year).

ACT (Payable)

19–5		£	19–5		£
July 14	Bank (6)	27,000	Jan 1	Balance b	27,000
Aug 11	ACT (Recov) (3)	6,000	June 30	ACT (Recov) (1)	15,000
Oct 13	Bank	9,000	Dec 31	ACT (Recov) (1)	30,000
	(15,000–6000)(6)				
Dec 31	Balance c/d	30,000			
		72,000			72,000
			19–6		
			Jan 1	Balance b/d	30,000

Proposed dividends

19–5		£	19–5		£
June 27	Bank (10)	63,000	Jan 1	Balance b/d	63,000
Dec 31	Balance c/d	70,000	Dec 31	Profit and Loss Appropn (9)	70,000
		133,000			133,000
			19–6		
			Jan 1	Balance b/d	70,000

Interim Dividend

19–5		£	19–5		£
Aug 22	Bank (10)	35,000	Dec 31	Profit and Loss Appropn	35,000
		35,000			35,000

Dividends Received

19–5		£	19–5		£
Dec 31	Profit and Loss – Investment Income(5)	20,000	Aug 11	Bank (2)	14,000
				Tax Credits (2)	6,000
		20,000			20,000

Tax Credits

19–5		£	19–5		£
Aug 11	Dividends Received	6,000	Dec 31	Profit and Loss (Taxation Section) (4)	6,000
		6,000			6,000

2.

Namtax PLC
Profit and Loss Account
for the year ended 31 December 19–5

	£	£
Trading profit (before tax)		400,000
Income from other fixed asset investments		
(Dividends are shown gross ie inclusive of tax credit.		
Interest is also shown gross (see 3.7))		20,000
Profit on ordinary activities before taxation		420,000
Less Taxation		
UK Corporation Tax at 35% on profits for year	140,000	
Over provision in 19–4	(7,500)	
Tax Credits on UK dividends received	6,000	
Irrecoverable ACT	NIL	
		138,500
Profit on ordinary activities after taxation		281,500
Less Appropriations		
Dividends (disclosed at net amount actually		
paid ie excluding ACT)		
Interim paid	35,000	
Final proposed	70,000	
		105,000
Retained profit for year		176,500

Namtax PLC
Balance Sheet (extract)
as at 31 December 19–5

	£	£
Debtors: (due after more than one year)		
Other debtors		
ACT Recoverable (This would have been deducted from Deferred Taxation account if in existence)		30,000
Creditors: amounts falling due within one year		
Other creditors		
Proposed Dividends	70,000	
Current Taxation		
Corporation Tax (Payable 1st Jan 19–6	92,500	
ACT Payable	30,000	
Creditors: amounts falling due after more than one year		
Other creditors		
Corporation tax (Payable 1st Jan 19–7)		104,000

DEFERRED TAXATION

5.0 The corporation tax which a company shows as a charge in its accounts is not necessarily the amount which it ultimately pays because, apart from the estimate aspect noted in 4.5, some of the tax may be deferred, that is, its payment is postponed for a long time or, in some cases, indefinitely.

5.1 Deferred taxation account is therefore an assortment of accumulated tax liabilities which may have to be discharged at various times in future accounting periods.

CIRCUMSTANCES GIVING RISE TO DEFERRED TAXATION LIABILITIES.

TIMING DIFFERENCES.

5.2 Taxable profit differs from accounting profit for a variety of reasons. Some of these differences are of a permanent nature - certain items of revenue are tax free and certain items of expense are not deductible for tax purposes. Most business entertaining expense, for example, is disallowed for tax purposes.

5.3 Other differences are simply phasing differences, that is, they affect taxable profit in a period different from that in which they affect accounting profit. Instances of this sort include interest receivable accrued in the financial accounts but not taxed until actually received, general provisions for bad debts not tax deductible until the debts become specific and capital allowances in excess of depreciation charges. These latter are termed accelerated capital allowances.

5.4 Differences in incidence are termed timing differences. Originating timing differences - transactions or events dealt with in a financial statement in a period different from that in which it is accounted for in the taxation assessment - give rise to deferred taxation entries.

5.5 These same originating differences are reversed in a later period or over a number of later periods.

5.6 Under this system, therefore, the taxation charge in the profit and loss account of a company is, as far as is possible, matched with the accounting profit to which that charge relates.

5.7 It achieves this objective by passing through the profit and loss account to deferred taxation account additional charges for taxation equivalent to the temporary tax savings resulting from the timing differences.

5.8 The effect of this is that these temporary tax savings do not benefit the profit and loss account of the period in which they arise but are carried forward for release in a later period or a number of later periods as an offset to the greater amount of tax payable when the differences reverse. The originating and reversing entries appear under the heading Taxation in the profit and loss account.

5.9 Permanent differences of the type noted in 5.2, by definition not being of a phasing nature, do not, of course, give rise to deferred taxation entries.

STOCK APPRECIATION RELIEF.

5.10 The Finance Act (No. 2) 1975 introduced tax relief on increased closing inventory values, to relieve companies of the effects of higher tax assessments stemming from profits enhanced by holding stocks acquired under inflationary conditions.

5.11 Such stock relief used to be available whether closing stock values were higher as the result of increased volume or of price or of a combination of both of these factors, but under the Finance Act 1981, the movement in an all stocks index was applied to opening stock. This relief was abolished completely in 1984.

5.12 When this relief was utilised the amount concerned was charged under the Taxation heading of the profit and loss account and credited to Deferred Taxation.

5.13 Stock appreciation relief was held in Deferred Taxation account pending possible clawback under the rules and regulations prevailing at the time.

SURPLUS ON REVALUATION OF FIXED ASSETS.

5.14 Companies may revalue their fixed assets to a current valuation figure. The uplift in value is regarded as a revaluation surplus and credited to a non distributable reserve account - Revaluation Reserve.

5.15 For taxation purposes, a chargeable gain does not arise until the fixed asset is sold and the gain is actually realised.

5.16 Nevertheless, the tax which, subject to 5.18 (below), might become payable on sale of the fixed asset at the revaluation figure, is debited to Revaluation Reserve and credited to Deferred Taxation.

SURPLUS ON SALE OF FIXED ASSETS.

5.17 When a fixed asset is sold at a figure above cost a chargeable gain might arise, thus increasing the corporation tax liability of the company.

5.18 If, however, the company is a continuing concern and provided certain conditions are satisfied, such liability can be deferred by reason of a special rollover relief.

5.19 Under these circumstances, the debit for deferred taxation would appear in the profit and loss account under Taxation if the surplus on sale of the asset is treated as an exceptional item or, if treated as an extraordinary item, as a deduction from that heading; the credit would of course go to Deferred Taxation. Exceptional and extraordinary items are defined in Chapter 4 3.33 and 3.34 respectively.

METHODS OF CALCULATING DEFERRED TAXATION PROVISIONS.

DEFERRAL METHOD.

5.20 Under this method, transfers to Deferred Taxation are calculated at the corporation tax rate operative at the date the originating timing difference occurs. Transfers out of this account in subsequent periods when reversing differences arise are at that same rate although the current tax rate may be different.

5.21 In any accounting period there can be both originating timing differences and reversing timing differences (of previous periods' originating differences).

5.22 Theoretically, when there is a change in the rate of corporation tax, the originating difference should be raised at the new rate and the reversing difference should be raised at the rate applicable when it originated.

5.23 As a practical expedient the two types of difference are netted. Net originating differences are provided at the new rate and net reversing differences released on a FIFO or average basis.

5.24 No adjustment to Deferred Taxation account is needed when the corporation tax rate changes when the provision is maintained under the deferral method.

5.25 The deferral method is illustrated and compared with the liability method in 5.31 and 5.32.

LIABILITY METHOD.

5.26 An alternative method of maintaining the Deferred Taxation account is the liability method. This is the only method now permitted under SSAP 15.

5.27 The originating and reversing differences are netted as in 5.23 but the current rate of corporation tax is used for calculation purposes.

5.28 On a change of rate of tax, an adjustment has to be put through to adjust the cumulative net differences to the current rate of tax.

5.29 Ideally, the provision should be maintained at the rate of tax which will be operative when the liability matures, but as this rate is not known and cannot be predicted, the current rate is used as an expedient.

5.30 An illustration to the liability and a comparison with the deferral method is given in 5.31 and 5.32. The liability method is preferred because the deferred taxation provision is maintained at an up-to-date figure.

EXAMPLE AND COMPARISON OF METHODS.

5.31 The timing differences for a company for three consecutive years were as follows:

Year	Timing differences Originating £	(Reversing) £	Net £	Corporation Tax Rate %
1	20,000	–	20,000	50
2	35,000	(5,000)	30,000	40
3	5,000	(15,000)	(10,000)	35

Required:

Show (with workings) the debits or credits in the Deferred Tax account for each of the three years, using

a. Deferral method, and

b. Liability method.

SOLUTION
5.32

Year	Net Timing Differences £	Tax Rate %	Deferred Taxation Debits £	Credits £
Deferral Method				
1	20,000	50		10,000
2	30,000	40		12,000
Balance	50,000	44 (Average)		22,000
3	(10,000)	50 (FIFO) (or 44 (Average))	5,000 (4,400)	
Balance (FIFO)	10,000 30,000	} 50		5,000 12,000 }
(Average)	(40,000)	(44)		(17,600)
Liability Method				
1	20,000	50		10,000
2	30,000	40		12,000
2 Rate adjustment	(20,000)	(50-40)	2,000	
Balance	50,000	40		20,000

3 Rate			
adjustment	(50,000)	(40-35)	2,500
3	(10,000)	35	3,500
Balance	40,000	35	14,000

At the end of year 3 the deferred taxation provision balance would be £17,000 under the deferral (FIFO) method, £17,600 under the deferral (average) method and £14,000 under the liability method.

SUMMARY OF ACCOUNTING ENTRIES

5.33 As has been stated in 5.2 to 5.19, Deferred Taxation Account is built up by a series of transfers most of which pass through the profit and loss account, mostly, but not exclusively, under the heading Taxation.

5.34 In outline, a profit and loss account appears, thus

	£
Profit on ordinary activities before tax	x
Less	
Taxation on profit on ordinary activities	x
Profit on ordinary activities after tax	x
Extraordinary items (less tax)	x
Profit for the financial year	x
Less	
Appropriations	x
Retained profit for the year	x

A breakdown of the heading Taxation, would disclose

	£
Taxation	
UK Corporation tax on profit for year at x%	x
(Over)/under provision in previous year	x
Tax credits on UK dividends received	x
Irrecoverable ACT	x
Overseas taxation relief	x
Overseas taxation	x
Transfers to/from deferred taxation	x

5.35 Sums included in the last item, Transfers to/from deferred taxation are those relating to short-term timing differences, accelerated capital allowances and chargeable gains on exceptional items.

5.36 Amounts in respect of deferred taxation on extraordinary chargeable gains appear as a deduction from the chargeable gain under the heading Extraordinary items.

5.37 Deferred taxation arising from revaluation surpluses on fixed assets is charged against Revaluation Reserve.

5.38 In the balance sheet, the credit balance of Deferred Taxation account is classified under the heading Provision for liabilities and charges.

5.39 Before inclusion in the balance sheet, the closing debit balance of ACT Recoverable account is deducted from the credit balance of Deferred Taxation and only the net balance is disclosed (see 4.36), but the details are shown by way of a note.

5.40 Further aspects of deferred taxation are considered when examining SSAP 15 Accounting for deferred taxation in Chapter 4.

MISCELLANEOUS

6.0 In addition to the items of taxation already covered in 2.0 to 5.0, the following items are encountered in financial accounting:

> Income Tax (PAYE)
> National Insurance contributions
> Vehicle Excise licences.

INCOME TAX (PAYE).

6.1 Under the Pay-As-You-Earn (PAYE) scheme the employer acts as collecting agent for the Inland Revenue. Income Tax is deducted from employees' wages and salaries at amounts calculated from tax tables provided by the Inland Revenue.

6.2 Wages/Salaries account is debited (inter alia) with the net remuneration actually paid to employees and with PAYE deducted. This latter amount is then credited to PAYE account.

6.3 Each month the PAYE account is debited with the amount paid over to the Collector of Taxes. The balances on PAYE account at the end of an accounting period is included in the balance sheet as Creditors: amounts falling due within one year.

NATIONAL INSURANCE CONTRIBUTIONS.

6.4 These are a tax in essence, but not in name, part of which is borne by the employer and part by the employee.

6.5 The combined employer/employee contribution is debited to Wages/Salaries account, as appropriate, and credited to National Insurance account.

6.6 The National Insurance account is debited each month when the amount is paid over. The balance on National Insurance account at the end of an accounting period is included in the balance sheet as Creditors: amounts falling due within one year.

VEHICLE EXCISE LICENCES

6.7 Before a motor vehicle can be used on the public roads it must have a current vehicle excise licence attached on display.

6.8 The cost of licences when acquired is debited to an expense account. At the end of an accounting period, the unexpired portion of the cost of the licences is carried forward to the succeeding accounting period and treated as a prepayment disclosed in the balance sheet as a current asset – Debtors.

STUDENT SELF TESTING
Test Exercises

1. The following balances have been extracted from the ledger of X.A.T. PLC on 31 December 19–5.

	DR £	CR £
Value Added Tax		38,000
Deferred Taxation		42,000
Provisions for Corporation Tax		
– Current		73,000
– Future		–
Advance Corporation Tax Recoverable	5,000	
Advance Corporation Tax Payable		–

The following matters have not yet been posted:

  i. VAT output tax £116,000, input tax £89,000, payments to revenue authorities £36,000

  ii. transfer to Deferred Taxation Account £7,000.

  iii. the balance of Provision for Corporation Tax (Current) shown above (£73,000) is the original unadjusted estimate based on 19–4 profit. The figure of £67,000 has now been agreed with the Inland Revenue and will be paid on the due date –

1 January, 19–6.

iv. corporation tax on the 19–5 profits is estimated at £94,000. Due date for payment is 1 January, 19–7.

v. there are proposed final ordinary dividends at 31 December 19–5 on which advance corporation tax of £21,000 is payable.

N.B. The balance of Advance Corporation Tax (Recoverable) (£5,000) relates to the interim ordinary dividend paid in August 19–5.

Required:

a. Complete and balance the above accounts.

b. Prepare extracts from the Profit and Loss Account for the year ended 31 December 19–5 and from the Balance Sheet as at 31 December 19–5, incorporating the effects of the above matters.

2. On 1 January 19–5 Chesil PLC had a credit balance on Income Tax account of £2,100. Basic rate of income tax is 30%.

The following transactions arose during the year 19–5.

			£
Jan	14	Paid income tax due (excluding on royalties paid Feb 1)	
Feb	1	Paid royalties (net) for second half year 19–4	1,400
April	14	Paid income tax due for March quarter	
May	30	Received investment income interest (net)	5,600
June	30	Paid debenture interest (net)	6,300
July	14	Paid income tax due for June quarter	
Aug	1	Paid royalties (net) for first half year 19–5	2,100
Sept	3	Received investment income interest (net)	7,000
Dec	31	Paid debenture interest (net)	6,300
Dec	31	Provided royalties (net) for second half year 19–5	3,500

Required:

a. Open, post and balance the appropriate accounts to record the above transactions.

b. Prepare the relevant profit and loss account and balance sheet extracts after (a) has been completed.

3. During 19–5, Chesil PLC also received dividends on investments and paid dividends as follows. In each case the amounts listed are net. Basic rate of income tax is 30%.

			£
May	30	Paid final dividend proposed at end of 19–4	70,000
July	14	Paid ACT for June quarter	
July	30	Received dividends on investments	1,400
Sept	19	Paid interim dividend in respect of first half year	35,000
Oct	14	Paid ACT for September quarter	
Nov	11	Received dividends on investments	2,100
Dec	31	Proposed final dividend for 19–5	105,000

Required:

a. Open, post and balance the appropriate accounts to record the above transactions.

b. Prepare the relevant profit and loss account and balance sheet extracts after (a) has been completed.

ACCA EXAMINATION QUESTIONS

4. **Required:**

a. Prepare the following Ledger Accounts to show the appropriate entries for 1983 in the books of Provincial Motor Spares Ltd:

> Debenture Interest
> Dividend Payable
> Investment Income
> Income Tax

Corporation Tax
Advance Corporation Tax
Deferred Tax

Note Assume that the debentures that have been redeemed have been held for re-issue. Assume Income Tax rate of 30%. Assume no ACT on inter group dividends. Assume Corporation Tax rate of 50%.

b. Prepare the Deferred Tax Account on the assumption that the Corporation Tax rate for 1983-84 has been increased from fifty per cent to fifty five per cent on the basis that:

i. Provincial Motor Spares Ltd uses the liability method, and

ii. Provincial Motor Spares Ltd uses the deferral method.
(ACCA 2.9(1) December 1984)

Appendix 1(a)
The Trial Balance of Provincial Motor Spares Ltd as at 31 December 1983

	Dr £000's	Cr £000's
Ordinary shares of £1 each		3,600
10% cumulative preference shares of £1 each		1,000
General reserve		1,820
Profit & Loss Account at 1 January 1983		2,250
8% debentures		500
Profit for 1983		3,780
Debenture redemption reserve		290
Creditors		4,130
Tax payable on 1 January 1984		700
Deferred taxation on 1 January 1983		1,655
Investment income (net)		14
Premises	7,200	
Equipment	3,800	
Investments	251	
Stock	6,580	
Debtors	1,480	
Bank	428	
	19,739	19,739

a. Profits accrue evenly throughout the year.

b. Provision is to be made for:
   i. Tax of £1,900,000 on the profits of the current year
   ii. The preference dividend
   iii. The proposed ordinary dividend of ten per cent.

c. A transfer of £170,000 is to be made to the General Reserve.

d. Sales for the year totalled £21,000,000 of which £1,000,000 consisted of sales to United Motor Spares Ltd. The sales are stated exclusive of Value Added Tax.

e. The Investment Income has suffered the deduction of Income Tax at the rate of thirty per cent.

Appendix 2
Further information relating to the debentures issued by Provincial Motor Spares Ltd.

a. The accountant has obtained a copy of the trust deed of the debentures which provides that:

   i. A debenture redemption reserve was to be created by the appropriation of £100,000 each year from otherwise distributable profits.

   ii. An amount equal to the appropriation, together with any income arising from previously invested appropriations, was to be invested on 31 December each year, commencing on 31 December 1980.

   iii. Investments in the redemption fund could be realised if the market price of the debentures was to fall below par and thus, under the terms of the trust deed, become eligible for purchase.

   iv. Debentures purchased in the open market may be held for possible re-issue.

b. In addition, the accountant has obtained information about the reserve fund and the related investments:

   i. the balance on the redemption reserve account was £290,000 on 1 January 1983.

   ii. Debenture fund investments which had cost £36,000 were realised on 31 March 1983 for £39,000 which was used to purchase some of the company's own debentures having a nominal value of £40,000.

   iii. Cash received from the debenture redemption fund investments amounted to £14,000 during 1983.

   iv. The bank figure of £428,000 in the trial balance contains the balances of both the General Bank Account and the Debenture Reserve Fund Bank Account.

Appendix 3
Further information about taxation in Provincial Motor Spares Ltd

a. *Deferred Tax*

   i. The company uses the deferral method.

   ii. The Equipment Register showed the following:

	1980 £000's	1981 £000's	1982 £000's	1983 £000's	Total £000's
Cost of equipment	1,700	400	2,000	1,000	5,100
Depreciation	680	120	400	100	1,300
Net book value	1,020	280	1,600	900	3,800

   iii. Assume Corporation Tax rate of fifty per cent.

   iv. Assume a 100% Capital Allowance in the year of acquisition.

b. Income Tax

Assume a rate of thirty per cent.

c. Advance Corporation Tax.

Assume a rate of thirty per cent.

Assume no Advance Corporation Tax is payable on inter group dividends.

5. Curtains Ltd was established prior to 1965 and has an accounting year ending 31 December. The issued share capital of the company at 1 January 1986 was 140,000 ordinary shares of 50p each and 70,000 7.1% preference shares of £1 each. On 1 July 1986 there was a bonus issue of ordinary shares of one new share for every share held at that date. A new issue for cash of 75,000 shares at a price of £1.50 each was made at the same time. The profits for corporation tax are calculated at £250,000 for 1986 and £220,000 for 1985. Corporation tax on the profits for 1984 was agreed at £65,000.

During 1985 preference dividends were paid on 31 March and 30 September. Ordinary dividends were paid - first and final for 1984 accounts at 10p per share paid 28 February, and interim of 3p per share paid 30 September.

During 1986 the final ordinary dividend for the year 1985 of 10p per share was paid on 28

February and an interim dividend of 5p per share was paid on 30 June, a second interim of 4p per share was paid on 31 October. On 31 March and 30 September the preference dividends were paid. A proposed ordinary dividend of 5p per share was included in the accounts for 1986. The company has a 10% debenture of £200,000 with interest payable 30 June and 31 December.

Fixed loan interest is received by the company on 1 May and 1 November each year. the total amount received in 1986 was £7,100.

Prior to payment of corporation tax for the 1985 accounts the figure was agreed by the authorities at £85,000 before deducting any relevant advance corporation tax. Advance corporation tax recoverable against the corporation tax on the 1984 profits was £9,750.

Curtains Ltd is entitled to dividends from a UK company and on 31 July 1986 the amount received was £7,100. No other dividends have been received during the period.

Required:

Prepare detailed corporation tax, advance corporation tax and income tax accounts for the year 1986.

Assume:

  i. all taxes are paid on the due dates;

  ii. corporation tax rate of 40% to 31 March 1986 and 35% thereafter.

  iii. advance corporation tax rate of 3/7ths of the dividend to 31 March 1986 and 29/71sts of the dividend thereafter;

  iv. basic rate income tax is 30% to 5 April 1986 and 29% thereafter.
     (ACCA 2.9(2) June 1987))

4 Final Accounts

GENERAL BACKGROUND

1.0 The preparation of final accounts of various forms of business (including limited companies) for internal reporting purposes, is a topic which will have been covered at a much earlier stage of study.

1.1 This chapter of the manual assumes that prior knowledge and, using it as a base, deals with the considerable body of detailed rules and regulations which have to be adhered to when these accounts are prepared for publication to external entities.

CONSTRAINTS

2.0 Apart from the normal accounting practices and procedures which are followed when final accounts are prepared, there are a number of legal and other requirements which have to be observed when the final accounts of limited companies are being prepared for publication purposes.

2.1 Originally, the Companies Acts of 1948 and 1981, and to a lesser extent of 1967, 1976 and 1980, specified the form and manner in which certain items have to be disclosed. The main statutory disclosure requirements are now included in the Companies Act 1985 and are summarised in Appendix 1 together with the relatively minor changes contained in the Companies Act 1989.

2.2 Secondly, the published accounts should also be prepared in accordance with Accounting Standards. A brief summary of the contents of the relevant ones, follows in the next subsection from 3.0 onwards.

2.3 Thirdly, the Council of the Stock Exchange has prescribed certain other disclosure requirements for listed companies, but these are not examinable in Paper 2.9.

STATEMENTS OF STANDARD ACCOUNTING PRACTICE (SSAPs) BACKGROUND

3.0 During the 1960s the accounting profession was severely criticised for the apparent ease with which financial results could be manipulated to give whatever figures were required.

3.1 In the course of takeover negotiations between two industrial giants, GEC and AEI, the latter company issued a forecast profit figure for year ended 31 December 1967 (and the forecast was approved by their accountants) of £10m. When the takeover had been effected, audited accounts produced for the GEC group for the 15 months to 31 March 1968 disclosed a loss of £5.9m.

3.2 Apart from shortcomings in forecasting, the reason for the massive discrepancy was the different accounting treatment which the two companies had accorded to the same transactions. In each case these different treatments were acceptable to their respective auditors.

3.3 Shortly after this, the Accounting Standards Steering Committee (ASSC) was formed in 1969/1970. It has since been re-designated the Accounting Standards Committee (ASC). Membership of the committee consists of representatives of the:

> Institutes of Chartered Accountants in England and Wales, in Scotland and in Ireland.
> Chartered Association of Certified Accountants
> Chartered Institute and Management Accountants
> Chartered Institute of Public Finance and Accountancy

The joint committee of these six bodies is called the Consultative Committee of Accountancy Bodies (CCAB).

PROCEDURE

3.4 The committee has first selected a topic for consideration and has carried out research into it. If the results of the research warranted it, an Exposure Draft (ED) was prepared and circulated to all interested parties for comment. The comments were considered and evaluated and if necessary the ED was amended before being approved by the Councils of the accountancy bodies in 3.3. After approval, the Statement of Standard Accounting Practice (SSAP), as it is now called, was published by the CCAB.

NATURE OF SSAPs.

3.5 A main aim of an SSAP is to restrict the choice of alternative accounting treatments where these exist, so that financial statements of reasonable comparability can be prepared.

3.6 SSAPs constitute a set of definitive principles to be followed when preparing financial statements.

3.7 Departures from principles and practices enunciated in SSAPs are permissible in exceptional circumstances, only where adherence would fail to give a true and fair view in a specific instance or because the SSAP would be obviously inappropriate, or because exemption from disclosure is granted by Statute.

APPLICATION AND ENFORCEMENT OF SSAPs

3.8 SSAPs apply to all financial statements intended to give a true and fair view of the financial position and of profit or loss. In some cases the standard is stated to apply only to business entities of a certain size or type.

3.9 Professional accountants, whether acting in the capacity of director, or other officer, or auditor, or reporting accountant etc. are expected to observe the standards and to ensure that their existence and purpose is understood by others. There is the additional onus on a professional accountant who acts as an auditor or reporting accountant etc to justify (in writing) his stated or implied concurrence in the event of significant non–compliance. Failure to do so renders that person liable to disciplinary proceedings for professional misconduct.

DEVELOPMENTS

3.10 In late May 1983 the ASC issued its report which reviewed the standard setting process. One of the report's suggestions was a streamlining of procedures. It proposed that after a topic had been selected a discussion paper might be issued, followed by a Statement of Intent (S.O.I.) outlining the proposed approach. An Exposure Draft would then follow which would be converted into a Standard for adoption by the CCAB bodies. SSAPs were to be restricted to matters of major and fundamental importance (and would therefore, become fewer in number). A new category of non-mandatory pronouncements, termed Statements of Recommended Practice (SORP), were to be introduced to deal with matters of widespread, but not fundamental, importance. Where a matter is of limited application (to a specific industry) an SORP approved by the ASC, and termed a Franked SORP, is now issued.

3.11 In August 1990 new arrangements, prescribed by the Companies Act 1989, came into force, based on the Dearing Committee's Report whereby the standard setting process is under the general oversight of the Financial Reporting Council. The Accounting Standards Board replaced the ASC and another new body, a Review Panel has been constituted to enquire into departures from Accounting Standards.

STANDARDS CURRENTLY IN FORCE
3.12

SSAP NO.	TITLE	Effective Date
1	Accounting for associated companies (revised)	17th December 1990
2	Disclosure of accounting policies	1st January 1972
3	Earnings per share (revised)	1 August 1974
4	Accounting for government grants	1st July 1990
5	Accounting for value added tax	1st January 1974
6	Extraordinary items and prior year adjustments (revised)	1st August 1986
8	The treatment of taxation under the imputation system in the accounts of companies	1st January 1975
9	Stocks and long-term contracts	1st July 1988
10	Statements of source and application of funds	1st January 1976
12	Accounting for depreciation (revised)	1st January 1987
13	Accounting for research and development (revised)	1st January 1989
14	Group accounts (revised)	17th December 1990
15	Accounting for deferred tax (revised)	1st April 1985
17	Accounting for post balance sheet events	1st September 1980
18	Accounting for contingencies	1st September 1980
19	Accounting for investment properties	1st July 1981
20	Foreign currency translation	1st April 1983
21	Accounting for leases and hire purchase contracts	1st July 1984 (part) 1st July 1987 (remainder)
22	Accounting for goodwill (revised)	1st January 1989
23	Accounting for acquisitions and mergers	1st April 1985
24	Accounting for pension costs	1st July 1988
25	Segmental reporting	1st July 1990

"Effective date" means that the standard applies to financial statements relating to accounting periods beginning on or after the date given.

SSAPs 7 (which was provisional only) and 11 have been withdrawn and the latter has been replaced by SSAP 15. The original SSAP 9 has now been withdrawn.

SSAPs 1, 14, 20, 21, 22 and 23 are dealt with in other chapters of this section and in Section IV and V. Full texts of the current standards are summarised at the appropriate points of this manual.

Although SSAPs are included in this section of the manual which is concerned with limited companies, the requirements of most of them apply equally to the accounts of other business formations.

SUMMARY OF CONTENTS OF SSAPs.

SSAP 2 DISCLOSURE OF ACCOUNTING POLICIES.

3.13 The standard states that in the absence of an explanatory statement to the contrary, four fundamental concepts (defined as broad basic assumptions which underlie the periodic financial accounts of business enterprises), namely, the going-concern, accruals, consistency and prudence concepts, are presumed to have been observed.

3.14 Accounting bases are the methods used for expressing or applying these concepts to financial trans-actions and items. Several possible and acceptable bases may exist for dealing with specific cases, for example, there are a number of recognised methods of writing off depreciation.

3.15 Accounting policies are the specific accounting bases followed for items judged to be material in determining profit or loss for the period and in stating the financial position. Such policies should be chosen by management as being most appropriate to the circumstances and best suited to present a true and fair view of the enterprise's results and financial position. Once chosen, the policies should be consistently applied.

DISCLOSURE

3.16 SSAP 2 stipulates that the policies adopted should be disclosed in succinct notes to the accounts.

SSAP 3 EARNINGS PER SHARE.

3.17 The widespread international use by investors and their advisers of the price earnings ratio as a stock market indicator requires that the components of that ratio be calculated on a comparable basis.

3.18 The "formula" for arriving at the price earnings (P/E) ratio is

$$\frac{\text{Market price per share}}{\text{Earnings per share.}}$$

3.19 In the absence of agreement on the content and method of calculation of the earnings per share (EPS) figure used as the denominator in the formula, the resultant P/E ratio could be a range of figures.

3.20 The standard seeks to remove as much subjectivity as possible by defining EPS within fairly narrow limits.

3.21 EPS is stated to mean the profit in pence attributable to each equity share, based on (group) profit after tax, after minority interests and after preference dividends but before extraordinary items (see 3.34) and divided by the number of equity shares in issue and ranking for dividend in respect of the period.

3.22 Unfortunately there are a number of complications. There are two methods of computing EPS, one taking account of all components of the tax charge and known as the "net" basis, the other taking account of only the constant components and known as the "nil" basis. In many cases, the net and nil bases give the same result, but where different, the net basis should be used (with a note of the figure using the nil basis, if materially different).

3.23 The denominator used to arrive at EPS is the number of equity shares in issue and ranking for dividend. Complications arise when equity share issues occur during the period. If issued for cash, the weighted average number of shares in issue should be used.

3.24 Where the issue consists of bonus shares, the previous year's EPS needs to be recalculated.

3.25 A rights issue produces a greater difficulty in that it is regarded as a part cash issue and part bonus issue.

3.26 If a company has either unissued shares and/or convertible loan stock in issue a figure of fully diluted EPS must be calculated if the dilution is more than 5%, using the number of shares which would be in issue if all the shares were issued and/or all the convertible loan stock converted to shares, this latter causing difficulty because the conversion terms differ according to the date of conversion.

DISCLOSURE

3.27 Standard practice requires that basic EPS (and if applicable, fully diluted EPS) be disclosed on the face of the profit and loss account together with a note of the basis of calculation with equal prominence. The full treatment is dealt with in Chapter 6 of this section.

SSAP 4 ACCOUNTING FOR GOVERNMENT GRANTS

3.28 This standard deals with grants made under the Industry Act 1972 by reference to capital expenditure. (Revenue based grants are credited to Revenue in the same period as the relative revenue expenditure is charged).

3.29 SSAP 4 requires that capital based grants be credited to revenue over the expected useful life of the asset by crediting part of the grant to profit and loss in each accounting period. The balance of this deferred credit should be shown in the balance sheet preferably as a deferred liability, but in any case not as part of the shareholders' funds.

SSAP 5 ACCOUNTING FOR VALUE ADDED TAX

3.30 This topic has been dealt with in Chapter 3 2.0 to 2.12.

3.31 The standard practice is that in the profit and loss account Turnover should be disclosed net of VAT. Irrecoverable VAT should, where material and practical, be included as part of the cost of the fixed asset or other item to which it is allocable.

SSAP 6 EXTRAORDINARY ITEMS AND PRIOR YEAR ADJUSTMENTS.

3.32 The objective of this standard is to achieve uniformity of accounting treatment for major items of revenue and expense, according to their incidence.

EXCEPTIONAL ITEMS

3.33 Items which arise from the ordinary activities of the business but which are abnormal in amount or incidence, are classed as exceptional items. Exceptional items are accounted for in the profit before tax figure for the period.

EXTRAORDINARY ITEMS

3.34 In contrast, those items of significant amount which arise from events or transactions outside the ordinary activities of the business and which are infrequent or irregular in occurrence, are classed as extraordinary items. They are accounted for (net of attributable taxation) under a separate heading "Extraordinary items" in the profit and loss account, immediately after the profit after tax figure.

PRIOR YEAR ITEMS

3.35 When annual accounts are prepared, there must, as a matter of necessity be a number of provisions raised for known liabilities, the amounts of which are not known precisely. In a following accounting period, when the actual figure becomes known, an adjustment is effected of the difference between the provision and the actual. If the item or transaction involved is of a routine type, the adjustment is a prior year item. The significance of this is that the adjustment falls into the accounting period in which it is corrected, not retrospectively into that to which it relates. In the profit and loss account the adjustment appears under the same heading as the original estimated figure. The same treatment also applies to the correction in one period of errors made in an earlier period.

PRIOR YEAR ADJUSTMENTS

3.36 Certain errors, however, originating from an earlier period may be of such magnitude that they affect the validity of the accounts for that period by destroying the true and fair view basis. Errors of this type are termed fundamental errors and are accounted for as prior year adjustments.

3.37 Whenever a business changes one of its accounting policies, for example, on the introduction of a new SSAP, the cumulative adjustments relating to prior years which have no connection with the results of the current year are also accounted for as prior year adjustments.

3.38 A prior year adjustment is effected by restating prior years' results so that the balance of retained profit brought forward then incorporates the adjustment net of attributable taxation. The effect of the adjustment should be given in a note reconciling the original and the amended opening balance of retained profit.

OTHER MATTERS

3.39 Another objective of SSAP 6 is to prevent certain transactions from being concealed by transfer against reserves. This practice is in some cases permitted by statute. For example, preliminary and issue expenses can be debited direct to Share Premium account under Section 130 Companies Act 1985.

3.40 In compliance with SSAP 6, such items should be disclosed in a statement of movements on reserves accompanying the profit and loss account.

3.41 The Appendix to SSAP 6 shows a suggested layout of the profit and loss account giving effect to 3.33 to 3.38. Explanatory notes should be appended when transactions constitute exceptional, extraordinary, prior year items or prior year adjustments.

SSAP 8 THE TREATMENT OF TAXATION UNDER THE IMPUTATION SYSTEM IN THE ACCOUNTS OF COMPANIES

3.42 The imputation system has already been fully described and illustrated in Chapter 3 4.15 to 4.40 of this section.

DISCLOSURE

3.43 SSAP 8 requires separate disclosure in the profit and loss account of

a. the amount (and rate) of UK corporation tax on the income of the year.

b. transfer to/from deferred taxation account, if material in amount, otherwise they should be included in a.

c. tax attributable to franked investment income (that is, tax credits)

d. irrecoverable ACT

e. relief for overseas taxation

f. total overseas taxation relieved and unrelieved, identifying that part of the unrelieved figure attributable to dividends paid or payable.

3.44 Dividends paid and/or payable should be shown net of the related ACT or attributable tax credit.

3.45 Dividends received and/or receivable should be shown gross of the related tax credit.

3.46 In the balance sheet, dividends proposed and/or payable should be included in current liabilities at their net amount. ACT payable on them, whether recoverable or not, should be included as a current taxation liability.

3.47 The recoverable amount of ACT on proposed and/or payable dividends should be deducted from the credit balance on deferred taxation account, if one exists, failing which it should be shown as ACT Recoverable under the heading Debtors.

SSAP 9 STOCKS AND LONG-TERM CONTRACTS

3.48 The amount at which stocks of raw materials and of finished goods and work in progress (process) but excluding long term contract work in progress, is the aggregate of the lower of cost and net realisable value of the individual items or groups of similar items of stock.

3.49 In this context, cost includes expenditure incurred in bringing the product or service to its present location and condition together with conversion costs, where appropriate.

3.50 Conversion costs are stated to include prime costs plus production and other attributable overheads (if any).

3.51 Profit deemed to have been realised on long-term contracts should be disclosed as the difference between contract turnover and the related cost of sales.

3.52 In the balance sheet amounts relating to long-term contracts are disclosed as amounts recoverable on contracts, payments on account of contracts, long-term contract balances and as provisions for liabilities and charges, as appropriate. The full treatment has been dealt with in Section II Chapter 5.

DISCLOSURE

3.53 The accounting policies adopted in calculating cost, net realisable value, attributable profit and foreseeable losses, where applicable, should be stated.

3.54 Stocks and work in progress should be suitably categorised in the balance sheet or in notes appended.

3.55 In the balance sheet there should be separately stated the amount of long term contract work in progress (at cost plus attributable profit and less foreseeable losses and progress payments received and receivable).

SSAP 10 STATEMENTS OF SOURCE AND APPLICATION OF FUNDS.

3.56 This standard applies to the financial accounts of all enterprises with an annual turnover or gross income of £25,000 or more.

3.57 Audited financial accounts should be accompanied by a statement of source and application of funds, the objective of which is to show the manner in which the operations of a business have been financed and the uses to which its financial resources have been put.

3.58 The statement should show the profit or loss for the period, with adjustments for non-cash items such as depreciation, and the following sources and applications where material - dividends paid, acquisitions and disposals of non-current assets, funds raised or expended on loans and share capital and increase or decrease in working capital, subdivided into its components. The full treatment is dealt with in Section IV Chapter 2.

SSAP 12 ACCOUNTING FOR DEPRECIATION

3.59 The general rule is that the cost (or valuation) of fixed assets, less estimated residual value, should be allocated on an equitable basis over the accounting periods expected to benefit from their use as a charge in the profit and loss account.

3.60 If the remaining useful life of an asset is revised, the unamortised cost should normally be allocated over the remaining useful life. Where material distortion of future financial results or position would result, the backlog should be recognised as an adjustment to profit on ordinary activities unless it is derived from an extraordinary event.

3.61 If, however, the unamortised cost is seen not to be fully recoverable, it should be written down at that point to the recoverable amount which should then be charged over the remaining useful life.

3.62 In the event of a change in method of calculating depreciation the unamortised cost should be written off over the remaining useful life on the new basis starting with the period in which the change is effected. The effect in that period should be disclosed, if significant.

3.63 The revaluation of assets requires that the depreciation provision be calculated on the revalued figure and on the latest estimate of remaining useful life. The effect in that period should be disclosed, if significant.

DISCLOSURE

3.64 For each main class of depreciable asset, the financial statements should show

   a. depreciation methods used.
   b. useful lives or depreciation rates used
   c. total depreciation for the period
   d. gross amount of depreciable assets and related cumulative depreciation to date

   Details of any changes in asset lives, depreciation methods or asset values should be disclosed in the year of occurrence.

SSAP 13 ACCOUNTING FOR RESEARCH AND DEVELOPMENT

3.65 The standard identifies three categories of activity

   a. pure research (work directed primarily towards the advancement of knowledge)
   b. applied research (work, other than at c., directed primarily at exploiting pure research)
   c. development (work directed primarily towards the introduction or improvement of specific products or processes).

3.66 The cost of fixed assets used for research and development activities should be capitalised and depreciated in the normal way. Such depreciation should form part of the research and development cost but also be included in the figure of depreciation disclosed in the profit and loss account.

3.67 Expenditure on pure and applied research (excluding the fixed assets in 3.66) should be written off in the period in which it is incurred.

3.68 Development expenditure should ordinarily be written off in the period in which it is incurred but it may be carried forward to future periods if it meets all the following criteria.

  a. there is a clearly defined project and the related expenditure is separately identifiable.

  b. the technical feasibility and the commercial viability have been assessed and adjudged to give the project a reasonably certain outcome.

  c. future revenues from the project will be more than adequate to cover further development costs and related production, marketing and administration costs.

  d. adequate resources (including extra working capital) are or will be available to enable the project to be completed.

3.69 If deferral takes place, amortisation should start when commercial production starts and should be allocated over the accounting periods of expected sale or use, with a periodic review of the justification for further deferral.

DISCLOSURE

3.70 Opening and closing balances of deferred expenditure and movements during the period should be disclosed. The closing balance should be shown separately, preferably under Deferred Assets, but in any case not as a Current Asset.

SSAP 15 ACCOUNTING FOR DEFERRED TAX

3.71 The subject of deferred taxation has been dealt with in Chapter 3 of this section. As has been seen, many transfers to Deferred Taxation affect profit after tax (see Chapter 3 5.35) and therefore affect earnings and its derivatives (EPS, P/E ratio, earnings yield).

3.72 By the beginning of 1979 when the original standard became operative, there was a massive build up of deferred taxation liabilities, some of which would never mature, but which had produced a deterioration in earnings and its above mentioned derivatives.

3.73 SSAP 15 relaxed the rules to the extent that, provided

  a. the business is a going concern

  b. on reasonable evidence the directors foresee that liability is unlikely to arise for at least three years ahead and probably not at all,

  it will be reasonable to assume that deferred taxation originating timing differences will not reverse and the deferred tax liabilities will not crystallise and need no longer be provided on certain types of transaction.

3.74 Deferred taxation should continue to be provided on all short term timing differences (see Chapter 3 5.3).

3.75 As regards accelerated capital allowances (see Chapter 3 5.3) provision need not be made on these timing differences if capital expenditure is regular and substantial, because under these conditions the originating timing differences will not reverse. Otherwise liability should be provided in full.

3.76 Deferred tax should be provided using the liability method.

3.77 No provision for deferred taxation need be made on a surplus on revaluation of fixed assets (Chapter 3 5.14 to 5.16) unless there is likely to be a sale under circumstances which give rise to a gain and rollover relief is unavailable.

3.78 Indefinite postponement of chargeable gains liability due to availability of rollover relief also absolves a company from responsibility to provide deferred taxation on sale of a fixed asset at a profit (Chapter 3 5.17 to 5.19).

DISCLOSURE

3.79 Deferred taxation passed through the profit and loss account should appear as part of the charge for taxation. The effects of accelerated capital allowances, other timing differences and tax rate changes (Chapter 3) 5.28) should be separately identified.

3.80 If, however, movements in deferred taxation are attributable to extraordinary items, they should be shown as part of these items (Chapter 3 5.36).

3.81 In the balance sheet deferred taxation must be shown as such under the heading Deferred Liabilities within Provision for Liabilities and Charges. The debit balance on ACT Recoverable account should be deducted (Chapter 3 5.39). The main components of Deferred Taxation should be disclosed in a note. The amount of deferred taxation not provided for in the accounts should also be disclosed by way of a note.

3.82 The deferred taxation aspects of movements in reserves (for example, revaluation reserves) should be separately shown as part of these movements (Chapter 3 115.37).

3.83 Where revaluations are not incorporated into the accounts but shown in memorandum accounts, the deferred taxation implications in the event of sale should also be disclosed.

SSAP 17 ACCOUNTING FOR POST BALANCE SHEET EVENTS.

3.84 An event occurring between balance sheet date and the date on which the accounts are prepared is a post balance sheet event for the purpose of this standard.

3.85 Such events may

a. concern conditions existing at balance sheet date, and/or
b. although occurring subsequently, may cast doubts upon the status of the business as a going concern, and/or
c. concern conditions not existing at balance sheet date, and/or
d. be the reversal or maturity of "window dressing" transactions.

3.86 Events a. and b. are regarded as adjusting events and c. and d. as non-adjusting events.

3.87 Adjusting events must be quantified, if material and incorporated into the relevant financial statements.

3.88 Non-adjusting events must be quantified, if material, and disclosed by way of notes to the financial statements.

DISCLOSURE

3.89 The disclosure mentioned in the previous paragraph should be of the event and of the pre-tax figures, accompanied by the taxation implications, or a statement if it is impracticable to make an estimate.

3.90 The date on which approval of the financial statements is granted by the board of directors (or by other officers) must be disclosed.

SSAP 18 ACCOUNTING FOR CONTINGENCIES

3.91 A condition existing at balance sheet date the outcome of which is dependent upon the happening, or failure to happen, of an uncertain future event or events. Uncertainties connected with accounting estimates do not give rise to contingencies within the definition of this standard.

3.92 Contingencies, as defined, give rise to contingent gains and contingent losses.

3.93 Contingent losses which are capable of quantification with reasonable accuracy, at date of approval of financial statements, should be accrued if the future event is probable. Except where the possibility of occurrence is remote, other contingent losses should be disclosed by way of note.

3.94 No accrual should be made for contingent gains, disclosure of which, if there is a probability that the gain will be realised, should be by way of note.

DISCLOSURE

3.95 For each disclosable contingency there should be stated in the appropriate financial statements

a. the nature of the contingency
b. the uncertainties which are expected to affect the eventual outcome
c. an estimate, at date of approval of the financial statements, of the net pre-tax financial effect and of the associated taxation implications, or, a statement that such an estimate is impracticable.

3.96 Individual disclosure of the separate contingencies common to a large group of like transactions, is not required. The financial effect can be calculated on a group of similar transactions.

SSAP 19 ACCOUNTING FOR INVESTMENT PROPERTIES

3.97 The standard, which is inapplicable to charities, defines investment properties as an interest in land and/or buildings in respect of which construction work and development have been completed and which is held for its investment potential, rental income being negotiated at arm's length.

3.98 Excluded from this definition is any property owned and occupied by a company for its own purposes or let to, and occupied by, another group company.

3.99 Investment properties should not be subject to periodic depreciation charges unless held on lease.

3.100 Open market value is the basis on which investment properties should be included in the balance sheet. Changes in value should be transferred to an investment revaluation reserve. If the reserve is insufficient to withstand a deficit, the shortfall should be charged to profit and loss account.

DISCLOSURE

3.101 The value of investment properties and the balance of the investment revaluation reserves should be prominently displayed in all financial statements. Reserve movements should be shown in the usual way.

3.102 Particulars (names and qualifications) of the valuers must be disclosed together with the bases of valuation and the fact that the valuer is an officer or employee of the company, if such is the case.

SSAP 24 ACCOUNTING FOR PENSION COSTS

3.103 Contributions payable to the pension scheme should be charged against profit and loss account for those schemes in which benefits are determined by the contributions paid (defined contribution schemes).

3.104 For those other schemes which are financed according to benefits to be paid (defined benefit schemes), the charge to profit and loss account should be an actuarially calculated level percentage of the current and expected pensionable payroll.

3.105 Variations from this regular cost should be allocated to the actual or average remaining service lives of the current employees.

3.106 Differences between pensions paid and cumulative pension cost charged in the profit and loss account should be shown in the balance sheet as either a pre-payment or as net pension provision.

DISCLOSURE

3.107 There should be stated the nature of the scheme, the accounting policy adopted, the pension cost charge for the period and any outstandings, provisions or prepayments at balance sheet date, together with information of an acturial nature.

PREPARATION OF FINAL ACCOUNTS OF LIMITED COMPANIES FOR PUBLICATION

4.0 The constraints under which accounts of limited companies are prepared for publication have already been noted in 2.0. These can be summarised as legal, standard and institutional.

4.1 Apart from a few notable exceptions, the form in which companies published these accounts was at their discretion. The advent of the Companies Act 1981 subsequently replaced by the 1985 Act, the main requirements of which are shown in Appendix 1, altered this situation somewhat in that the format of the profit and loss account and to an even greater extent, of the balance sheet, is prescribed by the statute.

4.2 Different formats are permitted under the Act and companies are free to adopt which they wish. However, two of the profit and loss account formats are more suited to the presentation of the results of trading companies and the other two formats to the results of manufacturing companies. In both cases a vertical or horizontal layout is allowed. In the past, companies have not favoured horizontal layouts. Throughout this manual, therefore, only vertical layouts will be illustrated but it must be remembered that, technically, a horizontal layout is equally acceptable.

4.3 The prescribed items, their sequence and content, as laid down by the 1985 Act, are displayed in Appendix 1 to which reference should be made. Profit and loss account formats 1 (and 3) are suitable for displaying the results of a trading company's activities and Formats 2 (and 4) for the results of a manufacturing company's operations. These are illustrated in 4.4. to 4.7 below. An example of the final accounts of a trading company and its solution then follows in 4.8 and 4.9.

4.4 Typical format of a profit and loss account for a trading company using Format 1 and including only the more common items:

Trading PLC
Profit and Loss account
for year ended 31 December 19–8

Notes		£
1	**Turnover**	X
2	Cost of sales	(X)
	Gross profit	X
2	Distribution costs	(X)
2	Administrative expenses	(X)
		X
2	Other operating income	X
	Operating profit	X
2	Income from other fixed asset investments	X
2	Other interest receivable	X
		X
2	Interest payable	(X)
	Profit on ordinary activities before taxation	X
3	Tax on profit on ordinary activities	(X)
	Profit on ordinary activities after taxation,	
	before extraordinary items	X
4	Extraordinary items, less taxation	X
	Profit for the financial year	X
5	Dividends	(X)
	Transfers to reserves	X
6	EPS	X

Corresponding figures would be shown in an adjoining column. Further statutory analysis/detail would be disclosed in the notes.

4.5 Typical format of a balance sheet for a trading company using Format 1, and including only the more common items:

Trading PLC
Balance Sheet
as at 31 December 19–8

Notes		£	£	£
	Fixed Assets			
7	Tangible assets			
	Land and buildings	X		
	Plant and machinery	X		
	Fixtures, fittings, tools			
	and equipment	X		
			X	
8	Investments		X	
			X	
	Current Assets			
9	Stocks	X		
10	Debtors	X		
	Cash at bank and in hand	X		
		X		
	Creditors: amounts falling due within one year			
11	Bank loans and overdrafts	X		
	Trade creditors	X		
	Bills of exchange payable	X		

12	Other creditors, including taxation and social security	X	
	Accruals	X	
			X
	Net current assets		X
	Total assets less current liabilities		X
	Creditors: amounts falling due after more than one year		
13	Bank loans and overdrafts	X	
14	Other creditors, including taxation and social security	X	
			(X)
	Provision for liabilities and charges		
15	Deferred taxation		(X)
			X
	Capital and Reserves		
16	Called up share capital		X
17	Share premium		X
18	Profit and loss account		X
	Shareholders' funds		X
			X

Corresponding figures would be shown in adjoining columns. Further statutory analysis/detail would be disclosed in the notes.

4.6 Typical format of a profit and loss account for a manufaturing company using Format 2 and including only the more common items.

Manufacturing PLC
Profit and Loss account
for the year ended 31 December 19–8

Notes		£	£
1	**Turnover**		X
	Change in stocks of finished goods and work in progress [increase/(decrease)]		X
	Own work capitalised		X
			X
	Raw materials and consumables		(X)
			X
2	Staff costs	X	
	Depreciation	X	
	Other operating charges	X	
			(X)
3	**Operating profit**		X
4	Income from other fixed asset investments		X
	Interest payable and similar charges		(X)
5	**Profit on ordinary activities, before taxation**		X
6	Tax on profit on ordinary activities		(X)
	Profit on ordinary activities, after taxation		(X)
7	Extraordinary items, less taxation		(X)
	Profit for the financial year		X
8	Dividends		(X)
	Transfers to reserves		X
9	EPS		X

Corresponding figures would be shown in an adjoining column. Further statutory analysis/detail would be disclosed in the notes.

4.7 Typical format of a balance sheet for a manufacturing company using Format 1.

Manufacturing PLC
Balance Sheet
as at 31 December 19–8

Notes		£	£	£
	Fixed Assets			
10	Intangible assets			
	Development costs		X	
	Tangible assets			
11	Land and buildings		X	
12	Plant and machinery		X̲	
				X
				X̲
	Current Assets			
13	Stocks		X	
15	Debtors		X	
	Cash at bank and in hand		X̲	
			X	
	Creditors: amounts falling due within one year			
	Trade creditors	X		
16	Other creditors, including taxation and social			
	security	X		
	Accruals	X̲		
			X	
	Net current assets			X̲
	Total assets less current liabilities			X
	Creditors: amounts falling due after more			
	than one year			
17	Debentures		X	
18	Other creditors, including taxation			
	and social security		X̲	
				(X)̲
				X̲
	Capital and Reserves			
19	Called up share capital		X	
20	Profit and loss account		X̲	
				X̲
	Shareholders' funds			X̲

Corresponding figures would be shown in adjoining columns. Further statutory analysis/detail would be disclosed in the notes.

4.8 There now follows an example of a trial balance and its adjusting and/or explanatory notes from which a set of final accounts suitable for publication has to be produced.

Mercator PLC
Trial Balance as at 31 December 19–8

	£	£
Trademarks	40,000	
Dividends received (excluding tax credits)		
– from listed investments in UK companies		7,700
– from unlisted investments in UK companies		3,500
Interest received (net) from unlisted investments		4,200
Cost of sales	2,281,830	

Turnover (including exports (to USA) £904,200)		3,573,930
Premises at cost (freehold)	1,199,000	
Furniture and equipment at cost	47,000	
Vehicles at cost	26,000	
Investments (long term) at cost		
– listed on London Stock Exchange	54,000	
– listed on an unrecognised stock exchange	20,000	
– unlisted (including 6% loan stock £100,000)	180,000	
Bank overdraft interest	5,600	
Selling and distribution expenses	355,700	
Provision for Corporation tax (on 19–7 profits)		108,400
Debenture interest paid (net)	2,800	
Administration expenses	201,900	
ACT recoverable	57,000	
4% Debentures 19–0/19–5 (secured on premises)		100,000
7% Preference share capital		100,000
Provisions for depreciation		
– premises		40,000
– furniture and equipment		19,850
– vehicles		12,510
Preference dividend paid	7,000	
ACT payable		3,000
Stocks	305,130	
Debtors (Trade)	400,600	
Bank and cash	92,652	
Creditors (Trade)		200,650
Profit and loss account 1st January 19–8		201,500
Provision for deferred taxation		100,972
Ordinary share capital		800,000
	5,276,212	**5,276,212**

Notes at 31st December 19–8

1. Authorised share capital:
   200,000 7% preference shares of £1.00 per share
   2,000,000 ordinary shares of £0.50 per share

2. Corporation Tax (UK) 35% basic rate of income tax 30%; ACT fraction 3/7; VAT should be ignored.

3. The dividends received and interest received on investments and the interest paid on debentures occurred in the last quarter of the financial year. No entries have yet been raised for the associated tax credits or for the income tax.

4. Bank overdraft interest was paid on a facility granted for a limited period ending in November 19–8. Items have been included in the trial balance as follows:
   Distribution £181,470, Selling £174,230 including in each case:

	Distribution £	Selling £
Depreciation (premises £29,000; furniture etc. £10,000; vehicles £11,100)	36,100	14,000
Plant hire	1,800	
Marketing director – salary		27,000
Other salaries	9,100	76,200
Wages	85,700	4,600
	Number	Number
Number of persons included above	26	23

	Administration £
Depreciation (premises)	5,300
Audit fees and expenses	12,200
Salaries – finance director	27,000
– staff manager	16,000
– company secretary	31,000
– managing director	36,000
– other salaries	25,300
Fees – managing director	3,000
– chairman	5,000
– finance director	2,000
– marketing director	2,000
– non-executive directors (two)	3,000
Directors' pension scheme contributions	5,900
Wages	3,600

	No.
Number of persons included above	18

	£
Social security costs (included in wages and salaries)	63,200

5. Fixed asset movements during the year, taken into account in the trial balance were:

	£
Acquisitions at cost	
Trademarks	Nil
Premises	Nil
Furniture and equipment	17,000
Vehicles	13,000
Investments – listed	30,000
– other	Nil
Sales and retirals at cost	
Trademarks	Nil
Premises	Nil
Furniture and equipment	13,000
Vehicles	8,000
Investments – listed	20,000
– other	Nil
Depreciation accumulated to date of sale or retiral	
Furniture	7,000
Vehicles	4,000

Profits and losses on sales and retirals of fixed assets were not material in amount and have been accounted for under the appropriate expense headings.

Market value of listed investments at 31st December 19–8 was:

	£
listed on London Stock Exchange	63,000
listed on an unrecognised stock exchange	28,000
Potential deferred taxation liability if listed investments were sold at market value	5,100

In no case did Mercator's holding exceed 10% of the allotted share capital or of any class of equity share capital.

6. The balance on ACT recoverable account comprises

		Dividend amount £	ACT fraction	Recoverable amount £
19–7	dividends paid in 19–7:			
	7% preference (see note 10)	14,000	3/7	6,000
19–7	dividends paid in 19–8:			
	ordinary	112,000	3/7	48,000
19–8	dividends paid in 19–8:			
	7% preference (see note 10)	7,000	3/7	3,000
				57,000

The balance on ACT payable account (£3,000) comprises the ACT payable on the 19–8 dividends paid in 19–8 on the 7% preference shares.

7. The directors have recommended a dividend of 9 pence per share on the ordinary shares. No entries have yet been made in the accounts either for the proposed dividend or for its associated ACT. General reserve is to be created by a transfer of £300,000.

8. Corporation tax on the 19–7 profits has now been agreed with the Inland Revenue at £103,300. Corporation tax of £177,000 should be provided on the 19–8 profits.

9. A provision should be raised for £100,000, the estimated legal costs and possible damages in a civil action which is pending against the company.

10. After the dividend had been paid in 19–7, 100,000 of the 200,000 7% preference shares then in issue were redeemed and replaced by an equivalent number of ordinary shares at par.

11. The provision for deferred taxation comprises accelerated capital allowances £57,500, other timing differences £43,472.

Required:

Prepare the profit and loss account of Mercator PLC for the year ended 31 December 19–8 and a balance sheet at that date in a form suitable for publication, so far as the necessary information is given.

SOLUTION

4.9 The solution which follows complies with the requirements of the Companies Act 1985 and with the applicable Statements of Standard Accounting Practice and, in so doing, is in a form suitable for publication.

Workings which are needed in building up certain figures, but which would not form part of the published accounts, are designated by a letter, thus, (a); notes, however, which form an integral part of the published accounts, are designated by a number, thus, (1), and are shown immediately after the balance sheet.

Mercator PLC
Profit and Loss Account
for the year ended 31 December 19–8

Note		£	£	Workings
1	Turnover		3,573,930	
	Cost of sales		2,281,830	(a)
	Gross profit		1,292,100	
	Distribution costs	355,700		(a)
	Administrative expenses	201,900		
			557,600	
2.3	Trading profit		734,500	
4	Income from other fixed asset investments		22,000	(b)
			756,500	
5	Interest payable and similar charges		9,600	(c)
1	Profit on ordinary activities before tax		746,900	
6	Tax on profit on ordinary activities		176,700	
	Profit on ordinary activities after tax		570,200	

314

7	Extraordinary charges		100,000	
	Tax (relief) on extraordinary charges		Nil	
			100,000	
	Profit for the financial year		470,200	
8	Dividends		151,000	
	Transfer to reserves		319,200	
9	EPS		35.2p	(d)

Mercator PLC
Balance Sheet
as at 31 December 19–8

	Fixed assets			
10	Intangible assets			
	Trademarks		40,000	
11	Tangible assets			
	Land and buildings	1,159,000		
	Plant and machinery	13,490		
	Fixtures, fittings, tools and equipment	27,150		
			1,199,640	
12	Investments			
	Other investments other than loans	154,000		
	Other loans	100,000		
			254,000	
				1,493,640
	Current assets			
	Stocks			
	Goods for resale		305,130	
	Debtors:			
	Trade debtors		400,600	
	Cash at bank and in hand		92,652	
			798,382	
	Creditors: amounts falling due within one year			
	Trade creditors	200,650		
13	Other creditors including taxation and social security	431,414		
			632,064	
	Net current assets			166,318
	Total assets less current liabilities			1,659,958
	Creditors: amounts falling due after more than one year			
14	Debenture loans		100,000	
	Provisions for liabilities and charges			(100,000)

16	Taxation including deferred taxation	39,258	
17	Other provisions	100,000	
			(139,258)
			1,420,700
18	Called up share capital		900,000
	Other reserves		
19	Other reserves		300,000
20	Profit and loss account		220,700
	Shareholders' funds		1,420,700

Notes to the accounts at 31 December 19–8

Accounting policies [the question does not give sufficient information for notes to be compiled under this heading].

1. Turnover

Turnover represents the invoiced amounts of goods sold net of value added tax (VAT). Turnover and profit on ordinary activities before tax is attributable to one activity only, namely the wholesale supply of automobile spare parts. An analysis of turnover by market is shown below.

£

United Kingdom	2,669,730
USA	904,200
	3,573,930

2. Trading profit

Trading profit is after charging:

£

Depreciation	55,400	(e)
Directors' remuneration:		
– for services as directors	15,000	(f)
– for other services (including pension contributions)	95,900	(g)
Auditors' remuneration	12,200	
Directors' remuneration (excluding pension contributions)		
Chairman	5,000	
Highest paid director	39,000	(h)

Other directors	No.	
£0 to £5,000	2	(h)
£25,001 to £30,000	2	(h)

3. Staff costs

£

Wages and salaries	283,300	(j)
Social security costs	63,200	
Other pension costs	5,900	
	352,400	

The average number of employees to which these figures relate:

	No.
Selling	23
Distribution	26
Administration and management	18
	67

4. **Investment Income**

	£	
from listed investments	11,000	(b)

5. **Interest payable**

	£	
On bank loans, overdrafts and other loans: repayable, other than by instalments, in full within 5 years	5,600	
On other loans	4,000	(c)

6. **Tax on profit on ordinary activities**

	£	
UK Corporation tax on profits for year at 35%	177,000	
Overprovision in 19–7	(5,100)	(k)
Tax credits on dividends received	4,800	(b)
	176,700	

7. **Extraordinary charges**

	£
Estimated legal costs and damages provided for impending civil action against the company	100,000

8. **Dividends**

	£	
7% preference paid	7,000	
Ordinary proposed	144,000	(l)
	151,000	

9. **EPS**

Earnings per share (35.2p) is based on earnings of £563,200 and on 1,600,000 ordinary shares of £0.50 per share in issue throughout the year and ranking for dividend	(d)

10. **Fixed assets – intangible assets**

£

Trademarks
– Cost

– at 1 January 19–8	40,000
– additions during year	Nil
– disposals during year	Nil
– at 31 December 19–8	40,000

Amortisation
 - at 1 January 19-8   Nil
 - provided during year   <u>Nil</u>
 - at 31 December 19-8   <u>Nil</u>

Net book value
 - at 1 January 19-8   40,000

 - at 31 December 19-8   40,000

11. Fixed assets – tangible assets

	Land and buildings (freehold)	Plant and machinery	Furniture fittings, equipment and tools	Total	Workings
	£	£	£	£	
Cost:					
- at 1 Jan 19-8	1,199,000	21,000	43,000	1,263,000	derived
- additions during year	–	13,000	17,000	30,000	
- disposals during year	–	(8,000)	(13,000)	(21,000)	
- at 31 Dec 19-8	1,199,000	26,000	47,000	1,272,000	
Depreciation					
- at 1 Jan 19-8	5,700	5,410	16,850	27,960	derived
- provided during year	34,300	11,100	10,000	55,400	
- disposals during year	–	(4,000)	(7,000)	(11,000)	
- at 31 Dec 19-8	40,000	12,510	19,850	72,360	
Net book value					
- at 1 Jan 19-8	1,193,300	15,590	26,150	1,235,040	derived
- at 31 Dec 19-8	1,159,000	13,490	27,150	1,199,640	

12. Fixed assets – investments

	£	
Cost - at 1 January 19-8	244,000	derived
- additions during year	30,000	
- disposals during year	(20,000)	
- at 31 December 19-8	254,000	

of which

	Cost	Market valuation
	£	£
- listed on a recognised stock exchange	54,000	63,000
- listed on an unrecognised stock exchange	20,000	28,000
Potential deferred taxation liability on capital gain if listed investments are sold at market valuation	5,100	

13. Other creditors (falling due within one year)

	£
Includes	
– Corporation tax on 19–7 profits	97,300 (m)
– Corporation tax on 19–8 profits	130,200 (o)
– Advance corporation tax payable	59,914 (n)
– Ordinary dividend proposed	144,000 (l)
	431,414

14. Debenture loans

Debenture loans are not wholly repayable within five years. They comprise an issue of £100,000 4% debentures secured on the company's freehold land and buildings and repayable at par at any time, at the company's option, between 1 January 19–0 and 31 December 19–5.

15. Other creditors (falling due after more than one year)

	£
Comprises Corporation tax payable 1 January 19– 0	130,200 (o)

16. Taxation including deferred taxation

	£
Comprises provision for deferred taxation analysed as follows:	
Accelerated capital allowances	57,500
Other timing differences	43,472
	100,972
Advance corporation tax recoverable	(61,714) (p)
	39,258

17. Other provisions

Comprises the provision for legal costs and damages dealt with in note 7.

18. Called up share capital

	Authorised		Issued and fully paid	
	No.	£	No.	£
7% preference shares of £1.00 per share	200,000	200,000	100,000	100,000
Ordinary shares of £0.50 per share	2,000,000	1,000,000	1,600,000	800,000
		1,200,000		900,000

19. Other reserves

	£
General reserve	
– at 1 January 19–8	Nil
– transfer from retained profit for the financial year	300,000
– at 31 December 19–8	300,000

20. Profit and loss account

	£
Profit and loss account	
– at 1 January 19–8	201,500
– retained profit for the year	319,200
– transferred to general reserve	(300,000)
– at 31 December 19–8	220,700

Workings

a. The accounting treatment of selling expenses is not specified in the Companies Act 1985. Until

319

the matter has been resolved by case law or by an amendment to the Act, the treatment will be a matter of conjecture and different companies will accord different treatments.

There appear to be two alternative treatments:

  i. to include selling expenses as part of the cost of sales figure.

  ii. to include selling expenses as part of the distribution costs figure (on the basis that this is intended to cover both selling and distribution costs).

     In this solution, alternative (ii) has been adopted.

b.

	£	£
Income from other fixed asset investments		
Dividends received		
– from listed investments in UK		
companies, per trial balance	7,700	
– tax credits [3/7 × 7,700]	3,300	
		11,000
– from unlisted investments in UK		
companies, per trial balance	3,500	
– tax credits [3/7 × 3,500]	1,500	
		5,000
Interest received		
– from unlisted investments	4,200	
– income tax suffered at source		
[3/7 × 4,200]	1,800	
		6,000
Per profit and loss account		22,000

c.

	£
Debenture interest paid, per trial balance	2,800
Income tax witheld [3/7 × 2,800]	1,200
	4,000
Bank overdraft interest	5,600
Per profit and loss account	9,600

d.

	£
Profit on ordinary activities after tax	570,200
less preference dividends	7,000
Earnings	563,200
Earnings per share $\left[\dfrac{563,200 \times 100}{1,600,000}\right]$	35.2p

e.

	£
Depreciation included in 4.8 note 4 as	
– distribution cost	36,100
– selling cost	14,000

– administration expense		5,300
– per 4.9 note 2		<u>55,400</u>

f.

	£
Fees per 4.8 note 4 (administration) (in total)	15,000

g.

	£
Salaries etc. per 4.8 note 4	
Salaries of Directors	
– marketing	27,000
– finance	27,000
– managing	36,000
Directors' pension scheme contributions	5,900
Per 4.9 note 2	<u>95,900</u>

h.

	Fees £	Salary £	Total £
Managing director	3,000	36,000	39,000
£25,001 to £30,000			
– finance director	2,000	27,000	29,000
– marketing director	2,000	27,000	29,000

j.

			£
Directors' fees per workings (f)			15,000
Directors' salaries etc. per workings (g)			95,900
Distribution	– wages per 4.8 note 4		85,700
	– salaries per 4.8 note 4		9,100
Selling	– wages per 4.8 note 4		4,600
	– salaries per 4.8 note 4		76,200
Administration	– salaries per 4.8 note 4		
	– staff manager		16,000
	– company secretary		21,000
	– others		25,300
	– wages per 4.8 note 4		3,600
			352,400
less, included above Other pension costs (directors' pension scheme contributions)			5,900
			346,500
Social security costs per 4.8 note 4			<u>63,200</u>
Wages and salaries per 4.9 note 3			<u>283,300</u>

k.

	£
Provision for Corporation tax on 19–7 profits	
– per trial balance	108,400
– per 4.8 note 8	<u>103,300</u>
– overprovision per 4.9 note 6	(5,100)

l.

		£
		Per 4.8 note 7
$\dfrac{800,000 \times 0.09}{0.50}$		144,000

m.

	£
Corporation tax on 19–7 profits per 4.8 note 8	103,300
Advance corporation tax recoverable on 19–7 dividends paid in 19–7 per 4.8 note 6	(6,000)
Per 4.9 note 13 (Mainstream corporation tax)	97,300

n.

	£
ACT payable per trial balance	3,000
ACT payable on ordinary dividends proposed $(3/7 \times 144,000)$	61,714
	64,714
Tax credits deductible per 4.9 workings (b) $(3,300 + 1,500)$	(4,800)
Per 4.9 note 13	59,914

o.

	£	£
Corporation tax on 19–8 profits per 4.8 note 8		177,000
ACT recoverable on 19–7 and 19–8 dividends paid in 19–8 per 4.8 note b. $(48,000 + 3,000)$	(51,000)	
Restriction for tax credits utilised in 4.9 workings (n)	4,800	
		(46,200)
		130,800
less		
Income tax suffered at source per 4.9 workings (b)	(1,800)	
Income tax withheld per 4.9 workings (c)	1,200	
		(600)
Per 4.9 note 15		130,200

p.

	£
ACT recoverable is equivalent to ACT payable in 4.9 workings (n)	61,714

The 1989 Annual Report and Accounts of B P P Holdings PLC is reproduced in Appendix II.

You should now refer to this to see how this well–known company has produced its accounts for publication.

STATEMENTS OF SOURCE AND APPLICATION OF FUNDS

5.0 Almost every company is obliged to include a statement of this sort in its Annual Report and Accounts. This is because the turnover/gross income threshold which triggers the SSAP 10 requirements is set at the low figure of £25,000.

5.1 The preparation and presentation of statements of source and application of funds is dealt with in Section IV Chapter 2 Cash Flow and Funds Flow Analysis, to which reference should be made.

DIRECTORS REPORT

6.0 Another of the essential contents of a company's Annual Report and Accounts is the Directors' Report. It is unlikely that Paper 2.9 would require such a report to be written but it could examine your knowledge of the contents of, and your familiarity with, Director's Reports.

6.1 The legal disclosure requirements are listed in Appendix I and a good example of an actual report is given in Appendix II of this manual.

STUDENT SELF TESTING

Test Exercises

1. SSAP 2 – Disclosure of accounting policies

    a. What are accounting bases?

    b. What are accounting policies?

    c. What are accounting concepts?

    d. Which four concepts are regarded as basic working assumptions?

    e. How must policies be disclosed?

2. SSAP 3 – Earnings per share

    a. Define EPS for a company which is not part of a group.

    b. What is the net basis of calculation?

    c. What is the nil basis of calculation?

    d. Which of these two bases is the standard practice?

    e. When a company pays arrears of preference dividend should these be deducted in arriving at earnings?

    f. On what basis is the number of shares used as the divisor calculated

        i. when there is an issue of shares during the year?

        ii. when a company has convertible loan stock in issue?

3. SSAP 4 – Accounting for government grants

    a. What is the acceptable method of crediting grants to revenue?

    b. How should any balance of grant not yet credited appear in the balance sheet?

4. SSAP 5 – Accounting for VAT

    a. How should input tax for exempt businesses, exempt activities and on non–deductible inputs be treated?

    b. On what basis should turnover be disclosed?

5. SSAP 6 – Extraordinary items and prior year adjustments

    a. Distinguish between
    Exceptional items
    Extraordinary items
    Prior year items
    Prior year adjustments

    b. Give examples of items for each of these classes.

    c. State the accounting treatment in the profit and loss account for each of these classes.

    d. What is the effect on earnings and its derivatives (EPS, earnings yield, P/E ratio) of each of these classes of item?

6. SSAP 8 – Treatment of taxation under the imputation system in the accounts of companies

    a. How are dividends received treated in the profit and loss account?

    b. How are dividends paid and/or proposed dealt with in the profit and loss account?

    c. What is the reason for this treatment?

   d. How is ACT payable shown in the balance sheet?

   e. How is ACT recouped?

   f. How is ACT recoverable shown in the balance sheet

      i. when the dividend (eg an interim dividend) has been paid before the year–end?

     ii. when the dividend has been proposed but not yet paid at the year–end?

   g. What is the correct treatment in the profit and loss account for unrelieved irrecoverable ACT?

7. SSAP 9 – Stocks and Long–term contracts

   a. On what basis should stock and w–i–p (excluding long term contract w–i–p) be valued?

   b. In the stock valuation context, what does "cost" mean?

   c. What comprises "cost"?

   d. What comprises net realisable value?

   e. On what basis should long term contract work be valued?

   f. What overheads should be allotted to the cost of long term contract w–i–p?

   g. For the purposes of this allotment, what level of activity should be assumed?

   h. How is the figure for attributable profit arrived at?

8. SSAP 10 – Statements of source and application of funds

   a. To what category of enterprise is this SSAP applicable?

   b. What is the objective of these statements?

   c. How do they achieve their objective?

   d. For which other accounting statements does it provide a link?

   e. Is the netting off of, say, acquisitions and disposals of fixed assets, permitted?

   f. Which items should be shown separately?

9. SSAP 12 – Accounting for depreciation

   a. If the useful life of an asset is discovered to be different from that originally estimated, how should the unamortised cost be written off?

   b. Where obsolescence has occurred, what should the accounting treatment be?

   c. If there is a change in method of providing for depreciation, how must the unamortised cost be written off?

   d. Do any of the three preceding circumstances constitute a prior year adjustment?

   e. Under what circumstances can depreciation constitute a prior year adjustment?

   f. What are the main disclosure requirements of SSAP 12?

10. SSAP 13 – Accounting for Research and Development

   a. How does the standard define

      i. pure research?

     ii. applied research?

    iii. development?

   b. What is the correct accounting treatment for expenditure on

      i. pure research?

     ii. applied research?

   c. For what reasons has this accounting treatment been stipulated?

   d. What is the correct accounting treatment for expenditure on development work?

   e. What conditions must be satisfied before development expenditure can be suspended?

   f. How is the suspended expenditure amortised?

   g. What is the correct accounting treatment for depreciation of fixed assets used for development work?

h. What research and development work is outside the scope of the standard?

i. What are the disclosure requirements of SSAP 13?

11. SSAP 15 – Accounting for deferred taxation

   a. Which key figures on a profit and loss account may be affected by deferred taxation provisions?

   b. Which main derivative figures are also affected?

   c. What purpose is served by raising a provision for deferred taxation?

   d. What does "permanent difference" mean?

   e. What does "timing difference" mean?

   f. What are originating timing differences?

   g. What are reversing timing differences?

   h. With which types of timing difference does this SSAP deal?

   i. On what criteria is a business absolved from providing for deferred taxation?

   j. What is the specific accounting treatment for:

      i. short term timing differences?

      ii. differences due to utilisation of capital allowances?

      iii. asset revaluation surpluses?

      iv. asset disposal surpluses?

   k. Which deferred taxation adjustments appear under the heading "Taxation" in the profit and loss account?

   l. By which method are deferred taxation transfers calculated?

   m. How does this method operate?

   n. On the introduction of this standard, how was the adjustment of opening balance of deferred taxation account dealt with?

   o. How is deferred taxation disclosed in the balance sheet?

12. SSAP 17 – Accounting for post balance sheet events

   a. What is a post balance sheet event, as defined by the standard?

   b. Which financial statements are covered by this standard?

   c. What are adjusting events and what is their effect?

   d. Give examples of adjusting events.

   e. What other events are treated as though they are adjusting events?

   f. What are non–adjusting events and what is their effect?

   g. Give examples of non–adjusting events.

   h. What other events are treated as though they are non–adjusting events?

   i. What must the notes on non–adjusting events disclose?

   j. What other disclosure(s) must be made?

13. SSAP 18 – Accounting for contingencies

   a. What is a contingency as defined by SSAP 18?

   b. What does the term "contingency" exclude?

   c. To what financial items to contingencies give rise?

   d. What financial statements are covered by this standard?

   e. What is the accounting treatment for contingent losses of material amount?

   f. What is the accounting treatment for contingent gains of material amounts?

   g. What are the disclosure requirements for each disclosable contingency?

14. a. Differentiate between:

    i. basic earnings per share; and

    ii. fully diluted earnings per share.

    b. From the information given below, calculate for B Ltd the earnings per share in respect of both i. and ii. above for year ended 30th September 19–8.

       If required, you are to assume corporation tax rate at 50% and all previous share conversions to have taken place on 1st October 19–7.

       (The information referred to above was, at 30th September 19–8.

	£000
Ordinary share capital (£0.25 per share)	123
8% Convertible Loan Stock	95
(convertible at 3 ordinary shares per £1.75 nominal value)	
Profit after tax (before extraordinary items)	48

       There were no preference shares in issue).

15. SSAP 19 – Accounting for investment properties

    a. How does the standard define an investment property?

    b. What property is specifically excluded from the definition?

    c. On what basis should investment properties be depreciated?

    d. At what figure should investment properties be included in the balance sheet.

    e. What is the accounting treatment for revaluation surpluses/deficits?

    f. What disclosure requirements apply in the case of investment properties?

16. After all the year end adjustments had been posted, the trial balance of Chaucer Enterprises PLC included the following balances at 31 December 19–4.

	Dr. £	Cr. £
Cost of sales	2,281,830	
Distribution costs	235,700	
Sales		3,273,930
Dividends received from trade investments (including tax credits)		22,000
Tax credits on dividends received	4,800	
Extraordinary loss	100,000	
Corporation tax – current year charge	177,000	
– previous year adjustment		5,100
Bank overdraft interest	5,600	
Administration expenses	285,900	
7% preference dividend (paid)	7,000	
Ordinary dividend (proposed)	144,000	

Required:

Prepare the profit and loss account of Chaucer Enterprises PLC for year ended 31 December 19–4 using Format 1.

17. The facts are the same as in 16 and these further balances were included.

	Dr. £	Cr. £
Creditors currently due		
– trade		196,400
– mainstream corporation tax		99,852
– advance corporation tax payable		59,914

– proposed dividends		144,000
– Other creditors		1,140
Accruals currently due		610
Land and buildings (net)	799,000	
Trade investments		
– shares	198,000	
– loans	56,000	
Deferred taxation		100,972
Advance corporation tax recoverable		
(on proposed dividends)	61,714	
Plant and machinery (net)	13,490	
Fixtures and fittings (net)	27,150	
Provision for extraordinary loss		100,000
Creditors not currently due		
– trade		2,500
– mainstream corporation tax		123,036
Stocks		
– consumables	2,700	
– goods for resale	302,430	
Ordinary share capital		800,000
Debtors currently due		
– trade	436,400	
– other	3,450	
Prepayments	750	
7% preference share capital		100,000
Profit and loss account		260,700
Bank balance	88,040	

Required:
Prepare the balance sheet of Chaucer Enterprises PLC as at 31 December 19–4, using Format 1.

18. The facts are the same as in 16. Total expenses comprises

	£
Cost of sales	2,281,830
Distribution costs	235,700
Administrative expenses	285,900
	2,803,430

This figure represents

	£
Decrease in work–in–progress and in stocks of finished goods	108,200
Usage of raw materials etc.	2,096,010
Depreciation	55,400
Staff costs	431,520
Other costs	112,300
	2,803,430

Required:
Prepare the profit and loss account of Chaucer Enterprises PLC for year ended 31 December 19–4 using Format 2.

19. After all the year end adjustments had been posted, the trial balance of Alexah PLC included the following balances at 31 December 19–5.

	Dr. £	Cr. £
Administrative expenses	241,100	
Cost of sales	1,542,100	

Sales		2,305,700
Distribution costs	207,300	
Investment grant (released)		22,800
Bank overdraft interest	18,700	
Proposed dividends	87,000	
Extraordinary income		94,600
Corporation tax		
– current year charge (on ordinary items)	130,000	
– previous year adjustment	12,700	
– current year charge (on extraordinary		
items)	28,200	

Required:

Prepare the profit and loss account of Alexah PLC for year ended 31 December 19–5 using Format 1.

20. The facts are the same as in 19. Total costs comprise:

	£
Cost of sales	1,542,100
Distribution costs	207,300
Administrative expenses	241,100
	1,990,500

This figure represents:

	£
Increase in stocks of finished goods and	
in work–in–progress	(36,700)
Raw materials and consumables used	1,520,100
Staff costs	392,100
Own work capitalised	(53,000)
Other operating charges	79,600
Depreciation	88,400
	1,990,500

Required:

Prepare the profit and loss account of Alexah PLC for year ended 31 December 19-5, using Format 2.

21. The facts are the same as in 19 and 20 and these further balances were included

	Dr.	Cr.
	£	£
Stocks		
– raw materials etc.	167,300	
– work–in–progress	25,600	
– finished goods and goods for resale	50,800	
Creditors currently due		
– proposed dividends		87,000
– trade		117,200
– mainstream corporation tax and		
ACT payable		118,400
Advance corporation tax recoverable (on		
proposed dividends)	37,300	
Land and buildings	98,000	
Pland and machinery	304,000	
Fixtures, fittings etc.	172,700	
Cash etc.	68,900	
Creditors not currently due		
– mainstream corporation tax		124,600

Ordinary shares of £1.00 per share		300,000
Debtors currently due		
– trade	152,400	
– other	1,500	
Profit and loss account		207,400
General reserve		62,400
Share premium account		18,500
Investment grant suspense		43,000

Required:

Prepare the balance sheet of Alexah PLC as at 31 December 19–5, using Format 1.

22. The following balances appeared in the books of Cellers PLC on 31 July 19–4, after being rounded to the nearest thousand pounds. The company's business was wholesaling electronic components.

	£000
Stock of goods for resale on 1 August 19–3	2,823
Purchases (net)	9,012
Sales (net)	15,832
Wages	847
Salaries	375
Social security costs	128
Directors' fees	24
Directors' salaries	97
Rentals received from subletting warehouse	127
Interest received on unlisted investments (gross)	35
Interest paid on short–term bank loans/overdrafts	30
Interest paid on 5% unsecured loan stock (gross)	25
Uninsured fire losses	176
Proposed ordinary dividend	700
Other selling and distribution costs	1,150
Other administrative expenses	395
Auditors fees and expenses	37
Directors' pension scheme contributions	18
Depreciation charge for year	904

Notes:

Other information at 31 July 19–4:

1. The average number of persons employed (including directors) was

	Number
Warehousing and distribution	161
Marketing	13
Management and administration	82

2.

	£000
Total taxation charge for the current year after accounting for	1,160
i. tax relief on extraordinary loss	62
ii. underprovision in previous year	85

3.

	£000
Stock of goods for resale on 31 July 19–4	3,754

4.

	£000
Turnover included exports to Europe	4,274

5.   £000

    Issued share capital comprised ordinary shares of £0.50
      per share (after bonus issue)   4,820

6.   £000

    Depreciation charged for the year had been provided on:
      – land and buildings   40
      – plant and machinery   495
      – fixtures and fittings etc.   369
                                         904

7. Various items appearing in the list of balances were analysed as follows:

	Selling and distribution	Administration	Total
	£000	£000	£000
Wages	826	21	847
Salaries	75	300	375
Directors' fees	–	24	24
Directors' salaries	19	78	97
Directors' pension scheme contributions	2	16	18
Social security costs	107	21	128
Depreciation	730	174	904

8. Corporation tax rate is 35% basic rate of income tax is 30% and ACT fraction is 3/7.
Required:
Prepare the profit and loss account for Cellars PLC for the year ended 31 July 19–4 in a form suitable for publication, so far as the information given permits.

23. The following balances appeared in the books of May–Kitt PLC at 30 June 19–4.

	£000
Stocks–work in progress	1,258
– finished goods	1,105
– raw materials and consumables	1,281
Sales (net)	7,347
Rent received from sub–letting storage space	17
Raw materials – purchases (net)	2,862
– external charges	18
Wages and salaries	906
Social security costs	84
Pension costs	28
Own work capitalised	25
Depreciation charged for year	
– buildings	41
– plant and machinery	594
– fixtures, fittings etc.	325
Rent, rates and insurance	390
Power, heat and light	674
General expenses	266
Audit fees and expenses	32
Sundry expenses	65
Franked investment income received on other fixed asset investments (listed)	80
Interest received on fixed asset investments (gross) (unlisted)	60
Interest paid on bank overdraft	20

Profit on sale of surplus plant	361
Rationalisation costs	217
Ordinary dividend proposed	637

Other information at 30 June 19–4

	£000
1. Stocks at 1 July 19–3	
– work in progress	978
– finished goods	1,153
– raw materials and consumables	1,080

	£000
2. Corporation tax	
– on total profit for the year	340
– liability on extraordinary items included above	45
– previous year underprovision	10

3. Share capital comprised

	Authorised	Issued
	£000	£000
Ordinary shares of £1.00 per share	10,000	6,300

4. The average number of persons employed (including directors) was

	Number
Manufacturing	64
Managerial and administrative	18

5. Directors received the following emoluments

	Fees	Salary	Pension Scheme contributions
	£000	£000	£000
Chairman	10	–	–
Other directors			
– managing	8	26	2
– production	7	16	1
– finance	7	14	1
– personnel and administration	7	12	1
	39	68	5

6. Turnover was derived from the sale of machine tools in the following areas:

	£000
UK	4,628
USA	932
Australasia	1,787
	7,347

7. Corporation tax rate is 35% and basic rate of income tax is 30%.

Required:

Prepare the profit and loss account for May–Kitt PLC for the year ended 30 June 19–4 in a form suitable for publication, so far as the information given permits.

24. In addition to the balance and information given in 22 concerning Cellers PLC, the following further information is available regarding this company.

1. Fixed assets

	Cost at 1 August 19–3 £000	Transactions during year	
		Additions £000	Disposals £000
Goodwill	171	–	–
Land and buildings (freehold)	2,384	–	–
Plant and machinery	2,034	839	121
Fixtures, fittings etc.	2,242	497	79
Unlisted investments – other loans	340	–	–

	Depreciation at 1 Aug 19–3 £000	Depreciation on disposals during year £000
Land and buildings	371	–
Plant and machinery	1,107	63
Fixtures, fittings etc.	926	55

2. Balances at 31 July 19–4

	£000
Debtors (trade) due within 1 year	2,678
Bank and cash	1,005
Creditors due within 1 year	
Trade creditors	2,987
Other creditors	141
Bank loans and overdrafts	141
Mainstream corporation tax based on agreed assessment	923
Creditors due after 1 year	
5% Unsecured loan stock 19–2/19–8	500
Bank loans and overdrafts	68
Other creditors	144
Advance corporation tax recoverable (in respect of dividends proposed at 31 July 19–3)	240
Provision for major repairs to buildings	390
Share premium account	90

3. Profit and Loss account balance at 1 August 19– 3   271

Transfers
– on 1 August 19–3 to capital redemption reserve   210
– on 31 July 19–4 to general reserve   200
Bonus issue of 2,600,000 ordinary shares of £0.50 per share on 31 July 19–4   1,300

4. Authorised share capital comprised:

500,000 7% preference shares of £1.00 per share	500
12,000,000 ordinary shares of £0.50 per share	6,000

Required:

Prepare the balance sheet of Cellers PLC at 31 July 19–4 in a form suitable for publication, so far as the information given permits.

25. In addition to the balances and information given in 23 concerning May–Kitt PLC, the following further information is available regarding this company.

1. Fixed assets

	Cost at 1 July 19–3 £000	Transactions during year	
		Additions £000	Disposals £000
Goodwill	50	–	–

Land and buildings (freehold)	1,546	–	–
Plant and machinery	6,337	853	302
Fixtures, fittings etc.	4,100	478	125
Investments in shares listed on a recognised UK stock exchange	202	35	–
Investment in loans (unlisted)	284	35	–

	Depreciation at 1 July 19–3	Depreciation on disposals during year
	£000	£000
Buildings	229	–
Plant and machinery	4,808	267
Fixtures, fittings etc.	3,116	91

2. Balances at 30 June 19–4

	£000
Cash at bank and in hand	921
Trade debtors due within 1 year	1,356
Other debtors due within 1 year	9
Creditors due for payment before 30 June 19–5	
– Trade creditors	1,285
– Bills of exchange payable	10
– Mainstream corporation tax (based on agreed assessment)	308
– Other creditors	206
Creditors due for payment after 1 July 19–5	
– 6% Debentures 20–6/20–9 (issued 30 June 19–4)	555
– Other creditors	68
Provision for deferred taxation	
– short–term timing differences	68
– accelerated capital allowances	236
Advance corporation tax recoverable (on dividends proposed at 30 June 19–3)	241
General reserve	50
Profit and loss account	74

3.	Market value of listed investments at 30 June 19–4	297
	Potential capital gains tax liability	18

Required:

Prepare the balance sheet of May–Kitt PLC as at 30 June 19–4 in a form suitable for publication, so far as the information given permits.

26. "Events arising after the balance sheet date need to be reflected in financial statement if they provide additional evidence of conditions that existed at the balance sheet date and materially affect the amounts to be included"

Extract from SSAP 17 Accounting for post balance sheet events.

Required:

Answer the following questions on SSAP 17:

a. In the context of the standard, what is a post balance sheet event?

b. What is meant by the terms

  i. adjusting event?

  ii. non–adjusting event?

c. To what extent, if any, are items classed under b.i. and b.ii. reflected in final accounts?

d. State, with reasons, whether the following unconnected circumstances should normally be classed as adjusting or non–adjusting events in the final accounts of the company whose year ended on 30 June 19–6. Approval of the accounts occurred on 26 September 19–6.

  i. the company contracted to buy additional premises for £200,000 on 3 September 19–6.

  ii. the company contracted to buy another business, as part of a rationalisation scheme, for £500,000 on 1 October 19–6.

  iii. a Finance Bill published on 12 September 19–6 reduced the rate of Corporation Tax (retrospectively) by 10%.

  iv. on 28th August 19–6 the company's auditors discovered that closing stock at 30 June 19–6 had been undervalued by £250,000.

  v. on 21 September 19–6 a writ was served on the company by the legal representatives of an employee who had been seriously injured whilst at work in January 19–6. An estimate of legal costs and probable damages payable in the event of the plaintiff's claim succeeding, is £120,000.

27. SSAP 18 (Accounting for contingencies) has now been in operation since 1980.
Required:
a. State the scope and coverage of the above Standard.
b. Explain the meaning which the Standard applies to the term "contingency".
c. Distinguish between the standard accounting treatment of contingent gains and contingent losses.
d. State the disclosure requirements relating to contingencies.
e. State, with reasons, how you would deal with each of the following circumstances in the final accounts of a limited company. (You may assume that the amounts stated are material).

  i. The company held maturing bills of exchange receivable £752,400. In addition it had received £861,700 (net of discount) from its bankers for bills receivable discounted.

  ii. As part of a rationalisation scheme, the company has vacated one of its depots which will be advertised for sale in the near future. A letter has been received from another company indicating that it might be interested in acquiring this depot and has tentatively suggested a price which, if accepted, would result in a profit on sale of about £600,000.

  iii. An overseas customer has indicated that he is to sue the company for losses sustained by the supply to him of goods which he alleges were of unmerchantable quality. The full amount of the claim, if successful, would cost the company about £900,000 (including legal costs). the company would counter–claim against its overseas agent alleging negligence in storing the goods whilst awaiting delivery to the customer. The net amount receivable if this action should succeed would be about £500,000.

28. Qwik–Freez (East Anglia) p.l.c. is a company which provides refrigerated storage facilities to local farmers.

Services offered include the collection of produce, the use of rapid freezing equipment, storage of the frozen produce and transport from frozen storage in refrigerated vehicles to any point within the country. Orders for these services are secured by the company's sales staff.

The company's revenue consists of charges for transport and freezing, and of storage rentals. Customers may hire storage space either on a long–term contract basis at advantageous charges (payable in advance) or on a casual basis (invoiced monthly).

A considerable amount of electricity from the public supply is used by the company in the freezing and storage operations. In the event of a sudden failure in this supply, the company is able to generate its own emergency supplies from standby generators kept for this purpose. An insurance policy has been taken out to protect the company against the claims which would arise should any of the frozen produce deteriorate as the result of power or equipment failure.

At the end of the company's financial year ended 30 September 19–2, the assistant accountant extracted the following balances from the ledgers.

Asset Accounts	£
Land and buildings (at cost)	390,000
Plant (at cost)	271,900
Vehicles (at cost)	82,600

Provision for depreciation (at 1 October 19–1):

Land and buildings	39,600
Plant	144,800
Vehicles	27,050

Stock of consumable stores (at 30 September 19–2):	23,449
Debtors –for rentals	18,204
– for charges	2,332
Bank	30,710
Cash	1,103

Liability Accounts

Trade Creditors	7,390
7% Debentures 20–4/20–2	80,000
Ordinary Share Capital (*see note 7*)	200,000
General reserve	25,000
Unappropriated profit (at 1 October 19–1)	108,284
Share Premium	15,000

Revenue Accounts

Storage rentals –long term contracts	302,090
– casual	85,063
Freezing charges	112,810
Transport charges	90,107

Expense Accounts

Wages, salaries and related expense	128,004
Rates	79,112
Electricity	76,860
Transport costs	43,271
Repairs	30,319
Consumable stores	29,800
Postages, stationery, telephones	15,604
Insurance premiums	7,800
Debenture interest	5,600
Sundries	9,176

Other Accounts

Suspense (credit balance)	8,650

Notes at 30 September 19–2

1. At the beginning of the 19–1/–2 financial year, the company had sold refrigeration plant (which had originally cost £26,000 and on which £20,800 had been provided as depreciation to date of disposal) for £4,000. The only accounting entries relative to this disposal which have been made so far, are a debit to Bank and a credit to Suspense of the amount of the sale proceeds.

2. In April 19–2, the compressor unit in No.7 storage unit failed and as a consequence the contents deteriorated to such an extent that they had to be disposed of by incineration. Compensation of £1,350 was paid to the farmer by Qwik–Freez by cheque and debited to Suspense. The insurance company has admitted liability under the policy but no further ledger entries have as yet been made.

3. During the 19–1/–2 financial year, the company replaced one of its refrigerated vehicles, which had originally cost £16,400 and on which £13,120 had been provided as depreciation to date of disposal. A trade–in (part exchange) allowance of £6,000 was granted in respect of this vehicle. A replacement vehicle was acquired at a list price of £27,000. The entries relating to the disposal of the old vehicle have not yet been made, except that the trade–in allowance has been debited to Vehicles and credited to Suspense. The balance of the price of the new vehicles has been paid by cheque and debited to Vehicles account.

4. It is the company's policy to provide for depreciation on a straight line basis calculated on the cost of fixed assets held at the end of each financial year and assuming no residual value. Annual depreciation

335

rates are:

	%
Buildings	2
Plant	10
Vehicles	25

The 'Buildings' content of the item Land and Buildings included in asset account balances is £120,000.

5. Adjustments, not yet posted to accounts, should be made for the following items:

£

Storage rentals received in advance	25,631
Insurance premium prepaid	600
Wages and Salaries accrued	1,920
Rates prepaid	28,820
Electricity accrued	5,757

6. Consumable stores include £4,131 and Repairs include £9,972 relating to vehicles.

7. The authorised and issued capital of the company consists of 400,000 Ordinary Shares of £0.50 per share. The directors have recommended a dividend for the year of £0.12 per share.

Required:

a. **Prepare, for internal circulation purposes, a Profit and Loss account for Qwik–Freez (East Anglia) p.l.c. for the year ended 30 September 19–2 and a Balance Sheet at that date. All workings must be shown.**

b. **Open the Suspense account and post the entries needed to eliminate the opening credit balance.**

29. Artic Haulage PLC is a general transport company. As an extra service to its customers, it provides storage facilities which can be hired on a semi–permanent basis under contract or casually as required.

At 31 December 19–5, the company's ledger included the following list of balances:

£

Assets	Premises (see note (5))	675,300
	Vehicles	1,141,700
	Plant and equipment	203,200
	Stock (closing) of repair materials, fuel oil, etc	154,031
	Trade debtors – storage	15,503
	– haulage	131,480
	Bank	42,356
	Cash	7,063
Liabilities		
	Provisions for depreciation at 1 January 19–5	
	– premises	117,800
	– vehicles	472,400
	– plant and equipment	51,100
	Trade creditors (see note (1))	125,607
	9% debentures 20–1/20–7	50,000
	Ordinary share capital (see notes (3) and (4))	800,000
	6% preference share capital (see note (4))	50,000
	General reserve	40,000
	Profit and loss account at 1 January 19–5	46,823
	Share premium	5,000
Revenues		
	Storage rentals – long term contracts	151,260
	– casual	29,752
	Haulage charges	1,734,611
Expenses		
	Wages, salaries and related charges (see note (5))	581,826
	Rates	62,500
	Power, heat and light	86,330

336

Repairs – vehicles	91,413
– other (see note(5)	156,494
Diesel oil, etc.	179,809
Postages, stationery, telephones	25,605
Insurance	21,480
Debenture interest	4,500
Sundry expenses	11,273
Other	
Suspense account (debit balance)	
(see notes(1),(2) and (3)	82,490

Notes at 31 December 19–5

1. In September 19–5, a consignment of perishable goods was delayed in transit due to the negligence of the transport manager. As a result, the entire consignment deteriorated to such an extent that it had to be destroyed on arrival at its destination.

   The total cost of this loss, which has been assessed at £84,680, has been claimed from the company by the consignor and has been debited to suspense account and temporarily credited to Trade Creditors prior to being settled *in contra* at 31 December 19–5. The claim is not covered by the company's insurance policy.

2. In October 19–5, one of the vehicles was seriously damaged in an accident. Repairs costing £37,810 were carried out in the company's own vehicle workshops. The cost has been held in suspense account pending the outcome of the claim under the insurance policy. This has now been agreed in full.

3. On 1 September 19–5, the company had declared a 1 for 20 bonus issue of ordinary shares (which do not rank for dividend until 19–6). The amount involved has been appropriated out of general reserve and credited to suspense account.

4. The issued share capital consists of 6% preference shares of £1.00 per share and ordinary shares of £0.50 per share. The directors have recommended payment of the preference dividend and an ordinary dividend of £0.075 per share.

5. During 19–5, the company had extended one of its warehouses and used its own labour and materials in the construction. The amounts expended are included in the above list under wages (£52,000) and repairs – other (£148,000).

6. Depreciation is provided on a straight line basis on the cost of fixed assets held at the end of each financial year and assuming no residual value.

   Assumed asset lives are:

Premises	50 years
Vehicles	5 years
Plant	8 years

7. The company's liability for corporation tax for the year 19–5 has been estimated at £90,000.

8. Adjustments, not yet posted to the accounts, should be made for:

	£
Storage rentals (long–term contracts) prepaid	13,644
Power charges accrued	5,005
Telephone rentals prepaid	207
Telephone calls accrued	548
Rates prepaid	16,730
Wages accrued	10,834
Insurance prepaid	1,747

   Required:

   a. **Open the suspense account and post the entries needed to eliminate the opening debit balance.**

   b. **Prepare, for internal circulation purposes, the profit and loss account for Artic Haulage PLC for year ended 31 December 19–5 and a balance sheet at that date.**

   Note: Marks will be awarded for workings which are an essential part of the anwers

   30. After all the year–end adjustments had been posted, the following balances were, amongst others, included in the trial balance as at 30 June 19–5 of Moulders plc.

	£
Closing stocks of: finished goods	2,081,400
work–in–progress	1,454,300
Raw materials and consumables used	5,361,000
Staff costs	583,400
Depreciation – provision for the year	349,200
Own work capitalised	61,200
Other operating charges	84,400
Sales	6,383,200
Corporation tax: current year charge including tax benefit (£44,000) of extraordinary loss	185,400
Royalties received (gross)	30,000
Proposed dividends	126,000
Extraordinary loss (before tax adjustment)	157,600
Bank overdraft interest	24,000

NOTES

(i) Included in the above figures were:

Distribution costs	380,600
Administrative expenses	167,200
Cost of sales	to be derived

(ii) Opening stocks had been:

of finished goods	1,296,700
of work in progress	1,476,400

Required

Prepare the published profit and loss account of Moulders plc for year ended 30 June 19–5, separately

a) using Format 1

b) using Format 2

The accompanying notes are not required.

31. After the proft and loss account of Estin PLC had been prepared for year ended 30 June 19–5, the following further information was available:

Balances at 1 July 19–4	£000
Profit and loss	126
Share premium account	12
Debenture redemption reserve	40
General reserve	66
Fixed assets (at cost)	
Land and buildings (freehold)	431
Plant and machinery	1,265
Investments	
: in shares listed on a recognised UK stock exchange	144
: in loans	33
Provision for depreciation	
: premises	38
: plant and machinery	551

Balance at 30 June 19–5	£000
ACT recoverable (on final dividends proposed)	120
ACT recoverable (on interim dividends paid 28 March 19–5)	24
ACT payable (on final dividends proposed)	120

Income tax (net amount recoverable)	
(debit balance)	16
Trade debtors	242
Bank and cash	136
Final dividends proposed	280

Creditors due for payment before 30 June 19–6

Trade creditors	359
Mainstream corporation tax (on previous	
year's profits)	87
Other creditors	30

Creditors due for payment after 1 July 19–6

8% Debentures 20–0/20–6	260
Corporation tax (on current year's profits)	275
Stocks	604
Ordinary share capital, authorised and paid up	750
(shares of £0.25 per share)	

Other information

Fixed asset movements

Additions during current year	£000
	Cost
: Land and buildings	52
: Plant and machinery	240

Disposals during current year	£000	£000
	Cost	Accumulated Depreciation
: Plant and machinery	73	34
: investments (shares)	28	–

Depreciation charge for current year	£
: Premises	9
: Plant and machinery	180

Listed investments at 30 June 19–5	
: market value	156
: potential capital gains tax liability	12

Retained profit for current year	57

Required:

Prepare the balance sheet of Estin PLC as at 30 June 19–5, <u>including such notes as are necessary</u>, in a form suitable for publication.

ACCA EXAMINATION QUESTIONS

32. Required:

a. Prepare for the Brighton Metal Company a forecast Profit and Loss account for the year ended 30 June 1983 and a Balance Sheet as at that date, both statements to comply as far as possible with the Companies Acts 1948–1981. [now Companies Act 1985] (ignore comparative figures.)

b. Prepare a forecast Source and Application of Funds Statement for the year ended 30 June 1983.

c. State FIVE further items of information that you would require in order to be able to produce a projected Profit and Loss Account for the year ended 30 June 1983 and a Balance Sheet as at that date that fully comply with the Companies Acts 1948–1981. [now Companies Act 1985] (ACCA 2.9(1) December 1982)

Appendix 1.
Trial Balance of Brighton Metal Company Limited as at 30 June 1982.

	Dr. £	Cr. £
Ordinary shares of £1 each		200,000
14% Redeemable Preference Shares (redeemable 1.1.83 at 110)		100,000
General reserve		40,000
Profit and Loss Account		52,000
12% Debentures (repayable at par 31.3.83)		100,000
Tax payable 1.1.84		40,000
Creditors		60,000
Tax payable 1.1.83		60,000
Proposed final ordinary dividend		21,000
Bank overdraft		80,000
VAT		18,000
Wages accrued		2,000
Distribution expenses accrued		3,000
Administration expense accrued		4,000
ACT payable on proposed final dividend		9,000
Long leasehold factory	360,000	
Plant and machinery (cost £500,000)	150,000	
Office equipment (cost £100,000)	50,000	
Motor vehicles (cost £240,000)	60,000	
Stock	100,000	
Debtors	60,000	
ACT recoverable	9,000	
	£789,000	£789,000

Appendix 2.
Expected Cash Movements for year to 30 June 1983.

The Budget Controller obtained the following additional details about proposed cash movements during the year ended 30.6.83 of the Brighton Metal Comapny.

a. Share Capital.
There is to be a Rights Issue of one ordinary share for every two shares held. The offer price is to be 80p per share. The difference between offer price and par value is to be transferred out of General Reserve.

b. Loan Capital.
There is to be an issue on 31 March 1983 of £160,000 of 10% Loan Stock, repayable in 1986. the issue price is to be £95.

c. Fixed Assets.

  i. The long leasehold factory is to be sold on 31 December 1982 for £500,000 and leased back at a rental of £40,000 per annum, payable half yearly in arrears. The tax liability on the capital gain is estimated at £42,000.

  ii. The tax liability on the capital gain is estimated at £42,000. An office block is to be purchased costing £280,000.

  iii. Machinery costing £140,000 which has been depreciated by £30,000 is to be sold for £30,000.

  iv. New plant and machinery is to be purchased for £184,000. VAT is recoverable.

  v. Vehicles are to be purchased for £69,000. VAT is recoverable.

d. Working Capital.
  (i) Estimated payments will be as follows:

	£
Paid to creditors	670,000
Paid to employees	246,000

Paid for distribution costs	172,000
Paid for admin. expenses	188,800
Paid for 1983 audit fee	10,000
VAT	47,000

Note: The leaseback charge of £20,000, the debenture interest and the loan interest to 30 June 1983 are included in the Administration expense)

(ii)   Estimated receipts will be: £
       Received from debtors   1,646,000

(iii) Accruals and stocks at 30.6.83   £
       Stock will increase by   20,000
       Creditors at 30.6.83 will total   80,000
       Debtors will increase by   10,000
       Wages accrued   6,000
       Distribution costs accrued   2,000
       Admin. expenses accrued   6,000
       Tax due on loan interest   1,200

e. **Dividends.**
   A dividend of £35,000 is proposed for 1982–83.

f. **Taxation**

   i. The Corporation Tax estimate for 1982–83 is £43,000

   ii. ACT is calculated at 3/7ths of dividend declared.

   iii. VAT is calculated at 15%. Assume all stock purchases, new plant and vehicles are subject to VAT which is recoverable. The VAT content of distribution expenses is £18,000 and the VAT content of administration expenses is £20,000.

g. **Depreciation charges for the year 1982–83.**
   New office block £20,000.
   Plant and machinery 25% of reducing balance.
   Vehicles 25% of reducing balance.
   Office equipment 20% of reducing balance.

33. Required:

Comment on the company accountant's proposal to write back the 1980 and 1981 Research & Development expenses in the 1982 accounts and to capitalise subsequent R & D expenditure.

Outline additional information you would request in order to be able to decide on the correct treatment in 1982.

(ACCA 2.9 (1) June 1982)

APPENDIX 7. *Note on Research and Development*
The expense of £36,721 for 1981 comprised the following:

	£
	£
Wages	9,479
Variable Overhead	10,484
Fixed Overhead	16,758
	£36,721

The wages were for industrial chemists and designers who have been working on a project to prepare and package chicken portions for the vending machine industry.

The project commenced in 1978 and the technical staff estimate that they will have a solution to the problem by the end of 1983.

Estimated expenditure on Research & Development for 1982 and 1983 are:

	1982	1983
	£	£
Wages	10,000	12,000

Variable overheads	11,000	13,000
Fixed overheads	17,700	21,000
Premises for test equipment	9,000	3,000
Plant and machinery for test runs		5,000
	£47,700	£54,000

The marketing staff are hopeful that 1984 sales will show an increase of 60% compared with 1983 as a result of the new processes.

The company accountant is proposing to change the treatment of R & D expenditure in 1982 and subsequent accounts as follows:

	1982 £	1983 £
Write back 1980 expenses	54,468	
Write back 1981 expenses	36,721	
Capitalise 1982 expenditure	47,700	
Capitalise 1983 expenditure		54,000
		138,889
Show in Balance Sheet as a Current Asset	£138,889	£192,889

The Sales Director estimates that the demand will remain, constant in 1982 and 1983 and that further growth will be dependent on being able to supply the vending machine industry with prepacked chicken portions. He forecast that sales would be:

	£
1981	287,968 (actual)
1982	320,000
1983	350,000
1984	500,000
1985	560,000

The Production Director estimates that the fixed assets required to supply such a demand would be:

	£
1981	11,950 (actual)
1982	15,000
1983	16,000
1984	24,000
1985	26,000

34. Prepare a draft profit and loss account for Prism PLC for the year ended 30 November 1983 and a draft balance sheet as at 30 November 1983 in accordance with the requirements of the Companies Acts 1948–1981 (now incorporated into the Companies Act 1985) together with the notes required.

Comparative figures are not required. Advance Corporation Tax may be assumed at 30% and stock relief is to be ignored.

All the relevant information available at the time of preparing the draft accounts is contained in appendices 1A, 2 and 3.

(ACCA 2.9 (1) December 1983)

Appendix 1A

Brief note on Prism PLC together with the Trial Balance as at 30 November 1983

Prism PLC is a public company that has its head office in London. It sells a range of educational toys through its own retail shops in the London area and through a branch shop in Manchester which is 200 miles from London.

The authorised share capital of the company consists of 8,000,000 ordinary shares of 25p each.

The following balances have been taken from the ledger and branch ledger of Prism PLC as at 30 November 1983:

4 : Final Accounts

Debits	Head Office £	Manchester Branch £
Fixed assets at cost at 1 December 1982:		
Freehold properties	500,000	45,000
Fixtures and fittings	1,032,000	18,000
Vehicles	86,000	25,000
Stocks at 1 December 1982 at cost	1,885,482	
Stocks at 1 December 1982 at transfer price		89,375
Debtors	500,165	18,170
Development expenditure	104,000	
Cash	29,618	13,532
Freehold property revalued on 1 January 1983 by	94,000	
Vehicles purchased during year	72,000	16,000
Quoted investments at cost at 1 December 1982	750,000	
Purchases	6,132,685	
Goods from head Office to branch at transfer price		350,000
Administration expense	1,020,800	111,900
Distribution expense	932,120	83,460
Interim dividend paid June 1983	35,000	
ACT paid on interim dividend	15,000	
Branch current account	360,615	
Remittances to head office		306,000
Bank overdraft interest paid	11,700	
	£13,561,185	£1,076,437

Credits	Head Office £	Manchester Branch £
Ordinary share capital	2,000,000	
Share premium	50,000	
Revaluation reserve	94,000	
Retained profits	124,000	
Value added tax	19,000	3,200
Bank overdraft	75,000	
Goods to Manchester Branch	360,615	
Remittances from Manchester Branch	300,000	
Sales (excluding VAT)	9,182,537	689,745
Creditors	388,133	3,697
Head Office current account		350,000
12% loan (repayable 1987)	100,000	
Income from investments (net of ACT)	92,155	
Proceeds from sale of vehicles	7,745	6,295
Corporation tax payable	64,000	
Deferred tax	150,000	
Provision for depreciation at 1 December 1982:		
Freehold properties	20,000	3,000
Fixtures and fittings	492,000	6,500
Vehicles	42,000	14,000
	£13,561,185	£1,076,437

Appendix 2
Information concerning Head Office and Branch transactions
The following information is relevant to the preparation of the Head Office, Branch and whole business Trading and Profit and Loss Accounts for the year ended 30 November 1983.

1. Head Office invoiced goods out to the Manchester branch at cost plus ten per cent.

2. The Retained Profits of £124,000 included in the Trial Balance given in Appendix 1 includes the provision for unrealised profits on the opening stock held at the Manchester branch.

3. There was stock in transit from Head Office to the branch at 30 November 1983 at an invoiced price to the branch of £10,615.

4. There was cash in transit from the branch to Head Office at 30 November 1983 of £6,000.

5. Stocks at 30 November 1983 were as follows:

	Head Office £	Branch £
At cost	1,250,000	
At transfer price		66,990

6. Depreciation is to be charged at the following rates:

Freehold properties	2% of revalued amount.
Fixtures and fittings	10% on original cost of assets held at 30 November 1983
Vehicles	25% of written down value of assets held at 30 November 1983

7. The company disposed of vehicles during the year. The details were as follows.

	Cost £	Cumulative Depreciation £
Head Office	28,000	14,500
Branch	12,000	8,000

Appendix 3
Further year end information on expenses and balance sheet items.
The following information may be relevant for the preparation of the published profit and loss account for the year ended 30 November 1983 and the balance sheet as at 30 November 1983.

1. The quoted investments are included in the trial balance at 30 November 1983 at cost. The details concerning the respective cost of each holding were not available at the date the draft accounts were being prepared. The Finance Director instructed that they should be treated as trade investments pending clarification and entered in the Balance Sheet at cost.

2. The 12% loan was raised on 1 June 1983 and is due for repayment on 31 May 1987. No loan interest has been paid or provided for.

3. The Administration Expenses included the following:

	£
Audit fee	56,000
Charitable donations	8,000
Salaries:	
Chairman	7,500
Managing Director	37,500
Finance Director	23,200

4. The Distribution Expenses included the following:

	£
Marketing Director's salary	28,000
Hire of vehicles	15,000

5. Corporation Tax for 1982–83 has been agreed at £67,000. The estimate for the current year on ordinary activities is £230,000. A transfer of £15,000 is to be made to the Deferred Taxation Account.

6. A final dividend of 1.5p per share has been proposed. It will be paid in March 1984.

7. The development expenditure has been incurred in a programme undertaken by the company to prepare an assembled prism toy that would, by rotating the prism, make pictures of footballers appear to move. the Finance Director has instructed that the expenditure of £104,000 should be treated as an asset in the Balance Sheet.

8. Notification of redundancy has been given to a number of staff to take effect from 31 December 1983. The cost to the company of redundancy payments will be £265,000. There will be an estimated reduction in tax payable by the company of £130,000 arising from this item.

9. The freehold of the Head Office premises in London was valued at current open market valuation on an existing use basis at £394,000. the original cost was £300,000. No adjustment is to be made to the accumulated depreciation provision to 1 December 1982 consequential upon the revaluation.

10. Dividends received during the year were as follows:

Shares	Date	Amount received £
AJAX	May 1983	78,655
SCRUBBER	July 1983	3,500
SCRAPER	August 1983	10,000
Total		£92,155

35. Required:

Prepare Balance Sheet extracts as at 31 December 1982 together with supporting notes for the investment in:

i. Southern Marketing Limited.

ii. Angular Limited.
   (Show clearly how you arrive at the amounts in both Balance Sheet and Notes.)

iii. Comment briefly on the correct treatment of the contingent gain on the shares in Southern Marketing Ltd.
   Your answer should comply with current accounting practice and the Companies Acts 1948–81 (now Companies Act 1985).
   (ACCA 2.9 (1) June 1983)

Appendix 7
Schedule of Investments

The company had trade investments in Southern Marketing Ltd, Angular Ltd, and Hartnell Ltd.

It also had funds invested on a short term basis in the shares of Plastics PLC which were sold when cash was required.

Details of the investments are given below:

Unquoted Shares	Issued Share Capital £	Date Acquired	Shares held	Cost of Shares £
Southern Marketing Ltd *(Note 1)*	100,000	1.1.1971	30,000	50,000
Angular Ltd. *Note 2)*	200,000	1.1.1982	20,000	22,600
Hartnell Ltd *(Note 3)*	1,000,000	1.2.1982	35,000	75,000
Total cost per Trial Balance				£147,600
Quoted Shares				
Plastics PLC	1,000,000	15.1.1982	(see appendix 2)	

Note 1 The shares in Southern Marketing Ltd. were acquired at the date of incorporation of that company. Profits have been healthy and there has been a regular dividend of 14% payable on 31 July (i.e. £4,200 was received by Easiglide). The Easiglide Company had received an offer in August 1982, for the whole of its holding in Southern Marketing Ltd. of £100,000. The Board of directors voted on 31 January 1983 not to accept the offer.

Note 2 The Balance Sheet of Angular Ltd is shown on Appendix 8. The PE ratio appropriate to the size and nature of the company is 8 and the appropriate gross dividend yield is 9%. A dividend of £2,000 was received from Angular on 31 October 1982.

Note 3 A dividend of £4,200 was received from Hartnell on 30 November 1982.

Appendix 8
Summarised balance sheet of Angular Ltd. as at 30 September 1982

	£	£
Fixed Assets		118,000
Current assets	398,000	
Current liabilities	216,000	
Working Capital		182,000
		£300,000

	£	£
Represented by:		
Ordinary share capital		200,000
Share premium		25,000
Revenue reserves:		
Brought forward	61,000	
Balance for 1982	14,000	75,000
		£300,000

Summarised balance sheet of Southern Marketing Ltd. as at 30 September 1982.

	£	£
Fixed Assets		145,000
Current assets	80,000	
Current liabilities	55,000	
Working Capital		25,000
		£170,000

	£	£
Represented by:		
Ordinary share capital		100,000
Revenue reserves		
Brought forward	40,000	
Balance for 1982	30,000	70,000
		£170,000

Summarised profit and loss account for Southern Marketing Ltd for year ended 30 September 1982

	£
Profit before tax	74,000
Tax	30,000
Profit after tax	44,000
Dividend	14,000
	30,000
Balance brought forward	40,000
Balance carried forward	£70,000

36. Required:
Prepare an historic cost Profit and Loss Account for The Easiglide Company for the year ended 31 December 1982 to comply as far as possible with the Companies Acts 1948–81 (now Companies Act 1985). Show clearly your calculation of Cost of Goods Sold.

(ACCA 2.9 (1) June 1983)
Appendix 1
The Easiglide Company Limited is a firm that sells a single product for cylinder lubrication.
The company employed 180 staff and in 1982 marketed their product solely in the home market.
The Accounts are made up to the 31 December 1982 and it is proposed to submit them to the directors for approval on 28 February 1983. The Trial Balance as at 31 December 1982 is given below:

Trial Balance of The Easiglide Company as at 31 December 1982

	£	£
Goodwill, at cost	711,500	
Ordinary share capital (50p shares		1,100,000
10% Debentures (1990)		150,000
10% Debentures (1985)		100,000
8% Preference shares		1,000,000
Debtors	612,000	
Creditors		115,000
Cash	20,000	
Bank		18,255
Freehold Land, at cost	650,000	
Freehold factory, at cost	1,400,000	
Plant and machinery, at cost	900,000	
Vehicles, at cost	100,000	
Office equipment, at cost	84,000	
General reserve		200,000
Income from quoted and unquoted investments		13,400
Debenture interest	25,000	
Unquoted investments, at cost	147,600	
Quoted investments, at cost	46,750	
Preference dividend paid (November 1982)	80,000	
Proceeds from sale of quoted investments		21,875
Profit and Loss Account balance		600,000
Share premium		300,000
Provision for bad debts		39,000
Provision for depreciation		
Freehold factory		40,000
Plant and machinery		400,000
Vehicles		32,000
Office equipment		38,000
Capital Redemption Reserve		50,000
Stock:		
Raw material, at invoice cost	160,000	
Work in progress, at standard cost	105,600	
Finished goods, at standard cost	364,800	
Sales at standard selling price		5,400,000
	5,407,250	9,617,530
Standard marginal cost of sales	3,283,200	
Fixed production overheads *(Note 1)*	1,046,000	
Variances		
Material price		9,540
Material usage	8,840	
Labour efficiency	80,640	

Labour rate	51,840	
Variable overhead	204,300	
Selling price		116,000
Bad debts	32,000	
Distribution expense *(Note2)*	110,000	
Administration expense *(Note 3)*	85,000	
Deferred tax		286,000
Provision for Corporation tax		300,000
Loss from expropriation of foreign assets	44,000	
ACT payable		24,000
	£10,353,070	£10,353,070

Note 1) Fixed production Overheads includes the following items: Depreciation of buildings £8,000; depreciation of plant £125,000; hire of plant £96,000; Chairman's salary £12,000; Managing director's salary £60,000; Works director's salary £42,000.

Note 2) Distribution expense includes the depreciation of motor vehicles £22,000, sales director's salary £32,000.

Note 3) Administration expense includes the depreciation of office equipment £16,000, hire of computer equipment £15,000, finance director's salary £32,000.

Note 4) Income tax is to be calculated at 30%.

Note 5) The loss from expropriation of foreign assets represents the loss after taking credit for compensation on the expropriation of the assets of a foreign branch.

Appendix 2
Transactions in the shares of Plastic PLC during the year ended 31 December 1982

15 January	Purchased 20,000 ordinary £1 shares for £40,000.
31 January	Sold 5,000 ordinary shares for £12,000 cum div.
31 March	Received an interim dividend of £0.05 per share.
30 April	Plastics PLC resolved to
	(a) Make a Bonus Issue of 1 share for every 5 held on 31 May, 1982
	(b) Give members the right to apply for a Rights Issue of 4 shares for every 10 held at 31 March payable in full on 30 June 1982. The issue price was £1.50 per share. Rights could be sold for £0.25 per share
31 May	Plastics PLC made Bonus Issue.
30 June	Company applied for three quarters of its Rights Issue and sold the rights to the remaining quarter.
30 September	Company sold 5,000 shares for £1.90 per share, ex div.
31 October	Company received a final dividend of £0.10 per share.
30 November	Plastics PLC converted the £1 shares to 25p Nominal Value.
31 December	The market price per share was £0.55

Appendix 5
Treatment of variances and overheads in stock valuation

	Raw Material £	Work in Progress* £		Finished Goods** £	
Amount in Trial Balance	160,000	105,600		364,800	
Adjustments	–	34,850	*(Note 1)*	139,142	*(Note 2)*
	£160,000	£140,450		£503,942	

*Work in Progress consisted of 30,000 units which were 100% complete for Material Content and 50% complete for Labour and Variable Overheads.

**Finished goods consisted of 60,000 units which were 100% complete.

Note 1 Work in Progress Adjustments

	Variable Cost £	Price Variance £	Usage Variance £	Basis £	Stock Adjustment £
Material: Oil	18,000	(1,500)		18,000 ÷ 108,000	(250)
			(2,500)	18,000 ÷ 108,000	(417)
Solvent	10,800	3,240		10,800 ÷ 64,800	540
			1,060	–	–
Labour	28,800	(17,280)		–	–
Variable Overhead	48,000	(68,000)		48,000 ÷ 576,000	(5,667)
Standard cost	£105,600				

Fixed Overheads
Actual Cost ÷ Total Standard Labour Cost × Labour in Work in Progess
1,046,000 ÷ 1,036,800 × 28,800 (29,056)
Adjustment to standard cost £34,850

Note 2 Finished Goods Adjustments

	Variable Cost £	Price Variance £	Usage Variance £	Basis £	Stock Adjustment £
Material: Oil	36,000	(1,500)		36,000 ÷ 108,000	(500)
			(2,500)	36,000 ÷ 108,000	(833)
Solvent	21,600	3,240		21,600 ÷ 64,800	1,080
			1,060	–	–
Labour	115,200	(17,280)	–	–	–
Variable Overheads	192,000	(68,000)		192,000 ÷ 576,000	(22,667)
Standard Cost	£364,800				

Fixed Overheads:
Actual Cost ÷ Total Standard Labour × Labour in Stock
1,046,000 ÷ 1,036,800 × 115,200
= (116,222)
Adjustment to standard cost £139,142

Note 3 Net Realisable Value

The company has carried out a comparison of cost with net realisable value and in all cases the costs as stated are lower than the relevant net realisable value.

Note 4 Cost of Sales

The company policy is to adjust the amount of the variances transferred to the Cost of Sales to take account of the proportion of the variances that have been applied to the stock valuation.

Appendix 6
Transactions not already recorded in the Trial Balance as at 31 December 1982

1. Provision is to be made for:

Auditors' remuneration on £41,000; Corporation tax on current year's profit of £425,000; a final dividend of 2.5p per share; a fall in value of investments by £15,000 (this relates to the shares in Hartnell Ltd).

2. Increase the bad debt provision on debtors as at 31 December 1982 to £42,000.

3. Transfer £75,000 from Deferred Tax Account to the Profit & Loss Account.

4. The Corporation Tax for 1982-83 has been agreed at £290,000.

Appendix 7
Schedule of Investments

The company had trade investments in Southern Marketing Ltd, Angular Ltd, and Hartnell Ltd.

It also had funds invested on a short term basis in the shares of Plastics PLC which were sold when cash was required.

Details of the investments are given below:

Unquoted Shares	*Issued Share Capital* £	*Date Acquired*	*Shares held*	*Cost of shares* £
Southern Marketing Ltd.*(Note 1)*	100,000	1.1.1971	30,000	50,000
Angular Ltd. *(Note 2)*	200,000	1.1.1982	20,000	22,600
Hartnell Ltd.*(Note 3)*	1,000,000	1.2.1982	35,000	75,000
Total cost per Trial Balance				£147,600

Quoted Shares

Plastics PLC	1,000,000	15.1.1982	(see appendix 2)

Note 1 The shares in Southern Marketing Ltd. were acquired at the date of incorporation of that company. Profits have been healthy and there has been a regular dividend of 14% payable on 31 July (i.e. £4,200 was received by Easiglide). The Easiglide Company had received an offer in August 1982, for the whole of its holding in Southern Marketing Ltd. of £100,000. the Board of directors voted on 31 January 1983 not to accept the offer.

Note 2 The Balance Sheet of Angular Ltd. is shown on Appendix 8. The PE ratio appropriate to the size and nature of the company is 8 and the appropriate gross dividend yield is 9%. A dividend of £2,000 was received from Angular on 31 October 1982.

Note 3 A dividend of £4,200 was received from Hartnell on 30 November 1982.

Appendix 8
Summarised balance sheet of Angular Ltd as at 30 September 1982

	£	£
Fixed Assets		118,000
Current assets	398,000	
Current liabilities	216,000	
Working Capital		182,000
		£300,000

		£
Represented by:		
Ordinary share capital		200,000
Share premium		25,000
Revenue reserves:		
Brought forward	61,000	
Balance for 1982	14,000	75,000
		£300,000

Summarised balance sheet of Southern Marketing Ltd as at 30 September 1982

	£	£
Fixed Assets		145,000
Current assets	80,000	
Current liabilities	55,000	
Working Capital		25,000
		£170,000

	£	£
Represented by:		
Ordinary share capital		100,000
Revenue reserves		
Brought forward	40,000	
Balance for 1982	30,000	70,000
		£170,000

Summarised profit and loss account for Southern Marketing Ltd for year ended 30 September 1982

	£
Profit before tax	74,000
Tax	30,000
Profit after tax	44,000
Dividend	14,000
	30,000
Balance brought forward	40,000
Balance carried forward	£70,000

37. Required:

Discuss briefly the treatment by The Easiglide Company of the variances and overheads in calculating its stock valuation as at 31 December 1982. State clearly the criteria you would apply when making such a decision in respect of:

i. Fixed production overheads.

ii. Material price variance.

Prepare Balance Sheet extract for stocks and work in progress as at 31 December 1982 and draft the Accounting Policy note in respect of such stocks and work in progress.

(ACCA 2.9(1) June 1983)

Appendix 1

The Easiglide Company Limited is a firm that sells a single product for cylinder lubrication.

The company employed 180 staff and in 1982 marketed their product solely in the home market.

The Accounts are made up to the 31 December 1982 and it is proposed to submit them to the directors for approval on 28 February 1983. The Trial Balance as at 31 December 1982 is given below:

Trial Balance of The Easiglide Company as at 31 December 1982

	£	£
Goodwill, at cost	711,500	
Ordinary share capital (50p shares)		1,100,000
10% Debentures (1990)		150,000
10% Debentures (1985)		100,000
8% Preference shares		1,000,000
Debtors	612,000	
Creditors		115,000
Cash	20,000	
Bank		18,255

Freehold land, at cost	650,000	
Freehold factory, at cost	1,400,000	
Plant and machinery, at cost	900,000	
Vehicles, at cost	100,000	
Office equipment, at cost	84,000	
General reserve		200,000
Income from quoted and unquoted investments		13,400
Debenture interest	25,000	
Unquoted investments, at cost	147,600	
Quoted investments, at cost	46,750	
Preference dividend paid (November 1982)	80,000	
Proceeds from sale of quoted investments		21,875
Profit and Loss Account balance		600,000
Share premium		300,000
Provision for bad debts		39,000
Provision for depreciation:		
Freehold factory		40,000
Plant and machinery		400,000
Vehicles		32,000
Office equipment		38,000
Capital Redemption Reserve		50,000
Stock: Raw material, at invoice cost	160,000	
Work in progress, at standard cost	105,600	
Finished goods, at standard cost	364,800	
Sales at standard selling price		5,400,000
Standard marginal cost of sales	3,283,200	
Fixed production overheads *(Note 1)*	1,046,000	
Variances		
Material price		9,540
Material usage	8,840	
Labour efficiency	80,640	
Labour rate	51,840	
Variable overhead	204,300	
Selling price		116,000
Bad debts	32,000	
Distribution expense *(Note 2)*	110,000	
Administration expense *(Note 3)*	85,000	
Deferred tax		286,000
Provision for Corporation tax		300,000
Loss from expropriation of foreign assets	44,000	
ACT payable		24,000
	£10,353,070	£10,353,070

Note 1) Fixed production Overheads includes the following items: Depreciation of buildings £8,000; depreciation of plant £125,000; hire of plant £96,000; Chairman's salary £12,000; Managing director's salary £60,000; Works director's salary £42,000.

Note 2) Distribution expense includes the depreciation of motor vehicles £22,000, sales director's salary £32,000.

Note 3) Administration expense includes the depreciation of office equipment £16,000, hire of computer equipment £15,000, finance director's salary £32,000.

Note 4) Income tax is to be calculated at 30%.

Note 5) The loss from expropriation of foreign assets represents the loss after taking credit for compensation on the expropriation of the assets of a foreign branch.

Appendix 3
Cumulative summary of the variances and fixed overheads that are shown in the Trial Balances as at 31 December 1982

	Material Price			Material Usage		
	Qtr 1-3	Qtr 4	Total	Qtr 1-3	Qtr4	Total
	£	£	£	£	£	£
Material:						
Oil	1,320	(1,500)	(180)	(9,620)	(2,500)	(12,120)
Solvent	6,480	3,240	9,720	2,220	1,060	3,280
Variances per Trial Balance			£9,540			£(8,840)

	Labour Efficiency			Labour Rate		
	Qtr 1-3	Qtr 4	Total	Qtr 1-3	Qtr 4	Total
	£	£	£	£	£	£
	(80,640)	–	(80,640)	(34,560)	(17,280)	(51,840)
Variances per Trial Balance			£(80,640)			£(51,840)

	Variable Overheads		
	Qtr 1-3	Qtr 4	Total
	£	£	£
	(136,300)	(68,000)	(204,300)
Variances per Trial Balance			£(204,300)

	Selling Price		
	Qtr 1-3	Qtr 4	Total
	£	£	£
	76,000	40,000	116,000
Variance per Trial Balance			£116,000

	Fixed Overheads		
	Qtr 1-3	Qtr 4	Total
	£	£	£
Budgeted Overheads	690,000	275,000	965,000
Variances	66,000	15,000	81,000
Total per Trial Balance			£1,046,000

Appendix 4

Budget/Actual Summary for 1982 and Quarter 4

	1982				Quarter Four					
	Original Budget	Flexed Budget	Actual Results	Variance	Original Budget	Flexed Budget	Volume Variance	Actual Results	Performance Variances	Total Variance
	£	£	£	£	£	£	£	£	£	£
Units	580,000	540,000	540,000		190,000	180,000	10,000	180,000		
Sales	5,800,000	5,400,000	5,516,000	(284,000)	1,900,000	1,800,000	(100,000)	1,840,000	40,000	(60,000)
Materials:										
Oil	348,000	324,000	336,300	11,700	114,000	108,000	6,000	112,000	(4,000)*	2,000
Solvent	208,800	194,400	181,400	27,400	68,400	64,800	3,600	60,500	4,300 *	7,900
Labour	1,113,600	1,036,800	1,169,280	(55,680)	364,800	345,600	19,200	362,880	(17,280)*	1,920
Variable Overheads	1,856,000	1,728,000	1,932,300	(76,300)	608,000	576,000	32,000	644,000	(68,000)*	(36,000)
Fixed Overheads	965,000	965,000	1,046,000	(81,000)	275,000	275,000	—	290,000	(15,000)*	(15,000)
Net Profit	£1,308,600	£1,151,800	£850,720		£469,800	£430,600		£370,620		

*Refer to appendix 3, for further analysis of the performance variances.

354

Appendix 5
Treatment of variances and overheads in stock valuation

	Raw Material £	Work in Progress* £		Finished Goods** £	
Amount in Trial Balance	160,000	105,600		364,800	
Adjustments	–	34,850	(Note 1)	139,142	(Note 2)
	£160,000	£140,450		£503,942	

*Work in Progress consisted of 30,000 units which were 100% complete for Material Content and 50% complete for Labour and Variable Overheads.

**Finished Goods consisted of 60,000 units which were 100% complete.

Note 1   Work in Progress Adjustments

	Variable Cost £	Price Variance £	Usage Variance £	Basis	Stock Adjustment £
Material: Oil	18,000	(1,500)		18,000 ÷ 108,000	(250)
			(2,500)	18,000 ÷ 108,000	(417)
Solvent	10,800	3,240		10,800 ÷ 64,800	540
			1,060	–	–
Labour	28,800	(17,280)		–	–
Variable Overhead	48,000	(68,000)		48,000 ÷ 576,000	(5,667)

Standard cost   £105,600

Fixed Overheads
Actual Cost   ÷   Total Standard
                Labour Cost × Labour in Work in Progress

1,046,000   ÷   1,036,800 × 28,800   (29,056)

Adjustment to standard cost   £34,850

Note 2   Note 2 Finished Goods Adjustments

	Variable Cost £	Price Variance £	Usage Variance £	Basis	Stock Adjustment £
Material: Oil	36,000	(1,500)		36,000 ÷ 108,000	(500)
			(2,500)	36,000 ÷ 108,000	(833)
Solvent	21,600	3,240		21,600 ÷ 64,800	1,080
			1,060	–	–
Labour	115,200	(17,280)		–	–
Variable Overhead	192,000	(68,000)		192,000 ÷ 576,000	(22,667)

Standard cost   £364,800

Fixed Overheads:
  Actual Cost ÷ Total Standard Labour × Labour in Stock
  $1,046,000 ÷ 1,036,800 × 115,200$

$$= (116,222)$$

Adjustment to standard cost $\qquad$ £139,142

Note 3 Net Realisable Value

The company has carried out a comparison of cost with net realisable value and in all cases the costs as stated are lower than the relevant net realisable value.

Note 4 Cost of Sales

The company policy is to adjust the amount of the variances transferred to the Cost of Sales to take account of the proportion of the variances that have been applied to the stock valuation.

38. Required:

a. Prepare a Profit and Loss Account for the year ended 31 December 1983 and a Balance Sheet as at 31 December 1983 for Health Sales Ltd. for internal use from the information provided in Appendices 1, 2, 3 and 4.

b. Prepare a Profit and Loss Account for the year ended 31 December 1983 for Health Sales Ltd to comply as far as possible with the requirements of the Companies Acts (1948-1981)

(ACCA 2.9(1) June 1984)

Appendix 1

Information about group structure

Black Root Ltd is a company that imports liquorice into the United Kingdom and sells to pharmaceutical companies and confectionery manufacturers. After a period of falling sales the company decided to acquire shares in a confectionery manufacturer and to acquire retail outlets in the health food market.

Accordingly on 1 January 1983 it paid £3,205,000 in cash to acquire 1,209,600 shares in Confectioners Ltd. On 31 December 1983 Confectioners Ltd made a Rights Issue for cash of 1 Ordinary £1 share for every 6 shares held at 250p per share, payable immediately. Black Root Ltd took up its full entitlement.

Also on 1 January 1983 Black Root Ltd. susbcribed for 1,190,000 Ordinary shares of £1 each, at par, in a newly formed company, Health Sales Ltd.

Health Sales Ltd. entered into an agreement on 1 January 1983 to acquire the retail business carried on by the partnership of Pharar, Khadir and Benson. The purchase consideration was 510,000 Ordinary shares of £1 each issued at a premium of 50p per share and a cash payment of £714,000. Health Sales Ltd. acquired all of the assets of the partnership and all of the liabilities, with the exception of the bank account. The freehold land was revalued at £1,020,000 otherwise the closing balance sheet values were accepted as those shown in Appendix 3.

Appendix 2

Summarised Profit and Loss Accounts for the year ended 31 December 1983 and summarised Balance Sheets as at 31 December 1983 of Black Root Ltd and Confectioners Ltd

	Black Root Ltd		Confectioners Ltd	
	1982	*1983*	*1982*	*1983*
	£000s	£000s	£000s	£000s
Turnover	27,968	34,523	2,492	3,536
Trading Profit	6,992	8,740	608	868
Depreciation	1,472	1,840	128	192
Debenture Interest	736	920	64	96
	4,784	5,980	416	580
Taxation	2,208	2,346	240	224
Profit after tax	2,576	3,634	176	356
Dividends paid:				
Ordinary	402.5	483	–	–
Preference	322	322	22	22
Dividends Proposed	805	1,041	100	235

356

Issued Ordinary Shares	8,050	10,410	2,016	2,352
Issued 7% Preference Shares	4,600	4,600	320	320
Share Premium	–	2,110	–	504
Retained Profits	3,680	5,468	300	399
10% Debentures	7,360	9,200	640	960
Creditors	736	1,044	320	384
Current Account with				
Black Root Ltd				57
Tax	1,897	2,070	230	257
ACT Payable	345	446	43	101
Proposed dividend	805	1,041	100	235
	27,473	36,389	3,969	5,569
Fixed assets	18,400	22,080	1,792	2,176
Investment in Confectioners Ltd.		3,709		
Investment in Health Sales Ltd.		1,190		
Stock	1,104	1,397	512	640
Current Account with				
Confectioners Ltd.		70		
Current Account with				
Health Sales Ltd.		140		
Debtors	2,530	5,060	1,404	1,600
ACT Recoverable	345	446	43	101
Cash at Bank	5,094	2,297	218	1,052
	27,473	36,389	3,969	5,569

Additional information.

1. Black Root Ltd's investment in Confectioners Ltd consisted of 1,209,600 Ordinary shares of £1 each acquired on 1 January 1983 and 201,600 Ordinary shares of £1 each acquired under the Rights Issue on 31 December 1983.

2. During the year ended 31 December 1983 Black Root Ltd purchased from Confectioners Ltd one of its fixed assets, a machine, for £126,000. Confectioners Ltd had invoiced the machine at book value plus 40%. Black Root Ltd has depreciated the machine at 20% of the invoiced price.

3. Black Root Ltd supplied goods to Confectioners Ltd at cost plus 25%. During the year ended 31 December 1983 Black Root Ltd despatched goods with an invoiced value of £485,000 and received cash of £415,000 from Confectioners Ltd.
   During the year Confectioners Ltd received goods from Black Root Ltd with an invoiced value of £475,000 and made payments to them totalling £418,000. At 31 December 1983 the stock of Confectioners Ltd included goods supplied by Black Root Ltd with an invoiced value of £50,000.

4. During the year ended 31 December 1983 Black Root Ltd sold fixed assets for £575,000 (net book value £460,000) and Confectioners Ltd sold fixed assets for £32,000 (net book value £48,000). The respective profit and loss have been included in the respective trading profit.

5. The proposed dividends from Confectioners Ltd have been included in the Black Root Ltd debtors in the Balance Sheet as at 31 December 1983.

6. It is group policy to disclose Goodwill on Consolidation in the Consolidated Balance Sheet.

Appendix 3
Draft Balance Sheet of Pharar, Khadir and Benson as at 31 December 1982

Capital Accounts	£	£	£	£
Pharar		368,000		
Khadir		552,000		
Benson		100,000	1,020,000	

Current Accounts			
Pharar	(120,800)		
Khadir	(56,000)		
Benson	(170,000)	(346,800)	673,200
			£673,200

Fixed Assets	Cost	Depreciation	Net Book Value	
	£	£	£	£
Freehold*	617,000	–	617,000	
Shop Fittings	602,000	301,000	301,000	
Total Fixed Assets				918,000
Current Assets				
Stock		212,400		
Debtors		265,200	477,600	
Current Liabilities				
Creditors		112,200		
Bank		610,200	722,400	
				(244,800)
				£673,200

Overseas candidates note: Freehold–land held in perpetuity

Appendix 4
Transactions by Health Sales Ltd during the year ended 31 December 1983.

a. During 1983 the following transactions took place:

   i.   Sales amounted to £1,254,000 and £500,400 for credit and cash respectively.

   ii. Purchases from Black Root Ltd totalled £816,000. This was the invoiced value to Health Sales Ltd.

   iii. Purchases from non-group suppliers were all acquired on credit. The credit terms were that Health Sales Ltd should receive 2% discount for payment within 1 month, 1% discount for payment within 2 months and no discounts for payment in the third month.

   iv. The position in respect of non-group purchases from 1 January 1983 to 30 September 1983 was that purchase invoices totalled £155,500, cheque payments totalled £140,856 and discounts received totalled £1,628.

   The records for payments in the period 1st October to 31 December 1983 showed as follows:

	August £	September £	October £	November £	December £
Invoiced	17,200	16,100	15,095	18,300	25,305
Payments for:					
August supplies	3,000	12,000	Balance		
September supplies		5,000	8,000	Balance	
October supplies			4,000	9,800	Balance
November supplies				3,300	14,100
December supplies					15,200

   Cheques had been drawn, awaiting signature, for payment of December supplies £8,000 and the balance of the November supplies. The cheques were dated 15 January 1984.

   v.   The company paid the creditors taken over from the partnership in full in January 1983. It collected all of the debtors taken over subject to a special discount of 10%.

All debtors of the partnership, subject to the discount, had been collected by 30 June 1983.

vi. Fixed assets were acquired as follows:

Freehold Land   £306,000
Shop fittings   £765,000

The directors have produced a five year plan which shows that there will be a regular programme of expansion at the same level each year.

vii. Shop fittings were disposed of for £105,000. Their book value at 1 January 1983 was £97,280 and their original cost to the parternship in 1977 had been £183,000.

viii. The expenses for the year were:

	Paid by cheque £	Invoiced £
Administration	150,000	161,853
Establishment	81,060	83,695
Selling	72,416	79,850
Distribution	27,148	28,960
Miscellaneous	16,193	17,500

ix. The Administration expense includes £25,000 for auditors remuneration and £42,000 for directors remuneration for services as a director and £8,000 for directors pension contributions. The miscellaneous expense includes interest on the bank overdraft of £13,000.

x. An interim dividend of 5% was paid in July 1983. The Advanced Corporation Tax was paid in November 1983. Assume an Advanced Corporation Tax rate of 30%.

b. At 31 December 1983 the following information was available:

i. The stock turnover for goods supplied by Black Root Ltd was ten to one, calculated on the invoiced price. The stock turnover for goods supplied by non-group suppliers was four to one, calculated on invoiced price.

ii. The debtor turnover rate was twelve to one.

iii. Depreciation of shop fittings was to be made at 12 1/2% of cost to the group.

iv. The Black Root Ltd Current Account was £100,000.

v. A final dividend of 2 1/2% was proposed.

39. Oldfield Enterprises Limited was formed on 1 January 1985 to manufacture and sell a new type of lawn mower. The book-keeping staff of the company have produced monthly figures for the first ten months to 31 October 1985 and from these figures together with estimates for the remaining two months, Barry Lamb, the managing director has drawn up a forecast profit and loss account for the year to 31 December 1985 and a balance sheet as at that date.

These statements together with the notes are submitted to the board for comment. During the board meeting discussion centres on the treatment given to the various assets. The various opinions are summarised by Barry Lamb who brings them, with the draft accounts, to you as the company's financial advisor.

Oldfield Enterprises Ltd
Draft profit and loss account for the year to 31 December 1985

	£000s	£000s
Sales		3,000
Cost of Sales		1,750
Gross profit		1,250
Administration overheads	350	
Selling and distribution overheads	530	
		880
Net profit before taxation		370

Draft balance sheet at 31 December 1985

Fixed assets-tangible	Cost £000s	Depreciation and Amortisation £000s	Net £000s
Leasehold land and buildings	375	125	250
Freehold land and buildings	350	–	350
Plant and machinery	1,312	197	1,115
	2,037	322	1,715

Fixed assets-intangible			
Research and development			375
Current assets			
Stock		375	
Debtors		780	
		1,155	

Current liabilities			
Creditors	250		
Bank Overdraft	125	375	
			780
			2,870

Share Capital			2,500
Net profit for year			370
			2,870

Notes

a. Administration overheads includes £50,000 written off research and development.

b. The lease is for 15 years and cost £75,000, buildings have been put up on the leasehold land at a cost of £300,000. Plant and machinery has been depreciated at 15%. Both depreciation and amortisation are included in cost of sales.

Opinions put forward

Leasehold land and buildings.

The works director thinks that although the lease provides for a rent review after three years the buildings have a 50 year life. The buildings should therefore be depreciated over 50 years and the cost of the lease should be amortised over the period of the lease.

The managing director thinks that because of the rent review clause the whole of the cost should be depreciated over three years.

The sales director thinks it is a good idea to charge as much as the profits will allow in order to reduce the tax bill.

Freehold land and buildings. The works director thinks that as the value of the property is going up with inflation no depreciation is necessary. The sales director's opinion is the same as for leasehold property. The managing director states that he has heard that if a property is always kept in good repair no depreciation is necessary. This should apply in the case of his company.

Plant and machinery. The managing director agrees with the 15% for depreciation and proposes to use the reducing balance method. The works director wants to charge 25% straight line.

Research and development. The total spent in the year will be £425,000. Of this £250,000 is for research into the cutting characteristics of different types of grass, £100,000 is for the development of an improved drive system for lawn mowers and £75,000 is for market research to determine the ideal lawn mower characteristics for the average garden. The managing director thinks that a small amount should be charged as an expense each year. The works director wants to write off all the market research and "all this nonsense of the cutting characteristics of grass". The sales director thinks that, as the company has only just started, all research and development expenditure relates to future sales so all this year's expenditure should be carried forward.

Stock. Both the managing director and the works director are of the opinion that stock should be shown at prime cost. The sales director's view is that stocks should be shown at sales price as the stock is virtually all sold within a very short period.

Required:

a. You are asked to comment on each opinion stating what factors should be taken into account to determine suitable depreciation and write off amounts.

b. Indicate what amounts should, in your opinion, be charged to profit and loss and show the adjusted profit produced by your recommendations, stating clearly any assumptions you may make.

(ACCA 2.9(2) December 1985).

40.

Required:

a. Prepare the following statements for Self Reliant Tours:
  bank reconciliation statements at 1 January 1984 and 31 January 1984.

b. Prepare the following accounts at 31 January 1984:

  i. Bank Account

  ii. Cash Account

  iii. Sales Ledger Control Account with balance brought down at 1 February 1984.

  iv. Current Account for Mr Anthony.

(ACCA 2.9(1) December 1985)

Appendix 5 Self Reliant Tours: receipts and payments information supplied by Mr Anthony at 31 January 1984

Receipts for period 1 January to 31 January 1984

Date	Narrative	Total £ p	Sales Ledger £ p	Sundries £ p
1 Jan	Alpha Associates	610.00	610.00	
1 Jan	B Arnold	110.30	110.30	
2 Jan	C Ayres	195.45	195.45	
2 Jan	B Benson	51.60	51.60	
3 Jan	S Solomon	79.20	79.20	
6 Jan	B Arnold	70.00	70.00	
8 Jan	B Benson	96.00	96.00	
9 Jan	S Randle	950.00		950.00
12 Jan	R Jayne	158.74		158.74
13 Jan	B Arnold	651.20	651.20	
15 Jan	C Ayres	103.50	103.50	
16 Jan	B Arnold	130.95		130.95
17 Jan	B Benson	98.64	98.64	
19 Jan	B Arnold	203.02	203.02	
20 Jan	Alpha Associates	191.75	191.75	
21 Jan	R Jayne	97.85	97.85	
22 Jan	B Arnold	105.23	105.23	
22 Jan	S Solomon	51.86	51.86	
23 Jan	S Solomon	21.95	21.95	
25 Jan	R Jayne	19.21	19.21	
27 Jan	S Solomon	33.75	33.75	

28 Jan	B Arnold	86.09	86.09
31 Jan	C Ayres	185.76	185.76
		4,302.05	3,062.36	1,239.69

Payments recorded for period 1 January to 31 January 1984

Date	Narrative	Bank £ p	Bought Ledger £ p	Cash Payments £ p	Sundries £ p	Wages £ p
1 Jan	British Tours	292.64	292.64			
	Iberian Tours	39.60	39.60			
	Advertising	139.04			139.04	
2 Jan	British Tours	210.50	210.50			
	Wages	393.02				393.02
3 Jan	Drawings (Anthony)	400.00			400.00	
	Motor expenses	54.00			54.00	
	Iberian Tours	305.04	305.04			
5 Jan	British Tours	9.75	9.75			
	Cash	900.00		900.00		
	Repairs	94.09			94.09	
8 Jan	Greek Tours	94.59	94.59			
	Wages	501.60				501.60
	Greek Tours	68.07	68.07			
10 Jan	British Tours	190.93	190.93			
	British Tours	69.60			69.60	
	Greek Tours	90.31	90.31			
12 Jan	Iberian Tours	63.60	63.60			
	Cleaning	5.90			5.90	
17 Jan	Iberian Tours	136.75	136.75			
	Wages	209.10				209.10
	Drawings (Anthony)	420.00			420.00	
29 Jan	Advertising	86.32			86.32	
	Greek Tours	258.99	258.99			
30 Jan	Wages	268.51				268.51
31 Jan	Cash	135.76			135.76	
	Copy typing			185.00		
	Staff bureau			267.95		
	Printing			306.86		
		5,437.71	1,760.77	1,659.81	1,404.71	1,372.23

Appendix 6 Self Reliant Tours: Bank statements for period 1 January to 5 February 1984

Date	Cheque number	Debit £ p	Credit £ p	Balance £ p
	Balance forward			709.44
1 Jan	Cash/cheques		1,116.55	1,825.99
4 Jan	10001	250.00		
	10008	139.04		
	10002	66.50		1,370.45
5 Jan	10007	39.60		
	10009	210.50		1,120.35
6 Jan	10013	305.04		
	10010	393.02		

	10003	125.30			
	10012	54.00		242.99	
7 Jan	10004	708.00			
	10011	400.00			
	10006	292.64			
	10014	9.75			
	10015	900.00		2,067.40	O/D
9 Jan	Cash/cheques		1,046.00	1,021.40	O/D
10 Jan	10005	174.52			
	10016	94.09			
	10017	501.60			
	10021	69.60			
	10019	68.07		1,929.28	O/D
14 Hab	19923	63.60			
	10024	5.90		1,998.78	O/D
16 Jan	10020	190.93			
	10017	94.59		2,284.30	O/D
17 Jan	Transfer		1,200.00	1,084.30	O/D
18 Jan	Cash/cheques		1,143.03	58.73	
21 Jan	Cash/cheques		492.62	551.35	
	10022	90.31		461.04	
22 Jan	10027	420.00		41.04	
25 Jan	10025	136.75		95.71	O/D
25 Jan	Cash/cheques		198.25	102.54	
27 Jan	10026	209.10		106.56	O/D
31 Jan	Standing Order	200.00		306.56	O/D
1 Feb	10030	268.51			
4 Feb	10031	135.76			
	10036	31.89			
	10033	91.48		834.20	O/D
5 Feb	10028	86.32			
	Cash/cheques		305.60		
	10035	111.09			
	10032	112.56			
	10029	258.99		1,097.56	O/D

Appendix 7 Self Reliant Tours: further information

1. Opening balances at 1 January 1984 as shown on the draft balance sheet:

Debtors	£12,100.53	Debit balance
	£350.76	Credit balance
Creditors	£16,500.81	Credit balance
	£210.34	Debit balance
Cash in hand	£520.60	
Current Account (Mr Anthony)	£5,000.00	Credit balance
Bank overdraft	£614.88	

2. Sundry receipts were analysed as follows:

   9 Jan   S Randle   £950.00   Sale of car
   12 Jan   R Jayne   £158.74   Sales ledger item
   16 Jan   B Arnold   £130.95   Sales ledger item

3. Sundry payments - further enquiry showed:

   10 Jan   British Tours   £69.60   Bought ledger item
   1 Jan   Advertising   £139.04   Payment to agent selling Mr Anthony's private yacht.

4. Payments not recorded-vouchers were produced as evidence of the following payments during January 1984:

   Cleaning   £51.85
   Gratuities   £20.50

5. Bank statement - further enquiry showed:

   17 Jan   Transfer   £1,200.00   A loan from Mr Anthony
   31 Jan   Standing Order   £200.00   Payment under a hire purchase agreement

6. Purchases and sales

The Sales Day Book totalled £15,200.25 for January The Purchases Day Book totalled £11,595.96 for January. The list of debtors totalled £23,597.07 at 31 January 1984. The list of creditors totalled £26,372.91 at 31 January 1984. There were also £316.85 debit balances in respect of creditors and no credit balances for debtors.

7. Cash in hand at 31 January 1984 was £224.20 and the bank overdraft was £1,056.14.

41. The draft accounts of Readycut Toys plc, a toy manufacturer, have been prepared for the year ended 30 September 1984, and are shown below.

The authorised share capital is 6,000,000 8% preference shares of 50p each and 36,000,000 ordinary shares of 25p each.

Draft Profit and Loss Account for the year ended 30 September 1984

	£000s	£000s
Turnover	318,000	
Operating profit	12,966	
Development grants	70	
Profit on sale of freehold	1,190	
		14,226
Less:		
Provision for bad debts	131	
Auditors remuneration	93	
Loan interest (net)	378	
Depreciation:		
Buildings	78	
Plant and machinery	774	
Fixtures and fittings	72	
Corporation tax	7,017	
Dividends:		
Interim-preference	120	
Interim-ordinary	370	
		9,033
Balance carried forward		5,193

Draft Balance Sheet as at 30 September 1984

	£		£
Creditors	2,160	Advance Corporation Tax	210
Profit & Loss account	10,659	Income tax on loan interest	162
Corporation tax	7,017	Plant and machinery	774
Loans	6,000	Goodwill	400
Preference shares (50p)	3,000	Trade debtors	6,017
Ordinary shares (25p)	4,500	Land - freehold	2,400
		Stock	9,828
		Buildings	3,360
		Bank balance	9,681
		Fixtures & fittings	504
	33,336		33,336

The following information was available at the time the accounts were drafted:

a. Acquisitions of fixed assets during 1984 were:
   Plant   £144,000
   Fixtures £120,000

b. Government grants have been received in respect of plant purchased during 1984. The whole amount of the grant has been credited to the Profit and Loss Account for the year ended 30 September 1984.

c. Freehold land costing £600,000 was sold for £1,790,000.

d. A contract has been entered into with a building contractor to extend the company's warehouse premises. The contract price was £6,000,000 and work is scheduled to commence on 1 February 1985.

e. The depreciation policy of the company is to provide depreciation at the following rates:
   Buildings   2% per annum on cost
   Plant & Machinery   20% per annum on cost
   Fixtures & Fittings 10% per annum on cost
   During the current year ended 30 September 1984 an additional 10% has been provided on plant and machinery to allow for the increased cost of replacement.

f. The loan is unsecured and repayable in the year 2000. It carries interest at 9% per annum.

g. Stock and work in progress consists of:
   Raw materials   £1,560,000
   Work in progress   £5,550,000
   Stock of finished goods £2,718,000

h. The Corporation Tax in the Profit and Loss Account is calculated at 52% of the taxable profits for the year. It is payable on 30 June 1985. The charge in the Profit and Loss Account includes £357,000 in respect of tax payable on the profit arising from the sale of the land.

i. Trade creditors and trade debtors are all payable and due within the next accounting year.

j. The Operating Profit is after charging the following:
   (i)   Obsolete stock written off   £2,460,000
   (ii) Directors' emoluments   £468,000

	Salary	Fees
This includes		
Managing Director	£146,000	£10,000
Chairman		£120,000
4 other directors		
each receiving	£25,000	£6,000

   (iii) Administration charges   £7,500,000
   (iv) Distribution costs   £29,250,000
   (v)   Hire of plant and machinery   £2,000,000

k. The issued share capital is fully paid up. The preference shares are redeemable at par on 1 October 1996.

The following information has become available since the draft accounts were prepared:

a. The following dividends are proposed: Preference shares - payment of second half year
   Ordinary shares - payment of a dividend of 24%.
   Assume an Advance Corporation Tax rate of 30%.

b. Goodwill is to be written off at 2% per annum.

c. An offer has been received by the company for its obsolete stock (see j above). The offer is for £500,000 provided the company repackages the stock with French instructions at an estimated cost to the company of £150,000 and allows a cash discount of 10% for payment by 31 March 1985.

Required:

Prepare a Profit and Loss Account for the year ended 30 September 1984 and a Balance sheet as at 30 September 1984, for publication in accordance with the requirements of the Companies Acts (1948-1981) (now consolidated into the Companies Act 1985)

(ACCA 2.9(2) June 1985)

42. The chief accountant of Uncertain Ltd is not sure of the appropriate accounting treatment for a number of events occurring during the year 1985-86.

a. A significant number of employees have been made redundant, giving rise to redundancy payments of £100,000 which have been included in manufacturing cost of sales.

b. One of Uncertain Ltd's three factories has been closed down. Closure costs amounted to £575,000. This amount has been deducted from reserves in the balance sheet.

c. The directors have changed the basis of charging depreciation on delivery vehicles. The difference between the old and new methods amounts to £258,800. This has been charged as a prior year adjustment.

365

d. During October 1986 a fire occurred in one of the remaining factories belonging to Uncertain Ltd and caused an estimated £350,000 of additional expenses. This amount has been included in manufacturing cost of sales.

e. It was discovered on 31 October 1986 that a customer was unable to pay his debt to the company of £125,000. The £125,000 was made up of sales in the period July to September 1986. No adjustment has been made in the draft accounts for this item.

Uncertain Ltd.
Draft profit and loss account for the year ended 30 September 1986

	£	£
Sales		5,450,490
Manufacturing cost of sales		3,284,500
Gross profit		2,165,990
Administration expenses	785,420	
Selling expenses	629,800	
		1,415,220
		750,770
Corporation tax (50%)		375,385
		375,385
Proposed dividend on ordinary shares		125,000
		250,385
Prior year adjustment	258,800	
Corporation tax	129,400	
		129,400
		120,985

Required:

a. Write a report to the chief accountant of Uncertain Ltd with suggestions for appropriate treatment for each of the items (a) to (e), with explanations for your proposals.

b. Amend the draft profit and loss account to take account of your proposals.

(Corporation tax should be taken at 50%.

(ACCA 2.9(2) December 1986)

43. **Required:**

a. Calculate a revised profit for Special Books for the year ended 31 December 1984 to reflect any adjustments you think necessary to the treatment of book tokens (see Appendix 7).

b. Prepare journal entries to correct both the 1983 and 1984 accounts in respect of any such adjustments.

(ACCA 2.9(1) December 1986)

Appendix 4: Special Books-draft profit and loss account for the year ended 31 December 1984

	£	£
Sales		610,085
Cost of sales:		
Stock at 1 January 1984	69,500	
Purchases	520,815	
	590,315	
Stock at 31 December 1984	129,368	

366

		460,947
Gross profit		149,138
Salaries	55,096	
Rent and rates	14,773	
Light and heat	1,529	
Repairs	319	
Printing and stationery	10,268	
Postage and carriage	3,994	
Telephone	2,765	
Travel and motor expenses	3,353	
Insurance	2,078	
Cleaning and shop expenses	1,079	
Computer rental	6,000	
Computer maintenance	1,227	
Security installation rental	752	
Advertising	1,081	
Trade subscriptions	750	
Fees (accountancy, surveyor)	989	
Bank charges	10,632	
Sundry expenses	555	
Depreciation: lease	1,903	
fixtures	301	
cars	1,138	
		120,582
Profit before extraordinary items		28,556
Loss on sale of fixed assets	9,593	
Amortisation of lease	8,408	
		18,001
		10,555

Note: No entries have been made for partners' loan interest or other appropriations.

Appendix 7: Further information about book tokens

Tokens Limited is an organisation that operates a scheme to provide booksellers with tokens for sale to the public.

Special Books became a member of this scheme on 1 January 1983 and takes part by:

a. Selling tokens to customers

b. Accepting tokens from customers in exchange for books

The scheme operates as follows:

a. *Selling tokens to customers* Special Books sells tokens for cash. At the end of the year it submits a return to Tokens Limited showing the total value of all the tokens it has sold. Special Books is entitled to deduct 12 1/2% commission and is accountable for the balance to Tokens Limited.

b. *Accepting tokens from customers*
Special Books submits a return (together with the cancelled tokens) at the end of each year showing the total value of the tokens accepted on the sale of books.

c. *Payment to and from Tokens Limited*
Tokens Limited sends Special Books a cheque for the face value of the tokens accepted in exchange for books less 12 1/2% commission deducted by Tokens Limited less the net value of tokens sold direct to customers by Special Books. If sales of tokens exceed the value of tokens exchanged, then Special Books makes payment to Tokens Limited.

Enquiries show that Special Books have included in the sales figure in the profit and loss accounts:

i. the cash proceeds from the sale of tokens.

ii. the face value of tokens exchanged during the year.

iii. the net reimbursement by Tokens Limited received during 1984.

A summary of relevant information is set out below:

	1983 £	1984 £
Stock of unsold tokens in the shop at 1 January	1100.00	1025.25
Stock of unsold tokens in the shop at 31 December	1025.25	350.50

No tokens were received from Tokens
Limited in 1983 or 1984

Tokens Accepted in exchange for Books:

1983 Number	Denomination	1984 Number	Denomination
6	25p	10	25p
30	50p	40	50p
120	£1	110	£1
145	£2	85	£2
180	£5	210	£5
60	£10	105	£10
7	£20	5	£20

The cash book showed that the partnership settled the 1983 account with Tokens Limited on 2 February 1984 and the 1984 account with Tokens Limited on 21 March 1985.

44. The following details have been extracted from the operating statement prepared by the cost accountant for the Hayes Toothpaste Co. Ltd for the month of May 1986.

Production   54,000 Tubes

	Standard £	Variances Adverse £		Favourable £
Materials –				
Powder	6,750	600	Usage	
Chemicals	2,700			180 Usage
Tube	1,350	6	Usage	
Labour	8,100	1,125	Efficiency	315 Rate
Factory overheads	8,100			
Production cost	27,000			

Sales during the month were 4,500 packs of 12 tubes per pack at the standard price of £7.20 per pack.

The company operates a system of absorption costing for factory overheads based on the standard hours worked. An overhead overabsorption of £900 is shown in the cost accounting records.

Price variances on the materials are based on materials purchased and the following details are relevant:

	Stock at 30 April 1986	Purchases during May 1986	Price Variance
Powder	1,500 kilos at cost £1,125	10,000 kilos at 70p	£500 favourable
Chemicals	1,200 litres at cost £2,880	1,200 litres at £2.40	nil
Tubes	2,000 tubes at cost £50	4,000 tubes at 3p each 50,000,000 tubes at 2.5p each	£20 adverse

The standard cost of a pack of 12 tubes is:

	£
Materials–	
Powder 2 kilos	1.50
Chemicals ¼ litre	60
Tubes 12	30
Direct labour (24 minutes)	1.80
	4.20
Factory overheads	1.80
	6.00

Other information available:

i. all sales and purchases in May are paid for in June. There are no other debtors or creditors;

ii. stocks of materials are carried in the balance sheet at cost on a first in first out basis (FIFO). Finished goods stocks are carried at standard factory cost. At the beginning of the month there were 2,500 packs of toothpaste in stock;

iii. administration overheads for the month amount to £750. Selling and distribution overheads were £1,350;

iv. the following figures have been extracted from the month end trial balance;

	£
Plant and machinery –	
cost	100,000
depreciation	54,000
50,000 Ordinary shares of £1 each	50,000
Share premium account	10,000
Profit and loss account at 30 April 1986	26,000
Balance at bank	2,735

Required:

a. A profit and loss account as prepared by the financial accountant showing actual costs and revenue for the month of May 1986.

b. A balance sheet as at 31 May 1986.

(ACCA 2.9(2) June 1986)

45. **Required:**

In the light of the information provided in Appendix 7, show clearly for the accounts for the year ended 31 December 1985:

a. The adjustments needed to the individual accounts to correct them.

b. The effect of the adjustments on the profit and loss account for the year ended 31 December 1985.

(ACCA 2.9(1) June 1986)

Appendix 7 Further information available after the preparation of Appendix 2

On examining the books and other records, the following were discovered:

1. a. One hundred items of £10 each were completely omitted from the physical stock count on 31 December 1985.

   b. The stock sheets at 31 December 1985 were undercast by £4,000.

2. a. The sales total in the sales day book for 31 May 1985 of £2,900 was not posted to the sales account or the sales ledger control account in the nominal ledger.

   b. One item for £750 in the sales day book was posted to the sales ledger control account in the nominal ledger as £1,400 and to the customer's account in the sales ledger as £850.

3. A balance of £6,250 was brought forward in the purchases day book on 1 January 1985. This amount had not been posted to the purchases account or the purchases ledger control account in the nominal ledger in 1984.

4. Included under the heading of investments were £10,000 of the company's own debentures, redeemed on 30 June 1985 for £9,000. It has been decided that these are to be cancelled.

5. The provision for depreciation on plant should have been brought forward as £48,680 not £47,880.

6. The figures of £38,022 for the overdraft was that shown by the bank statement on 4 January 1986. A comparison of the bank statements with the cash book showed the following differences:

   a. Cheques totalling £1,060 were paid into the bank on 30 December and credited to the bank statement on 3 January 1986.

   b. On 1 January 1986 one of the debtors paid £96 direct into the company's bank account.

   c. One of the cheques (for £135) paid into the bank on 19 December 1985 was dishonoured on 31 December 1985.

   d. Cheques for £87, £158 and £327 were drawn but not presented by 4 January 1986.

   e. A standing order for £255 was debited in December in payment of an insurance premium for 1986.

f. Bank charges of £156 were debited on 24 December 1985.

7. The company supplied an American customer with goods to a sales value of £162,720 in 1985 which were billed in US$. Details of the transactions were:

(a) *Sales*

Date	£invoice	Exchange rate
May 1985	£100,000	$1.95 = £1
November 1985	£62,720	$1.25 = £1

(b) *Remittances received*

July 1985	$195,000	$1.5 = £1

(c) Exchange rate at 31 December 1985 was $1.4 = £1.

(d) No entries have been made to deal with the exchange differences.

46. Required:

Prepare a draft profit and loss account for Pourwell Limited for the year ended 31 December 1985 and a draft balance sheet for Pourwell Limited as at 31 December 1985 together with supporting notes to comply as far as possible with the requirements run of the Companies Act 1985.

Note: The only information available at the time is set out in Appendices 1, 2 and 3.

(ACCA 2.9(1) June 1986)

Appendix 1 General introduction to Pourwell Limited

i. Pourwell Ltd is a company that manufactures plastic decanters.

ii. It was incorporated in 1974 with an authorised share capital of £500,000 consisting of 300,000 £1 ordinary shares and £200,000 7% cumulative preference shares of £1 each.

iii. The issued share capital is £300,000 consisting of 200,000 £1 ordinary shares and £100,000 7% cumulative preference shares. The preference shares are all held by an insurance company. The ordinary shares are held as follows:

75,000	Mr Albert (who is also managing director and chairman)
25,000	Mr Bryant (who is also a director)
12,500	Mr Chad (who is also a director)
87,500	held by 7 other shareholders, each with 12,500 shares.

200,000

iv. The company has incurred significant trading losses over the past five years.

v. The directors have been discussing with the company's accountants the advisability of either (a) arranging a merger with Willow Ltd or (b) carrying out a scheme of reorganisation.

vi. The directors estimate that the company will make profits in future years. The profits are estimated to be:

1986	£10,000
1987	£15,000
1988	£20,000

Appendix 2 List of balances extracted from the books of Pourwell Limited as at 31 December 1985

	£
Accrued interest on debentures	10,500
Administrative expenses	105,113
Audit fee accrual	2,850
Bank overdraft	38,022
Bank interest	7,100
Cost of sales	416,028
Creditors (trade)(control account total)	258,550
7% debentures (redeemable 1992)	75,000
Debtors (trade)(control account total)	89,505
Deferred development expenditure	87,500
Directors' loans	125,000
Dividend received (net)	3,500

Expense accrual	1,900
Fixtures and fittings	9,900
Goodwill	150,000
Insurance prepayment	4,000
Investment (at cost)	42,500
Land and buildings	100,000
Ordinary shares of £1 each	200,000
Plant	90,800
Preference shares (7% cumulative)	100,000
Profit and loss account (debit balance)	97,160
Profit on sale of land	15,000
Provision for depreciation of buildings	19,200
Provision for depreciation of plant	47,880
Provision for depreciation of fixtures	4,620
Sales	696,000
Selling and distribution expenses	200,101
Stock of raw material	20,210
Stock of work in progress	10,103
Stock of finished goods	170,102
Wages accrual	2,100

Appendix 3 Further information available when drafting the profit and loss account of Purwell Ltd for the year ended 31 December 1985 and a balance sheet as at that date

i. Directors received the following remuneration:

    Albert   £31,000
    Bryant   £22,000
    Chad   £15,000

    In addition, fees of £2,000 per annum were paid to each director.

ii. Depreciatiion has been provided for in the appropriate expense accounts for the year on the following basis:

	£	Estimated useful life
Land	Nil	
Buildings	1,600	50 years
Plant	4,540	20 years
Fixtures and fittings	660	15 years

iii. During the year the company sold land with a book value of £10,000 and purchased plant for £12,000.

iv. The goodwill arose on the purchase of the assets and liabilities of Mr Chad's business in 1980. The company are proposing to write if off over 10 years commencing 1985.

v. The preference dividend has not been paid for 1984 or 1985.

vi. The directors estimate that the company will return to profits in 1986 and given that they estimate profits will be £10,000 in 1986 rising to £20,000 in 1988 they propose to leave the development costs as an asset for the purpose of the 1985 accounts.

vii. The trade creditors aged analysis shows:

	£
Payable before 1 July 1985	93,490
Payable before 1 October 1985	50,060
Payable before 1 December 1985	30,000
Current	35,000
Payable in 1987	50,000

47. Required:

Draft headings with brief comments as the basis for a report to identify:

a. The major areas of potential improvements in accounting that might arise from the introduction of an electronic point of sale system.

b. The type of financial and numerical information that might be expected from the system.

c. The major problems that might be expected to be met on introducing such a system from an accounting point of view.

(ACCA 2.9(1) June 1987)

Appendix 7: Introduction of computer systems into Roadsports Limited

The finance director of Watersports Limited has been comparing operating performance of the subsidiary and associated companies.

He has produced the following comparative information from the 1986 accounts:

	Watersports Ltd £	Roadsports Ltd £	Speedsports Ltd DM	Propulsion Ltd £
Sales for year	605,850	565,000	475,000	524,790
Selling expenses	96,350	130,400	61,600	78,720
Selling expenses as % sales	15.9%	23.1%	12.9%	15.0%

In discussion with the finance director of Roadsports Limited, the following points were made about that company's activities:

i. The company operated through twenty branches.

ii. Many of their customers preferred to collect goods from the warehouses personally.

iii. Approximately 40% of the customers who collect personally paid on collection, the other 60% were issued with an invoice by the stores personnel for payment within 30 days.

iv. The company was preparing to invite a computer equipment supplier to submit a quotation for computerisation of existing sales and stock accounting systems.

After further discussion, it was decided by the two finance directors that there should be further preparation before inviting a supplier to quote. In particular, it was felt that the financial accountant should prepare a report to consider:

a. The major areas of potential improvement in accounting that might arise from the introduction of an electronic point of sale system.

b. The type of financial and numerical information that might be expected from the new system.

c. The major problems that might be expected to be met on introducing a computer system, from the accountant's point of view.

48. The accountant of Scampion plc a retailing company listed on the London Stock Exchange has produced the following draft financial statements for the company for the year to 31 May 1987.

Profit and loss account year to 31 May 1987

	£000	£000
Sales		3,489
Income from investments		15
		3,504
Purchase of goods and services	1,929	
Value added tax paid on sales	257	
Wages and salaries including pension scheme	330	
Depreciation	51	
Interest on loans	18	
General administration expenses – Shops	595	
– Head office	25	
		3,205
Net profit for year		299

Corporation tax at 40%		120
Profit after tax for year		179

Balance Sheet at 31 May 1987

	£000	£000
Fixed assets		
Land and buildings		1,178
Fixtures, fittings, equipment and motor vehicles		194
Investments		167
		1,539
Current assets		
Stock	230	
Debtors	67	
Cash at bank and in hand	84	
	381	
Current liabilities		
Creditors	487	
		(106)
		1,433
Ordinary share capital (£1 shares)		660
Reserves		703
Loans		70
		1,433

i. Fixed assets details are as follows:

	Cost	Depreciation	Net
	£000	£000	£000
Freehold land and buildings	1,212	34	1,178
Fixtures, fittings and equipment	181	56	125
Motor Vehicles	137	68	69

Purchases of fixed assets during the year were freehold land and buildings £50,000, fixtures, fittings and equipment £40,000, motor vehicles £20,000. The only fixed asset disposal during the year is referred to in Note (x). Depreciation charged during the year was £5,000 for freehold buildings, £18,000 for fixtures, fittings and equipment, and £28,000 for motor vehicles. Straight-line depreciation method is used assuming the following lives: Freehold buildings 40 years, fixtures, fittings and equipment 10 years and motor vehicles 5 years.

ii. A dividend of 10 pence per share is proposed.

iii. A valuation by Bloggs & Co. Surveyors shows the freehold land and buildings to have a market value of £1,350,000.

iv. Loans are:

£20,000 bank loan with a variable rate of interest repayable by 30 September 1987;

£50,000 12% debenture repayable 1995;

£100,000 11% debenture repaid during the year.

There were no other loans during the year.

v. The income from investments is derived from fixed asset investments (shares in related companies) £5,000 and current asset investment (government securities) £10,000.

vi. At the balance sheet date the shares in related companies (cost £64,000) are valued by the directors at £60,000. The market value of the government securities is £115,000 (cost £103,000).

vii. After the balance sheet date but before the financial statements are finalised there is a very substantial fall in share and security prices. The market value of the government securities had fallen to £50,000 by the time the directors signed the accounts. No adjustment has been made for this item in the accounts.

viii. Within two weeks of the balance sheet date a notice of liquidation was received by Scampion plc concerning one of the company's debtors. £45,000 is included in the balance sheet for this debtor and enquiries reveal that nothing is likely to be paid to any unsecured creditor. No adjustment has been made for this item in the accounts.

ix. The corporation tax charge is based on the accounts for the year and there are no other amounts of tax owing by the company.

x. Reserves at 31 May 1986 were:

	£
Revaluation reserve	150,000
Share premium account	225,000
Profit and loss account	149,000

The revaluation reserve represents the after tax surplus on a property which was valued in last year's balance sheet at £400,000 and sold during the current year at book value.

Required:
A profit and loss account for the year to 31 May 1987 and a balance sheet at that date for Scampion plc complying with the Companies Act 1985 in so far as the information given will allow.
Ignore advance corporation tax and related tax credit on investment income.
(ACCA 2.9(2) June 1987)

AAT EXAMINATION QUESTIONS

49. Popham plc has prepared its draft published accounts for the year to 30 September 19-9. Its turnover for the year was £45 million, and its net profit before taxation (before making any of the adjustments outlined below) was £10 million.

Before completing the accounts, the accounting treatment of a number of matters has still to be decided. These are as follows:

1. The company had incurred a net loss of £1 million on the disposal of its entire West African operations.

2. There was an underprovision of £25,000 for corporation tax in respect of the previous year.

3. A major customer had gone into liquidation owing the company £2 million.

   Required:

   a. Define the following terms:

      i. exceptional items;
      and

      ii. extraordinary items;
      and

   b. in accordance with SSAP 6 (Extraordinary items and prior year adjustments), state (being careful to give your reasons), how each of the above matters should be dealt with in the published accounts of Popham plc.

(AAT)

50. The following trial balance has been extracted from the books of account of Greet plc as at 31 March 19–8:

	Dr. £'000	Cr. £'000
Administrative expenses	210	
Called up share capital (ordinary shares of £1 fully paid)		600
Debtors	470	
Cash at bank and in hand	40	
Corporation tax (overprovision in 19–7)		25
Deferred taxation (at 1 April 19–7)		180
Distribution costs	420	
Extraordinary item		60
Fixed asset investments	560	
Franked investment income (amount received)		73
Plant and machinery:		
At cost	750	
Accumulated depreciation (at 31 March 19–8)		220
Profit and loss (at 1 April 19–7)		182
Purchases	960	
Stock (at 1 April 19–7)	140	
Trade creditors		260
Turnover		1,950
	£3,550	£3,550

Additional information:

1. Stock at 31 March 19–8 was valued at £150,000.
2. The following items (inter alia) *are already included* in the balances listed in the above trial balance:

	Distribution costs £'000	Administrative expenses £'000
Depreciation (for the year to 31 March 19–8)	27	5
Hire of plant and machinery	20	15
Auditors' remuneration	–	30
Directors' emoluments	–	45

3. The following rates of taxation are to be assumed:

	%
Corporation tax	35
Income tax	27

4. The corporation tax charge based on the profits on ordinary activities for the year is estimated to be £52,000.
5. A transfer of £16,000 is to be made to the credit of the deferred taxation account.
6. The extraordinary item relates to the profit made on the disposal of a factory in Belgium following the closure of the company's entire operations in that country. The corporation tax payable on the extraordinary item is estimated to be £20,000.
7. The company's authorised share capital consists of 1,000,000 ordinary shares of £1 each.
8. A final ordinary dividend of 50p per share is proposed.
9. There were no purchases or disposals of fixed assets during the year.
10. The market value of the fixed assets investments as at 31 March 19–8 was £580,000. There were no purchases or sales of such investments during the year.

Required:

Insofar as the information permits, prepare the company's published profit and loss account for the year to 31 March 19–8 and a balance sheet as at that date in accordance with the Companies Act

1985 and with related statements of standard accounting practice.

Relevant notes to the profit and loss account and balance sheet and detailed workings should be submitted with your answer, but a statement of the company's accounting policies is NOT required.

(AAT)

51. You are presented with the following information relating to Toy plc for the year to 30 June 19–8.

	£'000 Dr.	£'000 Cr.
Administrative expenses	90	
Advance corporation tax (paid on 14 April 19–8)	15	
Called up share capital (ordinary shares of £1 each)		980
Cash at bank and in hand	5	
Corporation tax (overprovision for the year to 30 June 19–7)		25
10% Debenture loan stock (repayable 2020)		300
Deferred taxation		200
Development costs (incurred during the year)	30	
Distribution costs	40	
Dividends paid (interim paid on 1 March 19–8)	49	
Dividends received (on 1 January 19–8)		14
Factory closure costs (before any tax relief)	150	
Interest paid (on debenture loan stock)	15	
Investments (listed)	45	
Land and buildings: at cost	4,200	
accumulated depreciation at 1 July 19–7		2,600
Plant and machinery: at cost	200	
accumulated depreciation at 1 July 19–7		75
Profit and loss account		70
Purchases (net of value added tax)	400	
Research expenditure	20	
Sales (net of value added tax)		980
Trade creditors		45
Trade debtors	16	
Stock at 1 July 19–7	35	
Value added tax account		21
	£5,310	£5,310

Additional information:

1. The company was incorporated in 1975.

2. The following rates of taxation are assumed to apply:

	%
Value added tax	15
Income tax	30
Corporation tax	35

3. Stock is valued at the lower of cost or net realisable value. At 30 June 19–8 it was estimated to be worth £55,000.

4. Fixed assets are depreciated on a straight line basis assuming no residual value. The following depreciation rates are to be applied:

	%
Buildings	5
Plant and machinery	20

The depreciation charge for the year is to be apportioned as follows:

	Cost of sales	Distribution costs	Administrative expenses
	%	%	%
Buildings	60	10	30
Plant and machinery	75	10	15

The cost of the land was £3,200,000. Land is not now depreciated. There were no purchases or sales of fixed assets during the year.

5. Development costs are to be amortised over a three year period. They are to be charged to cost of sales.
6. Corporation tax based on the profits for the year (before allowing for the factory closure costs) is estimated to be £95,000.
7. A transfer of £60,000 is to be made FROM the deferred taxation account.
8. Corporation tax relief on the factory closure costs is estimated to be £45,000.
9. The directors propose a final dividend of 5p per share.

Required:

Insofar as the information permits, prepare Toy plc's profit and loss account for the year to 30 June 19–8 and a balance sheet as at that date in accordance with the disclosure requirements of the Companies Act 1985 and related statements of standard accounting practice.

Formal notes to the accounts are NOT required, although detailed workings should be submitted with your answer.

(AAT)

52. The following information has been extracted from the books of Pick plc for the year to 31 March 19–9:

	Dr. £'000	Cr. £'000
Administrative expenses	175	
Called up share capital (ordinary shares of £1 each)		200
Cash at bank and in hand	15	
Corporation tax (under-provision for the year to 31 March 19–8)	10	
Deferred taxation (at 1 April 19–8)		90
Distribution costs	240	
Land and buildings: at cost	210	
accumulated depreciation (at 1 April 19–8)		48
Plant and machinery: at cost	125	
accumulated depreciation (at 1 April 19–8)		75
Profit and loss account (at 1 April 19–8)		350
Purchases	470	
Sales		1,300
Stock (at 1 April 19–8)	150	
Trade creditors		60
Trade debtors	728	
	£2,123	£2,123

Additional information:

1. Stock at 31 March 19–9 was valued at £250,000.
2. Buildings and plant and machinery are depreciated on a straight-line basis (assuming no residual value) at the following rates:

	On cost %
Buildings	5
Plant and machinery	20

Land at cost was £110,000. Land is not depreciated.
There were no purchases or sales of fixed assets during the year to 31 March 19–9.

The depreciation charges for the year to 31 March 19–9 are to be apportioned as follows:

	%
Cost of sales	60
Distribution costs	20
Administrative expenses	20

3. Included in the distribution costs and administrative expenses are the following items:

	£'000
Auditor's remuneration	67
Directors' emoluments	120
Entertaining overseas' customers	40
Hire of office furniture and fixtures	50
Political donations	5
Travelling expenses	65

4. Corporation tax for the year to 31 March 19–9 (based on profits for that year at a rate of 35%) is estimated to be £135,000.

5. The directors propose to pay a dividend of 150p per share. The basic rate of income tax is assumed to be 25%.

6. The balance of £90,000 on the deferred taxation account as at 1 April 19–8 is after deducting £50,000 ACT recoverable based on the proposed dividend for the year to 31 March 19–8.

7. The company's authorised share capital consists of 300,000 ordinary shares of £1 each.
   Required:
   Insofar as the information permits, prepare Pick plc's profit and loss account for the year to 31 March 19–9 and a balance sheet as at that date in accordance with the MINIMUM disclosure requirements of the Companies Act 1985 and related statements of standard accounting practice.
   [Note: A statement of accounting policies is NOT required.]

(AAT)

53. The following balances have been obtained from the books of account of Kuy public limited company for the year to 30 September 19–9:

	£'000
Accruals (amounts owing at 30 September 19–9)	8,000
Administrative expenses	20,000
Called up share capital: ordinary shares	20,000
preference shares	5,000
Cash at bank and in hand (debit)	7,300
Corporation tax (over provision for the year to 30 September 19–8)	600
Cost of sales	310,000
Distribution costs	8,000
Deferred taxation (credit at 1 October 19–8)	11,000
Extraordinary charges	4,000
Franked investment income (net amount received on 1 January 19–9)	900
Fixed asset investments	400
Interest paid during the year	3,800
Interim dividends: ordinary shares (paid on 31 March 19–9)	650
preference shares (paid on 30 April 19–9)	250
Land and buildings: at cost	22,000
accumulated depreciation (at 30 September 19–9)	2,000
Plant and machinery: at cost	48,000
accumulated depreciation (at 30 September 19–9)	28,000
Prepayments (amounts paid in advance at 30 September 19–9)	5,000
Profit and loss account (credit at 1 October 19–8)	24,000
Stock (at 30 September 19–9)	124,000
Trade creditors	98,000
Trade debtors	74,100
Turnover	430,000

Additional information:

1. The company's share capital structure is as follows:

	Authorised £'000	Issued and fully paid £'000
Ordinary shares of £1 each	80,000	20,000
10% Preference shares of £1 each	20,000	5,000
	£100,000	£25,000

2. Taxation rates:

	%
Value added tax	15
Basic rate of income tax	25
Corporation tax	35

3. Corporation tax based on the profit on ordinary activities for the year is estimated to be £6,200,000.

4. Corporation tax relief of £1,200,000 is available on the extraordinary charges.

5. A transfer of £11,000,000 is to be made to the deferred taxation account.

6. A final ordinary dividend of 6.5p per share is proposed.

7. The deferred taxation balance at 1 October 19–8 is shown after debiting ACT of £300,000 based on the proposed ordinary dividend for the year to 30 September 19–8, and the half year's preference dividend payable in respect of that year. The half year's preference dividend was paid on 31 October 19–8, and the proposed ordinary dividend on 15 December 19–8.

Required:

Insofar as the information permits, prepare Kuy's profit and loss account for the year to 30 September 19–9, and a balance sheet as at that date in accordance with the Companies Act 1985 and related statements of standard accounting practice.

(Note: formal notes to the accounts are NOT required, but detailed workings should be submitted with your answer.)

(AAT)

5 Value Added Statements

GENERAL BACKGROUND

1.0 The Corporate Report published in 1975 by the then Accounting Standard Steering Committee (ASSC) (subsequently redesignated the Accounting Standards Committee (ASC)), advocated the preparation by businesses of statements of their added value.

1.1 In this context, value added constitutes the difference between the monetary value of outputs and inputs of goods and services attributed to the business.

1.2 Many businesses now produce value added statements and publish them either as part of their Annual Report and Accounts or as part of the (internally circulated) Employee Report or as part of both these Reports. It must be stressed, however, that such disclosure is non-mandatory on companies, being required neither by statute nor by accounting standards.

1.3 The main reason adduced by companies for publishing these statements is that they focus attention away from those aspects of performance which are of particular interest to shareholders and directors (profit and derivatives), on to the broader concept of value added and illustrate the inter-dependence of the respective parties benefitting from it.

USERS

1.4 Potential and actual users of published accounting information, including value added statements, were identified in The Corporate Report as:

1. equity investors
2. loan creditors (long and short term)
3. employees
4. analyst-advisors
5. business contacts
6. government (local and national)
7. the public

The information needs of the above groups vary one from another and from the needs of management which publishes that information.

USES.

1.5 Possible uses to which value added information could be put were suggested in The Corporate Report as being:

1. a means of predicting managerial efficiency;
2. a means of evaluating the relative rewards of "stakeholders" of, or claimants against the company;
3. a means of indicating a company's wage paying ability in wages negotiations;
4. a means of evaluating what is nebulously referred to as the social performance of a company.

VALUE ADDED CONCEPT

2.0 Wealth in the economic sense can be calculated for an industry by aggregating value added at each production stage. For example, to use an oversimplified situation, the owner of a commercially run woodland supplies timber to a pulping mill where it is turned into sheet cardboard and sold to a carton manufacturer for production into document filing cartons which are bought by a stationer for resale to the public.

2.1 The output value of the woodland owner, as measured by the factor payments (profit, wages etc) becomes the input value of the pulp mill. After further factor payments this becomes the output value of the pulp mill and the input value of the carton manufacturer, whose output value then constitutes the input value of the stationer. The stationer's value comprises his input value plus his factor payments.

2.2 Because, as, has already been stated, value added is the difference between input value and output value, it can be seen to equal the factor payments. For an industry, it is equal to the aggregate of the factor payments made by all the producers in that industry. It is equal also to the output value of the final producer. Reverting to the example in 2.1, value added (in total) equals the aggregate factor payments of the woodland owner, the pulp mill, the carton manufacturer and the stationer. The resultant total coincides in amount with the output value of the stationer.

CONTENT AND FORMAT

3.0 Profit and loss accounts show the profit (loss) for a period and how it is arrived at and appropriated. In similar fashion, value added statements show the value added for a business for a particular period and how it is arrived at and appropriated to the previously mentioned stakeholders:

> the workforce - for wages, salaries and related expenses;
> the financiers - for interest on loans and for dividends on share capital;
> the government - for corporation tax;
> the business - for retained profits

3.1 Technically, it is possible to measure output value on either a production, or a sales, basis. Most, if not all companies calculate value added on the basis of sales value, for the same reasons that they arrive at profit or loss using a sales revenue figure rather than a value of production figure. Most companies use VAT exclusive sales figures.

3.2 Input value comprises the cost of goods and services bought in from external sources. As it is not usual to adjust the input value figure to a "cost of sales" basis, the resultant figure of value added is merely a balancing figure agreeing with total distributions to stakeholders (see 3.0). In line with sales, VAT is also excluded from the bought in figure.

DEPRECIATION

3.3 Another point of difficulty is the treatment of depreciation. One body of opinion (including The Corporate Report) advocates that depreciation should be regarded as a distribution to the company of value added for the purposes of reinvestment. The opposite viewpoint is that depreciation should be regarded as part of input value thereby reducing total value added, which is then described as net value added.

3.4 In fact only a small number of companies report a figure on the net basis; the great majority prefer to adopt the gross basis for reporting value added. In the former case, depreciation is regarded as a reduction in value added, whilst in the latter it is an appropriation of it. Surveys have shown that about 92% of companies use a gross basis.

FORMAT - SIMPLE CIRCUMSTANCES

3.5 After allowing for modifications due to use of the "net" basis, value added statements are prepared to a recognisable pattern, of which the following is a typical example for a small company. Amounts have been assumed but the percentages have been calculated on them. Corresponding figures for the previous year, which would ordinarily have been shown, have been omitted.

EXAMPLE

VAS PLC
Value Added Statement
for year ended 30 June 19-8

	£000	£000	%	%
Sales (excluding VAT)		15,000		
Less Cost of goods and services				
bought in (excluding VAT)		9,000		
Value added		**6,000**		**100.0**
Applied as follows:				
To pay employees:				
Salaries, wages, pensions				
and related costs		3,960		66.0
To pay providers of capital:				
Interest on loans	240		4.0	
Dividends to shareholders	300		5.0	
		540		9.0

Payable to government:			
Corporation tax		600	10.0
Retained in the business for			
maintenance of assets and			
for expansion:			
Depreciation		540	9.0
Retained profit		360	6.0
		—	—
		900	15.0
		6,000	100.0

On the gross basis, value added can be seen to be £6,000,000. If the net basis had been employed, the statement would have appeared thus:

VAS PLC
Value Added Statement
for year ended 30 June 19-8

	£000	£000	%	%
Sales (excluding VAT)		15,000		
Less Cost of goods and services				
bought in (excluding VAT)	9,000			
Depreciation	540			
		9,540		
Value added		5,460	100.0	
Applied as follows:				
To pay employees:				
Salaries, wages, pensions				
and related costs		3,960	72.5	
To pay providers of capital:				
Interest on loans	240		4.4	
Dividends to shareholders	300		5.5	
		540	9.9	
Payable to government:				
Corporation tax		600	11.0	
Retained in the business for				
expansion:				
Retained profit		360	6.6	
		5,460	100.0	

In the net basis version (above) it can be seen that, due to the reduction in value added following the alternative treatment accorded to depreciation, the relative shares of the claimants, as indicated by the percentages, have altered by comparison with the gross basis.

Many companies which publish value added statements also publish the same information but in a pictorial presentation which may take the form of a bar diagram or a pie chart or some equally graphic device.

CONTENTIOUS ITEMS
3.6 Certain difficulties which arise in compiling value added statements have already been mentioned, namely, the sales value/production value problem and the alternative treatment for depreciation giving rise to gross or net value added. Other points of contention are considered in the following sub- sections.

EXTRAORDINARY ITEMS
3.7 The question arises whether extraordinary items should be included on value added statements. By

definition, these items fall outside the normal operations of the business and include such items as profits or losses on disposal of fixed assets and gains or losses arising from certain foreign currency translations. (Note, however, that gains or losses from exchange differences on transactions in foreign currency are within the normal operations of a business but may be exceptional in amount). Extraordinary and exceptional items, inter alia, are defined in Chapter 4 and following and in SSAP 6. The preferred treatment is to include extraordinary items as a separate category, in arriving at value added (as illustrated in 3.13), in such a way as to disclose separately, value added as the result of normal manufacturing and trading activities.

INVESTMENT INCOME

3.8 In a manufacturing and/or trading business, investment income, in the form of interest and dividends, from trade investments also arises outside the normal operations. Separate disclosure is advocated in similar fashion to extraordinary items in 3.7. (This is also illustrated in 3.13).

SHARE OF PROFITS OR LOSSES OF ASSOCIATED COMPANIES

3.9 Where an investor company holds sufficient shares in an investee company, with the result that the latter company is classed as an associated company, the investor company should include, as a separate category. "Share of profits (or losses) of associated company." (This is also illustrated in 3.13) (Accounting for associated companies is dealt with in Section 2 Chapter 1, and in SSAP 1).

PAYE AND NATIONAL INSURANCE ETC CONTRIBUTIONS

3.10 It is a well established principle that, in preparing accounting statements, sums attributable to employees are disclosed gross, that is, before deduction of those items, comprising mainly income tax (PAYE) and national insurance contributions, for which a company acts in the capacity as a government collector. (The resultant net figure after deductions is generally referred to as "take-home pay".)

3.11 One viewpoint is that in the applications section of a value added statement, payments to employees should be shown net (that is, on a take- home basis) and the deductions referred to in 3.10 should be included under the payable to government heading. The main argument adduced to support this contention is that employees are interested more in what they actually receive than in the gross amount which they do not receive and that this distinction is important when evaluating the relative rewards of stake-holders (see 1.5).

3.12 The above viewpoint, however, has not impressed UK industry in general. A number of surveys have established that in a representative selection of value added statements, approximately 94% disclose payments to employees on a gross basis. The reasoning behind this is that liability to income tax and national insurance deductions is a personal liability of the employees as individuals and that the company is merely acting as a collection agent for the government.

FORMAT - COMPLICATED CIRCUMSTANCES

3.13 The simple format shown in the examples in 3.5 has to be modified when the complications outlined in 3.7 to 3.9 arise, thus (figures assumed):

VAS PLC
Value Added Statement
for year ended 30 June 19-8

	£000	£000	%	%
Sales (excluding VAT)		15,000		
Less Cost of goods and services bought in (excluding VAT)		9,000		
Value added by trading operations		6,000		
Investment income		430		
Share of profits of associated companies		710		
Extraordinary items: Loss on closure of regional depot	(350)			

Extraordinary losses including exchange translation losses (net) of overseas subsidiaries		(90)	
			(440)
Value added available for distribution		6,700	100.0
Applied as follows:			
To pay employees:			
Salaries, wages, pensions and related costs		3,960	59.1
To pay providers of capital:			
Interest on loans	240		3.6
Dividends to shareholders	300		4.5
		540	8.1
Payable to government:			
Corporation tax		600	8.9
Retain in business for maintenance of assets and for expansion:			
Depreciation	540		8.1
Retained profit	1,060		15.8
		1,600	23.9
		6,700	100.0

There is no standard format of universal agreement as regards the content of value added statements, but the above should serve as a useful model for examination question purposes.

STUDENT SELF TESTING
Test Exercises

1. The summarised trading and profit and loss account of Guthrie Ltd (for internal circulation) for year ended 30 September 19-4 was:

Guthrie Ltd
Trading and profit and loss account
for year ended 30 September 19-4

	£	£
Sales		3,027
less		
Cost of Sales		2,051
		976
Gross profit		976
less		
Wages and salaries		260
Interest paid	18	
Depreciation	97	
Other expenses	55	
		430
Profit before tax		546
less		
Corporation tax		119

Profit after tax	427
less	
Dividends paid and proposed	62
	—
Profit for the year retained	365
	—

Required:

Prepare a value added statement for the year, treating depreciation as an appropriation of value added.

2. The facts are the same as in 1.

Required:

Prepare a value added statement for the year, treating depreciation as an input value.

3. a. You are required to describe your understanding of the term "value added" as used in accounting.

   b. Using the following summarised information prepare:

   i. a conventional profit statement of a company

   ii. a value added statement.
   Summarised information for XYZ Ltd in respect of the year ended 31 December 19-9.

	£000
Salaries and wages	200
Purchased materials used in production	300
Sales	740
Corporation tax on the profit for the year	60
Dividend proposed	24
Services purchased	60
Depreciation of fixed assets	40
Loan interest paid and payable	20

   iii. There is an alternative view on the treatment of depreciation in value added statements. What is this view and how would it affect the answer you have produced in answer to question b.ii.

   c. What advantages are claimed for including a value added statement in a company's corporate report?

   (ACCA)

4. a. Many companies currently include a statement of 'value added' in their annual reports. From the information given below relating to SV Public Limited Company, you are required to prepare such a statement for each of the three years, 19-9, 19-0 and 19-1.

   Your statements should reveal how the value added was distributed in both monetary and percentage terms.

SV Public Limited Company

Year	19-1	19-0	19-9
	£000	£000	£000
10% Debentures	300.0	270.0	270.0
9% Preference shares	100.0	100.0	100.0
Ordinary shares (of £0.50 each, nominal value)	800.0	800.0	800.0
Auditors remuneration	2.5	2.1	1.7
Wages incurred	151.7	149.4	125.1
Depreciation	38.7	36.1	30.4
Debtors	217.4	192.3	178.1
Fuel consumed	72.5	60.4	47.6
Hire of plant and machinery	10.3	9.6	7.5
Provision for corporation tax	100.4	98.2	75.7
Creditors	132.5	112.1	106.6

Salaries incurred	50.8	49.5	41.7
Materials consumed	733.6	620.4	598.3
Sales	1,290.9	1,150.9	1,030.7
Fixed assets (net book value)	931.4	898.6	827.6
Ordinary Share dividend (per share)	3.9 pence	3.7 pence	3.1 pence

b. From the value added statements prepared in part (a), you are required to provide further ratios in respect of the employees interests and to comment thereon.

You are advised that the total number of employees were as follows:

Year	19-1	19-0	19-9
Number of employees	45	44	37

5. The following balances have been extracted from the books of the company for the year ended 30th June 19-9:

	£000
Customs and excise duties (included in the turnover)	160.4
Depreciation charge for the year	13.5
Dividends to ordinary shareholders	6.7
Interest on borrowed money	7.3
Investment income received	6.2
Minority interests in subsidiaries (including dividends 2.5 payable by the subsidiaries)	4.0
Profit retained	16.5
Purchases of plant	120.4
Raw materials and bought-in services used	325.1
Stock and work-in-progress at 30th June 19-9	62.7
Turnover (excluding value added tax)	642.7
United Kingdom and overseas corporation tax	15.4
Wages, salaries and retirement benefits	100.0

You are required to:

a. Prepare a value added statement for the year ended 30th June 1979, selecting the appropriate items from the list of balances, and

b. state the purpose(s) of the value added statement now being presented by many public companies.

ACCA EXAMINATION QUESTIONS

6. The Consolidated Profit and Loss Account of Value Ltd has been drafted for the year ended 30 June 1982 with supporting notes as set out below:

			1982
	£000	£000	£000
Sales		7,293	
Value Added Tax		432	6,861
Trading Profit (Note 1)		537	
Deduct:			
Depreciation	71		
Interest (Note 2)	40		
		(111)	
Add: Investment and rent income (Note 2)	12		
Surplus on property disposal	4	16	
Profit before tax		442	
Taxation		105	
Profit after tax		337	
Deduct: (Note 3)			

386

Foreign currency differences	3
Extraordinary items	7
	10
	327
Dividends	141
Retained Profit	__186__

Note 1. Trading Profit

	£000
After charging the following:	
Directors emoluments	3
Audit remuneration	1
Hire of equipment	56

Note 2. Interest, investment and rent income:

Interest paid on bank loans and overdrafts	43
Interest received	(3)
	40
Rent from let properties	12

Note 3. Extraordinary items:

	£'000
Surplus on sale and leaseback of properties	8
Reduction of interest in subsidiary to book value	(15)
	7

Note 4. Payment to employees for wages and pension contributions totalled £1,071,000.

Required:

a. Prepare a Value Added Statement for the year ended 30 June 1982.

b. Select three of the items that appear in a statement of value added and briefly discuss possible alternative methods of disclosing these items within the statement.

(ACCA 2.9 (2) June 1982)

7. **Required:**

a. Prepare a Value Added Statement for Confectioners Ltd for the year ended 31 December 1983 with comparative figures.

b. Provide five ratios from the Value Added Statement that you consider would be of interest to employees of the firm with a brief note on the information shown by each.

(ACCA 2.9(1) June 1984)

Appendix 2

Summarised Profit and Loss Account for the year ended 31 December 1983 and summarised Balance Sheets as at 31 December 1983 of Black Root Ltd and Confectioners Ltd.

	Black Root Ltd		Confectioners Ltd	
	1982	*1983*	*1982*	*1983*
	£000s	£000s	£000s	£000s
Turnover	27,968	34,523	2,492	3,536
Trading Profit	6,992	8,740	608	868
Depreciation	1,472	1,840	128	192
Debenture Interest	736	920	64	96

	4,784	5,980	416	580
Taxation	2,208	2,346	240	224
Profit after tax	2,576	3,634	176	356
Dividends paid:				
Ordinary	402.5	483	–	–
Preference	322	322	22	22
Dividends Proposed	805	1,041	100	235
Issued Ordinary Shares	8,050	10,410	2,016	2,352
Issued 7% Preference Shares	4,600	4,600	320	320
Share Premium	–	2,110	–	504
Retained Profits	3,680	5,468	300	399
10% Debentures	7,360	9,200	640	960
Creditors	736	1,044	320	384
Current Account with				
Black Root Ltd				57
Tax	1,897	2,070	230	257
ACT Payable	345	446	43	101
Proposed dividend	805	1,041	100	235
	27,473	36,389	3,969	5,569
Fixed assets	18,400	22,080	1,792	2,176
Investments in Confectioners Ltd.		3,709		
Investment in Health Sales Ltd.		1,190		
Stock	1,104	1,397	512	640
Current Account with				
Confectioners Ltd.		70		
Current Account with				
Health Sales Ltd.		140		
Debtors	2,530	5,060	1,404	1,600
ACT Recoverable	345	446	43	101
Cash at Bank	5,094	2,297	218	1,052
	27,473	36,389	3,969	5,569

Additional information.

a. Black Root Ltd's investment in Confectioners Ltd consisted of 1,209,000 Ordinary shares of £1 each acquired on 1 January 1983 and 201,600 Ordinary shares of £1 each acquired under the Rights Issue on 31 December 1983.

b. During the year ended 31 December 1983 Black Root Ltd purchased from Confectioners Ltd one of its fixed assets, a machine, for £126,000. Confectioners Ltd had invoiced the machine at book value plus 40%. Black Root Ltd has depreciated the machine at 20% of the invoiced price.

c. Black Root Ltd supplied goods to Confectioners Ltd at cost plus 25%. During the year ended 31 December 1983 Black Root Ltd despatched goods with an invoiced value of £485,000 and received cash of £415,000 from Confectioners Ltd.

During the year Confectioners Ltd received goods from Black Root Ltd with an invoiced value of £475,000 and made payments to them totalling £418,000. At 31 December 1983 the stock of Confectioners Ltd included goods supplied by Black Root Ltd with an invoiced value of £50,000.

d. During the year ended 31 December 1983 Black Root Ltd sold fixed assets of £575,000 (net book value £460,000) and Confectioners Ltd sold fixed assets for £32,000 (net book value £48,000). The respective profit and loss have been included in the respective trading profit.

e. The proposed dividends from Confectioners Ltd have been included in the Black Root Ltd debtors in the Balance Sheet as at 31 December 1983.

f. It is group policy to disclose Goodwill on Consolidation in the Consolidated Balance Sheet.

Appendix 6
Employee Productivity Statistics
The following information has been prepared by the management accountant of Black Root Ltd.

	Gross Wages		Sales/Wages		No. of Employees	
	1982	1983	1982	1983	1982	1983
	£'000s	£000s				
Black Root Ltd.	6,400	8,950	4.37	3.86	1164	1492
Confectioners Ltd.	628	891	3.97	3.97	143	197
Health Sales Ltd.	–	223	–	7.87	–	72

Note 1 No adjustment has yet been made to show the effect of the change in the Retail Price Index. The index was:

1	January 1982	120
31	December 1982	140
31	December 1983	154

Note 2 The summary appears to show that productivity of staff in Black Root Ltd is falling and that productivity in Health Sales Ltd is substantially better than in Black Root Ltd and in Confectioners Ltd.

Note 3 The employees are categorised as follows:

	Selling	*Distribution*	*Administration*
Black Root Ltd.	837	452	203
Confectioners Ltd.	93	44	60
Health Sales Ltd.	22	20	30

8. Manvers Ltd includes with its financial statements each year a statement of value added. The draft value added statement for the year ended 31 May 1986 is as follows:

	£	£
Revenue from sales		204,052
Bought in materials and services		146,928
Value added by the company		57,124
Applied to:		
The Benefit of Employees		
Salaries	16,468	
Deductions for income tax and national insurance	3,352	
	13,116	
Pension schemes	2,810	
Employees' profit sharing schemes	525	
Welfare and staff amenities	806	
		17,257
Central and Local Government		
Value added tax	30,608	
Corporation tax	985	
Local rates	325	
Tax etc. deducted from salaries and loan interest	3,832	
		35,750

The Providers of Capital

Interest on loan capital	1,600	
Income tax deducted	480	
	1,120	
Interest on bank overdrafts	250	
Dividends to shareholders of the company	500	
		1,870

The Replacement of Assets and the
Expansion of the Business

Depreciation	1,835	
Retained profits	412	
		2,247
		57,124

Discussion among the board of directors on the draft figures have revealed a wide variation of opinion on the usefulness of the value added statement to the readers of the accounts.

Some board members say that the value added statement is confusing as it is only a redrafting of the results which are shown in the profit and loss account, which gives all the information necessary. Another view is that the source and application of funds statement is far more important.

Required:

a. A report to the directors showing the advantages of the value added statement compared with the profit and loss account and the source and application of funds statement. Your report should deal specifically with the points raised in discussion by the directors.

b. Construct a profit and loss account from the information given.

c. Calculate the funds arising from operations for use in a source and application of funds statement.

(ACCA 2.9(2) June 1986)

6 Amalgamations and Absorptions

GENERAL BACKGROUND

1.0 The circumstances whereby one business gains control of one or more other businesses, is fairly common. Reasons for this occurrence are many and varied but are usually to enable advantages to be gained or disadvantages to be avoided.

1.1 Combination patterns range from the horizontal combination of businesses of a similar nature for the purposes of securing economies of scale and of reducing competition, to the vertical combination – a line combination from producer to retailer – aimed at securing the benefits of rationalisation. A combination is described as diverse when totally dissimilar businesses, with little or nothing in common, combine. The usual reason for this is to spread risk.

METHODS OF COMBINATION

2.0 The terminology in this area of accounting is imprecise. Different authors use different labels to describe identical circumstances. It is important, therefore, to understand that the terms used in this section of the manual need not necessarily mean the same in a different textbook. In particular, in the context of corporate bodies, the terms acquisition and merger have specific meanings and implications. These are dealt with in Section IV. The main methods by which combinations can be effected are described in the sub-sections which now follow.

AMALGAMATION

2.1 This involves the formation of a new business which then acquires the assets (and possibly the liabilities) of the two or more existing businesses, which are then wound up. Ideally suited to this method are similar sized businesses operating on a relatively small scale.

2.2 In diagram form this situation can be represented as:

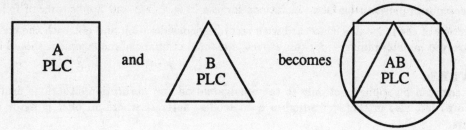

ABSORPTION

2.3 This applies when a relatively large, dominant, business acquires the assets (and possibly the liabilities) of the one or more existing businesses, which are then wound up. The diagrammatic representation of this situation is:

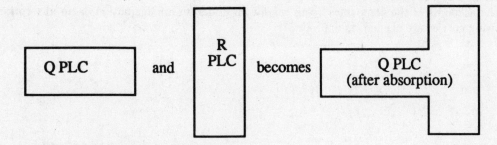

ACQUISITION OF CONTROLLING INTEREST

2.4 In 2.1 it was stated that the amalgamation method is employed when relatively small scaled businesses are concerned. Where this is not the case and large, complex businesses are involved, a holding company is usually established to acquire all, or a majority holding, of the voting shares of those companies which then continue in existence, but as subsidiaries of the holding company.

2.5 In diagram form, this situation can be represented as:

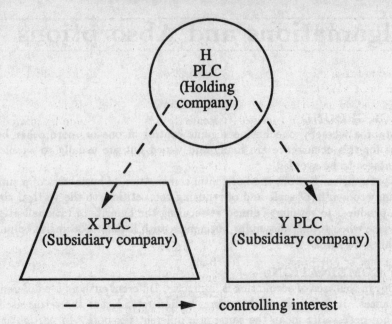

------▶ controlling interest

2.6 The acquisition of a controlling interest can also arise without the establishment of a holding company for the purpose, when an existing dominant company acquires a controlling interest in one or more other companies.

TYPES OF CONSIDERATION

2.7 Irrespective of the method of combination, the consideration can take one of several forms.

    a. payment of cash
    b. issue of shares
    c. issue of loan capital
    d. any composite permutation of a., b., c.

    This section of the manual is concerned with recording consideration and not with the complex considerations involved in determining it; for this aspect, a manual of financial management should be consulted.

TAKEOVERS

2.8 This term can be applied not only to the amalgamation and absorption situations dealt with in 2.1 to 2.3 (above) but also in the acquisition of a controlling interest where an offer is made direct to the shareholders.

ACCOUNTING ENTRIES

3.0 The accounting entries consequent upon a combination vary according to the combination method employed, each of which will now be considered.

AMALGAMATION AND ABSORPTION

3.1 In the accounts of the companies being wound up under an amalgamation or an absorption scheme, the following entries are needed, as appropriate:

Event	Account	
	Debited	Credited
1 Assets taken over (at book values)	Realisation	Individual assets
2 Realisation expenses	Realisation	Bank
3 Profit on realisation (derived) (alternative to 7)	Realisation	Sundry shareholders (or Capital)
4 Liabilities taken over	Individual liabilities	Realisation
5 Discount received from creditors	Creditors	Realisation
6 Purchase consideration agreed	New company	Realisation
7 Loss on realisation (derived) (alternative to 3)	Sundry shareholders (or Capital)	Realisation
8 Receipt of purchase consideration from new/ existing company	Bank and/or Shares in new company and/or Debentures in new company	New Company
9 Transfer of shareholders' funds	Share capital Reserves	Sundry shareholders
10 Distribution of purchase consideration to owners (shareholders or partners or sole proprietor, as appropriate)	Sundry shareholders (or Capital)	Bank and/or Shares in new company and/or Debentures in new company
11 Settlement of creditors	Creditors	Bank

When a company is in process of being liquidated a number of other accounts, additional to those shown above, would be prepared. For example, a Liquidator's and Liquidator's Remuneration account would be opened together with a Deficiency account (or Surplus account, as appropriate). To this latter account would be transferred the realisation profit or loss and the reserves and the liquidation costs would be debited. The Deficiency (Surplus) account would then be closed by transfer to Sundry Shareholders.

For the practical purposes of answering examination questions set in Advanced Accounting Practice papers, the refinements of the previous paragraph can be ignored in most cases and the short-cut expedient, outlined in the above table, used instead if the liquidation is consequent upon amalgamations or absorptions or reconstructions (see Chapter 7) of companies. If, however, the question is specifically concerned with liquidations as a main feature, the proper system should be followed.

3.2 If the business being wound up is either that of a sole trader or of a partnership, Capital should be substituted for Sundry Shareholders in 3, 7 and 10 above; entry 9 would not be made at all. If the closure is consequent upon an absorption, the name of the existing absorbing company should be substituted at 6, 8 and 10.

3.3 The entries needed on the establishment of a new company set up prior to an amalgamation being effected, have already been dealt with in Chapter 1 (Issue of shares and debentures). In an absorption situation the dominant company has been in existence for some time. It is therefore necessary to consider only the additional entries which arise in the books of the new or absorbing company.

3.4 When an amalgamation or an absorption takes place, the following extra entries are needed, as appropriate, in the books of the new or existing businesses, respectively.

Event	Account	
	Debited	Credited
1 Purchase consideration agreed	Acquisition of - - - - - - - - (name of business acquired)	Liquidator(s) of - - - - - - - - (name of business acquired)
2 Assets taken over (at current valuations)	Individual assets	Acquisition of - - - - - - - -
3 Liabilities taken over (at actual amounts to be liquidated)	Acquisition of - - - - - - - -	Individual liabilities
4 Transmission of purchase consideration to business(es) being wound up	Liquidator(s) of - - - - - - - -	Bank (Cash) and/or Share Capital and/or Debentures and possibly Share Premium

3.5 If the business being merged or absorbed is either a partnership or a sole proprietorship, the name of the firm or of the sole proprietorship should be substituted for Liquidator(s) of............in 1 and 4.

3.6 Sometimes goodwill is stated as an asset taken over (event 2). Any difference between the value of net assets (including goodwill) merged or absorbed, and the purchase consideration evaluated at the par value of any shares issued, represents share premium to be raised at event 4. However, in the case of a corporate merger, the share premium account transfer will not be necesssary if the merger relief provisions apply (see Section 2).

3.7 On the other hand, share premium is sometimes stated but goodwill is not. Any difference between the purchase consideration evaluated at the premium inclusive amount and the goodwill exclusive net assets merged or absorbed, is goodwill.

EXAMPLE

3.8 The partnership of CH and AS Jay and the company of Kay Ltd have agreed to amalgamate with effect from 1st July 19-8.

A new company Amalgam PLC has been established for this purpose. By the 30th June 19-8 Amalgam has issued 100,000 ordinary shares of £1.00 per share at par and £70,000 8% Debentures at par, in each case for cash.

At close of business on 30th June 19-8, the separate balance sheets of the partnership and of the old company were as set out below.

Balance Sheets
as at 30 June 19-8

CH & AS Jay			Kay Ltd.	
£	£		£	£
		Fixed Assets(at written down values)		
70,000		Freehold property	100,000	
–		Plant and machinery	95,000	
15,000		Vehicles	20,000	
46,000		Equipment	–	
	131,000			215,000
		Current Assets		
55,000		Stocks	109,000	
27,000		Debtors	64,000	
21,000		Bank/Cash	–	
103,000			173,000	

394

		Less		
		Current Liabilities		
31,000		Creditors	57,000	
–		Proposed dividends	22,000	
–		Bank Overdraft	49,000	
31,000			128,000	
	72,000	**Working Capital**		45,000
	203,000	**Net Assets Employed**		260,000

		Financed by		
		Capital Accounts		
120,000		C H Jay		
60,000		A S Jay		
	180,000			
		Current Accounts(credit)		
10,000		C H Jay		
13,000		A S Jay		
	23,000			
		Share Capital, fully paid		
		Ordinary shares of £1.00		200,000
		Reserves		
		Retained profit		60,000
	203,000			260,000

Under the terms of the agreement, Amalgam acquired all the assets of the partnership, except for bank and cash. This balance was retained by the partners in order to discharge some of the creditors. Other assets were taken over at the following values.

£

Freehold Property	120,000
Vehicle	8,000
Equipment	40,000
Stocks	50,000
Debtors	27,000

The agreed purchase consideration consisted of £23,000 in cash and 200,000 ordinary shares of £1.00 per share in Amalgam at a premium of £0.25 per share, of which 130,000 were taken by C H Jay and 70,000 by A S Jay. The partners then discharged the remaining creditors.

Partnership profits and losses were shared by the partners in capital account proportions.

Amalgam acquired all the assets of Kay Ltd and also assumed responsibility for discharging all the creditors, at the following agreed amounts.

£

Freehold Property	200,000
Plant and Machinery	80,000
Vehicles	20,000
Stocks	81,000
Debtors	62,000
Creditors	53,000

Goodwill was valued at £90,000.

The purchase consideration of £480,000 was discharged by the issue of 320,000 ordinary shares of £1.00

per share in Amalgam and the payment of £80,000 in cash to enable Kay Ltd to settle the outstanding bank overdraft balance and to pay the proposed dividends and liquidation expenses (£6,000).

Required:

a. Make the necessary entries in the main accounts affected, to dissolve the partnership of C H and A S Jay and to liquidate Kay Ltd;

b. Make the necessary entries, in the main accounts affected, to record the amalgamation in the books of Amalgam PLC;

c. Prepare a balance sheet for Amalgam PLC immediately after all the transactions have taken place on 1st July 19-8.

SOLUTION
3.9
a. Dissolution entries of C H and A S Jay

All the asset accounts, except bank and cash, are credited with an amount equal to their balance, to close them off, the corresponding debits appearing in Realisation account. This closure of the individual asset accounts is not illustrated here. Dissolution of partnership is dealt with in Section 3 Chapter 3.

In the accounts which follow, numbers in brackets () are the event numbers listed in 3.1 above.

Bank

	£		£
Balance b/d	21,000	Creditors(11)	31,000
Amalgam PLC (8)	23,000	Capital	
		- C H Jay (10)	7,500
		- A S Jay (10	5,500
	44,000		44,000

Realisation

	£		£
(Assets taken over at book values (1))		(Purchase consideration (6))	
Freehold Property	70,000	Amalgam PLC (6)	273,000
Vehicles	15,000		
Equipment	46,000	(200,000 ordinary £	
Stocks	55,000	shares @ £1.25 250,000	
Debtors	27,000	Cash 23,000	
		273,000)	
Profit on realisation c/d (derived)	60,000		
	273,000		273,000
Capital			
- C H Jay (3)	40,000	Profit on realisation b/d	60,000
- A S Jay (3)	20,000		
	60,000		60,000

Amalgam PLC

	£		£
Realisation (6)	273,000	Bank(8)	23,000
		Shares in Amalgam PLC (8)	250,000
	273,000		273,000

Shares in Amalgam PLC

	£		£
Amalgam PLC (8)	250,000	Capital - C H Jay (10)	162,500
		(130,000 × £1.25)	
		Capital - A S Jay (10)	87,500
		(70,000 × £1.25)	
	250,000		250,000

Capital Accounts

	CHJ	ASJ		CJH	ASJ
	£	£		£	£
Shares in Amalgam (10)	162.500	87,500	Balances b/d	120,000	60,000
Bank (10)	7,500	5,500	Current A/cs		
(derived figures)			transferred	10,000	13,000
			Realisation profit (3)	40,000	20,000
	170,000	93,000		170,000	93,000

Liquidation entries of Kay Ltd.

The closure of the individual asset and liability accounts (other than Bank) is not illustrated, and, in the absence of specific information, the liquidator's accounts have been omitted (see 3.1).

Realisation

	£		£
(Assets taken over at		(Liabilities taken over)	
at book value(1))		Creditors (4)	57,000
Freehold Property	100,000		
Plant and Machinery	95,000	(Purchase consideration)	
Vehicles	20,000	Amalgam PLC (6)	480,000
Stocks	109,000		
Debtors	64,000		
Bank - liquidation			
expenses(2)	6,000		
Sundry shareholders - profit			
on realisation (3)	143,000		
(derived)			
	537,000		537,000

Bank

	£		£
Amalgam PLC (8)	80,000	Balance b/d (overdraft)	49,000
		Proposed dividends	22,000
		Liquidation expenses (2)	6,000
		Sundry shareholders (10)	3,000
	80,000		80,000

Amalgam PLC

	£		£
Realisation (6)	480,000	Bank (8)	80,000
		Shares in Amalgam PLC (8)	40,000
	480,000		480,000

Shares in Amalgam PLC

	£		£
Amalgam PLC (8)	400,000	Sundry shareholders (10)	400,000

Sundry Shareholders

	£		£
Bank (10)	3,000	Ordinary share capital (9)	200,000
Shares in Amalgam		Retained profit (9)	60,000
PLC (10)	400,000	Realisation (3)	143,000
	403,000		403,000

b. Acquisition entries of Amalgam PLC

The new company, Amalgam, debits its asset accounts with the combined amounts of assets, acquired from the partnership and the old company, at the values agreed for the purposes of the amalgamation. Individual asset and liability accounts are not illustrated here.

In the accounts which follow, numbers in brackets () are the event numbers listed in 3.4 above.

Business Acquisition

	£		£
Creditors (3)	53,000	(Assets acquired (2))	
C H and A S Jay (1)	273,000	Goodwill (see below)	118,000
Liquidators of Kay Ltd. (1)	480,000	Freehold Property	320,000
		Plant and Machinery	80,000
		Vehicles	28,000
		Equipment	40,000
		Stocks	131,000
		Debtors	89,000
	806,000		806,000

Goodwill is a derived figure:

Goodwill

	£	£
Consideration agreed for partnership		
– cash	23,000	
– shares (200,000 × £1.25)	250,000	
	273,000	
less net value of partnership assets acquired	245,000	
Goodwill on acquisition of partnership		28,000
Goodwill on acquisition of company (given)		90,000
Goodwill (as above)		118,000

C H and A S Jay

	£		£
Bank (4)	23,000	Business Acquisition (1)	273,000
Ordinary share capital (4)	200,000		
Share premium (4)	50,000		
(200,000 × £0.25)			
	273,000		273,000

Liquidators of Kay Ltd

	£		£
Bank (4)	80,000	Business Acquisition (1)	480,000
Ordinary share capital (4)	320,000		
Share premium (4)	80,000		
(see below)			
	480,000		480,000

Share premium is a derived figure:

	£	£
Consideration agreed for company (given) (including goodwill)		480,000
less		
– cash	80,000	
– shares (nominal value) (320,000 × £1.00)	320,000	
		400,000
Share premium on acquisition		80,000

Bank

	£		£
8% Debentures	70,000	C H and A S Jay (4)	23,000
Ordinary share capital	100,000	Liquidators of Kay Ltd (4)	80,000
		Balance c/d	67,000
	170,000		170,000
Balance b/d	67,000		

Ordinary Share Capital

	£		£
		Bank	100,000
		C H and A S Jay	200,000
Balance c/d	620,000	Liquidators of Kay Ltd.	320,000
	620,000		620,000
		Balance b/d	620,000

Amalgam PLC
Balance Sheet as at 1 July 19-8

	£	£
Fixed Assets (at valuation)		
Freehold property	320,000	
Plant and machinery	80,000	
Vehicles	28,000	
Equipment	40,000	
		468,000
Goodwill (at valuation)		118,000
Current Assets		
Stocks	131,000	
Debtors	89,000	
Bank/Cash	67,000	
	287,000	

Less **Current Liabilities**			
Creditors		53,000	
			234,000
Net Assets Employed			820,000
Financed by:			
Share Capital, fully paid			
620,000 Ordinary shares of £1.00			
per share			620,000
Reserves			
Share Premium			130,000
Shareholders' funds			750,000
Loan capital 8% Debentures			70,000
			820,000

ACQUISITION OF CONTROLLING INTEREST.

3.10 No specific entries are needed in the accounts of the companies whose shares have been acquired under such a scheme. The only relative entries are those whereby the Register of Shareholders is altered for the changes in ownership of the shares.

3.11 In the accounts of the holding (acquiring) company, the shares of subsidiary, which the other company then is, constitute an investment. This is illustrated in Section 2 Chapter 1. The consideration for the investment, when discharged by the holding company, results in a reduction in cash/bank and/or an increase in share capital and/or loan capital.

3.12 The consolidation of the financial position of subsidiary companies is the subject matter of Section 2 Chapter 1 and nothing more need be added at this point.

STUDENT SELF TESTING

Test exercises

1. The partnership of P A Gee and M D Stephen and the company of Cathal Ltd. agreed to amalgamate with effect from 1 January 19-8.

   A new company, Aghad PLC was established for this purpose and had issued 80,000 ordinary shares of £1.00 per share at par and £50,000 7% Debentures at par, in each case for cash, by 31 December 19-7.

   At close of business on 31 December 19-7, the separate balance sheet of the partnership and of the old company were as set out below.

Balance Sheets
as at 31 December 19-7

Gee & Stephen			Cathal Ltd.	
£	£		£	£
		Fixed assets (at written down values)		
42,000		Freehold property	52,000	
9,000		Equipment	30,000	
–		Vehicles	17,000	
———			———	
	51,000			99,000
		Current assets		
34,000		Stock	38,100	
23,100		Debtors	35,000	
600		Bank and Cash	18,400	
———			———	
57,700			91,500	

		Less		
		Current Liabilities		
36,300		Creditors	46,500	
		Proposed dividends	18,000	
4,200		Bank overdraft	–	
40,500			64,500	
	17,200	**Net current assets**		27,000
	68,200	**Net assets employed**		126,000

		Financed by:	
		Capital accounts	
45,000		Gee	
15,000		Stephen	
	60,000		
		Current accounts	
2,900		Gee	
5,300		Stephen	
	8,200		

	Share capital	
	Ordinary shares of £1.00 per share	70,000
	Reserves	
	Profit and loss account	19,400
	Shareholders' funds	89,400
	Long-term loans	
	10% debentures	36,600
68,200		126,000

It was agreed that Aghad would acquire all the assets, except bank and cash, of the partnership and assume responsibility for the creditors (but not for the overdraft), at the following values.

	£
Freehold property	53,000
Equipment	7,400
Stock	28,200
Debtors	23,100
Creditors	36,300

The purchase consideration (£87,400) comprised £15,400 in cash and 60,000 ordinary shares of £1.00 per share in Aghad at a premium of £0.20 per share, of which 50,000 were taken by Gee and 10,000 by Stephen. The partners discharged the overdraft liability.

Partnership profits and losses are shared in capital account proportions.

Required:

Post and balance the following accounts on dissolution of the partnership.

    Bank and cash
    Realisation
    Aghad PLC
    Shares in Aghad PLC
    Capital accounts

2. The facts are exactly the same as in 1 but this further information is available. On amalgamation, Cathal Ltd retained the balance on bank and cash out of which it paid the proposed dividends, but transferred to Aghad all the other assets and liabilities at the undernoted agreed values, except for the 10% debentures which it redeemed at par. Liquidation expenses were £2,000.

	£
Goodwill	21,000
Freehold property	68,000
Equipment	23,600
Vehicles	14,100
Stock	34,200
Debtors	35,000
Creditors	46,500

The purchase consideration equalled the value of the net assets acquired (£149,400) and comprised £66,000 in cash and 70,000 ordinary shares of £1.00 per share in Aghad.

Required:

Post and balance the following accounts on the liquidation of Cathal Ltd.

> Bank and cash
> Realisation
> Aghad PLC
> Shares in Aghad PLC
> Sundry shareholders

3. The facts are exactly the same as in 2.

Required:

Post and balance the following accounts to record the amalgamation in the books of Aghad PLC

> Business acquisition
> Gee and Stephen
> Liquidators of Cathal Ltd.
> Bank and cash
> Ordinary share capital

4. The facts are exactly the same as in 3.

Required:

Prepare for internal use the balance sheet of Aghad PLC immediately after the amalgamation has taken place on 1 January 19-8.

5. A Limited and B Limited decided to amalgamate and form a new company to be named C Limited.

You are required to prepare:

    a. the ledger accounts closing the books of A Limited.

    b. the journal entries for the formation of C Limited.

The trial balances at the amalgamation date of the original two companies and the agreed values for amalgamation were:

	Trial balance	Agreed values for amalga- mation
	£	£
A Limited		
Share capital in shares of £1 each	8,000	
Reserves	11,000	
Creditors	3,700	3,600
	22,700	
Land and buildings	5,800	7,000
Plant and machinery	4,400	4,200
Investment in B Limited, at cost		
consisting of 2,000 shares	3,500	
Investment in D Limited, at cost, 6,000 shares	2,000	

Stock	1,000	900
Debtors	4,800	4,500
Cash	1,200	1,200
	22,700	

B Limited

Share capital in shares of £1 each	5,000	
Reserves	10,000	
Creditors	2,600	2,600
	17,600	

Land and buildings	8,000	10,000
Plant and machinery	4,000	4,100
Investment in D Limited, at cost, 8,000 shares	1,500	
Stock	2,000	1,800
Debtors	1,000	900
Cash	1,100	1,100
	17,600	

Under the terms of the amalgamation it was agreed that:

i. the values as shown above shall be used to decide the respective interest in the new company, C Limited.

ii. the share capital of C Limited shall consist of 13,000 ordinary shares of £1 each to be allotted to the shareholders of the existing companies on the basis of the new values agreed;

iii. the investments in D Limited shall be allotted as a scrip issue to the respective shareholders of A Limited and B Limited before the amalgamation takes place.

Note: Any problem arising from fractions of shares is to be ignored.

6. A new company, Sponge Ltd. was formed on the 30 April 19-8 to take over the business of each of the following companies, all of which went into voluntary liquidation on the following day. The new company was incorporated with a capital of £300,000 divided into 200,000 Ordinary £1 shares and 100,000 10% £1 Cumulative Preference shares.

Summary Balance Sheets as at 30 April 19-8

	Almond Ltd Ltd	Battenby Ltd	Cherry Ltd
Debit balances	£000	£000	£000
Bank	15		
Investments	10		
Trade Debtors	50	48	8
Stock	33	13	8
Plant and Machinery	22	8	4
Land and Buildings	20	6	
Goodwill	18		4
Preliminary Expenses		1	
Profit and Loss		12	
	168	88	24
Credit balances			
Trade Creditors	35	20	2
Bank Overdraft		18	1
Issued and paid up capital			
– Ordinary £1 shares	100	50	10

– 10% Cumulative Preference	–	–	10
	100	50	20
Profit and Loss	13		1
Revenue reserve	20		
	168	88	24

The basis of absorption of the three companies was:

Almond Ltd. All assets and liabilities to be taken over at book values and settlement to be by 5 fully paid ordinary shares in Sponge Ltd. to be issued for every 4 shares held in Almond Ltd.

Battenby Ltd. All assets and liabilities to be taken over at book values and settlement to be by 1 fully paid ordinary share and 3 cumulative preference shares paid £0.50 each in Sponge Ltd. to be issued for every 5 shares held in Battenby Ltd. Sponge Ltd. was to provide for doubtful debts of £9,000 and revalue the stock in hand at £10,000.

Cherry Ltd. Sponge Ltd, to purchase the assets and goodwill for £20,000 cash. Trade creditors to be paid by Cherry Ltd. Cherry Ltd also to pay liquidation expenses of £1,000 and to provide for and pay the outstanding current preference dividend. Sponge Ltd was to provide £2,000 for doubtful debts and to revalue stock at £7,000.

40,000 cumulative shares in Sponge Ltd. are offered to and subscribed for by the public, 50p being called and all but £1,000 being received by 30 June 19-8.

All Sponge Ltd shares are issued at par.

You are required to prepare:

1. The Liquidation accounts and Sundry Shareholders accounts of the three Vendor companies with the addition in the case of Cherry Ltd, of its Bank account showing the distribution of the available cash among the creditors and respective classes of shareholders.

2. The Balance Sheet of Sponge Ltd., as at 30 June 19-8, there being no transactions other than those above between 30 April and 30 June 19-8.

Workings must be submitted and should include the purchase of business a/c in the books of Sponge Ltd.

Taxation is ignored.

(ACCA)

7. The summarised balance sheets of PQ Limited and XY Limited at 31 December, 19-8 were as follows:

	PQ Limited		XY Limited	
	£	£	£	£
Authorised capital:				
7% cumulative preference shares of £1		–		150,000
6% cumulative preference shares of £1		25,000		
Ordinary shares of £0.25		150,000		200,000
Issued capital:				
7% cumulative preference shares of £1 fully paid		–		100,000
6% cumulative preference shares of £1 fully paid		25,000		–
Ordinary shares of £0.25		100,000		150,000
Profit and loss account balance		–		15,400
6% Debentures		40,000		–
Trade Creditors		39,000		37,000
Bank overdraft (secured)		24,000		–
Provision for doubtful debts (including £3,000 for PQ Ltd)		–		4,000
		228,000		306,400

Fixed assets at cost less depreciation

Buildings	54,000		61,000	
Plant and machinery	29,000		73,000	
		83,000		134,000
Goodwill		20,000		15,000
Investments:				
50,000 shares of £1 in MN				
Limited at cost		40,500		–
9,550 6% debentures in PQ				
Limited at cost		–		9,100
Current assets:				
Stocks	31,000		28,900	
Debtors	21,500		77,400	
Balance at bank	–		42,000	
		52,500		148,300
Profit and loss account balance		32,000		–
		228,000		306,400

PQ Limited owed XY Limited £9,000 on current trading and this is included in the debtors and creditors of the respective companies.

The necessary meetings of debenture holders, creditors and members having been held, it was agreed that PQ Limited should cease trading at 31st December and go into liquidation on 3rd January, 19-9 and XY Limited should take over the assets and liabilities of PQ Limited on the following terms and taking into account the following factors:

1. On 2nd January, 19-9 PQ Limited paid into its bank account the following sums:

	£
Collections from trade debtors	2,500
Bad debt recovered	300

2. MN Limited had gone into liquidation on 31st August 19-8 and on 3rd January, 19-9 a final repayment of £0.1 in the £ was paid which was paid to the purchasing company on 3rd January.

3. The assets of PQ Limited were to be taken over at the following valuations:

	£
Buildings	60,000
Plant	15,000
Stock	19,000
Goodwill	100
Trade debtors	At book value

4. The Bank overdraft as on 3rd January, 19-9 was to be paid off by XY Limited.

5. The debentures of PQ Limited (other than those held by XY Limited which were to be cancelled) were to be satisfied by an issue of 7 1/2% debentures in XY Limited which were to be issued at an agreed value of 102.

6. PQ Limited's debt of £9,000 to XY Limited was to be cancelled.

7. In settlement of each £1 of their claim the creditors of PQ Limited were to receive an immediate allotment of:

> two ordinary shares of £0.25 fully paid in XY Limited, followed by £0.3 cash,
> the latter to be paid by XY Limited on 1st February, 19-9.

8. Preference shareholders in PQ Limited were to receive two 7% cumulative preference shares of XY Limited for each five shares of their present holding.

9. Ordinary shareholders in PQ Limited were to receive one ordinary share in XY Limited for every fifty shares of their present holding.

You are required to prepare:

a. purchase of business account in the books of XY Ltd.

b. balance sheet of XY Ltd as at 3rd January, 19-9.

It should be noted that a recurring decimal of £1 is given in Note 7. above. Taxation to be ignored. (ICMA)

8. Cotton and Silk decided to amalgamate on 1 July 19-9, by selling their separate businesses to Modern Ltd., a new company formed for that purpose with an authorised capital of £40,000 in ordinary shares of £1 each. The following are the summarised balance sheets of the respective businesses as at 30 June 19-9:

	Cotton £	Silk £
Capital accounts	25,018	11,494
Loan		10,000
Creditors:		
Loan interest accrued		300
Sundry other creditors	16,182	17,820
	41,200	39,614
Freehold property	–	14,400
Plant & Furniture	12,462	4,864
Stocks	5,348	5,562
Debtors	13,750	4,014
Bank balance	9,640	10,774
	41,200	39,614

It was agreed that:

a. the company should take over the assets and assume the liabilities of the two businesses except (1) bank balances and (2) the loan and interest accrued thereon. The loan and accrued interest was settled by Silk who introduced the necessary additional cash for the purpose into his business:

b. the sale values should be the book amounts after adjustment for (1) an agreed value of £18,000 for the freehold property (2) obsolete stock of Cotton included at £720*(3) a debt of £350 owed to Silk but agreed to be irrecoverable and (4) an error of £440 in the accounts of Silk, being the omission of an invoice for goods supplied to him. Silk's stock figure is correct:

c. the company should take over a liability for formation costs of £240 incurred by Cotton (for which no provision had been made in his accounts); and

d. the company should issue 16,000 ordinary shares at par to Cotton, and 15,000 ordinary shares at par to Silk in consideration for (1) the amounts due to them respectively for the net assets acquired as above and (2) a cash payment from each vendor for the balance.

*This obsolete stock has zero value.

All the foregoing transactions were completed by the company as agreed on 1 July 19-9.

You are required to prepare:

a. i. a statement showing the amount of cash to be paid by Cotton and Silk in respect of the shares allotted to them; and

ii. the balance sheet of Modern Ltd, as it would appear immediately after the completion of the acquisition, assuming that there were no other transactions, and ignoring taxation and any further costs,

and

b. by way of ledger accounts, the closing of the books of Silk.

(ACCA)

9. It was agreed by all parties that Llewellyn Ltd, would acquire of Roberts Ltd., a small manufacturing company on 1 July 19-0. Roberts Ltd., was to be wound up and its books closed subsequent to the payment by Llewellyn Ltd of the net sum due in respect of its collection of the debtors and its payment of the creditors of Roberts Ltd on behalf of that company. The summary balance sheets of Roberts Ltd on 30 June 19-0 was as follows:

Roberts Ltd
Balance Sheet at 30 June 19-0

	£	£
Authorised and Issued Share Capital		
20,000 10% Preference shares of £1 each, fully paid		20,000
100,000 Ordinary shares of 50p each, fully paid	50,000	
Capital Reserves	35,000	
Profit and loss account	15,000	
		100,000
Shareholders' funds		120,000
12% Debenture		50,000
		£170,000
		£
Goodwill		14,000
Fixed Assets (Property, plant and machinery)		80,000
Current Assets		
Stock and work in progress	45,000	
Sundry debtors	60,000	
Cash	10,500	
	116,000	
Current Liabilities		
Sundry creditors	40,000	
		76,000
		£170,000

The takeover terms required that on 1 July 19-0, the agreed purchase consideration would be settled by:

a. the issue at par to the Preference shareholders of Roberts Ltd of 3 £1 12% Preference shares in Llewellyn Ltd fully paid, for every 2 held;

b. the issue to the Ordinary shareholders of Roberts Ltd of 8 Ordinary shares of £1 each in Llewellyn Ltd, credited as 75p paid, for every 5 held.

c. the issue to the Debenture holders of Roberts Ltd, of 176 Ordinary shares of £1 each in Llewellyn Ltd, credited as 75p paid, for every £100 Debenture stock held.

The purchase contract agreed that Llelwllyn Ltd. would take over only the Fixed Assets and the stock and work in progress of Roberts Ltd, the balance of the purchase price being a payment for Goodwill. It was agreed that Llewellyn Ltd would collect the debts and settle the creditors of Roberts Ltd, paying over the net balance in cash to that company after the retention of a service charge of 1% on the sums collected and 1/2% on the sums paid.

In completing these transactions, bad debts of £4,500 arose. Discounts received by Llewellyn Ltd for early payment of some creditors amounted to £1,200. Roberts Ltd debenture holders' interest had been paid to 30 June 19-0, but the preference divided for 19-0 which had not been provided for, was paid in the winding up. Roberts Ltd incurred and paid wind up costs of £4,451.

For the determination of the purchase price settled by Llewellyn Ltd., property included in Roberts Ltd Fixed assets was valued at £70,000 more than shown in the books. The remaining Fixed assets were subjected to additional depreciation of £5,500. The stock and work in progress was valued at £41,500. These values were to be reflected in the opening entries in the books of Llewellyn Ltd, but no adjusting entries were made in the books of Roberts Ltd.

You are required:

a. to show the final entries through the Realisation and other ledger accounts concerned in order to close the books of Roberts Ltd.

b. to show your calculation of and to state the cost of the Goodwill acquired by Llewellyn Ltd.

Ignore taxation.

(ACCA)

10. Following negotiations, Alpha Ltd and Beta Ltd who had commenced similar businesses on the

same day some years previously, decided to amalgamate.

It was agreed that a holding company would be formed on 1 April 19-9 to be called Gamma Ltd., which would acquire all the shares in both companies.

The basis of the agreement was as follows:

1. It was agreed that the accounts of Beta Ltd for the two years ended 31 March 19-9 should be adjusted to conform with the accounting practices of Alpha Ltd.

2. Beta Ltd's stock would have to be revalued to accord with the valuation basis adopted by Alpha Ltd. This would require a reduction in value of £1,500 at 31 March 19-8 and of £3,700 at 31 March 19-9.

3. The 21 year lease owned by Beta Ltd had a further 12 years to run from 31 March 19-9. The aggregate amortisation had been provided at £500 per annum. It was agreed that the valuation should be adjusted so as to reflect the effluxion of time.

4. The Plant and Equipment depreciation of both companies had been provided on the straight line basis. The Plant of both companies had been purchased on the same day.

5. In both 19-8 and 19-9, Beta Ltd had made a general provision against doubtful debts of 2% of debtors, whereas Alpha Ltd had made no such provision.

6. The Deferred Expenses in the Balance Sheet of Beta Ltd. represented new product development costs incurred in the year ended 31 March 19-8 which were being written off over 3 years. Alpha Ltd had written off similar expenditure as it had been incurred.

7. The unrealised gain on the necessary revaluation of Beta's investments was not to be credited to its profit and loss account for the purpose of 9.ii. below.

8. The pretax profits of the two companies were:

	Year ended 31 March	
	19-8	19-9
	£	£
Alpha Ltd	34,500	47,250
Beta Ltd	45,825	33,470

9. The settlement of the purchase price of each company's shares was to be:

i. £1 of 10% Convertible Loan Stock of Gemma Ltd for every £1 of Net Assets (as adjusted) owned by each company at 31 March 19-9.

ii. £0.25 Ordinary Shares of Gamma Ltd based on a two year purchase of the profits of each company before taxation, the profits to be the average profits of the two years with the year ended 31 March 19-9 being weighted on a 2:1 basis.

The Balance Sheets of both companies as at 31 March 19-8 and 19-9 are as follows:

Balance Sheets of as at 31 March	Alpha Ltd		Beta Ltd.	
	19-8	19-9	19-8	19-9
	£	£	£	£
Share Capital - Ordinary shares of £1 each fully paid	60,000	60,000	80,000	80,000
Reserves - Capital		8,000		
- Retained profits	12,820	26,200	26,900	40,180
Capital employed	72,820	94,200	106,900	120,180
	£	£	£	£
Freeholds, at cost	25,000	25,000		
Leaseholds, at cost			21,000	21,000
Less: Amortization			4,000	4,500
			17,000	16,500
Plant and Equipment, at cost	28,000	28,000	40,500	40,500
Less: Depreciation	7,000	8,400	8,100	9,720
	21,000	19,600	32,400	30,780
Total Fixed Assets	46,000	44,600	49,400	47,280
Quoted Investments - at market price		32,000		
at cost (market price £45,000)				43,500

Current Assets

Stocks, at cost	14,850	15,780	28,400	36,300
Trade Debtors	28,620	22,310	24,500	36,750
Deferred Expenses			9,000	6,000
Bank Balance	8,550	3,600	27,600	
	52,020	41,690	89,500	79,050

Current Liabilities

Sundry current liabilities	25,200	24,090	32,000	49,650
Working Capital	26,820	17,600	57,500	29,400
Capital employed	72,820	94,200	106,900	120,180

You are required:

a. to set out the calculations of:

    i. the adjusted profits and adjusted net assets of Beta Ltd.

    ii. the weighted profits of both companies.

    leading to the determination of the purchase price for the shares of both Gamma Ltd issued in settlement, and

b. prepare the Balance Sheet of Gamma Ltd as at 1 April 19-9 after the transactions have been completed. (A consolidated balance sheet is NOT required).

Ignore taxation and formation expenses.

(ACCA)

11. JD has been in business a number of years and on 31st December 19-8 formed a company, JD Limited, with an authorised capital of £100,000 in shares of 25 pence each to take over the business in terms set out below. On 31st March, 19-9 JD Limited purchased from CD, the controlling shareholder, the whole of the 40,000 ordinary shares in CD Limited for the sum of £50,000.

From the information given below you are required to prepare a profit and loss account showing a division of results between JD and JD Limited for the year ended 30th June, 19-9, and a balance sheet of JD Limited at that date.

Taxation is to be ignored. workings must be shown.

1. The balance sheet of JD at 1st July 19-8 was as follows:

	£	£
Freehold property, at cost		20,000
Plant, at cost	39,000	
less: depreciation	15,000	
		24,000
Net current assets		28,000
Capital account		72,000

2. The company took over the assets and liabilities, excluding the freehold property, at book values as at 30th September, 19-8. The purchase price of £56,000 was satisfied by an issue of fully paid up shares at par. It was agreed that JD should retain ownership of the freehold property and charge the company a rent of £3,200 per annum for its use. Also that he should be employed on a consultancy basis at a salary of £4,000 per annum. Both rent and fees would be payable from 1st October 19-8.

3. The purchase consideration of £50,000 for CD Limited was to be satisfied by £10,000 in cash and the balance by fully paid shares in JD Limited at a price of £0.625 per share.

4. JD Limited had taken over JD's books of account and did not open a new ledger. No entries had been made in the books in respect of the above transaction.

5. The following information was extracted from JD's books of account for the year ended 30th June 19-9.

    a. JD's drawings for the three months ended 30th September, 19-8 were £2,500.

    b. Sales for the six months ended 31st December, 19-8 totalled £60,000 and for the six months ended 30th June, 19-9 £120,000. In both half years the sales accrued at a uniform rate.

    c. The rate of gross profit to sales was 20% in the first six months and 22% in the last six months.

    d. Overhead expenditure for the year amounted to £19,000, of which normal overhead, varying directly with sales, totalled £17,400 and fixed overhead £1,600.

e. A debt of £120 in respect of a sale made in December 19-8 was found to be irrecoverable and written off.

f. On 1st May, 19-9 a new machine tool was purchased at a cost of £6,000. On 30th June, 19-9 plant with a book value of £60 at 1st July, 19-8 was sold for £900.

g. Depreciation is to be charged at the rate of 10% on book value and is to be regarded as accruing evenly throughout the year for the purpose of the sale agreement between JD and JD Limited.

6. On 1st April 19-9 JD Limited received a dividend of £6,000 from CD Limited.

ACCA EXAMINATION QUESTIONS

12. Required:

a. Calculate the number of shares that will be issued to the shareholders of the Brighton Metal Company by Brighton & Hove Ltd if the proposed absorption plan is put into effect.

b. Show the ledger accounts in the books of the Brighton Metal Company to record the closure following absorption.

c. Prepare an outline Balance Sheet for Brighton & Hove Ltd as at 30 June 1982 on the assumption that the absorption plan has been put into effect.

(ACCA 2.9(1) December 1982)

Appendix 1

Trial Balance of Brighton Metal Company Ltd as at 30 June 1982.

	Dr £	Cr £
Ordinary shares of £1 each		200,000
14% Redeemable Preference Shares (redeemable 1.1.83 at 110)		100,000
General reserve		40,000
Profit and Loss Account		52,000
12% Debentures (repayable at par 31.3.83)		100,000
Tax payable 1.1.84		40,000
Creditors		60,000
Tax payable 1.1.83		60,000
Proposed final ordinary dividend		21,000
Bank overdraft		80,000
VAT		18,000
Wages accrued		2,000
Distribution expenses accrued		3,000
Administration expense accrued		4,000
ACT payable on proposed final dividend		9,000
Long leasehold factory	360,000	
Plant and machinery (cost £500,000)	150,000	
Office equipment (cost £100,000)	50,000	
Motor vehicles (cost £240,000)	60,000	
Stock	100,000	
Debtors	60,000	
ACT recoverable	9,000	
	£789,000	£789,000

Appendix 3

Proposal for absorption with Hove Limited.

Hove Limited is a company in the same industry as the Brighton Metal Company. The directors of both companies have been having discussions for a number of years about a possible amalgamation.

The directors of Hove Limited have now proposed a firm proposal. The terms of the proposal are as follows:

a. A new company Brighton & Hove Limited should be formed to acquire the assets and liabilities of both the Brighton Metal Company and Hove Ltd.

b. Brighton & Hove Ltd would issue a total of 600,000 £1 ordinary shares. These are to be allocated to the shareholders of Brighton Metal Company and Hove Ltd in proportion to the net assets acquired from each company.

c. Tangible assets would be acquired by the new company at the following valuations:

	Brighton Metal Co.	Hove Ltd.
	£	£
Fixed Assets	490,000	597,000
Stock	80,000	300,000
Debtors (Trade and others)	57,000	288,000
Cash	−	380,000

d. Intangible assets. Goodwill would be purchased, calculated as one year's purchase of the weighted average profits of 1980, 1981, and 1982, using weights of 1, 2 and 3 respectively. The profits were:

	Brighton Metal Co.	Hove Ltd.
	£'000s	£000's
1980	190	170
1981	175	200
1982	160	230

e. All liabilities were to be assumed by the new company as follows:

i. The 12% debenture holders in Brighton Metal Company to accept £110,000 10% debentures in Brighton & Hove Ltd.

ii. The 14% preference shareholders in Brighton Metal Company to accept £120,000 10% debentures in Brighton & Hove Ltd.

iii. Other creditors to be assumed at their balance sheet values.

Financial Accounts

The Accounts to be used as a basis for the scheme were to be the data in the Trial Balance of Brighton Metal Company as at 30.6.82 in Appendix 1 and the Balance Sheet of Hove Ltd as at 30.6.82 in Appendix 4.

Appendix 4

Balance Sheet of Hove Ltd as at 30.6.82

	£	£
Fixed Assets		520,000
Current Assets		
Stock	320,000	
Debtors	200,000	
Cash	380,000	900,000
		£1,420,000
Share Capital		£
300,000 £1 ordinary shares	300,000	
Share premium	150,000	
Retained profit	695,000	1,145,000
Current Liabilities		
Creditors	100,000	
Current taxation	155,000	
Proposed dividend	20,000	275,000
		£1,420,000

13. Robert Ltd was incorporated with an authorised share capital of £200,000 divided into 600,000 ordinary shares of 25p each and 50,000 £1 10% cumulative preference shares to take over the existing businesses including cash of Alpha Ltd and Beta Ltd at 31 December 1982.

The draft balance sheets of Alpha Ltd and Beta Ltd at 31 December 1982 showed:

	Alpha £	Beta £		Alpha £	Beta £
Capital–Ordinary			Freehold property		
Shares of £1 each	30,000	20,000	at cost	28,000	12,000
Reserves	18,000	6,500			
Trade creditors	13,000	26,000	Plant at cost	32,000	25,000
Bank	14,000	–	Less Depreciation	(10,000)	(8,000)
			Development		
			Expenditure		10,000
			Stock	15,000	7,500
			Debtors	10,000	2,000
			Bank	–	4,000
	75,000	52,500		75,000	52,500

You are given the following information:

1. The purchase consideration for the businesses acquired is to be the amount which Robert Ltd would have to invest at 15% per annum to yield the weighted average profit of the past three years. The weights are to be 1, 2, 3 respectively.

Profits, which have been adjusted to take account of the adjustments required in Note 4 following, were:

	Alpha Ltd. £	Beta Ltd £
1980	8,000	17,000
1981	14,000	13,000
1982	16,500	6,500

2. The fixed assets have a fair value at 31 December 1982 as follows:

	Alpha Ltd £	Beta Ltd. £
Freehold property	35,000	18,000
Plant	17,500	22,000

3. The Development Expenditure of £10,000 has been reviewed. The project it relates to is technically viable but unless the new company is formed to acquire Beta Ltd and provide additional funds, there is doubt as to whether Beta Ltd is a going concern. However, subject to the amalgamation, it is felt that the carrying value should remain at £10,000.

4. Provision is to be made as follows:

	Alpha Ltd.	Beta Ltd
(a) for obsolete stock	5% of balance sheet value sheet value	–
(b) for doubtful debts	3% of debtors	$2\frac{1}{2}$% of debtors
(c) for warranty claims	£6,000	–

5. The purchase consideration is to be satisfied as follows:

   a. Preference shares are to be issued to the value of the freehold property.

   b. 75% of the remaining purchase consideration is to be satisfied by the issue of ordinary shares in Robert Ltd at a premium of 5p per share.

   c. The remainder of the purchase consideration is to be satisfied by cash.

6. Robert Ltd is to issue sufficient ordinary shares at a premium of 5p per share to establish a liquidity ratio of 1:1.

7. The shares received by Alpha and Beta are to be divided to the nearest whole number. If not exactly divisible the balance is to be sold for cash and the cash proceeds distributed.

Required:

a. Prepare journal entries to close the books of Beta Ltd.

b. Calculate for a shareholder with 100 £1 shares in Alpha Ltd what consideration he would receive from Robert Ltd, showing clearly the breakdown between shares and cash.

c. Prepare the Balance Sheet of Robert Ltd immediately after the amalgamation. (Ignore Taxation.)

(ACCA 2.9(2) December 1983)

7 Reorganisations and Reconstructions

GENERAL BACKGROUND

1.0 The share capital of company tends, with the passage of time, to get out of step with the assets which it finances.

1.1 Frequently, this means that the company has been accumulating substantial profits which, because they are undistributed, have swelled the company's reserves. This position gives rise to an ever-widening gap between the par value and market value of the company's ordinary shares.

1.2 In circumstances of this sort the company usually corrects this imbalance by capitalising some of the reserves by means of a bonus issue, the immediate effect of which is to reduce the ordinary share market value per share (but not necessarily proportionately).

1.3 However, a company may make losses as well as profits and when substantial losses have been accumulated and there are no immediate prospects of improvement, remedial measures have to be undertaken by way of a reorganisation or a reconstruction scheme.

CAPITAL REORGANISATION.

2.0 It may be possible to restore the company to a position of prosperity by injecting new capital. The success of a fresh issue would, however, almost certainly be jeopardized by the existence of accumulated losses, particularly if, as is often the case, there is a debit balance on the profit and loss account.

2.1 Prior to the issue of new capital, it is prudent and usual to eradicate these losses by putting a reorganisation scheme into effect.

2.2 A scheme of reorganisation involves carrying out an internal reconstruction of the company. Before this can be instituted certain formalities must be observed, including the passing of a special resolution which must then be confirmed by the High Court, because almost invariably a capital reduction is involved.

2.3 Several options are available to a company wishing to reorganise its capital structure. The reorganisation can be effected by

a. extinguishing or reducing the liability on share capital not paid-up; and/or

b. cancelling paid-up share capital not represented by assets; and/or

c. paying off paid-up share capital held surplus to the company's requirements.

2.4 In diagram form, a capital reorganisation can be depicted thus:

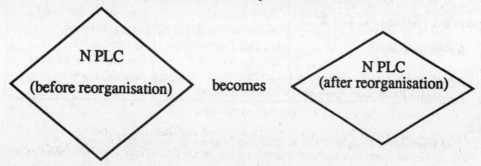

that is, the existing company retains its identity after reorganisation, but with a trimmed down capital structure reflecting the written off losses, borne by the shareholders.

CAPITAL RECONSTRUCTION

2.5 Sometimes the deterioration in the company's position is so marked that the relative superficiality of a reorganisation scheme is insufficient. A more fundamental approach is then needed in the form of a reconstruction scheme.

2.6 A new company with a different capital structure is formed to salvage the assets of the existing company, which is then wound up. Diagrammatically this can be represented as follows:

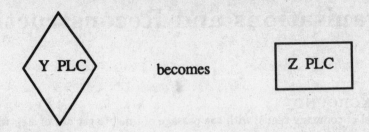

ACCOUNTING ENTRIES

3.0 The accounting entries are different for a reorganisation from that of a reconstruction, each of which will now be considered. The terminology in this area of accounting also is imprecise. Different authors use different labels to describe the same thing. It is important therefore to have regard to the substance of any particular scheme rather than its descriptive label.

CAPITAL REORGANISATION

3.1 A special account, called Capital Reorganisation (or Capital Reduction), is opened, through which are passed the amounts written off assets and share capital, accumulated losses etc as shown by the following table of entries.

	Event	Account Debited	Account Credited
1	Amounts written off assets on revaluation	Capital Reduction/ Reorganisation	Individual asset accounts
2	Adverse balance on reserve accounts, written off	Capital Reduction/ Reorganisation	Individual reserve accounts
3	Surplus on revaluation of fixed assets	Individual fixed asset accounts	Capital Reduction/ Reorganisation
4	Amounts written off called-up share capital	Individual share capital accounts	Capital Reduction/ Reorganisation
5	Settlement of liabilities by an issue of shares	Individual liabilities	Share capital; share premium (if appropriate)
6	Waiver of preference dividend arrears by an issue of shares/loan capital	Capital Reduction/ Reorganisation	Share capital/loan capital; Share premium (if appropriate)
7	Replacement of one class of shares by shares of a different class	Share capital (replaced shares)	Capital Reduction/ Reorganisation
		Capital Reduction/ Reorganisation	Share Capital (replacement shares)
8	Capitalisation of surplus on Capital Reduction account	Capital Reduction/ Reorganisation	Capital Reserve

EXAMPLE

3.2 The financial position of Phaylia PLC at 30th September 19-8 was as follows:

Balance Sheet
as at 30 September 19-8

	£ Cost	£ Depn	£ Net
Fixed Assets			
Freehold premises	100,000	20,000	80,000
Plant and equipment	250,000	60,000	190,000
Vehicles	45,000	15,000	30,000
	395,000	95,000	300,000

Current Assets

Stock	40,000	
Debtors	30,000	
Bank	10,000	
	80,000	

Less
Current Liabilities

Creditors	140,000	
		(60,000)
		240,000

Financed by
Share Capital

- authorised		
150,000 7% Preference shares of £1.00 per share	150,000	
400,000 Ordinary shares of £1.00 per share	400,000	
	550,000	
- issued and fully paid		
100,000 7% Preference shares of £1.00 per share	100,000	
400,000 Ordinary shares of £1.00 per share £0.75 paid	300,000	
		400,000

Reserves

Profit and loss (debit balance)		(160,000)
		240,000

The 7% Preference dividends are two years in arrears.

The company had formulated an approved scheme of reorganisation, to take effect on 1st October 19-8 which contained the following provisions.

1. the ordinary shares are to be written down to £0.25 per share and then to be converted into new ordinary shares of £1.00 per share fully paid.

2. The preference shareholders are to receive 50,000 ordinary shares of £1.00 per share, fully paid at par, in exchange for their preference shares.

3. In consideration for waiving their rights to arrears of preference dividend, the preference shareholders have agreed to accept 10,000 new ordinary shares of £1.00 per share, fully paid, in full and final settlement.

4. The creditors have agreed to take 100,000 new ordinary shares of £1.00 per share, fully paid at par, in part satisfaction of the sums due to them.

5. The adverse balance on profit and loss is to be written off.

6. The undernoted revaluations are to be incorporated into the accounts.

	£
Freehold premises	100,000
Plant and equipment	105,000
Vehicles	25,000
Stock	36,000

and a provision for bad debts is to be raised at £1,000.

Required:

a. Post the appropriate accounts to effect the reorganisation, and

b. Prepare the balance sheet of Phaylia PLC immediately after all the reorganisation entries have been posted.

SOLUTION

3.3 In the accounts which follow, numbers in brackets () are the event numbers listed in 3.1 above.

a.

Freehold Premises

	£		£
Balance b/d	100,000	Provision for depreciation	20,000
Capital Reduction (3)	20,000	Balance c/d	100,000
	120,000		120,000
Balance b/d	100,000		

Plant and Equipment

	£		£
Balance b/d	250,000	Provision for depreciation	60,000
		Capital Reduction (1)	85,000
		Balance c/d	105,000
	250,000		250,000
Balance b/d	105,000		

Vehicles

	£		£
Balance b/d	45,000	Provision for depreciation	15,000
		Capital Reduction (1)	5,000
		Balance c/d	25,000
	45,000		45,000
Balance b/d	25,000		

(N.B. As is usual when fixed assets are revalued, the provision for depreciation is transferred to the fixed asset account).

Stock

	£		£
Balance b/d	40,000	Capital Reduction(1)	4,000
		Balance c/d	36,000
	40,000		40,000
Balance b/d	36,000		

Provision for bad debts

	£		£
Balance c/d	1,000	Capital Reduction (1)	1,000
		Balance b/d	1,000

Creditors

	£		£
Ordinary share capital (5)	100,000	Balance b/d	140,000
Balance c/d	40,000		
	140,000		140,000
		Balance b/d	40,000

Profit and Loss

	£		£
Balance b/d	160,000	Capital Reduction (2)	160,000

7% Preference Share Capital

	£		£
Capital Reduction (7)	100,000	Balance b/d	100,000

Ordinary Share Capital

	£		£
Capital Reduction (4)	200,000	Balance b/d	300,000
(400,000 × (£0.75 − £0.25)		Capital Reduction (7)	50,000
Balance c/d	260,000	(preference share exchange)	
		Capital Reduction (6)	10,000
		Creditors (5)	100,000
	460,000		460,000
		Balance b/d	260,000

Capital Reserve

	£		£
Balance c/d	1,000	Capital Reduction (8)	1,000
		Balance b/d	1,000

Capital Reduction

	£		£
Plant and Equipment(1)	85,000	Freehold Premises (3)	20,000
Vehicles (1)	5,000	7% Preference Share	
Stock (1)	4,000	capital (7)	100,000
Provision for bad debts (1)	1,000	Ordinary share capital (4)	200,000
Profit and loss (2)	160,000		
Ordinary share capital (7)	50,000		
(preference share exchange)			
Ordinary share capital (6)	10,000		
Share premium (6)	4,000		
Capital Reserve (8)	1,000		
(derived)			
	320,000		320,000

Bank

	£		£
Balance b/d	10,000	Balance c/d	10,000
Balance b/d	10,000		

N.B. The question footnote stated that the preference dividends are two years in arrears. The amount involved is thus

$$7\% \times £100,000 \times 2 = £14,000$$

The preference shareholders agreed to accept £10,000 of ordinary shares in full settlement. Effectively, therefore, the extinguishing of the arrears by an issue of a lower nominal amount of ordinary shares has given rise to a share premium of £4,000 (14,000 - 10,000).

b.

Phaylia PLC
Balance sheet as at 1 October 19-8

	£	£
Fixed Assets at valuation		
Freehold premises	100,000	
Plant and equipment	105,000	
Vehicles	25,000	
		230,000

Current Assets

Stock	36,000	
Debtors	29,000	
Bank	10,000	
	75,000	

Less **Current Liabilities**

Creditors	40,000	
		35,000
		265,000

Financed By
Share capital
– authorised

150,000 7% Preference shares of £1.00 per share	150,000	
400,000 Ordinary shares of £1.00 per share	400,000	
	550,000	

– issued and fully paid

260,000 Ordinary shares of £1.00 per share		260,000

Reserves

Share Premium	4,000	
Capital Reserve	1,000	
		5,000
		265,000

CAPITAL RECONSTRUCTION

3.4 When a capital reconstruction scheme is put into effect, the winding up entries of the existing company are identical with those of a company being wound up under an amalgamation or an absorption scheme and are as set out in Chapter 6.

3.5 . The entries needed to establish the new company are as shown in Chapter 1, whilst the special entries for taking over the assets and liabilities of the existing company are as set out in Chapter 6.

3.6 It is not necessary therefore to give an example of a capital reconstruction because the principles have been illustrated already.

STRUCTURAL REORGANISATIONS AND RECONSTRUCTIONS

4.0 Apart from the capital reorganisations and reconstructions dealt with up to this point of the section, there is a further type which involves the reconstruction and reorganisation of various activities or segments of a business.

4.1 For example, the activities of a large company may be split up among a number of newly created companies (a demerger) or the activities of a private, family, company may be partitioned into a number of newly created companies. In both cases the original companies may continue (in their truncated form) or be wound up.

4.2 The accounting entries for the establishment of such new companies has been dealt with in Chapter 1 (Issue of shares and debentures). The accounting entries for the transfer of assets and liabilities between companies and for the winding up of the original companies are, according to circumstances, the same as for an amalgamation or an absorption dealt with in Chapter 6 of this manual.

4.3 If, at the time as the structural alterations, there is also a capital reorganisation or reconstruction as part of the same scheme, the accounting entries for that will be effected in accordance with 2.0 to 3.6 of this chapter.

STUDENT SELF TESTING
Test exercises
1. The financial position of Plummet PLC was as follows:

418

Balance Sheet
as at 30 September 19-6

	£	£
Fixed assets (at written down values)		
Freehold property	123,600	
Equipment	96,700	
Vehicles	47,200	
		267,500
Current assets		
Stock	82,300	
Debtors	44,500	
Bank and cash	12,400	
	139,200	
less		
Current liabilities		
Creditors	35,100	
Net current assets		104,100
Net assets employed		371,600

Financed by:

Share capital	Authorised	Issued and fully paid
	£	£
7% preference shares of £1.00 per share	100,000	100,000
Ordinary shares of £1.00 per share	500,000	350,000
	600,000	450,000
Reserves		
Profit and loss (debit balance)		(78,400)
		371,600

The preference dividends are two years in arrears.

A reorganisation scheme had been devised which had secured the necessary approval and contained the following provisions which were to become operative on 1 October 19-6.

1. The ordinary shares are to be written down to £0.40 per share and then to be converted into new ordinary shares of £1.00 per share, fully paid.
2. The preference shareholders are to receive 50,000 new ordinary shares of £1.00 per share, fully paid at par, in exchange for their preference shares.
3. The preference shareholders have also agreed to waive the rights to the dividend arrears and to accept in lieu 8,000 new ordinary shares of £1.00 per share, fully paid, in full settlement.
4. The creditors have agreed to accept 20,000 new ordinary shares of £1.00 per share, fully paid at par, in part satisfaction of the sums due to them.
5. The debit balance on profit and loss account is to be written off.
6. Certain assets are to be revalued at the undernoted amounts.

	£
Freehold property	102,600
Equipment	64,400
Vehicles	30,700
Stock	47,600
Debtors	41,600

Required:

Open, post and balance the capital reduction and share capital accounts to record the reorganisation arrangements.

2. The facts are exactly the same as in 1.

Required:

Prepare the balance sheet of Plummet PLC on 1 October 19-6 immediately after the reorganisation has been effected.

3. The balance sheet of SAD Limited as at 30th June, 19-0 was as follows:

	£		£
Share capital; authorised, issued and fully paid:		Freehold land and buildings	34,000
100,000 6% cumulative		Plant	96,000
preference shares	100,000	Tools and dies	27,300
300,000 ordinary shares		Investments	15,000
at £0.5 each	150,000	Current assets:	
		Stocks	42,500
	250,000	Debtors	53,400
Less Profit and loss		Research and development	
account; debit balance	98,000	expenditure	18,000
	152,000		
7% Debentures 60,000			
Interest due 4,200			
	64,200		
Bank overdraft, secured on freehold land and			
buildings and plant	20,000		
Creditors	50,000		
	£286,200		£286,200

The scheme of reorganisation detailed below has been agreed by all the interested parties and approved by the Court.

You are required to prepare:

a. the journal entries recording the transactions in the books, including cash; and

b. a balance sheet of the company as at 1st July, 19-0 after completion of the scheme

1. The following assets are to be revalued as shown below:

	£
Plant	59,000
Tools and dies	15,000
Stock	30,000
Debtors	48,700

2. The research and development expenditure and the balance on profit and loss account are to be written off.

3. A piece of land recorded in the books at £6,000 is valued at £14,000 and is to be taken over by the debenture holders in part repayment of principal. The remaining freehold land and buildings are to be revalued at £40,000.

4. A creditor for £18,000 has agreed to accept a second mortgage debenture of 10% per annum secured on the plant for £15,500 in settlement of his debt. Other creditors totalling £10,000 agree to accept a payment of £0.85 in the £1 for immediate settlement.

5. The investments, at a valuation of £22,000 are to be taken over by the bank.

6. The ascertained loss is to be met by writing down the ordinary shares to £0.05 each and the preference to £0.80 each. The authorised share capital to be increased immediately to the original amount.

7. The ordinary shareholders agree to subscribe for two new ordinary shares at par for every share held.

This cash is all received.

8. The costs of the scheme are £3,500. These have been paid and are to be written off. The debenture interest has also been paid.

4.

The Shires Property Construction Company Ltd found itself in financial difficulty. The following is a trial balance at 31st December 19-9 extracted from the books of the company.

	£
Land	156,000
Building(net)	27,246
Equipment (net)	10,754
Goodwill	60,000
Investment in shares, quoted	27,000
Stock and work in progress	120,247
Debtors	70,692
Profit and loss account	39,821
	511,760

	£
Ordinary shares of £1 each	200,000
5% Cumulative preference shares of £1 each	70,000
8% Debenture 19-2	80,000
Interest payable on debenture	12,800
Trade Creditors	96,247
Loans from directors	16,000
Bank Overdraft	36,713
	511,760

The authorised share capital is 200,000 ordinary shares of £1 each and 100,000 5% cumulative preference shares of £1 each.

During a meeting of shareholders and directors, it was decided to carry out a scheme of internal reconstruction. The following scheme has been agreed.

1. Each ordinary share is to be redesignated as a share of 25p.

2. The existing 70,000 preference shares are to be exchanged for a new issue of 35,000 8% cumulative preference shares of £1 each and 140,000 ordinary shares of 25p each.

3. The ordinary shareholders are to accept a reduction in the nominal value of their shares from £1 to 25p, and subscribe for a new issue on the basis for 1 for 1 at a price of 30p per share.

4. The Debenture holders are to accept 20,000 ordinary shares of 25p each in lieu of the interest payable. The interest rate is to be increased to $9\frac{1}{2}$%. A further £9,000 of this $9\frac{1}{2}$% Debenture is to be issued and taken up by the existing holders at £90 per £100.

5. £6,000 of directors loan is to be cancelled. The balance is to be settled by issue of 10,000 ordinary shares of 25p each.

6. Goodwill and the profit and loss account balance are to be written off.

7. The investment in shares is to be sold at the current market price of £60,000.

8. The bank overdraft is to be repaid.

9. £46,000 is to be paid to trade creditors now and the balance at quarterly intervals.

10. 10% of the debtors are to be written off.

11. The remaining assets were professionally valued and should be included in the books and accounts as follows:

Land	£90,000
Building	80,000
Equipment	10,000
Stock and work in progress	50,000

12. It is expected, that due to changed conditions and new management, operating profits will be earned at the rate of £50,000 pa after depreciation but before interest and tax. Due to losses brought forward

and capital allowances it is unlikely that any tax liability will arise until 19-7.

You are required to:

a. show the necessary journal entries including cash, to effect the reconstruction scheme.

b. prepare the balance sheet of the company immediately after the reconstruction.

c. show how the anticipated operating profits will be divided amongst the interested parties before and after the reconstruction, and

d. comment on the capital structure of the company subsequent to reconstruction.

5. The summarised balance sheet of Rejuvenated (19-9) Limited and of Rejuvenated (19-4) Limited from which it has recently emerged by way of a reorganisation are shown below.

	Rejuvenated (19-4)	Rejuvenated (19-9)
	£000	£000
Fixed assets	2,450	1,800
Current assets		
Stock	1,300	900
Work in progress	1,300	700
Debtors	400	350
	5,450	3,750
Share capital		
Ordinary shares of £1	1,000	200
Deferred shares of 5p	–	100
5% Preference shares of £1	1,000	–
8% Preference shares of £1	–	500
Reserves	350	50
15% Loan 20-2	–	1,000
10% Loan 19-1	1,000	–
Current liabilities		
Trade creditors	1,250	1,250
Overdraft	850	650
	5,450	3,750

The changes in share capital reflect the writing off of 90% of the ordinary share capital; the issue for cash of £100,000 of deferred shares at par to the existing ordinary shareholders; the writing-off of 50% of the preference share capital and the increase in the rate of interest from 5% to 8%; the issue for cash of 50,000 ordinary shares at par to the existing preference shareholders.

The debenture holders agreed to redate their loan from 19-2 to 20-2 in consideration of the increase in the rate of interest from 10% to 15%. They also purchased 50,000 ordinary shares at par.

The assets in the balance sheet of Rejuvenated (19- 9) reflect up to date valuations on a going concern basis.

It is expected that the profit available for payment of interest and dividends in the following year will amount to £300,000, and would have been available whether or not the new company had been organized.

The deferred shares do not participate in any dividend in any year until a dividend of 20% has been paid on the ordinary shares. Thereafter they rank equally with the ordinary shares on a "per share" basis.

You are required to:

a. show how the £300,000 available would have been paid to the interested parties if Rejuvenated (19-4) had survived.

b. show how the £300,000 available would be distributed by Rejuvenated (19-9).

c. calculate and state the amounts available to the original interested parties of Rejuvenated (19-4) following the reorganisation.

d. calculate one gearing ratio reflecting the capital position and one gearing ratio reflecting the income position, for both companies, and

e. comment on the balance sheet structure of Rejuvenated (19-9).

IGNORE ALL TAXATION MATTERS when answering this question. No credit will be given for reflecting current taxation legislation.

ACCA EXAMINATION QUESTIONS

6. The Merton Manufacturing Co. Ltd has been in business for many years making fitted furniture and chairs. During 1984 and 1985 substantial losses have been sustained on the manufacture of chairs and the directors have decided to concentrate on the fitted furniture side of the business which is expected to produce a profit of at least £22,500 per annum before interest charges and taxation. A capital reduction scheme has been proposed under which:

i. a new ordinary share of 50p nominal value will be created.

ii. the £1 ordinary shares will be written off and the shareholders will be offered one new ordinary share for every six old shares held;

iii. the £1, 6% redeemable preference shares will be cancelled and the holders will be offered for every three existing preference shares, one new ordinary share and £1 of a new 8% debenture;

iv. the existing $11\frac{1}{2}$% debenture will be exchanged for a new debenture yielding 8% and in addition existing debenture holders will be offered one new ordinary share for every £4 of the old debenture held;

v. existing reserves will be written off;

vi. goodwill is to be written off;

vii. any remaining balance of write off which is necessary is to be achieved by writing down plant and equipment; and

viii. existing ordinary shareholders will be invited to subscribe for two fully paid new ordinary shares at par for every three old shares held.

The balance sheet of the Merton Manufacturing Co. Ltd immediately prior to the capital reduction is as follows:

	£	£	£
Fixed intangible assets			
Goodwill at cost less amounts written off			50,000
Fixed tangible assets			
Freehold land and buildings at cost			95,000
Plant and equipment at cost		275,000	
Less: Depreciation to date		89,500	
			185,500
			330,500
Current assets			
Stocks		25,000	
Debtors		50,000	
		75,000	
Current liabilities	£		
Creditors	63,500		
Bank overdraft	15,850		
		79,350	
Excess of current liabilities			(4,350)
			326,150
Long term loan			
$11\frac{1}{2}$% debenture, secured on the freehold land and buildings			100,000
			226,150

	£
Share capital and reserves	
£1 ordinary shares fully paid	90,000
6% £1 redeemable preference shares fully paid	150,000
Share premium account	25,000
Profit and loss account	(38,850)
	226,150

On a liquidation freehold land and buildings are expected to produce £120,000, plant and equipment £40,000, stocks £15,000 and debtors £45,000. Goodwill has no value.

There are no termination costs associated with ceasing the manufacture of chairs.

Required:

a. Assuming that the necessary approval is obtained and that the new share issue is successful, produce a balance sheet of the company showing the position immediately after the scheme has been put into effect.

b. Show the effect of the scheme on the expected earnings of the old shareholders.

c. Indicate the points which a preference shareholder should take into account before voting on the scheme.

Corporation tax may be taken at $33\frac{1}{3}\%$

The tax credit on dividends may be taken at 25%.

(ACCA 2.9 (2) December 1986)

7. Required

a. Prepare the reduction and reconstruction account to give effect to the proposed reorganisation described in Appendix 6.

b. Prepare the draft balance sheet of Pourwell Limited as at 31 December 1985, after the reorganisation has been effected.

(ACCA 2.9(1) June 1986)

Appendix 1 General introduction to Pourwell Ltd.

i. Pourwell Ltd is a company that manufactures plastic decanters.

ii. It was incorporated in 1974 with an authorised share capital of £500,000 consisting of 300,000 £1 ordinary shares and £200,000 7% cumulative preferences shares of £1 each.

iii. The issued share capital is £300,000 consisting of 200,000 £1 ordinary shares and £100,000 7% cumulative preference shares. The preference shares are all held by an insurance company. The ordinary shares are held as follows:

75,000	Mr Albert (who is also managing director and chairman)
25,000	Mr Bryant (who is also a director)
12,500	Mr Chad (who is also a director)
87,500	held by 7 other shareholders, each with 12,500 shares
200,000	

iv. The company has incurred significant trading losses over the past five years.

v. The directors have been discussing with the company's accountants the advisability of either(a) arranging a merger with Willow Ltd or (b) carrying out a scheme or reorganisation.

vi. The directors estimate that the company will make profits in future years. The profits are estimated to be:

1986	£10,000
1987	£15,000
1988	£20,000

Appendix 2 List of balance extracted from the books of Pourwell Limited as at 31 December 19-5

	£
Accrued interest on debentures	10,500
Administrative expenses	105,113
Audit fee accrual	2,850
Bank overdraft	38,022
Bank interest	7,100
Cost of sales	416,028
Creditors (trade) (control account total)	258,550
7% debentures (redeemable 1992)	75,000
Debtors (trade)(control account total)	89,505
Deferred development expenditure	87,500
Directors' loans	125,000
Dividend received (net)	3,500
Expense accrual	1,900
Fixtures and fittings	9,900
Goodwill	150,000
Insurance prepayment	4,000
Investment (at cost)	42,500
Land and buildings	100,000
Ordinary shares of £1 each	200,000
Plant	90,800
Preference shares (7% cumulative)	100,000
Profit and loss account (debit balance)	97,160
Profit on sale of land	15,000
Provision for depreciation of buildings	19,200
Provision for depreciation of plant	47,880
Provision for depreciation of fixtures	4,620
Sales	696,000
Selling and distribution expenses	200,101
Stock of raw material	20,210
Stock of work in progress	10,103
Stock of finished goods	170,102
Wages accrual	2,100

Appendix 3 Further information available when drafting the profit and loss account of Pourwell Ltd for the year ended 31 December 1985 and a balance sheet as at that date

i. Directors received the following remuneration:

Albert	£31,000
Bryant	£22,000
Chad	£15,000

In addition, fees of £2,000 per annum were paid to each director.

ii. Depreciation has been provided for in the appropriate expense accounts for the year on the following basis:

	£	Estimated useful life
Land	Nil	
Buildings	1,600	50 years
Plant	4,540	20 years
Fixtures and fittings	660	15 years

iii. During the year the company sold land with a book value of £10,000 and purchased plant for £12,000.

iv. The goodwill arose on the purchase of the assets and liabilities of Mr Chad's business in 1980. The company are proposing to write it off over 10 years commencing in 1985.

v. The preference dividend has not been paid for 1984 or 1985.

vi. The directors estimate that the company will return to profits in 1986 and given that they estimate profits will be £10,000 in 1986 rising to £20,000 in 1988 they propose to leave the development costs as an asset for the purpose of the 1985 accounts.

vii. The trade creditors aged analysis shows:

	£
Payable before 1 July 1985	93,490
Payable before 1 October 1985	50,060
Payable before 1 December 1985	30,000
Current	35,000
Payable in 1987	50,000

Appendix 6 Proposed terms of reorganisation

The directors have produced the following information relating to the proposed reorganisations:

1. *Assets*

a. The land and buildings have been professionally valued. The valuer has quoted the following values:

	£
Open market in existing use	120,000
Existing user	62,000
Net replacement cost	179,000
Open market alternative use	156,000

b. The goodwill is thought to have no realisable value.

c. The deferred development expenditure was incurred in producing a collapsible decanter. The directors forecast that the project will produce sales as follows:

	£
1986	75,000
1987	125,000
1988	150,000
1989	150,000

and that the contribution margin will be 15%.

d. The valuation of stock of finished goods is to be reduced to a level which shows a stock turnover (based on sales) of 6 times per year.

e. Plant and machinery was revalued at £58,824.

f. A reduction of £19,200 was to be made to take account of irrecoverable trade debts.

2. *Liabilities*

g. The trade creditors payable prior to 1 July 1985 will require immediate payment.

h. The directors have agreed to waive £100,000 of their loans and to accept an issue of ordinary shares of 10p each to satisfy the balance.

i. The bank overdraft is to be repaid in full.

j. The preference shareholder is to be offered the right to convert the holding into a new issue of 10% cumulative preference shares or, alternatively, to accept ordinary shares of 10p each on a 6 for 1 (ordinary preference) basis. The initial response indicates that 50% of the holding will be converted into 10% cumulative preference shares and 50% into ordinary shares.

k. The cumulative unpaid dividend for 1984 and 1985 is to be paid immediately. (The accountant advised that legal advice would be required to ascertain whether it was legal to pay a dividend other than out of profits. For the immediate exercise it has been decided to treat the dividends as paid in cash but to take advice before making the final decision).

l. The debenture holder has agreed to convert the existing issue of debentures into a new issue carrying interest at 15% per annum. The accrued interest is to be paid immediately.

3. *Equity*

m. The ordinary shares are to be written down to 10p each.

n. The profit and loss account debit balance is to be eliminated.

o. A rights issue is to be made to raise sufficient cash to give the company a current ratio of 2:1 The shares are to be issued at 18p each.

8 Earnings per share

SSAP 3 – EARNINGS PER SHARE

1.0 This SSAP was originally issued in 1972 but was revised two years later consequent upon the introduction of the imputation system of corporation tax.

1.1 A proposed further revision to deal with practical problems associated with deferred taxation charges and with extraordinary items and prior year adjustments was abandoned in late 1984 in the light of revisions of SSAPs 15 and 6 then pending.

1.2 The basic requirements of this SSAP have been outlined in Chapter 4. These provisions and the complications to which they give rise, are considered in greater detail in the paragraphs which now follow.

SCOPE AND COVERAGE

1.3 Originally SSAP3 applied only to listed companies but subsequently this has been extended to include companies quoted on the Unlisted Securities Market (USM).

1.4 Earnings per share, (abbreviated to EPS) is the profit, expressed in pence, attributable to each ordinary share, based on the consolidated profit for the period (including that of associated companies) after deducting tax, minority interests and preference dividends but before adjusting for extraordinary items, divided by the number of equity shares in issue and ranking for dividend in the period. (NB. The preference dividends are those actually proposed/paid excluding the imputed tax credit. For cumulative preference shares, the dividend is taken whether paid/proposed or not and any arrears of such dividend are ignored when paid). A waiver of dividends by shareholders is to be disregarded in deciding whether a class of share ranks for dividend.

EPS–NIL BASIS

1.5 The tax charged in arriving at an earnings figure from which EPS is calculated includes certain elements which are constant irrespective of any dividend distribution. These include

  a. corporation tax on profits
  b. tax credits on dividends received
  c. unrelieved overseas tax arising from higher overseas tax rates.

  Where EPS calculated on this basis is significantly different from that on the net basis in 1.6 (below) it should be disclosed on the face of the profit and loss account.

EPS – NET BASIS

1.6 The tax charged in 1.5 (above) may additionally include elements which vary with the amount of profit distributed, viz.

  a. irrecoverable ACT
  b. unrelieved overseas tax arising from restricted double tax credits.

  The net basis of calculating EPS is to take account of these variable elements together with the constant elements in 1.5 (above).

1.7 Subject to the proviso in 1.5, standard practice requires that EPS on the net basis be disclosed on the face of the profit and loss account. The basis of the calculation must also be shown in the same place or as an annexed note. Corresponding period details must also be given.

NEGATIVE EPS

1.8 If earnings are negative the loss per share should be shown.

EXAMPLE

1.9 The issued and fully paid share capital of a company at 31 December 19–7 and 19–8 comprised

		£
800,000	7% preference shares of £1 per share	800,000
4,000,000	ordinary shares of £0.50 per share	2,000,000
		2,800,000

Post tax net profit for the years 19–7 and 19–8 was £256,000 and £244,000 respectively.

	19–7	19–8
	£	£
Earnings		
Net profit after tax	256,000	244,000
less preference dividends		
(7% × 800,000)	56,000	56,000
Earnings	200,000	188,000

	No.	No.
Equity shares in issue	4,000,000	4,000,000
EPS	5.0p	4.7p
	$\left[\dfrac{200,000 \times 100}{4,000,000}\right]$	$\left[\dfrac{188,000 \times 100}{4,000,000}\right]$

In the 19–8 accounts the two EPS figures would be shown on the profit and loss account (usually at the foot). There would also be a note:

EARNINGS PER SHARE

EPS has been calculated on earnings of £188,000 (19–7 £200,000) before extraordinary items and on 4,000,000 ordinary shares of £0.50 per share in issue throughout both years.

LOSSES BROUGHT FORWARD

1.10 If the current year's tax charge has been reduced by such losses, the EPS calculation should be accompanied by an explanation of the effects of tax relief on EPS for the current and preceding years.

TWO OR MORE CLASSES OF ISSUED EQUITY SHARES.

1.11 Where different classes of equity shares are in issue and/or some are only partly paid, earnings should be apportioned over the various classes in accordance with the dividend or other profit participatory rights.

2.0 CHANGES IN EQUITY CAPITAL DURING THE CURRENT YEAR.
NEW ISSUES OF SHARES
ISSUES FOR CASH AT FULL MARKET PRICE

2.1 Earnings should be apportioned over the weighted average number of shares ranking for dividend.

EXAMPLE

2.2 The issued and fully paid share capital of a company on 1 January 19–8 comprised:

		£
400,000	7% preference share of £1 per share	400,000
3,000,000	ordinary shares of £1 per share	3,000,000
		3,400,000

On 1 September 19–8 a further 600,000 of the ordinary shares were issued and fully paid in cash. Post tax net profit for the year to 31 December 19–8 was £197,600.

Earnings	£
Net profit after tax	197,600
less preference dividends	
[7% × 400,000]	28,000
Earnings	169,600

Equity shares in issue during 19–8	No.
January to August [$\frac{8}{12} \times 3,000,000$]	2,000,000
September to December [$\frac{4}{12} \times 3,600,000$]	1,200,000
Weighted average for 19–8	3,200,000

EPS $\left[\dfrac{169,600 \times 100}{3,200,000}\right]$	5.3p

The note to the accounts would state that 3,200,000 was the weighted average number of ordinary shares in issue during 19–8.

ISSUES IN EXCHANGE FOR THE ACQUISITION OF AN ASSET

2.3 As for 2.1 and 2.2. (above)

ISSUES FOR THE DISCHARGE OF A LIABILITY

2.4 As for 2.1 and 2.2 (above)

ISSUES AS PART OF A CAPITALISATION SCHEME (BONUS ISSUE)

2.5 Earnings should be apportioned over the increased number of shares ranking for dividend after the capitalisation. Corresponding figures for previous periods should be disclosed on a comparable basis.

EXAMPLE

2.6 The issued and fully paid share capital of a company on 1 January 19–8 comprised:

	£
4,800,000 ordinary shares of £0.25 per share	1,200,000

On 1 July 19–8 the company declared a 1 for 4 bonus (capitalisation) issue of fully paid shares out of reserves.

Post tax net profit for the year to 31 December 19–8 was £234,000. EPS for the previous year was 5.5p.

Earnings	£
Net profit after tax	234,000

Equity shares in issue during 19–8	No.
At 1 January 19–8	4,800,000
Bonus issue (1 July 19–8)(1 for 4)	1,200,000
Total number of shares after capitalisation	6,000,000
EPS 19–8 $\left[\dfrac{234,000 \times 100}{6,000,000} \right]$	3.9p

EPS 19–7

Originally 5.5p, this figure will now have to be adjusted per 2.5 (above). As the bonus issue was 1 for 4, the reduction fraction will be

$$\frac{4}{(4+1)} = \frac{4}{5}$$

The restated 19–7 EPS is thus $[\frac{4}{5} \times 5.5]$ 4.4p and a note to the accounts would state:

Earnings per share EPS has been calculated on earnings of £234,000 and on 6,000,000 ordinary shares of £0.25 per share after the capitalisation issue on 1 July 19–8. EPS for 19–7 has been adjusted accordingly.

EQUITY SHARES SPLIT INTO SHARES OF A LOWER NOMINAL VALUE

2.7 As for 2.5 and 2.6 (above)

ISSUES OF LOAN STOCK OR SHARES IN EXCHANGE FOR SHARES WHICH GIVE A CONTROLLING INTEREST IN A SUBSIDIARY COMPANY

2.8 This constitutes an acquisition or a merger situation. The controlling interest may be gained some time before the loan stock or shares are actually issued. The results of the subsidiary company are consolidated from the date control is gained and not from the date the consideration passes. For the EPS calculation the securities are deemed to have been issued from the (earlier) control gained date.

EXAMPLE

2.9 The issued and fully paid share capital of a company on 1 January 19–8 comprised:

		£
80,000	7% preference shares of £1 per share	80,000
4,200,000	ordinary shares of £1 per share	4,200,000
		4,280,000

On 1 August 19–8 the company issued 20,000 7% preference shares and 600,000 ordinary shares as consideration for an 80% (controlling) interest in another company which had become a subsidiary on 1 January 19–8.

Post tax net profit for the year to 31 December 19–8 was £273,200 for the group of which £7,400 was attributable to minority interests in the subsidiary, the profit of which had been consolidated for the whole year.

All the shares in issue at 31 December 19–8 ranked for dividend.

Earnings	£
Group net profit after tax	273,200
less Minority interests	7,400
	265,800
less preference dividends	
[7% × (80,000 + 20,000)]	7,000
(i.e. full year effect)	
Earnings	**258,800**

Equity shares in issue during 19–8	No.
At 1 January 19–8	4,200,000
Issued 1 August 19–8 (assumed to have been in issue throughout the year)	600,000
At 31 December 19–8	**4,800,000**

$$\text{EPS} \left[\frac{258,800 \times 100}{4,800,000} \right] \qquad 5.4\text{p}$$

The note to the accounts would state:

Earnings per share EPS has been calculated on earnings of £258,800 after adjustment for a full year's dividend on the increased preference capital of 100,000 shares and on 4,800,000 ordinary shares on the basis that the 600,000 shares issued on 1 August 19–8 had been issued for the whole of 19–8.

If any part of the consideration had consisted of loan stock, the full year's interest charge would have been reflected in the earnings figure for the purpose of the EPS calculation.

RIGHTS ISSUES

2.10 When equity shares which rank equally with an existing class are issued as a rights issue, the concessionary price at which they are issued reflects the bonus element of the rights issue. In other words, the rights issue is regarded partly as an issue for cash at full market price and partly as a bonus issue on the combined number of original and assumed rights shares.

EXAMPLE

2.11 A company had 4,000,000 ordinary shares of £1 per share in issue, the market value of which were £3.50 per share, termed the actual cum rights price.

It then declared a 1 for 4 rights issue at the concessionary price of £2.80 per share. The total issue is then valued thus

No. of shares		£
4,000,000	ordinary shares at the cum rights price of £3.50 per share	14,000,000
1,000,000	(1 for 4) ordinary shares at the rights price of £2.80 per share	2,800,000
5,000,000	**Total issued capital (post rights)**	**16,800,000**

The value of the post rights capital (£16,800,000) divided by the new number of shares (5,000,000) gives a value of £3.36 per share, termed the theoretical ex rights price.

The actual post rights price would almost certainly be different from this figure of £3.36 per share as various other complicated factors would affect the market for them.

2.12 An alternative view of the transactions in 2.11 (above) is that the proceeds of the rights issue (£2,800,000) represents a number of shares at the full actual cum rights price of £3.50 per share, that is 800,000 shares (2,800,000/3.5). The balance between the aggregate of the original share capital (4,000,000 shares) plus the notional rights shares (800,000 shares) and the total number of post rights shares in issue (5,000,000) is 200,000 shares and this represents a bonus issue of 1 for 24 on the 4,800,000 aggregate, thus.

No.of shares   £

No. of shares		£
4,000,000	ordinary shares at the actual cum rights price of £3.50 per share	14,000,000
800,000	notional rights issue of 1 for 5 ordinary shares at the actual cum rights price of £3.50 per share	2,800,000
4,800,000		16,800,000
200,000	notional bonus issue of 1 for 24 ordinary shares	–
5,000,000	Total issued capital per 2.11 (above)	16,800,000

2.13 The significance of this is that when a rights issue is made, two adjustments have to be made simultaneously in arriving at the number of shares used as the divisor in the EPS calculation.

2.14 Firstly, as the issue is for cash, the number of shares in issue are weighted on a time basis as in 2.1 and 2.2 (above).

2.15 Secondly, the bonus element aspect has to be dealt with as in 2.5 and 2.6 (above). This is achieved by the application of an adjusting factor to the number of pre-rights shares in issue.

2.16 In calculating EPS for the year in which the rights issue is made, the weighted average shares in issue must be adjusted by applying the factor

$$\frac{\text{actual cum rights price (on last day of cum rights quotation)}}{\text{theoretical ex rights price}}$$

to the time weighted shares in issue before the rights issue and adding to this figure the time weighted shares in issue after the rights issue has occurred.

2.17 Under the circumstances in 2.16 (above) EPS for previous years must be disclosed on a comparable basis by taking the EPS figures as originally calculated and applying the inverted version of the adjusting factor in 2.16 (above), thus,

$$\frac{\text{theoretical ex rights price}}{\text{actual cum rights price (on last day of cum rights quotation)}}$$

EXAMPLE

2.18 The issued and fully paid capital of a company on 1 January 19–8 comprised

		£
100,000	7% preference shares of £1 per share	100,000
4,000,000	ordinary shares of £1 per share	4,000,000
		4,100,000

On 1 October 19–8 the company declared a 1 for 4 rights issue of ordinary shares at £1.40 per share.

The market price of the ordinary shares on the last day of quotation on a cum rights basis, was £2.40 per share.

Post tax net profit for the year to 31 December 19–8 was £115,540. EPS for the previous year was 2.8p.

Earnings	£
Net profit after tax	115,540
less preference dividends [7% × 100, 000]	7,000
Earnings	108,540

Theoretical ex rights price

No. of shares		£
4,000,000	ordinary shares at the actual cum rights price of £2.40	9,600,000
1,000,000	rights issue (1 for 4) at the rights price of £1.40 per share	1,400,000
5,000,000	total issued ordinary share capital (ex rights) at the theoretical ex rights price of £2.20 per share [£11,000,000/5,000,000]	11,000,000

Adjusting factor for 19–8 pre-rights weighting

$$\frac{2.4}{2.2} = \frac{12}{11}$$

Adjusting factor for pre 19–8 EPS figures
Invert previous figures, thus

$$\frac{2.2}{2.4} = \frac{11}{12}$$

Equity shares in issue during 19–8	No.
January to September $[\frac{12}{11} \times \frac{9}{12} \times 4,000,000]$	3,272,727
October to December $[\frac{3}{12} \times 5,000,000]$	1,250,000
Weighted average for 19–8	**4,522,727**

$$\textbf{EPS 19–8} \left[\frac{108,540 \times 100}{4,522,727} \right] \qquad 2.4p$$

EPS 19–7 The adjusting factor for pre 19–8 EPS figures would be applied to the original figure of 2.8p thus

$$\frac{11}{12} \times 2.8 = 2.6p$$

Notional equivalents
The view stated in 2.12 (above) can be expressed as

No. of shares		£
4,000,000	ordinary shares at the actual cum rights price of £2.40 per share	9,600,000
583,333	notional rights issue at the actual cum rights price of £2.40 per share	1,400,000
4,583,333		11,000,000
416,667	notional bonus issue (1 for 11)	–
5,000,000	**Total post rights issued capital (per above)**	11,000,000

In the equity share calculation above, the application of the adjusting factor to the pre- rights shares reflects the notional bonus element thus

	No.
Pre-rights shares time weighted $[\frac{9}{12} \times 4,000,000]$	3,000,000
Notional bonus issue (1 for 11)	272,727
Total as above	**3,272,727**

Conversely, the 1 for 11 bonus element is also the basis of the adjusting reduction factor applied to previous years EPS figures. The effect of applying a factor of $\frac{11}{12}$ is to reduce the original figure by $\frac{1}{(11 + 1)}$.

EPS – FULLY DILUTED BASIS

3.0 The calculations of EPS from 1.9 to 2.18 (above) have been made on the basis of actual shares in issue and ranking for dividend. This is termed basic EPS.

3.1 Where however a company has incurred obligations which may at some specified or unspecified future time result in the issue of additional equity shares, further calculations must be made to arrive at the figure of earnings which would result, should these issues be made.

3.2 The resultant figure is termed fully diluted EPS and should be disclosed on the face of the profit and loss account with equal prominence to basic EPS.

3.3 Fully diluted EPS need not, however, be shown if the dilution is immaterial, that is, less than 5% of basic EPS or if a higher figure of EPS results as can happen when earnings are increased by interest added back.

3.4 The circumstances which occasion the disclosure of a fully diluted EPS figure are where a company has issued:

a. a separate class of equity shares which will rank for dividend at some future time;
b. debentures and/or loan stock and/or preference shares convertible into equity shares of the company.
c. options and/or warrants to subscribe for equity shares of the company

SEPARATE CLASS OF EQUITY SHARE

3.5 Fully diluted EPS should be calculated on the assumption that this class of share ranked for dividend from the start of the period (or such later date) as they were issued or were assumed to have been issued.

EXAMPLE

3.6 The issued and fully paid share capital of a company on 31 December 19–7 comprised:

		£
8,000,000	ordinary shares of £0.25 per share	2,000,000

On 1 January 19–8 the company issued 2,000,000 ordinary 'A' shares of £0.25 per share which do not rank for dividend until December 19–9.

Post tax net profit for the year to 31 December 19–8 was £248,000

Earnings	£
Net profit after tax	248,000

Equity shares in issue during 19–8	No.
At 1 January 19–8 brought forward	8,000,000
Issue of class 'A' shares (not ranking for dividend until 19–9)	2,000,000
At 31 December 19–8	10,000,000

EPS-basic $\left[\dfrac{248,000 \times 100}{8,000,000}\right]$ 3.1p

EPS-fully diluted $\left[\dfrac{248,000 \times 100}{10,000,000}\right]$ 2.5p

The note would state:

Earnings per share Basic EPS has been calculated on earnings of £248,000 and on 8,000,000 ordinary shares of £0.25 per share. Fully diluted EPS is based on the same earnings but on 10,000,000 ordinary shares of £0.25 per share, including 2,000,000 class 'A' shares not ranking for dividend until 19–9.

CONVERTIBLE SECURITIES

3.7 The terms of the issue specify the date(s) and number of equity shares to be issued. If the conversion rate varies according to the date of occurrence, it should be assumed, for the purpose of calculating fully diluted EPS, that the conversion takes place at the maximum number of shares available at the date.

3.8 Furthermore, the shares in 3.7 (above) are assumed to have been issued at the start of the financial year, or at date of issue of the security, if later.

3.9 The effect of this assumption is that the basic earnings for the year have to be adjusted by the notional interest (net of corporation tax) deemed to have been saved on the basis of 3.8 (above).

EXAMPLE

3.10 The issued and fully paid share capital of a company on 31 December 19–8 comprised:

		£
400,000	7% preference shares of £1 per share	400,000
4,000,000	ordinary shares of £1 per share	4,000,000
		4,400,000

Post tax net profit for the year to 31 December 19–8 was £372,000

On 1 October 19–0 the company had issued £1,200,000 6% convertible loan stock 19–9/19–3, convertible per £100 of loan stock into ordinary shares of £1 per share as follows:

30 September	19–9	120
	19–0	115
	19–1	110
	19–2	108
	19–3	105

Earnings	£	£
Net profit after tax		372,000
less preference dividends		
[7% × 400,000]		28,000
Basic earnings		344,000
add back		
6% convertible loan stock		
interest [6% × 1,200,000]	72,000	
less corporation tax [35%]	25,200	
		46,800
Fully diluted earnings		390,800

Equity shares in issue	No.
At 31 December 19–8 (basic)	4,000,000
Convertible loan stock equivalent	1,440,000
[120/100 × 1,200,000]	
At 31 December 19–8 (fully diluted)	5,440,000

EPS-basic $\left[\dfrac{344,000 \times 100}{4,000,000}\right]$ 8.6p

EPS-fully diluted $\left[\dfrac{390,800 \times 100}{5,440,000}\right]$ 7.2p

At the end of the following year 19–9, the next available conversion date will be 30 September 19–0 when the rate will have dropped to 115 per £100. The convertible loan stock equivalent shares will therefore then be 1,380,000 [115/100 × 1,200,000].

The note to the 19–8 accounts would state:

Earnings per share Basic EPS has been calculated on earnings of £344,000 and on 4,000,000 ordinary shares of £1 per share.

Fully diluted EPS has been calculated on the adjusted earnings of £390,800 after adding back interest (less corporation tax) on 6% convertible loan stock issued on 1 October 19–0. The maximum number of shares into which this stock becomes convertible on 30 September 19–9 is 1,440,000 making a total of 5,440,000 ordinary shares issued and issuable at 31 December 19–8.

3.11 If a partial conversion of loan stock has taken place during the year, basic EPS is calculated on the weighted average number of shares in issue during the year.

3.12 Under the circumstances of 3.11, fully diluted EPS is calculated on the adjusted earnings and on the total number of shares in issue at the end of the year plus the maximum number of ordinary shares issuable under the conversion terms.

EXAMPLE

3.13 The issued and fully paid share capital of a company on 1 January 19–9 comprised

		£
400,000	7% preference shares of £1 per share	400,000
4,000,000	ordinary shares of £1 per share	4,000,000
		4,400,000

Post tax net profit for the year to 31 December 19–9 was £407,040. On 1 October 19–0 the company had issued £1,200,000 6% convertible loan stock 19–9/19–3, convertible per £100 of loan stock into ordinary shares of £1 per share as follows:

434

$$
\begin{array}{llr}
\text{30 September} & \text{19--9} & 120 \\
& \text{19--0} & 115 \\
& \text{19--1} & 110 \\
& \text{10--2} & 108 \\
& \text{19--3} & 105 \\
\end{array}
$$

On 30 September 19–9 the company converted £400,000 of the 6% convertible loan stock at the rate of 120 shares per £100 stock into 480,000 ordinary shares of £1 per share which ranked for dividend in 19–9.

Earnings	£	£
Net profit after tax		407,040
less preference dividends		
[7% × 400,000]		28,000
		———
Basic earnings		379,040
add back		
6% convertible loan stock interest	66,000	
[6% × 400,000 × $\frac{9}{12}$ = 18,000		
6% × 800,000 = 48,000]		
less corporation tax (35%)	23,100	
		———
		42,900
Fully diluted earnings		421,940

Equity shares in issue during 19–9	No.
January to September [$\frac{9}{12}$ × 4,000,000]	3,000,000
October to December [$\frac{3}{12}$ × 4,480,000]	1,120,000
Weighted average for 19–9 (basic)	4,120,000
At 1 January 19–9	4,000,000
Issued 30 September 19–9 (and	
ranking for dividend)	480,000
	———
At 31 December 19–9	4,480,000
Convertible loan stock equivalent	
[(1,200,000 − 400,000) × 115/100]	920,000
At 31 December 19–9 (fully diluted)	5,400,000

If the shares issued on 30 September 19–9 did not rank for dividend in 19–9, the divisor for basic EPS would be 4,000,000 shares.

$$
\textbf{EPS-basic} \qquad \left[\frac{379,040 \times 100}{4,120,000} \right] \quad 9.2\text{p}
$$

$$
\textbf{EPS-fully diluted} \qquad \left[\frac{421,940 \times 100}{5,400,000} \right] \quad 7.8\text{p}
$$

The note to the 19–9 accounts would state:

Earnings per share Basic EPS is calculated on earnings of £379,040 and on the weighted average of 4,120,000 ordinary shares ranking for dividend.

Fully diluted EPS is based on adjusted earnings of £421,940 after adding back interest (less corporation tax) on 6% convertible loan stock. £400,000 of the loan stock was converted into 480,000 ordinary shares on 30 September 19–9, leaving £800,000 of the loan stock outstanding. The maximum number of shares into which the remaining stock is convertible on 30 September 19–0 is 920,000 making a total of 5,400,000 ordinary shares issued and issuable.

3.14 When the final conversion takes place, it will be necessary to show fully diluted EPS for that year, unless final conversion occurred on the first day and the new shares have ranked for dividend.

EXAMPLE

3.15 The issued and fully paid share capital of a company on 1 January 19–8 comprised:

		£
400,000	7% preference shares of £1 per share	400,000
4,480,000	ordinary shares of £1 per share	4,480,000
		4,880,000

Post tax net profit for the year ended 31 December 19–8 was £380,080.

On 1 October 19–0, the company had issued £1,200,000 6% convertible loan stock 19–7/19–1 convertible into ordinary shares at variable rates.

On 30 September 19–7, £400,000 of the loan stock had been converted into ordinary shares at 120 per £100 stock.

The remainder of the stock was converted on 30 September 19–8 at 115 per £100 stock into 920,000 ordinary shares which ranked for dividend in 19–8.

Earnings	£	£
Net profit after tax		380,080
less preference dividends		
[7% × 400,000]		28,000
Basic earnings		352,080
add back		
6% convertible loan stock interest	36,000	
[6% × 800,000 × $\frac{9}{12}$]		
less corporation tax [35%]	12,600	23,400
Fully diluted earnings		375,480
Equity shares in issue during 19–8		No.
January to September [$\frac{9}{12}$ × 4,480,000]		3,360,000
October to December [$\frac{3}{12}$ × 5,400,000]		1,350,000
Weighted average for 19–8		4,710,000
At 1 January 19–8		4,480,000
Issued on 30 September 19–8		920,000
At 31 December 19–8		5,400,000

If the shares issued on 30 September 19–8 did not rank for dividend in 19–8, the divisor for basic EPS would be 4,480,000 and a figure of fully diluted EPS would be required:

EPS-basic   (assuming new shares ranked for dividend in 19–8)

$$\frac{352,080 \times 100}{4,710,000} \quad 7.5p$$

(assuming new shares did not rank for dividend in 19–8)

$$\frac{352,080 \times 100}{4,480,000} \quad 7.9p$$

EPS-fully diluted   (assuming new shares did not rank for dividend in 19–8)

$$\frac{375,480 \times 100}{5,400,000} \quad 6.9p$$

The note to the 19–8 accounts, assuming that the shares did not rank for dividend in that year, would state:

Earnings per share Basic EPS has been calculated on earnings of £352,080 and on 4,480,000 ordinary shares of £1 per share.

Fully diluted EPS has been calculated on the adjusted earnings of £375,480 after adding back interest (less corporation tax) on the remaining 6% convertible loan stock to date of final conversion. This remaining stock was converted on 30 September 19–8, making a total of 5,400,000 ordinary shares ranking for dividend in 19–9.

OPTIONS OR WARRANTS TO SUBSCRIBE FOR EQUITY SHARES

3.16 Where a listed company has granted options, for example, to executives or has issued warrants to subscribe for equity shares of the company, certain assumptions should be made when calculating fully diluted EPS:

1. that the options or warrants were exercised at the beginning of the period so that the proceeds were received on the first day of the financial year;
   and

2. that the proceeds in (1) were invested in 2 1/2% Consolidated Stock.

3.17 In view of these assumptions, earnings for the year will need to be increased by the yield from the investment as though they had been invested in the first day of the period at the closing price of the previous day. The yield is calculated net of corporation tax.

EXAMPLE

3.18 The issued and fully paid share capital of a company on 1 January 19–8 comprised:

		£
600,000	7% preference shares of £1 per share	600,000
8,000,000	ordinary shares of £0.25 per share	2,000,000
		2,600,000

Post tax net profit for the year to 31 December 19–8 was £346,000.

On 1 May 19–4 the company had granted options, exercisable on or before 31 December 19–1, on 800,000 ordinary shares of £0.25 per share on payment of £1,200,000.

The closing price of $2\frac{1}{2}$% Consols on 31 December 19–7 was £29.75

Earnings	£	£
Net profit after tax		346,000
less preference dividends		42,000
[7% × 600,000]		
Basic earnings		304,000
add back		
Assumed yield on subscription proceeds	100,800	
[2.5 × 100)/29.75 = 8.4% (yield)		
8.4% × 1,200,000]		
less corporation tax [35%]	35,280	65,520
Fully diluted earnings		369,520

Equity shares in issue in 19–8	No.
At 31 December 19–8 (basic)	8,000,000
Issuable on or before 31 December 19–1	800,000
At 31 December 19–8 (fully diluted)	8,800,000

$$\text{EPS-basic} \quad \frac{304,000 \times 100}{8,000,000} \quad 3.8\text{p}$$

$$\text{EPS-fully diluted} \quad \frac{369,520 \times 100}{8,800,000} \quad 4.2\text{p}$$

In this particular instance, fully diluted EPS would not be disclosed because it is greater than basic EPS (see 3.3)

The note to the 19–8 accounts would state:

Earnings per share Basic EPS has been calculated on earnings of £304,000 and on 8,000,000 ordinary shares of £0.25 per share in issue during the year.

On 1 May 19–4 the company had granted options, exercisable on or before 31 December 19–1 to subscribe for 800,000 ordinary shares of £0.25 per share at £1.50 per share. The fully diluted EPS, based on the assumption that the option had been exercised on 1 January 19–8 and that the proceeds of the subscription had been invested in 2 1/2% Consolidated Stock and on 8,800,000 ordinary shares issued and issuable, exceeds basic EPS and is not therefore disclosed.

STUDENT SELF TESTING Test Exercise

1. Summarised balance sheet, profit and loss account and statement of source and application of funds for Northern Manufacturing Co. Ltd. follow.

	31 December	
	19-9	19-8
	£000	£000
Balance Sheet		
Fixed assets	1,900	1,400
Current assets		
Stocks	1,000	600
Debtors	800	500
Cash	–	40
	3,700	2,540
Share capital		
ordinary shares of £1	1,000	600
Reserves	600	300
Convertible 8% loan	500	500
12% Loan repayable 19-0	600	600
Current liabilities		
Trade creditors	700	350
Overdraft	300	190
	3,700	2,540
Profit and loss account		
Turnover	7,000	5,000
Trading profit, before depreciation	800	500
Depreciation	600	400
Advance corporation tax paid and written off	60	33
Dividends paid, as interim and only one for year	140	67
Retained	–	–
Statement of source and application of funds		
Profit before taxation and depreciation	800	500
Share issues	700	–
Increase in creditors	350	100
	1,850	600
Purchase of Plant	1,100	200
Dividends paid	140	67
Advance corporation tax paid and written off	60	33
Increase in debtors	300	100
Increase in stock	400	200
	2,000	600
Increase (Decrease) in net bank and cash balance	(150)	–

The overdraft has been renewed every three months since 1st January 19-0. Since that time the maximum overdraft each year has varied between £750,000 and £250,000.

The 8% loan is convertible into ordinary shares at the rate of 1 ordinary share for each £1 of loan stock on 31st December 19–5.

There was an issue of new shares to existing shareholders on the basis of 4 new shares for every six held at a price of £1.75 each on 1st May 19–9.

The 19–9 accounts were published on 31st May, 19–0 and since that date the share price has fluctuated between £2.00 and £1.10. The current price is £1.80.

No taxation is provided as planned expansion of activities indicates that none will be payable in the foreseeable future.

You are required to:

Calculate earnings per share as disclosed in the accounts of 19–8 and 19–9.

ACCA EXAMINATION QUESTIONS

2. On 30 September 1979, Purbeck Ltd had an issued share capital of £1,500,000 in ordinary shares of 25p each. On 31st March 1980 the company made a Rights Issue of 1:3 at 80p per share. The Rights Issue was fully taken up. The stock exchange quoted price for the existing shares on the day before the shares went ex rights was 140p per share. The new shares were not entitled to the 10% dividends declared for the year ended 30 September 1980.

The consolidated profits of Purbeck Ltd and its subsidiaries for the year ended 30 September 1980 were £880,000 before deducting taxation £460,000 and profits attributable to minority interests in a subsidiary of £25,000. The earnings per share disclosed for the year ended 30 September 979 was 6.5p per share.

During the year ended 30 September 1981 Purbeck acquired the minority interest in the subsidiary by issuing 500,000 10% cumulative preference shares. It also issued £1,000,000 8% convertible debenture stock 1991. The debenture stock was convertible into ordinary shares as follows:

31 May 1982 200 ordinary shares per £100 of debenture stock
31 May 1983 180 ordinary shares per £100 of debenture stock
31 May 1984 160 ordinary shares per £100 of debenture stock

The terms of conversion included the clause that shares issued under the agreement would rank for dividend in the accounting year following the exercise of the conversion. Holders of £400,000 debenture stock exercised their conversion right on 31 May 1982. The profit and loss accounts for the years ended 30 September 1981 and 1982 are as follows:

		1981		1982
	£	£	£	£
Trading profit for the year		940,000		1,200,000
Less debenture interest		80,000		80,000
		860,000		1,120,000
Less taxation				
Corporation Tax		480,000		530,000
Transfer to (from)				
Deferred Tax		(30,000)		50,000
Profit after tax		410,000		540,000
Extraordinary items		(35,000)		20,000
		375,000		560,000
Less dividends				
Preference	50,000		50,000	
Ordinary	200,000	250,000	200,000	250,000
Profit retained		£125,000		£310,000

Assume Corporation Tax at 52%

Required:

a. Calculate the earnings per share figures for disclosure in the profit and loss account of Purbeck Ltd for the year ended 30 September 1980 and the comparative figure for the year ended 30 September 1979.

b. Show the earnings per share calculation for disclosure in the profit and loss account of Purbeck plc (name changed from Purbeck Ltd in 1981) for the year ended 30 September 1982 and the comparative figure for 1981.

(ACCA 2.9(2) December 1983)

3. The draft Profit and Loss Account of Pilum PLC for the year ended 31st December 1984 is set out below:

Pilum PLC

Draft Profit & Loss Account for year ended 31 December 1984

	£	£
Profit before tax and extraordinary items		2,530,000
Less: Taxation		
Corporation tax	1,058,000	
Under provision for 1983	23,000	
Irrecoverable Advance		
Corporation Tax	69,000	
		1,150,000
		1,380,000
Less: Extraordinary loss	207,000	
Less Taxation	92,000	
		115,000
		1,265,000
Less: Transfer to reserves	115,000	
Dividends		
Paid - Preference interim dividend	138,000	
Paid - Ordinary interim dividend	184,000	
Proposed - Preference final		
dividend	138,000	
Proposed - Ordinary final dividend	230,000	
		805,000
Retained		£460,000

On 1 January 1984 the issued share capital of Pilum PLC was 4,600,000 6% preference shares of £1 each and 4,140,000 ordinary shares of £1 each.

Required:

Calculate the earnings per share (on basic and fully diluted basis) in respect of the year ended 31 December 1984 for each of the following circumstances. (Each of the five circumstances (a) to (e) is to be dealt with separately):

a. On the basis that there was no change in the issued share capital of the company during the year ended 31 December 1984.

b. On the basis that the company made a bonus issue on 1 October 1984 of one ordinary share for every four shares in issue at 30 September 1984.

c. On the basis that the company made a rights issue of £1 ordinary shares on 1 October 1984 in the proportion of 1 for every 5 shares held, at a price of £1.20. The middle market price for the shares on the last day of quotation cum rights was £1.80 per share.

d. On the basis that the company made no new issue of shares during the year ended 31 December 1984 but on that date it had in issue £1,150,000 10% convertible loan stock 1988-1991. This loan stock will be convertible into ordinary £1 shares as follows:

> 1988 90 £1 shares for £100 nominal value loan stock.
> 1989 85 £1 shares for £100 nominal value loan stock.
> 1990 80 £1 shares for £100 nominal value loan stock.
> 1991 75 £1 shares for £100 nominal value loan stock.

e. On the basis that the company made no issues of shares during the year ended 31 December 1984 but on that date there were outstanding options to purchase 460,000 ordinary £1 shares at £1.70 per share.

Assume where appropriate that:

i. Corporation Tax rate is 50%.

ii. The Quotation for 2 1/2% consolidated stock was £25.

(ACCA 2.9(2) June 1985)

9 Changing Price Levels

GENERAL BACKGROUND

1.0 The constant and unremitting rise in prices in the United Kingdom after the end of the Second World Ward in 1945 was accompanied by an increasing awareness of the need for a system of accounting relevant to such inflationary conditions.

1.1 By the early 1970s the search for such a system had progressed to the point where an Exposure Draft was published (1973) and followed by a provisional standard entitled "Accounting for changes in the purchasing power of money" in 1974.

1.2 At about the same time that this system was first exposed, the government of the day instituted an inflation Accounting Committee under the chairmanship of (the now) Sir Francis Sandilands. Its report, published in 1975, rejected the current purchasing power system and advocated a form of replacement cost accounting which it termed current cost accounting.

1.3 Work was immediately started to convert the proposals into a workable standard and in 1976, ED18 Current Cost Accounting, was published, but proved to be too controversial and was rejected by the membership of the Institute of Chartered Accountants in England and Wales.

1.4 As an interim, stop-gap, measure the Accounting Standards Committee in late 1977 issued "Inflation Accounting – An Interim Recommendation" which became widely known as the Hyde Guidelines, so-called after the chairman of the committee which produced them.

1.5 ED 24 Current Cost Accounting was published in 1979 and after a longer than usual exposure period, was converted into a standard of that name (SSAP 16) in April 1980. This is dealt with in 6.4.0 and following sub-sections.

1.6 On publication, SSAP 16 was given an effective life of three years, after which it was intended to issue a replacement standard aimed at resolving identified problem areas and responding to the reactions of companies and users of their CCA information. SSAP 16 has now been withdrawn.

1.7 An Exposure Draft (ED 35) Accounting for the effects of changing prices was issued in July 1984 but withdrawn in May 1985. This is dealt with in 7.0 to 7.4. In 1986 the ASC issued a handbook, representing the latest thinking on the subject, and bearing the same title as the withdrawn ED 35.

DEFECTS OF HISTORICAL COST SYSTEM

2.0 Traditionally, assets have appeared in the balance sheet at historical cost, less, in the case of fixed assets, depreciation; profit has been measured as the difference between current period revenue and past periods' costs.

2.1 It is readily apparent that financial statements prepared in accordance with the historical cost concept have always been defective to the extent that

    a. they fail to reflect the impact of changing price levels:

    b. assets are disclosed in the balance sheet at unrealistic values;

    c. the profit and loss account does not bear proper charges, particularly for depreciation and cost of materials consumed.

2.2 The situation was aggravated throughout the 1970s by the accelerated rate of inflation; as a consequence, products and services undercosted, thus producing fictitiously high "paper" profits which the company then shared out between its employees as wages, its shareholders as dividends and the taxation authorities as corporation tax.

ADVANTAGES OF CURRENT COST ACCOUNTING (CCA) SYSTEM

3.0 In general, the advantages of a CCA system are that it overcomes the defects of a historical cost system, in that, being a current value system of accounting, its aim is to represent, as far as is feasible, the commercial reality of the situation to which it refers.

3.1 Particular advantages are that

    a. Current costs are matched with current revenues, for example

        i. depreciation is calculated on the value to the business of the assets concerned; in the majority of cases, such value is the net current replacement cost;

   ii. cost of sales is calculated on actual or assumed date-of-sale cost prices;

b. the balance sheet shows assets at their value to the business;

c. as the result of a. and b. users of accounts have available more realistic information on costs, profits/losses, asset values and the return on capital and on assets;

d. the system identifies profits and losses arising from business operations separately from those arising from price level changes.

e. current basis figures lead to better quality long-term and short-term decisions.

SSAP 16 – CURRENT COST ACCOUNTING

4.0 Current cost accounting principles have found practical exposition in SSAP 16 whose contents are summarised in the sub-sections which follow. To allow for experimentation with the basic framework of the standard it was not reviewed, for the purposes of alteration, until a period of three years had elapsed from the operative date (January 1980) but is not now mandatory for companies to observe. Its principles are expected to be embodied in a future standard and for that reason are dealt with in this section.

SCOPE

4.1 The standard applied to all business enterprises whose annual financial statements are intended to give a true and fair view of the financial position and of profit or loss.

4.2 Included in the coverage are:

a. listed companies

b. unlisted companies, provided that they satisfy at least two of the following requirements.

   i. a turnover exceeding £5,000,000 per annum;

   ii. net book value (at historical cost) in the balance sheet of fixed assets, investments and current assets exceeding £2,500,000 at the beginning of the period.

   iii. average number of employees in the UK exceeding 250.

4.3 Specifically excluded from the coverage

a. wholly owned subsidiaries, unless the parent is exempted under b. to e. below;

b. authorised insurers.

c. property investment and dealing entities except those entities holding properties of another entity within the group affected by the standard;

d. investment trust companies, unit trusts and other similar long-term investment entities;

e. non-profit making entities, including charities, building societies, friendly societies, trade unions and pension funds.

BASIS OF DISCLOSURE

4.4 Both historical cost and current cost information must be disclosed, either by

a. maintaining historical cost based accounts with supplementary current cost based accounts; or

b. maintaining current cost based accounts with supplementary historical cost based accounts; or

c. maintaining current cost based accounts with supplementary historical cost based information.

CURRENT COST PROFIT AND ADJUSTMENTS

4.5 Current cost profit is determined in two stages. At the first stage, current cost operating profit is arrived at and represents the surplus contributed by the ordinary activities of the business, before interest and taxation but after allowing for changes on the funds needed to continue the existing business and to maintain its operating capability. At the second stage, that part of the current cost profit attributable to shareholders is ascertained by taking cognisance of the way the business is financed.

4.6 At the first stage, historical cost operating profit is converted to a current cost basis by the application of three main adjustments for:

   i. depreciation

   ii. cost of sales

   iii. monetary working capital

      and one secondary adjustment for:

   iv. fixed asset disposals.

4.7 The second stage involves the application of a gearing adjustment to the current cost operating profit to convert it to a figure of current cost profit attributable to shareholders.

4.8   The purpose of the adjustments is to make allowance for the impact of price changes on the funds needed to maintain the net operating assets of the business.

4.9   The depreciation adjustment is the difference between the proportion of the value to the business of the fixed assets consumed and depreciation calculated on the historical cost basis.

4.10   The cost of sales adjustment is the difference between the value to the business of stock consumed in the period and its cost calculated on the historical basis.

4.11   The monetary working capital adjustment is the variation in finance needed for monetary working capital purposes as a result of changes in the input prices of goods and services used and financed by the business. (Monetary working capital is defined as trade debtors, prepayments, trade bills receivable and stocks not subject to a cost of sales adjustment, less the aggregate of trade creditors, accruals and trade bills payable, to the extent to which all these items arise from everyday operating activities. Items of a capital nature are excluded).

4.12   Together, the cost of sales and monetary working capital adjustments allow for the impact of price changes on the total amount of working capital used by the business in day to day operations.

4.13   The fixed assets disposals adjustment is the difference between the historical cost and the current cost value to the business of the assets disposed less the proceeds of disposal in each case.

4.14   The gearing adjustment is the amount by which the foregoing current cost adjustments are abated by an amount representing that proportion of the adjustments financed by borrowing.

CURRENT COST PROFIT AND LOSS ACCOUNT

4.15   The standard specifies the minimum disclosures as:

> current cost operating profit/loss
> interest/income on net borrowing used in the gearing calculation;
> gearing adjustments;
> taxation
> extraordinary items
> current cost profit/loss attributable to shareholders;
> a reconciliation between (historical cost) profit before interest
>   and tax and current cost operating profit/loss
> individual adjustments
>   depreciation
>   cost of sales
>   monetary working capital

CURRENT COST BALANCE SHEET.

4.16   Where current cost accounts are supplementary to historical cost accounts a summarised current cost balance sheet is permissible, disclosing the various items on the following basis:

Item	Basis
Land, buildings, plant etc and stock subject to a cost of sales adjustment	at value to the business
Investment in associated companies	either (a) at appropriate proportion of their net assets, or (b) at directors' estimate of (a)
Other investments	at directors' valuation
Intangible assets (excluding goodwill)	at estimated value to the business
Goodwill/capital reserve on consolidation of subsidiary companies accounts	various bases according to circumstances - see SSAP 16
Liabilities current assets (excluding stock dealt with above)	on historical cost basis

CURRENT COST RESERVE

4.17 In the current cost balance sheet, reserves should include revaluation surpluses (or deficits) together with the previously mentioned current cost adjustments. Further amplification is given later in 6.1 to 6.7

GROUP ACCOUNTS

4.18 The parent company of a group falling within the scope of SSAP 16 should prepare current cost group accounts but need not produce such accounts for itself where historical based accounts are the main accounts.

CALCULATION OF CURRENT COST ADJUSTMENTS

5.0 Different considerations apply in the calculation of each of the adjustments mentioned previously, as shown in the following sub-sections.

DEPRECIATION ADJUSTMENT

5.1 Under the historical cost convention, depreciation is calculated on the basis of the original cost. The defect of this approach is that in ascertaining a figure of profit, historical cost is matched with current revenue.

5.2 The purpose of the depreciation adjustments is to eradicate this defect, as far as depreciation is concerned, by matching current cost with current revenue; the adjustment effectively converts the depreciation charge from a historical cost to a current cost basis.

5.3 It achieves this objective by making an adjustment to historical cost profit of an amount equal to the difference between depreciation calculated on the value to the business of the fixed assets concerned and the corresponding historical cost depreciation.

5.4 In the context of current cost accounting, value to the business means either net current replacement cost or the recoverable amount, if a permanent diminution in value, as a consequence of reduction in service potential, has been recognised.

5.5 Where an asset continues in use, but with a shortened life, recoverable amount is the estimated cash flows from future use and from eventual scrapping. If, however, an asset is to be sold or scrapped immediately, recoverable amount is the net realisable amount.

5.6 A difficulty arises when current replacement cost is to be used as the basis for the depreciation charge, in that the current replacement cost of fixed assets may not be readily available.

5.7 Ideally, current replacement cost should be obtained from suppliers' price lists but it is rarely practical to use them because of the work involved in detailed calculations.

5.8 The acceptable alternative is to apply relevant indices to existing gross book values. A variety of indices may be used. An enterprise may maintain its own indices; alternatively, it may employ indices compiled by an outside agency - a trade association, for example, or the government, which publishes, through the Central Statistical Office, a booklet of price index numbers for current cost accounting (PINCCA) containing indices for specific types of asset and for specific industries.

5.9 The depreciation charge in a particular period should be the estimated value to the business of fixed asset consumption during that period. The value to the business for the purpose of this calculation should be that subsisting at the date of consumption, SSAP 16 allows either the average (that is, mid-period) or end of period values to be used. In the case of buildings such as petrol stations, hotels etc which are usually bought and sold as going concerns, value to the business is the open market value. Other buildings, however, which are not normally sold apart from the business in which they are used, are evaluated as in 5.4 above, in the same way as plant and machinery. (For this purpose, all physical assets, other than the "going concern" buildings are treated as plant and machinery).

5.10 The method employed is to analyse the historical cost of plant and machinery, and its accompanying depreciation, by year of acquisition. These figures are then converted to a current cost basis by means of the previously mentioned indices. In subsequent years, the current cost figures are updated on the basis of the indices then available. CCA depreciation adjustment is the different between the current cost and historical cost depreciation figures for the year concerned. Asset life for CCA purposes need not necessarily coincide with that used for historical cost calculations. SSAP 12 (Revised 1987) requires that asset lives for CCA and historical cost purposes are identical.

5.11 An extension of the workings in 5.10 readily gives figures for the transfer of the revaluation surplus (that is, the difference between net book value on a CCA and on a historical cost basis) to current cost reserve and for the transfer of the CCA net book value to the CCA balance sheet. In subsequent years only the variation between opening and closing net book values is transferred to or from current cost reserve together with that year's depreciation adjustment.

EXAMPLE

5.12 At the end of year 4, the following figures were available for plant and machinery.

Depreciation is calculated at 10% straight line, assuming no residual value, for both historical and current cost purposes.

Year of acquisition	Historical cost £
1	100,000
3	150,000
	250,000

Year	Index
1	120 (mid-year)
3	150 (mid/year)
4	180 (end of year)

Required:

Calculate the

a. depreciation adjustment

b. revaluation surplus transferred to current cost reserve.

c. net book value included in the current cost balance sheet.

SOLUTION

5.13 Historical cost figures are converted using the formula

$$\frac{\text{Index at end of year 4 (see 5.9)}}{\text{Average index for year of acquisition}}$$

	Historical cost			**Current cost**
Year of acquisition	Cost	Depreciation for year 4	Conversion ratio	Depreciation for year 4
	£	£		£
1	100,000	10,000	180/120	15,000
3	150,000	15,000	180/150	18,000
		25,000		33,000
		────────────────────────────➤		25,000

a. Depreciation adjustment — 8,000

	Cost	Accumulated depreciation		Accumulated depreciation	Replacement cost
	£	£		£	£
1	100,000	40,000	180/120	60,000	150,000
3	150,000	30,000	180/150	36,000	180,000
	250,000	70,000		96,000	330,000
		70,000 ◄────────┘		┌────────➤	96,000
WDV	180,000		c. Net book value (CCA)		234,000
				└──────────────➤	180,000

b. Revaluation surplus transferred to current cost reserve — 54,000

COST OF SALES ADJUSTMENT (COSA)

5.14 Under the historical cost convention, cost of sales is calculated on the basis of original cost. In this context original cost is usually taken to be FIFO cost. The defect of this approach is that in ascertaining a figure of profit, historical (FIFO) cost is matched with current revenue.

5.15 The purpose of the cost of sales adjustments is to eradicate this defect, as far as cost of sales is concerned, by matching current cost with current revenue; the adjustment effectively converts the cost of sales from a historical cost to a current cost basis. (Certain classes of stock, for example, non-routine work-in-progress and seasonal items, are excluded from stock for the purposes of this calculation because they do not have a meaningful current replacement cost, and are classed as monetary working capital).

5.16 The combined effect of the historical cost of sales figure and the CCA cost of sales adjustment represents the current replacement cost, at point of sale, of goods sold.

5.17 It is not usually feasible to ascertain the precise replacement cost because the enormous amount of research into price lists and catalogues and of the calculations arising from that research.

5.18 As an alternative to aggregating the replacement cost of each individual item of stock used up, current cost basis cost of sales can be arrived at by converting historical cost opening and closing stock figures to an average current cost figure for the period by the use of index numbers (as noted in 5.8 previously).

5.19 If transactions have occurred evenly throughout the year, CCA cost of sales can be calculated using the mid-year index; if they have not, separate calculations should be made for each accounting period within the accounting year and then aggregated to a total for the year. The use of indices in this manner is termed averaging. Where there is a wide variation in price movements between different stock classifications, separate indices may have to be used for individual clasifications. The source of the indices has been dealt with in 5.8.

5.20 The method employed is to convert opening and closing stock values from a historical cost basis to a current cost basis by the use of the previously mentioned index numbers. The converted figures are then used to calculate cost of sales on a current cost basis, the excess of which over the comparable historically based figure, constitutes the cost of sales adjustment.

5.21 An extension of the workings in 5.20 readily gives figures for the transfer of the revaluation surplus (that is, the difference between the value of stock on a historical cost and a current cost basis) to current cost reserve and for the transfer of the CCA closing stock value to the CCA balance sheet. In subsequent years, only the variation between opening and closing stock values is transferred to or from current cost reserve together with that year's cost of sales adjustment.

EXAMPLE

5.22 At the end of year 4, the following figures were available for stocks on a historical cost basis.

	£
Opening stocks	94,800
Purchases	419,600
Closing stocks	63,000

An average of three months' sales is held in stock. For simplicity, it is assumed that a single index is appropriate to all stocks.

		Index
Mid-month–year 3	October	238.2
	November	239.6
	December	241.0
– year 4	October	273.2
	November	275.0
	December	276.8
– year 5	January	279.2
Average for year 4		260.2

Required: Calculate the

a. cost of sales adjustment

b. revaluation surplus transferred to current cost reserve

c. closing stock included in the current cost balance sheet.

SOLUTION

5.23 Historical cost figures are converted using the formula

$$\frac{\text{Average index for year 4}}{\text{index for stock}}$$

for the purpose of the cost of sales adjustment, and

$$\frac{\text{Index at end of year 4}}{\text{Index for closing stock}}$$

to arrive at the current replacement cost for the CCA balance sheet.

The starting point is the determination of the index numbers to be used as the denominators in the above formulae. The age of the stocks is given as an average of three months. The index applicable to the mid-point of the middle of the three months, that is, the November year 3 and year 4 indices, can be used for the opening and closing stock indices, respectively. Thus, 239.6 will be the opening stock index, and

275.0 the closing stock index, for year 4.

If there had been only two months' purchases in stock at the end of year 4, the closing stock index would have been 275.9, that is, the simple average of the mid-November and mid-December indices for year 4. This figure would then have represented the end of November (year 4) index number.

In similar fashion the index at the end of year 4 is the simple average of the December year 4, and January year 5, indices, 278.0 ($\frac{1}{2}$ × (276.8 plus 279.2).

	Historical cost	Conversion ratio	Current cost
	£		£
Opening stock	94,800	260.2/239.6	102,950
Purchases	419,600		419,600
	514,400		522,550
Less Closing stock	63,000	260.2/275.0	59,610
Cost of sales	451,400		462,940
			451,400
(a) **Cost of sales Adjustment** **(COSA)** (balancing figure)			11,540

Another way of regarding the COSA is that it represents that part of the current cost stock variation attributable to price; this is the residual after elimination of the volume variation:

	Historical cost	Conversion ratio	Current cost
	£		£
Opening stock	94,800	260.2/239.6	102,950
Closing stock	63,000	260.2/275.0	59,610
Stock variation Increase/(decrease)	(31,800)		
Volume variation increase/(decrease)			(43,340)
Price variation (COSA) Increase/(decrease) (balancing figure)			11,540
			(31,800)

The value to the business, assumed for this example to be the current replacement cost, of closing stock is:

	Historical cost	Conversion ratio	Current cost
	£		£
Closing stock	63,000	278.0/275.0	63,687 (b)
			63,000
(c) **Revaluation surplus** **transferred to current** **cost reserve**			687

MONETARY WORKING CAPITAL ADJUSTMENT (MWCA)

5.24 The term monetary working capital includes trade debtors, bills receivable, prepayments, trade creditors, bills payable, accruals, cash and bank balances and bank overdrafts. Certain items of stock and work-in-progress, whose replacement cost is difficult or impossible to ascertain, are included in monetary working capital (and included in MWCA) instead of being included in stock subject to COSA.

5.25 In arriving at a figure of monetary working capital, the items noted in 5.24 should be included only to the extent that they are employed in the day-to-day operating activities of the business. For example, debtors and creditors relating to fixed asset acquisitions and disposals are excluded from monetary working capital, as also may some cash and bank balances and bank overdraft which are then regarded as a component of net borrowing (see 5.40 and following).

5.26 Together with physical assets such as plant and stock, which are, respectively subject to depreciation and cost of sales adjustments, monetary working capital is an operating asset which must be maintained to allow the operating capability of a business to remain unimpaired.

5.27 The monetary working capital adjustment represents the variation in finance needed for monetary working capital purposes as a result of changes in the input prices of goods and services used and financed by the business.

5.28 The COSA and MWCA amounts are complementary in that their combined effects allow for the impact of price changes on day-to-day operations. For this reason, SSAP 16 allows these two adjustments to be merged in the current cost profit and loss account if the business so wishes.

5.29 Monetary working capital adjustment can be calculated by the system of averaging already explained at 5.19 in relation to the COSA.

5.30 Theoretically, a separate index should be applied to the debtors and creditors components of monetary working capital. The debtors index should reflect that element, of changes in current cost of goods and services sold, attributable to changes in input prices over the period the debt is outstanding. The index applied to creditors should reflect changes, during the credit period, in the cost of items which they finance.

5.31 From a practical standpoint, a single index can be used where the debtors and creditors indices are similar. In view of the need to index input values, many businesses use the same index as for stock.

5.32 The method employed is to convert opening and closing monetary working capital from a historical cost basis to a current cost basis by the use of the appropriate index numbers. The excess of the current cost figure over the historically based figure constitutes the monetary working capital adjustment.

5.33 Unlike fixed assets subject to a depreciation adjustment and stock subject to a cost of sales adjustment, monetary working capital is included in the current cost balance sheet on a historical cost basis. Consequently, no further adjustment is needed, in respect of monetary working capital items, to the current cost reserve comparable with the adjustments needed in respect of fixed assets and of stock subject to a cost of sales adjustment.

EXAMPLE

5.34 At the end of year 4 the following figures were available for monetary working capital items.

	Opening £	Closing £
Debtors (including prepayments etc)	920,000	1,040,000
Creditors (including accruals etc)	560,000	640,000

The average age of each of these items is two months.

It is assumed that the same single index used in the cost of sales adjustment calculation can be applied to monetary working capital items. The appropriate index numbers are:

		Index
Mid-month - year 3	November	239.6
	December	241.0
- year 4	November	275.0
	December	276.8
Average for year 4		260.2

Required:

Calculate the monetary working capital adjustment.

SOLUTION

5.35 Historical cost monetary working capital figures are converted using the formula.

$$\frac{\text{Average index for year 4}}{\text{Index for monetary working capital}}$$

The example stated that the average age of the items was two months. Accordingly, the index to be used as the denominator in the above formula is the simple average of the mid-November and mid-December indices for the opening and closing monetary working capital respectively, viz.

Index for opening monetary working capital

		Index
Mid-month – year 3	November	239.6
	December	<u>241.0</u>
		<u>480.6</u>
Simple average		240.3

Index for closing monetary working capital

		Index
Mid-month – year 4	November	275.0
	December	<u>276.8</u>
		<u>551.8</u>

| | Simple average | 275.9 |

It is now possible to carry out the calculations.

	Historical cost £	Conversion ratio	Current cost £
Opening monetary working capital			
Debtors etc	920,000		
Creditors etc	(560,000)		
	360,000	260.2/240.3	389,813
Closing monetary working capital			
Debtors etc	1,040,000		
Creditors etc	(640,000)		
	400,000	260.2/275.9	377,238
MWC variation increase/(decrease)	40,000		
Volume Variation increase/(decrease)			(12,575)
Monetary working capital adjustment (balancing figure)			52,575
			40,000

GEARING ADJUSTMENT

5.36 Under inflationary conditions, the value to a business of its operating assets, rises; however, the monetary value of funds which the business originally borrowed to finance these assets remains fixed.

5.37 One significance of this is that the benefit realised by the business by sale or use of that proportion of the operating assets financed by borrowing, can be applied to the benefit of the shareholders. In other words, there is a transference of the realised enhanced values from lenders to shareholders.

5.38 The mechanism by which this is carried out is the gearing adjustment, so called because this adjustment is a function of the capital gearing of the company. It achieves its objective by restricting the full effect of the operating adjustments (depreciation, fixed asset disposals, COSA and MWCA) in arriving at a figure of current cost profit attributable to shareholders.

5.39 Calculation of gearing involves two separate stages. Firstly the gearing proportion is calculated. This is then applied to the previously noted operating adjustments to give the gearing adjustment which, subject to interest payable (less interest receivable), is then used to arrive at current cost profit attributable to shareholders.

5.40 **Stage 1 – Calculation of gearing proportion**

The gearing proportion is calculated on average figures for the year on a current cost basis and is the proportion of net borrowing to net operating assets.

Net operating assets include fixed assets, trade investments, stock and monetary working capital. Alternatively, the same figure can be arrived at by aggregating net borrowing, shareholders interest and proposed dividends. In both instances the figures are taken from the current cost balance sheet.

Net borrowing comprises the aggregate of convertible debentures, deferred taxation and other liabilities and provisions fixed in monetary terms (but excluding proposed dividends and other liabilities included in monetary working capital) minus the aggregate of those current assets not classed as monetary working capital or subject to a cost of sales adjustment.

EXAMPLE

5.41 The following figures appeared in the current cost balance sheets of a company.

	As at end of	
	Year 3 £000	Year 4 £000
Current assets		
Bank and cash balances (not included in MWC)	900	1,140
Current liabilities		
HP creditors	300	240

Proposed dividends	400	400
Taxation	800	900
Bank overdraft	600	900
(not included in MWC)		
net assets employed	14,800	15,900
Shareholders funds	10,800	11,600
Long-term liabilities		
Debentures	2,400	2,800
Deferred liabilities		
Deferred taxation	1,600	1,500

Required: Calculate the gearing proportion

SOLUTION
5.42

	Year 4		
	Opening £000	Closing £000	Mean £000
Net borrowing			
Debentures	2,400	2,800	
Deferred taxation	1,600	1,500	
HP creditors	300	240	
Taxation	800	900	
Bank overdraft	600	900	
Bank and cash balances	(900)	(1,140)	
	4,800	5,200	5,000
Shareholders funds	10,800	11,600	
Proposed dividends	400	400	
	11,200	12,000	11,600
Net operating assets	16,000	17,200	16,600

The other method of arriving at net operating assets is to start with net assets employed and to eliminate those current assets and current liabilities which do not comprise stock or monetary working capital:

	Year 4		
	Opening £000	Closing £000	Mean £000
Net assets employed	14,800	15,900	
add back			
HP creditors	300	240	
Proposed dividends	400	400	
Taxation	800	900	
Bank overdraft	600	900	
Bank and cash balances	(900)	(1,140)	
Net operating assets	16,000	17,200	16,600

Gearing proportion =

$$\frac{\text{Average net borrowing}}{\text{Average net operating assets}} = \frac{5,000}{16,600} \times \frac{100}{1} = 30.12\%$$

5.43 Stage 2 – Calculation of gearing adjustment

The gearing proportion arrived at in 5.42 is applied to the current cost adjustments in total to give the gearing adjustment which, being an abatement, has the effect of increasing current cost operating profit.

EXAMPLE

5.44 The current cost adjustments of the company in 5.41 were:

	£000
Depreciation	1,260
Disposal of fixed assets	180

451

COSA	1,020
MWCA	740

Required:
Calculate the gearing adjustment, using the gearing proportion in 5.42.

SOLUTION
5.45

	£000
Current cost adjustment:	
Depreciation	1,260
Disposal of fixed assets	180
COSA	1,020
MWCA	740
Total	3,200
Gearing adjustment	
$(30.12\% \times 3,200)$	964

5.46 Monetary assets held by a business surplus to operating requirements are not regarded as part of the operating assets of the business. This situation gives rise to two implications. Firstly, income from such assets should be included in the current cost profit and loss account after the current cost operating profit line. Secondly, such surplus assets should be offset against net borrowing for the purposes of calculating the gearing adjustment.

5.47 If monetary assets exceed monetary liabilities resulting in a negative figure of net borrowing, the gearing adjustment is zero.

PREPARATION AND PRESENTATION OF CURRENT COST ACCOUNTS
6.0 The minimum disclosures (and where appropriate, the basis of disclosure) have been summarised in 15 and 16. Examples of presentation of current cost accounts are contained in an appendix to SSAP 16.

CURRENT COST RESERVE
6.1 Current cost reserve appears in the current cost balance sheet. It has no counterpart in historically based accounts.

6.2 Through the current cost reserve are passed net revaluation surpluses or deficits of the operating assets. The net amounts transferred are the restatement of gross current replacement cost of fixed assets (excluding land and buildings carried at open market value) stocks and investments minus backlog depreciation. Backlog depreciation arises from the restatement of the accumulated depreciation and represents the effect of current price changes on past consumption. Land and buildings valued on the gross current replacement cost basis minus accumulated depreciation includes those buildings of a specialist nature which would not ordinarily be sold apart from the business. Included in this category would be the repair workshops of a garage business.

6.3 Land and buildings bought as continuing businesses cannot be revalued by indexing as their replacement cost fluctuates with open market forces, not with rebuilding costs. Accordingly, their open market value coincides with net current replacement cost. When this latter figure is restated for current cost purposes, the whole of the uplift is transferred to current cost reserve, because open market value is itself net of depreciation.

6.4 Foreign currency translation differences arising from the consolidation in group accounts of subsidiaries whose accounts are denominated in foreign currencies are also passed through current cost reserve.

6.5 The surpluses and deficits described in 6.2 to 6.4 are regarded as unrealised. The cumulative current cost adjustments for depreciation, fixed asset disposals, COSA, MWCA and gearing are also transferred to the credit of current cost reserve but, by virtue of having been passed through the current cost profit and loss account, are regarded as realised amounts and, in effect, represent the difference between historically based and current cost profits on a cumulative basis since current cost accounts were first prepared for the company concerned.

6.6 An analysis of current cost reserve should be shown by way of note to the current cost accounts. A suggested layout for the analysis is appended to the standard and repeated in 6.7 for convenience of reference.

6.7 Analysis of current cost reserve

	£	£	£
Balance at beginning of period			X
Revaluation surpluses/deficits reflecting price changes			
Land and buildings	X		
Plant and machinery	X		
Stocks and work-in-progress	X		
		X	
Currency adjustments		X	
Monetary working capital adjustment		X	
Gearing adjustment		(X)	
Balance at end of period			X
of which:			
Realised			X
Unrealised			X
			X

ED 35 Accounting for the effects of changing prices

7.0 This ED was issued in July 1984 but subsequently withdrawn in May 1985. Its purpose was to alleviate the harshness of the original standard, SSAP 16, by allowing companies to maintain either current cost based accounts or historically based accounts supplemented by current cost notes.

Gearing

7.1 By way of greater flexibility, three different methods of gearing were permitted. These are described in 7.2 to 7.4 below. It is possible that a future standard will embody these principles and for that reason they are now described.

Method 1

7.2 In essence this is the SSAP 16 method described in 5.38 to 5.43 (above), whereby the total current cost adjustments are abated by the amount attributable to net borrowing.

Method 2

7.3 This is identical to Method 1 above, except that the abatement is applied to the aggregate of the current cost adjustments plus the net surplus on asset revaluations. This would result in an element of unrealised profit being recognised in the profit and loss account.

Method 3

7.4 Under this method, account would be taken of the effect of general price changes on net borrowing or on net monetary assets excluding those included in monetary working capital. This would involve the use of a CPP (Current Purchasing Power) type of adjustment using the RPI (Retail Price Index). CPP principles are explained in 9.0 to 9.14 below.

CURRENT PURCHASING POWER (CPP) SYSTEM

9.0 In 1974 in the UK a provisional statement of standard accounting practice (PSSAP 7) was issued which set out a method for dealing with the accounting aspects of changes in the purchasing power of money.

9.1 PSSAP 7 fell out of use when CCA methods gained the ascendancy, culminating in the issue of SSAP 16.

9.2 However, the case for CPP has been kept alive by its leading proponents and in the light of 8.1 to 8.3 (above) may well return, albeit in modified form. In view of this distinct possibility, the following paragraphs explain and illustrate the system.

FEATURES OF CPP

9.3 The main features of CPP are that it demonstrates the changes in the purchasing power of money on accounts prepared on the traditional historical cost basis and that the conversion of historical pounds of varying purchasing powers into figures of approximate current purchasing power should be by means of a general index of the purchasing power of the pound. The general index of retail prices, the RPI (Retail Price Index), in fact, is employed.

9.4 In other words CPP is concerned with maintaining the purchasing power of the company's shareholders. CCA on the other hand seeks to maintain the operating capability of the company. CPP is concerned with financial capital, CCA with physical capital.

MONETARY AND NON MONETARY ITEMS

9.5 A distinction is drawn between monetary and non-monetary items. Monetary items are those which are fixed irrespective of price level changes. Examples include cash, debtors, loans etc. Non–monetary items include assets such as fixed assets and stock. Ordinary shareholders' interest, being a residual, is neither a monetary nor a non-monetary item.

9.6 Businesses which have monetary liabilities gain general purchasing power in a period of inflation because the pounds used to extinguish those liabilities have a lesser purchasing power than the pounds in which those same liabilities were incurred in the first instance. The converse considerations apply to holders of monetary assets.

9.7 A gain in purchasing power arising out of the circumstances of 9.6 (above) needs separate disclosure as it may be accompanied by a dangerously illiquid position or by excessively high gearing.

9.8 The conversion of non–monetary items in a balance sheet involves increasing the amounts in proportion to the inflation that has occurred since their acquisition or revaluation. Monetary items, however, remain at the same figure.

9.9 The preparation of accounts on a CPP basis is performed in a series of stages, each of which will be illustrated in later paragraphs of this section:

Stage 1	Figures for items in a balance sheet on a conventional historical cost basis at the start of the period are converted into pounds of current purchasing power at that same date. (Conversion is the act of translating units of current purchasing power).
Stage 2	The Stage 1 figures on a converted basis are updated to a CPP basis at the *end* of the period (updating is the act of translating units of current purchasing power at one date to those at another later date).
Stage 3	Figures for items in a balance sheet on a conventional historical cost basis at the *end* of the period are converted into pounds of current purchasing power at that same date.
Stage 4	The profit or loss for the period can be derived as the difference between equity interest at the start and end of the period, in each case on an end of period CPP basis (Stages 2 and 3) adjusted for dividends, taxation and capital introduced (if any)
Stage 5	Calculation of gain or loss of purchasing power as the result of holding net monetary liabilities or net monetary assets
Stage 6	Production of a profit and loss account for the period on a CPP basis.

EXAMPLE – STAGE 1

9.10 The simplified, historical cost based accounts of CPP Ltd are as shown below:

CPP Ltd
Balance sheets as at end of

	Period 5 £	Period 5 £		Period 5 £	Period 5 £
	250,000		Fixed assets at cost (note 1)	260,000	
	74,500		less Accumulated depreciation (note 1)	99,000	
		175,500			161,000
			Current assets		
	35,000		Stock	61,000	
	43,500		Trade Debtors	52,000	
	6,600		Bank/Cash	16,800	
	85,100			129,800	
			less		
			Current liabilities		
	15,000		Trade creditors	18,200	
	18,000		Taxation	21,300	
	5,000		Dividends	7,500	
	38,000			47,000	
		47,100	Working capital		82,800
		222,600	Net assets employed		243,800
			Financed by:		
	150,000		Share capital	150,000	
	42,600		Retained profit	63,800	
		192,600			213,800
		30,000	Long–term loan		30,000
		222,600			243,800

Note 1

Period of acquisition	Fixed assets at cost	Depreciation (by period of acquisition) accumulated to end of	
		Period 5	Period 6
	£	£	£
1	120,000	55,000	66,000
4	70,000	14,000	21,000
5	60,000	5,500	11,000
	250,000	74,500	
6	10,000		1,000
	260,000		99,000

CPP Ltd
Trading and Profit and Loss Account
for period 6

	£	£
Sales		447,500
less		

Opening stock	35,000	
Purchases	328,000	
Closing stock	(61,000)	
	————	
Cost of sales		302,000
Gross profit		145,500
less		
Depreciation [99,000–74,500]	24,500	
Other expenses	71,000	
	————	
		95,500
Net profit before tax		50,000
less		
Taxation	21,300	
Dividends	7,500	
	————	
		28,800
Retained profit for year		21,200

Monetary items, by definition, (see 9.5) are already expressed in terms of pounds of purchasing power at the start of the period and do not therefore require to be converted.

Non–monetary items are adjusted for changes in the purchasing power of the pound since acquisition or revaluation by applying the Retail Price Index in the formula:

$$\text{item} \times \frac{\text{index at start of period}}{\text{index at date of acquisition or revaluation}}$$

For the purpose of these examples, an extract from a hypothetical RPI has been assumed thus:

Period	Start	End	Average for period	Average for closing stock
1	100.0			
4	109.8			
5	112.2	115.6	113.9	114.9
6	115.6	120.4	118.0	119.7

It is usual to calculate conversion factors based on the above formula for fixed assets which are assumed to have been acquired at the start of their respective periods, these are, for start of period 6 (end of period 5) figures:

Period of acquisition		Conversion factor
1	$\frac{115.6}{100.0}$	1.156
4	$\frac{115.6}{109.8}$	1.053
5	$\frac{115.6}{112.2}$	1.030

Stock will be converted using the period 5 average index for closing stock.

	$\frac{115.6}{114.9}$	1.006

Monetary items are not converted as stated above.

CPP Ltd
Balance sheet as at start of period 6, converted to CPP basis as at start of period 6

Conventional basis			CPP basis	
£	£		£	£
250,000		Fixed assets at cost (see below)	274,230	
		less Accumulated		
74,500		depreciation (see below)	83,987	
	175,500			190,243
		Current assets		
35,000		Stock (see below)	35,210	
43,500		Trade Debtors	43,500	
6,600		Bank/Cash	6,600	
85,100			85,310	
		less		
		Current liabilities		
15,000		Trade creditors	15,000	
18,000		Taxation	18,000	
5,000		Dividends	5,000	
38,000			38,000	
	47,100	Working capital		47,310
	222,600	Net assets employed		237,553
		less		
	30,000	Long–term loan		30,000
	192,600	Equity interest (residue)		207,553

Fixed Assets and Depreciation

Period of acquisition	Conversion factor	Fixed asset bases Conventional	CPP	Depreciation bases Conventional	CPP
	(a)	(b)	(c)=(a)x(b)	(d)	(e)=(a)x(d)
		£	£	£	£
1	1.156	120,000	138,720	55,000	63,580
4	1.053	70,000	73,710	14,000	14,742
5	1.030	60,000	61,800	5,500	5,665
		250,000	274,230	74,500	83,987

Stock $1.006 \times £35,000 = £35,210$

EXAMPLE–STAGE 2
9.11 The facts are as in 9.10

The figures at the end of Stage 1, that is items in the balance sheet at the start of the period on a CPP basis at the start of the period are updated to a CPP basis at the end of the period by applying the RPI in the formula

$$\text{item x} \quad \frac{\text{index at end of period}}{\text{index at start of period}}$$

In this instance the resultant conversion factor would be

$$\frac{120.4}{115.6} = 1.042$$

As a practical expedient, however, a short–cut can be taken by eliminating Stage 1 altogether and applying a modified version of the above updating process. Instead of updating the Stage 1 figures, the historical cost items in the balance sheet at the start of the period can be converted direct to a CPP basis at the end of the period by applying the RPI in the formulae:

Non–monetary items:

$$\text{Item x} \quad \frac{\text{index at end of period}}{\text{index at date of acquisition or revaluation.}}$$

Monetary items:

$$\text{Item x} \quad \frac{\text{index at end of period}}{\text{index at start of period}}$$

Conversion factors will therefore be, for start of period 6 (end of period 5) figures.

	Period of acquisition		Conversion factor
Fixed assets and depreciation	1	$\frac{120.4}{100.0}$	1.204
	4	$\frac{120.4}{109.8}$	1.096
	5	$\frac{120.4}{112.2}$	1.073

Period 6 opening (acquired in period 5) at period 5 closing stock average index.

$$\frac{120.4}{114.9} = 1.048$$

Monetary items at start of period 6 closing index

$$\frac{120.4}{115.6} = 1.042$$

CPP Ltd
Balance sheet as at start of period 6, converted to
CPP basis as at end of Period 6

Conventional basis			Conversion factor	CPP basis	
£	£		(see below)	£	£
250,000		Fixed assets at cost less Accumulated	(see below)	285,580	
74,500		depreciation	(see below)	87,466	
	175,500				198,114
		Current assets			
35,000		Stock	1.048	36,680	
43,500		Trade Debtors	1.042	45,327	
6,600		Bank/Cash	1.042	6,877	
85,100				88,884	
		less			
		Current liabilities			
15,000		Trade creditors	1.042	15,630	
18,000		Taxation	1.042	18,756	
5,000		Dividends	1.042	5,210	
38,000				39,596	
	47,100	**Working capital**			49,288
	222,600	**Net assets employed**			247,402
		less			
	30,000	**Long–term loan**	1.042		31,260
	192,600	**Equity interest (residue)**			216,142

Fixed assets and depreciation

Period of acquisition	Conversion factor	Fixed asset bases		Depreciation bases	
		Conventional	CPP	Conventional	CPP
	(a)	(b)	(c)=(a)x(b)	(d)	(e)=(a)x(d)
		£	£	£	£
1	1.204	120,000	144,480	55,000	66,220
4	1.096	70,000	76,720	14,000	15,344
5	1.073	60,000	64,380	5,500	5,902
		250,000	285,580	74,500	87,466

EXAMPLE – STAGE 3

9.12 The facts are as in 9.10

The figures for items in the balance sheet at the end of the period on a historical cost basis are converted to a CPP basis at the end of the period by applying the RPI in the formulae

$$\text{item} \times \frac{\text{index at end of period}}{\text{index at date of acquisition or revaluation}}$$

and to work out conversion factors.

As in Stage 1, and for the same reason, monetary items do not require to be converted.

Conversion factors for end of period 6 figures will be

	Period of acquisition		Conversion factor
Fixed assets and depreciation	1	$\frac{120.4}{100.0}$	1.204
	4	$\frac{120.4}{109.8}$	1.096
	5	$\frac{120.4}{112.2}$	1.073
	6	$\frac{120.4}{115.6}$	1.042
Closing stock for period 6 at average index for stock		$\frac{120.4}{119.7}$	1.006

CPP Ltd

Balance sheet as at end of period 6, converted to CPP basis as at end of period 6

Conventional basis			CPP basis	
£	£		£	£
260,000		Fixed assets at cost (see below)	296,000	
99,000		less Accumulated depreciation (see below)	115,325	
	161,000			180,675
		Current assets		
61,000		Stock (see below)	61,366	
52,000		Trade Debtors	52,000	
16,800		Bank/cash	16,800	
129,800			130,166	
		less		
		Current liabilities		
18,200		Trade creditors	18,200	
21,300		Taxation	21,300	

7,500	Dividends	7,500
47,000		47,000

82,800	Working capital	83,166
243,800	Net assets employed	263,841
	less	
30,000	Long–term loan	30,000
213,800	Equity interest (residue)	233,841

Fixed assets and depreciation

Period of acquisition	Conversion factor	Fixed asset bases Conventional	CPP	Depreciation bases Conventional	CPP
	(a)	(b)	(c)=(a)x(b)	(d)	(e)=(a)x(d)
		£	£	£	£
1	1.204	120,000	144,480	66,000	79,464
4	1.096	70,000	76,720	21,000	23,016
5	1.073	60,000	64,380	11,000	11,803
6	1.042	10,000	10,420	1,000	1,042
		260,000	296,000	99,000	115,325

Stock $1.006 \times £60,000 = £61,366$

EXAMPLE – STAGE 4
9.13 The facts are as in 9.10

The difference between the residual equity interest at the start and end of period on an end of period CPP basis, increased by the taxation charge and dividend appropriation for the period but reduced by any capital introduced during the period, gives the net profit or loss for the period.

In the practical terms of the example, this involves using the equity interest residue in Stage 3 (9.12), deducting the comparable Stage 2 (9.11) figure from it and adjusting the resultant figure by the Stage 3 taxation and dividends, thus

	End of period 6 CPP basis £
Equity interest	
at end of period 6 (Stage 3)	233,841
at start of period 6 (Stage 2)	216,142
Retained profit for period 6	17,699
add, at end of period 6(Stage 3)	
Taxation	21,300
Dividends	7,500
Net profit before tax	46,499

The limited amount of information available at Stage 4 is insufficiently informative to be of much use. This situation can be remedied by the production of a full profit and loss account on a CPP basis. This is done in Stage 6 (9.15 below). A pre–requisite is to calculate the gain or loss in purchasing power in the period in Stage 5 below.

EXAMPLE – STAGE 5
9.14 The facts are the same as in 9.10.

The net monetary items at the start of the period on an end of period CPP basis, adjusted by receipts and payments during the period, are compared with net monetary items at the end of the period, to disclose a gain or loss in purchasing power as the result of holding monetary items, thus

Calculation of gain or loss in purchasing power as the result of holding monetary items

	Conventional basis		CPP basis	
	£	£	£	£
Monetary items at start of period 6 (Stage 2(9.11 above))				
Trade debtors		43,500		45,327
Bank/cash		6,600		6,877
		50,100		52,204
less Trade creditors	15,000		15,630	
Taxation	18,000		18,756	
Dividends	5,000		5,210	
Long–term loan	30,000		31,260	
		(68,000)		(70,856)
Net monetary liabilities		(17,900)		(18,652)
add Payments during period 6				
Purchases (see below)	328,000		334,560	
Expenses (see below)	71,000		72,420	
Assets acquired (Stage 3 (9.12 above))	10,000		10,420	
Taxation (Stage 3 (9.12 above))	21,300		21,300	
Dividends (Stage 3 (9.12 above))	7,500		7,500	
		(437,800)		(446,200)
		(455,700)		(464,852)
less Receipts during period 6 Receipts during period 6				
Sales (see below)		447,500		456,450
		(8,200)		(8,402)

For sales and expense items, adjustments are made for changes in purchasing power between occurrence and end of period by applying the RPI in the formula

$$\text{item} \times \frac{\text{index at end of period}}{\text{average index for period}}$$

For period 6 items this becomes $\frac{120.4}{118.0}$, a conversion factor of 1.020 which is applied as follows:

	Conventional basis	Conversion factor	End of period 6 CPP basis
	£	£	£
Purchases	328,000	1.020	334,560
Expenses (requiring payment in cash, i.e. excluding depreciation)	71,000	1.020	72,420
Sales	447,500	1.020	456,450

	Conventional basis		CPP basis	
	£	£	£	£
Monetary items at end of period 6 (Stage 3(9.12 above))				
Trade debtors		52,000		52,000
Bank/Cash		16,800		16,800
		68,800		68,800

less Trade creditors	18,200	18,200
Taxation	21,300	21,300
Dividends	7,500	7,500
Long-term loan	30,000	30,000
	(77,000)	(77,000)
Net monetary liabilities at end of period 6	(8,200)	(8,200)
less		
Net monetary liabilities at start of period 6 (above)	(8,200)	(8,402)
Gain/(loss) in purchasing power from holding net monetary assets/(liabilities)	–	202

EXAMPLE – STAGE 6

9.15 The facts are the same as in 9.10

The figures obtained in Stages 2, 3, 4 and 5 are now used to produce a profit and loss account for the period on an end of period 6 CPP basis.

CPP Ltd
Trading and profit and loss account for period 6, converted to a CPP basis as at end of period 6

Conventional basis			CPP basis	
£	£		£	£
	447,500	**Sales**		456,450
		less		
35,000		Opening stock	36,680	
328,000		Purchases	334,560	
(61,000)		Closing stock	(61,366)	
	302,000	**Cost of sales**		309,874
	145,500	**Gross profit**		146,576
		add		
		Gain in purchasing power from holding net monetary liabilities (Stage 5(9.14 above))		202
				146,778
		less		
24,500		Depreciation [115,325–87,466]	27,859	
71,000		Other expenses	72,420	
	95,500			100,279
	50,000	**Net profit before tax**		46,499
		less		
21,300		Taxation	21,300	
7,500		Dividends	7,500	
	28,800			28,800
	21,200	**Retained profit for year**		17,699

STUDENT SELF TESTING

Test exercises

1. At the end of year 4, a business had the following figures for vehicles. Depreciation, for both historical and current cost purposes, is calculated at 20% on a straight line basis, assuming no residual value.

Year of acquisition	Historical cost £	Current cost index	
1	80,000	130	
2	70,000	150	mid year
3	20,000	160	
4	30,000	180	
4		200	end of year

Required:
Calculate the current cost depreciation adjustment for year 4.

2. The facts are exactly the same as in 1.
Required:
Calculate the revaluation surplus to be transferred to current cost reserve at the end of year 4.

3. The facts are exactly the same as in 1.
Required:
Calculate the net book value of vehicles for inclusion in the current cost balance sheet at the end of year 4.

4. At the end of year 3, the following figures were available on a historical cost basis. The company's year ends in June.

	£
Opening stock	172,800
Purchasing for year	601,500
Closing stock	149,200

An average of three months' sales is held in stock
A single index is used for stocks for current cost purposes.

				Index
Mid–month:	Year 2	April	301.2	
		May	303.4	
		June	304.8	
	3	April	360.6	
		May	362.6	
		June	363.8	
	4	July	365.0	
Average for		3	334.2	

Required:
Calculate the current cost of sales adjustment for year 3.

5. The facts are exactly the same as in 4.
Required:
Calculate the revaluation surplus transferred to current cost reserve at the end of year 3.

6. The facts are exactly the same as in 4, except that an average of two months' sales is held in stock.
Required:
Calculate the closing stock figure included in the current cost balance sheet at the end of year 3.

7. The facts are exactly the same as in 4, except that an average of two months' sales is held in stock.
Required:
State the conversion ratios which would be used to arrive at current cost opening and closing stock at the end of year 3.

8. At the end of year 3, the monetary working capital of a business was composed of

	Opening £	Closing £
Debtors	873,600	962,100
Creditors	531,400	587,400

The average age of these items is two months.

The index numbers given in 4 above apply also to monetary working capital items.

Required:

Calculate the current cost monetary working capital adjustment for year 3.

9. The facts are exactly the same as in 8, except that

	Opening £	Closing £
Debtors	962,100	873,600
Creditors	587,400	531,400

Required:

Calculate the current cost monetary working capital adjustment for year 3.

10. The facts are exactly the same as in 8, except that

	Opening £	Closing £
Debtors	531,400	587,400
Creditors	873,600	962,100

Required:

Calculate the current cost monetary working capital adjustment for year 3.

11. The current cost balance sheet of a company contained the following figures.

	£000
Current assets	
Bank & cash (not included in MWC)	450
Current liabilities	
Hire purchase creditors	170
Taxation	210
Proposed dividends	250
Bank overdraft (not included in MWC)	190
Net assets employed	3,540
Shareholders' funds	2,680
Long term loans	
Debentures	540
Deferred liabilities	
Deferred taxation	320

Required:

Calculate the current cost gearing proportion.

12. The facts are exactly the same as in 11 and the current cost adjustments were:

	£000
Depreciation	870
Fixed asset disposals	80
Cost of sales	1,050
Monetary working capital	320

Required:

Calculate the current cost gearing adjustment.

13. RS Limited, a manufacturer of construction equipment, has decided to comply with the requirements of Statement of Standard Accounting Practice No.16 in respect of the year ended 31st December, 19–0, by presenting its accounts on a historic cost basis supplemented by a current cost profit and loss account and balance sheet.

From the information given below you are required to prepare a current cost profit and loss account for the year ended 31st December, 19–0 and a current cost balance sheet as at that date.

Comparative figures are not required; all workings must be shown.

1. The historic cost accounts for the period were as follows:

Profit and Loss Account

	19–0 £	19–0 £	19–9 £	19–9 £
Turnover		6,633,000		5,559,000
Trading profit		594,980		618,600
Depreciation				
Freehold property	–		4,000	
Plant and machinery	64,670		53,650	
	64,670		57,650	
Auditors' remuneration	7,450		6,400	
Bank interest	8,160		2,950	
Directors' emoluments	92,400		84,400	
		172,680		151,400
Profit before taxation		422,300		467,200
Taxation		176,000		260,000
Profit after taxation		246,300		207,200
Dividends		78,000		70,000
Retained profit for year		168,300		137,200

Balance Sheets at 31 December

	19–0 £	19–0 £	19–9 £	19–9 £
Fixed assets:				
Freehold property, at valuation		300,000		180,000
Plant and machinery, at cost	770,600		651,600	
Less: depreciation	228,600		181,600	
		542,000		470,000
		842,000		650,000
Current assets:				
Stocks	1,286,000		1,025,600	
Work–in–progess	350,300		310,000	
Debtors	973,200		776,400	
	2,609,500		2,112,000	
Current liabilities:				
Creditors	792,300		591,000	
Taxation	107,000		153,000	
Bank overdraft	148,200		6,300	
Proposed dividend	48,000		48,000	
	1,095,500		798,300	
		1,514,000		1,313,700
		2,356,000		1,963,700
Share capital:				
Ordinary shares of £1 each				
issued and fully paid		800,000		800,000
Capital reserves		120,000		–
Retained profits		726,000		557,700

Deferred taxation	710,000	606,000
	2,356,000	1,963,700

2. The freehold property was professionally valued at 31st December 19–0 at £300,000 and no depreciation is to be provided in 19–0.

3. On average, stocks and unallocated work–in–progress represent three months purchases.

4. £152,400 of the work–in–progress was specifically allocated to customers at 31st December, 19–0. At 31st December, 19–9 the figure was £136,000.

5. For the purpose of calculating the gearing adjustment you may assume that the current cost reserve at 31st December, 19–9 would have been £226,200 made up as follows:

	£
Stock (cost of sales)	5,200
Plant	221,000
	226,200

This is additional to the retained profits of £557,700 but in the absence of full information this notional figure of £226,200 is not required to be brought forward for incorporation into the balance sheet at 31st December, 19–0.

6. An analysis of the plant into years of acquisition gave the following figures.

	£
19–5	223,400
19–6	190,200
19–7	111,000
19–8	42,000
19–9	85,000
19–0	119,000
	770,600

Plant has been depreciated at 10% on a straight line basis calculated from the date of acquisition or the date put into use whichever was the later. For current cost purposes, however depreciation is to be calculated on the assumption that plant was acquired and put into use at the beginning of each financial year.

7. The relevant indices which are average or mid–period are set out below:

Plant and machinery		Stocks	
19–5	962	Oct 19–9	136.1
19–6	1179	Nov 19–9	137.0
19–7	1354	Dec 19–9	137.2
19–8	1557	Jan 19–0	139.7
19–8	1758	Oct 19–0	158.5
19–0	1970	Nov 19–0	160.8
		Dec 19–0	161.3
		Jan 19–1	162.1

The actual index at 31st December, 19–0 for plant and machinery was 2000.

14. SSAP 16 – CURRENT COST ACCOUNTING

a. In what form could current cost information be supplied?

b. For what purpose are adjustments made to historical cost profit from trading (before interest)?

c. What are the adjustments referred to in b. above?

d. What are the net operating assets of a business?

e. What items comprise monetary working capital?

f. On what basis should the main assets and liabilities be included in the current cost balance sheet?

g. Which items should be separately stated in the current cost profit and loss account?

h. In what form should the current cost balance sheet be presented?

ACCA EXAMINATION QUESTIONS

15. Required:

a. Prepare a current Cost Profit & Loss Account for year ended 31 December 1981 in accordance with the Statement of Standard Accounting Practice on Current cost accounting.

b. Prepare a Current Cost Balance Sheet as at 31 December 1981.

c. Discuss the reasons for the Current Cost Adjustments made to the Profit & Loss Account in arriving at Profit before Tax.

(ACCA 2.9(1) June 1982)

APPENDIX 1. *Draft Balance Sheets and Profit & Loss Accounts for years ended 31 December 1979, 1980, 1981.*

BALANCE SHEETS

	1979 £	1980 £	1981 £
Share Capital	2,860	13,500	13,500
Profit & Loss Account	8,557	14,996	19,992
Loan Capital	–	20,262	18,174
	11,417	48,758	51,666

		1979	1980	1981
Capital Employed				
Fixed Assets				
Land and Buildings			1,240	380
Plant and Machinery			5,360	5,255
Net Fixed Assets		4,496	6,600	5,635

Current Assets	£	£	£
Stock	20,000	35,000	36,000
Debtors	12,000	20,000	25,000
Cash	1,000	2,000	1,800
	33,000	57,000	62,800
Creditors	(7,000)	(13,342)	(15,769)
Tax	(1,200)	(1,500)	(1,000)
Overdraft	(17,879)	–	–
Working Capital	6,921	42,158	46,031
	£11,417	£48,758	£51,666

PROFIT & LOSS ACCOUNTS

	1979 £	£	1980 £	£	1981 £	£
Income		171,649		261,789		287,968
Less: Material	31,600		46,697		63,076	
Labour	28,341		36,522		46,075	
Variable Overheads	28,378		43,404		51,000	
Fixed Overheads	69,000		70,259		81,500	
Research and Development	10,000	167,319	54,468	251,350	36,721	278,372
Profit from trading		4,330		10,439		9,596
Interest		1,500		2,000		2,000
		2,830		8,439		7,596
Tax		430		1,200		1,000

	2,400	7,239	6,596
Dividends	800	800	1,600
	1,600	6,439	4,996
Balance b/f	6,957	8,557	14,996
	£8,557	£14,996	£19,992

APPENDIX 2 *Fixed Asset Summary*

	Land and Buildings £	Plant and Machinery £	Total £
Cost of Valuation			
At 1.1.81	1,400	10,195	11,595
Additions	–	1,600	1,600
Disposals	(1,000)	(245)	(1,245)
At 31.12.81	400	11,550	11,950
At cost	–	11,550	11,550
At Valuation	400	–	400
	400	11,550	11,950
Depreciation			
At 1.1.81	160	4,835	4,995
Charge for year	20	1,702	1,722
Disposal	(160)	(242)	(402)
At 31.12.81	20	6,295	6,315
Net Book Value			
At 1.1.81	1,240	5,360	6,600
At 31.12.81	380	5,255	5,635

APPENDIX 3. *Land and Buildings Schedule*

	Freehold North Street 3(a) £	Leasehold East Street 3(b) £	Total £
Cost or Valuation			
At 1.1.81			
Buildings	800	200	1,000
Land	200	200	400
	1,000	400	1,400
Disposals	(1,000)	–	(1,000)
At 31.12.81	–	400	400
Depreciation			
At 1.1.81	150	10	160
Charge	10	10	20

Disposal	(160)	–	(160)
At 31.12.81	–	20	20

3 *(a) North Street*

This was a freehold office shown in the books at cost less depreciation at 2% per annum.

The company had acquired a leasehold office in East Street in 1980 and the staff and records were transferred to East Street in the early part of 1981. The North Street premises were sold on 15 August 1981 for £1,100 which represented £900 for the building and £200 for the land.

3 *(b) East Street*

The lease was acquired on this property on 1.1.80. The company required funds for expansion and it was decided to sell the freehold premises in North Street. The lease was for a period of 40 years and was valued at £400 on 1.1.80 (buildings £200, land £200). The Directors estimate that the buildings are worth £270 on 31.12.81.

APPENDIX 4 *Plant and Machinery Schedule*

4(a) Plant and Machinery at 31.12.81

Year of Purchase	Cost at 1.1.81 £	Disposal in 1981 £		Additions in 1981 £	Cost at 31.12.81 £	Dep'n at 1.1.81 £	Charge for 1981 £	Dep'n on Dis'l £	Dep'n at 31.12.81 £
1976	7,195	245	(4b)	–	6,950	4,385	1,000	230	5,155
1980	3,000	–		–	3,000	450	450	–	900
1981	–	–		1,600	1,600	–	240	–	240
	£10,195	£245		£1,600	£11,550	£4,835	£1,690	£230	£6,295

4(b) Plant Disposed of in 1981

There was a depreciation charge (not included in the Plant and Machinery Table above) of 15% for the four months from 1 January to 30 April 1981 on the plant purchased in 1976 for £245 and scrapped at nil value on 30.4.81. Use end of year index for current cost adjustment on disposal.

APPENDIX 5 *Index Numbers (average for year unless indicated othersie)*

Year	Retail Price Index	Plant and Machinery Index	Stock
1976	112	110	
1980	158	150	
1981	200	160	193
31.12.80	162	155	189
31.12.81	210	165	199

Average Acquisition date for 1981 Opening stock and Monetary Working Capital	188
Average Acquisition date for 1981 Closing stock and MWCA	198

APPENDIX 6. *Current Cost Balance Sheet as at 31.12.80*

	£	£
Shares		13,500
Profit and Loss Account		14,996
Current Cost Reserve		1,175
Loan		20,262
		49,933

Fixed Assets

Land and Buildings		1,478
Plant and Machinery	12,513	
Depreciation	6,402	6,111

Current Assets

Stock	35,186	
Debtors	20,000	
Cash	2,000	
	57,186	
Creditors	(13,342)	
Tax	(1,500)	
Working Capital		42,344
		£49,933

16. Required:

a. Calculate the Gearing Adjustment for Scraper Ltd. for the Current Cost Profit and Loss Account for the year ended 30 November 1983.

b. Restate the Profit and Loss Account of Scraper Ltd. for the year ended 30 November 1983 to show the calculation of the Current Cost Profit attributable to shareholders.

(ACCA 2.9 (1) December 1983)

Appendix 5

The Profit and Loss Account of Scraper Ltd for the year ended 30 November 1983 and Balance Sheet as at 30 November 1983.

	£	£
Sales		3,066,000
Cost of sales		2,055,000
Gross Profit		1,011,000
Administration expense *(Note 2)*	220,000	
Distribution expense *(Note 1)*	200,000	420,000
Operating profit		591,000
Tax		182,000
Profit after tax		409,000
Dividend 10p per share		40,000
		369,000
Balance brought forward		(113,000)
		£256,000

Note 1
Depreciation on the freehold property was £3,888 calculated at 2% of valuation.
One of the properties was revalued from £30,000 to £124,400 on 1 December 1982
Note 2
Includes debenture interest paid.

Scraper Ltd–Balance Sheet as at 30 November 1983

Fixed Assets	Cost/Valuation £	Depn £	NBV £	£
Freehold property	194,400	14,400	180,000	
Vehicles	300,000	60,000	240,000	
Fixtures and fittings	28,000	12,000	16,000	436,000

Current Assets			
Stock		395,000	
Debtors		176,000	
Cash		232,000	803,000

Creditors–amounts due less than 1 year			
Trade creditors		112,000	
HP Creditors		89,100	
Bank Overdraft		17,043	218,143

Net current assets		584,857

Total assets less current liabilities		1,020,857

Creditors–amounts due more than 1 year		
10% debentures (convertible 1986)	100,000	
Other creditors including tax	174,857	274,857

Net assets	£746,000

Capital and Reserves	£
Share Capital	400,000
Share premium	50,000
Capital redemption reserve fund	100,000
Revaluation deficit	(130,000)
General reserve	70,000
Profit and loss account	256,000
	£746,000

Note:

The revaluation deficit results from a reappraisal on 1 December 1982 of the fixed asset register of fixtures and fittings within one of the London properties. There was no general programme of revaluation. The gain on the freehold of £94,400 has been netted off against the loss on revaluation of fixtures.

Appendix 6
Extract from the Balance Sheet of Scraper Ltd at 30 November 1983 which has been prepared under the the current cost convention.

1982 £	Fixed Assets	£	£	£
210,000	Freehold property	250,000		
276,000	Vehicles	282,000		
19,000	Fixtures and fittings	22,000		
505,000			554,000	

	Current Assets		
175,000	Stock	400,000	
106,000	Debtors	176,000	
32,000	Cash	232,000	
313,000			808,000
	Creditors–amounts due in less than 1 year		
15,000	HP Creditors	89,100	
60,000	Trade Creditors	112,000	
57,000	Tax	–	
14,000	Bank overdraft	17,043	218,143
167,000	Net current assets		589,857
672,000	Total assets less current liabilities		1,142,857
	Creditors–amounts due in more than 1 year		
100,000	10% Debentures	100,000	
9,000	Other creditors including tax	174,857	
96,000	HP creditors	–	274,857
£467,000	Capital employed		£869,000

The current cost adjustments appearing in the current cost profit and loss account were:

	£
Cost of sales adjustment	29,000
Depreciation adjustment	6,766
Monetary working capital adj.	9,334
	£45,100

17. Required:

a. Calculate the following adjustments to comply with SSAP 16 *(Current Cost Accounting)*:

   i. Depreciation Adjustment on Plant and Machinery.

   ii. Disposal Adjustment on Plant and Machinery.

   iii. Monetary Working Capital Adjustment.

b. Explain briefly and critically discuss the reasons for making the following adjustments.

   i. Depreciation Adjustment.

   ii. Monetary Working Capital Adjustment.

(ACCA 2.9(1) June 1983)

Appendix 9
Data for current cost adjustments
Comparative Balance Sheet data for debtors and creditors

	1.1.1982	31.12.1982
Debtors	£330,000	£612,000
Creditors	£64,000	£115,000

Assume collection and payment period is the same at 31 December 1981 as at 31.12.1982.

Analysis of Plant and Machinery

Year of purchase	Cost 1981 £	Cost 1982 £	Net Book Value 1981 £	Net Book Value 1982 £
1975	200,000		50,000	
1977	327,000	327,000	194,000	150,000

472

1980	463,000	463,000	321,000	250,000
1982		110,000	–	100,000
	£990,000	£900,000	£565,000	£500,000

On 31 October 1982 all plant acquired in 1975 was sold for book value. Plant acquired in 1982 was purchased during the year for £110,000.

The following specific indices have been selected by the company as relevant to its particular industry and business:

	Stock & Monetary Working Capital	Plant & Machinery
1975 average		102
1976 average		105
1977 average		109
1978 average		110
1979 average		112
1980 average		114
1981 average		126
31 October 1981	115	134
30 November 1981	117	136
31 December 1981	119	138
1982 average	125	145
31 October 1982	128	150
30 November 1982	130	152
31 December 1982	132	155

Section IV

Analysis of Financial Statements

Chapter

1   Ratio analysis

2   Cash flow and funds flow analysis

1 Ratio Analysis

GENERAL BACKGROUND

1.0 Financial statements, including the final accounts of businesses, are produced not merely for their own sakes but for the uses to which they can be put by the various parties interested in different aspects of these statements.

1.1 The Corporate Report, issued by the (then) Accounting Standards Steering Committee (since redesignated the Accounting Standards Committee) as a consultative document, identified many of these user groups.

1.2 Within a company the directorate, as the apex of the management "pyramid", is interested in overall figures which indicate whether the company is profitable and whether it is on a sound financial footing.

1.3 At workshop level in a manufacturing business are the foremen and chargehands who are concerned only with those matters which relate to the particular section for which they are responsible, for example, time taken to complete a job or task, material usage etc.

1.4 Between these two levels of management are the intermediate stages ranging from departmental managers to the General Manager, each concerned about measurements relating to the matters which fall within their individual responsibilities.

1.5 From the point of view of the ownership of a company, shareholders, actual and prospective, are interested in its earnings (current and future) out of which dividends can be paid, the security of their dividends (dividend cover), return on their investment (yield) and so on.

1.6 External interested parties include loan creditors, for example, debenture holders who are concerned that the company is solvent and that there is adequate cover for their interest, and trade creditors (actual and prospective) who want to be assured that the company is both solvent and liquid, that is, that it has adequate cash or cash convertible resources to meet all current liabilities as they fall due.

ANALYTICAL METHODS

2.0 Examination questions involving analysis, which appear on Financial Accounting papers, are concerned only with income statements (trading and profit and loss accounts), with statements of financial position (balance sheets) and with statements of changes in financial position (cash flow statements, funds flow statements). The remainder of this section is thus confined exclusively to trading and profit and loss accounts and to balance sheets.

2.1 The analytical technique employed is known as ratio analysis. A ratio is simply one number expressed in terms of another number to show the relationship between the two numbers. For example, the relationship between 12 and 3 is 12/3 or 4:1, indicating that the former figure is four times as great as the latter figure. An alternative way of stating this relationship would be to omit stating the base of 1 and merely to give the ratio as 4 (the word "times" being understood). If the number order is reversed to 3 and 12, the ratio is $\frac{3}{12}$ or 0.25:1 (or 0.25 times).

2.2 A variation is to use a base of 100. This is termed a percentage. Using the figures 3 and 12, the percentage is

$$\frac{3}{12} \times \frac{100}{1} = 25\%$$

2.3 It can be seen therefore that ratios, by using a common base of 1 or 100, afford a means of comparing figures prepared on different bases.

2.4 In financial statement analysis, it is recognised that there are certain important relationships (expressed by means of ratios) between items within the trading account, within the profit and loss account and within the balance sheet.

2.5 There are also equally, if not more, important relationships between items in the trading account and in the profit and loss account, between items in the trading account and in the balance sheet and between items in the profit and loss account and in the balance sheet.

2.6 Calculation of the ratios is a relatively easy and straightforward task. The "formulae" for arriving at the ratios commonly employed are given in 3.0 to 3.7 and illustrated in 4.5 to 4.6.

2.7 The art of ratio analysis is firstly in the selection of those ratios most appropriate under the circumstances and subsequently in the interpretation of the position which they reveal. This aspect is dealt with in 4.0 to 4.4

RATIOS IN COMMON USE

3.0 It was stated in 2.4 and 2.5 that there are important relationships within and between the various financial statements. The specific ratios which express these relationships now follow under statement classified headings in 3.1 to 3.7 and are illustrated in 4.5 and 4.6. They are reclassified according to the aspect of the business which they are devised to highlight, in 4.0 to 4.4.

TRADING ACCOUNT RATIOS

3.1

a. **Gross profit %** $\dfrac{\text{Gross profit}}{\text{Sales}} \times \dfrac{100}{1}$

Indicates the average gross margin on sales of goods. Sales margins vary widely between products and between different trades/industries but tend to be similar within specific trades/industries. The sales figure is VAT exclusive.

A high gross profit percentage does not result in a large (absolute) figure of gross profit unless it is accompanied by a large volume of sales.

b. **Stock turnover** $\dfrac{\text{Cost of sales}}{\text{Average stock}}$

Indicates the velocity, in number of times per period, at which the average figure of trading stock is being "turned over", that is, sold.

The denominator, average stock, is often a simple average of opening stock plus closing stock. If, however, stock has fluctuated throughout the period to any great extent, as happens in businesses where the nature of the trade is seasonal, a weighted average figure should be used.

PROFIT AND LOSS ACCOUNT RATIOS.

3.2

a. **Expense %** $\dfrac{\text{Individual expense}}{\text{Total expenses}} \times \dfrac{100}{1}$

Indicates the relative weight of each item of expense in relation to total expenses.

This ratio is rarely used since the same objective can be achieved by an expense to sales percentage illustrated in 3.4 b.

b. **Fixed interest cover** $\dfrac{\text{Net operating profit}}{\text{Fixed interest}}$

Indicates the number of times fixed interest is covered by profit. Profit in this context is net profit before charging such interest and before taxation; such a figure is termed net operating profit.

c. **Fixed dividend cover** $\dfrac{\text{Net profit after tax}}{\text{Fixed dividends}}$

Indicates the number of times fixed dividends are covered by taxed profit.

BALANCE SHEET RATIOS

3.3

a. **Current (or working capital) ratio** $\dfrac{\text{Current assets}}{\text{Current liabilities}}$:1

Indicates, in a general sort of way, the ability of a business to meet its short–term liabilities, as they fall due, out of its short–term assets.

For practical purposes, more refined calculations are needed such as 3.3b., 3.5a. and 3.5b.

b. **Liquidity (or acid test or quick assets) ratio** $\dfrac{\text{Liquid assets}}{\text{Current liabilities}}$:1

Indicates the relative amount of assets in cash, or which can be quickly converted into cash, available to meet short–term liabilities. Liquid assets consist of cash and bank balances, debtors and marketable securities.

c. **Total debt to shareholders' funds** $\dfrac{\text{Total external liabilities}}{\text{Shareholders' funds}}$

Indicates whether the business is solvent and the extent of "cover" for the external liabilities. It is therefore a test of financial stability.

d. **Long–term debt to shareholders' funds** $\dfrac{\text{Fixed external liabilities}}{\text{Shareholders' funds}}$

Indicates the extent of "cover" for fixed liabilities (loans, debentures).

e. **Proprietary ratio** $\dfrac{\text{Shareholders' funds}}{\text{Total assets (tangible)}}$

Indicates the degree to which unsecured creditors are protected aganst loss in the event of liquidation.

f. **Gearing** $\dfrac{\text{Fixed interest loans plus preference share capital}}{\text{Ordinary share capital}}$:1

Indicates the degree of vulnerability of earnings available for ordinary shareholders.

There are various alternatives to the formula given. Some companies use ordinary shareholders' funds as the denominator, that is, ordinary share capital plus reserves, some use the book value of loans and shares whilst others include them at their market values. Textbooks usually state that a gearing of greater than 1:1 is high and less then 1:1 is low. In practice, however, greater than 0.6:1 is regarded as high and less than 0.2:1 is low, with the range between these two extremes being regarded as relatively high or relatively low.

g. **Net book value per ordinary share** $\dfrac{\text{Net book value of ordinary shares}}{\text{No. of ordinary shares.}}$

Indicates the historical cost base to which the price per ordinary share relates.

Net book value consists of fixed assets plus working capital less debentures and preference share capital; an alternative way of arriving at the same figure is to deduct preference share capital from shareholders' funds.

TRADING ACCOUNT/PROFIT AND LOSS ACCOUNT RATIOS.
3.4

a. **Net profit to sales %** $\dfrac{\text{Net profit (before tax)}}{\text{Sales}} \times \dfrac{100}{1}$

Indicates the relative efficiency of the business after taking into account all revenues and expenses. For this purpose extraordinary items are sometimes eleminated. Sometimes also, net operating profit is used in substitution for net profit (see 3.2b). The sales figure is VAT exclusive.

b. **Expense to sales%** $\dfrac{\text{Individual expense}}{\text{Sales}} \times \dfrac{100}{1}$

Indicates where the improvement (or deterioration) of 3.4.a. (above) has occurred. The figures are VAT exclusive.

TRADING ACCOUNT/BALANCE SHEET RATIOS
3.5

a. **Debtor collection**

   i. **Turnover** $\dfrac{\text{Credit sales}}{\text{Trade debtors}}$

   Indicates where the improvement (or deterioration) of 3.4.a. (above) has occurred.
   Both figures must be VAT inclusive.

   ii. **Collection period** $\dfrac{\text{Trade debtors}}{\text{Credit sales}} \times \dfrac{12}{1} \left(\dfrac{\text{or } 52 \text{ or } 365}{1)} \right)$

Indicates the average period (measured in months, if 12 is used as the numerator, or in weeks if 52 is used, or in days if 365 is used) for which debtors remain uncollected. Both figures must be VAT inclusive.

b. **Creditor payment period** $\dfrac{\text{Trade creditors}}{\text{Credit purchases}} \times \left(\dfrac{12}{1} \dfrac{\text{or } 52 \text{ or } 365}{1)} \right)$

Indicates the average period (measured in months, if 12 is used as the numerator, or in weeks if 52 is used, or in days, if 365 is used) for which creditors remain unpaid. Both figures must be VAT inclusive.

c. **Sales to total assets ratio** $\dfrac{\text{Sales}}{\text{Total assets}}$

Indicates efficiency of utilisation of assets in generating revenue.

d. **Sales to capital employed ratio** $\dfrac{\text{Sales}}{\text{Capital employed}}$

Indicates efficiency of utilisation of capital employed in generating revenue.

e. **Sales to assets ratio** $\dfrac{\text{Sales}}{\text{Individual assets}}$

Indicates the effect of individual assets (or groups of assets or of working capital) on the overall figures in 3.5.c. and 3.5d. above.

PROFIT AND LOSS ACCOUNT TO BALANCE SHEET RATIOS.

3.6

a. **Net profit to capital employed %** $\dfrac{\text{Net profit before tax}}{\text{Capital employed}} \times \dfrac{100}{1}$

Indicates the overall profitability of the business. Sometimes net operating profit is used in substitution for net profit (see 2.3.2.b.).

b. **Earnings per share (EPS)** $\dfrac{\text{Total Earnings (in pence)}}{\text{No. of ordinary shares}}$

Indicates the amount of net profit after tax (but before taking account of extraordinary items) attributable to each ordinary share in issue and ranking for dividend during the period. It is a component of the price earnings ratio (see 3.7.a. (below) and is always calculated in pence. Earnings per share is the subject of SSAP 3.

The earnings figure is arrived at thus:

	£	£
Net profit after tax (before extraordinary items)		X
Less		
Minority interests	X	
Preference dividends	X	
		X
Earnings (attributable to ordinary shares)		X

and represents the fund which supports the distribution of profit by way of dividend to ordinary shareholders.

c. **Dividend per share** $\dfrac{\text{Total Dividend (in pence)}}{\text{No. of ordinary shares}}$

Indicates the dividend and retention policy of the company when used in conjunction with EPS (above). Total dividend is usually taken to mean the net dividend proposed (or actually paid) plus the associated tax credits.

OTHER RATIOS

3.7 There are many other ratios which the various parties interested in a business might calculate according to circumstances. The less common ones are not listed here but will be dealt with as they arise. Three useful ratios are

a. **Price/earnings ratio** $\dfrac{\text{Market price per ordinary share}}{\text{Earnings per share}}$

Indicates the number of years' purchase of the earnings and is regarded internationally as an indicator of future performance.

b. **Earnings yield** $\dfrac{\text{Earnings per share}}{\text{Market price per ordinary share}} \times \dfrac{100}{1}$

Indicates potential return on investment. Like the P/E ratio (above), of which it is the inverse expressed as a percentage, it highlights the amount earned on the shares relative to their market price.

c. **Dividend yield** $\dfrac{\text{Dividend per share}}{\text{Market price per share}}$

Indicates current return on investment. Dividend per share is usually taken to mean the net dividend plus its associated tx credits.

CLASSIFICATION OF RATIOS ACCORDING TO TYPE

4.0 All the ratios listed in 3.1 to 3.7 are designed to illustrate the various facets of a business which fall into the following broad groupings:

a. long–term solvency and stability;
b. short–term solvency and liquidity;
c. efficiency and profitability;
d. potential and actual growth,

each of which will now be considered.

LONG–TERM SOLVENCY AND STABILITY.

4.1 The ratios which measure this include

	Subsection
Fixed interest cover	3.2.b.
Fixed dividend cover	3.2.c.
Total debt to shareholders' funds	3.3.c.
Long–term debt to shareholders' funds	3.3.d.
Gearing	3.3.f.

SHORT–TERM SOLVENCY AND LIQUIDITY

4.2 The ratios which measure this include

	Subsection
Stock turnover	3.1.b.
Current ratio	3.3.a.
Liquidity ratio	3.3.b.
Debtor collection	3.5.a.
Creditor payment period	3.5.b.

EFFICIENCY AND PROFITABILITY

4.3 The ratios which measure this include

	Subsection
Gross profit %	3.1.a.
Expense %	3.2.a.
Net profit to sales %	3.4.a.
Expense to sales %	3.4.b.
Sales to total assets ratio	3.5.c.
Sales to capital employed ratio	3.5.d.
Sales to (individual) assets ratio	3.5.e.
Net profit to capital employed %	3.6.a.

POTENTIAL AND ACTUAL GROWTH

4.4 The ratios which measure this include

	Subsection
Net book value per ordinary share	3.3.g.
Earnings per share	3.6.b.
Dividends per share	3.6.c.
Price/earnings ratio	3.7.a.
Earnings yield	3.7.b.
Dividend yield	3.7.c.

EXAMPLE

4.5 A simple example, from which some of the above ratios can be calculated, now follows.

The summarised results of S, M & Co Ltd for the year ended 31st December 19–1 were as shown below.

Trading and Profit and Loss Account
for year ended 31 December 19–1
(for internal circulation)

	£	£
Sales		358,400
Less Opening stock	13,400	
Add Factory cost of finished production	315,835	
	329,235	
Less Closing stock	11,100	
Cost of sales		318,135
Gross profit		40,265
Less Expenses (in total)		20,415
Net profit		19,850
(Purchases totalled £262,900)		

Balance Sheet
as at 31 December 19–1
(for internal circulation)

	£	£
Fixed assets (in total) (net)		105,600
Current assets		
Stocks–Raw materials	7,900	
Work–in–progress	10,500	
Finished goods	11,100	
	29,500	
Debtors	19,400	
Bank and Cash	3,250	
	52,150	
Less Current liabilities		
Creditors	16,800	
Accruals	850	
	17,650	
Working capital		34,500
Net assets employed		140,100
Financed by		
Ordinary shares of £1.00 per share		60,000
Reserves		60,100
Shareholders' funds		120,100
Long–term liabilities 8% Loan		20,000
Capital employed		140,100

Required:

Calculate suitable ratios which will indicate the financial strength and profitability of S, M & Co Ltd and comment briefly on your findings.

SOLUTION

4.6 The first step is to identify those areas for which ratios should be calculated. Fairly obviously, these should be those concerned with long–term and short–term strength and with efficiency and profitability, that is, the ratios listed in 4.1 to 4.3 (above).

It is not desirable (or even possible in this instance) to calculate every ratio listed. The financial analyst should be selective in approach.

Applying tests for long–term solvency and stability:–

$$\frac{EL}{SF} \quad \frac{37,650}{120,100} = 0.31 \quad \frac{LTD}{SF} \quad \frac{20,000}{120,100} = 0.17$$

$$\frac{SF}{TA} \quad \frac{120,100}{157,750} = 0.76 \quad \frac{NOP}{FI} \quad \frac{(19,850 + 1,600)}{1,600} = 13.41 \text{ times}$$

In absolute terms, the excess of total assets over external liabilities, as represented by the shareholders' funds, indicates that the business is solvent. It can be seen that the business relies heavily on "internal" sources of funds (share capital and reserves); this is shown by a low ratio of 0.31 indicating that the business depends for less than one third on external funds for its finance.

Reliance on long–term loans, compared with shareholders' funds, is even lower at 0.17 and as these funds amount to 0.76 of total tangible assets, there is good cover for external liabilities in general.

Multiplying 0.17×0.76 we get a proportion of long–term debt to total assets of 0.13 which shows that the long–term creditors are well protected. (The lower the proportion the better the protection).

The interest commitment to these long–term loan creditors is adequately covered (13.4 times) by profits.

All the pointers show that the business is solvent and very stable, financially, in the long–term. Applying some tests of short–term solvency and liquidity we get

$$\frac{CA}{CL} \quad \frac{52,150}{17,650} \quad :1 \quad = \quad 2.95:1 \qquad \frac{QA}{CL} \quad \frac{(19,400 + 3,250)}{17,650} \quad :1 \quad = \quad 1.28:1$$

$$\frac{C \text{ of } S}{\text{Avge SK}} \qquad \frac{318,135}{(13,400 + 11,100)/2} \quad = \quad 25.97 \text{ times}$$

$$\frac{\text{Drs} \times 12}{\text{Credit sales}} \qquad \frac{19,400 \times 12}{358,400} \quad = \quad 0.65 \text{ months}$$

$$\frac{\text{Crs} \times 12}{\text{Credit purchases}} \qquad \frac{16,800 \times 12}{262,900} \quad = \quad 0.76 \text{ months}$$

(It has been assumed that all purchases and sales have been on credit. If they had not, the cash transactions would have had to be eliminated from the denominator, otherwise the period calculation would have been distorted).

Overall there is an adequate amount of current assets out of which to meet current liabilities; in fact the figures of 2.95 requires further investigation to see whether it is too high. It is not possible to lay down an optimum figure applicable to all businesses but as a general rule this figure should not normally exceed about 1.8:1 without good reason. If no such reason exists, the implication is that too many current assets are being tied up in working capital and, as they are not bringing in any sort of return, the profits and profitability of the businesses are being unduly depressed.

In this instance, current assets include stocks of both raw materials and work–in–progress as well as of finished goods and this fact largely accounts for the current ratio of 2.95:1.

Liquidity, at 1.28:1, appears to be very adequate. Unless a business has a substantial amount of cash sales, a liquidity ratio of more than 1:1 is desirable, particularly when, unlike this company, the timing of creditor settlement occurs before debtor collection or, in other words, when the business has to meet its obligations to creditors before receiving cash from its debtors. Here, on average, the debtors pay in 0.65 months whilst the creditors are settled in 0.76 months, thus there is a very comfortable liquidity margin. (One very well–known retail chain, selling on a cash only basis, survives quite comfortably on a liquidity ratio of 0.88 to 0.93:1).

There is an unusually fast turnover of finished goods stock of 25.97 times per annum, that is, once every two weeks, on average (52/25.97). Rates of stock turnover of this velocity are usually to be found in the retail perishables sector. In the case of S, M & Co Ltd this is unlikely to be the explanation because it is obviously a manufacturing company; more likely it is in the fortunate position of being able to gear its output to a predictable demand.

$$\frac{NP}{CE} \quad \frac{19,850}{140,100} \quad \times \quad \frac{100}{1} \quad = \quad 14.2\% \qquad \frac{S}{CE} \quad \frac{358,400}{140,100} \quad = \quad 2.56 \text{ times}$$

$$\frac{GP}{S} \quad \frac{40,265}{358,400} \quad \times \quad \frac{100}{1} \quad = \quad 11.23\% \qquad \frac{NP}{S} \quad \frac{19,850}{358,400} \times \frac{100}{1} \quad = \quad 5.54\%$$

Relationships between these four indicators can be expressed diagrammatically in the following manner.

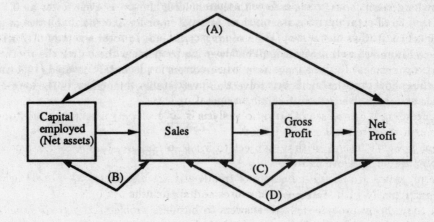

The diagram shows that capital employed generates sales from which firstly gross profit, and then net profit, is derived.

There are, therefore, relationships between capital employed and net profit (A), between capital employed and sales (B), between sales and gross profit (C) and between sales and net profit (D).

These relationships are reflected in the four ratios already calculated:

$$\frac{NP}{CE} = \text{(A)} \quad \frac{S}{CE} = \text{(B)} \quad \frac{GP}{S} = \text{(C)} \quad \text{and} \quad \frac{NP}{S} = \text{(D)}$$

At 11.23% (C) (GP/S) is very low. A reasonable amount of gross profit can only be achieved if there is a compensatory fast turnover of stock. This, as has already been seen, is the case, the rate of turnover being abnormally high at 25.97 times.

Net profit % (D) is low (5.54%) in line with the gross profit %.

However S/CE (B) is 2.56 times per annum and reflects, inter alia, the fast stock turnover. The figure shows that each £1.00 of capital employed has generated £2.56 of sales during the year.

On an overall view NP/CE% (A) is 14.2% and can be seen to consist of the effects of both (B) and (D). This can be proved by multiplying (B) and (D) together, thus 2.56 times 5.54% equals 14.2%.

If S, M & Co Ltd are seeking to improve (A) (overall profitability) they can do so by improving either (B) (CE/S) or (D) (NP/S) or,better still, both (B) and (D).

From the foregoing we can see that S, M & Co Ltd's profitability is probably reasonable and that the company's strategy is to achieve a very fast turnover induced by low selling prices.

Sometimes net operating profit is substituted for net profit in (A) and (D) and total tangible assets for capital employed in (A) and (B).

The term primary ratio is applied to (A) and secondary ratios to (B) and (D).

VALIDITY OF RATIO ANALYSIS

5.0 When employing ratio analysis, the analyst must always be aware of the major dangers.

5.1 Firstly, the figures resulting from the calculations are often given to a number of decimal places, thereby creating a false impression of absolute accuracy, but for reasons given in 5.3 and 5.4 (below) and because they are only as good as the basic figures on which they have been calculated, such accuracy is spurious.

5.2 Secondly, the interpretation of the ratios must not be divorced from an examination of the surrounding circumstances. For example, in a retailing business a low stock turnover figure would ordinarily be regarded as a bad situation. An acceptable explanation might be that average stock (the denominator in the calculation) has been artificially inflated by reason of a build- up of stock at the end of the period in readiness for a major sales promotional campaign in the ensuing period. Under these circumstances an unusually high closing stock would be essential to satisfy the sudden expected demand stimulated by advertising.

5.3 Thirdly, a business may carry out an analysis of its results, on a comparative basis, at different points in time. If, as is usually the case, figures are used which have been prepared on the historical cost convention, the effects of inflation will have been ignored and the resultant ratios will be of limited value; additionally, they suffer from two further drawbacks, namely that they are of little value in predicting future results and by the time they have been calculated it is too late for any action to be taken. These criticisms do not apply when comparisons are made between actual and budgeted or forecast figures.

5.4 Fourthly, even greater problems arise when an attempt is made to compare the ratios of one business with those of another or other businesses. The main reason is that there are a variety of available accounting bases and unless the businesses being compared have uniform accounting policies, the figure cannot be meaningfully compared. Similar problems arise when comparing businesses whose accounting policies are identical but whose operating methods are different. For example, one business may have bought its plant whilst the other one may have leased it under an operating lease.

5.5 From the foregoing it can be seen that ratio analysis is, at best, only a general indicator of performance on which too much reliance must not be placed.

5.6 Ratios are, however, useful in that, subject to 5.1 to 5.4 above, they afford a means of comparing otherwise incomparable absolute figures.

5.7 Furthermore, ratios are useful indicators of trends and are also useful when used in conjuction with other figures, particularly with statements of source and application of funds.

5.8 Although they rarely provide definite answers to business problems the great value of ratios is the questions which they suggest should be answered if, for example, any ratios are markedly different at different points in time.

STUDENT SELF TESTING
Test Exercises

1. The following summarised data was extracted from the published accounts of Colwick Castings Ltd for the year 19–1.

	£
Fixed assets	1,300,000
Net current assets	100,000
	1,400,000
Ordinary shares of £1 per share	700,000
7% Preference shares of £1 per share	200,000
Revenue reserves	300,000
Shareholders' funds	1,200,000
8% Debentures	200,000
	1,400,000
Net profit before tax	440,000
Taxation	(230,000)
Net profit after tax	210,000
Dividends paid and proposed	
Ordinary shares	(90,000)
7% Preference shares	(14,000)
Retained profit for year	106,000

Price per ordinary share (19–1 closing quotation) 220p.

Required:

Calculate for each ordinary share

  a. Book value of net assets per share

  b. Earnings per share (EPS).

  c. Earnings yield

  d. Dividend yield

  e. Price/Earnings ratio

2. a. Explain the term "gearing" in relation to the capital structure of a limited company.

  b. The capital employed by two different companies was as shown below:

	Ess Ltd £	Tee Ltd £
Ordinary shares of £1 per share	300,000	900,000
6% Preference shares of £1 per share	300,000	–
	600,000	900,000
Retained profits	400,000	600,000
Shareholders funds	1,000,000	1,500,000
9% Debentures	1,000,000	500,000
Capital employed	2,000,000	2,000,000

Required:

i. Calculate the gearing ratios of each company, stating in each case whether the gearing is high or low.

ii. Calculate the maximum % dividend on Ordinary shares which each company could declare, without utilising, or adding to, accumulated retained profits, if profit for 19–1 was:

	A £	B £
Net profit (before debenture interest and corporation tax)	250,000	500,000

Assume Corporation Tax to be 52% of Net profit

iii. State what conclusion you can draw from your calculation in b.ii.

3. The summarised final accounts of a small trading business for year ended 31st December 19–1 were as follows:

Trading and Profit and Loss Account for year ended 31st December 19–1

	£
Sales	52,000
Less Cost of sales	38,000
Gross profit	14,000
Less Overhead expenses	8,300
Net Profit	5,700

Balance Sheet as at 31st December 19–1

	£		£	£
Capital	18,000	Fixed Assets		27,000
Add Retained Profits	7,000	Current Assets		
	25,000	Stock	4,300	
Long term loan from		Debtors	1,200	
business associate	5,000	Bank/cash	1,500	
Current liabilities	4,000			7,000
	34,000			34,000

N.B. Stock on 1st January 19–1 was £5,100.
The average figures of performance for that type and size of business in that area (as obtained from trade association sources) were:

Gross profit/Turnover	31.2%
Net profit/Turnover	12.4%
Net profit/Net capital employed	14.2%
Stock turnover	11.8 times
Current ratio	1.6:1

Required:

a. Calculate the above ratios for the above business.

b. Suggest possible reasons for the differences revealed between the ratios in a. and the "average" ratios.

4. a. It is widely recognised that, in order to succeed, a business must pay regard not only to its profitability but also to its financial stability.

Required:

i. State briefly what you understand to be the meaning of the terms "profitability" and "financial stability".

ii. Name three ratios which can be used for measuring profitability and three ratios for measuring financial stability.

b. The figures shown below relate to a medium sized company.

	£
For year ended 31st October, 19–3:	
Gross Profit	797,000
Net Profit	255,000
Turnover (Sales)	2,743,000
As at 31st October, 19–3:	
Shareholders' funds	1,335,000
Total tangible assets	2,008,000
Total current assets	32,000
Current liabilities	25,000
Long–term loans	648,000
Non–liquid current assets	19,000

Required:

Using such of the above figures and their derivatives as are relevant, calculate each of the ratios which you have named in your answer to (a) (ii) above.

5. The latest Balance Sheet and Profit and Loss Account summary of Sunlight Ltd, a manufacturing company for internal circulation is as follows:

Sunlight Ltd
Balance Sheet as at 31 March 19–9

	£		£	£
Authorised Share Capital–		*Fixed Assets*		
400,000 £1 Ordinary Shares	400,000	Freehold Property (book value)		240,000
Issued and fully paid–		Plant and Machinery		
200,000 £1 Ordinary Shares	200,000	(cost *less* depreciation)		400,000
Capital Reserves	100,000	Motor Vehicles (cost *less*		
Revenue Reserves	400,000	depreciation)		100,000
Shareholders' funds employed	700,000	Office Furniture (cost *less*		
Loan Capital		depreciation)		100,000
200,000 10% Debentures				840,000
(secured on Freehold Property				
– repayable 20–1)	200,000	*Current Assets*	£	
Book value of Long				
Term Funds	900,000	Stocks	500,000	
Current Liabilities	£	Debtors	200,000	
Trade Creditors	119,200	Investments	60,000	760,000
Bank overdraft				
(secured)	439,200			
Current taxation	88,000			
Dividends payable	53,600	700,000		
		£1,600,000		£1,600,000

Summary Profit and Loss Account for the year ended 31 March 19–9

	£
Sales (all on credit)	2,000,000
Profit after charging all expenses except debenture interest	220,000
Less: Debenture interest (gross)	20,000
Profit before taxation	200,000
Less: Corporation tax on the taxable profit for the year	88,000
Profit after taxation	112,000
Less: Ordinary dividend proposed	53,600
Retained profits transferred to revenue reserve	£58,400

Notes:

Purchases for the year were £1,080,000 Cost of sales for the year was £1,500,000. The market price of a Sunlight Ltd ordinary share at 31 March 19–9 was £4.00. Income tax is to be taken at 33% A.C.T is ignored. The company estimates the current value of its Freehold property at £440,000. The Managing Director has suggested that a figure representing the company's goodwill be computed and included in the Balance Sheet under the heading with the Shareholders' funds increased by its value.

You are required:

a. to compute the following ratios:

  i. Primary ratio (using the BOOK value of total assets as capital employed).

  ii. Secondary ratio – the profit margin.

  iii. Secondary ratio – the turnover of capital.

  iv. Current ratio.

  v. Liquid ratio.

  vi. Debtors ratio.

  vii. Proprietary ratio.

  viii. Stock turnover ratio.

  ix. Dividend yield.

  x. Price Earnings ratio and its reciprocal.

b. To write a brief comment on the *liquidity* of Sunlight Ltd, stating the reference points to which relevant ratios can be compared.

(ACCA)

6. The summarized final accounts for the year ended 31st December, 19–1, for two retailing companies in the same line of business are shown below:–

Trading and Profit and Loss Accounts
for year ended 31st December, 19–1

	Company 'A'		Company 'B'	
	£	£	£	£
Sales		200,000		200,000
Opening Stock	32,000		8,000	
Purchases	156,000		150,000	
	188,000		158,000	
Less Closing Stock	48,000		12,000	
Cost of Sales		140,000		146,000
Gross Profit		60,000		54,000
Less Expenses		47,400		42,480
Net Profit		12,600		11,520

Balance Sheets as at 31st December, 19–1

	£	£	£	£
Fixed Assets at written down values		130,000		80,000
Current Assets				
Stock	48,000		12,000	
Debtors	17,000		4,250	
Bank	5,000		19,750	
	70,000		36,000	
Less Current Liabilities	20,000		20,000	
		50,000		16,000
		180,000		96,000
Financed by:				
Share Capital		80,000		80,000
Reserves		100,000		16,000
		180,000		96,000

Required:

Copy out the following table and insert the appropriate figures (with workings)

	Company 'A'	Company 'B'
Current Ratio		
Acid test Ratio		
Rate of Stock Turnover		
Gross Profit to Turnover %		
Net Profit to Turnover %		
Net Profit to Capital Employed %		

b. One of the companies is Cutpryce Stores Ltd. which has adopted the policy of selling goods as cheaply as possible to increase the volume of sales. The other company is Hiclass Merchandising Ltd which occupies a prestige site, gives special attention to customer service and charges top prices for its goods.

Required:

State with reasons, which of these companies is Company 'A' and which is Company 'B' in part a. of this question.

7. The financial information provided below is for two companies which operate in similar retail fields, using the same business and accounting policies.

Balance Sheets at 30.6.–5

	Barlow Ltd £000	Watt Ltd £000
Share Capital and Reserves		
Issued Capital	350	470
Capital Reserves	65	35
Revenue Reserves	185	287
10% Debentures	55	64
Current Liabilities		
Bank Overdraft	21	20
Trade Creditors	97	132
Other Current Liabilities and Provisions	42	48
	815	1,056
Fixed Assets (at Book Values)		
Land and Buildings	286	381
Plant and Equipment	218	342
Motor Vehicles	59	62

Current Assets

Stock	122	97
Trade Debtors	124	166
Cash	6	8
	815	1,056

Profit and Loss Accounts for year ended 30 June 19–5

	Barlow Ltd		Watt Ltd	
	£000	£000	£000	£000
Sales		747		570
Cost of Sales				
Opening Stock	102		92	
Purchases	588		381	
	690		473	
Closing Stock	122		96	
		568		377
Gross Profit		179		193
Operating Expenses				
Selling and Distribution	64		60	
Administration and Management	31		29	
Financial	9		8	
		104		97
Net Profit		75		96
Provision for Taxation		37		45
		38		51
Provision for Dividend		24		37
Transfer to Revenue Reserve		14		14

You are required to:

a. Calculate for each company six ratios which you consider most appropriate for indicating the efficiency of operations and short term financial strength of the two firms, showing the figures you have used and pointing out any weakness in the figures, and alternatives that might be taken had more information been available.

b. Using the financial information provided above and the ratios you have calculated prepare a report which analyses and compares the efficiency of operations and short term financial strength of the Barlow and Watt companies.

(ACCA)

8. Mosich Supply Company, a medium sized manufacturer of surgical supplies and equipment has recently reorganised the management team, due in the main to low profitability in recent years.

You have been requested to make an analysis of the firm's financial position and the most recent financial statements are reproduced below, together with average ratios for the industry.

Industry Average Ratios

Current Ratio	2:1
Quick rato	1:1
Debt to total assets	30%
Times interest earned	7x
Fixed charges coverage	5x
Stock turnover	10x
Average collection period	15 days
Fixed assets turnover	6x
Total assets turnover	3x
Net profit on sales	3%
Return on total assets	9%
Return on net worth	12.8%

Mosich Supply Company
Income Statement for the year ended 31 December 19–5

		£000
Sales		7,950
Less: Cost of Goods Sold		6,600
Gross Profit		1,350
Operating Expenses	735	
Depreciation	120	
Interest	45	
		900
Net Profit before tax		450
Taxation (50%)		225
Undistributed Profits after tax		£225

Balance Sheet as at 31 December 19-5
(for internal circulation)

	£000	£000	£000
Fixed Assets			
Plant and Equipment			2,250
Less Depreciation			780
			1,470
Current Assets			
Stock	1,590		
Debtors	660		
Marketable Securities	330		
Cash	450		
		3,030	
Less **Current Liabilities**			
Sundry liabilities	210		
Creditors	450		
Notes payable (6%)	450		
		1,110	
			1,920
			£3,390
Represented by:			
Ordinary Share Capital			1,140
Undistributed profits			2,010
			3,150
5% Debenture Stock			240
			£3,390

You are required to:

1. Calculate ratios which you feel would be useful in your analysis.
2. Examine the income statement and balance sheet with a view to ascertaining the reasons for low profits.
3. State with reasons which specific ratios seem to be most out of line in their relationships to other firms in the industry.
   (ACCA)

9. The summarised balance sheet of MacSuit and Coat Limited, together with extracts from its revenue account for the year ended 31 March 19–6 are given below:

This small company manufactures clothing and is managed by two young capable, energetic directors with a good knowledge and experience of the trade.

They have made loans to the company to the full extent of their personal resources and currently require funds to finance a large contract worth £60,000 from reputable first class buyers for a quantity of suits.

They have applied to their bank for an unsecured overdraft limited of £15,000 to finance the contract. They have offered the bank manager their personal guarantees and postponement of their own loans. They do not wish to offer a secured debenture as they feel this would precipitate action from the company's creditors.

You are employed by the bank in its regional office as accountant advisor to bank managers in the region in respect of requests such as this.

You are required to write a report to the bank manager:–
   a. analysing the information available to you, in the context of the request made,
      and
   b. advising him of the risk to the bank, in granting the overdraft.

MacSuit and Coat Limited
Balance sheet as at 31 March 19–6

	£	£
Share Capital – Ordinary Shares of £1 fully paid		3,000
Profit and Loss account		500
		3,500
Loans by Directors		5,500
Current Liabilities		
Accrued expenses	5,000	
Trade creditors	55,000	
		60,000
		£69,000
Fixed Assets		
Plant and Machinery (cost *less* depreciation)		10,500
Motor Vehicles (cost *less* depreciation)		1,500
Goodwill		1,800
		13,800
Current Assets		
Cash and Bank	11,800	
Trade debtors	17,000	
Stocks and work in progres	23,500	
Prepayments	2,000	
Preliminary expenses	900	
		55,200
		£69,000

Extracts from the profit and loss account for the year ended 31 March 19–6:
   Sales   £230,000   Purchases of stock   £140,000

	£
Profit for the year (after all expenses including those below)	4,550
Provision for Corporation Tax	Nil
Provision for depreciation of fixed Assets	1,800
Provision for Directors' remuneration	6,400

(ACCA)

10. The outline balance sheets of the Nantred Trading Co. Ltd were as shown below:

Balance Sheets
as at 30 September

19–5			19–6	
£	£		£	£
		Fixed assets (at written down values)		
40,000		Premises	98,000	
65,000		Plant and equipment	162,000	
	105,000			260,000
		Current assets		
31,200		Stock	95,300	
19,700		Trade debtors	30,700	
15,600		Bank and cash	26,500	
66,500			152,500	
		Current Liabilities		
23,900		Trade Creditors	55,800	
11,400		Corporation tax	13,100	
17,000		Proposed dividends	17,000	
52,300			85,900	
	14,200	*Working capital*		66,600
	119,200	*Net assets employed*		326,600
		Financed by		
100,000		Ordinary share capital	200,000	
19,200		Reserves	26,600	
	119,200	*Shareholders' funds*		226,600
	–	7% Debentures		100,000
	119,200			326,600

The only other information available is that the turnover for the years ended 30 Septembr 19–5 and 19–6 was £202,900 and £490,700, respectively, and that on 30 September 19–4 Reserves were £26,100.

Required:

a. Calculate for each of the two years, six suitable ratios to highlight the financial stability, liquidity and profitability of the company.

b. Comment on the situation revealed by the figures you have calculated in your answer to (a) above.

(ACCA)

11. The net assets of three unconnected companies are financed as follows, as at 31 December 19–4:

	Company					
	X PLC		Y PLC		Z PLC	
	£000	£000	£000	£000	£000	£000
Share capital						
Authorised						
Ordinary shares of £1.00 per share	12,000		–		–	
Ordinary shares of £0.25 per share	—		6,000		6,000	
8% preference shares of £1.00 per share		–	4,000		4,000	
		12,000		10,000		10,000

Called up and issued

Ordinary shares of £1.00 per share £0.75 paid	6,000	—	—
Ordinary shares of £0.25 per share fully paid	–	4,000	1,000
9% preference shares of £1.00 per share, fully paid	–	4,000	2,000
	6,000	8,000	3,000

Reserves

Share premium account (raised on issue of ordinary shares)		500	200
General reserve	1,000	—	1,300
Fixed asset revaluation reserve	2,000	—	—
Fixed asset replacement reserve	—	1,000	—
Profit and loss account	1,000	500	1,500
	4,000	2,000	3,000
Shareholders' funds	10,000	10,000	6,000
10% Debenture stock	—	—	4,000
	10,000	10,000	10,000

For all three companies, the profit before interest and tax is estimated at £5,000,000 for the next 12 months ended 31 December 19–5. The capital structure of each company will remain unaltered.

Taxation on profits after interest is an effective rate of 40%. Assume that an ordinary dividend of 12% of the paid up share capital will be paid.

Required:

For each of the three companies,

a. prepare the estimated profit and loss accounts for the year ended 31 December 19–5,

b. calculate

   i. basic earnings per share for the year ended 31 December 19–5,

   ii. gearing ratio as at 31 December 19–4,

c. briefly explain, in relation to gearing, the effects on earnings of substantial changes in profit after tax.

Marks will be awarded for workings which must be shown.

12. Company financial statements, including profit and loss accounts, balance sheets and statements of source and application of funds, are used by a variety of individuals and institutions for a wide variety of purposes.

Required:

Specify six different types of users of financial statement and explain in each case the aspects of performance or position in which they are interested.

13. Loxley PLC requires £1 million to invest in a new project. The directors intend to finance the project either by a rights issue at £1.25 per share or by raising a 12% loan at par. Over the two years the company's share price has increased from £1.50 to £1.60.

A summary of the annual accounts for 19–5 and 19–6 is given below.

Profit and Loss Account

	19–5 £000's	19–6 £000's
Turnover	12,350	12,658
Operating Profit	700	640
Less interest payable	60	60
	640	580

Less taxation	256	232
Profits after taxation	£384	£348

Balance Sheets

Assets	19–5	19–6
Fixed assets	1,802	2,128
Stocks	894	852
Debtors	616	642
Cash	104	22
	£3,416	£3,644
Funded by		
Ordinary Shares of £1 each	1,000	1,000
Reserves	1,050	1,298
Loans – 10% Debentures 20–6	600	600
Trade Creditors	410	414
Taxation payable	256	232
Dividends	100	100
	£3,416	£3,644

It is expected that profit earned on existing assets will be repeated in 19–7 and that the new project will earn £200,000 before interest and corporation tax. If a rights issue is made the dividend will be increased to £200,000.

Required:

a. Identify two ratios which you consider to be of particular interest to shareholders, two of interest to lenders and two of financial interest.

b. Advise the directors which method of finance to adopt, basing your advice on calculations of the company's gearing ratios.

14. Mr Big has been approached by Volatile Ltd for a loan to the company of £100,000 for 5 years at an interest rate of 10% p.a.

Mr Big has given to you the following information from the company's audited accounts:
Balance Sheet as at 30 June

	19–3	19–4	19–5
	£	£	£
Share Capital	100,000	120,000	120,000
Revenue	82,000	115,000	152,000
12% Debenture	75,000	110,000	110,000
	£257,000	£345,000	£382,000
Fixed Assets			
Freehold Property	66,000	66,000	66,000
Plant and Machinery	67,000	120,000	145,000
	133,000	186,000	211,000
Current Assets			
Stocks and work in progress	136,000	220,000	290,000
Debtors	91,000	138,000	166,000
	227,000	358,000	456,000
Current Liabilities			
Creditors	23,000	35,000	50,000
Corporation Tax	28,000	31,000	35,000
Bank overdraft (secured)	52,000	133,000	200,000
	103,000	199,000	285,000
Net Current Assets	124,000	159,000	171,000
	£257,000	£345,000	£382,000

Profit and Loss Account
for the year ended 30 June

	19–3	19–4	19–5
	£	£	£
Sales	578,000	761,000	890,000
Less cost of sales	434,000	586,000	694,000
	144,000	175,000	196,000
Other costs	67,000	87,000	100,000
	77,000	88,000	96,000
Corporation Tax	(28,000)	(31,000)	(35,000)
Dividends	(20,000)	(24,000)	(24,000)
Profits retained	£29,000	£33,000	£37,000

Notes

1. Sales of fixed assets have been insignificant.
2. Mr Big is told the following as to the reason for the need for further capital:

a. The additional plant will cost £150,000.

b. Sales will be increased by 40%. Two months' credit will be given to customers and one month's credit will be extended by suppliers. Stocks and work in progress will represent 3 months' cost of sales. The anticipated rate of gross profit will be 20%.

c. The directors state that overhead expenses will not increase significantly as a result of the increased activity.

REQUIRED

Prepare a report advising Mr Big on the proposition.

15. In December, 19–3 the directors of XY Limited, a firm of wholesale merchants, raised additional capital in the form of a debenture of £80,000 at 10% p.a. to facilitate expansion of the business.

From the information given below you are required to assess the financial success of the expansion following the injection of a debenture fund and the efficiency of the company's operations by means of internal accounting ratios covering profitability, use of capital, liquidity and gearing (the figures to be calculated to one decimal place).

1. The annual accounts for the years ended 31st December, 19–3 and 19–4 are set out below:

Trading and Profit and Loss Accounts

	£	£	£	£
Sales: Credit		550,000		660,000
Cash		50,000		40,000
		600,000		700,000
Cost of sales		468,000		553,000
Gross margin		132,000		147,000
Expenses:				
Administration	27,000		27,500	
Selling	39,500		40,000	
Warehouse and distribution	28,000		32,500	
Depreciation	3,000		3,500	
Debenture interest	–		8,000	
		97,500		111,500
		34,500		35,500

Balance Sheets as at 31st December

	£	£	£	£
Fixed assets:				
Cost	70,000		90,000	
Depreciation	15,000		18,500	
		55,000		71,500
Net current assets:				
Stock	136,000		150,000	
Debtors	96,000		156,000	
Cash	2,000		22,000	
	234,000		328,000	
Creditors	64,000		84,500	
		170,000		243,500
		225,000		315,000
Share capital		150,000		150,000
Reserves		75,000		85,000
Debentures		–		80,000
		225,000		315,000

2. The product range and buying prices were unchanged over two years.
3. The debenture loan was received on 1st January, 19–4 and the additional warehouse facilities became available on that date. Taxation is to be ignored.

16. In November, 19–8 the directors of LM Limited, an engineering company incorporated in 19–5 manufacturing files and small tools, decided to raise additional capital in the form of a 13% debenture of £100,000 to be taken up on 1st January 19–9, in order to provide additional funds for expansion.
From the information given below you are required to:

a. prepare a cash flow statement for internal use for the year ended 31st December, 19–9;
b. assess the progress and efficiency of the company in 19–9 by means of internal accounting ratios covering profitability, use of capital, liquidity and gearing;
c. comment, using the foregoing information on whether or not, the additional finance has been wisely used.

1. The accounts for the two years ended 31st December, 19–9 are set out below:

Trading and Profit and Loss Accounts

	19–8		19–9	
	£	£	£	£
Sales:				
Credit		820,000		998,000
Cash		80,000		60,000
		900,000		1,058,000
Cost of sales		702,000		830,000
Gross margin		198,000		228,000
Overhead expenditure				
Administration		36,000		39,500
Selling		58,500		60,000

Warehouse and distribution	42,500	48,500
Depreciation	5,000	8,000
Debenture interest	–	13,000
	142,000	169,000
Profit before taxation	56,000	59,000
Taxation	26,000	28,000
Profit after taxation	30,000	31,000
Dividends:		
Preference	4,000	4,000
Ordinary	15,000	16,500
	19,000	20,500
Retained profit	11,000	10,500

Balance Sheets as at 31st December

	19–8		19–9	
	£	£	£	£
Fixed Assets:				
Cost	105,000		130,000	
Depreciation	25,000		28,000	
		80,000		102,000
Net current Assets:				
Stocks	219,000		240,000	
Debtors	142,000		234,000	
Bank	4,000		7,000	
	365,000		481,000	
Creditors	86,000		100,000	
Taxation	42,000		54,000	
Dividend	15,000		16,500	
	143,000		170,500	
		222,000		310,500
		302,000		412,500
Share Capital:				
150,000 Ordinary shares of £1		150,000		150,000
50,000 8% Preference of £		50,000		50,000
		200,000		200,000
Retained profits		102,000		112,500
13% Debentures		–		100,000
		302,000		412,500

2. Capital expenditure in the year totalled £36,000. On 31st December, 19–9 fixed assets, which had cost £11,000 and which at that date had a book value of £7,000, were sold for £6,000. The loss on sale of £1,000 is included in the depreciation charge for the year.

3. The preference dividend is paid on 30th June and 31st December and the ordinary dividend in the March following the year end.

17. T Limited and H Limited were each incorporated five years ago and entered the same market. They have now decided that it would be in both their interests to amalgamate. You are asked to advise whether the performance of either company compared with that of the other, will justify the inclusion of a goodwill

value in the final price to be agreed for the amalgamation.

a. study carefully the following accounts of each company covering the period since formation and state clearly the adjustments you would propose to make the two sets of accounts comparable

b. prepare a statement to show accounting results adjusted as proposed in a. together with a precise explanation of the adjustments made;

c. comment on factors relating to goodwill disclosed by your statement of adjusted results. You are not required to establish a figure for goodwill.

T Limited: Balance Sheets

As at 31st December

	19-9 £	19-0 £	19-1 £	19-2 £	19-3 £
Ordinary share capital	100,000	100,000	100,000	100,000	100,000
Reserves	25,000	40,000	60,000	90,000	116,000
	125,000	140,000	160,000	190,000	216,000
Freehold buildings at cost	20,000	20,000	20,000	20,000	20,000
Plant at cost	40,000	40,000	30,000	45,000	45,000
less depreciation to date	4,000	8,000	9,000	12,000	16,500
	36,000	32,000	21,000	33,000	28,500
Stock	63,500	50,000	60,000	40,000	80,000
Debtors	84,000	96,000	104,000	139,600	124,000
Balance at bank	1,500	2,000	5,000	7,400	3,500
	149,000	148,000	169,000	187,000	207,500
less Creditors	80,000	60,000	50,000	50,000	40,000
	69,000	88,000	119,000	137,000	167,500
	125,000	140,000	160,000	190,000	216,000

Profit and Loss Appropriation Accounts
for year ended 31st December

	19-9 £	19-0 £	19-1 £	19-2 £	19-3 £
Balance brought forward	nil	25,000	40,000	60,000	90,000
Total profit for year	31,000	28,000	35,000	47,000	46,000
	31,000	53,000	75,000	107,000	136,000
Dividends paid	6,000	13,000	15,000	17,000	20,000
Per Balance sheet	25,000	40,000	60,000	90,000	116,000
Notes:					
Stock at prime cost	63,500	50,000	60,000	40,000	80,000
Stock at variable cost	80,000	70,000	72,000	60,000	120,000

At the beginning of 19-1, plant originally costing £10,000 in 19-9 was sold for £8,000. At the beginning of 19-2 plant originally costing £5,000 in 19-9 was sold for £3,400.

H Limited: Balance Sheets

As at 31st December

	19–9 £	19–0 £	19–1 £	19–2 £	19–3 £
Ordinary share capital	75,000	75,000	75,000	75,000	75,000
Reserves	28,100	40,100	48,600	75,600	109,500
	103,100	115,100	123,600	150,600	184,500
Freehold buildings at cost	16,000	16,000	16,000	16,000	16,000
Plant at cost	30,000	30,000	22,500	33,800	33,800
less depreciation to date	6,000	10,800	10,980	14,060	18,010
	24,000	19,200	11,520	19,740	15,790
Stock	60,000	52,500	54,000	45,000	90,000
Debtors	62,000	71,000	77,000	104,000	92,000
Balance at bank	1,100	1,400	2,580	3,360	710
	123,100	124,900	133,580	152,360	182,710
less Creditors	60,000	45,000	37,500	37,500	30,000
	63,100	79,900	96,080	114,860	152,710
	103,100	115,100	123,600	150,600	184,500

Profit and Loss Appropriation Accounts
for year ended 31st December

	19–9 £	19–0 £	19–1 £	19–2 £	19–3 £
Balance brought forward	nil	28,100	40,100	48,600	75,600
Total profit for year	32,600	21,800	19,700	39,700	48,900
	32,600	49,900	59,800	88,300	124,500
Dividends paid	4,500	9,800	11,200	12,700	15,000
Per Balance sheet	28,100	40,100	48,600	75,600	109,500
Notes:					
Stock at prime cost	47,600	37,500	45,000	30,000	60,000
Stock at variable cost	60,000	52,500	54,000	45,000	90,000

At the beginning of 19–1, plant originally costing £7,500 in 19–9 was sold for £4,800. At the beginning of 19–2, plant originally costing £3,800 in 19–9 was sold for £2,000.

18. You are required to give your interpretation of the results of A Limited, as shown in schedule A issued with this paper. Your comments should, where possible, be supported by ratios and grouped under suitable 'user' groups (eg management, shareholders, creditors and employees).

19. The management of B Limited wishes to compare its ratio of profit before tax to total assets employed with that of A Limited. After studing carefully both schedules A and B and the information given below, you are required as a first step:

a. to state clearly the adjustments which should be made to the figures of B Limited to facilitate such a comparison; and

b. to make these adjustments to the figures for the two years 19–7 and 19–8 only. Do not calculate the ratios themselves.

The following information is given:

1. Stocks:	19–6 £000	19–7 £000	19–8 £000	19–9 £000
A Limited				
at prime cost	46,540	51,670	58,720	66,700
at cost of production	81,940	94,860	111,500	125,200
B Limited				
at prime cost	15,600	18,200	20,000	22,000
at cost of production	28,000	35,200	39,000	43,500

2. A Limited is known to write off fully research and development expenditure in the year in which it is incurred, whereas B Limited writes it off evenly over a period of five years.

3. The premises initially rented by B Limited have now been acquired on a ten years lease.

4. The cash cost of acquiring the plant on hire would have been £10 million and it has a five year life with no residual value.

SCHEDULE A:

Information extracted from the published accounts of A Limited.

Year	19–6	19–7	19–8	19–9
	£000	£000	£000	£000
Sales	374,000	408,000	442,000	476,000
Profit before tax	47,600	55,400	55,000	65,360
After charging:				
Directors' emoluments	950	950	1,000	1,100
Depreciation	29,100	23,980	19,984	16,607
And crediting:				
Gross dividends	3,400	7,100	9,500	13,600
Profit on sale of plant	–	–	–	10,000
Taxation on profits	22,000	26,000	28,000	30,000
Taxation on dividends received	1,020	2,130	2,850	4,080
Profit after tax	24,580	27,270	24,150	31,280
Purchases of materials and services	239,992	283,190	309,342	327,499
Employees' remuneration	56,100	62,900	69,700	73,800
Ordinary share capital	200,000	200,000	200,000	220,000
Reserves	55,000	58,270	58,420	39,700
Equity capital employed	255,000	258,270	258,420	259,700

	Persons	Persons	Persons	Persons
Number of employees	27,200	30,600	34,000	37,400
	£000	£000	£000	£000
Assets Employed:				
Leasehold premises, at cost	35,000	35,000	35,000	35,000
Depreciation	(7,000)	(10,500)	(14,000)	(17,500)
Plant and machinery, at cost	160,000	160,000	160,000	120,000
Depreciation	(57,600)	(78,080)	(94,464)	(80,678)
Total fixed assets	130,400	106,420	86,536	56,822
Investments, at cost	34,000	70,000	80,000	115,000
Current assets:				
Stock	81,940	94,860	111,500	125,200
Debtors	62,330	76,120	91,540	106,900
Cash	31,790	26,000	17,800	2,000
Total	176,060	196,980	220,840	234,100
Current liabilities:				
Trade creditors	48,460	65,930	77,956	85,222
Current Tax	17,000	25,200	27,000	31,000
Proposed dividends	20,000	24,000	24,000	30,000
Total	85,460	115,130	128,956	146,222
Net current assets	90,600	81,850	91,884	87,878
Net assets employed	255,000	258,270	258,420	259,700

You may assume that prices have remained stable over the four years period, advance corporation tax on the proposed dividends has been ignored. All sales are zero rated for value added tax.

SCHEDULE B: Information relating to B Limited

Year	19-6	19-7	19-8	19-9
	£000	£000	£000	£000
Sales	75,000	82,000	90,000	95,000
Depreciation	4,800	4,800	4,800	8,500
Rent of premises	3,000	3,000	3,000	–
Hire of plant	–	2,500	2,500	2,500
Research and development	–	60	100	170
Interest on loan stock	2,000	2,000	2,000	–
Premium on repayment of loan stock	–	–	–	3,000
profit on sale of plant	–	–	–	(2,400)
Other costs	55,200	57,640	63,600	67,830
Total	65,000	70,000	76,000	79,600
Profit before tax	10,000	12,000	14,000	15,400
Taxation	5,000	6,500	7,000	7,500
Profit after tax	5,000	5,500	7,000	7,900
Dividends	3,500	3,500	3,500	4,500
Retained earnings	1,500	2,000	3,500	3,400
Ordinary share capital	40,000	40,000	40,000	55,000
Share premium	5,000	5,000	5,000	15,000
Reserves	2,200	4,200	7,700	6,100
10% unsecured loan stock	20,000	20,000	20,000	–
	67,200	69,200	72,700	76,100
Assets Employed:				
Leasehold premises at cost		–	–	25,000
Depreciation	–	–	–	(2,500)
Plant and machinery at cost	48,000	48,000	48,000	60,000
Depreciation	(9,600)	(14,400)	(19,200)	(18,800)
Total fixed assets	38,400	33,600	28,800	63,700
Research and development	–	240	340	520
Current assets:				
Stock	15,600	18,200	20,000	22,000
Debtors	13,200	15,700	18,100	20,000
Cash in hand	16,000	22,060	26,960	–
Total	44,800	55,960	65,060	42,000
Current liabilities:				
Trade creditors	10,000	12,000	14,000	20,000
Current tax	4,000	6,600	5,500	5,800
Proposed dividends	2,000	2,000	2,000	2,500
Bank overdraft	–	–	–	1,820
Total	16,000	20,600	21,500	30,120
Net current assets	28,800	35,360	43,560	11,880
Net assets employed	67,200	69,200	72,700	76,100

You are advised that:

i. During 19-9 and prior to the rights issue, the company made a bonus issue of one new share for every eight shares already held.

ii. At the beginning of 19–9, plant and machinery which had originally cost £16,000 and had a book value of £9,600 was sold and replaced with more modern equipment.

20. The summarised balance sheets of Cedar PLC for the years ended 31st December 9–7 and 31 December 19–8 follow:

Cedar PLC Balance Sheets

	Year ended 31st December	
	19–7	19–8
	£000	£000
Issued Share Capital in £1 Ordinary Shares, fully paid	1,200	1,200
General Revenue Reserve	240	260
Profit and Loss Account	572	510
8% Debenture Stock	–	600
Corporation Tax (payable 1 January 19–8)	148	–
Corporation Tax (payable 1 January 19–9)	178	178
Corporation Tax (payable 1 January 19–0)	–	62
Proposed Dividend	180	180
Sundry Creditors	738	1,080
	3,256	4,070
	£000	£000
Plant, at cost	1,620	1,990
Less: Depreciation	616	736
	1,004	1,254
Freehold Property	400	480
Goodwill	300	300
Stocks	990	1,276
Sundry Debtors	484	736
Bank	78	24
	3,256	4,070

The following information is relevant to the profits for the years ended 31 December 19–7 and 19–8:

	Year ended 31 December	
	19–7	19–8
	£000	£000
Sales	6,000	6,600
Net profit before Corporation Tax	560	200
Among the items charged in the calculation of net profit before Corporation Tax were:		
Depreciation of plant	100	120
Bad debts	46	164
Directors' emoluments	50	52
Advertising and sales promotion	216	324

Cedar PLC shares have been quoted on the London Stock Exchange since January 19–6. It had started business some 20 years ago and has had a continuous expansion record under the control of its Chairman and major shareholder. Currently the main business is the manufacture of high quality furniture of which 45% is exported.

In February 19–9, the Chairman asked the company's bankers for overdraft facilities of £400,000 during the succeeding twelve months (the overdraft limit in the year ended 31 December 19–8 had been £100,000).

In making this request, the Chairman indicated:

1. That in the year ended 31 December 19–8, the company had expanded its production capacity and the sales organisation was extended by the acquisition of retail distribution outlets in Europe.

2. Initial difficulties with the European acquisitions and increasingly severe competition in both home

and overseas markets were the cause of the fall in profits in the year ended 31 December 19-8.

3. These were unprecedented setbacks, but his board were hopeful that conditions would prove more favourable in the coming year.

4. The requested overdraft facility is necessary if the company is to continue to offer delivery and credit terms comparable with its competitors in the export market.

You are required as an investigating accountant in the bank's regional office:

a. to draw up a memorandum for the bank manager commenting on the financial condition of Cedar PLC as disclosed in the above statements, and

b. to set out matters on which you would require further information before making a recommendation in respect of the proposed overdraft level.

(ACCA).

ACCA EXAMINATION QUESTIONS

21. The managers of Bubblegum Ltd are having their annual conference in January 1983 to discuss the company's past year's performance. There is concern over the decline in the company's profitability although the turnover figures have remained constant. The quarterly reports are set out below:

	Quarter 1 31.3.82		Quarter 2 30.6.82		Quarter 3 30.9.82		Quarter 4 31.12.82	
Profit & Loss Statement	£	£	£	£	£	£	£	£
Sales		6,000		6,200		5,700		6,000
Cost of Sales:								
Materials	1,200		1,250		1,250		1,200	
Labour	900		910		920		1,200	
Production overheads	750		750		760		770	
		2,850		2,910		2,930		3,170
		3,150		3,290		2,770		2,830
Administration	1,500		1,540		1,200		1,300	
Development	400		430		380		380	
Distribution	1,000		1,040		970		1,000	
		2,900		3,010		2,550		2,680
Profit		£250		£280		£220		£150
Fixed assets		2,500		2,300		2,100		1,900
Stock Finished Goods	600		615		595		600	
Stock Work in Progress	390		375		400		395	
Stock Raw Materials	590		600		590		590	
Debtors	730		750		850		800	
		2,310		2,340		2,435		2,385
Capital Employed		£4,810		£4,640		£4,535		£4,285

Required:

a. Prepare an outline report with headings and brief comment, illustrated by appropriate ratios, to present to the meeting, analysing the performance of Bubblegum Ltd over the year and suggest possible causes for the decline in profitability.

b. Comment on the advantages and disadvantages of ratio analysis as a technique for interim and interperiod comparisons.

(ACCA 2.9(2) December 1982)

22. Required:

a. Comment on the trends shown in the data of Competition Limited.

b. Briefly indicate additional information you would require in order to be able to use the data for inter-company comparison.

c. Produce a graph from the data on Competition Limited in a form which you think will assist in the interpretation of the relationship between turnover and the return on capital employed.
(ACCA 2.9(1) December 1982)

Appendix 6

Summary of data prepared by Competition Ltd, a company in the same industry as Brighton Metal Co. Ltd.

	Actual				Current			Forecast	
	1979	1980	1981	1982	1983	1984	1985	1986	1987
Sales £000s	1,650	1,700	1,750	1,850	1,900	2,160	2,400	2,600	3,100
% change		3	3	6	3	14	11	8	19
INDEX	100	100	100	100	100	100	100	100	100
Cost of Sales									
£000s	990	1,020	1,085	1,185	1,250	1,400	1,500	1,600	1,850
% change		3	6	9	5	12	7	7	16
% to sales	60	60	62	64	66	65	63	62	60
Overheads,									
£000's	395	440	455	480	440	475	460	450	550
% change		11	3	5	(8)	8	(3)	(2)	22
% to sales	24	26	26	26	23	22	19	17	18
Profit	265	240	210	185	210	285	440	550	700
% change		(9)	(12)	(12)	14	36	54	25	27
% to sales	16	14	12	10	11	13	18	21	23
Capital Employed									
£000s	1,750	1,850	1,900	2,050	2,100	1,670	1,900	2,040	2,250
Rate of Return on Capital Employed	15	13	11	9	10	17	23	27	31
Sales/Capital Employed	94	92	92	90	90	129	126	127	138

23. **Required:**

Analyse the position of the company, identify any further information you would seek to obtain and draft notes to be included in a report to a client who is proposing to acquire 3,000 of the 13,500 issued shares.
(ACCA 2.9 (a) June 1982)

APPENDIX 1 *Draft Balance Sheets and Profit & Loss Accounts for years ended 31 December 1979, 1980, 1981*

BALANCE SHEETS

	1979 £	1980 £	1981 £
Share Capital	2,860	13,500	13,500
Profit & Loss Account	8,557	14,996	19,992
Loan Capital	–	20,262	18,174
	11,417	48,758	51,666
Capital Employed			
Fixed Assets			
Land and Buildings		1,240	380
Plant and Machinery		5,360	5,255
Net Fixed Assets	4,496	6,600	5,635

Current Assets	£		£		£	
Stock	20,000		35,000		36,000	
Debtors	12,000		20,000		25,000	
Cash	1,000		2,000		1,800	
	33,000		57,000		62,800	
Creditors	(7,000)		(13,342)		(15,769)	
Tax	(1,200)		(1,500)		(1,000)	
Overdraft	(17,879)		–		–	
Working Capital		6,921		42,158		46,031
		£11,417		£48,758		£51,666

PROFIT AND LOSS ACCOUNTS

		1979		1980		1981
		£		£		£
Income		171,649		261,789		287,968
Less: Material	31,600		46,697		63,076	
Labour	28,341		36,522		46,075	
Variable						
Overheads	28,378		43,404		51,000	
Fixed Overheads	69,000		70,259		81,500	
Research and						
Development	10,000	167,319	54,468	251,350	36,721	278,372
Profit from trading		4,330		10,439		9,596
Interest		1,500		2,000		2,000
		2,830		8,439		7,596
Tax		430		1,200		1,000
		2,400		7,239		6,596
Dividends		800		800		1,600
		1,600		6,439		4,996
Balance b/f		6,957		8,557		14,996
		£8,557		£14,996		£19,992

APPENDIX 2 Fixed Asset Summary

	Land and Buildings	Plant and Machinery	Total
	£	£	£
Cost of Valuation			
At 1.1.81	1,400	10,195	11,595
Additions	–	1,600	1,600
Disposals	(1,000)	(245)	(1,245)
At 31.12.81	400	11,550	11,950
At Cost	–	11,550	11,550
At Valuation	400	–	400
	400	11,550	11,950
Depreciation			
At 1.1.81	160	4,835	4,995
Charge for year	20	1,702	1,722
Disposal	(160)	(242)	(402)

At 31.12.81	20	6,295	6,315
net Book Value			
At 1.1.81	1,240	5,360	6,600
At 31.12.81	380	5,255	5,635

24. The Good Fortune Printing Company Limited was a member of an Interfirm Comparison scheme. They have recently received the comparative summary for the year ended 31 July 1982 set out below with the company's own ratios compared with the first quartile, median and third quartile results of other members. Note: 'Mgmt' is abbreviation for 'Management'.

No.	Ratio	Your ratios	Quartiles	No.	Ratio	Your ratios	Quartiles
1	Operating Profit / Operating Capital	0.8%	1 / 5 / 9	16	Production Cost (Net) / Cost of Output	57%	42 / 48 / 53
2	Operating Profit / Net Sales	1.0%	0 / 4 / 6	17	Factory Wages / Production Cost (Net)	68%	62 / 65 / 68
3	Value of Output / Net Sales	101%	99 / 100 / 101	18	Factory Mgmt, Salaries / Production Cost (Net)	4%	5 / 7 / 8
4	Production Cost (Gross) / Cost of Output	85%	82 / 85 / 87	19	Depreciation / Production Cost (Net)	3%	8 / 11 / 13
5	Distribution Cost / Cost of Output	2%	1 / 2 / 3	20	Other Factory Expenses / Production Cost (Net)	15%	14 / 18 / 20
6	Selling Cost / Cost of Output	3%	4 / 5 / 6	21	Factory Wages / Factory Employees	£785	680 / 756 / 874
7	Administration Cost / Cost of Output	10%	6 / 8 / 9	22	Male Factory Employees / Factory Employees	76%	58 / 69 / 76
8	Net Sales / Operating Capital	77%	108 / 123 / 155	23	Factory Mgmt. Salaries / Factory Mgmt. Staff	£1,360	1,333 / 1,515 / 1,718
9	Fixed / Operating Capital	60%	52 / 61 / 62	24	Plant / Factory Employees	£1,210	943 / 1,192 / 1,433
10	Plant / Fixed Assets	78%	85 / 93 / 97	25	Sales Staff Salaries / Sales Staff	£2,000	1,466 / 1,959 / 2,366
11	Value Added / Plant	£120	109 / 152 / 196	26	Admin. Expenses / Administration Cost	31%	25 / 34 / 43
12	Materials / Stock	5 times	3 / 4 / 5	27	General Mgmt Salaries / Administration Cost	6%	7 / 13 / 20
13	Debtors / Sales per Day	124 days	55 / 60 / 70	28	Admin. Staff Salaries / Administration Cost	63%	39 / 53 / 60

No.	Ratio	Your ratios		No.	Ratio	Your ratios	
14	Value Added / Factory Employees	£1,460	1,470 / 1,680 / 1,840	29	Administration Cost / Printing Jobs	£5	4 / 6 / 12
15	Value Added / Factory Wages	2 times	1.9 / 2.0 / 2.3	30	General Mgmt. Salaries / General Mgmt. Staff	£5,200	2,245 / 2,967 / 3,988
31	Admin. Staff Salaries / Administrative Staff	£699	616 / 690 / 755	32	Male Admin. Staff / Administrative Staff	61%	31 / 44 / 57

When the Board of Directors discussed the Interfirm Comparative Ratios in the previous year the non–executive director on the Board expressed the view that each member of the Board could compare individual ratios perfectly easily but what they really required was a brief report from the accountant with an explanation of why the Rate of Return on Capital Employed was low, with possible reasons ranked in order of importance.

Required:

a. Draft a report to the Board of Directors of The Good Fortune Printing Company Ltd interpreting the comparative ratios for the year ended 31 July 1982 in a form that will satisfy the non– executive director.

b. Briefly indicate further information you would request in order to satisfy yourself that the data in the comparative survey allowed you to make a valid assessment of the company's results.
(ACCA 2.9 (2) December 1983)

25. B Quick & Co., a firm of Certified Accountants, has recently acquired as a new client Mr Jones, the proprietor of 'The Ice Cream Parlour'. Mr Jones has produced draft accounts for the year ended 31 May 1983 which include a Trading Account as follows:

Trading Account for year ended 31 May 1983

	£
Sales	144,000
Cost of Sales	90,720
Gross Profit	£53,280

He has noticed from reading his trade association journal that the average gross profit is 40% on sales and he requests that an investigation be carried out to explain why his gross profit appears to be lower than the average and also apparently worsening.

An analysis is carried out by B Quick & Co. of the make–up of the Sales for the last two months. This analysis is shown below:

	April £	May £
Ice Creams	3,000	3,900
Coffee–percolated	2,800	3,300
Coffee–prepacked cups	1,700	1,500
Lemonade	1,200	900
Orangeade	2,000	1,800
Blackcurrent cordial	1,100	900
	£11,800	£12,300

A comparison of the purchase invoices with the price list showed the gross profit % on sales to be Coffee–percolated 33%, Coffee– prepacked cups 40%, Lemonade 46%, Orangeade 48%, Blackcurrent Cordial 42%.

The gross profit % on the Ice Creams was calculated as an average based on comparing total monthly cost of Ice Creams with total monthly sales of Ice Creams–the result was 25%.

Required:

a. Draft a letter to Mr Jones with supporting data to explain why the gross profit % appears to be worsening from April to May.

b. Draft a note to the partner quantifying any possible loss and specifying any further work you think should be carried out to confirm the reason why the gross profit percentage of The Ice Cream parlour is lower than the industry average.

(ACCA 2.9(2) June 1983)

26. **Required:**

a. Briefly explain the possible reasons for selecting each of the five variables that have been included in the formula given in Appendix 4.

b. Calculate the Z score for Provincial Motor Spares Ltd using the formula provided.

c. Briefly give your own views, with supporting calculations, of the company's liquidity and suggest what further reports you would advise the company to prepare.

(ACCA 2.9(1) December 1984)

Appendix 1(a) The Trial Balance of Provincial Motor Spares Ltd as at 31 December 1983

	Dr £000's	Cr £000's
Ordinary shares of £1 each		3,600
10% cumulative preference shares of £1 each		1,000
General reserve		1,820
Profit & Loss Account at 1 January 1983		2,250
8% debentures		500
Profit for 1983		3,780
Debenture redemption reserve		290
Creditors		4,130
Tax payable on 1 January 1984		700
Deferred taxation on 1 January 1983		1,655
Investment income (net)		14
Premises	7,200	
Equipment	3,800	
Investments	251	
Stock	6,580	
Debtors	1,480	
Bank	428	
	19,739	19,739

a. Profits accrue evenly throughout the year.

b. Provision is to be made for:

   i. Tax of £1,900,000 on the profits of the current year.

   ii. The preference dividend.

   iii. The proposed ordinary dividend of ten per cent.

c. A transfer of £170,000 is to be made to the General Reserve.

d. Sales for the year totalled £21,000,000 of which £1,000,000 consisted of sales to United Motor Spares Ltd. The sales are stated exclusive of Value Added Tax.

e. The Investment Income has suffered the deduction of Income Tax at the rate of thirty per cent.

Appendix 4
Further information concerning the liquidity of Provincial Motor Spares Ltd

One of the directors had recently read an article on methods of predicting company failure. One of the methods combined five variables and calculated a Z score by multiplying each variable by a discriminant coefficient.

The five variables (labelled X_1, X_2, X_3, X_4, X_5) were as follows:

X_1 = net working capital/total assets

X_2 = retained earnings/total assets

X_3 = earnings before interest and taxes/total assets

X_4 = market value of equity/book value of total debt

X_5 = sales/total assets

The Z score was calculated using the following formula:

$$Z \text{ score} = 0.012X_1 + 0.014X_2 + 0.033X_3 + 0.006X_4 + 0.999X_5$$

The score was interpreted on the basis that all companies with a score less than 1.81 were likely to become bankrupt; all companies with a score greater than 2.99 were unlikely to become bankrupt; companies with scores between 1.81 and 2.99 were likely to consist of companies that may become bankrupt.

The market value of the equity is calculated using a PE ratio of 5:1 applied to Earnings before Tax.

27. A client of Jones & Co., Certified Accountants, has inherited 1,000 shares in Portslade Joinery Ltd and has requested a brief report advising him as to whether to retain or sell the shares.

One of Jones & Co.'s trainee accountants, was instructed to analyse the company's accounts and to draft a report.

The accounts of Portslade Joinery Ltd have been obtained for the years 1980-83 and are summarised below:

	1980 £000s		1981 £000s		1982 £000s		1983 £000s
Sales	506,000		566,720		623,390		673,260
Profit before tax	58,800		68,400		68,470		78,370
After charging:							
Depreciation	41,330		34,800		29,620		25,360
After crediting:							
Gross dividends							
(grossed at 33%)	5,200		10,900		14,500		20,800
Tax	28,860		33,090		32,450		29,740
Profit after tax	29,940		35,310		36,020		48,630
Share Capital (£1 shares)	200,000		200,000		200,000		200,000
Reserves	172,910		174,220		176,240		182,870
	372,910		374,220		376,240		382,870
Represented by:							
Goodwill		18,000		18,000		18,000		18,000
Leasehold Premises	60,000		60,000		60,000		60,000	
Depreciation	30,000	30,000	36,000	24,000	42,000	18,000	48,000	12,000
Plant and Machinery	250,000		250,000		250,000		250,000	
Depreciation	90,000	160,000	118,800	131,200	142,420	107,580	161,780	88,220
Investments		52,000		100,000		140,000		176,740
Total Fixed Assets		260,000		273,200		283,580		294,960
Current Assets							
Stock	109,910		127,780		149,000		166,440
Debtors	83,600		102,540		121,160		142,970
Cash	42,680		26,040		6,500		6,000
	236,190		256,360		276,660		315,410
Current Liabilties							
Creditors	65,780		87,070		118,000		155,800
Tax	29,900		34,270		32,000		29,700
Dividend	27,600		34,000		34,000		42,000
	123,280		155,340		184,000		227,500

Working Capital	112,910	101,020	92,660	87,910
Capital Employed	372,910	374,220	376,240	382,870
Employees No.	17,500	18,750	20,000	21,000
Employees Remuneration £000s	79,000	89,000	98,000	106,000

The trainee accountant prepared the following analysis and comments:

		1980	1981	1982	1983
(1)	*Sales* These are showing a steady growth	506,000	566,720	623,390	673,260
(2)	*Capital Employed* This is showing a slight growth	372,910	374,220	376,240	382,870
(3)	*Profit after tax* This is showing uneven but substantial growth % growth	29,940	35,310 18%	36,020 2%	48,630 35%
(4)	*Return on Capital Employed* Profit after tax to Capital Employed is showing a steady increase	8%	9.4%	9.6%	12.7%
(5)	*Dividends per share* These are growing in line with profit after tax	14p	17p	17p	21p

The analysis shows a company which is well managed and achieving steady growth in sales, capital employed, profit percentage, rate of return and dividends paid to shareholders.

The client should be advised to retain his shares and, if he has surplus funds from his legacy, should possibly consider increasing the number of shares he owns in Portslade Joinery Ltd.

Required:

a. Comment on the analysis and conclusions of the trainee accountant.

b. Prepare notes, with supporting detail, of further matters that you would raise for discussion with the trainee.

(ACCA 2.9(2) June 1984)

28.

Required:

a. Draft a report interpreting the interfirm comparison data available for Hopeful Booksellers Ltd.

b. State the questions you would put to the directors when attempting to establish how the rate of return on capital employed might be improved.

(ACCA 2.9(1) June 1985)

Appendix 5

Interfirm comparison data for the year ended 30 September 1984 for Hopeful Booksellers Ltd

Plural Publishers Ltd has been approached by the directors of Hopeful Booksellers Ltd to initiate discussions for a possible takeover by Plural Publishers Ltd. The directors of Hopeful Booksellers Ltd produced copies of the accounts for the five years 1980-1984 together with copies of the Interfirm Comparison Report comparing their company with a group of similar companies.

The comparative data is set out below:

			1983	1984	Group average
1	Net profit/Operating assets	%	5	5	10
2	Net profit/Sales	%	5	5	3 1/3
3	Sales/Operating assets	No of times	1	1	3
4	Gross profit/Sales	%	40	40	27
5	Total costs/Sales	%	35	35	23 2/3
6	Sales/Current assets	No of times	1.5	1.5	3.5
7	Sales/Fixed assets	No of times	2.5	2.5	15

8	Sales/Other stock	No of times	-	-	5
9	Sales/Retail books stock	No of times	1.5	1.5	4
10	Sales/Debtors	No of times	50	50	20
11	Retail sales/Sales	%	100	100	75
12	Retail gross profit/Retail sales	%	40	40	27
13	Library sales/Sales	%	0	0	2
14	Library gross profit/Sales	%	N/A	N/A	10
15	Agent sales/Sales	%	0	0	5
16	Agent gross profit/Agent sales	%	N/A	N/A	8
17	School sales/Sales	%	0	0	5
18	School gross profit/School sales	%	N/A	N/A	15
19	Other sales/Sales	%	0	0	13
20	Other sales gross profit/Other sales	%	N/A	N/A	12
21	Fixed assets/Area in sq ft	£000s	30	30	4
22	Sales/Area in sq ft	£	79	80	71
23	Labour costs/Sales	%	10	10	15
24	Overheads/Sales	%	25	25	8 2/3
25	Interest/Sales	%	0	0	2
26	Rent & rates/Sales	%	18	18	4
27	Other overheads/Sales	%	7	7	6
28	Power/Sales	%	1	1.5	1
29	Phone/Sales	%	0.7	0.7	0.7
30	Postage/Sales	%	0.03	0.03	0.03
31	Printing/Sales	%	0.3	0.35	0.35
32	Advertising/Sales	%	0.75	0.8	0.75
33	Repairs/Sales	%	0.9	0.6	0.9
34	Travel/Sales	%	1.2	0.7	1.2
35	Depreciation/Sales	%	1.8	1.9	0.75
36	Other expenses/Sales	%	0.32	0.42	0.32
37	Sales/Wages	No of times	11	11	9
38	Sales/Staff	£000	19	19	14
39	Wages/Staff	£000	3.5	3.5	3.1

29. **Required:**

a. Calculate the same ratios for Speedsports Limited from draft accounts for the year ended 31 December 1986 as those prepared for the competitors in Appendix 6.

b. Draft headings with brief comments for the finance director of Watersports Limited to highlight the major points arising from your comparison of the ratios calculated for Speedsports Limited with its three competitors and identify any further information you would seek to obtain.

c. Identify the major problems likely to confront the directors of East Limited and Speedsports Ltd during 1987.

(ACCA 2.9(1) June 1987)

Appendix 5: Draft balance sheet and profit and loss account of Speedsports Limited for the year ended 31 December 1986

Balance sheet as at 31 December 1986

	DM	DM
Fixed assets		
Tangible assets (net book value)		1,950,000
Current assets		
Stock	320,800	
Debtors	224,950	
Cash	17,600	
	563,350	

Creditors (due within one year)		
Trade and other creditors	361,450	
Dividends	70,000	
	431,450	
Net current assets		131,900
Total assets less current liabilities		2,081,900
Creditors (due after one year)		
7% Debentures		450,000
Net assets		1,631,900

Capital and reserves		
Ordinary shares of 1DM each	1,400,000	
Revaluation reserve	170,000	
Profit and loss account	61,900	
		1,631,900
		1,631,900

Profit and Loss Account for the year ended 31 December 1986

	DM	DM
Sales		475,000
Cost of sales		135,500
Gross profit		339,500
Administration expenses	82,900	
Selling expenses	61,600	
		144,500
Trading profit		195,000
Interest paid		4,500
		190,500
Taxation		69,240
		121,260
Dividends proposed		70,000
Retained		51,260
Reserve movement		
Profit brought forward		10,640
Profit retained		51,260
		61,900

Note

i. The revaluation reserve was created on 1 January 1986 and the assets were accepted as being at fair value when Watersports Limited acquired their holding.

ii. The exchange rates for DMs to the £ were:

1 January	3.20
31 December	3.25
Average for 1986	3.22

Appendix 6: Interfirm comparison data on German competitors

Speedsports Limited is one of four specialist wholesalers in Germany. The following statistics have been compiled relating to its three competitors.

Ratio		Competitor North Ltd	Competitor South Ltd	Competitor East Ltd
R(1)	Return on total capital employed (%)	6.00	4.50	5.60
R(2)	Sales: Total capital employed	.18	.15	.19
R(3)	Profit before interest and tax: Sales (%)	33	30	30
R(4)	Sales: Fixed assets	.25	.2	.23
R(5)	Sales: Net working capital	3.9	4.1	4.2
R(6)	Current assets: Current liabilities	1.7:1	2.5:1	1.4:1
R(7)	Current assets – stock: Current liabilities	1 :1	1.5:1	0.75:1
R(8)	Stockturn (times per annum)	2	1.5	1
R(9)	Av. credit period allowed to customers (days)	75	95	90
R(10)	Earnings per share(DM)	.08	.05	.04
R(11)	Loan:Capital and reserves(%)	40	35	25
R(12)	Interest payable: Trading Profit (%)	5%	4%	2%

Sales in DM for each company for the year ended:

	North Ltd	South Ltd	East Ltd	Speedsports Ltd
31 December 1985	600,000	400,000	100,000	500,000
31 December 1986	550,000	400,000	150,000	475,000

Enquiries have established that the ratios have been prepared after adjusting the competitors figures to apply the same accounting policies as are employed in Speedsports Ltd. A comparison of each firm's catalogues showed no evidence that there were material differences in the selling prices.

Mr Johnson, the managing director of Watersports Limited, has been discussing the comparative statistics with the financial director and asked that a report be drafted to highlight the major points that are disclosed from the comparison and to identify the the major problems likely to confront each company during 1987.

AAT EXAMINATION QUESTIONS

30. You are presented with the following information for three quite separate and independent companies:

Summarized balance sheets at 31 March 19–7

	Chan plc £'000	Ling plc £'000	Wong plc £'000
Total assets *less* current liabilities	600	600	700
Creditors: amounts falling due after more than one year 10% Debenture stock	–	–	(100)
	£600	£600	£600
Capital and reserves: Called up share capital			
Ordinary shares of £1 each	500	300	200
10% Cumulative preference shares of £1 each	–	200	300
Profit and loss account	100	100	100
	£600	£600	£600

Additional Information:

1. The operating profit before interest and tax for the year to 31 March 19–8 earned by each of the three companies was £300,000.

2. The EFFECTIVE rate of corporation tax for all three companies for the year to 31 March 19–8 is 30%. This rate is to be used in calculating each company's tax payable on ordinary profit.

3. An ordinary dividend of 20p for the year to 31 March 19–8 is proposed by all three companies, and any preference dividends are to be provided for.

4. The market prices per ordinary share at 31 March 19–8 were as follows:

	£
Chan plc	8.40
Ling plc	9.50
Wong plc	10.38

5. There were no changes in the share capital structure or in long-term loans of any of the companies during the year to 31 March 19–8.

Required:

  a. Insofar as the information permits, prepare the profit and loss account for each of the three companies (in columnar format) for the year to 31 March 19–8 (formal notes to the accounts are NOT required);

  b. calculate the following accounting ratios for each company;

    i. earnings per share;

    ii. price earnings;

    iii. gearing [taken as total borrowings (preference share capital and long term loans) to ordinary shareholders' funds];

    and

  c. using the gearing ratios calculated in answering part b) of the question, briefly examine the importance of gearing if you were thinking of investing in some ordinary shares in one of the three companies assuming that the profits of the three companies were fluctuating.

(AAT)

31. Aled is in business as a sole trader. You are presented with the following summarised information relating to his business for the year to 31 October 19–8:

Trading, profit and loss account for the year to 31 October 19–8

	£'000	£'000
Sales: cash	200	
: credit	600	800
Less: cost of goods sold –		
Opening stock	80	
Purchases	530	
	610	
Less: closing stock	70	540
Gross profit		260
Expenses		205
Net profit for the year		£55

Balance sheet at 31 October 19–8

	£'000	£'000
Fixed assets		
Plant and machinery at cost	1,000	
Less: accumulated depreciation	450	550
Current assets		
Stocks	70	
Trade debtors	120	
Cash	5	
	195	
Less: Current liabilities		
Trade creditors	130	65
		£615
Capital		
As at 1 November 19–7		410
Net profit for the year	55	
Less: drawings	50	5
		415
Loan		200
		£615

Required:

a. Based on the above information, calculate EIGHT recognised accounting ratios; and

b. list what additional information you would need in order to undertake a detailed ratio analysis exercise of Aled's business for the year to 31 October 19–8.

Note that in answering part a) of the question, each ratio must be distinct and separate. Marks will NOT be awarded for alternative forms of the same ratio.

(AAT)

32. You are presented with the following information relating to Messiter public limited company:

Year to 31 December	19–4	19–5
	£'m	£'m
Profit and loss accounts:		
Turnover, all on credit terms	1,300	1,400
Cost of sales	650	770
Gross profit	650	630
Profit before taxation	115	130
Balance sheets at 31 December:		
Fixed assets at cost	850	850
Less: Accumulated depreciation	510	595
Net book value	340	255
Stock at cost	105	135
Trade debtors	142	190

Required:

a. Using the historic cost accounts and stating the formulas you use, calculate the following accounting ratios for both 19–4 and 19–5:

    i. Gross profit percentage;

    ii. Net profit percentage;

    iii. Stock turnover, stated in days;

    iv. Trade debtor collection period, stated in days;
        and

    v. Fixed Asset turnover.

b. Using the following additional information:

    i. Restate the turnover for 19–4 and 19–5 incorporating the following average retail price indices:

Year to 31/12/19–4	85
Year to 31/12/19–5	111

    ii. Calculate the additional depreciation charge required to finance the replacement of fixed assets at their replacement cost. The company's depreciation policy is to provide 10% per annum on original cost, assuming no residual value.

        The replacement cost of fixed assets at 31 December were as follows:

	£millions
19–4	1,140
19–5	1,200

    iii. Based upon these two inflation adjustments, why may it be misleading to compare a company's results for one year with that of another without adjusting for changes in general (R.P.I.) or specific inflation?

(AAT)

2 Cash Flow and Funds Flow Analysis

GENERAL BACKGROUND

1.0 In analysing the performance of a business it is a useful exercise to compare its financial structure at two different dates and to relate the structural changes to the profit or loss made in the intervening period.

1.1 The results of such a comparison are set out in a classified format on a statement of source and application of funds.

1.2 It is now obligatory, under SSAP 10 for all enterprises having a turnover or gross income in excess of £25,000 per annum, to produce an audited statement of source and application of funds as part of their final published accounts. This standard therefore applies equally to companies, partnerships, non-profit making organisations etc. In common, however, with other standards which do not have exclusive application to companies, SSAP 10 tends nevertheless to be examined only in a company context.

1.3 It is useful, also to analyse the flow of cash to and from a business because many businesses have failed through lack of cash even when earning a substantial profit. Cash flow statements, which are not required either by Statute or by an SSAP, are considered in 5.0 onwards.

FUNDS FLOW ANALYSIS

NATURE

2.0 Business enterprises depend upon an adequate supply of financial resources (funds) in order (initially) to acquire, and then to maintain, an appropriate level of physical resources which they use to generate profit.

2.1 Non-technical users of accounting information often find it puzzling that a business which is making a substantial profit may nevertheless be short of cash. The reason is that profit need not necessarily be matched by an increase in cash. During any accounting period

$$\text{Profit} = \text{Revenues minus Expenses}$$

but closing Cash balance = Opening Cash balance plus Receipts minus Payments.

2.2 In order to discover where the funds have come from (sources) and how they have been utilised (applications), we employ funds flow analysis. The analysis may take one of several forms. This section of the manual is however concerned only with the type of analysis required by SSAP 10 and explained in 3.0 onwards.

2.3 The funds of a business may be supplied by

	the owners	eg capital; loans
and/or	external parties	eg Trade creditors (ie suppliers on credit);
		loan creditors
and/or	the business itself	eg. internally generated profit

and may be used, for example,

	to acquire fixed assets
and/or	to redeem long term liabilities
and/or	to pay dividends
and/or	to increase working capital.

2.4 Statements of source and application of funds are effectively classified lists of changes both in the sources of supply of funds and in the uses to which these same funds are applied.

2.5 From such a list an insight can be gained into the strengths and weaknesses of the financial position of the enterprise concerned. In particular, these statements can be used in conjunction with ratio analysis to understand and interpret the performance of an enterprise.

CONSTRUCTION

3.0 Excluded from this sub-section is the preparation of statements of source and application of funds for groups of companies; that aspect is covered in Section 2 Chapter 1.

3.1 As has been stated in 1.2, these statements are obligatory for all enterprises above a £25,000 turnover/gross income threshold. At professional level, examiners tend to set questions involving companies; thus the examples, and questions which follow, concern only limited companies but it must be remembered that a question may occasionally be set involving a different sort of business enterprise.

518

3.2 Statements of source and application of funds are constructed from balance sheets at the beginning and end of a financial period and from the profit and loss account for the period, to disclose movements in capital, liabilities and assets.

3.3 It follows from what has been stated in 2.3 that sources of funds can consist of:

> liability increases   eg an injection of capital in cash;
> > an increase in trade creditors etc.

> and   asset decreases   eg proceeds of sale of assets;
> > a decrease in trade debtors
> > (following settlement of sums due
> > from them) etc.

and that application of funds can consist of

> asset increases   eg purchase of assets;
> > an increase in debtors etc

> and   liability decreases   eg a decrease in creditors (following
> > payment of sums due to them);
> > redemption of debentures for cash etc.

3.4 The first stage in the construction of a statement of source and application of funds is the isolation and quantification of the individual sources and applications of funds using the profit and loss account and balance sheets mentioned in 3.2

EXAMPLE

3.5 The balance sheets of Fabis Ltd for the years ended 31st December 19–1 and 19–2 were summarised thus:

	19–2	19–1
	£	£
Ordinary shares of £1.00 per share	60,000	50,000
Reserves		
Profit and Loss	5,000	4,000
Current liabilities		
Creditors	4,000	2,500
Taxation	1,500	1,000
Proposed dividends	2,000	1,000
	72,500	58,500
Fixed Assets (at w.d.v.)		
Premises	10,000	10,000
Fixtures	17,000	11,000
Vehicles	12,500	8,000
Current Assets		
Stock	17,000	14,000
Debtors	8,000	6,000
Bank and Cash	8,000	9,500
	72,500	58,500

and the profit and loss account for the year 19–2 disclosed

	£
Profit before tax	4,500
Taxation	(1,500)
Profit after tax	3,000
Proposed dividends	(2,000)
Retained profit	1,000

Required:
Prepare a Funds Flow Statement for Fabis Ltd for year ended 31 December 19–2.

SOLUTION

3.6 The differences between the two years' balance sheet figures are then analysed into sources of funds and applications of funds, using the principles set out in 3.3.

	19–2 £	19–1 £	Sources Liability increases Asset decreases £	Applications Liability decreases Asset increases £
Ordinary Shares	60,000	50,000	10,000	
Profit and Loss	5,000	4,000	1,000	
Creditors	4,000	2,500	1,500	
Taxation	1,500	1,000	500	
Proposed dividends	2,000	1,000	1,000	
	72,500	58,500		
Premises	10,000	10,000		–
Fixtures	17,000	11,000		6,000
Vehicles	12,500	8,000		4,500
Stock	17,000	14,000		3,000
Debtors	8,000	6,000		2,000
Bank/Cash	8,000	9,500	1,500	
	72,500	58,500		
			15,500	15,500

It follows that, as the assets and liabilities figures in each balance sheet agree, so the differences between those two sets of figures (as represented by sources and applications) must also agree. In fact these differences total £15,500 for each column.

3.7 As they stand, some of the source and application figures in 3.6 are not yet usable because they represent the net effect of certain transactions. Netting off must be avoided because it masks the true position by understating the gross source and gross application figures. The second stage in construction is building up gross figures from net figures.

3.8 Taxation, for example, is shown as a source of £500. However, the taxation provision at the end of 19–0 is a source of £1,500 (inasmuch as it is a component of the profit before tax figure of £4,500) whilst the provision at the end of 19–1 is an application of £1,000 when paid during 19–2.

3.9 Similar considerations apply to proposed dividends. Instead of a (net) source of £1,000, the true position (for the same reasons as in 3.8) is a source of £2,000 and an application of £1,000.

3.10 The fixed assets present a more complicated situation because the figures quoted are at written down values. This further information is available:

	Fixtures £	Vehicles £
Depreciation for year	1,000	2,500
Disposals at written down value	–	1,000
Proceeds on disposal		1,700
Profit on disposal		700

3.11 Using this information in conjunction with the figures in 3.5 it is possible to derive the fixed asset acquisitions (applications), thus:

	Fixtures £	Vehicles £
W.D.V. at 31/12/19–2	17,000	12,500
Add back		
Depreciation for year	1,000	2,500
Disposals	–	1,000
	18,000	16,000
Less W.D.V. at 31/12/19–1	11,000	8,000
Acquisitions during 19–2	7,000	8,000

3.12 The figures in 3.10 and 3.11 are reconcilable with the (net) applications figures disclosed in 3.6 in the following manner:

	Fixtures £	Vehicles £
Applications		
Acquisitions during 19–2 (3.11)	7,000	8,000
Sources		
Depreciation during 19–2 (3.10)	(1,000)	(2,500)
Disposals during 19–2 (3.10)	–	(1,000)
Net applications per (3.6)	6,000	4,500

3.13 Strictly speaking, an increase in a provision, in this case the provision for depreciation, is not a source of funds, as it gives rise merely to internal accounting entries unaccompanied by an inflow of funds. Depreciation is simply the write off over time of the cost of assets. The movement of funds occurred at the time the assets were acquired and constituted an outflow, that is, an application, of funds in that period.

3.14 Depreciation charged in a period is simply a quasi source of funds, in that, in arriving at the figures of funds generated from operations, the increase in provision for depreciation, which has reduced the net profit figure from what it would otherwise have been, is added back as a non–cash expense.

3.15 Reverting to the figures in 3.6 (as modified in 3.8 and 3.9) it is now possible to build up a figure of funds generated by operations.

	Sources £
Profit and loss (3.6)	1,000
Taxation (3.8)	1,500
Proposed dividends (3.9)	2,000
Net Profit before tax (3.5)	4,500
Add/(deduct) non–cash items included	
Depreciation (3.12)	3,500
Profit on disposal of vehicles (3.10)	(700)
Total funds generated from operations	7,300

The profit on disposal (£700) was included in the net profit before tax figure (£4,500) but does not represent a cash inflow and so is taken out in arriving at total funds (inflow) generated. The inflow represented by the sale proceeds (£1,700, including the profit of £700) is a non– operational inflow which is dealt with separately, as noted in 4.2 and 4.6 as funds from other sources.

3.16 On the basis of the figures in 3.6 used in conjunction with those in 3.8, 3.9, 3.11 and 3.15, it is now possible to construct a funds flow statement, thus:–

Fabis Ltd
Funds Flow Statement
for year ended 31 December 19–2

	£	£
During the year, the company		
Generated funds	7,300	
Issued shares for cash	10,000	
Sold fixed assets	1,700	
Increased creditors	1,500	
thus producing funds of		20,500
which were utilised to		
Pay tax	1,000	
Pay dividends	1,000	
Purchase fixed assets	15,000	
Increase stock	3,000	
Increase debtors	2,000	
		22,000
This left a deficit of		(1,500)
which was financed by a reduction		
in cash balances.		

It should be noticed that the items sub–totalling to £20,500 are sources, whilst those sub–totalling to £22,000 are applications.

The shares issued for cash are a source of funds. This would not have been the case if they had been issued as bonus shares. A bonus issue is made out of reserves and involves an internal accounting transfer, not an inflow of funds. (The inflow occurred when the profits, out of which the reserves have been created, were earned).

3.17 The statement illustrated in 3.16 does not follow the groupings and layout suggested by SSAP 10. This is the next matter to be considered.

DISCLOSURE AND FORMAT

DISCLOSURE

4.0 Explanatory notes to SSAP 10 state that the objective of a statement of source and application of funds is to show the manner in which the operations of a company have been financed and in which its financial resources have been used.

4.1 Funds generated or absorbed by business operations should be distinguished clearly as also should long–term and short–term items. The manner in which any resulting surplus of liquid assets has been applied (or any deficiency has been financed) should also be made obvious.

4.2 In particular, the following items should be shown separately (where material):–

> dividends paid
> acquisitions of non–current assets
> disposals of non–current assets
> funds raised by increasing medium or long term loans or issued share capital.
> funds expended in repaying or redeeming long term loans or issued share capital
> increase or decrease in working capital, subdivided into its components, and movements in
> net liquid funds.

(N.B. This latter item, net liquid funds, is defined in the standard as comprising cash at bank and in hand, marketable securities (held as current assets) less overdrafts and other borrowings repayable within one year of the accounting date).

4.3 Netting–off of items is to be avoided, wherever possible, as has already been noted in 3.7. Thus the issue and redemption of shares should be shown as separate items and not as a single netted item.

4.4 Wherever possible the figures in the statement of source and application of funds should be identifiable with figures in the profit and loss account, balance sheet and their related notes.

FORMAT

4.5 An appendix to SSAP 10 gives an example of a possible format for producing such a statement for a company without subsidiaries. The proforma, which is by way of illustration only and is not mandatory, is in the following form except that it also includes columns for comparative (previous period) figures to inserted.

4.6 (Proforma)

**Statement of Source and Application of Funds
for year ended.......**

	This period		
	£	£	£
Source of funds			
Profit before tax		x	
Adjustments for items not involving movements of funds			
Depreciation	x		
Other	x		
		x	
Total generated from operations			x
Funds from other sources			
Issue of shares for cash		x	
Other		x	
			x
			x
Application of funds			
Dividends paid		x	
Tax paid		x	
Purchase of fixed assets		x	
Other		x	
			x
Increase/(decrease) in working capital			x
Increase/(decrease) in stock		x	
debtors		x	
(Increase)/decrease in creditors		x	
Movement in net liquid funds			
Increase/(decrease) in cash balances		x	
			x

4.7 The statement for Fabis Ltd in 3.16 can now be rewritten, substituting figures at the appropriate point of the proforma in 4.6:

**Fabis Ltd
Statement of source and application of funds
for year ended 31 December 19–2**

	£	£	£
Source of funds			
Profit before tax		4,500	
Adjustments for items not involving movement of funds			
Depreciation	3,500		
Profit on disposal of assets	(700)		
		2,800	
Total generated from operations			7,300
Funds from other sources			
Issue of shares for cash		10,000	
Sale of fixed assets		1,700	
			11,700
			19,000

Application of funds

Dividends paid	1,000	
Tax paid	1,000	
Purchase of fixed assets	15,000	
		17,000
Increase/(decrease) in working capital		2,000
Increase/(decrease) in stock	3,000	
debtors	2,000	
(Increase)/decease in creditors	(1,500)	
Movement in net liquid funds		
Increase/(decrease) in cash balances	(1,500)	
		2,000

CASH FLOW ANALYSIS

NATURE

5.0 Cash flow statements are somewhat similar to funds flow statements. The essential difference between them is that whereas funds flow reports are a mixture of both cash and accruals based figures, the cash flow statement attempts to report only cash movements.

5.1 The sources from which cash is obtained – share issues, loans, internally generated profit – and the uses for which it is applied – fixed asset acquisitions, dividend and taxation payments – are identical with funds flow reports. The resultant difference between these sources and applications of cash represents the net increase or decrease during the period.

CONSTRUCTION

6.0 There is no statutory or standard obligation upon any business to prepare a cash flow statement at all. Those which do so use them for internal report purposes only. For these reasons there is no universally accepted format, but it is generally aggred that it is desirable to distinguish cash inflows outflows associated with financing (share issues, borrowings), finance servicing (interest, dividends), government (taxation), investment (fixed asset acquisitions/disposals), and operations.

6.1 The starting point for the construction of a cash flow statement is a funds flow statement, if one exists. In its absence, a balance sheet for the start and end of the period, together with a profit and loss account for the period, are used.

6.2 Differences are derived between the balance sheet figures at the two points in time as in 3.6. These raw figures are then modified along the same lines as 3.7 to 3.15. These results can then be marshalled into a statement similar to that in 3.16.

EXAMPLE

6.3 The facts are the same as in 3.5 and 3.10

    Required:

Prepare a cash flow statement for Fabis Ltd for year ended 31 December 19–2.

SOLUTION

6.4 The basic workings are exactly the same as in 3.7 to 3.15 and are not repreated here, but the manner in which they are used is different in that movements in stock, debtors, creditors, accruals and prepayments are assumed, in the absence of information to the contrary, to affect only funds generated from operations, thus:

Fabis Ltd
Cash Flow Statement
for year ended 31 December 19–2

	£	£
During the year, the company		
Generated cash [7.300 + 1,500 – 3,000 – 2,000]	3,800	
Issued shares for cash	10,000	
Sold fixed assets	1,700	
thus producing cash of		15,500
which was utilised to		

Purchase fixed assets	15,000	
Pay tax	1,000	
Pay dividends	1,000	
		17,000

This resulted in a deficit of	(1,500)

DISCLOSURE AND FORMAT

6.5 The solution given in 6.4 is arithmetically correct but, like its funds flow counterpart in 3.16, is insufficiently informative. It could be re–arranged to embrace the desirable attributes noted in 6.0.

6.6 The cash flow statement for Fabis Ltd. in 6.4 can now be rewritten:

Fabis Ltd
Cash Flow Statement
for year ended 31 December 19–2

	£	£
Cash inflows/(outflows)		
Financing:		
Issue of shares for cash	10,000	
		10,000
Investment:		
Sale of fixed assets	1,700	
Purchases of fixed assets	(15,000)	
		(13,300)
Finance servicing		
Dividends	(1,000)	
		(1,000)
Government		
Taxation	(1,000)	
		(1,000)
Operations		
Cash generated from operations	3,800	
		3,800
Net cash inflow/(outflow)		(1,500)

6.7 The example and its solution based on a very simple set of circumstances, but other complications can be catered for within the basic framework.

6.8 If, for example, the fixed assets had been sold on credit and the amount was still outstanding, the item sale of fixed assets would not appear under Investment. Cash generated from operations would then become £5,500[7,300 + 1,500 − 3,000 − (2,000 − 1,700)]. If £1,000 of the fixed assets had been bought on credit and the amount had not been settled, the item Purchase of fixed assets would appear under Investments as £14,000 and Cash generated from operations would be disclosed as £2,800[7,300 + (1,500 − 1,000) − 3,000 − 2,000].

OTHER MATTERS

6.9 One of the shortcomings of cash flow statements is that they ignore the timing of cash flows. The overall position for a period may be that a satisfactory net inflow has resulted. This may, however, mask the fact that at intervening points during the periodic cycle there has been a massive outflow causing the business to go into overdraft.

6.10 Recording such a situation after the event is of little value. It is far more useful for a business to be aware of the likelihood of its occurrence before it actually arises so that measures can be put into effect to avoid (or to cater for) it.

6.11 A specialised form of cash flow statement operates prospectively, that is, a statement is drawn up for (say) one year ahead on a month by month basis. In critical cases the interval may be weekly instead of monthly. This statement is known as a Cash Forecast or Cash Budget and forms part of the Master Forecast or Master Budget system.

6.12 Budgeting generally is outside the scope of Paper 2.9 and is not further developed in this manual.

STUDENT SELF TESTING

Test exercises

1. A friend of yours who owns a newsagent's business has asked for your help. He is very worried because he suspects that a shop assistant is stealing money from his till. He comments as follows.

"For the year to 31st March 19–5 my shop made a profit of £8,600 and yet I have had to ask the bank for an overdraft", and then adds "Will you check the figures for me please?". You agree to help and he supplies the following information.

Nick's Newsmart
Balance Sheets as at 31st March

	19–4			19–5	
	£	£	**Fixed Assets**	£	£
	16,000		Premises at cost	16,000	
	3,600		Less Depreciation	3,900	
		12,400			12,100
	3,000		Fixtures and Fittings at cost	8,200	
	1,000		Less Depreciation	1,300	
		2,000			6,900
		14,400			19,000
			Current Assets		
	5,400		Stocks –magazines, periodicals etc.	8,060	
	1,480		–sweets, tobacco etc.	3,240	
	2,200		Debtors – trade	4,900	
	140		–other	420	
	6,400		Bank	–	
	280		Cash	500	
	15,900			17,120	
			Less		
			Current Liabilities		
	4,200		Creditors – trade	3,600	
	100		–other	120	
	–		Bank overdraft	4,000	
	4,300			7,720	
		11,600	**Working Capital**		9,400
		26,000	**Net Assets Employed**		28,400
	24,600		Opening Capital	26,000	
	6,800		Add Net Profit	8,600	
	31,400			34,600	
	5,400		Less Drawings	6,200	
		26,000	Closing Capital		28,400

You confirm that he has not disposed of any fixed assets during the year.

Required:

Prepare a Statement of Source and Application of Funds (Funds Flow Statement), to show Nick where his profit has gone, in any format other than that illustrated in SSAP 10.

2. The facts are the same as in 1.

Required: Prepare the Statement of Source and Application of Funds (Funds Flow Statement) in the format illustrated in SSAP 10.

3. The balance sheets of Grimston Ltd, for internal circulation at 31 March 19–5 and 1986, disclosed

Grimston Ltd
Balance Sheets as at 31 March

	19–5				19–6	
Cost £	Depn £	Net £		Cost £	Depn. £	Net £
			Fixed Assets			
46,000	18,000	28,000	Land and buildings	62,000	20,000	42,000
87,000	39,000	48,000	Plant and equipment (see note(1))	103,000	51,000	52,000
133,000	57,000	76,000		165,000	71,000	94,000
			Current assets			
			Stocks			
	42,400		– raw materials etc.		37,000	
	29,800		– work-in-progress		18,400	
	21,700		– finished goods		36,700	
	34,100		Debtors and prepayments		29,600	
	800		Cash in hand		1,200	
	5,300		Bank balance		7,500	
	134,100				130,400	
			Current liabilities			
67,200			Creditors and accruals	55,200		
11,400			Corporation tax	13,300		
5,000			Dividends proposed	6,000		
83,600				74,500		
		50,500	**Working capital**			55,900
		126,500	**Net assets employed**			149,900
			Financed by:			
		100,000	Ordinary share capital (see note (2))			120,000
		6,500	Profit and loss account			4,900
		10,000	General Reserve			5,000
		116,500	Shareholders' funds			129,900
		10,000	9% Debentures			20,000
		126,500				149,900

Notes:

1. Plant originally costing £21,000 and on which £15,000 had been provided as depreciation, was sold for £7,500 during the year.

2. During the year, Grimston Ltd. made a 1 for 20 bonus issue of ordinary shares from general reserve followed by an issue of 15,000 ordinary shares of £1.00 per share for cash at par.

Required:

Prepare a statement of source and application of funds for Grimston Ltd. for year ended 31 March 19–6, in any format other than that illustrated in SSAP 10.

4. The facts are the same as in 3.
   Required:
   Prepare a statement of source and application of funds in the format illustrated in SSAP 10.

5. From the following information you are required to prepare a source and application of funds statement for the year ended 31st March 19–9, complying with Statement of Standard Accounting Practice (SSAP) No 10. Advance corporation tax is to be ignored.

| | Trial balances as at: | |
	1st April 19–8 £	31st March 19–9 £
Credits		
6% Debentures 20-7	30,000	20,000
Ordinary shares of £0.25 each	20,000	45,000
Share premium	–	15,000
Sales	–	107,006
Creditors	7,520	9,050
Reserves and retained profit	35,963	18,963
Corporation tax due 1st January 19–9	4,200	–
Bad debt provision	9	11
Depreciation provision:		
Freehold buildings	4,023	5,164
Machinery and vehicles	9,671	10,732
Profit on redemption of debentures	–	1,700
Profit on sale of machinery	–	95
Proposed final dividend	1,567	–
Provision for maintenance of properties	325	268
Bank overdraft	85	–
	113,363	232,989
Debits		
Stock	8,853	10,625
Cost of sales	–	95,042
Debtors	9,577	12,024
Trade loans to customers	3,750	4,950
Fixed assets at cost:		
Freehold land	13,200	16,200
Freehold buildings	56,075	58,760
Machinery and vehicles	18,422	20,652
Investment at cost	3,486	4,024
Interim dividends	–	1,383
Balance at bank	–	9,329
	113,363	232,989

During the year:

  i. There was a bonus issue of shares of one for one to the ordinary shareholders, followed by a rights issue of one share for every eight shares held at a price of £1 per share.

  ii. The freehold land was revalued from £13,200 to £16,200, the increase in valuation being transferred to reserves.

  iii. Machinery costing £2,700 and with a book value of £600 was sold at a profit of £95.

  iv. Part of the debentures were redeemed at a profit of £1,700.

  v. £100 was spent on the maintenance of properties.

6. B Limited is a company engaged in brewing and the wholesale and retail selling of beers, wines, spirits and tobacco. From the information given below you are required to prepare a source and application

of funds statement for the year ended 30th September 19–8 in accordance with the requirements of Statement of Standard Accounting Practice No. 10. Advance corporation tax (ACT) is to be ignored.

Profit and Loss Account, year ended 30th September

	19–8		19–7	
	£000	£000	£000	£000
Sales		852		695
Costs		758		626
Trading Profit		94		69
Corporation tax	42		18	
Deferred tax	4		14	
		46		32
Profit after tax before extraordinary item		48		37
Extraordinary item, less tax		14		–
Profit after extraordinary item		34		37
Dividends: interim paid	5		4	
final proposed	7		6	
		12		10
Profit retained		22		27

Balance Sheets as at 30th September

	19–8		19–7	
	£000	£000	£000	£000
Ordinary share capital £0.25 each		123		120
Share premium		19		15
Reserves		279		154
8% Convertible loan stock		95		102
6% Debentures		90		176
Deferred taxation		50		46
Corporation tax		73		51
Property maintenance provision		18		20
		747		684
Fixed assets		717		704
Investments		8		7
Trade loans		39		38
Assets held by debenture trustees		14		12
Stocks	88		56	
Debtors	95		61	
	183		117	
Less: Creditors	(198)		(176)	
Proposed dividends	(7)		(6)	
Bank overdraft	(9)		(12)	
		(31)		(77)
		747		684

Movements on Fixed Assets

	Land and property	Machinery and vehicles
	£000	£000
1st October 19–7, at cost or valuation	680	156
Additions during year, at cost	108	22
	788	178

Disposals	<u>115</u>	<u>54</u>
	673	124
Revaluation during year	23	–
30th September 19–8, at cost or valuation	<u>696</u>	<u>124</u>
1st October 19–7, depreciation to date	37	95
Disposals	<u>–</u>	<u>48</u>
	37	47
Charge for year	8	11
30th September 19–8, depreciation to date	<u>45</u>	<u>58</u>

Investments on Reserves

	Debenture reserve fund £000	Other reserves £000
1st October 19–7 balance	28	126
Profit on redemption of debentures	33	–
Transfer under debenture trust deed	20	(20)
Revaluation of properties		23
Write down of investments		(2)
Retained profits		22
Profit on sale of vehicles		4
Profit on sale of land		45
	<u>81</u>	<u>198</u>

	Assets held by Debenture Trustees 19–8 £000	19–7 £000
At bank	9	5
Loan to local authorities	5	7
	<u>14</u>	<u>12</u>

These are held by the trustees pending substitution of other properties in place of properties released from charge.

8% Convertible loan stock

During the year the holders of £7,000 nominal value of convertible loan stock exercised their option to convert into ordinary shares. The terms of conversion were three ordinary shares for every £1.75 nominal value of convertible loan stock.

7. From the following information you are to prepare a source and application of funds statement for the year, complying with Statement of Standard Accounting Practice (SSAP) No. 10.
   All workings should be shown.

Summary Cash Account

	£000		£000
Opening balance, at 1st January	276	Payments: Trade creditor	3,875
Receipts:		VAT	326
Trade debtors	8,342	Final dividend	156
Sales of fixed assets	220	Interim dividend	104
Rent	98	ACT	140
Rights issue	1,500	Corporation tax	380
		Wages and salaries, net	2,760
Closing balance, at 31st December	42	Wages and salaries, deductions	922

	Bank interest	15
	Loan stock repaid	1,800
10,478		10,478

Transactions:	£000
Sales excluding VAT	8,600
VAT on sales	688
Purchases on credit:	
Raw materials for stock	2,400
Other expenditure charged to overhead	1,200
Fixed assets	500
Major repairs to fixed assets	100
VAT on purchases	336
Direct wages charged to work-in-progress	1,358
Wages, salaries and deductions charged to overhead	2,472
Opening stock of raw materials	230
Opening stock of work-in-progress	421
Prime cost of sales	3,738
Bad debts written off	14
Provision for corporation tax on year's profit	416
Decrease in bad debt provision	8
Items cancelled by contra, between bought and sales ledgers	36
Fixed assets sold:	
Original cost	900
Depreciation provision	740
Direct materials issued to production	2,350
Discount received	80
Discount allowed	120
Provision for major repairs to fixed assets	133
Depreciation charge for the year	224

Further information:

1. The rights issue consisted of a one for four offer of ordinary shares, nominal value £0.25, at a price of £1.50 per share. The issued ordinary share capital before the rights issue was 4,000,000 shares.

2. For the purpose of this question the work–in–progress stocks are valued at prime cost, all other expenses are written off against the current year sales.

3. During the year £800,000 of convertible loan stock was converted into 400,000 ordinary shares.

4. Proposed final dividend is £169,000.
   Advanced corporation tax may be assumed at 35%

8. The latest balance sheet of Telrad (UK) Ltd prepared for internal use is as shown below.

Balance Sheet as at 30 June 19–4

Fixed Assets	Cost £	Depreciation £	£
Premises	15,000	6,000	9,000
Tools and equipment	10,000	5,450	4,550
Vehicles	8,000	6,800	1,200
	33,000	18,250	14,750

Current Assets	£	£
Stocks		4,109
Debtors and prepayments		3,381
Bank balance		1,208
Cash		83
		8,781

Less: Current Liabilities

Creditors and accruals	3,534	
Corporation tax	2,257	
Proposed dividends	200	
	5,991	

Working Capital — 2,790

Net assets employed — £17,540

Financed by:
Issued share capital

Ordinary shares of £0.50 per share	4,000	
6% preference shares of £1.00 per share	3,000	
		7,000

Reserves

General reserve	5,000	
Profit and loss	2,540	
		7,540
		14,540

Loan Capital

8% Debentures		3,000
		£17,540

The directors are in process of making certain forecasts for the year ended 30 June 19–5 and have been considering the following statement from the chief accountant.

Forecast Statement of Source and Application of Funds
for year ended 30 June 19–5

	£	£
Profit before tax		33,470
Adjustments for items not involving movement of funds:		
depreciation	6,750	
loss on disposal of equipment	360	
profit on disposal of vehicles	(780)	
		6,330
Total funds generated from operations		39,800
Funds from other sources		
Issue of ordinary shares for cash	2,000	
Issue of 8% debentures	5,000	
Proceeds of sale of fixed assets:		
equipment	1,440	
vehicles	1,980	
		10,420
		50,220

Application of funds
Cost of acquisition of

premises	30,000	
equipment	6,000	
vehicles	11,000	
Tax paid *(see Note 5)*	2,205	
Dividends paid (see Note 6)	540	
		49,745

Increase/(decrease) in working capital		475
Increase/(decrease) in stocks	1,167	
in debtors/prepayments	273	
(Increase)/decrease in creditors and accuals	(551)	
Movement in net liquid funds		
Increase/(decrease) in bank balance	(448)	
in cash	34	
		475

Additional information:

The above statement has been prepared on the following assumptions:

(1) Fixed assets will be sold as follows during the year.

	Original cost	Aggregate depreciation
	£	£
Tools and equipment	4,000	2,200
Vehicles	8,000	6,800

(2) Fixed assets will be acquired as follows:

	Cost
	£
Premises (at end of year)	30,000
Tools and equipment (during year)	6,000
Vehicles (during year)	11,000

(3) The charge for depreciation comprises:

	£
Premises	1,500
Tools and equipment	3,050
Vehicles	2,200
	£6,750

(4) Additional ordinary shares will be issued at the end of the year, but will not rank for dividend until 19–6, as follows:

	£
Bonus issue (3 for 4)	3,000
For cash	2,000
	£5,000

The bonus issue will be appropriated from the credit balance on general reserve after a further £1,000 has been transferred to that account from profit and loss account.

(5) Tax paid is corporation tax after adjustment of an overprovision of £52 in 19–4. Corporation tax liability at 30 June 19–5 is forecast at £819.

(6) Dividends paid comprise:

	£
Ordinary share final dividend proposed at 30 June 19–4	
but since paid during current year	200
6% preference share dividend paid	180

Ordinary share interim dividend paid (4%)	160
	£540

An ordinary share final dividend of 6% will be proposed at 30 June 19–5 on those ordinary shares in issue excluding the new share issues (*see Note 4* above).

(7) The additional 8% debentures will be issued on 1 January 19–5.

The directors now require a forecast profit and loss account for the period and a forecast balance sheet at 30 June 19–5.

Required:

a. Comment briefly on the apparent plans of Telrad (UK) Ltd. for the year ended 30 June 19–5, as far as they can be deduced from the forecast Statement of Source and Application of Funds.

b. Prepare, from the information and data given, a forecast profit and loss account for the year ended 30 June 19–5 in the following format:

	£	£
Profit before items listed below		
Add: Profit on disposal of vehicles		
	___	
Less: Loss on disposal of equipment		
Depreciation		
Debenture interest		
	___	
Profit before tax		33,470
Less: Corporation tax		___
Profits after tax		
Less:		
Transfer to general reserve		
Dividends–paid:		
6% preference		
ordinary interim (4%)		
– proposed		
ordinary final (6%)		
	___	___
Retained profits for		
current year		
previous year b/f		
c/f		£ ___

c. Prepare a forecast balance sheet as at 30 June 19–5 in the same format as that given for 30 June 19–4.

All workings must be shown

(ACCA)

9. You are required to prepare for B Limited a source and application of funds statement for 19–9, complying with Statement of Standard Accounting Practice No.10 from the information given schedule B issued with this paper.

SCHEDULE B:

Information relating to B Limited

Year	19–6	19–7	19–8	19–9
	£000	£000	£000	£000
Sales	75,000	82,000	90,000	95,000
Depreciation	4,800	4,800	4,800	8,500

Rent of premises	3,000	3,000	3,000	–
Hire of plant	–	2,500	2,500	2,500
Research and development	–	60	100	170
Interest on loan stock	2,000	2,000	2,000	–
Premium on repayment of loan stock stock	–	–	–	3,000
Profit on sale of plant	–	–	–	(2,400)
Other costs	55,200	57,640	63,600	67,830
Total	65,000	70,000	76,000	79,600
Profit before tax	10,000	12,000	14,000	15,400
Taxation	5,000	6,500	7,000	7,500
Profit after tax	5,000	5,500	7,000	7,900
Dividends	3,500	3,500	3,500	4,500
Retained earnings	1,500	2,000	3,500	3,400
Ordinary share capital	40,000	40,000	40,000	55,000
Share premium	5,000	5,000	5,000	15,000
Reserves	2,200	4,200	7,700	6,100
10% unsecured loan stock	20,000	20,000	20,000	–
	67,200	69,200	72,700	76,100
Assets Employed:				
Leasehold premises at cost	–	–	–	25,000
Depreciation	–	–	–	(2,500)
Plant and machinery at cost	48,000	48,000	48,000	60,000
Depreciation	(9,600)	(14,400)	(19,200)	(18,800)
Total fixed assets	38,400	33,600	28,800	63,700
Research and development	–	240	340	520
Current assets:				
Stock	15,600	18,200	20,000	22,000
Debtors	13,200	15,700	18,100	20,000
Cash in hand	16,000	22,060	26,960	–
Total	44,800	55,960	65,060	42,000
Current liabilities:				
Trade creditors	10,000	12,000	14,000	20,000
Current tax	4,000	6,600	5,500	5,800
Proposed dividends	2,000	2,000	2,000	2,500
Bank overdraft	–	–	–	1,820
Total	16,000	20,600	21,500	30,120
Net current assets	28,800	35,360	43,560	11,880
Net assets employed	67,200	69,200	72,700	76,100

23

You are advised that:

i. During 19–9 and prior to the rights issue, the company made a bonus issue of one new share for every eight shares already held.

ii. At the beginning of 19–9, plant and machinery which had originally cost £16,000 and had a book value of £9,600 was sold and replaced with more modern equipment.

10. The Balance Sheet of Excelsior Ltd as at 31 March 19–8 (with comparative figures as at 31 March 19–7) together with other pertinent information, are given below:

Balance sheets as at	31 March 19–8		31 March 19–7	
	£000	£000	£000	£000
Share Capital – Ordinary Shares of £1 each fully paid		1,200		1,000
Reserves –				
Share Premium		550		600
Retained Profits		3,725		3,500
		5,475		5,100
Debentures–8% £1 Convertible		2,000		–
Current Liabilities				
Bank overdraft	1,750		1,500	
Creditors	1,450		1,550	
Taxation	820		1,150	
		4,020		4,200
		11,495		9,300
	£000	£000	£000	£000
Fixed Assets				
Land and Buildings at cost		3,500		1,800
Plant and Machinery at cost	6,100		5,800	
Less depreciation	3,900		3,850	
		2,200		1,950
		5,700		3,750
Current Assets				
Stock and Work in Progress	3,435		3,150	
Debtors	2,200		1,900	
Cash and Bank Balance	160		500	
		5,795		5,550
		11,495		9,300

Notes:

1. The profit for the year 19–8 after charging all expenses including the loss on the sale of the plant, but before depreciation and taxation, was £1,715,000. The Corporation tax of £820,000 charged in the profit and loss account on the profits for the year was reduced by the over– provision for Corporation tax on the 19–7 profit, ie by £150,000. The Ordinary Dividend paid during the year and charged against the profit after tax, was £180,000.

2. During the year, Plant and machinery which had cost £1,200,000 and in respect of which depreciation of £590,000 had been provided, was sold for £565,000. There had been a rights issue of ordinary shares at the rate of 1 for 10 at a price of £1.50 per share payable in full on 1 April 19–7. Subsequently, a scrip (bonus) issue of 1 for 11 had been made utilising Share Premium Account. The convertible debentures had been issued at par on 1 April 19–7, payable in full. The conversion terms exercisable on 31 March 19–1 are 1 ordinary share for every 4 £1 Debentures. £1 million agreed Corporation tax on the 19–7 profits had been paid on the due date.

You are required to:

a. Prepare a Source and Application of Funds Statement for the year ended 31 March 19–8 bearing in mind the recommendations of SSAP 10.

b. Tabulate briefly SEVEN points of comment on the prepared statement.

c. Calculate i. Basic, and ii. Diluted Earnings per Share for the year ended 31 March 19–8.

Your workings should be submitted
(ACCA)

ACCA EXAMINATION QUESTIONS

11. Required:

a. Prepare a Source and Application Statement at 31 December 1981 using Historic Cost data in accordance with the Statement of Standard Accounting Practice on Statements of source and application of funds. (Ignore comparative figures.)

b. Discuss the uses and limitations of the statement which you have prepared to the users of the Accounts.

(ACCA 2.9(1) June 1982)

APPENDIX 1. *Draft Balance Sheets and Profit & Loss Accounts for years ended 31 December 1979, 1980, 1981*

BALANCE SHEETS

		1979		1980		1981
		£		£		£
Share Capital		2,860		13,500		13,500
Profit & Loss						
Account		8,557		14,996		19,992
Loan Capital		–		20,262		18,174
		11,417		48,758		51,666

	1979 £		1980 £		1981 £
Capital Employed					
Fixed Assets					
Land and					
Buildings			1,240		380
Plant and					
Machinery			5,360		5,255
Net Fixed Assets		4,496	6,600		5,635

Current Assets	£		£		£	
Stock	20,000		35,000		36,000	
Debtors	12,000		20,000		25,000	
Cash	1,000		2,000		1,800	
	33,000		57,000		62,800	
Creditors	(7,000)		(13,342)		(15,769)	
Tax	(1,200)		(1,500)		(1,000)	
Overdraft	(17,879)		–		–	
Working capital		6,921	42,158		46,031	
		£11,417	£48,758		£51,666	

PROFIT & LOSS ACCOUNTS

	1979 £		1980 £		1981 £	
Income		171,649		261,789		287,968
less: Material	31,600		46,697		63,076	
Labour	28,341		36,522		46,075	
Variable						
Overheads	28,378		43,404		51,000	
Fixed Overheads	69,000		70,259		81,500	
Research and						
Development	10,000	167,319	54,468	251,350	36,721	278,372

Profit from trading	4,330	10,439	9,596
Interest	1,500	2,000	2,000
	2,830	8,439	7,596
Tax	430	1,200	1,000
	2,400	7,239	6,596
Dividends	800	800	1,600
	1,600	6,439	4,996
Balance b/f	6,957	8,557	14,996
	£8,557	£14,996	£19,992

APPENDIX 2 *Fixed Asset Summary*

	Land and Buildings £	Plant and Machinery £	Total £
Cost or Valuation			
At 1.1.81	1,400	10,195	11,595
Additions	–	1,600	1,600
Disposals	(1,000)	(245)	(1,245)
At 31.12.81	400	11,550	11,950
At Cost	–	11,550	11,550
At Valuation	400	–	400
	400	11,550	11,950
Depreciation			
At 1.1.81	160	4,835	4,995
Charge for year	20	1,702	1,722
Disposal	(160)	(242)	(402)
At 31.12.81	20	6,295	6,315
Net Book Value			
At 1.1.81	1,240	5,360	6,600
At 31.12.81	380	5,255	5,635

APPENDIX 3 *Land and Buildings Schedule*

	Freehold North Street 3(a) £	Leasehold East Street 3(b) £	Total £
Cost or Valuation			
At 1.1.81			
Buildings	800	200	1,000
Land	200	200	400
	1,000	400	1,400
Disposals	(1,000)	–	(1,000)
At 31.12.81	–	400	400

Depreciation

At 1.1.81	150	10	160
Charge	10	10	20
Disposal	(160)	–	(160)
At 31.12.81	–	20	20

3 (a) North Street

This was a freehold office shown in the books at cost less depreciation at 2% per annum.

The company had acquired a leasehold office in East Street in 1980 and the staff and records were transferred to East Street in the early part of 1981.

The North Street premises were sold on 15 August 1981 for £1,100 which represented £900 for the building and £200 for the land.

3 (b) East Street

The lease was acquired on this property on 1.1.80. The company required funds for expansion and it was decided to sell the freehold premises in North Street. The lease was for a period of 40 years and was valued at £400 on 1.1.80 (buildings £200, land £200). The directors estimate that the buildings are worth £270 on 31.12.81.

APPENDIX 4 *Plant and Machinery Schedule*

4 (a) Plant and Machinery at 31.12.81

Year of Purchase	Cost at 1.1.81 £	Disposal in 1981 £		Additions in 1981 £	Cost at 31.12.81 £	Dep'n at 1.1.81 £	Charge for 1981 £	Dep'n on Dis'l £	Dep'n at 31.12.81 £
1976	7,195	245	(4b)	–	6,950	4,385	1,000	230	5,155
1980	3,000	–		–	3,000	450	450	–	900
1981	–	–		1,600	1,600	–	240	–	240
	£10,195	£245		£1,600	£11,550	£4,835	£1,690	£230	£6,295

4 (b) Plant Disposed of in 1981

There was a depreciation charge (not included in the Plant and Machinery Table above) of 15% for the four months from 1 January to 30 April 1981 on the plant purchased in 1976 for £245 and scrapped at nil value on 30.4.81. Use end of year index for current cost adjustment on disposal.

APPENDIX 5 *Index Numbers* (average for year unless indicated otherwise)

Year	Retail Price Index	Plant and Machinery Index	Stock
1976	112	110	
1980	158	150	
1981	200	160	193
31.12.80	162	155	189
31.12.81	210	165	199

Average Acquisition date for 1981 opening stock and Monetary Working Capital	188
Average Acquisition date for 1981 closing stock and MWCA	198

12. The accountant of the Gorgon Company Ltd prepared a forecast profit and loss account for the six months ended 31 March 1985 together with a forecast balance sheet as at 31 March 1985.

The forecast profit and loss account and balance sheet are set out below together with the achieved comparative figures for the two half year periods to 31 March 1984 and 30 September 1984:

	Half year to 31 March 1985		Half year to 31 March 1984		Half year to 30 Sept 1984	
	£	£	£	£	£	£
Sales		79,000		60,000		99,500
Cost of sales		48,000		30,000		45,000
Gross profit		31,000		30,000		54,500
Less:						
Establishment expenses	4,000		3,500		3,700	
Administration expenses	5,000		4,500		10,900	
Selling & Distribution expenses	5,000		4,000		21,000	
Depreciation expenses	3,000	17,000	2,000	14,000	5,900	41,500
Net profit before tax		14,000		16,000		13,000
Tax	2,000		3,000		1,000	
Deferred tax	5,000	7,000	2,000	5,000	–	1,000
Net profit after tax		7,000		11,000		12,000
Dividends						
Ordinary shares	10,000			7,500	–	
Preference shares	3,000	13,000		–	–	–
		(6,000)		3,500		12,000
Balance brought forward		37,000		21,500		25,000
Balance carried forward		31,000		25,000		37,000

Balance sheets as at:

	31 March 1985		31 March 1984		30 Sept 1984	
	£	£	£	£	£	£
Share Capital						
Ordinary shares of £1 each		150,000		100,000		100,000
Share premium		18,000		–		–
10% Preference shares		30,000		–		–
General reserve		31,000		25,000		37,000
Revaluation reserve		10,000		–		10,000
Deferred tax		13,000		8,000		8,000
10% Debentures		75,000		–		55,000
Unsecured loan		–		50,000		–
		327,000		183,000		210,000

Represented by:

Fixed Assets

Freehold premises	98,000		70,000		80,000	
Fixtures	92,000		45,000		95,000	
Vehicles	21,000	211,000	15,000	130,000	14,000	189,000

Current assets

Stock	42,000		41,000		20,000	
Debtors	32,000		21,000		24,000	
Bank	81,000		16,500		–	
	155,000		78,500		44,000	

Current liabilities

Creditors	20,500	12,000	21,000
Accrued expenses	2,500	3,000	–
Dividend payable	13,000	7,500	–
Tax due	3,000	3,000	1,000
Overdraft	–	–	1,000
	39,000	25,500	23,000
Working capital	116,000	53,000	21,000
	327,000	183,000	210,000

Further information:

a. There were two sales of fixtures

   i. On 30 April 1984 items with a book value of £8,000 were sold for £6,000.

   ii. On 31 August 1984 items with a book value of £3,000 were sold for £4,500.

b. On 28 February 1984 a company vehicle was damaged in an accident. The vehicle, which had a book value of £6,000, was sold for £1,000 on 31 March 1984. The company's insurance company made a payment of £2,000 to the company on 30 April 1984 in full settlement of their claim.

c. The unsecured loan of £50,000 was redeemed under the terms of the loan agreement on 31 August 1984 at a premium of ten per cent satisfied by the issue of £35,000 10% debentures at par and the balance in cash.

d. The stock was written down by £15,000 on 31 August 1984 following a detailed review by the company's auditors.

e. The company had entered into an agreement to acquire the assets of a small business in the same industry. The assets acquired at fair values were: Freehold premises £18,000. Fixtures £2,000; Stock £6,000. The purchase consideration was satisfied by the issue of 20,000 £1 ordinary shares on 31 October 1984.

Required:

a. Prepare a Forecast Source and Application Statement for the year to 31 March 1985.

b. Prepare a Cash Flow Statement in columnar form to show cash movements for the year to 31 March 1985.

Note: Ignore Advance Corporation Tax.

(ACCA 2.9 (2) December 1984)

13. **Required:**

Prepare a Statement of Source and Application of Funds for the Plural Publishers Group for the year ended 30 September 1983 in accordance with the principles set out in the relevant Statement of Standard Accounting Practice.

(ACCA 2.9(1) June 1985)

Appendix 1

Notes on the group structure

Plural Publishers Ltd was incorporated on 1 October 1972 to publish computer magazines. In 1979 it acquired a 40% interest in Computer Software Texts Ltd, a company which specialised in publishing self instruction texts on computer programming.

On 1 April 1983 Plural Publishers Ltd acquired a majority holding in Video Hire Ltd by purchasing 80% of the issued share capital. The purchase consideration was £625,000. The purchase consideration was settled in full by the payment by Plural Publishers Ltd of £250,000 in cash and the issue of 250,000 £1 ordinary shares.

At the date of acquisition Video Hire Ltd had net assets of £575,000.

Video Hire Ltd had a financial year ended on 30 September. The draft profit and loss account of Video Hire Ltd for the year ended 30 September 1984 disclosed a loss of £300,000. Enquiries indicated that profits and losses accrued evenly throughout the year.

Appendix 2

Plural Publishers Group
Draft Consolidated Profit and Loss Account for the year ended 30 September 1983

	£000s	£000s
Operating profit		3,300
(after charging depreciation of £700,000)		
Share of profits in Computer Software Texts Ltd		400
		3,700
Less Taxation		
Plural Publishers Ltd & Video Hire Ltd	1,800	
Computer Software Texts Ltd	150	
		1,950
		1,750
Extraordinary items less tax		45
		1,705
Minority interest		30
		1,735
Less Dividends		
Interim paid	450	
Final proposed	800	
		1,250
		485
Retained profit held in:		
Plural Publishers Ltd	555	
Video Hire Ltd	(120)	
Computer Software Texts Ltd	50	
		485

Appendix 3
Draft Consolidated Balance Sheets for the Plural Publishing Group as at 20 September 1982 and 1983

1982 £000's		1983 £000's
	Capital and Reserves	
3,450	Share capital	3,700
2,375	Share premium	2,500
7,615	Retained earnings	8,100
	Minority interest	85
13,440		14,385
	Fixed assets	
–	Intangible asset	165
5,685	Tangible assets (Note 1)	6,400
490	Investment in Computer Software Texts Ltd	540

	Current assets	
7,305	Stocks	8,135
4,150	Debtors	3,600
390	ACT Recoverable	470
1,200	Cash	1,015
	Creditors (due within 1 year)	
2,010	Creditors	2,150
1,700	Taxation	1,640
745	Proposed dividends	800
	Creditors (due after more than 1 year)	
515	Debentures	500
810	Deferred Taxation Account	850
$\overline{13,440}$		$\overline{14,385}$

Note 1: Fixed assets with a book value of £75,000 were sold for £100,000 during the year.

AAT EXAMINATION QUESTION

14. You are presented with the following summarised information relating to Clinic plc:

Profit and loss account for the year to 30 June 19–8

	£'000
Net profit for the year before taxation	900
Taxation (see Note 1)	(651)
Profit for the year after taxation	249
Extraordinary item (after tax relief of £35,000)	(90)
Profit for the year after taxation and extraordinary item	159
Dividends paid and proposed	(119)
Retained profit for the year	£40

543

Balance sheet at 30 June 19–8

	19–7 £'000	19–8 £'000
Fixed assets (see Note 2)	1,515	1,810
Investments	40	40
Current assets		
Stocks	175	200
Debtors	100	60
Cash at bank and in hand	20	–
	295	260
Creditors: amounts falling due within one year		
Bank loans and overdrafts	–	(30)
Trade creditors	(130)	(100)
Other creditors including taxation and social security (see Note 3)	(500)	(619)
	(630)	(749)
Creditors: amounts falling due after more than one year		
Debenture loans	(200)	(50)
Provisions for liabilities and charges		
Taxation, including deferred taxation (see Note 4)	(120)	(211)
	£900	£1,100
Capital and reserves		
Called up share capital	750	910
Profit and loss account	150	190
	£900	£1,100

NOTES

1. The taxation charge in the profit and loss account includes the following items:

	£'000
Corporation tax based on the profit for the year	542
Overprovision of last year's corporation tax	(15)
Tax credit on franked investment income	24
Transfer to deferred taxation account	100
	£651

2. During the year to 30 June 19–8, Clinic sold an asset originally costing £150,000 for £5,000 in cash. The depreciation on this asset was £135,000. The total depreciation charged in the profit and loss account for the year to 30 June 19–8 was £384,000.

3. Other creditors including taxation and social security includes the following items:

	19–7 £'000	19–8 £'000
Corporation tax	400	489
Proposed dividend	70	91
Advance corporation tax on the proposed dividend	30	39
	£500	£619

4. The deferred taxation balances include the following items:

	19–7 £'000	19–8 £'000
Opening balance	100	120
Transfer from the profit and loss account	50	100
ACT paid offset against corporation tax	–	30
Advance corporation tax on the proposed dividend	(30)	(39)
	£120	£211

5. The basic rate of income tax is assumed to be 30%.

   Required:

   Insofar as the information permits, prepare Clinic plc's statement of source and application of funds for the year to 30 June 19–8 in accordance with Statement of Standard Accounting Practice 10 (Statements of source and application of funds).

   (AAT)

Section V

The Accounts of Groups of Companies

Chapter

1   Final accounts

2   Acquisitions and mergers

1 Final Accounts

GENERAL BACKGROUND

1.0 There are various ways by which one company can gain control over other companies.

1.1 One method is for the company to acquire the assets (or net assets) of the companies concerned thereby securing control by ownership of such assets. Such an arrangement is termed an amalgamation or an absorption, according to circumstances, and is dealt with in Section 1 Chapter 6 of this manual.

1.2 Another method is for one company to gain control of other companies by acquiring a majority holding of the voting shares of these companies. Majority holding effectively means more than 50% of the voting rights, but in order to secure the passing of special resolutions, a holding in excess of 75% is needed. The rights acquisition manoeuvres usually result in a seat on the Board of Directors of the "acquired" companies for a nominee director (or directors) of the acquiring company. Unlike the situation in 1.1. (above) all the companies which are party to these transactions retain their individual and separate identities. A majority holding constitutes what is termed a controlling interest. The Companies Act 1989 extended this to include control contracts and control provisions included in a Memorandum of Association or Articles of Association and to other undertakings, defined as unincorporated associations, including partnerships.

HOLDING AND SUBSIDIARY UNDERTAKINGS

1.3 The company acquiring the control is referred to as the parent or holding undertaking; those over whom control has been acquired in this manner are subsidiary undertakings.

1.4 Subsidiary undertakings can themselves acquire subsidiaries. In relation to the holding company, these latter are termed sub-subsidiaries.

1.5 Collectively, a holding company together with its subsidiaries and subsubsidiaries, is labelled a group.

REGULATORY FRAMEWORK OF GROUP FINANCIAL ACCOUNTS AND STATEMENTS

2.0 The form and content of financial accounts and financial statements published by a group and its individual constituent undertakings is governed by various constraints.

LEGAL CONSTRAINTS

2.1 The manner in which group accounts are to be drawn up and the items to be disclosed and the way in which they are to be disclosed, were originally laid down principally by the Companies Act of 1948, as extended or modified by the Companies Acts of 1967, 1976, 1980 and 1981. A summary of the main requirements which have now been consolidated into the Companies Act 1985 and modified by the Companies Act 1989 appears as Appendix 1 of this manual.

STANDARD ACCOUNTING PRACTICE (SSAP) CONSTRAINTS.

2.2 In addition to the legal requirements, certain Statements of Accounting Practice (SSAPs) affect the preparation of group financial statements. These are SSAP 1 (Accounting for associated companies) and SSAP 14 (Group Accounts). Both SSAPs are summarised in 6.0 to 6.8 and 3.3. to 3.9 respectively.

2.3 All other SSAPs apply generally to companies whether part of a group or not but several are of special relevance in that they contain sections which concern groups specifically. Included in this category are SSAP 3 (Earnings per share) SSAP 16 (Current Cost Accounting), SSAP 20 (Foreign Currency Translation) and SSAP 22 (Accounting for Goodwill).

STOCK EXCHANGE CONSTRAINTS.

2.4 At various times the Council of the Stock Exchange has prescribed a number of requirements for companies whose securities are included on the official list. These requirements embrace routine matters, such as preliminary profits announcements and the annual report and accounts, and non-routine matters such as prospectus and offer for sale particulars.

OTHER CONSTRAINTS

2.5 As a Member State of the European Economic Community (the EEC), the United Kingdom is bound to incorporate into its legislation the Directives of the Council of the EEC which are promulgated from time to time.

The EEC therefore represents an indirect constraint on the presentation of company accounts (including group accounts).

The EEC's Fourth Directive on disclosure in the final accounts of limited companies has now been incorporated into the (UK) Companies Act 1985.

The EEC's Seventh Directive on Consolidated Accounts has been incorporated into UK legislation in the Companies Act 1989.

PREPARATION AND PRESENTATION OF GROUP FINANCIAL ACCOUNTS AND STATEMENTS

3.0 This section of the manual deals with the form and content of:

a. Group balance sheets in 4.0 and following.

b. group profit and loss accounts in 5.0 and following.

c. treatment in group accounts of associated undertakings in 6.0 and following.

d. group statements of source and application of funds in 7.0 and following.

e. the presentation of group accounts for publication in 8.0 and following.

3.1 Under SSAP 16 the parent company of a group was required to produce current cost group accounts but not for itself where historical based accounts are the main accounts.

3.2 Technically, it is possible to produce the final accounts of a group of undertakings in various ways. In the UK, however, the Companies Act 1985 specifies that group accounts shall take the form of consolidated financial statements as a general rule. It is considered that, by consolidating (that is aggregating) the financial results of the holding and subsidiary undertakings into statements as of a single entity, a truer and fairer view of the profit or loss and of the state of affairs of the group is thereby attained. Exceptions from consolidation requirements are dealt with in Appendix I (Summary of legal requirements of Companies Act 1985) and in 3.3 to 3.9 below.

SSAP 14 – GROUP ACCOUNTS

3.3 This standard applies to all financial statements produced with the intention of giving a true and fair view of financial position and profit or loss. Within its scope, therefore, are covered balance sheets, profit and loss accounts, statements of source and application of funds, notes and other statements.

3.4 Group accounts should be prepared in the form of a single set of consolidated statements compiled on an item by item basis. Adjustments should be made for intra group balances and transactions and for intra group unrealised profit.

3.5 Consolidated financial statements should be prepared using uniform accounting policies. Where possible, adjustments should be made to achieve this objective; failing that, the policies and their effect should be disclosed.

3.6 All undertakings within a group should prepare financial statements to the same date as the holding company. If this is impracticable, suitable adjustments should be made for abnormal transactions which have occurred between the various accounting year ends.

3.7 Subsidiary undertakings should be excluded from consolidation on the grounds of dissimilarity of activities or lack of effective control by the holding company or the temporary nature of the control. Different accounting treatments apply according to the reason for this exclusion. Special disclosure requirements applying to subsidiaries so excluded are contained in paragraph 23 to 27 of the standard.

3.8 Where there is a substantial change in the composition of the group as the result of acquisition or disposal of subsidiary undertakings, group accounts should contain sufficient information to enable shareholders to assess the effect on consolidated results; in addition, details of each main subsidiary should be scheduled in the annual accounts of the group.

3.9 Interests of outside or minority shareholders (see 4.17) should be separately disclosed in the balance sheet, but not as part of group shareholders' funds. In the profit and loss account, outside and minority interests are disclosed after the group profit after tax line but before extraordinary items; these latter are then disclosed net of minority interests.

GROUP BALANCE SHEETS

4.0 In considering the preparation of consolidated accounts it is easier to follow the principles involved if the starting point is taken as the preparation of the group balance sheet at date of acquisition. For the purposes of the examples and questions in this section, unless specifically stated otherwise, the balance sheet presentation is, for simplicity, in a form suitable only for internal circulation. The presentation of group balance shsets for publication is dealt with in 8.0 and following.

4.1 When one company acquires a controlling interest in another company, that fact will be reflected in the balance sheet of the acquiring company. It does not, however, affect the balance sheet of the company whose

whose shares have been acquired; the reason for this is that a company's balance sheet does not reflect changes of ownership of its shares - this circumstance is recorded in the (statutory) Register or Shareholders.

FULL HOLDING ACQUIRED

EXAMPLE

4.2 The balance sheets of H PLC and S PLC, at the date on which the former company acquired the whole of the share capital of the latter, were summarised thus, before the acquisition of the controlling interest was effected.

H PLC
Balance Sheet as at 31.12.19-7

	£000		£000
Ordinary shares of £1	600	Fixed assets	500
Reserves	130	Current assets	300
Shareholders' funds	730		
Current liabilities	70		
	800		800

S PLC
Balance Sheet as at 31.12.19-8

	£000		£000
Ordinary shares of £1	150	Fixed assets	180
Reserves	50	Current assets	60
Shareholders' funds	200		
Current liabilities	40		
	240		240

Required:

Show the effect on the balance sheet of H PLC if the consideration for the shares of S PLC comprised:

a. a cash payment on the open market of £210,000; or alternatively,

b. an issue of 200,000 Ordinary shares in H of £1.00 per share at a premium of £0.05 per share.

SOLUTION
4.3
   a.

H PLC
Balance Sheet as at 1.1.19-8

	£000		£000
Ordinary shares of £1	600	Fixed assets	500
Reserves	130		
Shareholders' funds	730	Investment in subsidary company	
Current liabilities	70	(150,000 shares of £1 per share, at cost)	210
		Current assets	90
		(300 - 210 (cash consideration for shares))	
	800		800

The only change from the original position is a switch of £210,000 from one asset heading to another. As regards S, that company does not receive the £210,000 paid by H for the shares. That sum is received by the shareholders of S who have sold their shares to H on the open market.

H PLC
Balance Sheet as at 1.1.19-8

	£000		£000
Ordinary shares of £1	800	Fixed assets	500
(600 + 200)			
Reserves	140	Investment in	
(130 + 10 (share premium))		subsidiary company	
	—	(150,000 shares of £1 per	
		share, at cost)	210
Shareholders' funds	940		
Current liabilities	70	Current assets	300
	1,010		1,010

The changes from the original position comprise an increase in share capital and reserves, with a corresponding increase in assets in the form of Investment in subsidiary company.

Neither circumstance a. nor circumstance b. would result in any changes in the balance sheet of the subsidiary company, S PLC (see 4.1).

4.4 Preparation of a group balance sheet from the individual balance sheets of the members of a group involves, basically, the aggregation of figures for individual assets and liabilities into total figures.

4.5 This is not invariably the case, however, and each exception will be considered separately as it arises. As circumstances become more complex, so the exceptions become more numerous.

4.6 The first exception is that the item Investment in subsidiary company/companies which appears in the holding company's balance sheet is not included as such, in the group balance sheet. The reason for this apparent anomaly is that the individual assets and liabilities represented by this figure, are aggregated to a group figure and to include this figure as well would result in a "double count".

4.7 The amount of the item Investment in subsidiary company/companies, being the cost to the holding company of acquiring the controlling interest, need not, and in fact rarely does, coincide with the book value of the net assets over which control has been gained.

4.8 The second exception, therefore, is that an excess of cost of investment over net book value of the assets to which it relates is shown in the group balance sheet as Goodwill on acquisition of subsidiary company/companies or, as Cost of Control of subsidiary company/companies. The reverse situation, the excess of net book value of the assets over the cost of investment, is shown in the group balance sheet as Capital Reserve on acquisition of subsidiary company/companies. Fair values are used in substitution for book values, if different.

4.9 The reason that this constitutes an exception is that it results in a group asset (Goodwill/Cost of control) or a group liability (Capital Reserve) which does not exist in the balance sheet of any individual member company of the group. It is unusual in the sense that it is a group asset (or liability) which does not have an existence separate from the group. The standard treatment of accounting for goodwill is the subject of SSAP 22, dealt with in this chapter in 9.0 to 9.8.

4.10 Another exception is that the shareholders' funds of the subsidiary company/companies, that is, the share capital and reserves, are not aggregated with those of the holding company in arriving at group share capital and reserves.

4.11 This third exception arises to avoid a further double count and is associated with the circumstances noted in 4.6. The item, Investment in subsidiary company/companies, is the cost incurred by the holding company in acquiring the controlling interest in the subsidiary company/companies. From a group viewpoint the acquisition is an internal transaction both aspects of which, the shareholders' funds on the one hand and the cost of acquiring control over them on the other, must be eliminated to avoid artificially inflating group assets and liabilities.

4.12 Preparation of the group balance sheet can then proceed, taking the above matters into account.

CONSOLIDATION AT DATE OF ACQUISITION

EXAMPLE

4.13 Taking the facts as stated in 4.2 assume that the consideration was paid in cash to the existing shareholders for the sale of their shares on the open market.

Required: Prepare the group balance sheet immediately after the acquisition had taken place on 1st January 19-8.

SOLUTION

4.14 It is not usual for a group balance sheet to be prepared at that point in time specified, but the justification for it here is that in so doing, certain other complications are avoided at this stage of study.

H Group
Consolidated Balance Sheet as at 1.1.19-8

	£000		£000
Ordinary shares of £1	600	Fixed assets (500 + 180)	680
Reserves	130	Goodwill on acquisition of	
Shareholders' funds	730	subsidiary (see note)	10
Current liabilities	110	Current assets(90 + 60)	150
(70 + 40)			
	840		840

Notes:

1. H has gained 100% control of S whose net assets at the material date were:

	£000
Fixed assets	180
Current assets	60
Current liabilities	(40)
Net assets	200

Alternatively,. this could be viewed as

	£000
Ownership of ordinary share capital	150
Attributable reserves	50
Shareholders' funds	200

The purchase consideration was £210,000, which is £10,000 greater than the book value of the net assets/shareholders' funds. This £10,000, therefore, constitutes goodwill on acquisition. The term cost of control may also be used as an alternative description.

2. The items "Investment in subsidiary company, £210,000" in the balance sheet of H PLC and "Shareholders' funds, £200,000" in the balance sheet of S have now disappeared for the reasons advanced in 4.6 and 4.10 respectively.

PARTIAL HOLDING ACQUIRED

4.15 In order to acquire a controlling interest in a subsidiary undertaking, a holding company is not obliged to secure a full (100%) holding (see 1.2). Where a holding company has acquired a less than full holding, the subsidiary undertaking is described as partly (or partially) owned.

4.16 The question then arises as to how this circumstance should be reflected in the group balance sheet. Technically, if a holding company acquired an 80% holding, the group balance sheet could be prepared by consolidating the assets and liabilities of the holding company with 80% of those of the subsidiary. The resultant figures, though arithmetically correct, would be absurd and would not accord with the true and fair view principle.

4.17 With relative ease this difficulty can be overcome by consolidating the assets and liabilities of the subsidiary as though it were wholly owned but at the same time introducing an extra item on to the liabilities side of the balance sheet. This item is labelled Minority Interest and represents the share capital owned by the shareholders outside the group (who must of necessity be in the minority) together with attributable undistributed reserves.

CONSOLIDATION AT DATE OF ACQUISITION.

EXAMPLE.

4.18 H PLC acquired 120,000 Ordinary shares of (£1.00 per share) in S PLC on the open market at a cost of £172,000.

Individual balance sheets of the two companies produced immediately after the acquisition had taken place on 1st January 19-8 were.

H PLC
Balance Sheet as at 1.1.19-8

	£000		£
Ordinary shares of £1	600	Fixed assets	500
Reserves	130	Investment in subsidiary	
Shareholders' funds	730	company	172
Current liabilities	70	(120,000 shares of £1 per share, at cost)	
		Current assets	128
	800		800

S PLC
Balance Sheet as at 1.1.19-8

	£000		£000
Ordinary shares of £1	150	Fixed assets	180
Reserves	50	Current assets	60
Shareholders' funds	200		
Current liabilities	40		
	240		240

Required:

Prepare the group balance sheet immediately after the acquisition had taken place on 1st January 19-8.

SOLUTION

4.19 As has been noted in 4.14 the preparation of the balance sheet for the group at date of constitution is a useful but artificially contrived device for illustrating basic principles.

H Group
Consolidated Balance Sheet as at 1.1.19-8

	£000		£
Ordinary shares of £1	600	Fixed assets	680
Reserves	130	(500 + 180)	
Shareholders' funds	730	Goodwill on acquisition	12
Minority interests	40	(see notes 1. and 3.)	
(see note 2.)		Current assets	188
Current liabilities	110	(128 + 60)	
(70 + 40)			
	880		880

Notes: £000 £000

1. Cost of investment 172

Net value of assets at acquisition date (as represented by shareholders' funds over which control has been gained) 200

Proportion acquired $\frac{120,000}{150,000} \times 200$ (160)

Goodwill on acquisition 12

2. Net value of assets at acquisition date (as above) 200

Proportion retained by outside shareholders 40

$\frac{30,000}{150,000} \times 200$

and shown as Minority interests

3. The figure derived for goodwill in 1. (£12,000) is not an absolute figure of the value of goodwill but simply the amount applicable to H's 80% holding. A greater or lesser holding would have produced a different figure.

CONSOLIDATION SUBSEQUENT TO DATE OF ACQUISITION

4.20 Once a group has been constituted, consolidated accounts must be prepared, as occasion demands, throughout the life of the group.

4.21 In the group balance sheet the reserves figure comprises the reserves of the holding company plus the post-acquisition reserves of the subsidiaries and the minority interests figure consists of the share capital and reserves attributable to the "outside" shareholders. The goodwill/capital reserve on acquisition figure, however, remains unaltered; events subsequent to the acquisition of subsidiaries have no effect on the premium/discount, represented by the goodwill/capital reserve figure, originally expended by the holding company in order to secure a controlling interest. However, goodwill is written off, either at once or gradually (see SSAP 22 in 9.4).

EXAMPLE.

4.22 The summarised balance sheets of H PLC and S PLC at 31st December 19-8 were:

	H PLC	S PLC
	£000	£000
Fixed assets	794	190
Investment in S PLC (60,000 shares)	126	–
Net current assets	250	30
	1,170	220
Financed by		
Share Capital		
Ordinary shares of £1.00 per share	800	100
Reserves		
Profit and loss	150	60
General	220	60
	1,170	220

When H had acquired its holding on 1st January 19-8, S's profit and loss account had a credit balance of £40,000 and general reserve £50,000.

Required:

Prepare the balance sheet of the H Group at 31st December 19-8.

SOLUTION.

4.23 The only problem here, additional to those already encountered, is the identification and segregation of individual post-acquisition reserves (for inclusion in group reserves) from those whose arose in the pre-acquisition period and which are used in the cost of control calculation. This can be achieved by analysis:

Reserves held by:

←		S PLC		→	H PLC	Group
			Attributable to:			
Pre-acqun	Post-acqun	Total	Min.Ints.	H PLC (Post-acqun)		
(i) (given)	(ii) (derived) = (iii) - (i)	(iii) (given)	(iv) (derived) = 40% X (iii)	(v) (derived) = 60% X (ii)	(vi) (given)	(vii) (derived) (v) + (vi)
£000	£000	£000	£000	£000	£000	£000
Profit and loss 40	20	60	24	12	150	162
General reserve 50	10	60	24	6	220	226

An alternative form of analysis will be introduced later for more complicated circumstances.

The calculation to determine cost of control/capital reserve on acquisition then becomes

	£000	£000
Cost of investment		126
Less net book value of shares acquired:		
Share capital	60	
Attributable pre-acquisition reserves		
– profit and loss (60% X (i) above)	24	
– general (60% X (i) above)	30	
		114
Cost of control		12

An implicit or explicit requirement of some examination questions is the preparation of ledger accounts (or their journal entries) for minority interests and for cost of control. Using figures calculated up to this point, the consolidation adjustments in the form of ledger accounts prepared by H PLC as the parent company would be:

Cost of control in S PLC

	£		£
Investment in S PLC	126,000	S PLC	
		– Ordinary shares	60,000
		– Profit and Loss (pre-acquisition)	24,000
		– General reserve (pre-acquisition)	30,000
		Cost of control (balance)	12,000
	126,000		126,000

Minority Interest in S PLC

	£		£
Minority Interests	88,000	S PLC	
		– Ordinary shares	40,000
		– Profit and loss (iv) above)	24,000
		– General reserve (iv) above)	24,000
	88,000		88,000

Utilising all the figures given and derived up to this point, it is now possible to prepare the group balance sheet.

H Group
Consolidated Balance Sheet as at 31 December 19-8

	£000	£000
Fixed assets (794 + 190)		984
Cost of control on consolidation (see above)		12
Net current assets (250 + 30)		280
		1,276
Financed by		
Share Capital		
Ordinary shares of £1.00 per share		800
Reserves		
Profit and loss (vii) above)	162	
General reserve (vii) above)	226	

$$388$$

Shareholders' funds	1,188
Minority interest (above)	88
	1,276

TRANSACTIONS WITHIN A GROUP. (INTRA GROUP TRANSACTIONS)

4.24 A common feature of groups is that member undertakings have business dealings not only with external parties but also with each other.

4.25 Common examples of this are that one or more undertakings may supply trading stock to another or other members of the group, or a manufacturing member may supply some of its products to other member undertakings either as trading stock for sale outside the group or to become fixed assets of the recipient undertakings. The payment of dividends by a subsidiary to its parent (holding) company is another example of an intra group transaction.

4.26 Transactions of the sort noted in the previous paragraph have a number of different implications, each of which will be considered in the following paragraphs 4.27 to 4.58.

INTRA GROUP INDEBTEDNESS

4.27 If at the balance sheet date one member undertaking is owed a sum of money by another member undertaking (as the result, for example, of the supply of goods, products, finance or services) the amount involved will appear as part of the debtors and creditors (or loans to/loans from) of the respective parties, but are eliminated on consolidation so that the amounts shown for debtors and creditors in the group balance sheet are the externally owed by/to amounts. Similarly, inter undertaking current account balances cancel out at group level.

EXAMPLE

4.28 Included in the separate balance sheets of H PLC and S PLC are the following items:

Notes: (Assets)		**H PLC**	**S PLC**
		£000	£000
	Trade investments		
1.	Loans	170	
	Current assets		
	Stock	190	60
2.	Debtors and prepayments	120	40
	Bank and cash	50	20
	(Liabilities)		
	Long-term liabilities		
3.	Loans		150
	Current liabilities		
4.	Creditors and accruals	100	30
	Other	80	30

Notes

The following amounts are included in the figures on the lines indicated.

1.	loan to S PLC	120	
	other loans	50	
2.	owed by S PLC for goods	20	
3.	loan from H PLC		120
4.	owed to H PLC for goods		20

557

Required:

Prepare an extract from the H Group balance sheet to show how the above matters would be included.

SOLUTION

4.29

H Group

Consolidated Balance Sheet (extract)

	£000	£000
Assets		
Trade investments		
Loans (170 - 120)		50
Current assets		
Stock (190 + 60)	250	
Debtors etc (120 - 20 + 40)	140	
Bank and cash (50 + 20)	70	
	――	
		460
Liabilities		
Long-term liabilities		
Loans (150 - 120)		30
Current liabilities		
Creditors etc (100 + 30 - 20)	110	
Other (80 + 30)	<u>110</u>	
		220

INTRA-GROUP UNREALISED PROFIT.

4.30 It was stated in 4.25 that there may be internal trading transactions within a group, goods and/or services and/or fixed assets, for example, may be transferred between member undertakings. The transfer price used on these occasions may be at cost (to the transferor) but is frequently at a price above cost. In other words, it gives rise to a transfer profit to the selling undertakings. As regards the accounts of the separate undertakings, no action is needed. The transferor correctly takes credit for what it regards as a sale (at the transfer price), the transferee regards the transfer price as an input cost.

4.31 From a group viewpoint, however, transfers from one member of the group to another member merely constitute an internal transfer and not a sale. (The implications of this for turnover are considered in 5.13 and 5.14, because group sales is a term confined to sales to parties outside the group).

4.32 Where internally transferred items are subsequently sold to parties outside the group, the profit on them, that is, any internal transfer profit plus any further profit added by the transferee undertaking when selling externally, can legitimately be regarded as having been realised.

4.33 To the extent, however, that such items have not been sold but are still held by a transferee under-taking, for example, as trading stock and/or as fixed assets, the internal transfer profit has not been realised from a group point of view. Consequently a provision for unrealised profit must be raised, the calculation and effects of which on the accounts are considered in the following subsections. It should also be noted that the intra group transfers of stock may be in transit at balance sheet date (and thus included in the unrealised profit calculation). (This is a situation similar to that encountered by branches – see Section II Chapter 3).

UNREALISED PROFIT ON TRADING STOCKS.

4.34 Calculation of unrealised profit is a relatively straightforward matter, when one member transfers trading stock to a fellow member company at a transfer price in excess of cost.

EXAMPLE

4.35 H PLC sold goods for resale to S PLC for £2,000, which represented cost plust 25%. At balance sheet date, goods (valued at the transfer price) of £1,200 were still unsold and included in S PLC's stock.

Required:

Calculate the amount of unrealised profit included in the closing stock valuation for the group.

SOLUTION

4.36 S's closing stock includes goods, transferred from H at cost plus 25% amounting to £1,200. The unrealised profit element contained within this figure is:

$$\frac{1}{(4+1)} \times \frac{1,200}{1} = £240$$

(Note that if the question had stated that transfer profit represent 25% of selling price, unrealised transfer profit would have been $25\% \times £1,200 = £300$).

Calculation of unrealised profit for a group becomes more difficult when there is a "chain" of these transactions, that is, when member companies transfer, at profit to themselves, some of the stock which has been transferred to them.

UNREALISED PROFIT ON FIXED ASSETS

4.37 If a member company transfers fixed assets to another member or transfers current assets (stock) which become fixed assets of the transferee company and the transaction results in a transfer profit to the transferor, a similar, but not identical, problem arises as that seen in connection with trading stock transfers.

4.38 The transaction has a twofold effect at group level. Firstly, the transferor company has made an unrealised profit vis-a-vis the group, but secondly this profit must be abated by the additional depreciation which has automatically been calculated by the transferee company on the enhanced input cost of the fixed assets. In these instances, group unrealised profit is the net of the two calculations.

EXAMPLE

4.39 H PLC sold machinery, which it had manufactured at a cost of £70,000 to S PLC for £100,000. S PLC depreciated plant and machinery at the rate of 10% per annum, (charging a full year's depreciation in the year of acquisition) on a straight line basis assuming no residual value.

Required:

Calculate the amount of unrealised profit included in the closing figure of fixed assets.

SOLUTION

4.40 It is readily apparent that fixed assets of S contain an amount of £100,000 for plant and machinery transferred by H at a profit of £30,000. As far as the group is concerned, this is an unrealised profit for which a provision must be raised.

However, S has charged depreciation at 10% per annum on its input cost of £100,000 which, from a group viewpoint, is a figure inflated by internal profit.

The "gross" figure of unrealised profit in the first paragraph above is restricted by the excess depreciation in the second, thus:

	£
"Gross" provision for unrealised profit (100,000 - 70,000)	30,000
Less	
Excess provision for depreciation (10% × 30,000)	3,000
"Net" provision for unrealised profit	27,000

ACCOUNTING FOR UNREALISED PROFIT.

4.41 Examples 4.35 and 4.39 have dealt solely with the calculation of unrealised profit.

In the case of unrealised profit on trading stocks (Example 4.35) the general rule is that group stocks and unappropriated profits are reduced.

Where fixed assets are the subject of the transaction (Example 4.39), the general rule is that group fixed assets are reduced, in total and for the class of asset concerned.

- at cost stage by the "gross" provision
- at the accumulated depreciation stage by the excess depreciation.
- at the net (written down value) stage by the "net" provision.

Accounting arrangements for these provisions for unrealised profit are to a certain extent determined by the origin and destination of the items concerned.

No difficulty arises when the items are sold by the holding company to a wholly owned subsidiary – the whole of the unrealised profit is deducted from the group asset affected and from group profit.

When, however, the transaction originates from a partly owned subsidiary company to another subsidiary or to the holding company, several different accounting treatments are possible:

Treatment 1	–	the whole amount of unrealised profit is deducted from the appropriate group asset and from group profit.
Treatment 2	–	the group proportion of unrealised profit is deducted from the appropriate group asset and from group profit.
Treatment 3	–	the whole amount of unrealised profit is deducted from the appropriate group asset but only the group proportion is deducted from group profit; the minority interest proportion is deducted from minority interests.

EXAMPLE

4.42 S PLC, 60% of whose share capital is owned by H PLC sold goods for resale to its parent company at a profit of £10,000. All of these goods were in stock at the year end and included as such in H PLC's balance sheet.

Required:

Show the possible accounting treatments of this unrealised profit.

SOLUTION

4.43 Applying the treatments outlined in subsection 4.41, the following results are obtained.

Reduce the following items by the amounts shown:

	Stock (group)	Minority Interests	Profit (group)
	£	£	£
Treatment 1	10,000	–	10,000
Treatment 2	6,000	–	6,000
(60% × 10,000)			
Treatment 3	10,000	4,000	6,000

The question then arises as to which treatment to adopt when preparing group accounts. Sometimes explicit instructions are given but in their absence Treatment 1 is recommended for general application. This practice is followed consistently in answers throughout this manual.

Similar considerations apply when fixed assets are involved.

EXAMPLE

4.44 S PLC also sold plant, which had cost £160,000 to manufacture, to H PLC for £200,000. H PLC's policy is to depreciate plant over ten years on a straight line basis assuming no residual value.

Required:

Using Treatment 1, show the effects on items in the group balance sheet.

SOLUTION

4.45 In year 1 the following items will be reduced by the amounts shown:

	Plant and Machinery (group)			Minority Interests	Profit (group)
	Cost	Depreciation	WDV		
	£	£	£	£	£
(200,000 - 160,000)	40,000				
(10% × 40,000)		4,000			
(40,000 - 4,000)			36,000	–	36,000

In years 2 to 10 group profit will be increased by £4,000 per annum as a result of the progressive release of the provision for unrealised profit to counteract the depreciation charge calculated on the £200,000 cost to H.

INTER-COMPANY DIVIDENDS

4.46 One result of a holding company's investment in shares of a subsidiary company is that the former is likely to receive dividends on its shareholding from the latter. Such dividends may be paid, wholly or partly, out of pre-acquisition or post acquisition profits.

DIVIDENDS RECEIVED OUT OF PRE-ACQUISITION PROFITS.

4.47 If a holding company acquires its shares in a subsidiary on a cum. div. basis, the subsequent receipt of dividends in respect of the pre–acquisition period is usually regarded as a reduction in the capital cost of acquiring the investment.

4.48 The holding company should therefore credit the dividends concerned to the investment account in which the cost of acquiring the shares in the subsidiary is recorded. This does not, however, alter the amount of group goodwill or capital reserve arising on acquisition of the subsidiary.

EXAMPLE.

4.49 H PLC acquired 60% of the ordinary share capital of S PLC, whose shareholders' funds at the date of acquisition comprised:

	£
Ordinary shares of £1.00	100,000
Reserves(various)	40,000
Shareholders' funds	140,000

Cost of acquisition was £98,000.
Required:

1. Calculate the amount of goodwill or capital reserve arising on acquisition.
2. Calculate the amount, if any, by which the figure in 1. would alter if S PLC subsequently declares and pays a dividend of 12% out of pre–acquisition profits.

SOLUTION
4.50

	1. £	2. £
Cost of acquisition	98,000	98,000
Less:		
Dividends received out of pre-acquisition profits (60% × 12% × 100,000)	–	7,200
Net cost of acquisition	98,000	90,800
Ordinary shares acquired	60,000	60,000
Reserves (60% X 40,000)	24,000	24,000
Dividends paid out of pre-acquisition profits	–	(7,200)
Net book value of shares acquired	84,000	76,800
Goodwill on acquisition	14,000	14,000

If at date of acquisition S had already proposed a dividend of 12%, total reserves would then have been £28,000 (40,000 - 12,000) and shareholders' funds, £128,000. Such proposed dividends would be added back, on the grounds that they constitute profits retained. The calculations at 1. would then have been modified to:

	On acquisition £	On payment £
Net cost of acquisition (as above)	98,000	90,800
Ordinary shares acquired	60,000	60,000
Reserves (60% X 28,000)	16,800	16,800

Dividends proposed out of pre-acquisition profits (60% × 12% × 100,000)	7,200	–
Net book value of shares acquired	84,000	76,800
Goodwill on acquisition	14,000	14,000

4.51 If the acquisition occurs part-way through the financial year of the subsidiary, in the absence of contrary indications, it is usual to apportion dividends (and profits) paid in respect of that year, between the pre-acquisition and post- acquisition periods on a time basis.

DIVIDENDS RECEIVED AND RECEIVABLE OUT OF POST-ACQUISITION PROFITS

4.52 Dividends received by a holding company from a subsidiary out of profits arising in the post–acquisition period, are treated as investment income in the books of the holding company. Within the group, however the dividends are simply an intra group transaction resulting in an increase in retained profits in the holding company accompanied by a simultaneous reduction in retained profits in the subsidiary.

4.53 When a subsidiary company proposes a dividend, its holding company may credit Dividends Receivable and debit Debtors (or Current Account) but to do so creates problems with the tax credit aspects of the transaction, unless a group election is in force.

4.54 More frequently, the holding company does not take credit for dividends from subsidiary companies until those dividends have been received.

4.55 The result under these circumstances, is that the dividends are recorded by the subsidiary as proposed but not recorded by the holding company at all at that stage. From the group viewpoint, however, such proposed dividends constitute profits retained within the group and as such are included in group reserves.

4.56 Dividends proposed by a subsidiary which are attributable to minority interests are included in the group balance sheet as a current liability and not as part of the item Minority Interests.

EXAMPLE

4.57 H PLC owned 60% of the ordinary share capital of S PLC whose shareholders' funds at balance sheet date were:

	£
Ordinary shares of £1.00	100,000
Reserves	
Pre-acquisition	40,000
Post-acquisition	90,000
Shareholders' funds	230,000

The post-acquisition reserves are after a dividend of £30,000 had been proposed. H PLC's reserves were £500,000.

Required: Calculate the group reserves and amount attributable to minority interests.

SOLUTION
4.58

	£	£
H PLC Reserves		500,000
S PLC Reserves		
– Post acquisition	90,000	
– Proposed dividends	30,000	
– Total	120,000	
– Attributable to group		
(60% × 120,000)		72,000
Group reserves		572,000

The group's share of S's pre-acquisition profits, that is 60% of £40,000 (£24,000) is transferred to Cost of control in S account and does not form part of group reserves.

	£	£
S PLC Reserves		
– Pre-acquisition	40,000	
– Post-acquisition	90,000	
	130,000	
– attributable to minority interests		
(40% × 130,000)		52,000
Proposed dividends		
– minority interests (Current liability)		
(40% × 30,000)		12,000

ACQUISITION OF CONTROL BY DEGREES.

4.59 A holding company may acquire control of a subsidiary by degrees, that is, gradually by a series of acquisitions. The subsidiary does not become such, of course, until control has actually been gained.

4.60 For the purposes of calculating goodwill/capital reserve on acquisition for inclusion in the group balance sheet the intention of the holding company must be taken into account. In any event no post-acquisition profit can be attributed to the group until after control has been gained. Until this occurs, dividends received constitute normal income.

4.61 If the holding company had originally intended to gain such control and had achieved its objective by acquiring shares according to a plan, the final goodwill/capital reserve figure should be the grand total of such figures calculated separately on the occasion of each acquisition.

4.62 In contrast where no plan of that sort had been in operation and control of a subsidiary has been gained without the existence of an original intention, the goodwill/capital reserve calculation is calculated on the position at the date control is gained (and subsequently in the event of further acquisitions).

EXAMPLE

4.63 H PLC acquired 40,000 (40%) of the £1.00 ordinary shares in S PLC, whose reserves at that date totalled £60,000, for £70,000.

H PLC subsequently acquired a further 30,000 of these shares when S PLC's reserves totalled £90,000, for £75,000.

Required:

Calculate goodwill/capital reserve on acquisition on the assumption

a. that H PLC intended from the outset to gain control of S PLC

b. that H PLC did not originally intend to gain control of S PLC.

SOLUTION

4.64 It is readily apparent from the facts given that H did not gain control over S until the second acquisition had been effected.

	Assumption (a) £	Assumption (b) £
1st Acquisition		
Cost of investment in subsidiary company	70,000	Not
Share capital	40,000	calculated
Reserves (40% × 60,000)	24,000	at
		this
Net book value of shares acquired	64,000	stage
Goodwill/(capital reserve)	6,000	
2nd Acquisition		
Cost of investment in subsidiary company	75,000	145,000
Share capital	30,000	70,000
Reserves (30% × 90,000)	27,000	
(70% × 90,000)		63,000
Net book value of shares acquired	57,000	133,000
Goodwill/(capital reserve)	18,000	12,000
Total goodwill on acquisition	24,000	12,000

The total ordinary share capital of S is not stated but can be deduced as £100,000 from the percentage holding acquired in the first transaction.

CHANGES IN PROPORTION OF MINORITY INTERESTS.

4.65 When a holding company, which has partial control of a subsidiary company, acquires further amounts of that company's shares, there is an automatic effect on the proportion attributable to minority interests. The amount shown in a group balance sheet for minority interests is calculated on the proportion of their holding at that date and ignores the differing proportions which may have existed previously. This principle applies also in the reverse situation where a holding company reduces its holding and there is a simultaneous and corresponding increase in minority interests.

EXAMPLE

4.66 H PLC acquired a 70% holding of the shares of S PLC and subsequently acquired a further 10%.

At the material dates, the shareholders' funds of S PLC comprised:

	At date of 1st Acquisition £	2nd Acquisition £
Share capital	100,000	100,000
Reserves	50,000	70,000
Shareholders' funds	150,000	170,000

Required:

Calculate the amounts attributable to minority interests and to the group immediately after each acquisition had taken place.

SOLUTION
4.67

	Attributable to				
	Minority interests		Group		Total
	Amount £	%	Amount £	%	Amount £
After 1st Acquisition	45,000	30	105,000	70	150,000
After 2nd Acquisition	34,000	20	136,000	80	170,000

These percentages continue to apply subsequently until a further change in holding, if any, takes place. Proof of the correctness of the above figures can be obtained by analysing the changes which have taken place.

	Attributable to				
	Minority interests		Group		Total
	Amount	%	Amount	%	Amount
After 1st Acquisition	£	%	£	%	£
Share capital	30,000	30	70,000	70	100,000
Reserves (pre-acquisition)	15,000	30	35,000	70	50,000
Shareholders' funds (as above)	45,000	30	105,000	70	150,000
On 2nd Acquisition					
Transfer of holding from minority interests to group					
Share capital	(10,000)	(10)	10,000	10	–
Reserves (pre-1st acquisition	(5,000)	(10)	5,000	10	–
	30,000	20	120,000	80	150,000
Increase in post 1st acquisition pre 2nd acquisition reserves (70,000 – 50,000)	4,000	20	16,000	80	20,000
Shareholders' funds (as above)	34,000	20	136,000	80	170,000

ACQUISITION OF PREFERENCE SHARES IN SUBSIDIARY COMPANY

4.68 A holding company may also acquire preference shares in a subsidiary company. On this occurrence, goodwill/capital reserve on acquisition is calculated, in the normal way, by comparing the nominal value of the shares acquired with the net cost of acquiring them.

4.69 In carrying out this calculation, none of the subsidiary company's reserves are attributed to these shares. The resultant figure of goodwill/capital reserve on acquisition of the preference shares is merged with that arising on previous acquisitions of ordinary shares and need not be separately identified.

4.70 The extent to which a holding company has not acquired control of the preference shares of its subsidiary company is usually described as Outside Interests. In the group balance sheet this item is combined with Minority Interests as Minority and Outside Interests, or simply, Outside Interests.

COMPREHENSIVE EXAMPLE

4.71 A comprehensive example, incorporating the various points encountered so far, now follows.

H PLC has two subsidiary companies. ESS 1 PLC and ESS 2 PLC to which the following information relates.

	ESS 1 PLC	ESS 2 PLC
	£	£
1. On 31st March 19-7 H PLC acquired		
a. 60% of ordinary share capital for	121,000	
and b. 75% of preference share capital for	65,000	
in each case ex div.		
At that date there were credit balances attributable to ordinary shareholders		
a. on profit and loss account	40,000	
and b. on other reserves	50,000	
2. On 1st February 19-8 H PLC acquired		
a. an additional 20% of ordinary capital for	53,000	
	(cum div)	
On 31st December 19-7 there were credit balances		
a. on profit and loss account	50,000	
and b. on other reserves	60,000	
after an ordinary dividend of 10% had been proposed	10,000	

and the 6% preference dividend had been paid   4,800

3.   On 1st January 19-8 H PLC acquired
     a. 70% of ordinary share capital for   150,000
    At that date there were credit balances
     a. on profit and loss account   30,000
     and b. on other reserves   10,000

4.   In April 19-8 ESS 1 PLC paid the 19-7
    proposed dividend of 10% (above)   10,000
    and on 31st December 19-8
     a. paid the 6% preference dividend   4,800
     and b. proposed a 12% ordinary dividend   12,000

5.   On 31st December 19-8
     a. ESS 2 PLC proposed an ordinary
    dividend of $2\frac{1}{2}$%   5,000
     and b. H PLC proposed an ordinary dividend
    of 10% (£90,000)

6.   During the year 19-8 H PLC has transferred
    goods
     a. to ESS 1 PLC at cost plus 20% for   36,000
    of which one third were still in stock at
    31st December 19-8 at transfer price   12,000
     and b. to ESS 2 PLC at cost plus 25% of which
    there was an amount in stock on 31st
    December 19-8 at transfer price   10,000

7.   It is the policy of H PLC not to take credit in
    its accounts for dividends receivable from
    subsidiary companies until they are actually
    received

8.   At 31st December 19-8
     a. ESS 1 PLC owed H PLC   50,000
     and b. ESS 2 PLC owed ESS 1 PLC   22,000

The individual balance sheets of H PLC and of its two subsidiary companies are summarised below.

Summarised Balance Sheets
as at 31 December 19-8

	H PLC £000	H PLC £000	ESS 1 PLC £000	ESS 1 PLC £000	ESS 2 PLC £000	ESS 2 PLC £000
Fixed Assets		615		249		205
(as written down value)						
Investment in subsidiary companies		389		–		–
Current Assets						
Stock	92		43		15	
Debtors	60		41		26	
Bank/cash	32		21		14	
	184		105		55	
Less						
Current Liabilities						
Creditors	42		28		25	
Proposed dividends	90		12		5	
	132		40		30	

Working capital		52		65		25

Net assets employed		<u>1,056</u>		<u>314</u>		<u>230</u>

Financed by
Share Capital, fully paid shares
of £1.00 per share

6% Preference shares		–		80		–
Ordinary shares	<u>900</u>		<u>100</u>		<u>200</u>	
		900		180		200

Reserves

Profit and loss	78		62		20	
Other	<u>78</u>		<u>72</u>		<u>10</u>	
		156		134		30
		<u>1,056</u>		<u>314</u>		<u>230</u>

SOLUTION

4.72 The first step is to identify the respective amounts of pre-acquisition and post-acquisition reserves. This can be achieved by analysing the figures.

		Reserves		
	ESS 1 PLC		**ESS 2 PLC**	
	Profit & Loss	Other	Profit & Loss	Other
	£000	£000	£000	£000
At 31st December 19-7	50	60		
January 19-8 $[\frac{1}{12} \times (62-50)]$	1			
$[\frac{1}{12} \times (72-60)]$		1		
At 2nd Acqun (1st February 19-8)	51	61		
Less				
At 1st Acqun (31st March 19-7)	40	50		
Post 1st Acqun and pre 2nd Acqun increase in reserves	11	11		
At 31st December 19-8	62	72	20	10
Less				
At 2nd Acqun (1st February 19-8)	51	61		
1st Acqun (1st January 19-8)			30	10
Post 1st Acqun decrease in reserves			(10)	–
Post 2nd Acqun increase in reserves	11	11		

Further calculations are then needed, based on the above, before the figures for goodwill/capital reserve, minority interest and group profit/loss can be arrived at.

There is no single way of setting these out but one possibility is in the form of a grid, as illustrated below.

	ESS 2 PLC		**ESS 1 PLC**		**H PLC**	Group
Note	Minority Interests	H PLC	Minority Interests	H PLC		
	£	£	£	£		
Investment in subsidiary companies						
1st Acqun						
–Ordinary shares		150,000		121,000		
–Pref.shares				65,000		

		£	£	£	£
	2nd Acqun				
	–Ordinary shares		–		53,000
1	Divs received ex pre-acqun profits		–		(2,900)
	Net		150,000		236,100
		%	%	%	%
	Holding				
	1st Acqun				
	–Ordinary shares	30	70	40	60
	–Pref.shares	–	–	25	75
	2nd Acqun				
	–Ordinary shares	–	–	20	80

		£	£	£	£
	1st Acqun				
3	**Shr Cap**				
	–Ordinary	60,000	140,000	40,000	60,000
	–Pref.			20,000	60,000
	Pre-acqun reserves				
3	Profit and loss	9,000	21,000	16,000	24,000
3.	Other	3,000	7,000	20,000	30,000
	2nd Acqun				
4	**Shr Cap Transfer**			(20,000)	20,000
	Pre-acqun reserves transfers				
4	Profit and loss			(8,000)	8,000
4	Other			(10,000)	10,000
	Post 1st Acqun.pre-2nd Acqun increase in reserves				
1,5	Profit and loss			2,200	2,200
5	Other			2,200	2,200
	Proposed dividend ex pre-acqun profits				
2	$(20\% \times \frac{1}{12} \times 12{,}000)$				200
	Net book value of shares on acquisition	72,000	168,000	62,400	216,600
	Goodwill/(Capital Reserve) on acquisition		(18,000)		19,500	1,500
	1st Acqun				
	Post acqun increase (decrease) in reserves				
5	Profit and Loss	(3,000)	(7,000)		6,600
5	Other				6,600
	2nd Acqun				
	Post acqun increase in reserves				
	Profit and Loss			2,200	8,800
	Other			2,200	8,800

2	Subsidiary companies' proposed dividends (added back)	1,500	3,500	2,400	9,400
		70,500		69,200	
2	*Less* Minority interests' dividends transferred to current liabilities	1,500		2,400		3,900
	Minority Interests	69,000		66,800		135,800
	Reserves Other	–		15,400	78,000	93,400
	Profit and Loss	(3,500)		24,800	78,000	99,300
1	Adjustments Elimination of Divs. received ex pre-acqun profits					(2,900)
6	Unrealised profits					(4,000)
	Profit and Loss	(3,500)		24,800	78,000	92,400

The adjustments, although effected by H, arise only on consolidation and for this reason are shown in the group column.

Notes

1. Dividends received by H out of pre-acquisition profits comprise

	£
Share of 10% ordinary dividend proposed by ESS 1 in December 19-7 and paid in April 19-8 (20% × £10,000)	2,000
Share of 6% preference dividend paid in December 19-7 (75% × £4,800 × $\frac{3}{12}$)	900
	2,900

The correct accounting treatment would have been for H to have credited the £2,900 to Investment in Subsidiary Companies but this has not been done as is evident from the summarised balance sheet where this item (£389,000) is the sum of cost of the individual acquisitions:

	£
Investment in ESS 1 PLC	
1st Acquisition	
ordinary shares	121,000
preference shares	65,000
2nd Acquisition	
ordinary shares	53,000
Investment in ESS 2 PLC	
1st (only) Acquisition	
ordinary shares	150,000
Total per balance sheet	389,000

These dividends must therefore have been credited to revenue erroneously and the transfer of £2,900 is now necessary to correct the situation.

ESS 1's pre 1st acquisition reserves on 31st March 19-7 do not need to be reduced (by the amount of the pre-acquisition preference dividend) as they have already been adjusted for the purposes of this question which states that they are at the amount "attributable to ordinary shareholders", nor does the figure of post 1st pre 2nd acquisition reserves need to be reduced as the proposed ordinary dividend has been taken out already. (This follows the accounting treatment outlined in 4.50 in the "on payment" example).

2. Different considerations apply in respect of the 12% ordinary dividend proposed by ESS 1 on 31.12.19-8 for the year 19-8. Part of this dividend is attributable to pre 2nd acquisition profits.

	£
Total proposed ordinary dividend (12%)	12,000
Attributable to	
Minority interests $(20\% \times 12,000)$	2,400
Pre 2nd Acqun profits $(20\% \times 12,000 \times \frac{1}{12})$	200
Post acquisition profits	
Post 1st Acqun $(60\% \times 12,000 \times \frac{1}{12})$	600
Post 2nd Acqun $(80\% \times 12,000 \times \frac{11}{12})$	8,800
	12,000

The dividend attributable to pre 2nd Acqun profits (£200) is added back for the same reason in 4.50 in the "on acquisition" example, namely that it represents retained profit of the group. When the dividend, of which this £200 is part, is paid.

a. the item Investment in Subsidiary Companies will reduce by a further £200 to £235,900.

b. the item Net book value of shares on acquisition (attributable to H) will also reduce by £200 to £216,400

leaving goodwill on acquisition of ESS 1 at its present figure of £19,500.

The group proportion of dividends from post acquisition profits, £9,400 (600 + 8,800 above) for ESS 1 and £3,500 for ESS 2 is also added back as post acquisition retained profits but the minority interests portion is excluded (£3,900 in total) and classed as a current liability.

3. On the occasion of the first acquisition of ESS 1's shares, which (incidentally), gave H immediate control (and therefore does not give rise to "control by degrees" problems, see 4.59 et. seq.) minority interests were 40% and the relevant items have been apportioned on that basis.

4. The effect of the second acquisition was that the minority shareholders gave up half their shareholding (and accompanying reserves to H). This is shown by the transfers of 20% of the original figures, this being the amount needed to bring the holding company's share up to 80%. In place of the calculations explained in this and the previous note, the short method shown in 4.65 et. seq., could have been used.

5. The post 1st acqun, pre 2nd acqun increases in reserves are calculated.

	£
Minority interests $(20\% \times 11,000)$	2,200
Pre 2nd acquisition $(20\% \times 11,000)$	2,200
Post 1st acquisition $(60\% \times 11,000)$	6,600
	11,000

In this instance the calculations are identical for both profit and loss and for other reserves.

6. Unrealised profits for which H has raised a provision are, on goods transferred

	£
from H to ESS 1	
$\left(\frac{1}{5+1} \times \frac{12,000}{1} \right)$	2,000
from H to ESS 2	
$\left(\frac{1}{4+1} \times \frac{10,000}{1} \right)$	2,000
	4,000

The figures appearing in the group column of the grid are then used in the group balance sheet which now follows:

H PLC and Subsidiaries
Consolidated balance sheet as at 31 December 19-8

	£	£
Fixed Assets(at w.d.v.)(615 + 249 + 205)		1,069,000
Goodwill on acquisition of subsidiary companies		1,500
(per grid)		
Current Assets		
Stock [92 + 43 + 15 - 4 (unrealised profit)]	146,000	
Debtors [60 + 41 + 26 - (50 + 22)		
intra group debtors)]	55,000	
Bank/cash (32 + 21 + 14)	67,000	
	268,000	
Less		
Current Liabilities		
Creditors [42 + 28 + 25 - (50 + 22)		
(intra group creditors) + 3.9 (minority dividends)]	26,900	
Proposed dividends	90,000	
	116,900	
Working capital		151,100
Net assets employed		1,221,600
Financed by		
Share Capital, issued and fully paid		
900,000 Ordinary shares of £1.00 per share		900,000
Reserves		
Profit and loss (per grid)	92,400	
Other (per grid)	93,400	
		185,800
Shareholders' funds		1,085,800
Minority and outside interests(per grid)		135,800
		1,221,600

CONSOLIDATION OF FINANCIAL POSITION OF SUB- SUBSIDIARY COMPANIES

4.73 Up to this point all the examples and questions have dealt with the situation whereby the figures of holding companies and the subsidiaries are consolidated into group figures.

4.74 An added complication arises when a subsidiary company itself owns a controlling interest in another undertaking. Suppose that X PLC owns 60% of the ordinary share capital of Y PLC which, in turn, owns 80% of the ordinary share capital of Z PLC.

4.75 The relationship of Y to Z is that of holding company and subsidiary, respectively. An identical relationship clearly exists also between X and Y.

4.76 Effectively X, through its direct controlling interest in Y, is able to control Z indirectly. In this sort of situation Z is termed a sub-subsidiary of X. The law requires that X publishes group accounts consolidating the figures of both subsidiary and sub–subsidiary companies.

4.77 In view of the foregoing, Y would prepare consolidated accounts for the group comprising itself and Z. Only rarely, however, do examination questions require this to be done, almost invariably they would require the consolidated accounts for the X group of companies, namely, X, Y and Z.

4.78 There are two methods available for effecting the consolidation. Under the first, the figures for the sub-subsidiary are consolidated with those of the subsidiary (its holding company) and then the figures for the group are consolidated with those of the holding company. In other words, Z would be consolidated with Y to give the Y group balance sheet which itself would be consolidated into X group balance sheet. This is called the direct method.

4.79 The alternative is termed the indirect method, and derives its name from the fact that goodwill (or capital reserve) on consolidation, reserves and minority interests figures of the subsidiary are consolidated on the basis of the holding company's indirect interest. Using the facts in 4.79, in preparing the group balance sheet X would consolidate the assets and liabilities in the usual way but, for the items mentioned above, would consolidate 60% in respect of Y and 48% (60% of 80%) in respect of Z.

EXAMPLE

4.80 On 31st December 19-7 H PLC acquired 80% of the equity share capital of ESS 1 PLC when there was a debit balance of £10,000 on profit and loss account and a credit balance on other reserves of £15,000.

At that same date ESS 1 PLC acquired 60% of the equity share capital of Essess 2 PLC when there were credit balance of £12,000 and £21,000 respectively, on profit and loss and other reserves.

The individual balance sheets of H PLC and of its two subsidiary companies are summarised below.

Summarised balance sheets
as at 31 December 19-8

	H PLC £000	H PLC £000	ESS 1 PLC £000	ESS 1 PLC £000	Essess 2 PLC £000	Essess 2 PLC £000
Fixed Assets (at written down values)		590		300		378
Investment in subsidiary companies		355		220		–
Net current assets		80		26		54
Net assets employed		1,025		546		432
Financed by:						
Share capital, fully paid shares of £1.00 per share						
Ordinary shares		800		400		300
Reserves						
Profit and loss	150		100		60	
Other	75		46		72	
		225		146		132
		1,025		546		432

Required:

Prepare the balance sheet for the H PLC Group as at 31st December 19-8, using

a. the direct, and

b. the indirect

methods of consolidation.

SOLUTION

4.81

a. Direct method

Workings

	Essess 2 PLC Minority Ints	Essess 2 PLC ESS 1 PLC	ESS 1 PLC Minority Ints	ESS 1 PLC H PLC	H PLC	Group
Investment in subsidiary companies	%	%	%	%		
–Holding	40	60	20	80		
	£	£	£	£	£	£
– Cost		220,000		355,000		
On acquisition						
Share Capital	120,000	180,000	80,000	320,000		
Profit and loss	4,800	7,200	(2,000)	(8,000)		
Other reserves	8,400	12,600	3,000	12,000		
Net book value of shares on acquisition		199,800		324,000		
Goodwill/(Capital Reserve) on acquisition		20,200		31,000		51,200

Post acquisition
Profit and loss

[60,000 − 12,000]	19,200	28,800				
[100,000 − (10,000)]			22,000	88,000		
Transfer		(28,800)	5,760	23,040		
Profit and loss		−		111,040	150,000	261,040
Other reserves						
(72,000-21,000)	20,400	30,600				
(46,000 - 15,000)			6,200	24,800		
Transfer		(30,600)	6,120	24,480		
Other reserves		−		49,280	75,000	124,280
Minority interests	172,800		121,080			293,880

The acquisition by ESS 1 of a controlling interest in Essess 2 gave rise to a goodwill figure of £20,200. Although ESS 1 itself is owned partly by H and partly by minority interests, no attempt is made to split the £20,200 between the two sets of shareholders in ESS 1. The reason for this is that the goodwill is treated in the same way as all the other assets owned by the ESS 1 (and subsidiary) group, and shown gross, that is, at their full amount, minority interests being shown as a separate figure; to treat goodwill otherwise would be inconsistent with the treatment of these other assets.

An apparent contradiction arises in the converse situation when the net book value of the shares on acquisition exceeds the cost of acquiring them (the cost of investment in subsidiary companies). The resultant capital reserve is apportioned between the subsidiary's immediate holding company and its minority shareholders. In this instance a capital reserve arising on acquisition of ESS 1's controlling interest in Essess 2 would have been apportioned 20/80 between the minority shareholders and H. Justification for this seeming anomaly is the fact that whereas goodwill on acquisition is regarded as an extra asset, capital reserve on the other hand is regarded as a reduction in the value of existing assets, part of which must be borne by the minority shareholders.

Post-acquisition profits/(losses) of Essess 2 belong partly to minority interests and partly to ESS 1. Insofar as they belong to this latter company, they must be apportioned between the minority interests of ESS 1 and between H which has the controlling interest, so that they are ultimately correctly attributed to the appropriate set of shareholders. The "transfer" item in the workings has been inserted to effect this.

The balance sheet incorporating the figures from the direct consolidation method is shown after the workings for b.

Indirect method

	Essess 2 PLC		ESS 1 PLC		H PLC	Group
	Minority Ints	H PLC	Minority Ints	H PLC		
Investment in subsidiary companies	%	%	%	%		
– Holding (see note 1.)	52	48	20	80		
	£	£	£	£	£	£
– Cost (see note 2.)	44,000	176,000		355,000		
On acquisition						
Share capital	156,000	144,000	80,000	320,000		
Profit and loss	6,240	5,760	(2,000)	(8,000)		
Other reserves	10,920	10,080	3,000	12,000		
Net book value of shares on acquisition		159,840		324,000		
Goodwill/(Capital Reserve) on acquisition)		16,160		31,000		47,160
Post-acquisition						
Profit and loss						
[60,000 − 12,000]	24,960	23,040				
[100,000 − (10,000)]			22,000	88,000		
Profit and loss		23,040		88,000	150,000	261,040

Other reserves							
(72,000-21,000)	26,520	24,480					
(46,000-15,000)				6,200	24,800		
Other reserves		24,480			24,800	75,000	124,280
Minority interests (see note 2.)	180,640			109,200			289,840

Notes

1. Under this method, the figures for Essess 2 are consolidated into the group on the basis of H's financial interest in that company, 80% of 60%, namely 48%. The outside interest is the balance of 52% comprising

	%
Direct interest of minorities in Essess 2	40
Indirect interest of ESS 1's minority in Essess 2	
(20% of 60%)	12
	52

At first sight it seems strange that H's interest is less than 50%. However, it must be remembered that by virtue of its 48% indirect interest it has a 60% control of Essess 2 as the result of ESS 1's holding in that company.

2. The indirect method requires that the cost of the investment by ESS 1 in Essess 2 is apportioned in such a way that the minority shareholders bear the appropriate proportion, thus.

	£
Total cost of investment by ESS 1 in Essess 2	220,000
attributable to	
H (80% × 220,000)	176,000
Minority interest (20% × 220,000)	44,000
	220,000

In the grid workings the £44,000 has been deducted in arriving at the indirect minority interest figure of £180,640.

The balance sheet for the H Group can now be prepared by aggregating those figures for which workings have not been shown.

In order to highlight the points at which the two methods coincide and differ, balance sheets prepared under each of the methods a. and b. are shown in juxtaposition.

H PLC and subsidiaries
Consolidated Balance Sheet as at 31 December 19-8

	Method a. (Direct)		Method b. (Indirect)	
	£	£	£	£
Fixed assets		1,268,000		1,268,000
Goodwill on acquisition of				
subsidiary companies (per workings)		51,200		47,160
Net current assets		160,000		160,000
		1,479,200		1,475,160
Financed by:				
Share capital, fully paid shares of £1.00 per share				
Ordinary shares		800,000		800,000
Reserves				
Profit and loss (per workings)	261,040		261,040	
Other (per workings)	124,280		124,280	
		385,320		385,320

Minority Interests	293,880	289,840
	1,479,200	1,475,160

CONSOLIDATION OF FINANCIAL POSITION OF A MIXED GROUP.

4.82 The term mixed group is applied in the situation where a holding company and one or more of its subsidiaries together hold a controlling interest in another undertaking although their individual holdings are less than 50%.

EXAMPLE.

4.83 Wimbourne PLC owns 75% of the equity share capital of Birkin PLC and 30% of the equity share capital of Palin PLC, a further 40% of which is owned by Birkin PLC.

It is apparent that neither Wimbourne nor Birkin individually have a controlling interest in Palin but together have a majority (70%) holding. As Wimbourne is Birkin's holding company it has effective control of Palin, as shown by the following table.

	Palin PLC	
	Minority interests %	Wimbourne PLC interest %
Wimbourne - direct		30
[100 − (30 + 40)]	30	
– indirect		
(ie via Birkin)		
(75% × 40%)		30
(25% × 40%)	10	
Extent of interest	40	60

4.84 Consolidation techniques for a mixed group are identical with those of a vertical group.

GROUP PROFIT AND LOSS ACCOUNTS

5.0 It has already been stated that the Companies Act 1985 compels holding companies to publish group accounts annually, along with their own final accounts. The group profit and loss account must be presented in the form of a consolidated profit and loss account in respect of the holding company and its subsidiaries. For the purposes of the examples and questions in this Section, unless specifically stated otherwise, the profit and loss account presentation is, for simplicity, in a form suitable only for internal circulation. The presentation of group profit and loss accounts is dealt with in 8.0 and following.

5.1 Theoretically, it is possible to prepare a group profit and loss account by aggregating the figures of the holding company with the appropriate proportions of the same items of the subsidiaries. This practice, however, is not adopted because it would prevent meaningful analyses and comparisons of performance from being carried out.

5.2 The usual method of consolidation is to aggregate the holding and subsidiary companies' figures, on an item by item basis, and to deduct, as appropriate, amounts relating to minority and outside interests and to pre-acquisition profit and loss.

EXAMPLE

5.3 The respective retained profits as at 31st December 19-7 of H PLC and S PLC were £120,000 and £50,000 when the former company acquired 70% of the ordinary share capital of the latter company. During the following twelve months H made a trading profit of £90,000 and S £40,000 on which their respective corporation tax liability was £36,000 and £16,000. Turnover, Cost of Sales and other expenses of H were £377,000, and £264,000 and £23,000 respectively and of S these same items were £142,000, £87,000 and £15,000. As at 31 December 19-8 H proposed an ordinary dividend of £35,000 and S £10,000.

Required:

Prepare the H Group consolidated profit and loss account for the year 19-8.

SOLUTION

5.4 The group figures are basically the aggregation of the individual companies figures but the following special points must be noted.

a. Dividends proposed by S are ignored because

    i. the profit out of which they have been proposed has been consolidated.

    ii. the holding company's shares of dividends is merely an internal transfer.

    iii. the minority interests' share of dividends is included in the minority interests deduction (but see 4.56 for the treatment of minority interests dividends in the balance sheet):

    iv. in the light of i, ii, and iii above, group profit and group dividends would be inflated by doubly counted figures if such dividends were not ignored.

b. the same considerations as in a. above would also have applied if S had actually paid dividends.

c. In the profit and loss account of H (as opposed to H Group) it is a matter of accounting policy as to whether the dividends proposed by S are taken into account as dividends receivable. Some companies would ignore such dividends until actually received. In either event, group profit would be unaffected for the reasons stated in a. above.

d. In the group profit and loss account, pre- acquisition profits/losses are eliminated from current year and/or retained profit brought forward figures, as appropriate. In this instance, as the acquisition occurred immediately preceding the start of the current year, only retained profit brought forward is affected.

H PLC and subsidiary
Consolidated Profit and Loss Account
for year ended 31 december 19-8

	£
Turnover	519,000
Cost of Sales	351,000
Gross profit	168,000
Other expenses	38,000
Profit before tax (90,000 + 40,000)	
(see notes a. and c.)	130,000
Less	
Taxation (36,000 + 16,000)	52,000
Profit after tax	78,000
Less	
Minority interests [30% × (40,000 − 16,000)]	7,200
Profit attributable to holding company shareholders	70,800
Less:	
Dividends proposed (see note a.)	35,000
Retained profit for year	35,800
Retained profit brought forward	120,000
(see note d.)	
Retained profit carried forwad	155,800

OUTSIDE HOLDINGS OF PREFERENCE SHARES.

5.5 Part of the share capital of a subsidiary company may consist of preference shares, some or all of which may be owned by outside interests.

5.6 In the group profit and loss account, preference dividends paid and/or proposed by the subsidiary have a two-fold effect. Firstly, the preference dividend attributable to outside interests is deducted from profit after tax and secondly, minority interests are calculated on a figure of profit after tax minus total preference dividend.

EXAMPLE

5.7 The facts are the same as in 5.3 except that S PLC also had £100,000 8% Preference Shares in issue. H PLC had acquired 80% of these on 31st December 19-7.

Required:

The consolidated profit and loss account for the H Group for the year ended 31st December 19-8.

SOLUTION
5.8

H PLC and subsidiary
Consolidated Profit and Loss Account
for year ended 31 December 19-8

	£
Turnover	519,000
Cost of Sales	351,000
Gross profit	168,000
Other expenses	38,000
Profit before tax (90,000 + 40,000)	
(see notes a. and c.)	130,000
Less	
Taxation	52,000
Profit after tax	78,000
Less	
Outside and Minority Interests (see below)	6,400
Profit attributable to holding company shareholders	71,600
Less	
Dividends proposed	35,000
Retained profit for year	36,600
Retained profit brought forward	120,000
Retained profit carried forward	156,600

Calculation of minority and outside interests (see above)

	£
– in preference shares (20% × 8,000)	1,600
– in ordinary shares (30% × (24,000 − 8,000))	4,800
	6,400

ACQUISITION OF INTEREST IN SUBSIDIARY DURING THE YEAR

5.9 As has already been explained (see 4.21), the group can take credit/debit in the profit and loss account for only the post-acquisition profit/loss of the subsidiary company. The usual way in which this is done is for the whole of the pre and post–acquisition profit/loss to be consolidated and an adjusting entry to be made which eliminates the pre- acquisition portion from group profit after tax.

EXAMPLE

5.10 The facts are the same as in 5.7 except that the acquisition of all the shares occurred on 1st April 19-8.

Required:

Prepare the H Group consolidated profit and loss account for the year ended 31st December 19-8.

SOLUTION.

5.11 The solution is the same as 5.8 in many respects, except that there is a separate deduction for pre-acquisition profits with a consequent difference in sub-totalled figures.

Pre-acquisition profit arising between 1st January 19-8 and 31st March 19-8 is calculated thus for the group.

	£
attributable to 8% Preference shares	
[80% × (3/12 × 8,000)]	1,600
attributable to Ordinary shares	
[70% × (3/12 × (24,000 − 8,000))]	2,800
Pre-acquisition profit (current year)	4,400

H PLC and subsidiary
Consolidated Profit and Loss Account
for year ended 31st December 19-8

	£	£
Turnover		519,000
Cost of Sales		351,000
Gross profit		168,000
Other expenses		38,000
Profit before tax (90,000 + 40,000) (see notes a. and c.)		130,000
Less		
Taxation (36,000 + 16,000)		52,000
Profit after tax		78,000
Less		
Outside and Minority interests	6,400	
Pre-acquisition Profit (current year) (see above)	4,400	
		10,800
Profit attributable to holding company shareholders		67,200
Less Dividends proposed		35,000
Retained profit for year		32,200
Retained profit brought forward		120,000
Retained profit carried forward		152,200

MISCELLANEOUS MATTERS

PUBLISHING DISPENSATION

5.12 The Companies Act 1985 requires holding companies to publish their own accounts, in addition to those of the group, as has been noted in 5.1.0. However, by Section 228(7) of that Companies Act, a holding company need not publish its own profit and loss account provided that the consolidated profit and loss states the amount of group profit dealt with in the accounts of the holding company. The holding company's profit to be disclosed is profit after tax after taking account (as appropriate) of dividends received and receivable from subsidiary companies and of provision for unrealised profit on transfer stocks. Dividends are restricted to those arising from post-acquisition profits and some holding companies would not take credit for dividends receivable until actually received.

TURNOVER

5.13 The figure of turnover disclosed in the consolidated profit and loss account is after inter company sales have been eliminated.

EXAMPLE

5.14 An analysis of turnover of H PLC and its subsidiary S PLC for year ended 31st December 19-8 was

Sales to	Sales by		
	H PLC	S PLC	Total
	£	£	£
H PLC	–	100,000	100,000
S PLC	200,000	–	200,000
External customers	3,500,000	1,800,000	5,300,000
	3,700,000	1,900,000	5,600,000

The figure of group turnover for the purposes of the consolidated profit and loss account is £5,300,000.

DIRECTORS' REMUNERATION

5.15 If a holding company publishes its own profit and loss account, it must disclose details of remuneration of directors in order to comply with the law. These details, of emoluments (subdivided between for services as directors and for other services) of directors' and past directors' pensions and compensation for loss of office, need not be disclosed in the consolidated profit and loss account except where, relying on Section 228 of the Companies Act 1985, the holding company does not publish its own profit and loss account.

5.16 The remuneration disclosed under these circumstances in the consolidated profit and loss account is the remuneration paid to those directors who are directors of the holding company.

EXAMPLE

5.17 An analysis of directors' emoluments of H PLC and its subsidiary S PLC for year ended 31st December 19-8 was

Paid to (Name of director) for services as directors	Paid by H PLC	S PLC	Group emoluments
	£	£	£
Anderson	9,000	–	9,000
Bardell	8,000	4,000	12,000
Cornwall	7,000	3,500	10,500
Dewsbury	16,000	2,500	18,500
Exton	–	7,500	–
	40,000	17,500	50,000

An amount of £50,000 would be disclosed as directors' emoluments (for services as directors) in either the holding company's profit and loss account or in the consolidated profit and loss account, as appropriate.

EXTRAORDINARY ITEMS

5.18 SSAP 6 defines extraordinary items as those material items which arise outside the ordinary activities of the business and whose incidence is both infrequent and irregular. In the group profit and loss account extraordinary items are taken into account after the profit attributable to group line. It should be noted that items which are regarded as extraordinary in the subsidiary company's own accounts may not be regarded as sufficiently material to be so regarded in the consolidated profit and loss account.

GROUP ELECTION FOR ACT PURPOSES

5.19 It is common practice for a group election to be made under Section 256 Income and Corporation Taxes Act 1970, whereby dividends paid by a subsidiary to a holding company are regarded not as franked investment income but as group income. The significance of this is that the dividends are accounted for by the holding company without the incidence of ACT; that is, such dividend income is shown as its ACT-exclusive amount and there is no charge under the taxation heading for tax credits on those dividends. The proforma which follows in 5.20 has been prepared on this basis and, unless otherwise stated, so have the solutions to the questions which appear throughout this manual.

PROFORMA PROFIT AND LOSS ACCOUNT

5.20 A proforma consolidated profit and loss account for a group, and reflecting the matters dealt with in 5.12 to 5.19, is shown below.

X PLC and subsidiary
Consolidated Profit and Loss Account
for year ended

	£	£
Turnover		X
Cost of Sales		X
Gross profit		X
Other expenses		X
Profit before tax		X
Less		
Taxation		X
Profit after tax		X
Less		
Minority and outside interests	X	
Pre-acquisition profits (current year)	X	

		X
Profit attributable to holding company		
shareholders (of which £X has been accounted		
for in the books of X PLC)		X
Less/add		
Extraordinary items (after tax)		X
Profit after extraordinary items		
attributable to group		X
Dividends paid and proposed		X
Retained profit – for year		X
– brought forward		X
– carried forward		X
Profit retained by X PLC (holding company)		X
Profit retained by subsidiary undertaking		X
(Retained profit as shown above)		X

COMPREHENSIVE EXAMPLE

5.21 The separate profit and loss accounts of H PLC and ESS PLC for the year ended 31st December 19-8 were:

	H PLC	ESS PLC
	£	£
Turnover	5,300,000	2,700,000
Profit before tax	770,000	440,000
Taxation	(309,000)	(200,000)
Profit after tax	461,000	240,000
Extraordinary items	92,000	(100,000)
	553,000	140,000
Appropriations		
Preference dividends paid	(70,000)	(30,000)
Ordinary dividends proposed	(230,000)	(60,000)
Retained profit		
– for year	253,000	50,000
– brought forward	189,000	104,000
– carried forward	442,000	154,000

Notes:

1. H had acquired 80% of the ordinary share capital of ESS on 1st April 19-8.

2. Turnover of H includes sales of £220,000 to ESS; turnover of ESS includes sales of £58,000 to H. Cost of Sales, Distribution costs and Administrative expenses of H were £4,419,000, £80,000 and £67,000 respectively and these same items for S £2,164,000, £56,000 and £40,000.

3. Included in the profit before tax of H are dividends (£36,000) receivable from ESS out of post-acquisition profits. A group election is in force whereby dividends are paid by ESS to H without the incidence of ACT.

4. Profit before tax is after charging:

	H PLC	ESS PLC
	£	£
Directors' emoluments - for		
services as directors	60,000	28,000
Depreciation	110,000	60,000
Auditors' fees	18,000	6,000
Interest on long term loans	–	11,000
Bank interest	1,000	–

None of the directors of ESS are also directors of H.

5. Extraordinary item of ESS is a provision for the uninsured portion of the loss resulting from a major fire at the company's warehouse in November 19-8.

Required:

Prepare the consolidated profit and loss account of the H group for the year ended 31st December 19-8.

SOLUTION

5.22 It is very useful to use the figures given in a question as the workings for the answer. This can be achieved by carrying out slight modifications, in this instance for reasons which are explained in the notes following the consolidated profit and loss account.

H PLC and subsidiary
Consolidated profit and loss account
for year ended 31 December 19-8

Workings H PLC £	ESS PLC £	Note		£
5,300,000 (278,000)	2,700,000	1		
5,022,000	2,700,000		Turnover	7,722,000
4,419,000 (278,000)	2,164,000	1		
4,141,000	2,164,000		Cost of Sales	(6,305,000)
881,000	536,000		Gross profit	1,417,000
(80,000)	(56,000)		Distribution costs	(136,000)
(67,000)	(40,000)		Administrative expenses	(107,000)
734,000	440,000	2	**Profit before tax**	1,174,000
36,000		2		

			after accounting for	£
60,000	28,000		Directors' emoluments	60,000
110,000	60,000		Depreciation	170,000
18,000	6,000		Auditors' fees	24,000
–	11,000		Interest – long-term	11,000
1,000	–		Bank interest	1,000

			Less	
(309,000)	(200,000)		**Taxation**	(509,000)
461,000	240,000		**Profit after tax**	665,000
			Less	
			Minority and outside interests	(72,000)
	(30,000)		(Preference 100% × 30,000)	
	(42,000)		Ordinary 20% × (240,000 − 30,000)	
			Pre-acquisition profits during year	(42,000)
	(42,000)		[3/12 × 80% × (240,000 − 30,000)]	
461,000	126,000		**Profit before extraordinary items**	551,000
92,000	(80,000)	4	**Extraordinary items** attributable to group holding company shareholders	12,000
553,000	46,000	5	**Profit attributable to holding company shareholders** after extraordinary items (of which £553,000 has been accounted by H PLC)	563,000

Workings H PLC £	ESS PLC £	Note		£
(230,000) (70,000)	(36,000)	2, 6	**Dividends paid and proposed**	(300,000)
253,000	10,000	8	**Group retained profit** – for current year	263,000
189,000	Nil	7	– brought forward	189,000
442,000	10,000		– carried forward	452,000
			Group profit for year	
			Retained by parent	253,000
			Retained by subsidiary	10,000
		9		263,000

Notes

1. Intra group sales and Cost of Sales are eliminated so that group turnover and group cost of sales relate solely to transactions with external parties.

2. Dividends receivable by H from ESS, have been eliminated from group profit before tax because they are an intra group transfer. They are, however, correctly shown under H; consequently from this point the group figures will be £36,000 less than the sum of the corresponding figures of H and ESS. The contra, cancelling, entry occurs in the ESS column at the dividend proposed line, after which point the sub-totals for H and ESS add across to the group figure. See note 6. for calculations.

3. The fees of only those directors who are holding company directors are disclosed for the group. As none of ESS' directors are involved, their fees are excluded from group fees.

4. The figure is arrived at by taking the group's share of ESS' extraordinary item ($80\% \times £100,000$). It is readily apparent from the date given (November 19-8) that the occurrence is post-acquisition. If it had happened prior to 1st April 19-8, it would have affected pre-acquisition profit instead.

5. The statement of H's profit at this stage is necessary if, as has been assumed, H does not publish its own profit and loss account. Included in the amount declared, £553,000, is the amount of dividends receivable, £36,000.

6. Only the dividends paid and/or proposed by the holding company are shown at this point. The total amount of profit attributable to minority interests (including that which is the subject of a dividend) has already been eliminated. The dividend payable by ESS to H is £48,000 ($80\% \times 60,000$) in total but part of this relates to the pre-acquisition period. The balance, £36,000 ($9/12 \times 48,000$) representing dividend out of post-acquisition profits serves as the contra entry (see note 2.). Pre-acquisition dividend, £12,000 ($3/12 \times 48,000$) has reduced the cost of H's investment in ESS.

7. Group retained profit comprises profit (or loss) of the holding company and the group's share of post-acquisition profit (or loss) of the subsidiary. However, in this example, the whole of the retained profit brought forward by ESS (£104,000) was earned prior to date of acquisition, therefore none of it is consolidated, leaving the brought forward figure for the group to consist solely of the amount brought forward by H (£189,000).

8. The group total (£263,000) can also be viewed as comprising

	£
H PLC - profit retained from operations (ie excluding dividends receivable from ESS, which for consolidation purposes are regarded as being retained within the group)	217,000
ESS PLC - group share of post-acquisition profit $[9/12 \times (80\% \times (240,000 - 30,000)) = 126,000$ less group share of extraordinary item (note 4) $(12/12 \times (80\% \times 100,000) = (80,000)]$	46,000
Group retained profit for year	263,000

9. These figures are obtained by reading off from the workings at the retained profit for year line.

ACCOUNTING FOR ASSOCIATED COMPANIES

6.0 An investing group or company may be able to participate in the policy decisions of another company (other than of a subsidiary company) either because there is effectively a partnership or other joint venture relationship, or because the former owns a substantial, long-term, holding or, unless the significant influence presumption can be rebutted, any holding of between 20% and 50% of the equity voting rights of the latter. Under these circumstances the latter (investee) is termed an associated company. Accounting for associated companies is the subject matter of SSAP 1, summarised below. Within the Companies Act 1989, associated companies are included in the term participating interest.

SSAP 1. ACCOUNTING FOR ASSOCIATED COMPANIES.

6.1 The investing company should bring into its own accounts dividends received and receivable from associated companies in respect of periods of account ending on or before that date and declared prior to the approval of the accounts by the directors of the investing company.

6.2 In the case of the group accounts, the investing group (or company) should consolidate the investing group's share of profits less losses of the associated companies.

6.3 Adjustments similar to those made when consolidating the results of subsidiary companies, should be made, when appropriate, in the case of associated companies. Elimination of unrealised profit on stock is an example of such an adjustment.

6.4 The group's share of turnover and depreciation of the associated company should not be consolidated. If these items are significant in relation to the investing group's accounts, separate disclosure should be by way of note.

6.5 The profit and loss account of the investing group or company should incorporate, as individual items, the attributable share of the associated companies' profit before tax, taxation, extraordinary items and retained profits. This is illustrated in 6.9 and 6.10 below.

6.6 In the balance sheet, the group's interest in associated companies is the aggregate of the group's share of the goodwill in the associated companies' financial statements and the premium paid or discount on acquisition of the interest and, to be separately disclosed, the net assets (excluding goodwill).

6.7 Where consolidated accounts are not prepared for any reason the required information should be shown in a separate balance sheet, or as a supplement to its own balance sheet.

6.8 SSAP 1 was re-issued in a revised version in April 1982.

PROFORMA PROFIT AND LOSS ACCOUNT

6.9 The proforma which follows is one of a number of formats which comply with the requirements of SSAP 1 which does not prescribe a specific layout but gives companies the freedom to experiment with alternative layouts provided that they disclose the items stated in 6.5 above. The proforma is for a group comprising a holding company which has invested in subsidiary and associated companies.

Zed PLC and subsidiaries
(Proforma) Consolidated Profit and Loss Account
for year ended

	£	£
Turnover (of investing company and subsidiaries)		X
Cost of Sales (of investing company and subsidiaries)		X
Gross profit (of investing company and subsidiaries)		X
Other expenses (of investing company and subsidiaries)		X
Profit before tax (of investing company and subsidiaries)		X
Profits, less, losses, of associated companies (group share only)		X
Profit before tax		X
Less		
Taxation (of investing company and subsidiaries)	X	
Taxation of associated companies (group share only)	X	
		X
Profit after tax		X
Less		
Minority Interests		X

Pre-acquisition profits during year (of subsidiaries)	X
	X̲
Profit after tax, before extraordinary items	X
Add/Less	
Extraordinary items (of investing company and group share of subsidiaries and, if not material, of associated companies)	X
Extraordinary items of associated companies (if material in amount) (group share only)	X̲
	X̲
Profit attributable to members of the investing company (of which £X has been dealt with in the accounts of the investing company)	X
Less	
Dividends paid and proposed (of investing company)	X̲
Retained profit – current year	X
– brought forward	X̲
– carried forward	X̲
Profit retained	
By investing company	X
By subsidiary undertakings	X
In associated undertakings	X̲
	X̲

EXAMPLE

6.10 The facts are the same as in 5.21 except that H PLC acquired 30% of the equity share capital of A PLC on 1st October 19-7 at a cost of £307,000. There were retained profits of £263,000 at acquisition date and an equity share capital of £500,000.

The total results for A for the year ended 31st December 19-8 are summarised thus:

	£
Profit before tax	420,600
Taxation	150,000
Extraordinary loss	60,300
Retained profit at January 19-8	303,400
Proposed dividends	100,000

Required:

Prepare the consolidated profit and loss account of the H group for the year ended 31 December 19-8 and an extract from the balance sheet at that date showing the inclusion of the results of the associated company, A.

SOLUTION

6.11 The answer follows the proforma given in 6.9 above. Workings for H and ESS would be as already shown in 5.21 but with slight modifications. Workings for the associated company are shown in a separate column on the right of the profit and loss account, thus:

H PLC and subsidiary
Consolidated profit and loss account
for year ended 31 December 19-8

Workings H PLC £	ESS PLC £	Note		£	Workings A PLC £
5,300,000	2,700,000				
(278,000)		1			
5,022,000	2,700,000		Turnover	7,722,000	N/A
4,419,000	2,164,000				
(278,000)		1			
4,141,000	2,164,000		Cost of Sales	(6,305,000)	N/A
881,000	536,000		Gross profit	1,417,000	N/A
(80,000)	(56,000)		Distribution costs	(136,000)	N/A
(67,000)	(40,000)		Administrative expenses	(107,000)	N/A
734,000	440,000	2	**Profit before tax**	1,174,000	420,600
36,000		1	**Share of profit of**		
₡30,000		2, 5	**associated company** (30% × 420,600)	126,180	126,180
				1,300,180	
			Less		
(309,000)	(200,000)	5	**Taxation**	(509,000)	
			Share of taxation of associated company 30% × 150,000)	(45,000)	(45,000)
491,000	240,000		**Profit after tax**	746,180	81,180
			Less		
	(30,000)		**Minority and outside interests**	(72,000)	
	(42,000)		(workings as in 5.22)		
	(42,000)		**Pre-acquisition profits during year** (workings as in 5.22)	(42,000)	
491,000	126,000		**Profit before extraordinary items**	632,180	81,180
92,000	(80,000)		**Extraordinary items**	12,000	
			Share of extraordinary loss of associated company (30% × 60,300)	(18,090)	(18,090)
583,000	46,000		**Profit attributable to holding company shareholders** (of which £583,000 has been accounted) for by H PLC)	626,090	63,090

Workings H PLC £	ESS PLC £	Note		£	Workings A PLC £
			Less		
(300,000)	(36,000)	2	Dividends proposed	(300,000)	(30,000)¢
			Group retained profit		
283,000	10,000	4	– for current year	326,090	33,090
189,000	Nil	3	–brought forward	201,120	12,120
472,000	10,000		–carried forward	527,210	45,210
			Group profit for current year retained (see note 4.)		
			By H PLC	283,000	
			By subsidiary company	10,000	
			In associated company	33,090	
				326,090	

N/A denotes Not Applicable

Notes

1. In the workings, dividends receivable by H from ESS are isolated from profit before tax for reasons stated in 5.22 (note 2).

2. SSAP 1 requires that dividends received and receivable from associated companies should be credited in the investing company's profit and loss account. This answer assumes that this has not been done already aı d that this further adjustment of £30,000 (30% × £100,000) is necessary together with the contra entry in A's workings column. From this point downwards the cross additions of the workings totals exceed the group totals by £66,000 (the amount of the dividends receivable) until the current year retained profit line is reached.

3. For consolidation purposes, there is no post–acquisition profit brought forward for ESS, as stated in 5.22 (note.7). The total retained profit brought forward for A at 1st January 19-8 was given as £303,400. Of this figure £263,000 was stated to have been the figure at acquisition date. Post-acquisition profit brought forward is thus £40,400 (303,400 - 263,000); the group share is thus £12,120 (30% × £40,400).

4. The workings totals at this line provide the figures for this table.

5. The consequences of a group election (see 5.19) are inapplicable to an associated company. For simplicity, however, and because the tax credit used to gross up the actual dividends received to a franked investment income figure then counteracts itself by inclusion as a component of the taxation charge, and because both the dividend and the tax credit have no effect on the group figures, the grossing up aspect has been ignored.

H PLC and subsidiary
Consolidated balance sheet (extract)
as at 31 December 19-8

	£
Fixed assets	
Investments	
Associated companies	352,210
[307, 000 + 45, 210]	

Notes to balance sheet: £

Investments
Associated companies
This figure comprises
Goodwill   78,100   [see workings]

Group's share of net assets of associated companies	274,110	
	352,210	

Reserves
Associated companies Group share

– at 1 January 19-8	12,120	
– retained profit for year	33,090	
– at 31 December 19-8	45,210	

£

Workings:

	£
Cost of investment	307,000
Share capital (30% × 500,000)	150,000
Reserves (pre-acquisition) (30% × 263,000)	78,900
Group share of net assets at date of acquisition	228,900
Goodwill	78,100

GROUP STATEMENTS OF SOURCE AND APPLICATION OF FUNDS

7.0 The general nature of statements of source and application of funds and their construction and format, are dealt with in Section IV Chapter 2. The following subsections show the modifications which need to be made to the basic format when a group of companies is involved.

GROUP FORMAT

7.1 When a holding company with subsidiary companies (and possibly, associated companies as well) prepares a statement of source and application of funds statement for the group as a whole, certain additional items have to be superimposed on the basic format illustrated in Section IV Chapter 2.

7.2 In particular, there must be incorporated, as separate items, minority interests and profits (less losses) of associated companies.

7.3 Additionally, if a subsidiary has been acquired during the year, the effects of the acquisition must be incorporated and separately identified. There are two ways by which this can be achieved, either.

a. the individual assets and liabilities of the acquired subsidiary are merged with the individual assets and liabilities of the rest of the group; or

b. the net assets acquired are included as a single, separately identified application of funds.

In both cases the effects of the acquisition of the subsidiary are summarised, (if 7.3a is used) or analysed (if 7.3b. is used.)

7.4 A proforma statement for a group, illustrating the matters noted in 7.1 to 7.3, now follows. Columns for previous period figures have been omitted.

(Proforma)
Exe PLC and subsidiaries
Statement of source and application of funds

	£000	£000	£000
Source of funds			
Profit before tax and extraordinary items			
less minority interests		X	
Extraordinary items		X	
Adjustment for items not involving movement of funds			
Minority interests in retained profits of the year	X		
Depreciation	X		
(Profits)/losses retained in associated companies	(X)		
		X	
Total generated from operations			X

Funds from other sources
(itemised as appropriate)

	X		
	X̲		
		X	
		X	

Application of funds
(Itemised as appropriate)

	X		
	X		
(Purchase of subsidiary Wye PLC (if method 7.3b. is employed))	X		
		X̲	
Increase/decrease in working capital		X	(A)
(Itemised as appropriate)	X		
	X		
	X̲		
		X̳	(B)

Subtotals at (A) and (B) agree.

Analysis/Summary of the effects of the acquisition of Wye PLC

£000

Net Assets acquired
(Itemised as appropriate)

(assets)	X	
	X	
	X	
	X	
	X	
(liabilities)	(X)	
	(X)̲	
	X̳	(C)

Purchase consideration

Cash paid	X	
Shares issued	X̲	
	X̳	(D)

Sub-totals at (C) and (D) agree.

The above proforma closely follows an example given in an Appendix to SSAP 10. (Statement of sources and application of funds). The standard states that there is no standard format and that businesses are free to devise the form of their own statements and that in doing so the overriding factor should be the production of a statement which shows clearly "the manner in which the operations of the company have been financed and in which its financial resources have been utilised...".

EXAMPLE

7.5 The summarised consolidated accounts of the A Group were as shown below:

A Group
Consolidated profit and loss account
for year ended 31 December 19-8

	£000
Profit before depreciation	735
Depreciation	(254)
Profit before tax	481
Corporation tax	(120)
Profit after tax	361
Minority and outside interests	(34)
	327

Extraordinary losses		(135)
Profit for year attributable to A PLC		192
Dividends proposed		(50)
Retained profit – for year		142
– brought forward		26
– carried forward		168

A PLC had acquired a majority holding during 19-8 in its subsidiary J. PLC when that company's net assets comprised:

	£000
Tangible fixed assets	92
Stock	76
Debtors	40
Creditors	(54)
Net	154

Of this net figure, £24,000 was attributable to minority interests. The purchase consideration, £20,000, was satisfied by A. issuing ordinary shares, £150,000 and 9% debentures, £50,000.

A Group
Consolidated balance sheet as at 31 December

19-7			19-8	
£000	£000		£000	£000
		Goodwill	70	
	491	Tangible fixed assets	784	
				854
		Current assets		
120		Stock	217	
182		Debtors	246	
97		Bank and cash	113	
399			576	
		Current liabilities		
83		Creditors	168	
30		Proposed dividends	50	
115		Taxation	120	
228			338	
	171	Net current assets		238
	662	Net assets employed		1,092
		Financed by:		
£000	£000		£000	£000
	450	Ordinary share capital		600
		Reserves:		
26		– profit and loss	168	
36		other	36	
	62			204
	512	Shareholders' funds		804
	–	Minority and outside interests		58
	150	9% debentures		230
	662			1,092

(NB. ACT has been ignored for simplicity)

Required:

Prepare the group statement of source and application of funds for year ended 31 December 19-8 on each of the following bases.

a. individual assets and liabilities of A. and J. are merged.
and

b. net assets of J are shown as a single application.

SOLUTION

7.6 For convenience the solutions to a. and b. are arrayed on the left and right respectively. The narrative, where appropriate, applies to both.

A Group
Statement of source and application of funds
for year ended 31 December 19-8

a. £000	a. £000		b. £000	b. £000
447		Profit before tax, less minority and outside interests [481 − 34]	447	
(135)		Extraordinary items	(135)	
	312			312
		Adjustments for items not involving use of funds:		
254		Depreciation	254	
34		Minority and outside interests	34	
	288			288
	600	**Total generated from operations**		600
		Funds from other sources		
		Issues in consideration for acquisition of J. PLC		
150		—shares	150	
50		—debentures	50	
30		Other debentures issues [230 − (150 + 50)]	30	
24		Interest of outside shareholders in J.PLC on acquisition		
	254			230
	854			830
		Application of funds		
		Acquisition of assets		
70		—goodwill		
547		—tangible fixed assets [(a) 784 + 254 − 491]	455	
		—purchase of J.PLC.	200	
30		Dividends paid	30	
115		Tax paid	115	
	762			800
	92	**Increase/(decrease) in working capital**		30
97		Increase/decrease in – stock	21	
64		– debtors	24	
(85)		(Increase)/decrease in – creditors	(31)	
		Movement in net liquid funds		
16		Increase/(decrease) in bank and cash	16	
	92			30

Summary (a) Analysis (b) of the effects of the
acquisition of J.PLC

	£000
Net assets acquired	
Goodwill	70
Tangible fixed assets (itemised)	92
Stock	76
Debtors	40
Creditors	(54)
Minority and outside interests	(24)
	200

Consideration

Ordinary shares in A. PLC	150
9% debentures in A. PLC	50
	200

PRESENTATION OF GROUP ACCOUNTS FOR PUBLICATION

8.0 Up to this point in this chapter, the profit and loss accounts and balance sheets have, as stated in 4.0 and 5.0 been prepared in a form suitable only for internal circulation in that their content and formats do not comply with current legislation.

8.1 Disclosure requirements applicable to the published accounts of companies generally, appear in Appendix 1.

PROFIT AND LOSS ACCOUNT FORMAT

8.2 As explained in Section 1 Chapter 4, companies are free to adopt any one of the four formats available under Schedule 4, Companies Act, 1985. In fact, companies have almost exclusively opted to use Formats 1 or 2, both of which result in a vertical presentation.

8.3 Basically, the format of a consolidated profit and loss account is a modified version of that of a non-group (individual) company, as illustrated in Section 1 Chapter 4 paragraphs 4.4 and 4.6.

8.4 However, within a group profit and loss account, items arise which are not to be found within that of a non-group undertaking. These items include share of profits/(losses) of associated undertakings, share of the taxation charge of associated undertakings and minority interests in profits/(losses) of subsidiary undertakings. The majority of undertakings, for published purposes at least, tend not to disclose pre-acquisition profits/(losses) arising during the current year (see 5.20). Instead, the usual practice is to consolidate, in the case of newly acquired subsidiaries, profits/(losses) from date of acquisition, or, in the case of subsidiaries disposed of during the current year, the profit(loss) to date of cessation.

8.5 Typical format of a consolidated profit and loss account (Format 1).

Mercantile Holdings (19-1) PLC
Profit and loss account
for year ended 31 December 19-X.

	£000	£000
Turnover		X
Cost of sales		(X)
Gross profit		X
Distribution costs	(X)	
Administrative expenses	(X)	
Other operating income	X	
		(X)
Trading profit		X
Income from interests in associated undertakings	X	
(i.e. group share of profit of associated undertakings)		
Income from other participating interests	X	
Income from other fixed asset investments	X	
Interest payable	(X)	
		X
Profit on ordinary activities before tax		X
Tax on profit on ordinary activities		
(including group share of tax of associated undertakings)		(X)
Profit on ordinary activities after tax		X
Minority interests		(X)
		X
Extraordinary loss net of taxation benefit		(X)
Profit for the financial year attributable to shareholders		X
Dividends		(X)
Profit retained		X

8.6 Typical format of a consolidated profit and loss account (Format 2).

Fabri-Kayshun Holdings PLC
Profit and loss account
for year ended 31 December 19-X

	£000	£000
Turnover		X
Change in stocks of finished goods and work in progress (increase)		X
Own work capitalised		X
		X
Raw materials and consumables		(X)
		X
Staff costs	(X)	
Depreciation	(X)	
Other operating charges	(X)	
		(X)
Operating profit		X
Income from interests in associated undertakings	X	
(i.e. group share of profit of associated undertakings)		
Income from other participating interests	X	
Income from other fixed assets investments	X	
Interest payable	(X)	
		X
Profit on ordinary activities before tax		X
Tax on profit on ordinary activities		(X)
(including group share of tax of associated undertakings)		—
Profit on ordinary activities after tax		X
Minority interests		(X)
Profit for the financial year attributable to shareholders		X
Dividends		(X)
Profit retained		X

BALANCE SHEET FORMAT

8.7 Companies are free also to adopt either of the two formats available under Schedule 4, Companies Act 1985. As a matter of fact, companies have almost exclusively opted to use Format 1 vertical presentation.

8.8 The format of a consolidated balance sheet is, in essence, a modified version of that of a non- group (individual) company, as illustrated in Section III Chapter 4 paragraphs 4.5 and 4.7

8.9 As was noted in relation to group profit and loss accounts, items arise within a group balance sheet also which are not to be found within that of a non-group undertaking. These items include goodwill on consolidation, participating interests, loans to and from participating interests, trading balances owing to and from participating interests, the group's share of post acquisition reserves of participating interests, minority interests. A typical pro-forma group balance sheet using Format 1 is given in 8.10 and a modified version in 8.11.

8.10 Typical format of a consolidated balance sheet (Format 1)

Mercantile Holdings (19-1) PLC
Balance Sheet
as at 31 December 19-X

	£000	£000	£000
Fixed assets			
Intangible assets			
Goodwill on consolidation		X	
Tangible assets			
(itemised)		X	
Investments			
Shares in related companies		X	
			X

Current assets

Stocks (Itemised)		X	
Debtors			
Trade debtors	X		
Amounts owed by undertakings in which			
the company has a participating interest	X		
Other debtors	X		
Cash at bank and in hand	X̲		
		X̲	

Creditors: amounts falling due within one year X

Bank loans and overdrafts	X	
Trade creditors	X	
Amounts owed to undertakings in which		
the company has a participating interest	X	
Other creditors	X̲	
		(X)̲

Net current assets	X̲
Total assets less current liabilities	X̲

Creditors: amounts falling due after more than one year

Debenture loans	X	
Amounts owed to undertakings in which		
the company has a participating interest	X̲	
		(X)̲

Provisions for liabilities and charges

Deferred taxation		(X)̲
		X̳

Capital and Reserves

Called up share capital		X
Share premium account		X
Other reserves		
Capital redemption reserve	X	
Other reserves	X̲	
		X
Profit and loss account		X
Minority interests		X̲
		X̳

8.11 A common modification to 8.10 above is to interpose minority interest between the items provisions for liabilities and charges and capital and reserves. Additionally, a company may opt to arrive at a grand total after the item total assets less liabilities, thus:

Mercantile Holdings (19-1) PLC
Balance Sheet
as at 31 December 19-X

	£000	£000
Fixed assets (details as in 8.10)		X
Current assets (details as in 8.10)	X	
Creditors: amounts due within one year		
(details as in 8.10)	(X)̲	
Net current assets (as in 8.10)		X̲
Total assets less current liabilities (as in 8.10)		X̳
Creditors: amounts falling due after		
more than one year		
(details as in 8.10)		X
Provisions for liabilities and charges		
(details as in 8.10)		X
Minority interests		X
Capital and reserves (details as in 8.10)		X̲
		X̳

GOODWILL

9.0 The difference which can arise between the fair value of the consideration and that of the separable net assets was first noted in para 4.7 of this section and in subsequent paragraphs throughout.

9.1 An Exposure Draft on accounting for goodwill (ED30) achieved standard status in late 1984 and became effective, from 1 January, 1985, as SSAP 22, and revised from 1 January 1989.

SSAP 22 ACCOUNTING FOR GOODWILL

9.2 Companies or groups should not bring non–purchased goodwill into their accounts. Purchased goodwill representing the difference between the fair value of the consideration and that of the aggregate of the fair values of the separable net assets (including identifiable intangibles but excluding separable intangibles), can be either negative or positive.

9.3 Negative purchased goodwill should be credited directly to reserves.

9.4 Positive purchased goodwill should be written off,
  either

  a. against reserves on acquisition, or

  b. by amortisation on a systematic basis over its useful economic life in arriving at profit or loss
     on ordinary activities.

9.5 If the method in 9.4 (b) is selected.

  a. any subsequent permanent diminution in value should be written off at once

  b. the useful economic life should be calculated at acquisition but may subsequently be shortened.

9.6 The alternative treatments in 9.4 are both available to a company or group at all times and for different acquisitions.

9.7 There were transitional arrangements for goodwill existing at the date the standard became operative.

STUDENT SELF TESTING

Test exercises

Special Note: The exercises which follow are designed to test the techniques of calculating figures for use in group accounts. The answers are not therefore necessarily in a form suitable for publication.

1. The summarised balance sheets of C PLC and D PLC at 31st December 19-5 were:

	C PLC		D PLC	
	£000	£000	£000	£000
Ordinary shares of £1.00 per share		400		100
Reserves				
– profit and loss	100		50	
– general	50		40	
		150		90
		550		190
Tangible fixed assets		317		120
Investment in D PLC (70,000 shares)		118		–
Net current assets		115		70
		550		190

C had acquired its shareholding during 19-3 when D's profit and loss account had a credit balance of £30,000 and general reserve, £20,000.

Required:

Prepare the consolidated balance sheet of the C Group as at 31st December 19-5.

2. The facts are exactly the same as in 1, except that C's investment in D cost £71,000 and C's net current assets were £162,000.

Required:

Prepare the consolidated balance sheet of the C Group as at 31st December 19-5.

3. . The summarised balance sheets of G PLC and H PLC at 31 August 19-5 were:

	G PLC		H PLC	
	£000	£000	£000	£000
Ordinary shares of £1.00 per share		840		200
Reserves: profit and loss		250		140
Shareholders' funds		1,090		340
Long-term loans		–		170
		1,090		510
Tangible fixed assets		110		350
Trade investments: loans		220		
Investments in H PLC (200,000 shares)		240		
Current assets				
Stock	300		190	
Debtors	270		90	
Bank and cash	160		50	
	730		330	
Current liabilities				
Creditors	210		170	
		520		160
		1,090		510

G had acquired its holding when H's profit and loss account had a credit balance of £100,000. Since that date G has made a long-term loan of £130,000 and, as a separate arrangement, has supplied trading stock to H for £125,000 (at cost) for which H has not yet paid.
Required:
Prepare the consolidated balance sheet of the G Group as at 31 August 19-5.

4. The facts are exactly the same as in 3, except that the goods supplied to H for £125,000 had cost G £100,000 and H still had four fifths of these goods in stock at 31 August 19- 5.
   Required:
   Specify the items in your answer to 3 which would be affected by these circumstances and the amounts by which they would alter.

5. The facts are exactly the same as in 4, except that, additionally G had also supplied H with machinery which H retained as a fixed asset. The machinery had cost G £140,000 but the transfer price was £190,000. H depreciates machinery over a 10 year life using the straight line method and assuming no residual value.
   Required:

   a. Specify the items in the consolidated balance sheet which would be affected by these circumstances and the amounts by which they would alter.

   b. Prepare the consolidated balance sheet of the G Group as at 31 August 19-5 incorporating the above matters.

6. The facts are exactly the same as in 3 except that H subsequently declared and paid a dividend of 10% from pre-acquisition profits.
   Required:

   a. Specify how this circumstance would affect the balance sheet of G PLC given in 3. Ignore the taxation implications.

   b. Rewrite the balance sheet of G PLC given in 3, incorporating the above matters.

7. The facts are exactly the same as in 3 except that H subsequently declared a dividend of 10% out of post-acquisition profits. It is the policy of G not to take credit for investment income until it is actually received.
   Required:

   a. State the effects of H's dividend declaration on the balance sheet of

      i. G PLC

      ii. H PLC

      iii. G Group

b. State the effects on your answer to 7a., of H's actual payment of the dividend, on the balance sheet of

    i. G PLC

    ii. H PLC

    iii. G Group

8. The facts are exactly the same as in 7 except that G holds only 150,000 ordinary shares in H and G has also proposed a dividend of 10%.

Required:

Prepare the consolidated balance sheet of the G Group after the dividends have been proposed. Ignore the taxation implications.

9. The summarised balance sheets of three companies at 31 December 19-5 were:

	J PLC	K PLC	L PLC
	£000	£	£
Tangible fixed assets	972	843	406
Investment in subsidiary companies			
– J in K (700,000 shares)	356	–	–
– K in L (300,000 shares)	–	248	–
Net current assets	205	229	164
	1,533	1,320	570
Ordinary shares of £1.00 per share	1,200	1,000	400
Reserves			
– profit and loss	233	200	100
– other	100	120	70
	1,533	1,320	570

At the date of acquisition by J of its holding, K's profit and loss account had a credit balance of £100,000 and other reserves, £50,000. L's profit and loss account had a debit balance of £40,000 when K acquired its holding on the same day.

Required:

Prepare separate consolidated balance sheets of the J Group as at 31 December 19-5, using.

    a. the direct method and

    b. the indirect method

of consolidation.

10. M PLC had acquired a 60% holding of the ordinary share capital of P PLC during 19-4. For the year ended 31 December 19-5 their individual summarised profit and loss accounts disclosed:

	M PLC	P PLC
	£000	£000
Profit before tax	520	270
Corporation tax	(210)	(70)
Profit after tax	310	200
Proposed dividends	(100)	(40)
Retained profit		
- for year	210	160
- brought forward	150	120
- carried forward	360	280

The retained profit brought forward by P included £100,000 pre-acquisition profit.

Required:

Prepare the consolidated profit and loss account for the M Group for the year ended 31 December 19-5.

11. The facts are exactly the same as in 10, except that P also had 100,000 10% preference shares of £1.00 per share in issue (of which 30,000 had been acquired by M in 19-3) and on which the dividends had been paid.

Required:

Prepare the consolidated profit and loss account for the M Group for the year ended 31 December 19-5.

12. Details of the turnover and directors' emoluments relating to Q PLC and its subsidiaries R PLC and S PLC for year ended 31 October 19-5 are as shown below:

Sales to

		Sales by		
	Total	Q PLC	R PLC	S PLC
	£000	£000	£000	£000
Q	726	–	94	632
R	1,189	608	–	581
S	198	121	77	–
External customers	8,925	7,095	1,534	296
	11,038	7,824	1,705	1,509

Directors' emoluments
Paid to

		Paid by		
	Total	Q PLC	R PLC	S PLC
	£000	£000	£000	£000
Forster	42	32	6	4
Garfield (Chairman)	31	28	3	–
Harrow	28	25	–	3
Idris	20	20	–	–
Jackson	19	–	19	–
Kelly	20	–	–	20
	160	105	28	27

Required:

State the amounts which would appear in the consolidated profit and loss account of the Q Group for

a. turnover and

b. directors' emoluments

so far as information is available

13. The facts are exactly the same as in 10, except that M PLC had also acquired 40% of the £100,000 equity share capital of T PLC during 19-4, when the company's reserves stood at £60,000 at a cost of £85,000.

For the year ended 31 December 19-5, data relating to T included:

	£000
Retained profit at 1 January 19-5	100
Profit before tax	200
Corporation tax	70
Extraordinary loss (after tax)	80
Proposed dividends	10

Required:

a. Prepare the consolidated profit and loss account of the M Group for the year ended 31 December 19-5.

b. Prepare extracts from the M Group consolidated balance sheet as at 31 December 19-5, showing how the relevant data for T PLC would be incorporated. Ignore the taxation aspects.

14. The summarised consolidated accounts of the W Group were as shown below.

W Group
Consolidated profit and loss account
for year ended 31 December 19-6

	£000
Profit before tax (after charging depreciation £160,000)	395
Corporation tax	(137)
Profit after tax	258
Minority and outside interests	(56)
	202
Extraordinary gain	90
Profit for year attributable to W PLC shareholders	292
Dividends proposed	(180)
Retained profit – for year	112
– brought forward	29
– carried forward	141

W Group
Consolidated balance sheet
as at 31 December

19-5		19-6
£000		£000
–	Goodwill	10
510	Tangible fixed assets (at written down values)	980
510		990
	Current assets	
240	Stock	381
231	Debtors	350
106	Bank and cash	184
577		915
	Current liabilities	
293	Creditors	328
70	Proposed dividends	180
42	Taxation	137
405		645
172	Net current assets	270
682	Net assets employed	1,260
600	Ordinary shares of £1.00 per share	700
29	Reserves – profit and loss	141
53	– other	53
682		894
–	Minority and outside interests	206
–	10% debentures	160
682		1,260

N.B. For simplicity, ACT has been ignored.

During 19-6, W had acquired a controlling interest in Z PLC, thus.

Net assets acquired	£000	Consideration	£000
Goodwill	10	Issue of	
Tangible fixed assets	312	– ordinary shares	100
Stock	90	– 10% debentures	160

Debtors	30	
Creditors	(32)	
Minority interests	(150)	
	260	260

Required:

Prepare the group statement of source and application of funds for year ended 31 December 19- 6, on each of the following bases.

    a. individual assets and liabilities of W and Z are merged
        and

    b. net assets of Z are shown as a single application.

15. SSAP 1 - Accounting for results of associated companies.

    a. How is an associated company defined?

    b. How is investment income from an associated company accounted for in the accounts of the investing company?

    c. How is investment income from an associated company accounted for in the accounts of the investing group?

    d. On what grounds may the results of an associated company be omitted from the consolidated accounts?

    e. On what grounds may adjustments be made to the accounts of associated companies prior to their inclusion in the accounts of the investing group?

    f. What specific items relating to associated companies should be separately shown in the profit and loss account?

    g. On what basis should the interests in associated companies be disclosed in the balance sheet of the investing group?

    h. What particulars regarding associated companies should be disclosed in the accounts of the investing company or group?

    i. On what basis should the interests in associated companies be disclosed in the balance sheet of the investing company?

16. SSAP 14 - Group Accounts

    a. In what form should a holding company prepare group accounts?

    b. On what basis should a holding company prepare group accounts?

    c. If it is impractical to adopt uniform accounting policies, what disclosures must be made?

    d. What procedure should be followed where the accounts of a subsidiary are not co-terminous with those of the holding company?

    e. On what grounds may subsidiary companies be excluded from group accounts?

    f. What particulars should be disclosed in respect of excluded subsidiaries?

    g. When shares in companies are acquired or sold, what information should be included in consolidated financial statements?

    h. What items should be included in the consolidated profit and loss account when a material disposal occurs?

    i. What particulars of the principal subsidiaries should be included in the group accounts?

    j. How should outside or minority interests be dealt with in the consolidated accounts?

17. In preparing the consolidated balance sheet of L Limited as at 31st December 19-9 you are required to show clearly what amounts, if any, you would include in respect of W Limited with regard to:

    a. cost of control or capital reserve:

    b. profit or loss;

    c. minority interests;

under each of the following assumptions:

a. 48,000 of the shares then in issue of W Limited were acquired at a cost of £75,000 on 1st March 19-7; L Limited participated in the proposed dividend of £8,000;

b. 40,000 of the shares then in issue of W Limited were acquired at a cost of £60,000 on 31st December, 19-7; L Limited participated in the bonus issue but not the proposed dividend of £9,000

c. 60,000 of the shares then in issue of W Limited were acquired at a cost of £80,000 on 1st July, 19-9; L Limited did not participate in the proposed dividend of £6,000.

The balance sheet of W Limited as at 31st December 19-9 showed:

	£
Share capital, authorised and issued:	
Ordinary shares of £1 each, fully paid	80,000
Undistributed profits	24,000
7% Debentures 20-1/20-8	40,000

The profit and loss appropriation account, for the years ended 31st December, was as follows:

	19-6	19-7	19-8	19-9
	£	£	£	£
Balance at beginning of year	16,000	22,000	43,000	28,000
Bonus issue of one for four – 1st January 19-8			16,000	
			27,000	
Profit for the year	14,000	30,000	7,000	Loss (4,000)
	30,000	52,000	34,000	24,000
Proposed dividends	8,000	9,000	6,000	Nil
Balance carried forward	£22,000	£43,000	£28,000	£24,000

The only increase in issued share capital during this period has been from the bonus issue on 1st January, 19-8.

18. Grip Ltd, which has an authorised and issued share capital of 100,000 ordinary shares of £1 each fully paid, had a balance on revenue reserve of £16,200 on 31st December 19-3, after paying a dividend for the year ended on that date.

You are also given the following information:

a. On 31st October 19-4, Grip Ltd purchased 9,000 of the 10,000 issued ordinary shares of £1 each fully paid in Hand Ltd for £14,250. The balance on revenue reserve of Hand Ltd as on 31st December 19-3 had been £3,450 after paying a dividend for the year ended on that date.

b. For the year ended 31st December 19-4 Grip Ltd made a trading profit of £18,640 and paid a dividend of 15%, whilst Hand Ltd made a trading profit of £4,000 and paid a dividend of 20%.

c. For the year ended 31st December 19-5 Grip Ltd made a trading profit of £26,540 and paid a dividend of 20% whilst Hand Ltd incurred a trading loss of £4,100 and no dividend was paid.

d. During the year ended 31st December 19-5 Hand Ltd had manufactured and sold to Grip Ltd an item of plant for £8,000 which included a profit on selling price to Hand Ltd of 25%. The plant had been included in the fixed assets of Grip Ltd and a full year's depreciation had been provided thereon at 20% on cost.

You are required to show how the above items would be reflected in the consolidated Balance sheet of Grip Ltd as on 31st December 19-5, together with corresponding figures for the preceding year, and to provide detailed schedules showing the compilation of the figures contained therein.

19. From the information given below you are required to prepare the consolidated balance sheet of X Limited and its subsidiary companies as at 31st December 19-1:

	X Limited £	Y Limited £	Z Limited £
Share capital:			
Ordinary shares of £1 each	100,000	50,000	30,000
7½% Preference shares of £1 each	–	10,000	–
General reserve	65,000	–	–
Retained profit (or loss)	41,000	7,000	(10,000)
	206,000	67,000	20,000
Due to group companies	–	11,700	5,000
Creditors	37,500	11,000	7,500
Taxation	28,000	7,000	–
Preference dividend half-year	–	375	–
Bank overdraft	–	–	5,000
	£271,500	£97,075	£37,500

	X		Y		Z	
Fixed assets:						
Freehold land and buildings, at cost	80,000			–		–
less depreciation	15,000					
		65,000				
Plant and machinery, at cost	60,000		26,000		20,000	
less depreciation	16,000		6,000		6,000	
		44,000		20,000		14,000
Subsidiary companies:						
shares, at cost		65,500	–		–	
amounts due		14,000	–		4,000	
Stocks, at cost		43,500	35,400		12,500	
Debtors		26,000	22,300		7,000	
Bank balance		13,500	19,375		–	
		£271,500	£97,075		£37,500	

The following information is relevant:

i. X Limited acquired shares in its subsidiary companies as follows:

> 10,000 ordinary shares in incorporation, at par;
> 20,000 ordinary shares at 1st January, 19-9 for £28,000;
> 8,000 preference shares at 1st July 19-0 for £7,500;
> Z Limited
> 30,000 ordinary shares on 1st July 19-0 for £20,000.

ii. On 1st January, 19-9 there was a debit balance of £2,000 on the profit and loss account of Y Limited, and on 1st July, 19-0 there was a credit balance of £3,000 on the profit and loss account of Z Limited.

iii. Inter company balance at 31st December, 19–1 were as under:

		£			£
X Limited debtors	Y Limited	8,000		Z Limited	6,000
Y Limited creditors	X Limited	7,700		Z Limited	4,000
Z Limited debtors	Y Limited	4,000 creditors		X Limited	5,000

iv. A remittance of £1,000 from X Limited to Z Limited was not received and recorded by the latter company until after the books had been closed.

v. Included in the stocks of X Limited are goods for which it paid Y Limited £9,600, which the latter company sold at cost plust 20%.

20. H Limited acquired 60% of the ordinary share capital of S Limited on 1st January, 19-5 at a price of £0.50 per share and a further 20% on 1st July, 19-5 at a price of £0.60 per share.

From the information given below you are required to prepare a consolidated balance sheet for H Limited as at 31st December, 19-5.

Workings must be shown.

1. The balance sheets of H Limited and S Limited at 31st December, 19-5 were as follows:

	H Limited £	H Limited £	S Limited £	S Limited £
Ordinary share capital:				
800,000 shares of £0.25 fully paid		200,000		
400,000 shares of £0.25 fully paid				100,000
Capital reserve		84,000		27,000
Retained profits		69,000		35,000
Loan from S Limited		35,000		–
Taxation		60,000		37,000
Creditors		25,800		19,000
Proposed dividend		30,000		18,000
S Limited, current account		1,200		–
		£505,000		£236,000
Land and buildings, at cost	92,000		54,000	
less Depreciation	26,000		18,000	
		66,000		36,000
Plant and machinery, at cost	165,000		99,000	
less Depreciation	61,000		44,000	
		104,000		55,000
Shares in S Limited at cost		168,000		–
Loan to H Limited		–		35,000
Stocks and work-in-progress		91,000		54,600
Debtors		60,000		39,000
Bank		1,600		15,000
Dividend receivable from S Limited		14,400		–
H Limited, current account		–		1,400
		£505,000		£236,000

2. Capital and reserves in S Limited amounted to £144,000 on 1st January, 19-5 and to £156,000 on 30th June 19-5.

3. The summarised profit and loss accounts of H Limited and S Limited for the year ended 31st December, 19-5 are summarised below:

	H Limited £	S Limited 1st six months £	S Limited 2nd six months £	S Limited Total £
Trading profits	105,600	24,000	48,000	72,000
Dividend ex S Limited	14,400	–	–	–
	120,000	24,000	48,000	72,000
less: Taxation	60,000	12,000	24,000	36,000
	60,000	12,000	24,000	36,000
less: Dividend	30,000	–	18,000	18,000
	£30,000	£12,000	£6,000	£18,000

4. Cash of £200 remitted by H Limited to S Limited on 29th December, 19-5 was not received by S Limited until 2nd January 19-6.

21. As on 30 June 19-5 the Balance Sheets of three companies showed the following position.

	Fig Ltd		Run Ltd		Trot Ltd	
	£	£	£	£	£	£
Fixed Assets						
Freehold land and buildings, at cost		40,000		100,000		65,000
Plant and machinery, at cost	130,000		56,000		87,000	
Less aggregate depreciation	50,000		22,000		60,000	
		80,000		34,000		27,000
		120,000		134,000		92,000
Investments						
Shares in Run Ltd, at cost	115,000					
Shares in Trot Ltd, at cost	70,000					
		185,000				
Current Assets						
Stocks on hand	57,000		68,000		54,140	
Debtors	96,340		43,245		42,190	
Balances at bank	44,250		110,425		11,409	
		197,590		221,670		107,739
		502,590		355,670		199,739
Deduct Current Liabilities						
Creditors	32,396		61,710		34,287	
Corporation Tax	72,450		52,000		24,400	
Proposed dividends	120,000		80,000		10,000	
		224,846		193,710		68,687
		277,744		161,960		131,052
Financed by: Share capital: authorised and issued						
Ordinary shares of £1 each fully paid		200,000		80,000		100,000
Capital reserve		20,000		40,000		–
Revenue reserve		57,744		41,960		31,052
		277,744		161,960		131,052

You are also given the following information:

1. Fig Ltd acquired 50,000 shares in Run Ltd in 19-0 when the balance on capital reserve had been £20,000 and on revenue reserve £16,000. A further 20,000 shares were purchased in 19-2 when the balances on capital reserves and revenue reserve had been £40,000 and £24,000 respectively.

2. Fig Ltd had purchased 75,000 shares in Trot Ltd in 19-1 when there had been an adverse balance on revenue reserve of £6,000.

3. During the year ended 30th June 19-5 Fig Ltd had purchased a machine from Run Ltd for £10,000 which had yielded a profit on selling price of 30% to that company. Depreciation on the machine had been charged in the accounts at 20% on cost.

4. Run Ltd purchases goods from Fig Ltd providing Fig Ltd with a standard gross profit on invoice price on $33\frac{1}{3}$%. On 30th June 19-5, the stock valuation of Run Ltd included an amount of £16,000 being goods purchased from Fig Ltd. for £18,000.

5. The proposed dividends from subsidiary companies have been included in the figure for debtors in the accounts of the parent company.

You are required to prepare the consolidated Balance Sheet of Fig Ltd. and its subsidiaries as on 30th June 19-5, together with your consolidation schedules.

22. The following are the summarised trial balances of a group of three companies for the year ended 30th April 19-7. Taxation in all its aspects has been and is to be ignored.

	Fletcher Ltd £	Major Ltd £	Palma Ltd £
Debit Balances			
Plant and Machinery (cost or valuation)	241,200	84,960	144,200
Stocks	61,904	28,060	10,984
Sundry debtors	57,520	24,800	4,980
Land and buildings (cost)	18,700	26,400	11,210
Dividends paid (on 15 November 19-6)			
on Ordinary shares	35,000	3,000	6,000
Cash	12,620	–	1,616
Investment in Subsidiary companies	50,000	–	24,000
Goodwill	34,636	–	–
Inter-group current accounts	92,000	–	–
	£603,580	£167,220	£202,990
Credit Balances			
Profit and Loss A/c at 1 May 19-6	93,470	4,680	17,400
Profit for 19–6/19–7	40,280	12,400	19,920
Ordinary shares of £1 each, fully paid	200,000	30,000	60,000
Sundry creditors	86,080	17,760	21,108
Dividends received	7,500	–	2,400
Provision for depreciation of Plant and Machinery	149,250	20,140	56,162
Bank overdraft	–	4,240	–
Capital reserves	11,000	2,000	–
10% Debentures	16,000	–	10,000
Inter-group current accounts	–	76,000	16,000
	£603,580	£167,220	£202,990

The profits for the year 19–6/19–7 are after charging all expenses including debenture interest. Fletcher Ltd had acquired 50,000 Ordinary shares of £1 each in Palma Ltd for £50,000 and Palma Ltd 24,000 Ordinary shares of £1 each in Major Ltd for £24,000. Both these transactions took place on 1 August 19–7. The ordinary shares and capital reserves are unchanged since 1 May 19-6.

The following information should be taken into account:

1. Fletcher Ltd propose to pay a final dividend on its Ordinary shares of $2\frac{1}{2}$%.

2. On 6 August 19-6 Palma Ltd paid a final dividend of 5% for the year ended 30 April 19-6. This had been provided for at that date (30 April 19-6) in the paying company's accounts.

You are required to prepare a consolidated balance sheet for the group at 30 April 19-7.

Your workings must be submitted.

(ACCA)

23. The following are the balance sheets of Llewellyn Ltd and its subsidiaries Dilwyn Ltd and Grove Ltd, as at 31 March 19-8.

	Llewellyn Ltd. £	Dilwyn Ltd. £	Grove Ltd. £
Ordinary Share capital £1 shares fully paid	400,000	360,000	320,000
General revenue reserve 1 April 19-7	120,000		
Profit and loss account	170,000	54,400	40,000
	690,000	414,400	360,000
Debenture 10% – Secured	350,000	260,000	80,000
Current liabilities			
Current accounts with Llewellyn Ltd.		30,000	2,000
Sundry creditors	300,000	120,000	80,000
Current taxation	100,000	80,000	60,000
Bank overdraft	200,000	80,000	
	1,6440,000	984,400	582,000

Fixed assets

Plant & Machinery cost *less* depreciation	342,500	245,500	191,000
Freehold property - cost	300,000	150,000	91,500
Furniture & Fittings - cost *less* depreciation	51,500	30,500	25,450
	694,000	426,000	307,950
Investment in Dilwyn Ltd –			
240,000 Ordinary shares at cost	350,000		
Investment in Grove Ltd –			
80,000 Ordinary shares at cost	148,000		
Investment in Grove Ltd –			
200,000 Ordinary shares at cost		340,000	
Current assets			
Current account with Dilwyn Ltd	40,000		
Current account with Grove Ltd	5,000		
Stocks	170,500	103,800	125,010
Sundry debtors	232,500	114,600	146,040
Cash			3,000
	1,640,000	984,400	582,000

Notes:

1. Llewellyn Ltd purchased its shares in Dilwyn Ltd on 31 March 19-5 when Dilwyn Ltd profit and loss account had a credit balance of £42,000.

2. Both Llewellyn Ltd and Dilwyn Ltd purchased their shares in Grove Ltd on 31 March 19-6, when Grove Ltd profit and loss account had a credit balance of £32,000.

3. Cheques of £10,000 from Dilwyn Ltd to Llewellyn Ltd and of £3,000 from Grove Ltd to Llewellyn Ltd were in transit at 31 March 19-8.

4. Llewellyn Ltd sold goods to Dilwyn Ltd during the year ended 31 March 19-8 at cost plus 33 1/3 per cent. Dilwyn Ltd had £49,600 in value of these stocks in hand at the year end.

You are required to prepare the Consolidated Balance Sheet of Llewellyn Ltd and its subsidiaries as at 31 March 19-8.

Your workings must be submitted.

(ACCA)

24. The draft balance sheets of Rip Ltd., Van Ltd, and Winkle Ltd., as on 31st March 19-3 are as under:

	Rip Ltd	Van Ltd	Winkle Ltd
	£	£	£
Share capital - issued and fully paid:			
Ordinary shares of £1 each	100,000	60,000	50,000
8% Preference shares of £1 each	–	80,000	–
Share premium account	–	–	20,000
Reserves	80,000	30,000	dr.(18,000)
Inter-company accounts	10,000	6,500	3,400
Taxation	18,000	12,000	–
Creditors	69,200	31,000	14,000
Dividend proposed	20,000	5,000	2,000
Overdraft at Red Bank	23,000	–	–
	320,200	224,500	71,400
Plant at cost	68,000	71,500	36,000
Less: Depreciation	33,200	31,100	15,280
	34,800	40,400	20,720
Freehold premises at cost	40,000	61,000	–
Shares in subsidiary companies at cost:			
Van Ltd - Ordinary	94,500	–	–
- Preference	50,400	–	–
Winkle Ltd	18,000	22,000	–

Inter-company accounts	7,000	12,100	2,680
Stocks at cost	38,000	47,500	28,000
Debtors	37,500	33,500	17,000
Cash at Black Bank	–	8,000	3,000
	320,200	224,500	71,400

The following information is ascertained:

1. The following acquisitions of shares had taken place:

   a. On 1st April 19-2 Van Ltd purchased 20,000 shares in Winkle Ltd for £22,000.

   b. On 1st October 19-2 Rip Ltd purchased 54,000 ordinary shares in Van Ltd for £94,500 and 48,000 preference shares for £50,400.

   c. Also on 1st October 19-2 Rip Ltd purchased 19,500 ordinary shares in Winkle Ltd from outside shareholders, for £18,000.

2. The only movements in the reserves during the year to 31st March 19-3 were in the Profit and Loss Accounts which showed:

	Rip Ltd	Van Ltd	Winkle Ltd
	£	£	£
Pre-tax profit/loss	45,000	32,000	19,000 (loss)
Corporation Tax	18,000	12,000	–
Dividends payable	20,000	15,400	–

   Van Ltd paid the first half of the preference dividend and its interim ordinary dividend on 30th September 19-2.

3. a. The preference dividend for the six months ended on 31st March 19-3 was declared and payable by Van Ltd on that date. Cheques were sent to the outside shareholders, and Rip Ltd was appropriately credited. When preparing the draft accounts, the accountant of Rip Ltd was not aware of the position.

   b. No book entries had been made by Rip Ltd in respect of the final dividend proposed by Van Ltd.

   c. A group election is in force.

4. The proposed dividend of Winkle Ltd had been provided in the accounts for the year ended 31st March 19-2, but in view of the deteriorating trading position had not been paid. It was decided to write back this provision to the opening reserves.

5. A machine, which originally cost £5,000 was transferred from Van Ltd to Rip Ltd at its written down value of £3,000. The transaction has only been recorded in the books of Van Ltd.

6. On 31st March 19-3, Winkle Ltd sent a cheque for £800 to Van Ltd, which was not received until 3rd April 19-3.

7. In general, inter-company trading was minimal. However, on 20th March 19-3 Rip Ltd sold goods for £10,000 to Van Ltd, earning its usual profit of 25% calculated on cost price. 50% of these goods were in stock on 31st March 19-3.

You are required to prepare the Consolidated Balance Sheet of Rip Ltd and its subsidiary companies as on 31st March 19-3. Working schedules are to be presented.

25. A Limited acquired 60% of the ordinary share capital of B Limited on 1st January 19-2 and a further 10% on 1st July, 19-2. It later acquired 75% of the ordinary share capital of C Limited on 1st October, 19-2.

From the information given below you are required to prepare the consolidated profit and loss account of A Limited for the year ended 31st December, 19-2.

Workings and adjustments must be given.

Corporation Tax is to be taken at 40% and turnover and profits are assumed to have accrued equally throughout the year.

1. The profit and loss accounts for the three companies for the year ended 31st December, 19-2 are as follows:

	A Limited	B Limited	C Limited
	£	£	£
Turnover	1,680,000	1,320,000	720,000
Profit	193,000	144,000	21,000
less			
Depreciation	47,000	35,000	26,000
Bank interest	3,000	–	7,000
Debenture interest	–	13,000	–
Audit fees	5,000	4,000	2,000
Directors' emoluments:			
Fees	9,000	7,000	2,000
Remuneration	12,000	15,000	8,000
	76,000	74,000	45,000
Trading profit,(loss)	117,000	70,000	(24,000)
Dividends from subsidiaries	24,000	–	–
Profit before taxation	141,000	70,000	(24,000)
Taxation	57,000	28,000	–
	84,000	42,000	(24,000)
Brought forward, 1st January 19-2	28,800	76,000	(8,000)
	112,800	118,000	(32,000)
Dividends:			
Interim paid: 3%	15,000	12,000	–
Final proposed: 7%	35,000	–	–
Final proposed: 6%	–	24,000	–
	50,000	36,000	–
	£62,800	£82,000	(£32,000)

2. Turnover of A Limited included sales of £97,000 to B Limited and £67,000 to C Limited, while that of B Limited included £42,000 to C Limited.

3. At 31st December, 19-2 B Limited held stock valued at cost of £9,900 ex A Limited on which the latter had taken a profit of 10% on cost. C Limited held stock valued at cost of £11,250 ex B Limited on which the latter had taken $12\frac{1}{2}$% on cost.

4. The directors of A Limited received fees of £5,000 from B Limited and £1,500 from C Limited.

26. The issued capitals, in ordinary shares of £1 each, of Film Ltd, Tape Ltd and Edit Ltd, were £300,000, £100,000 and £90,000 respectively.

On 31st March 19-8 the summarised profit and loss accounts of the companies showed the following:

	Film Ltd		Tape Ltd		Edit Ltd	
	£	£	£	£	£	£
Trading profits for the year		528,000		162,000		65,000
Interim dividend received		8,000				
Proposed dividends receivable		34,000				
Directors' fees received		20,000				
		590,000		162,000		65,000
Less:						
Directors' fees	45,000		27,500		15,000	
Depreciation	42,000		27,000		10,000	
Audit fees	2,500		2,000		1,000	
Provision for corporation tax	239,000		54,800		20,400	

Interim dividend paid, actual	30,000	10,000	
Proposed dividends, actual	150,000	30,000	15,000
	508,500	151,300	61,400
Retained profits	81,500	10,700	3,600
Add:			
Balance brought forward 1st April 19-7	78,600	40,000	29,700
	160,100	50,700	33,300

You are also given the following relevant information:

1. Film Ltd acquired 80,000 shares in Tape Ltd on 1st April 19-6 when there had been a debit balance on profit and loss account of £20,000.

2. Film Ltd buys goods for resale from Tape Ltd which yield a profit to Tape Ltd of 25% on selling price. Goods purchased by Film Ltd during the year ended 31st March 19-8 at a cost of £40,000 were unsold at that date and included in stocks at a value of £37,500.

3. On 1st July 19-7, Film Ltd acquired 60,000 shares in Edit Ltd, whose profits accrue evenly throughout the year.

4. Edit Ltd manufactures for resale plant of the type used by Film Ltd. On 1st October 19-7 Edit Ltd sold plant to Film Ltd. for £40,000 on which Edit Ltd earned its normal profit of 35% on selling price. Depreciation of £4,000 has been charged on this plant in the accounts of Film Ltd.

5. The directors' fees paid by the subsidiary companies to directors who are on the board of Film Ltd are all credited to the profit and loss account of the holding company.

You are required to prepare a consolidated Profit and Loss Account of film Ltd and its subsidiary companies for the year ended 31st March 19-8, together with your consolidation schedules.

27. XY Limited is a holding company, which does not publish its own profit and loss account, holding 80% of the ordinary share capital of B Limited and 75% of the ordinary share capital of C Limited.

From the information given below you are required to prepare the consolidated profit and loss account for the year ended 31st December 19-6.

1. XY Limited acquired its holding of 80,000 ordinary shares in B Limited on 1st April 19-5. In the year ended 31st December, 19-5 B Limited made a profit after tax of £20,000 and declared a final dividend of £0.10 per share.

2. XY Limited acquired its holding of 90,000 ordinary shares in C Limited on 1st July, 19-6.

3. XY Limited owns £50,000 10 $\frac{1}{2}$% Treasury Stock 19-8 purchased in 19-5.

4. The profit and loss accounts of the three companies for the year ended 31st December, 19-6 are set out below:

	XY Limited		B Limited	C Limited
	£	£	£	£
Trading profits		63,000	36,000	46,000
Interest on Treasury Stock	5,250			
Dividends received	15,600		1,200	–
		20,850		
		83,850	37,200	46,000
Corporation tax		34,000	19,000	24,000
		49,850	18,200	22,000
Dividends proposed		30,000	12,000	8,000
		19,850	6,200	14,000
Balance brought forward		71,150	30,800	22,000
Balance carried forward		91,000	37,000	36,000

608

5. Trading profits are assumed to accrue evenly over the year.

6. Goods to the value of £10,000 purchased from B Limited were held in stock by XY Limited at the year end. The cost of B Limited was £8,000.

28. The summarised profit and loss accounts of Kestrel Ltd, Sparrow Ltd, Thrush Ltd and Osprey Ltd for the year ended 31st March 19-5, and the issued share capitals as on that date, were as follows:

	Kestrel Ltd £	Sparrow Ltd £	Thrush Ltd £	Osprey Ltd £
Balance brought forward 1st April 19-4	45,000	30,000		
Trading profits	416,000	126,000	10,000	210,000
Interim dividend received from Sparrow Ltd.	16,000			
Proposed dividend from Osprey Ltd.	27,000			
Directors' fees from Thrush Ltd	6,000			
Balance carried forward			29,800	
	510,000	156,000	39,800	210,000
Balance brought forward 1st April 19-4			20,000	
Directors fees	24,000	12,000	10,000	20,000
Depreciation	20,000	18,000	9,000	15,000
Audit fees	1,500	1,000	800	1,000
Provision for corporation tax	188,000	47,000		87,000
Transfer to reserve	50,000			
Written off shares in Thrush Ltd	8,000			
Proposed dividends, actual	150,000			60,000
Interim dividend paid, actual		20,000		
Balance carried forward	68,500	58,000		27,000
	510,000	156,000	39,800	210,000
	£	£	£	£
Issued ordinary share capital in £1 shares	250,000	100,000	80,000	120,000

You also obtain the following information:

1. Kestrel Ltd had acquired the following shares:

  Sparrow Ltd   60,000 shares on 1st April 19-2
                20,000 shares on 1st April 19-4
  Thrush Ltd   60,000 shares on 1st April 19-3
  Osprey Ltd   54,000 shares on 1st April 19-4

2. Osprey Ltd commenced trading on 1st April 19-4.

3. The profit and loss account of Sparrow Ltd had a debit balance of £40,000 on 1st April 19-2. On 1st April 19-3 the credit balance on the profit and loss account of Thrush Ltd had been £4,000.

4. An election had been made for dividends between subsidiary companies and the holding company to be treated as group income without the incidence of advance corporation tax.

5. During the year Kestrel Ltd had purchased goods from Sparrow Ltd which had yielded a profit of 25% on selling price to Sparrow Ltd. Goods purchased by Kestrel Ltd from that company for £20,000 were included in the closing stock as on 31st March 19-5 at a valuation of £19,000.

6. The directors of Sparrow Ltd and Thrush Ltd are also directors of the holding company.

You are required to prepare a consolidated Profit and Loss Account of Kestrel Ltd and its subsidiary companies incorporating the results of its associated company for the year ended 31st March 19- 5, together with your consolidation schedules.

29. On 1st February 19-6 Abstract Ltd purchased 150,000 ordinary shares and 50,000 preference shares in Bran Ltd, and on 1st March 19-6 purchased 45,000 ordinary shares in Corn Ltd. All three companies

make up their accounts to 30th June in each year. The following figures were extracted from the companies' records for the year ended 30th June 19- 6:

	Abstract Ltd	Bran Ltd	Corn Ltd
	£	£	£
Sales	900,000	850,000	500,000
Purchases	497,990	482,580	221,100
Selling expenses	45,000	67,500	45,000
Overhead expenses	115,000	52,500	65,000
Interim dividends paid 1st January			
19-6 on ordinary shares	75,000	40,000	
on preference shares		4,500	
Stocks on hand as on 30th June 19- 5	49,650	100,280	34,500
Issued share capital			
Ordinary shares of £1 each	300,000	200,000	100,000
9% Preference shares of £1 each		100,000	
Revenue reserves as on 30th June			
19-5 after deducting all dividends to			
that date	26,750	32,000	48,000

You also obtain the following additional information:

1. Profits of Bran Ltd and Corn Ltd accrued evenly throughout the year.
2. Stocks on hand at 30th June 19-6 were: Abstract Ltd £87,640; Bran Ltd £92,860; and Corn Ltd £45,600.
3. Provision for corporation tax based on the profits for the year at 52% is to be made as follows:

Abstract Ltd	£150,000
Bran Ltd	£108,000
Corn Ltd	£86,400

4. Abstract Ltd proposes to pay a final dividend on ordinary shares of 25%; Bran Ltd a half-year's dividend on the preference shares and a final dividend on ordinary shares of 30%; and Corn Ltd a dividend on ordinary shares of 60%.

You are required to prepare a consolidated Profit and Loss Account of Abstract Ltd and its subsidiary company incorporating the results of its associated company for the year ended 30th June 19-6, together with your consolidation schedules.

30. The following are the draft profit and loss accounts of Anton Ltd, its subsidiary Condor Ltd and its associated company Tenor Ltd, for the year ended 31 December 19-9:

	Anton Ltd	Condor Ltd	Tenor Ltd	
	£	£	£	£
Turnover (after excluding inter group sales)		2,600,000	1,400,000	1,800,000
Net operating profit before tax		340,000	130,000	200,000
Dividends receivable (franked investment income including tax credit)		62,550		
		402,550	130,000	200,000
less:				
Corporation tax on the operating profit for the year	130,000		50,000	90,000
Tax on dividends receivable	20,850	150,850		
Profit after tax		251,700	80,000	110,000

Ordinary dividends proposed (net amount)	140,000	36,000	49,000
Profit unappropriated	£111,700	£44,000	£61,000

Anton Ltd acquired 75% of the ordinary share capital of Condor Ltd on 1 May 19-9. On 1 January 19-9, it had acquired 30% of the ordinary share capital of Tenor Ltd. A director of Anton Ltd was then appointed to the board of Tenor Ltd, and took an active part in its management.

Anton Ltd had no other investments.

Included in the stock of Condor Ltd is £120,000 for goods purchased from Anton Ltd. Anton Ltd's profit margin on these goods was 25% of the selling price.

Anton's policy is to make a full provision in the consolidated accounts for unrealised inter-group profit without reference to minority interests.

You are required to prepare the consolidated profit and loss account of Anton Ltd for the year ended 31 December 19-9 with appropriate notes thereto, including a reconciliation of the group's retained profit for the year.

Assume a basic rate of income tax of $33\frac{1}{3}\%$. Your workings must be submitted.

(ACCA)

31. The following are the draft consolidated accounts of Roadway Ltd.

Summarised Consolidated Balance Sheet as on 31st May 19–5

			19–4	
	£000	£000	£000	£000
Net assets employed				
Fixed assets and loose tools		3,088		2,257
Goodwill		190		–
		3,278		2,257
Current assets:				
Stock and work in progress	1,128		492	
Debtors	3,684		2,291	
Cash at bank	–		359	
	4,812		3,142	
Less Current liabilities:				
Creditors	1,365		790	
Overdraft	402		–	
Corporation tax	998		497	
Dividends payable	209		260	
ACT payable on dividends	158		113	
	3,132		1,660	
		1,680		1,482
		4,958		3,739
Financed by:				
Share capital 5,200,000 ordinary shares of 25p each		1,300		1,200
Share premium account	280		–	
Undistributed profit	2,653		2,119	
		2,933		2,119
		4,233		3,319
Deferred taxation		725		420
		4,958		3,739

Summarised Consolidated Profit and Loss Account
for the year ended 31st May 19-5

	£000	£000	£000	19–4 £000
<u>Turnover</u>		<u>9,540</u>		<u>6,266</u>
Profit for the year before taxation (after charging £192,000 for depreciation)		1,781		1,225
Taxation at 52%		926		637
Profit after taxation		855		588
Less dividends				
Interim	112		36	
Final	209		260	
		321		296
Retained profit for the year		534		292
Balance from previous year		2,119		1,827
Undistributed profit		2,653		2,119

You ascertain that:

1. On 1st December 19-4 Roadway Ltd acquired Pavement Ltd. The effects of the acquisition are summarised as:

	£000
Net assets acquired	
Fixed assets	450
Goodwill	190
Stock and work in progress	230
Debtors	480
	1,350
Less Creditors	490
	860
Consideration	
Shares issued	380
Cash	480
	860

2. Machinery having a written down value of £130,000 was sold on 1st November 19-4 for £92,000.

3. There was no change in the issued share capital during the year 31st May 19-4.

You are required to prepare a statement of source and application of funds for the year ended 31st May 19-5 in a form consistent with current practice as far as the information given permits, and explain the usefulness of this statement.

32. From the information given below you are required to prepare a statement of source and disposition of funds in respect of AB Limited, a holding company, for the year ended 31st December, 19-7, in accordance with the principles laid down in Statement of Standard Accounting Practice (SSAP) No.10.

AB Limited

1. Profit and Loss Account for the year ended 31st December 19–7:

	£000	£000
Group profit before taxation and extraordinary items		2,490
Taxation		1,294
Profit before extraordinary items		1,196
Extraordinary items less taxation relating thereto		33
		1,163
Outside interests in losses of subsidiary		18
		1,181
Less: Dividends paid	375	
proposed	600	
		975
Balance transferred to reserves		206

2. Balance Sheets as at 31st December.

	19-7		19-6	
	£000	£000	£000	£000
Issued share capital		3,067		3,067
Share premium		1,827		1,827
Reserves and retained profits		7,167		6,961
		12,061		11,855
Deferred taxation		1,880		813
Surplus on consolidation		345		517
		14,286		13,185
Fixed assets		6,876		6,213
Loans		1,482		3,404
Current Assets:				
Stocks and work-in progress	7,644		7,379	
Debtors	4,229		3,898	
Bills receivable	84		261	
ACT recoverable	459		214	
Cash on deposit	1,863		–	
Bank and cash balances	103		66	
	14,382		11,818	

	19-7		19-6	
	£000	£000	£000	£000
Current liabilities:				
Bank borrowing	1,275		836	
Creditors and provision	5,100		5,315	
Taxation	1,014		1,184	
Dividend	600		500	
	7,989		7,835	
		6,393		3,983
		14,751		13,600

Debenture stocks	407	415
Outside shareholders interests	58	–
	465	415
	14,286	13,185

3. On 1st July 19-7 the company acquired a new subsidiary by purchasing 75% of the issued ordinary share capital of CD Limited for £400,000. At that date the net assets of CD Limited totalled £304,000. For the six months ended 31st December, 19-7 CD Limited lost £72,000.

4. All subsidiary companies other than CD Limited were wholly owned.

5. Depreciation charged in the year totalled £672,000.

6. Sales of fixed assets during the year were £77,000.

33. The following summarised accounts have been prepared by Furniture Ltd and its subsidiary Chairs Ltd for the years ended 31st May 19-9, and 19-8.

	Furniture Ltd		Chairs Ltd	
	£000	£000	£000	£000
Balance sheet at 31st May				
Issued ordinary share capital	6,000	4,000	550	500
Issued preference share capital	3,000	3,000	400	400
Retained profits	2,490	2,000	117	100
10% Debentures	5,000	4,000	1,000	500
Trade creditors	600	400	300	250
Current taxation	1,695	1,446	127	60
Proposed dividend	600	500	55	–
Overdraft	–	–	1,392	1,304
	19,385	15,346	3,941	3,114
Land and buildings	2,500	2,000	700	600
Plant and machinery	9,500	8,000	1,000	800
Investment in Chairs Ltd at cost	440	400	–	–
Stock and work-in-progress	750	600	600	400
Debtors	2,500	2,000	1,500	1,250
ACT recoverable	546	497	41	14
Cash and bank balances	3,149	1,849	100	50
	19,385	15,346	3,941	3,114
Profit and loss account for year to 31st May				
Trading profit for the year	3,500	3,000	300	150
Debenture interest	500	400	100	50
Taxation (treated as current taxation)	1,400	1,200	100	60
Dividends paid				
Ordinary	300	300	–	–
Preference	210	210	28	28
Dividends proposed, ordinary	600	500	55	–
Retained	490	390	17	12
The trading profit for the year is stated after charging depreciation of	1,000	800	150	100

Furniture Ltd acquired the ordinary shares of Chairs Ltd on two dates; 400,000 of £1 each on 31st January 19-0 for £400,000 and 40,000 of £1 each for £40,000 on 31st January 19-9 on the occasion of a rights issue to all ordinary shareholders.

Neither company sold any fixed assets during the year.

You are required to:

a. prepare a consolidated statement of source and application of group funds for the year ended 31st May 19-9.
b. state what difference it would make to the statement if Furniture Ltd had acquired its holding of 400,000 ordinary shares on 1st June 19-8 instead of on 31st January 19-0.

34. As on 30 September 19-8 the balance sheets of three companies showed the following position:

	Sun Ltd		Sea Ltd		Sky Ltd	
	£000	£000	£000	£000	£000	£000
Fixed Assets						
Equipment and fittings, at cost	146,720		79,290		220,400	
Less aggregate depreciation	72,490		46,230		82,360	
		74,230		33,060		138,040
Investments						
Shares in Sea Ltd, at cost	67,500					
Shares in Sky Ltd, at cost	175,000					
		242,500				
Current Assets						
Stocks on hand	49,068		88,860		76,292	
Debtors	101,558		64,275		79,758	
Bills receivable	14,600		–		–	
Balances at bank	76,408		98,540		74,062	
		241,634		251,675		230,112
		558,364		284,735		368,152
Deduct Current Liabilities						
Creditors	49,467		27,406		41,086	
Corporation tax	56,490		37,409		41,206	
Bills payable	–		3,900		–	
Proposed dividends	125,000		60,000		50,000	
		230,957		128,715		132,292
		327,407		156,020		235,860

Note: There is a contingent liability of £3,000 for bills receivable discounted.

Financed by:						
Share capital: authorised and issued ordinary shares of £1 each fully paid		250,000		100,000		150,000
Capital reserve		40,000		–		–
Revenue reserves		37,407		56,020		85,860
		327,407		156,020		235,860

You are also given the following information.

1. Sun Ltd acquired 60,000 shares in Sea Ltd in 19-2 when there had been an adverse balance on revenue reserve of £20,000. A further 25,000 shares were purchased in 19-6 when the credit balance on revenue reserve had been £45,000.

2. Sun Ltd had purchased 120,000 shares in Sky Ltd in 19-7 when there had been a credit balance on revenue reserve of £65,000.

3. Bills receivable by Sun Ltd include £1,500 from Sea Ltd. Bills payable by Sea Ltd include £2,000 to Sun Ltd.

4. The proposed dividends from subsidiary companies have been included in the figure for debtors in the accounts of the parent company.

5. On 1st October 19-8 Sky Ltd utilised part of its reserves to make a bonus issue of one ordinary share for every three held.

You are required to prepare the Consolidated Balance Sheet of Sun Ltd and its subsidiaries as on 1st October 19-8, together with your consolidation schedules.

35. Greater Combinations Ltd, and its subsidiary Cooperative Ltd, have produced the following summarised balance sheets as on 30th November 19-5 and profit and loss accounts for the year ended on that date.

Summarised balance Sheets as on 30th November 19-5

	Greater Combinations £000	Cooperative £000
Issued share capital, ordinary shares of £1	500	100
Reserves and unappropriated profits	800	260
Deferred taxation	100	90
	1,400	450
Fixed assets	600	100
Shares in subsidiary, 75,000 shares of £1	25	–
Patents and trade marks	75	20
Net current assets	700	330
	1,400	450

Summarised Profit and Loss Accounts for year ended 30th November 19-5

	Greater Combinations £000	Cooperative £000
Trading profit	300	80
Taxation at 55%	165	44
	135	36
Proposed dividend	75	20
Retained	60	16

You have ascertained that:

1. The entire issued share capital of Cooperative Ltd was acquired on 1st August 19-0 at £1 per share. At this date total reserves and unappropriated profits of Cooperative Ltd were equivalent to £0.80 per share. There have not been any changes in the issued share capital since that date.
2. On 31st May 19-5 25,000 shares of Cooperative were sold at £3 per share.
3. The sale had been recorded in the books of Greater Combinations Ltd by crediting the receipt against the cost of purchase.
4. Trading and profit of Cooperative Ltd arise evenly throughout the year.
5. Greater Combinations Ltd sells to Cooperative Ltd on the normal trade terms of cost plus 25%, goods to the value of £100,000 per month. Stock held by Cooperative Ltd at the end of the year represents one month's purchases.
6. Both companies maintain the deferred taxation account under the deferral method.
7. Greater Combinations Ltd does not take credit in its own accounts for dividends until they have been received.

You are required to:

a. prepare a consolidated balance sheet at 30th November 19-5 which complies with the best current practice in so far as the information provided will allow.
b. prepare a detailed analysis of the movements in the group reserves and unappropriated profits, and
c. write a *brief* note with numerical illustration comparing the alternatives available to reflect

in the group accounts the trading between parent and subsidiary.

36. The summarised profit and loss accounts of Roller Ltd, Grind Ltd and Sift Ltd for the year ended 31st March 19-0, and the issued share capitals as on that date, were as follows:

	Roller Ltd £	Grind Ltd £	Sift Ltd £
Balance brought forward 1st April 19-9	62,000	22,000	50,000
Trading profits	364,000	74,500	210,000
Dividends received from Grind Ltd:			
preference shares	5,400		
ordinary shares	7,500		
Proposed dividend from Sift Ltd	27,000		
	465,900	96,500	260,000
Directors' fees	26,000	10,000	20,000
Depreciation	19,000	7,000	12,000
Audit fees	3,200	1,500	2,000
Provision for corporation tax	161,000	29,000	89,000
Dividends paid:			
preference shares			
– 30th September 19-9		3,000	
– 31st March 19-0		3,000	
ordinary shares			
– 30th September 19-9		10,000	
– 31st March 19-0		10,000	
Proposed dividends	200,000		60,000
Balance carried forward	56,700	23,000	77,000
	465,900	96,500	260,000
Issued share capital			
6% preferences shares of £1 each		100,000	
Ordinary shares of £1 each	450,000	200,000	120,000

You also obtain the following information.

1. Roller Ltd had acquired the following shares:

Grind Ltd	90,000	preference shares on 1st April 19-9
	150,000	ordinary shares on 1st October 19-9
Sift Ltd	54,000	ordinary shares on 1st April 19-6

The preference shares carry no voting rights.

2. The profits of Grind Ltd are deemed to accrue evenly throughout the year.

3. On 1st October 19-9 the directors of Grind Ltd resigned and were replaced by the directors of Roller Ltd, who received remuneration of £5,000 from Grind Ltd.

4. On 1st April 19-6 the credit balance on the profit and loss account of Sift Ltd had been £30,000.

You are required to prepare a consolidated profit and loss account of Roller Ltd and its subsidiary company incorporating the results of its associated company for the year ended 31st March 19-0, together with your consolidation schedules. Ignore advance corporation tax.

37. Whole Ltd purchased 80,000 shares in Fragment Ltd in 19-6, and a further 20,000 shares in 19-8. In 19-6 Fragment Ltd had no capital reserve and a balance on revenue reserve of £15,000 and in 19-8 the balances on capital and revenue reserves were £60,000 and £30,000 respectively.

Whole Ltd purchased 120,000 shares in Part Ltd in 19-7 when there had been an adverse balance on revenue reserve of £40,000.

As on 31st March 19-0 the balance sheets of the three companies showed the following position:

1 : Final Accounts

	Whole Ltd £	Whole Ltd £	Fragment Ltd £	Fragment Ltd £	Part Ltd £	Part Ltd £
Fixed Assets						
Freehold land, at cost		89,000		30,000		65,000
Buildings, at cost	100,000		120,000		40,000	
Less aggregate depreciation	36,000		40,000		16,400	
		64,000		80,000		23,600
Plant and equipment, at cost	102,900		170,000		92,000	
Less aggregate depreciation	69,900		86,000		48,200	
		33,000		84,000		43,800
		186,000		194,000		132,400
Investments						
Shares in Fragment Ltd, at cost	135,000					
Shares in Part Ltd, at cost	75,000					
		210,000				
Current Assets						
Stocks on hand	68,740		76,490		81,070	
Debtors	196,420		123,732		45,660	
Balances at bank	81,520		42,760		31,470	
		346,680		242,982		158,200
		742,680		436,982		290,600
Deduct Current Liabilities						
Creditors	160,014		113,722		59,638	
Corporation tax	56,900		47,620		22,490	
Proposed dividends	90,000		48,000		16,000	
		306,914		209,342		98,128
		435,766		227,640		192,472
Financed by:						
Share capital: authorised and issued ordinary shares of £1 each fully paid		300,000		120,000		160,000
Capital reserve		70,000		60,000		–
Revenue reserve		65,766		47,640		32,472
		435,766		227,640		192,472

You are also given the following additional information:

1. The proposed dividends from subsidiary companies have been included in the figure for debtors in the accounts of the parent company.

2. On 1st April 19-9 Part Ltd had purchased a warehouse from Whole Ltd for £50,000 apportioned as to £30,000 for the land and £20,000 for the building. Whole Ltd had originally acquired the warehouse on 1st April 19-5 for £30,000 (building £15,000 and land £15,000). The group policy is to depreciate buildings on a straight line basis over fifty years. The surplus over cost on the sale of land and building has been credited to capital reserve.

You are required to prepare the consolidated balance sheet of Whole Ltd and its subsidiaries as on 31st March 19-0, together with your consolidation schedules.

38. Bear Ltd has an authorised share capital of £155,000 divided into 80,000 7% (net) preference shares of £1 each and 150,000 ordinary shares of 50p each.

Draft accounts for the year ended 31st December 19-6 showed the following position:

Profit and Loss Account

	£		£
Corporation tax	122,998	Trading profit	276,000
Depreciation on plant and machinery	24,000		
Dividends paid			
Preference shares	5,600		
Ordinary shares (interim)	7,500		
Final dividend proposed			
Ordinary shares	37,500		
Undistributed profit			
– carried forward	78,402		
	276,000		276,000

Balance Sheet

	£		£
Preference share capital	80,000	Stock	295,631
Ordinary share capital	75,000	Balance at bank	81,915
Profit and loss account	147,402	Freehold land and buildings	70,000
Corporation tax	249,998	Plant and machinery	135,000
Creditors	87,300	Debtors	87,600
Proposed dividends	37,500	Advance corporation tax on	
		dividends paid	7,054
	677,200		677,200

You also obtain the following information:

1. On 1st October 19-6, Able Ltd acquired 100,000 ordinary shares in Bear Ltd for £150,000.
2. Profits of Bear Ltd accrue evenly over the year.

You are required to prepare the consolidation schedules and to indicate how the resulting figures would be included in the consolidated accounts of Able Ltd.

39. The following is the draft consolidated balance sheet of Llewellyn Limited and its subsidiary Roberts Limited at 30th June 19-4.

Llewellyn Limited paid £68,000 for its interest in Roberts Limited on 1st July, 19-3.

	£	£
Ordinary share capital of £1 shares, issued and fully paid		100,000
Profit and loss account:		
Llewellyn Limited	20,000	
Roberts Limited (since acquisition)	12,000	
		32,000
Current liabilities:		
Sundry creditors		54,000
		186,000
		£
Fixed Assets:		
Freehold Property (cost)		30,000
Plant and machinery at cost less accumulated depreciation		80,000

		110,000
Cost of Control - Goodwill		16,000
Current Assets:		
Stock	32,000	
Debtors	24,000	
Cash	4,000	
		60,000
		186,000

The following facts have been ascertained since the draft balance sheet was prepared:

1. Llewellyn Limited acquired only 80% of the Ordinary share capital of Roberts Limited whereas it was assumed by the Assistant Accountant who drew up the draft consolidated balance sheet that the whole of it had been acquired:

2. Stock shown in the balance sheet of Roberts Limited was undervalued by £1,000 at 30th June, 19-3, and by £1,600 at 30th June 19-4.

3. Plant shown in the balance sheet of Roberts Limited at 30th June, 19-3 was overvalued by £2,000. (Rate of depreciation - 10% per annum).

4. Stock held by Roberts Limited at 30th June 19-4 includes £800 transferred from Llewellyn Limited which cost the latter £600.

Roberts Limited has no preference capital, no reserves other than the Profit and Loss account balance and had paid no dividends since the acquisition of the shares by Llewellyn Limited.

You are required to:

a. present working papers in the form *either* of ledger accounts *or* journal entries showing the adjustments necessary to correct the Consolidated balance sheet, and.

b. present the revised Consolidated balance sheet as at 30th June 19-4.

Ignore taxation.

(ACCA)

40. The following statements are reproduced from the published accounts of two companies, Alpha and Beta.

ALPHA LTD

Source and Application of Group Funds

	19-4 £000	19-3 £000
SOURCE OF FUNDS		
Profit before taxation	3,241	2,662
Less: Profit of associated company	15	46
	3,226	2,616
Surplus on sale of goodwill, patents and trade marks	–	60
Depreciation	660	551
Sale of fixed assets	61	61
Government grants	26	6
	3,973	3,294
APPLICATION OF FUNDS		
Capital expenditure	1,588	974
Additional working capital	1,297	1,026
Taxation	1,154	662
Dividends	531	279

	4,570	2,941
Unrealised gains (losses) arising from changes in exchange rates	73	153
	4,497	2,788
INCREASE (DECREASE) IN GROUP FUNDS	(524)	506

Note: Group funds comprise bank and short term deposits, less short term borrowings:

BETA LTD

Source and Application of Group Funds

	19-4 £000	19-3 £000
SOURCE OF FUNDS		
Retained profit (including minority interests)	5,866	9,248
Depreciation	15,214	18,319
Deferred tax	2,302	2,645
Internal cash flow	23,382	30,212
Loan capital	(774)	15,024
Bank overdrafts and loans repayable within one year	8,715	2,997
Increases in capital and share premium	1,515	–
Other	(951)	19
	31,887	48,252
APPLICATION OF FUNDS		
Expenditure on fixed assets(net)	23,908	25,145
Increase in working capital	3,183	16,548
Increase in investments	2,864	5,059
Goodwill arising on acquisitions	1,932	1,500
	31,887	48,252

You are required to discuss critically and constructively these two statements having due regard for Statement of Standard Accounting Practice No.10 (Statements of source and application of funds). Your answer should deal with both presentation and interpretation.

41. Hover Ltd, which has an authorised and issued share capital of 200,000 ordinary shares of 50p each, fully paid, had a balance carried forward on revenue reserve of £62,000 on 31st March 19-7.
You also receive the following information:

1. On 1st October 19-7, Hover Ltd purchased 60,000 shares of 50p each in Drove Ltd for £80,000. Drove Ltd had an issued share capital of 80,000 ordinary shares of 50p each, fully paid, and a balance brought forward on revenue reserve of £44,000 as on 31st March 19-7.
2. In the year ended 31st March 19-8 Hover Ltd made a trading profit of £46,000 and had paid a dividend of 25p per share whilst Drove Ltd made a trading profit of £28,000 and in February 19-8 had paid a dividend of 20p per share.
3. On 1st December 19-8 Hover Ltd purchased 90,000 of 100,000 issued ordinary shares of £1 each, fully paid, in Worker Ltd for £80,000. On the 31st March 19-8 Worker Ltd had an adverse balance on revenue reserve of £20,000 carried forward.
4. In the year ended 31st March 19-9 the trading profits of the three companies were: Hover Ltd £52,000; Drove Ltd £36,000; and Worker Ltd £10,000. Hover Ltd and Drove Ltd had paid respectively dividends of 35p per share and 25p per share. Worker Ltd has not paid a dividend.
5. Included in the stock of Worker Ltd on 31st March 19-9 was an amount of £5,000 which had been purchased from Hover Ltd at a profit of 25% on its selling price.

You are to assume that profits of both Drove Ltd and Worker Ltd accrue evenly throughout the year. You are required to show how the above items would be reflected in the consolidated Balance sheet of Hover Ltd as on 31st March 19-9, together with corresponding figures for the previous year, and to provide detailed schedules showing the make up of the relevant figures.

42. The balance sheets of Argos Ltd, and its subsidiaries Bodmin Ltd and Carter Ltd at 31st March 19-9 are summarised as follows:

	Argos Ltd		Bodmin Ltd		Carter Ltd	
	£	£	£	£	£	£
Freehold property		154,352		92,886		–
Plant and machinery						
(net book value)		93,854		14,758		542
Motor vehicles (net book value)		21,258		1,002		–
		269,464		108,646		542
Subsidiary Companies						
Shares at cost	81,604		2,114			
Loan account	–		1,900			
Current accounts	5,030		6,102			
		86,634		10,116		
Goodwill		–		–		1,026
Investment in government bonds		40,000		70,000		
Current Assets						
Stocks and work in progress	218,096		24,214		4,756	
Patterns	–		390		36	
Debtors	143,380		49,536		778	
Cash and bank balances	61,776		16,512		4,154	
	423,252		90,652		9,724	
Deduct:						
Current Liabilities						
Creditors	129,294		43,670		294	
Due to Argos Ltd	–		4,942		88	
Due to Bodmin Ltd.	–		–		8,002	
Taxation	37,530		5,762			
Unclaimed dividends	332		–		–	
Proposed dividends	40,000					
	207,156		54,374		8,384	
Net current assets		216,096		36,278		1,340
		612,194		225,040		2,908
Represented by:						
Ordinary share capital		20,000		2,000		6,000
General revenue reserve		250,000		–		–
Profit and loss account		162,194		223,040	(Loss)	3,092
		612,194		225,040		2,908

Argos Ltd had acquired 75% of the shares in Bodmin Ltd in 19-4 when the credit balance on the profit and loss account of that company was £46,216; no dividends had been paid since that date. Bodmin Ltd acquired all the shares in Carter Ltd in 19-6 when the balance on its profit and loss account was £2,928 (Dr). Subsequently £204 was received by Carter Ltd and credited to its profit and loss account representing recovery of a bad debt which had been wholly written off at the time of Bodmin's acquisition. Argos Ltd and Bodmin Ltd sell product X which is made by Argos. During the year Bodmin Ltd had purchased 10,000 units from Argos at a price of £0.60 (being cost plus 20%) of which 4,000 units were in stock at 31 March 19-9. Group Policy is to make a full provision for unrealised inter company profits.

You are required to prepare a consolidated balance sheet of Argos Ltd and its subsidiaries as at 31st March 1979.

Your workings must be submitted.

(ACCA)

43. The summarised profit and loss accounts of Figure Ltd, Loop Ltd, Rocker Ltd and Edge Ltd for the year ended 28th February 19-9, and the issued share capitals as on that date, were as follows:

	Figure Ltd £	Loop Ltd £	Rocker Ltd £	Edge Ltd £
Turnover	2,462,000	850,000	240,400	830,600
Balance brought forward 1st March 19-8	60,000	80,000	20,000	35,000
Trading profits	482,000	147,700	39,400	165,025
Extraordinary amount received for legal damages		40,000		
Interim dividend received from Loop Ltd	15,000			
Proposed dividends from Loop Ltd and Edge Ltd	57,500			
Debenture interest from Loop Ltd (gross)	5,000			
	619,500	267,700	59,400	200,025
Directors' fees	62,000	16,000	12,000	30,000
Depreciation	59,000	19,500	8,500	16,000
Audit fees	4,500	1,800	1,000	2,100
Debenture Interest (gross)		10,000		
Provision for corporation tax	185,000	52,000	8,000	60,800
Proposed dividends, actual	201,000	50,000		50,000
Interim dividend paid, actual		20,000		
Balance carried forward	108,000	98,400	29,900	41,125
	619,500	267,700	59,400	200,025
Issued ordinary share capital in £1 shares	300,000	100,000	120,000	80,000

You also obtain the following information.

1. On 1st March 19-5 Loop Ltd purchased 80,000 shares in Rocker Ltd.

2. Figure Ltd purchased 75,000 shares in Loop Ltd on 1st March 19-6, and 32,000 shares in Edge Ltd on 1st March 19-8.

3. The balances on profit and loss account on the respective dates had been:

	1st March 19-5 £		1st March 19-6 £	
Figure Ltd	72,000		80,000	
Loop Ltd	60,000		40,000	
Rocker Ltd	(80,000)	Debit	(70,000)	Debit
Edge Ltd	27,000		32,000	

4. The chairman of the board of Figure Ltd is the only director of that company to serve as a director also of the other three companies, and in return receives directors' fees of £2,000 per annum from each company.

You are required to prepare a consolidated Profit and Loss Account of Figure Ltd and its subsidiary companies, incorporating the results of its associated company, for the year ended 28th February 19-9, together with your consolidation schedules.

44. The following are the trial balances of McTavish Ltd, and its subsidiary company Patel Ltd, as at 31 March 19-9:

	McTavish Ltd £000	Patel Ltd £000
Authorised and Issued Ordinary Share Capital of £1 shares	30,000	15,000
Sales	128,000	36,000
Creditors	5,550	2,960
Profit and Loss Account - balance at 31 March 19-8	3,600	4,000
	167,150	57,960
Cost of Goods sold	87,000	27,320
Freehold Land and Buildings (Net book value)	12,300	7,500
Plant and Machinery (Net book value)	5,875	8,100
Motor Vehicles (Net book value)	–	900
Expenses including depreciation of Fixed Assets	23,000	5,440
Trade Debtors	6,125	3,750
Balance at Bank	8,482	770
Stock at 31 March 19-9	7,320	4,180
Investment: 12 million Ordinary £1 shares in Patel Ltd at cost	16,600	
Interim dividend paid	300	
Advance Corporation Tax (A.C.T.) recoverable, on Interim dividend paid	148	
	167,150	57,960

The following information should be taken into account:

i. McTavish Ltd, acquired the shares in Patel Ltd on 1 April 19-8.

ii. Included in the stock of Patel Ltd, at 31 March 19-9 is an amount of £2,400,000 for goods purchased from McTavish Ltd, which had cost the latter 70% of that figure.

iii. Sales by McTavish Ltd, to Patel Ltd, during the year ended 31 March 19-9 amounted to £8,400,000.

iv. Both companies proposed to pay a dividend of 10% in respect of the year ended 31 March 19-9.

v. The estimated Corporation Tax on the profits for the year is:

McTavish Ltd – £8,000,000
Patel Ltd – £1,400,000

vi. The ACT on the McTavish Ltd, interim dividend has been paid.

vii. ACT calculations should be made to the nearest thousand pounds. Income Tax is at 33%.

You are required to prepare a Consolidated Profit and Loss Account for the year ended 31 March 19-9 and a Consolidated Balance Sheet as at that date.

Your workings must be submitted.

(ACCA)

45. A new company, Z Ltd, formed on 1 October 19-9 and starting operations on that day, became a subsidiary of Y Ltd, on 1 April 19-0 when the latter obtained 60% of the ordinary shares of Z Ltd, for £25,520.

X Ltd was Y Ltd's holding company, having purchased 80% of Y Ltd ordinary shares on 1 June 19-9 for £53,600. Subsequent to Z Ltd becoming a member of the group, X Ltd purchased 25% of the Z Ltd ordinary shares on 1 July 19-0 for £12,200. The following are summarised balance sheets of the three companies as at 30 September 19-0, their accounting year end:

	X Ltd		Y Ltd		Z Ltd	
	£	£	£	£	£	£
Ordinary share capital		100,000		60,000		36,000
Profit and Loss Account						
Balances 1 October 19-9	60,000		(9,000)*		–	
Profit/(Loss) year ended						
30 September 19-0	40,000		26,000		6,400	
		100,000		17,000		6,400
		200,000		77,000		42,400
Net Assets						
(including for X Ltd and Y Ltd,						
Investment in Subsidiary company						
A/Cs)		200,000		77,000		42,400

*Y Limited had made a loss of £18,000 during the year ended 30 September 1979.

You are required to prepare a summary consolidated balance sheet of the XYZ group as at 30 September 19-0.

Workings which must be submitted should include a proof of the net asset figure shown in the consolidated balance sheet.

(ACCA)

46. On 1st January 19-9 RS Limited acquired 96,000 ordinary shares in TV Limited at a cost of £107,000 and on 1st April, 19-9 300,000 ordinary shares in XY Limited at a cost of £524,000. Directors were appointed to the boards of both companies by RS Limited so as to take an active part in their management.

From the information given below, you are required to prepare a consolidated balance sheet for RS Limited as at 31st December, 19-9.

Workings must be shown.

1. The closing balances of the three companies at 31st December 19-9 are as follows:

	RS Limited	TV Limited	XY Limited
	£	£	£
Share capital:			
£1 ordinary shares authorised, issued and			
fully paid	1,000,000	320,000	400,000
Share premium	200,000	24,000	
Capital reserve	300,000		56,000
Retained profit at 1st January 19-9	534,000	76,000	152,000
Profit for year after tax	252,000	102,000	128,000
Creditors	590,600	135,400	149,000
Current account, XY Limited	36,000		
Depreciation on plant, 31st December 19- 9	521,200	115,000	124,600
Taxation	190,000	90,000	114,000
Bank overdraft, Jones Bank	55,000		
	3,678,800	862,400	1,123,600
Freehold property, at cost	721,000		200,000
Plant and machinery, at cost	1,372,000	448,600	326,400
Stock and work-in-progress	514,600	220,400	360,200
Debtors	440,200	185,200	149,000
Current account, RS Limited			48,000
Investments	631,000		
Bank balances, Smiths Bank		8,200	40,000
	3,678,800	862,400	1,123,600

2. No interim dividends have been paid during the year but final dividends are proposed as follows:

	%
RS Limited	10
TV Limited	12
XY Limited	8

3. No transfer to reserves have been made during the year.

4. Profits are to be assumed to have accrued equally throughout the year.

5. Included in the stock and work-in-progress of RS Limited were goods supplied by XY Limited valued at £40,000, which XY Limited had invoiced at cost plus 25%

6. A remittance of £12,000 from RS Limited on 29th December, 19-9 to XY Limited was not received by the latter until 2nd January, 19-0.

7. Advance corporation tax is to be taken at 3/7.

47. A limited owns 80% of the issued ordinary share capital of B Limited, 75% of that of C Limited and 45% of that of X Limited.

From the information given below you are required to prepare a consolidated profit and loss account for the year ended 31st December 19-9, which should comply with the requirements of Statements of Standard Accounting Practice Nos 1 (Accounting for the results of associated companies) and 14 (Group accounts).

All workings should be shown.

1. The summarised profit and loss accounts of the four companies for the year ended 31st December, 19-9 are set out below:

	A Ltd £	B Ltd £	C Ltd £	X Ltd £
Balance brought forward at 31st December, 19-8	90,000	60,000		
Trading profits	832,000	252,000	20,000	415,400
Dividend ex B Limited	32,000			
Dividend ex X Limited	54,000			
Balance carried forward			50,000	
	1,008,000	312,000	70,000	415,400
Balance brought forward, at 31st December 19-8			40,000	
Directors' fees	36,000	20,000	10,000	35,000
Depreciation	40,000	36,000	18,000	30,000
Audit fees	4,000	2,000	2,000	2,400
Corporation Tax	380,000	94,000		174,000
Proposed dividend	300,000			120,000
Interim dividend paid		40,000		
Balance carried forward	248,000	120,000		54,000
	1,008,000	312,000	70,000	415,400

2. The issued ordinary share capital in £1 shares was

	£
A Limited	500,000
B Limited	200,000
C Limited	160,000
X Limited	240,000

3. A Limited acquired its shares on the following dates:

	Shares	
B Limited	120,000	1st January, 19-6
	40,000	1st January, 19-9
C Limited	120,000	1st January, 19-7
X Limited	108,000	1st January, 19-9

4. X Limited commenced trading on 1st January, 19-9.

5. The profit and loss account of B Limited showed a debit balance of £80,000 on 1st January, 19-6,

and that of C Limited showed a credit balance of £8,000 on 1st January 19-7.

6. The holding company and the subsidiaries have elected for inter company dividends to be paid without the incidence of advance corporation tax.

7. During the year A Limited had purchased goods from B Limited which gave the latter company a profit of 25% on selling price. Goods purchased by A Limited from B Limited for £30,000 were included in the closing stock at 31st December at a valuation of £27,500.

8. The directors of B Limited are also directors of A Limited. Two of the directors of A Limited are also directors of X Limited.

48. On 1st January, 19-8 PQ Limited purchased 80,000 ordinary shares in RS Limited for the sum of £108,000 and on 1st April 19-8 300,000 ordinary shares in TV Limited for the sum of £504,000. PQ Limited appointed directors to the boards of both companies in order to take an active part in their management.

From the information given below you are required to prepare a consolidated balance sheet for PQ Limited as at 31st December 19-8.

1. The balance sheets of the three companies at 31st December, 19-8 are set out below.

	PQ Limited £	TV Limited £	RS Limited £
Share capital:			
Authorised and issued in £1 shares fully paid	1,000,000	400,000	320,000
Share premiums	100,000	–	24,000
Retained profits at 1st January, 19-8	524,000	208,000	76,000
Creditors	626,600	149,000	135,400
Bank overdraft (Smiths Bank)	55,000	–	–
Depreciation on plant, at 31st December 19-8	521,200	124,600	115,000
Profit for 19-8, including dividends received	252,000	128,000	102,000
	3,078,800	1,009,600	772,400
Freehold property, at cost	570,000	200,000	–
Plant and machinery, at cost	1,142,000	326,400	448,600
Stocks and work-in-progress	504,600	324,200	190,400
Debtors	250,200	95,000	125,200
Bank balances (Jones Bank)	–	64,000	8,200
Investments	612,000	–	–
	3,078,800	1,009,600	772,400

2. In May 19-8 TV Limited paid a final dividend of 4% provided out of profits for 19–7.

3. Final dividends are proposed as follows:

> PQ Limited   8%
> TV Limited   6%
> RS Limited   10%

4. Profits of TV Limited are assumed to have accrued equally throughout the year.

5. Taxation is to be ignored. Workings must be shown.

49. A Limited holds 75% of the ordinary share capital of B Limited (acquired on 1st June, 19-8) and 40% of the ordinary share capital of C Limited (acquired on 1st April, 19-8).

A director of A Limited has been appointed to the board of C Limited to take an active part in the management of that company.

A Limited has no other investments, and none of the companies has any preference capital.

From the information given below you are required to prepare a consolidated profit and loss account for A Limited for the year ended 31st December, 19-8, with the appropriate notes.

1 : Final Accounts

1. The profit and loss accounts for the year ended 31st December, 19–8 are set out below:

		A Limited £	B Limited £	C Limited £
Turnover (excluding inter-group sales)		4,600,000	2,280,000	3,200,000
Trading profit		480,000	234,000	380,000
Dividends receivable		128,400	–	–
		608,400	234,000	380,000
Corporation tax	£			
Trading profit	230,000		102,000	160,000
Dividends receivable	42,800			
		272,800		
Profit after tax		335,600	132,000	220,000
Proposed dividends		214,000	64,000	94,000
Retained profit		121,600	68,000	126,000

2. Included in the stock of B Limited at 31st December, 19–8 was £72,000 for goods purchased from A Limited which the latter company had invoiced a cost plus 20%. It was the policy of A Limited to make full provision for unrealised profit without reference to minority interests.

50. The Balance Sheets as at 30 June 19–8, of A Ltd, and its subsidiary companies, B Ltd, C Ltd, and D Ltd, are summarised below:

Credit Balances	A Ltd £	B Ltd £		C Ltd £		D Ltd £	
Capital:							
Authorised, issued and fully paid in Ordinary Shares of £1 each	40,000	8,000		3,000		1,000	
Profit and Loss account	–	3,000	Dr	6,000	Cr	2,000	Dr
Trade Creditors	–	28,000		38,000		14,000	
Current Account with D Ltd	–	4,000		–		–	
Current Account with B Ltd	–	–		2,000		–	
Bank Overdraft	–	6,000		–		–	
	40,000	43,000		49,000		13,000	

Debit Balances				
Fixed Assets	–	2,000	6,000	1,000
Investment in Subsidiary companies at cost	20,000	–	–	–
Stock	–	18,000	15,000	2,000
Trade Debtors	–	21,000	24,000	2,800
Current Account with C Ltd	–	2,000	–	–
Current Account with B Ltd	–	–	–	6,000
Bank balance	20,000	–	4,000	1,200
	40,000	43,000	49,000	13,000

Note:

1. A Ltd was incorporated on 1 January 19–8 and on that date acquired all the issued shares of D Ltd and three-quarters of the issued shares of B Ltd by the allotment to the shareholders in those companies of an equal number of shares in A Ltd at par.

2. On the same day, the balance of the authorised capital of A Ltd was subscribed for in cash and all the issued shares of C Limited were purchased for £13,000.

3. D Ltd was incorporated on 1 July 19-7.

4. The accounts of B Ltd and C Ltd prepared as on 30 June 19-7 showed balances on profit and loss account of £8,000 (Debit) and £4,000 (Credit) respectively. It may be assumed that profit and/or losses of B Ltd, C Ltd and D Ltd, accrue evenly. No appropriations of profit have been made.

5. On 30 June 19-8, there was cash in transit from B Ltd to D Ltd of £2,000.

6. On 30 June 19-8, the stock of B Ltd included £5,000 of goods purchased from C Ltd, C Ltd had invoiced these goods at cost plus 25%. A Ltd established a policy of providing for the whole of the unrealised inter-company profit without regard for Minority interests.

7. Taxation and preliminary expenses have been ignored.

You are required to prepare the consolidated balance sheet of A Ltd and its subsidiaries as on 30 June 19-8.

Your workings must be submitted.

(ACCA)

51. On 1st April 19-3 three companies, Mountain Ltd, Plain Ltd and Peninsula Ltd, decided to develop a new method of transportation through a new company, Isthmus Ltd, in which each of them hold one third of the ordinary shares.

The summarised results of Isthmus Ltd for the four years ended on 31st March 1907 were:

	19-4	19-5	19-6	19-7
	£000	£000	£000	£000
Sales	2,000	10,000	21,000	25,500
Costs	5,000	11,500	15,000	18,000
Profit/(Loss)	(3,000)	(1,500)	6,000	7,500
Dividend	–	–	–	3,000
Retention	(3,000)	(1,500)	6,000	4,500
Fixed Assets	3,000	6,000	9,000	12,000
Net Current assets	3,000	(1,500)	1,500	3,000
	6,000	4,500	10,500	15,000
Share Capital	9,000	9,000	9,000	9,000
Retained Profit/(Loss)	(3,000)	(4,500)	1,500	6,000
	6,000	4,500	10,500	15,000

Mountain Ltd has always considered and treated its interest as a trade investment, Plain Ltd treated it as an associated company and Peninsula Ltd treated it as a trade investment for the first two years and then as an associated company.

The directors of Mountain Ltd, Plain Ltd and Peninsula Ltd obtained professional advice and agreed, as each year's accounts became available, that the value of a shareholding of one-third of the issued share capital of Isthmus Ltd was £3m, £5m, £5m and £7m respectively on 31st March 19-4, 19-5, 19-6 and 19-7. These valuations were relied upon for purposes of disclosure in accounts. Taxation should be ignored. You are required to:

a. show how Mountain Ltd, Plain Ltd and Peninsula Ltd recorded the investment and its results in their own accounts for the three years ended 31st March 19-7.

b. calculate the effect of the different treatment on the earnings per share in 19-7 of Mountain Ltd and Plain Ltd if both companies have other net profits of £2 million and an issued share capital of 10m ordinary shares of £1 each, and

c. describe the conditions that are used to determine whether or not an investment should be treated as an associated company.

52. You are required to prepare a consolidated profit and loss account for the year ended 31st December 19-0 suitable for incorporation in the published accounts of A Limited, which will not include a separate profit and loss account for the holding company. Workings should be submitted.

	A Limited	B Limited
	£	£
Profit and loss account, balance at 1st January 19-0	36,000	15,000
Trading profit	71,000	40,000
Dividends from B Limited		
Preference	5,400	–
Ordinary	7,500	–
	119,900	55,000
Depreciation	12,000	4,000
Debenture interest	10,000	–
Directors' emoluments	7,000	3,000
Taxation	22,000	15,000
Dividends paid:		
Date of Payment		
6% Preference: 30th June	–	3,000
31st December	–	3,000
Ordinary:		
Interim 30th June	12,000	5,000
Final 31st December	12,000	5,000
Profit and loss account, balance at 31st December, 19-0	44,900	17,000
	119,900	55,000

The following information relates to share capital:

	A Limited	B Limited
	£	£
Ordinary shares of £1 each fully paid	400,000	200,000
6% Preference shares of £1 each, fully paid		100,000
Shares in B Limited held by A Limited:		
Ordinary shares acquired 1st July 19-0		150,000
Preference shares acquired 1st January, 19-0		90,000

Income and expenditure are deemed to accrue evenly throughout the year. All dividends are payable out of the current year's profits. The directors of B Limited resigned on 1st July 19-0 and were replaced on that day by directors of A Limited who are to receive the same remuneration as the former directors.

53. The balance sheets and profits and loss accounts of Transport Enterprise Ltd and its two subsidiaries, Motor Cycles Ltd and Aircraft Ltd, are summarised below:

Balance sheets at 31st December 19-9	Transport Enterprises	Motor Cycles	Aircraft
	£000	£000	£000
Share capital			
10% preference shares of £1	1,000	–	–
8% preference shares of £1	1,000	500	1,000
Ordinary shares of £1	4,000	500	2,000
Reserves	2,500	600	400
Long term loans			
12% repayable 20-9	1,000	–	–
10% repayable 20-0	2,000	700	1,000
10% repayable 20-5	–	500	600
Current liabilities			
Trade creditors	3,427	1,364	2,593
Taxation	625	222	476

Dividends payable (ordinary)	1,000	400	100
Overdraft	527	220	347
	17,079	5,006	8,516
Fixed assets at cost	13,492	3,627	5,876
less depreciation	1,728	1,549	2,931
	11,764	2,078	2,945
Investment in			
Motor Cycles Ltd			
300,000 ordinary shares	600	–	–
Aircraft Ltd			
1,500,000 ordinary shares	750	–	–
Current assets			
Stock	1,629	1,794	2,243
Debtors	1,547	1,206	2,728
Cash	789	(72)	600
	17,079	5,006	8,516

The shares in Motor Cycles Ltd were acquired in two stages; 100,000 at £1 per share on 1st January 19-4, the date of incorporation, and 200,000 at £2.50 per share on 1st January 19-8, when the reserves totalled £100,000. There has been no change in the issued share capital of Motor Cycles Ltd since incorporation.

The shares in Aircraft Ltd were acquired on 1st January 19-6 at 50p per share. The reserves at this date were nil.

Plant and machinery bought by Transport Enterprises Ltd for £50,000 on 1st January 19-6, and depreciated on a straight line basis over 5 years, was transferred to Aircraft Ltd at its written down and fair market value on 1st January 19-9. This transaction has not been recorded in the books of either company.

Another item of plant, purchased by Aircraft Ltd, on 1st January 19-7 for £100,000 and depreciated on the straight line basis over 10 years, was sold to Transport Enterprises Ltd for £150,000 on 1st January 19-9. Transport Enterprises Ltd paid for it on 1st February 19-9, and assumed that the plant would last for another 8 years.

Dividends are not recorded by Transport Enterprises Ltd until received.

You are required to:

a. prepare a consolidated balance sheet of the group at 31st December 19-9 and

b. discuss briefly the alternative consolidation adjustments which could have been appropriate if Motor Cycles Ltd had sold £100,000 worth of goods, including £20,000 profit to Transport Enterprises Ltd, assuming they were in the latter company's stock at 31st December 19-9.

54. SSAP 22 Accounting for goodwill

a. How is goodwill defined?
b. What does the term 'separable net assets' include?
c. What is 'fair value'?
d. What is 'purchased goodwill'?
e. What accounting treatment is prescribed for:
    i. negative goodwill?
    ii. positive goodwill?

55. As the accountant of Parent PLC you are preparing the annual accounts. The company has both subsidiary and related (associated) companies but you are NOT concerned with the preparation of group (consolidated) accounts.

a. In the course of your task you discover that the following transactions have arisen:

1. A dividend of £14,000 (plus tax credit, £6,000) has been received from Lyne PLC, an associated company.

2. Interest (less income tax at 30%) for the second half year, has been received from its holding of £100,000 (nominal) 12% Debentures acquired as a long term investment at an original cost of £95,000.

3. An invoice for £35,000 for publicity and advertising in the newspapers and on television during the last quarter of the year.

REQUIRED
State the accounting treatment you would apply to the above items in Parent PLC's own final accounts.

56. At 30 June 19-5, the summarised balance sheets of Dorset plc, Chesil plc and Bridport plc were:

	Dorset plc £000	Chesil plc £000	Bridport plc £000
Tangible Fixed Assets	852	687	504
Investment in subsidiary companies			
Dorset in Chesil (640,000 shares)	461	–	–
Chesil in Bridport (360,000 shares)	–	206	–
Net Current Assets	305	227	146
	1,618	1,120	650
Ordinary Shares of £1.00 per share	1,000	800	600
Reserves			
Profit and Loss Account	418	220	50
Other	200	100	–
	1,618	1,120	650

At the date of the acquisition by Dorset of its holding, Chesil's profit and loss account had a credit balance of £120,000 and other reserves of £40,000.

Bridport's profit and loss account had a debit balance of £60,000 when Chesil acquired its holding on the same day.

REQUIRED:
Prepare separate consolidated balance sheets of the Dorset Group at 30 June 19-5, (for internal circulation only), using:

a. the direct method
b. the indirect method
of consolidation

57. The balance sheets (for internal circulation only) of three companies as at 31 December 19-5, were

	Exe PLC £000	£000	Wye PLC £000	£000	Zed PLC £000	£000
Fixed Assets						
(At written down values)						
Premises	631		425		502	
Plant	252		171		281	
Vehicles	114		83		54	
		997		679		837
Investments at cost						
Shares in Wye and Zed		467		–		–
Current Assets						
Stocks	116		189		154	
Debtors – trade	96		78		85	
Dividends receivable						
from Zed PLC	27		–		–	

Bank and cash	55	47	56
	294	314	295
Creditors due within 1 year			
Creditors – trade	80	151	130
Taxation	39	48	28
Proposed dividends	100	80	90
	219	279	248
Net current assets	75	35	47
Total assets less current liabilities	1,539	714	884
Creditors due in more than 1 year			
Debentures	600	150	61
Provision for liabilities & charges			
Deferred taxation	48	24	43
Capital and Reserves			
Called up share capital	700	400	600
Other reserves	70	35	62
Profit and loss account	121	105	118
	891	540	780
	1,539	714	884

Notes:
1. Exe had acquired an 80% holding in Wye's share capital for £250,000. At that date there was a debit balance on Wye's profit and loss account of £40,000 and no reserves.
2. Exe had acquired a 30% holding in Zed's share capital for £217,000. At that date there were credit balances on other reserves of £21,000 and on profit and loss account of £39,000.
3. During the year Exe had supplied goods at a transfer price of cost plus 25% to Wye. At 31 December 19-5 Wye had such goods in stock amounting to £45,000 (at cost to Wye).
4. Included in the above balance sheets are sums owed:

By	To			
	Exe	Wye	Zed	Total
	£000	£000	£000	£000
Exe	–	7	15	22
Wye	10	–	9	19
Zed	12	5	–	17
Total	22	12	24	58

REQUIRED:

Prepare the consolidated balance sheet of the Exe Group as at 31 December 19-5 together with relevant notes to the extent of the available information.

58. The individual draft profit and loss accounts of three companies X PLC, Y PLC and Z PLC for the year ended 31 March 19-6, were as follows:

1 : Final Accounts

	X PLC £	X PLC £	Y PLC £	Y PLC £	Z PLC £	Z PLC £
Turnover	7,063,100		4,264,500		2,037,000	
Cost of sales	4,790,400		1,853,200		1,009,200	
Gross profit		2,272,700		2,411,300		1,027,800
Less:						
Interest payable	1,400		–		600	
Directors' emoluments	48,500		29,100		18,200	
Depreciation	65,000		32,700		25,800	
Audit fees	13,900		9,400		2,600	
Other expenses	867,000		1,030,000		640,000	
		995,800		1,101,200		687,200
Profit before tax		1,276,900		1,310,100		340,600
Corporation tax on profits for year		197,300		240,000		8,000
Profit after tax		1,079,600		1,070,100		332,600
Extraordinary items (adjusted for tax)						
:gains		655,000				
:losses				700,000		
Profit after extraordinary items		1,734,600		370,100		332,600
Proposed dividends		500,000		200,000		100,000
Retained profit						
: for year		1,234,600		170,100		232,600
: brought forward		408,700		145,300		128,000
: carried forward		1,643,300		315,400		360,600

1. X had acquired an 80% holding in the equity share capital of Y on 1 July 19-5 and a 40% holding in the equity share capital of Z on 1 January 19-5. You are to assume that profits were earned evenly throughout the years (on ordinary activities) and that the extraordinary loss in Y's accounts arose in January 19–6. Z had been incorporated on 1 April 19–4.

2. X had sold goods to Y during the year at a transfer price of £440,000, being cost (to X) plus 10%. One quarter of these goods were still held in stock by Y at 31 March 19-6. It is X's policy to provide for unrealised profit without reference to minority interests.

3. It is the policy of X not to take credit for dividends from the subsidiary company until actually received.

4. The ACT fraction to be used is $\frac{3}{7}$.

5. Directors' emoluments paid by Y and Z to those directors who are also directors of X amount to £15,600 and £8,200 (respectively).

REQUIRED:

a. Prepare the profit and loss account of the X Group of companies (for internal use) for the year ended 31 March 19-6.

b. State the items and amounts which appear in the published profit and loss account of the group, for

  i. Directors' emoluments,

  ii. Profit attributable to shareholders of X accounted for by X.

ACCA EXAMINATION QUESTIONS

59. The following information is provided:

a. Extracts from the Profit and Loss Accounts for the year ended 30 September 1982 of Group Ltd, Subsidiary Ltd and Associate Ltd.

b. Details of the capital structure as at 1 October 1981 for each of the companies.

c. Information relating to the purchase of shares and debentures by Group Ltd.

a. Extracts from the Profit & Loss Accounts for year ended 30 September 1982:

	Group £000s	Subsidiary £000s	Associate £000s
Turnover	7,000	2,000	1,000
Trading Profit (before Directors' Fees, Depreciation and Debenture Interest	1,000	382	215
Interim Dividend from Subsidiary	40		
Proposed Final Dividend from Subsidiary	80		
Proposed Final Dividend from Associate	24		
Debenture Interest from Subsidiary	10		
Directors' Fees	115	35	60
Depreciation	120	47	30
Debenture Interest		25	
Provision for Corporation Tax	400	105	55
Interim Dividend Paid		50	
Final Dividend Proposed	300	100	60

b. The capital structures at 1 October 1981 were as follows:

	Group	Subsidiary	Associate
Issued Ordinary Shares	750	250	150
Reserves	280	160	50
10% Debentures		250	
	£1,030	£660	£200

c. Information relating to purchase of shares and debentures by Group Ltd.

  i. Group Ltd acquired 200,000 £1 Ordinary shares in Subsidiary Ltd for a cash payment of £285,000 on 1 October 1980. At the date of acquisition the Reserves in Subsidiary Ltd had a credit balance of £125,000.

  ii. Group Ltd acquired 60,000 £1 Ordinary shares in Associate Ltd for a cash payment of £72,000 on 1 October 1981.

  iii. Group Ltd subscribed for £100,000 Debentures in Subsidiary Ltd on 1 October 1981. It acquired the debentures for a cash payment of £100,000.

Required:

a. Prepare a Consolidated Profit and Loss Account for Group Ltd and its subsidiary for the year ended 30 September 1982, together with supporting workings.

b. Calculate the values that would be disclosed in the Consolidated Balance Sheet as at 30 September 1982 for:

  Investment in Associate Ltd.
  Cost of Control
  Minority Interest
  Debentures

(ACCA 2.9(2) December 1982)

60. The following accounts are the Consolidated Balance sheet and Parent Company Balance Sheet for Alpha Ltd as at 30 June 1982:

	Consolidated Balance Sheet	Parent Company
	£	£
Ordinary Shares	140,000	140,000
Capital Reserve	92,400	92,400
Profit and Loss Account	79,884	35,280
Minority Interest	12,320	
	324,604	267,680
Fixed Assets		
Freehold Premises	127,400	84,000
Plant and Machinery	62,720	50,400
Goodwill	85,680	–
Investment in subsidiary (50,400 shares)		151,200
Current Assets		
Stock	121,604	71,120
Debtors	70,420	46,760
Dividends Receivable	–	5,040
Cash at Bank	24,360	–
	216,384	122,920
Current liabilities		
Creditors	128,660	69,720
Corporation Tax	27,160	20,720
Bank Overdraft	–	39,200
Proposed Dividend	11,760	11,200
	167,580	140,840
Working Capital	48,804	(17,920)
	£324,604	£267,680

Notes:

i. There is only one subsidiary company called Beta Ltd.

ii. There are no capital reserve in the subsidiary.

iii. Alpha produced stock for sale to the subsidiary at a cost of £3,360 in May 1982. The stock was invoiced to the subsidiary at £4,200 and is still on hand at the subsidiary's warehouse on 30 June 1982. The invoice had not been settled at 30 June 1982.

iv. The Profit and Loss of the subsidiary had a credit balance of £16,800 at the date of acquisition.

v. There is a right of set-off between overdrafts and bank balances.

Required:

a. Prepare the Balance Sheet as at 30 June 1982 of the subsidiary company from the information given above.

b. Briefly discuss the main reasons for the publication of consolidated accounts.

(ACCA 2.9(2) June 1982)

61. Required:

a. Explain and demonstrate the effect on the Profit and Loss Account and Balance Sheet of Prism PLC as at 30 November 1983 of any revision you consider necessary in the treatment of the investment in Scraper Ltd arising from the additional information contained in Appendix 4 and Appendix 5.

Assume that Prism PLC does not exercise its option to purchase the additional 200,000 existing ordinary shares in Scraper Ltd on 30 November 1983. (Show your calculations but do not reproduce the whole of the Profit and Loss Account and Balance Sheet of Prism PLC.)

b. Calculate the cost of control and the value of the interest of Prism PLC in Scraper Ltd on the assumption that the management of Prism PLC intended to gain control of Scraper Ltd from the time it acquired its initial interest and that it now proceeds to exercise the option as at 30 November 1983.

(ACCA 2.9 (1) December 1983)

Appendix 4
Further information relating to the quoted investments.

The following information became available after the draft accounts had been prepared for Prism PLC.

The quoted investments shown in the Trial Balance at a cost of £750,000 consisted of holdings in three companies.

Date of acquisition	Company	Issued share capital	Shares held by Prism PLC	Cost
				£
1.1.80	AJAX	10,000,000 ordinary shares of £1	786,550	595,000
1.3.81	SCRUBBER	150,000 ordinary shares of £1	–	–
		50,000 7% preference shares of £1	50,000	75,000
1.3.83	SCRAPER	400,000 ordinary shares of £1	100,000	80,000
				£750,000

The market price of the shares at 30 November 1983 was:

AJAX LTD   £1.10 for each £1 ordinary share.
SCRUBBER LTD   £1.45 for each £1 preference share.
SCRAPER LTD   £1.66 for each £1 ordinary share.
PRISM PLC   £0.30 for each 25p ordinary share.

The fixed assets of Scraper Ltd had a market value as follows:

	£
Freehold properties	250,000
Vehicles	182,000
Fixtures and fittings	12,000

Prism PLC has an option to acquire an additional 200,000 of the existing ordinary shares in Scraper Ltd with effect from 30 November 1983.

The option was acquired in March 1983 in anticipation of the fact that Scraper Ltd was tendering for extremely profitable contracts in the export market. The terms of the option were that Prism PLC would issue 10 ordinary shares of 25p each for each of the £1 ordinary shares in Scraper Ltd. Scraper Ltd had a record of low profitability in the year to 30 November 1982, when a new management team was recruited.

Appendix 5
The Profit and Loss Account of Scraper Ltd for the year ended 30 November 1983 and Balance Sheet as at 30 November 1983

	£	£
Sales		3,066,000
Cost of sales		2,055,000
Gross profit		1,011,000
Administration expense (Note 2)	220,000	
Distribution expense (Note 1)	200,000	420,000
Operating profit		591,000
Tax		182,000
Profit after tax		409,000
Dividend 10p per share		40,000

Balance brought forward	369,000
	(113,000)
	£256,000

Note 1

Depreciation on the freehold property was £3,888 calculated at 2% of valuation. One of the properties was revalued from £30,000 to £124,400 on 1 December 1982.

Note 2

Includes debenture interest paid.

Scraper Ltd – Balance Sheet as at 30 November 1983

Fixed Assets	Cost/Valuation £	Depn £	NBV £	£
Freehold property	194,400	14,400	180,000	
Vehicles	300,000	60,000	240,000	
Fixtures and fittings	28,000	12,000	16,000	436,000
Current Assets				
Stock			395,000	
Debtors			176,000	
Cash			232,000	803,000
Creditors-amounts due less than 1 year				
Trade creditors			112,000	
HP creditors			89,100	
Bank overdraft			17,043	218,143
Net current assets				584,857
Total assets less current liabilities				1,020,857
Creditors-amounts due more than 1 year				
10% debentures (convertible 1986)			100,000	
Other creditors including tax			174,857	274,857
Net assets				£746,000

Capital and Reserves	£
Share capital	400,000
Share premium	50,000
Capital redemption reserve	100,000
Revaluation deficit	(130,000)
General reserve	70,000
Profit and loss account	256,000
	£746,000

Note: The revaluation deficit results from a reappraisal on 1 December 1982 of the fixed asset register of fixtures and fittings within one of the London properties. There was no general programme of revaluation. The gain on the freehold of £94,400 has been netted off against the loss on revaluation of fixtures.

62. Triple Holdings Ltd had acquired shares in 1977 in First Sub Ltd and Second Sub Ltd. The position at 31 December 1981 is given in the Balance Sheet extracts that follow.

1 : Final Accounts

Extracts from Balance Sheets as at 31.12.1981

	Triple Holdings £000s	First Sub £000s	Second Sub £000s
Share capital	2,000	500	1,000
Capital reserves	200	300	–
Profit and Loss balance	500	400	(200)
Goodwill		(480)	
	2,700	720	800
Sundry net assets	2,000	720	800
500,000 £1 shares in First Sub	100		
800,000 £1 shares in Second Sub	600		
	2,700	720	800

The Balance Sheets of the subsidiaries at the date of acquisition by Triple Holdings are shown below:

	First Sub £000s	Second Sub £000s
Shares	500	1,000
Profit & Loss balance	–	200
Goodwill	(480)	–
Net tangible assets	20	1,200

On 1 January 1982 Triple Holdings purchased 750,000 £1 ordinary shares in Third Sub Ltd for £1,875,000. At that date the share capital of Third Sub consisted of 1,000,000 £1 ordinary shares and there was a credit balance of £200,000 on the Profit and Loss Account.

Third Sub Ltd already had a subsidiary, Subsub Ltd, in which it had acquired 280,000 of the 400,000 £1 ordinary shares issued for a purchase consideration of £840,000. On 1 January 1982, Subsub Ltd had a credit balance of £300,000 on its Profit and Loss Account.

Extracts from the Balance Sheets at 31 December 1982 are as follows:

	Triple £000s	First Sub £000s	Second Sub £000s	Third Sub £000	Subsub £000s
Share capital	2,000	500	1,000	1,000	400
Capital reserve	200	400			
Profit & Loss Balance	700	400	(500)	600	1,100
Goodwill	–	(480)	–	–	–
Net tangible assets	2,900	820	500	1,600	1,500

On 31 December 1982 Third Sub Ltd proposed to sell 40,000 of the shares it held in Subsub Ltd for a total of £260,000.

Required:

a. Prepare a Consolidated Balance Sheet for Triple Holdings as at 31 December 1982 on the basis that the sale of shares has occurred.

b. Prepare a Consolidated Balance Sheet for Triple Holdings as at 31 December 1982 on the basis that the sale of shares has NOT occurred.

(ACCA 2.9(2) June 1983.)

63. Required:

Prepare a draft Consolidated Profit and Loss Account for United Motor Spares Ltd and its subsidiary for the year ended 31 December 1983 and a draft Consolidated Balance Sheet for United Motor Spares Ltd and its subsidiary as at 31 December 1983.

Note: The only information available at the time the draft Consolidated Profit and Loss Account and Balance Sheet were to be prepared is set out in Appendix 1 and Appendix 1(a).

(ACCA 2.9(1) December 1984)

Appendix 1
The Trial Balance of United Motor Spares Ltd as at 31 December 1983

	Dr £000's	Cr £000's
Ordinary shares of £1 each		6,750
10% preference shares of £1 each		900
General reserve		1,665
Deferred taxation at 1 January 1983		1,800
Profit & Loss Account at 1 January 1983		7,290
Trading profit for 1983		6,030
Creditors		3,250
Tax payable on 1 January 1984		1,225
Debenture interest (net)		14
Goodwill	600	
Premises	5,600	
Equipment	4,800	
Investment in Provincial Motor Spares Ltd	6,250	
Stock	8,504	
Debtors	2,410	
Bank	760	
	28,924	28,924

a. The investment in Provincial Motor Spares Ltd consists of:

   i. £250,000 8% debentures acquired at par on 1 January 1980.

   ii. Sixty per cent of the 10% preference shares of £1 each acquired at par on 1 January 1983.

   iii. Seventy five per cent of the ordinary shares of £1 each acquired for cash on 1 April 1983.

b. The stock of £8,504,000 includes stock supplied by Provincial Motor Spares Ltd at an invoice price of £120,000. The cost price to Provincial Motor Spares Ltd was £80,000. The group policy is to adjust the Profit and Loss Account of the selling company for the group proportion of the unrealised profits.

c. The proposed final dividends for 1983 on the ordinary shares and preference shares in Provincial Motor Spares Ltd have not been included in the books of United Motor Spares Ltd.

d. Provision to be made for:

   i. Tax of £3,150,000 for the current year.

   ii. The preference dividend.

   iii. The proposed ordinary dividend of twenty per cent.

e. A transfer of £450,000 is to be made to the General Reserve.

f. Sales for 1983 totalled £70,000,000 excluding Value Added Tax.

g. A transfer of £300,000 is to be made from deferred taxation account.

Appendix 1(a) The Trial Balance of Provincial Motor Spares Ltd as at 31 December 1983

	Dr £000's	Cr £000's
Ordinary Shares of £1 each		3,600
10% cumulative preference shares of £1 each		1,000
General reserve		1,820
Profit and Loss Account at 1 January 1983		2,250
8% debentures		500
Profit for 1983		3,780
Debenture redemption reserve		290
Creditors		4,130
Tax payable on 1 January 1984		700
Deferred taxation on 1 January 1983		1,655

Investment income (net)		14
Premises	7,200	
Equipment	3,800	
Investments	251	
Stock	6,580	
Debtors	1,480	
Bank	428	
	19,739	19,739

a. Profits accrue evenly throughout the year.

b. Provision is to be made for:

    i. Tax of £1,900,000 on the profits of the current year.

    ii. The preference dividend

    iii. The proposed ordinary dividend of ten per cent.

c. A transfer of £170,000 is to be made to the General Reserve.

d. Sales for the year totalled £21,000,000 of which £1,000,000 consisted of sales to United Motor Spares Ltd. The sales are stated exclusive of Value Added Tax.

e. The Investment Income is net of tax credits at the rate of 3/7ths.

64. Required:

Prepare a summarised Consolidated Balance Sheet as at 31 December 1983 for Black Root Ltd and the subsidiary Confectioners Ltd.

Note: You are **NOT** required to include Health Sales Ltd in the Consolidation, or use the equity accounting method.

(ACCA 2.9(1) June 1984).

Appendix 1

Information about group structure

Black Root Ltd is a company that imports liquorice into the United Kingdom and sells to pharmaceutical companies and confectionery manufacturers. After a period of falling sales the company decided to acquire shares in a confectionery manufacturer and to acquire retail outlets in the health food market.

Accordingly on 1 January 1983 it paid £3,205,000 in cash to acquire 1,209,600 shares in Confectioners Ltd. On 31 December 1983 Confectioners Ltd made a Rights Issue for cash of 1 Ordinary £1 share for every 6 shares held at 250p per share, payable immediately. Black Root Ltd took up its full entitlement.

Also on 1 January 1983 Black Root Ltd subscribed for 1,190,000 Ordinary shares of £1 each, at par, in a newly formed company, Health Sales Ltd.

Health Sales Ltd entered into an agreement on 1 January 1983 to acquire the retail business carried on by the partnership of Pharar, Khadir and Benson. The purchase consideration was 510,000 Ordinary shares of £1 each issued at a premium of 50p per share and a cash payment of £714,000. Health Sales Ltd. acquired all of the assets of the partnership and all of the liabilities, with the exception of the bank account. The freehold land was revalued at £1,020,000 otherwise the closing balance sheet values were accepted as those shown in Appendix 3.

Appendix 2

Summarised Profit and Loss Accounts for the year ended 31 December 1983 and summarised Balance Sheets as at 31 December 1983 of Black Root Ltd and Confectioners Ltd.

	Black Root Ltd		Confectioners Ltd	
	1982	*1983*	*1982*	*1983*
	£000s	£000s	£000s	£00s
Turnover	27,968	34,523	2,492	3,536
Trading profit	6,992	8,740	608	868
Depreciation	1,472	1,840	128	192
Debenture Interest	736	920	64	96
	4,784	5,980	416	580
Taxation	2,208	2,346	240	224

Profit after tax	2,576	3,634	176	356
Dividends paid:				
Ordinary	402.5	483	–	–
Preference	322	322	22	22
Dividends Proposed	805	1,041	100	235
Issued Ordinary Shares	8,050	10,410	2,016	2,352
Issued 7% Preference Shares	4,600	4,600	320	320
Share Premium	–	2,110	–	504
Retained Profits	3,680	5,468	300	399
10% Debentures	7,360	9,200	640	960
Creditors	736	1,044	320	384
Current Account with Black Root Ltd				57
Tax	1,897	2,070	230	257
ACT Payable	345	446	43	101
Proposed dividend	805	1,041	100	235
	27,473	36,389	3,969	5,569
Fixed assets	18,400	22,080	1,792	2,176
Investments in Confectioners Ltd		3,709		
Investment in Health Sales Ltd		1,190		
Stock	1,104	1,397	512	640
Current Account with Confectioners Ltd		70		
Current Account with Health Sales Ltd		140		
Debtors	2,530	5,060	1,404	1,600
ACT Recoverable	345	446	43	101
Cash at Bank	5,094	2,297	218	1,052
	27,473	36,389	3,969	5,569

Additional information.

1. Black Root Ltd's investment in Confectioners Ltd consisted of 1,209,600 Ordinary shares of £1 each acquired on 1 January 1983 and 201,600 Ordinary shares of £1 each acquired under the Rights Issue on 31 December 1983.

2. During the year ended 31 December 1983 Black Root Ltd purchased from Confectioners Ltd one of its fixed assets, a machine, for £126,000. Confectioners Ltd had invoiced the machine at book value plus 40%. Black Root Ltd has depreciated the machine at 20% of the invoiced price.

3. Black Root Ltd supplied goods to Confectioners Ltd at cost plus 25%. During the year ended 31 December 1983 Black Root Ltd despatched goods with an invoiced value of £485,000 and received cash of £415,000 from Confectioners Ltd.

   During the year Confectioners Ltd received goods from Black Root Ltd with an invoiced value of £475,000 and made payment to them totalling £418,000. At 31 December 1983 the stock of Confectioners Ltd included goods supplied by Black Root Ltd with an invoiced value of £50,000.

4. During the year ended 31 December 1983 Black Root Ltd sold fixed assets for £575,000 (net book value of £460,000) and Confectioners Ltd sold fixed assets of £32,000 (net book value of £48,000). The respective profit and loss have been included in the respective trading profit.

5. The proposed dividends from Confectioners Ltd have been included in the Black Root Ltd debtors in the Balance Sheet as at 31 December, 1983.

6. It is group policy to disclose Goodwill on Consolidation in the Consolidated Balance Sheet.

65. On 1 April 1981 Machinery Limited bought 80% of the ordinary share capital of Components Limited and on 1 April 1983 Machinery Limited was itself taken over by Sales Limited who purchased 75% of the ordinary shares in Machinery Limited.

The balance sheets of the three companies at 31 October 1985 prepared for internal use showed the following position:

1 : Final Accounts

	Sales Ltd £	Sales Ltd £	Machinery Ltd £	Machinery Ltd £	Components Ltd £	Components Ltd £
Fixed assets						
Freehold land at cost		89,000		30,000		65,000
Buildings at cost	100,000		120,000		40,000	
Less:						
Accumulated depreciation	36,000		40,000		16,400	
		64,000		80,000		23,600
Plant and equipment at cost	102,900		170,000		92,000	
Less:						
Accumulated depreciation	69,900		86,000		48,200	
		33,000		84,000		43,800
		186,000		194,000		132,400
Investments						
Shares in Machinery at cost		135,000				
Shares in Components at cost				96,000		
Current assets						
Stocks	108,500		75,500		68,400	
Debtors	196,700		124,800		83,500	
Cash at bank	25,200		–		25,400	
		330,400		200,300		177,300
		651,400		490,300		309,700
Current liabilities						
Creditors	160,000		152,700		59,200	
Bank overdraft	–		327,400		–	
Corporation tax	57,400		47,200		24,500	
Proposed dividends	80,00		48,000		12,000	
		297,400		285,300		95,700
		£354,000		£205,000		£214,000
Ordinary shares		200,000		120,000		100,000
10% Preference shares		–		–		40,000
Revenue reserves		154,000		85,000		74,000
		354,000		205,000		214,000

Additional information

a. All ordinary shares are £1 each, fully paid.

b. Preference shares in Components Ltd are 50p each fully paid.

c. Proposed dividends in Components Ltd are:

643

on Ordinary shares   £10,000

on Preference shares   £2,000

d. Proposed dividends receivable by Sales Ltd and Machinery Ltd are included in debtors.

e. All creditors are payable within one year.

f. Items purchased by Machinery Ltd from Components Ltd and remaining in stock at 31 October 1985 amounted to £25,000. The profit element is 20% of selling price for Components Ltd.

g. Depreciation policy of the group is to provide for:

     i. buildings - at the rate of 2% on cost each year.

     ii. plant and equipment - at the rate of 10% on cost each year including full provision in the year of acquisition.

These policies are applied by all members of the group.

Included in the plant and equipment of Components Ltd is a machine purchased from the manufacturers, Machinery Ltd on 1 January 1984 for £10,000. Machinery Ltd recorded a profit of £2,000 on the sale of the machine.

h. Intra group balances are included in debtors and creditors respectively and are as follows:

			£
Sales Ltd	Creditors	– Machinery Ltd	45,600
		– Components Ltd	28,900
Machinery Ltd	Debtors	– Sales Ltd	56,900
Components Ltd	Debtors	– Sales Ltd	28,900

i. A cheque drawn by Sales Ltd for £11,300 on 28 October 1985 was received by Machinery Ltd on 3 November 1985.

j. At 1 April 1981, reserves in Machinery Ltd were £28,000 and in Components Ltd £20,000. At 1 April 1983 the figures were £40,000 and £60,000 respectively.

Required:

Prepare a group balance sheet at 31 October 1985 for Sales Limited and its subsidiaries complying, so far as the information will allow, with the accounting requirements of the Companies Acts.

(ACCA 2.9(2) December 1985)

66. **Required:**

a. Prepare a Value Added Statement for the Plural Publishers Group for the year ended 30 September 1984.

b. Discuss the use of such a statement to an existing shareholder of Plural Publishers Ltd.

c. Discuss alternative treatments for:

     i. Minority interest

     ii. Depreciation

(ACCA 2.9(1) June 1985)

Appendix 1

Notes on the group structure

Plural Publishers Ltd was incorporated on 1 October 1972 to publish computer magazines. In 1979 it acquired a 40% interest in Computer Software Texts Ltd, a company which specialised in publishing self instruction texts on computer programming.

On 1 April 1983 Plural Publishers Ltd acquired a majority holding in Video Hire Ltd by purchasing 80% of the issued share capital. The purchase consideration was £625,000. The purchase consideration was settled in full by the payment by Plural Publishers Ltd of £250,000 in cash and the issue of 250,000 £1 ordinary shares.

At the date of acquisition Video Hire Ltd had net assets of £575,000.

Video Hire Ltd had a financial year ending on 30 September. The draft profit and loss account of Video Hire Ltd for the year ended 30 September 1983 disclosed a loss of £300,000. Enquiries indicated that profits and losses accrued evenly throughout the year.

Appendix 4

Information relating to the Profit and Loss Account of Plural Publishers Ltd, Video Hire Ltd and Computer Software Texts Ltd for the year ended 30 September 1984

644

	Plural Publishers Ltd £000's	Video Hire Ltd £000's	Computer Software Texts Ltd £000's
Balance brought forward at 1 October 1983	8,080	(150)	125
Sales	17,280	7,560	3,825
Purchase of materials	10,368	4,158	2,056
Purchase of services	3,430	936	431
Salaries and Wages	1,322	1,386	573
Profit on trading	2,160	1,080	765

The Profit on Trading was before taking the following information into account:

Directors' emoluments	225	78	68
Auditors' fees	58	7	4
Depreciation	360	180	93
Debenture interest	60	5	
Tax on trading profit	630	360	315
Proposed dividends on ordinary shares	900	300	150

	£000
Retained profit for the group at 30 September 1984	401

67. Required:

Prepare a Consolidated Profit and Loss account for the Plural Publishers Group for the year ended 30 September 1984.

(ACCA 2.9(1) June 1985)

Appendix 1

Notes on the group structure

Plural Publishers Ltd was incorporated on 1 October 1972 to publish computer magazines. In 1979 it acquired a 40% interest in Computer Software Texts Ltd, a company which specialised in publishing self instruction texts on computer programming.

On 1 April 1983 Plural Publishers Ltd acquired a majority holding in Video Hire Ltd by purchasing 80% of the issued share capital. The purchase consideration was £625,000. The purchase consideration was settled in full by the payment by Plural Publishers Ltd of £250,000 in cash and the issue of 250,000 £1 ordinary shares.

At the date of acquisition Video Hire Ltd had net assets of £575,000.

Video Hire Ltd had a financial year ending on 30 September. The draft profit and loss account of Video Hire Ltd for the year ended 30 September 1983 disclosed a loss of £300,000. Enquiries indicated that profits and losses accrued evenly throughout the year.

Appendix 4.

Information relating to the Profit and Loss Account of Plural Publishers Ltd, Video Hire Ltd and Computer Software Texts Ltd for the year ended 30 September 1984

	Plural Publishers Ltd £000's	Video Hire Ltd £000's	Computer Software Texts Ltd £000's
Balance brought forward at 1 October 1983	8,080	(150)	125
Sales	17,280	7,560	3,825
Purchase of materials	10,368	4,158	2,056
Purchase of services	3,430	936	431

Salaries and wages	1,322	1,386	573
Profit on trading	2,160	1,080	765

The Profit on Trading was before
taking the following information
into account:

Directors' emoluments	225	78	68
Auditors' fees	58	7	4
Depreciation	360	180	93
Debenture interest	60	5	
Tax on trading profit	630	360	315
Proposed dividends on ordinary shares	900	300	150

68. On 30 June 1980 the Overseas Trading Co. Ltd in London set up a wholly owned subsidiary, Internal Trading Ltd in Bongoland.

The latest balance sheet of Internal Trading Ltd is as follows:

Balance Sheet at 30 September 1986

	Cost fcs	Depreciation fcs	fcs
Fixed assets	850,000	395,000	455,000
Current assets			
Stock		425,000	
Debtors		858,000	
Bank		125,000	
		1,408,000	
Less: Current liabilities			
Trade creditors	395,000		
Current account with parent company (head office)	123,000		
Taxation	54,000		
		572,000	
			836,000
			1,291,000
Financed by:			
Ordinary shares at par			750,000
Reserves			541,000
			1,291,000

You ascertain the following additional information:

i. Fixed assets are made up as follows:

	Cost fcs	Depreciation fcs	Net fcs
Plant			
Balances at 30 September 1985	695,000	486,000	209,000
Disposals in December 1985	248,000	199,000	49,000
	447,000	287,000	160,000

Additions in June 1986	273,000	108,000	165,000
	720,000	395,000	325,000
Land and buildings	130,000	–	130,000
	850,000	395,000	455,000

ii. Stocks are shown at cost and are analysed as:

			fcs
Finished goods	– current prices		215,000
Material and parts	– current prices		87,000
	– bought in June 1986		123,000
			425,000

Stocks at 30 September 1985 were shown at 450,000 fcs, all at current prices at that date.

iii. A debtor for 70,000 fcs is considered to be in financial difficulties and unlikely to be able to pay the debt. No adjustment has been made for this in the accounts.

iv. The net profit after taxation for the year to 30 September 1986 was 300,000 fcs before adjustment.

v. The current account with Overseas Trading Co. Ltd in the parent company (head office) books shows a debtor of £175,500. An amount of 20,000 fcs was sent to the parent company on 28 September 1986 and this did not reach London until 3 October 1986.

vi. Depreciation has been charged at 15% of cost.

vii. Rates of exchange are:

30 June 1980	.70	fcs to the £1 sterling
date of original purchase of		
plant	.80	
land and buildings	.90	
30 September 1985	1.25	
December 1985	1.40	
June 1986	.95	
30 September 1986	.80	
Average for year to 30 September 1986	1.30	

Required:

a. Prepare a balance sheet for Internal Trading Ltd at 30 September 1986 in sterling, suitable for use in preparing the consolidated balance sheet for the group.

b. Prepare a balance sheet using the same foreign currency figures but on the assumption that they relate to a branch of the Overseas Trading Co. Ltd which has been financed by a loan from head office of 991,000 fcs made up as follows:

500,000 fcs raised in Bongoland - cost £350,000 on 30 June 1980

250,000 fcs sent from London at the same time as the original purchase of plant

241,000 fcs sent from London on 30 September 1985.

(Assume that the adjustments necessary do not affect the charge for taxation).

(ACCA 2.9(2) December 1986)

69. Bryon Ltd has held 1,500,000 shares in Carlyle Ltd for many years. At the date of acquisition, the reserves of Carlyle Ltd amounted to £800,000. On 31 March 1986 Carlyle Ltd bought 400,000 shares in Doyle Ltd for £600,000 and a further 400,000 shares were purchased on 30 June 1986 for £650,000.

At 30 September 1986 the balance sheets of the three companies were:

	Bryon Ltd		Carlyle Ltd		Doyle Ltd	
	£	£	£	£	£	£
Freehold land and buildings – Cost		950,000		1,375,000		300,000
Plant and equipment						
Cost	500,000		10,000,000		750,000	
Depreciation	280,000		7,500,000		500,000	
		220,000		2,500,000		250,000
		1,170,000		3,875,000		550,000

Investments						
1,500,000 shares in Carlyle Ltd		1,600,000				
800,000 shares in Doyle Ltd			1,250,000			
Stocks	50,000		2,050,000		850,500	
Debtors	325,000		2,675,000		1,700,000	
Cash at bank	25,500		–		16,500	
		400,500		4,725,000		2,567,000
		3,170,500		9,850,000		3,117,000
Creditors under 1 year	91,500		2,385,750		1,395,800	
Proposed dividend	200,000					
Bank overdraft	–		1,450,850		–	
		291,500		3,836,600		1,395,800
		2,879,000		6,013,400		1,721,200
10% Debenture				2,000,000		–
		2,879,000		4,012,400		1,721,200
		£		£		£
Ordinary shares of £1 each		2,000,000				1,200,000
50p each				1,000,000		
8% Redeemable preference shares of £1 each				2,000,000		
Reserves		879,000		1,013,400		521,200
		2,879,000		4,013,400		1,721,200

Proposed dividends have not yet been provided for on the shares in Carlyle Ltd and Doyle Ltd although Bryon Ltd has included dividends of 5p per share as receivable from Carlyle Ltd in debtors. Dividends on the preference shares were paid for one half year on 1 April 1986, the next payment date was 1 October 1986. Dividends on the ordinary shares in Doyle Ltd are proposed at the rate of 10p per share and on Carlyle's shares as anticipated by Bryon.

Profits for the year in Doyle Ltd were £310,000, before making any adjustments for consolidation, accruing evenly through the year.

The directors of Bryon Ltd consider that the assets and liabilities of Carlyle Ltd are shown at fair values but fair values for Doyle Ltd for the purposes of consolidation are:

			£
Freehold land and building			500,000
Plant and equipment	– Valuation	968,400	
	– Depreciation	639,600	
			328,800

Other assets and liabilities are considered to be at fair values in the balance sheet.

Additional depreciation due to the revaluation of the plant and equipment in Doyle Ltd amounts to £40,000 for the year to 30 September 1986.

Included in stocks in Carlyle Ltd are items purchased from Doyle Ltd during the last three months of the year, on which Doyle Ltd recorded a profit of £80,000.

On 30 September 1986 Carlyle Ltd drew a cheque for £100,000 and sent it to Doyle Ltd to clear the current account. As this cheque was not received by Doyle Ltd until 3 October, no account was taken of it in the Doyle Ltd balance sheet.

Required:

Prepare a balance sheet as at 30 September 1986 for Bryon Ltd and its subsidiaries, conforming with the Companies Act 1985, so far as the information given will permit.

Ignore taxation.
(ACCA 2.9(2) December 1986)

70. The following figures for the year to 30 April 1986 have been extracted from the books and records of three companies which form a group:

	Old plc	Field Ltd	Lodge Ltd
	£	£	£
Revenue reserves at 1 May 1985	30,000	40,000	50,000
Stocks at 1 May 1985	90,000	150,000	80,000
Sales	1,250,000	875,000	650,000
Purchases	780,000	555,000	475,000
Distribution expenses	125,000	85,000	60,000
Administration expenses	28,000	40,000	72,000
Interim dividends:			
Paid 31 July 1985 ordinary	45,000	35,000	15,000
Paid 31 October 1985, preference		4,000	
Share capital – fully paid			
ordinary shares of £1 each	450,000	350,000	200,000
8% preference shares of £1 each		100,000	
Stocks at 30 April 1986	110,000	135,000	85,000

Profits are deemed to accrue evenly throughout the year.
Other information:

a. Corporation tax of the following amounts is to be provided on the profits of the year:

Old plc	£125,000
Field Ltd	75,000
Lodge Ltd	20,000

b. Final dividends proposed are:
   Old plc   15p per share
   Field Ltd   12.5p per share on the ordinary shares
                   and a half year's dividend on the preference shares
   Lodge Ltd   7.5p per share

c. Field Ltd sells goods for resale to both Old plc and Lodge Ltd. At 30 April 1986, stocks of goods purchased from Field Ltd are:

           in Old plc   £40,000
           in Lodge Ltd   £28,000

   The net profit percentage for Field Ltd on sales of these goods is 25%. Old plc had £36,000 of these goods in stock at 1 May 1985. Total sales in the year by Field Ltd to Old plc were £150,000 and to Lodge Ltd £120,000.

d. Old plc acquired the whole of the ordinary shares in Field Ltd many years ago. 50,000 of the preference shares were acquired on 1 August 1985. Old plc acquired 120,000 shares in Lodge Ltd on 1 August 1985.

Required:
A consolidated profit and loss account for Old plc and its subsidiaries for the year ended 30 April 1986, together with any relevant notes.
(ACCA 2.9(2) June 1986)

71. **Required:**

a. Translate the balance sheet and profit and loss account of Speedsports Limited using the closing rate method. It is group policy to translate the profit and loss account using the closing rate.

b. In accordance with the 'net investment' concept as per SSAP 20 for consolidated financial statements:

   i. calculate the translation difference, and

   ii. state how any such difference should be treated in the accounts of the holding company.

c. Calculate the profits for inclusion in the consolidated balance sheet of Watersports Limited and subsidiaries for the year ended 31 December 1986 if Speedsports Ltd's profit and loss account is translated using:

   i. the average rate

  ii. the closing rate

d. Calculate the goodwill or reserve arising on consolidation that will be entered in the consolidated balance sheet as at 31 December 1986 in respect of the investment in Speedsports Ltd.

(ACCA 2.9(1) June 1987)

Appendix 5: Draft balance sheet and profit and loss account of Speedsports Limited for the year ended 31 December 1986.

Balance Sheet as at 31 December 1986

	DM	DM
Fixed assets		
Tangible assets (net book value)		1,950,000
Current assets		
Stock	320,800	
Debtors	224,950	
Cash	17,600	
	563,350	
Creditors (due within one year)		
Trade and other creditors	361,450	
Dividends	70,000	
	431,450	
Net current assets		131,900
Total assets less current liabilities		2,081,900
Creditors (due after one year)		
7% Debentures		450,000
Net assets		1,631,900
Capital and reserves		
Ordinary shares of IDM each	1,400,000	
Revaluation reserve	170,000	
Profit and loss account	61,900	
		1,631,900
		1,631,900

Profit and Loss Account for the year ended 31 December 1986

	DM	DM
Sales		475,000
Cost of sales		135,500
Gross profit		339,500
Administration expenses	82,900	
Selling expenses	61,600	
		144,500
Trading profit		195,000
Interest paid		4,500

	190,500
Taxation	69,240
	121,260
Dividends proposed	70,000
Retained	51,260

Reserve movement	
Profit brought forward	10,640
Profit retained	51,260
	61,900

Note

i. The revaluation reserve was created on 1 January 1986 and the assets were accepted as being at fair value when Watersports Limited acquired their holding.

ii. The exchange rates for DMs to the £ were:

1 January 1986	3.20
31 December 1986	3.25
Average for 1986	3.22

AAT EXAMINATION QUESTION

72. You are presented with the following summarised information relating to Block plc for the year to 30 September 19–8:

	Block plc £'000	Chip ltd £'000	Knot ltd £'000
Fixed assets	8,900	3,240	2,280
Investments			
Shares in group companies:			
Chip ltd	2,500	–	–
Knot ltd	1,600	–	–
	4,100	–	–
Current assets			
Stocks	300	160	80
Trade debtors	1,600	130	50
Cash at bank and in hand	400	110	120
	2,300	400	250
Creditors: amounts falling due within one year			
Trade creditors	(200)	(90)	(110)
Proposed dividend	(100)	(50)	(20)
	(300)	(140)	(130)
	£15,000	£3,500	£2,400
Capital and reserves			
Called up share capital (ordinary shares of £1 each	10,000	3,000	2,000
Profit and loss account	5,000	500	400
	£15,000	£3,500	£2,400

Additional information:

1. Block purchased 80% of the share capital of Chip on 1 October 19–3 when Chip's profit and loss account balance was £200,000 credit.

2. On 1 October 19–7, Block purchased 60% of the share capital of Knot. Knot's profit and loss account balance at that date was £500,000 credit.

3. Goodwill is written off against reserves immediately on acquisition.

4. During the year to 30 September 19–8, Block sold goods costing £200,000 to Chip for £300,000. Half of these goods remained in stock at the year end.

5. Inter-company debts at the year end were as follows:

	£'000
Chip owed Block	20
Knot owed Chip	30

Required:

Prepare the Block plc group of companies consolidated balance sheet as at 30 September 19–8. (Formal notes to the accounts are NOT required, although detailed working should be submitted with your answer.)

(AAT)

2 Acquisitions and mergers

1.0 When one company becomes the subsidiary of another, the combination may constitute an acquisition or a merger. The criterion for deciding the form is the means by which the combination is effected.

1.1 An acquisition is deemed to have occurred when there is a significant outflow of material resources (in the form of cash), from the offeror (acquiring) company to the offeree (acquired) company's shareholders as consideration for their holdings.

1.2 In contrast, a merger is said to have occurred where there is no such outflow, or merely an insignificant one. In this instance the offeror company acquires the offeree company's shares by giving its own shares in exchange in full consideration, or accompanied by no more than 10% of the nominal value of the consideration in the form of cash and/or loan stock. (Until the passing of the Companies Act 1989, the 10% restriction was calculated on the fair value of the consideration).

1.3 Whilst the result in both instances is that the offeror company gains control of the offeree company, each of the two methods outlined above, acquisition (also known as the purchase method) and merger (also known as the pooling of interests methods) have distinguished features which are tabulated below:

Method of treatment in offeror company's books

Item	Acquisition	Merger
Offeree company's shares	Included at the fair value, that is, at the cost of acquisition	Included at their nominal value.
Difference between the fair value of the purchase consideration and that of the separable net assets underlying the shares acquired	An excess of the former constitutes goodwill (which is dealt with according to SSAP 22) whilst an excess of the latter constitutes negatibe goodwill which is credited to reserves.	Not applicable
Difference between the nominal values of the shares transferred and shares exchanged (plus other consideration if applicable)	Not applicable	Primarily adjusted against unrealised reserves, failing which, adjusted against realised reserves
Asset revaluation	The separable net assets of the subsidiary are revalued to a fair value, thus giving rise to higher depreciation charges	Not usually applicable
Consolidation date	From date of acquisition. Thus, pre–acquisition reserves are capitalised. Corresponding figures for previous year are not restated on a post acquisition basis	Deemed always to have been effective. Thus pre and post merger reserves are pooled and regarded as distributable. Corresponding figures for pre merger year are restated on a post merger basis.

MERGER RELIEF PROVISIONS

2.0 In the UK. merger accounting methods were thought to be illegal because there was no requirement to make a share premium account entry (mandatory under the (then) Section 56 Companies Act, 1948) when the nominal value of the shares exchanged exceeded that of the shares transferred (see 1.3 above).

2.1 This situation was remedied by Sections 36 to 41 of the Companies Act 1981 (now sections 131-134 of the 1985 Act), by what are known as the merger relief provisions.

2.2 The otherwise mandatory transfer to share premium account in respect of the shares allotted to the offeree company is not required if,

a. the offeror company has acquired at least 90% of the nominal value of each class of the offeree company's equity capital. (Prior holdings are included in the 90%)

b. equity shares in the offeror company are issued to the offeree company's shareholders.

c. the consideration in (b) above can take the form of the issue or transfer to the offeror company of equity shares in the offeree company or the cancellation of offeree company equity shares not held by the offeror company.

Shares held in the offeree company by other companies in the offeror company's group are regarded as though held by the offeror company itself.

2.3 Merger relief is extended to an accompanying issue or transfer of non-equity shares (in the offeree company) to the offeror company.

ACQUISITION AND MERGER ACCOUNTING METHODS

3.0 The principles of these two methods have been tabulated in 1.3. The examples which follow are a practical exposition of these principles under various circumstances.

EXAMPLE

3.1 The summarised balance sheets of AR PLC and JM PLC immediately prior to their combination were summarised as shown below:

	AR PLC	JM PLC
	£000	£000
Ordinary shares (£1 per share)	10,000	4,000
Revenue reserves	2,000	1,000
	12,000	5,000
Fixed assets	8,000	3,000
Net current assets	4,000	2,000
Separable net assets	12,000	5,000

AR then acquired the entire share capital of JM by the issue of one new ordinary share for one share in JM.

The fair value of the consideration was £5,600,000, this being the market value of JM's share (£1.40 per share).

The fair value of JM's separable net assets was £5,000,000.

Required:

Prepare summarised balance sheets for AR PLC immediately after combination, for

1. AR PLC (the company) and
2. AR Group

using

a. the acquisition method and
b. the merger method

SOLUTION
3.2

AR PLC Balance Sheets

	Acquisition Company	Acquisition Group	Merger Company	Merger Group
	£000	£000	£000	£000
Ordinary share capital	14,000	14,000	14,000	14,000
Reserves				
Share premium [5,600-4,000]	1,600	1,600	–	–
Revenue	2,000	2,000	2,000	3,000
	17,600	17,600	16,000	17,000
Goodwill [5,600-5,000]	–	600	–	–
Investment in JM PLC	5,600	–	4,000	–
Fixed assets	8,000	11,000	8,000	11,000
Net current assets	4,000	6,000	4,000	6,000
	17,600	17,600	16,000	17,000

Note:

If, as is likely, AR PLC utilises the merger relief to which it is entitled, the amounts shown above as share premium would instead be shown as merger reserve.

EXAMPLE

3.3 The facts are the same as in 3.1 except that the consideration is three new shares in AR for four in JM.

Required:
The same as in 3.1

SOLUTION
3.4

AR PLC Balance Sheets

	Acquisition		Merger	
	Company	Group	Company	Group
	£000	£000	£000	£000
Ordinary share capital	13,000	13,000	13,000	13,000
Reserves				
Share premium (see 3.2 note)	2,600	2,600	–	–
[5,600 – 3,000]				
Revenue	2,000	2,000	2,000	3,000
Capital	–	–	–	1,000
[4,000 – 3,000]				
	17,600	17,600	15,000	17,000
Goodwill [5,600 – 5,000]	–	600	–	–
Investment in JM PLC	5,600	–	3,000	–
Fixed assets	8,000	11,000	8,000	11,000
Net current assets	4,000	6,000	4,000	6,000
	17,600	17,600	15,000	17,000

EXAMPLE

3.5 The facts are the same as in 3.1 except that the consideration is five new shares in AR for four shares in JM.

Required:
The same as in 3.1

SOLUTION
3.6

AR PLC Balance Sheets

	Acquisition		Merger	
	Company	Group	Company	Group
	£000	£000	£000	£000
Ordinary share capital	15,000	15,000	15,000	15,000
Reserves				
Share premium (see 3.2 note)	600	600	–	–
[5,600 – 5,000]				
Revenue				
[see note below]	2,000	2,000	2,000	2,000
	17,600	17,600	17,000	17,000

Goodwill [5,600 − 5,000]	–	600	–	–
Investment in JM PLC	5,600	–	5,000	–
Fixed assets	8,000	11,000	8,000	11,000
Net current assets	4,000	6,000	4,000	6,000
	17,600	17,600	17,000	17,000

In the merger situation group revenue reserves have been arrived at as follows:

	£000
AR PLC	2,000
JM PLC	1,000
less difference in nominal share values (no unrealised reserves available) [5,000 − 4,000]	(1,000)
	2,000

EXAMPLE

3.7 The facts are the same as in 3.1 except that £400,000 is in cash and the balance of the consideration comprises 3,600,000 shares in AR for the shares in JM.

Required:
The same as in 3.1

SOLUTION
3.8

AR PLC Balance Sheets

	Acquisition		Merger	
	Company	Group	Company	Group
	£000	£000	£000	£000
Ordinary share capital	13,600	13,600	13,600	13,600
Reserves				
Share premium (see 3.2 note) [(5,600 − 400) − 3,600]	1,600	1,600	–	–
Revenue	2,000	2,000	2,000	3,000
	17,200	17,200	15,600	16,600
Goodwill [5,600 − 500]	–	600	–	–
Investment in JM PLC	5,600	–	4,000	–
Fixed assets	8,000	11,000	8,000	11,000
Net current assets [AR 4,000 − 400]	3,600	5,600	3,600	5,600
	17,200	17,200	15,600	16,600

SSAP 23 ACCOUNTING FOR ACQUISITIONS AND MERGERS

4.0 This standard deals with accounting for business combinations in group accounts only. Methods to be applied in the offeror company's own books are contained in an appendix to the standard by way of guidance but are not mandatory. The full standard became effective on 1 April, 1985.

4.1 In group accounts, merger accounting principles may be applied only if a number of conditions are satisfied. These are that;

a. the combination is the result of an offer to holders of all equity and all voting shares not already held by the offeror;

b. as the result of (a) above, the offeror has obtained a holding of not less than 90% of each class of equity share and of not less than 90% of the offeree's voting shares;

c. immediately prior to the offer, the offeror holds less than 20% of each class of equity share and less than 20% of the offeree's voting shares;

d. at least 90% of the fair value of the total consideration for the equity shares of the offeree is in the form of equity share capital;

e. at least 90% of the fair value of the total consideration for the voting non-equity shares of the offeree is in the form of equity and/or voting non-equity capital.

4.2 If the conditions set out in 4.1 (above) are not met in full, acquisition accounting principles must be applied in the group accounts. In view of the fact that the application of merger accounting principles is optional, acquisition accounting principles may still be applied even when all the 4.1 conditions have been observed.

4.3 In accounting for a business combination as an acquisition, the difference between the fair value of the consideration and that of the aggregate of the separable net assets (including identifiable intangibles) constitutes goodwill in the consolidated accounts. Such goodwill is then accounted for according to the provisions of SSAP 22.

4.4 The results of the acquired company should be brought into account only from the date of acquisition when 4.3 applies.

4.5 In accounting for a business combination as a merger the assets and liabilities of the subsidiary are not valued at fair value, therefore goodwill does not arise.

4.6 The results of the company are brought into account for the whole accounting period. Corresponding figures for the previous period should be restated as if the merger has existed throughout that period.

4.7 Any consolidation difference arising between the nominal value of shares exchanged (plus the fair value of any other consideration) and the nominal value of shares transferred should be shown as a reserve or as a reduction in reserves, as appropriate.

DISCLOSURE

4.8 The acquiring company is required, in the year in which the combination takes place, to disclose the following details, whether acquisition or merger methods have been applied:

a. the names of the companies combining;

b. the number and class of securities issued together with details of any other consideration;

c. whether acquisition or merger principles have been adopted;

d. the nature and amount of any material adjustments effected to harmonise accounting policies.

4.9 Additionally, where any significant acquisition has taken place the consolidated financial statements should give sufficient detail about the subsidiaries' results to enable their impact on the consolidated results to be appreciated. The effective date of acquisition should also be stated.

4.10 If a significant merger has occurred, the following additional information should be given for that year:

a. the fair value of the consideration;

b. a pre and post merger analysis of the current year's profit before extraordinary items;

c. a pre merger analysis, for the current year and previous year, of profit before extraordinary items, between each combining company;

d. an analysis of extraordinary items between pre and post merger events and between each combining company.

STUDENT SELF TESTING
Test Exercises

1. SSAP 23 Accounting for acquisitions and mergers.

   a. What are the features of accounting for a business combination as

   i. an acquisition?

   ii. a merger?

   b. What is the scope of applicability of SSAP 23?

   c. What criteria must be satisfied in order to constitute a merger situation?

2. The summarised balance sheets of Predator Ltd and Victim Ltd immediately prior to their combination, are summarised below:

	Predator Ltd	Victim Ltd
	£000	£000
Ordinary shares of £1 per share	6,000	3,000
Revenue reserves	3,000	2,500
	9,000	5,500
Fixed assets	7,000	4,000
Net current assets	2,000	1,500
Separable net assets	9,000	5,500

Predator then acquired the entire share capital of Victim by the issue of one ordinary share for one share in Victim.

The fair value of the consideration was £4,800,000.

Victim's separable net assets are at fair values.

Required:

Prepare the summarised balance sheets for Predator Ltd immediately after combination for

(1) Predator Ltd (the company) and (2) Predator Group

using

    a. the acquisition method and

    b. the merger method

3. The facts are the same as in 2, except that the consideration is two shares in Predator for three in Victim.

   Required:

   As in 2.

4. The facts are the same as in 2, except that the consideration is four shares in Predator for three in Victim.

   Required:

   As in 2.

5. The facts are the same as in 2, except that the consideration is £900,000 in cash and 2,400,000 in shares.

   Required:

   As in 2.

ACCA EXAMINATION QUESTIONS

6. Required

    a. Using the additional information supplied in Appendices 4 and 5, prepare a consolidated balance sheet for Willow Ltd as at 31 December 1985 on the basis that Willow Ltd merged with Pourwell Limited on 31 December 1985.

    b. Show the capital and reserves section and the change in the composition of the assets of the consolidated balance sheet prepared on the basis that the acquisition of shares by Willow Ltd is treated as a parent acquisition.

    c. Comment on the proposed merger from the viewpoint of a shareholder whom you may assume to currently own 100 ordinary shares in Pourwell Ltd.

(ACCA 2.9(1) June 1986)

Appendix 1 General introduction to Pourwell Ltd

    i. Pourwell Ltd is a company that manufactures plastic decanters.

   ii. It was incorporated in 1974 with an authorised share capital of £500,000 consisting of 300,000 £1 ordinary shares and £200,000 7% cumulative preference shares of £1 each.

  iii. The issued share capital is £300,000 consisting of 200,000 £1 ordinary shares and £100,000 7% cumulative preference shares. The preference shares are all held by an insurance company. The ordinary shares are held as follows:

      75,000   Mr Albert (who is also managing director and chairman)

      25,000   Mr Bryant (who is also a director)

      12,500   Mr Chad (who is also a director)

87,500   held by 7 other shareholders, each with 12,500 shares
200,000

iv. The company has incurred significant trading losses over the past five years.

v. The directors have been discussing with the company's accountants the advisability of either (a) arranging a merger with Willow Ltd or (b) carrying out a scheme of reorganisation.

vi. The directors estimate that the company will make profits in future years. The profits are estimated to be:

1986	£10,000
1987	£15,000
1988	£20,000

Appendix 2 List of balances extracted from the books of Pourwell Limited as at 31 December 1985

	£
Accrued interest on debentures	10,500
Administrative expenses	105,113
Audit fee accrual	2,850
Bank overdraft	38,022
Bank interest	7,100
Cost of sales	416,028
Creditors (trade)(control account total)	258,550
7% debentures (redeemable 1992)	75,000
Debtors (trade) (control account total)	89,505
Deferred development expenditure	87,500
Directors' loans	125,000
Dividend received (net)	3,500
Expense accrual	1,900
Fixtures and fittings	9,900
Goodwill	150,000
Insurance prepayment	4,000
Investment (at cost)	42,500
Land and buildings	100,000
Ordinary shares of £1 each	200,000
Plant	90,800
Preference shares (7% cumulative)	100,000
Profit and loss account (debit balance)	97,160
Profit on sale of land	15,000
Provision for depreciation of buildings	19,200
Provision for depreciation of plant	47,880
Provision for depreciation of fixtures	4,620
Sales	696,000
Selling and distribution expenses	200,101
Stock of raw material	20,210
Stock of work in progress	10,103
Stock of finished goods	170,102
Wages accrual	2,100

Appendix 5 Proposed terms of the merger with Willow Ltd

(a) The estimated market value of a £1 ordinary share in Pourwell Limited is 50p

(b) The estimated market value of a £1 share in Willow Ltd is £2.50.

(c) The merger is to be effected by the offer of ordinary shares to be issued by Willow Ltd to all of the ordinary shareholders of Pourwell Limited in exchange for their shares.

(d) The shares are to be exchanged in proportion to their estimated market values.

(e) It is anticipated that there would be a 100% acceptance.

(f) The authorised share capital of Willow Ltd is sufficient to accommmodate the transaction.

Appendix 3 Further information available when drafting the profit and loss account of Pourwell Ltd for the year ended 31 December 1985 and a balance sheet as at that date

i. Directors received the following remuneration:

    Albert   £31,000
    Bryant   £22,000
    Chad   £15,000

    In addition, fees of £2,000 per annum were paid to each director.

ii. Depreciation has been provided for in the appropriate expense accounts for the year on the following basis:

	£	Estimated useful life
Land	Nil	
Buildings	1,600	50 years
Plant	4,540	20 years
Fixtures and fittings	660	15 years

iii. During the year the company sold land with a book value of £10,000 and purchased plant for £12,000.

iv. The goodwill arose on the purchase of the assets and liabilities of Mr Chad's business in 1980. The company are proposing to write it off over 10 years commencing in 1985.

v. The preference dividend has not been paid for 1984 or 1985.

vi. The directors estimate that the company will return to profits in 1986 and given that they estimate profits will be £10,000 in 1986 rising to £20,000 in 1988 they propose to leave the development costs as an asset for the purpose of the 1985 accounts.

vii. The trade creditors aged analysis shows:

	£
Payable before 1 July 1985	93,490
Payable before 1 October 1985	50,060
Payable before 1 December 1985	30,000
Current	35,000
Payable in 1987	50,000

Appendix 4 Draft balance sheet of Willow Ltd as at 31 December 1985

Fixed Assets Tangible assets:	Cost £	Aggregate Depreciation £	£
Freehold land and buildings	360,000	120,000	240,000
Plant and machinery	348,000	240,000	108,000
	708,000	360,000	348,000

Current assets		
Stocks of raw material		56,200
Stock – work in progress		63,000
Stock – finished goods		97,360
Debtors		168,760
Cash		45,636
		430,956

Creditors: amounts due in less than one year		
Creditors	137,148	
Corporation tax	97,600	
Proposed dividends	40,000	

		274,748
Net current assets		156,208
		504,208

Share capital and reserve
Share capital

Ordinary shares of £1 each	250,000
Retained earnings	254,208
	504,208

7. **Required:**

    a. Using the information in appendices 1-4: prepare for consolidation as at 31 December 1986 by preparing a consolidated balance sheet for Watersports Limited, Roadsports Limited and Propulsion Limited.

       N.B. the consolidation is to be carried out (i) using the merger method for Roadsports Limited and (ii) treating Propulsion Limited as an associate.

    b. Show the effects on:

       i. the balance sheet of Watersports Ltd, and

       ii. the consolidated balance sheet if the directors of Watersports Limited had decided to include the investment in Roadsports Ltd in the parent company's own accounts at the fair value of the shares issued.

(ACCA 2.9(1) June 1987)

Appendix 1: General introduction to Watersports Limited

Watersports Limited was incorporated in 1975 to carry on business as a wholesaler of sports equipment.

The company has decided to pursue a policy of growth by acquisition and made the following investments:

Date of purchase	Shares acquired	Consideration provided by Watersports Ltd	Carrying value of the investment in the Balance Sheet £
31.12.86	945,000 ordinary shares in Roadsports Limited	700,000 ordinary shares in Watersports Limited	350,000
1.1.86	441,000 ordinary shares in Propulsion Limited	Cash	332,500
1.1.86	1,050,000 ordinary shares in Speedsports Limited, a wholesaler operating in Germany	Cash	400,000

Note

    i. It is the group policy to write off goodwill at the rate of 20% per annum commencing in the year of acquisition.

    ii. A recent valuation of the ordinary shares of Watersports Limited carried out by the company's auditors places a value of 75p per share on each ordinary share.

Appendix 2: Draft balance sheet and profit and loss account of Watersports Limited for the year ended 31 December 1986.

Balance Sheet as at 31 December 1986

	£	£
Fixed assets		
Tangible assets (net book value)		550,000
Investments		1,082,500
Current assets		
Stock	259,000	
Debtors	238,000	
Cash	7,000	
	504,000	
Creditors (due within one year)		
Trade and other creditors	246,200	
Bank overdraft	227,000	
Proposed dividends	21,000	
	494,200	
Net current assets		9,800
Total assets less current liabilities		1,642,300
Creditors (due after one year)		
9% Debentures	245,000	
Deferred tax	52,500	
		297,500
Net assets		1,344,800
Capital and reserves		
Ordinary shares of 50p each		
(fully paid up)	700,000	
Share premium account	320,000	
Revaluation reserve	225,000	
Other reserves	30,000	
Profit and loss account	69,800	
		1,344,800
		1,344,800

Profit and Loss account of Watersports Limited
for the year ended 31 December 1986

	£	£
Sales		605,850
Cost of sales		245,000
Gross profit		360,850
Administration expenses	160,200	
Selling expenses	96,350	
		256,550
Trading profit		104,300
Interest payable		25,200

	79,100
Taxation	27,000
	———
	52,100
Dividends	28,000
	———
Retained	24,100

Reserve movement
Profit brought forward	45,700
Profit retained	24,100
	———
Profit carried forward	69,800

Note

Dividends receivable for 1986 have not been taken into account in the profit and loss account.

Appendix 3: Draft balance sheet and profit and loss account of Roadsports Limited for the year ended 31 December 1986

Balance Sheet as at 31 December 1986

	£	£
Fixed assets		
Tangible assets (net book value)		1,100,000
Current assets		
Stock	175,250	
Debtors	132,500	
Cash	74,750	
	———	
	382,500	
Creditors (due within one year)		
Trade and other creditors	236,000	
Bank overdraft	283,300	
Proposed dividend	14,000	
	———	
	533,300	
Net current assets		(150,800)
		———
Total assets less current liabilities		949,200
Creditors (due after one year)		
10% Debentures	106,750	
Deferred tax	23,450	
	———	
		130,200
		———
Net assets		819,000
Capital and reserves		
Ordinary shares of 50p each		
(fully paid up)	525,000	
Reserves	140,000	
Profit and loss account	154,000	
		———
		819,000
		———
		819,000

664

Profit and Loss Account of Roadsports Limited
for the year ended 31 December 1986

	£	£
Sales		565,000
Cost of sales		232,500
		332,500
Administration expenses	110,300	
Selling expenses	130,400	
		240,700
Trading profit		91,800
Interest payable		20,950
		70,850
Taxation		24,000
		46,850
Dividends		14,000
Retained profit		32,850
Reserve movement		
Profit brought forward		121,150
Profit retained		32,850
Profit carried forward		154,000

Note

i. During 1986 Watersports Limited had sold goods to Roadsports Limited to an invoiced value of £80,500.

   At 31 December 1986 Roadsports Limited still held in stock such goods with an invoiced value of £21,500.

   Watersports Limited invoiced goods to Roadsports Limited at 25% on cost.

ii. The fair value of the tangible fixed assets in Roadsports Limited was £1,250,000.

Appendix 4: Draft balance sheet and profit and loss account of Propulsion Limited for the year ended 31 December 1986.

Balance Sheet as at 31 December 1986

	£	£
Fixed assets		
Tangible assets		2,090,000
Current assets		
Stock	300,250	
Debtors	160,200	
Cash	11,000	
	471,450	
Creditors (due within one year)		
Trade and other creditors	491,130	
Bank overdraft	68,950	
	560,080	

Net current assets		(88,630)
Total assets less current liabilities		2,001,370
Creditors (due after one year)		
10% Debentures	350,000	
Deferred tax	103,250	
		453,250
Net assets		1,548,120

Capital and reserves

Ordinary shares of 50p each	1,050,000	
Share premium account	70,000	
Revaluation reserve	300,000	
Profit and loss account	128,120	
		1,548,120
		1,548,120

*Profit and Loss Account of Propulsion Limited
for the year ended 31 December 1986*

	£	£
Sales		524,790
Cost of sales		215,130
		309,660
Administration expenses	138,400	
Selling expenses	78,720	
		217,120
Trading profit		92,540
Interest payable		36,000
		56,540
Taxation		35,000
Retained		21,540

Note

i. Propulsion Limited revalued its assets on 31 December 1985 and created a revaluation reserve of £250,000 in order to show its assets at fair value at that date.

ii. During 1986 Propulsion Limited increased the revaluation reserve by £50,000 which represented an increase in asset valuation that occurred during 1986.

Section VI

Questions without answers

SECTION I Chapter 3

QUESTION 1

Two sole traders, Bentinck and Hartley amalgamated their businesses and formed a partnership, Hyson Factors, on 1 March 19-5.

At the date of amalgamation, their separate balance sheets were

Balance Sheets as at 1 March 19-5

Bentinck £	Bentinck £		Hartley £	Hartley £
		Fixed Assets (at written down values)		
39,000		Premises	28,500	
17,200		Fixtures etc.	14,300	
	56,200			42,800
		Current Assets		
9,400		Stock	12,300	
2,100		Debtors	3,000	
1,700		Bank and Cash	2,600	
13,200			17,900	
		less		
		Current Liabilities		
4,400		Creditors	5,500	
3,800		Bank overdraft	-	
8,200			5,500	
	5,000	**Working Capital**		12,400
	61,200	**Net Assets Employed**		55,200
		Financed by:		
	61,200	Capital		45,000
	-	Loan from Gregory		10,200
	61,200			55,200

For the purposes of the partnership the following valuations were agreed for the assets

	Bentinck £	Hartley £
Premises	50,000	35,000
Fixtures etc	15,000	
Stock	8,000	

All other assets were taken over by Hyson Factors at book values.

Hartley agreed to pay creditors of £2,500 privately. The partnership assumed responsibility for the remainder and for the loan and, by agreement with the bank, for the overdraft.

It was agreed that the capital of Hyson Factors should be subscribed by the partners in equal shares.

Required:

Prepare the balance sheet of Hyson Factors immediately after the amalgamation had taken place.

QUESTION 2

Bridgend, Chester and Dorset were in partnership sharing profits and losses 1/2, 1/3 and 1/6 respectively.

Following a review of the relative contributions to partnership activities, it was mutually agreed to change the proportions to 3/8, 3/8 and 1/4 respectively.

Goodwill which was not to be retained in the books was valued at £24,000. Partners fixed capital account balances were Bridgend £20,000, Chester £30,000 and Dorset £30,000.

Required:

Post the entries in capital accounts to introduce, and then to write back, goodwill.

QUESTION 3

The facts are the same as in Question 2 (above) except that the partners decided that a full revaluation was necesary. It was decided that the new values, with the exception of goodwill, should be retained in the books.

Item	Value prior to change £	Revalued at £
Premises	80,000	104,000
Fixtures	22,000	25,500
Goodwill	-	24,000
Stock	27,500	25,000
Debtors	16,800	15,800

Required:

Post and balance the revaluation and capital accounts to record the above revaluations.

QUESTION 4

On 31 May 19-5, the balance sheet of Berridge and Noel who were in partnership sharing profits and losses equally, was

Balance Sheet as at 31 May 19-5

	£	£
Fixed assets (at written down values)		
Premises	39,000	
Fixtures	18,500	
		57,500
Current assets		
Stock	17,100	
Debtors	4,200	
Bank	5,600	
	26,900	
Less		
Current liabilities		
Creditors	7,400	
Working Capital		19,500
Net assets employed		77,000
Financed by:		
Capital-		
Berridge		50,000
Noel		27,000
		77,000

On that date the partnership was converted into a limited company, Goodall Ltd. The partners were to receive cash of £3,000 (Berridge) and £5,000 (Noel). The balance owing to the partners was then satisfied by the issue of 50,000 ordinary shares of £1.00 per share in Goodall Ltd at a value of £75,000. The company undertook to discharge the creditors in full.

Required:

Prepare the Realisation, Goodall Ltd and capital accounts of the partnership to record the conversion.

QUESTION 5

The facts are as in Question 4 above, except that on conversion Goodall Ltd revalued Premises at £50,000 and Stock at £19,000. It also contained an overdraft in order to discharge the liabilities to the creditors and partners.

Required:
Prepare the balance sheet of Goodall Ltd immediately after the above arrangements had been affected.

QUESTION 6

The facts are as in Question 4 (above) except that on 31 May 19-5 the partnership was dissolved and the assets were sold publicly and realised:

	£
Premises	47,000
Fixtures	10,000
Stock	11,700

Debtors realised £4,100, dissolution expenses were £800, creditors were paid in full and the remaining stock was taken over personally by Berridge at an agreed valuation of £5,000.

Required:
Prepare the Realisation, Bank and Capital accounts to record the dissolution.

QUESTION 7

Acourt, Bright and Cobden had been in partnership for many years, trading as Redoubt and Co. and sharing profits and losses in the ratio of 1 : 1 : 2 respectively.

Their capital account balances were:

	£
Acourt	20,000
Bright	10,000
Cobden	5,000

Following a decline in business they decided to dissolve the partnership. This produced a terminal loss of £16,000 to be shared between the partners. At this point it was discovered that Cobden was insolvent and unable to contribute towards his deficiency.

Required:
Prepare the partners' capital accounts to record the above matters.

QUESTION 8

Dale, Fell and Hill were in partnership sharing profits and losses in the ratio 3:3:2 after allowing interest on capitals at 5% per annum. A summarised version of their balance sheet at 1 January 19-9 showed:

	£
Capital accounts (Dale £40,000, Fell £40,000, Hill £20,000)	100,000
Current accounts (Dale £200, Fell £100, Hill £100)	400
Loan account - Fell (8% p.a. interest)	5,000
Life assurance fund	26,000
	131,400
Fixed and current assets *less* liabilities	105,400
Life assurance policies	26,000
	131,400

Fell died during December 19-9 and the other partners then decided to sell the business.

The life assurance contract was represented by 'with profits' whole life policies on the three lives and a total premium of £3,000 was paid annually in March. The policies account and the fund account were annually adjusted to surrender values. The sum payable on Fell's death was £36,000 and the surrender value immediately afterwards was £15,000. It has been agreed that all proceeds from the life assurance policies be apportioned in profit sharing ratios.

The profit for the year after charging all trading expenses was £37,200 and the partners had withdrawn £12,600, £13,500 and £7,900 respectively.

At the close of trading there was a bank balance of £800 together with the £36,000 received from the insurance company. All of the remaining assets were sold and, after settling the liabilities to the creditors, the proceeds were £124,000. £320 was paid in legal fees and other expenses. The life assurance contract was to be re-assigned and new policies issued to Dale and Hill at values of £9,000 and £6,000 respectively.

Required:

Prepare ledger accounts to show the closing entries, assuming that all the transactions, including final payments to Dale, Hill and to Fell's estate, were completed on 31 December 19-9.

(ACCA)

QUESTION 9

Henry and Peter were partners in a wholesale and retail paint business. They shared profits three-fifths and two-fifths respectively. From 1 April 19-0 Roger, previously an employee earning £8,000 per annum, became a partner and the new profit sharing ratio was: Henry two-fifths, Peter two-fifths and Roger one-fifth. Roger's salary as an employee ceased but he was to be credited with £6,000 per annum partnership salary. He agreed to bring in £10,000 as capital and it was also mutually agreed that at 1 April 19-0, the book value of the land and buildings should be increased by £30,000 and that of the equipment and vehicles reduced by £4,000. Goodwill was to be valued at the same date by reference to expected future earnings (agreed as £30,000 per annum after allowing for partners' services) and an acceptable yield on capital (agreed as 20% per annum). The capital accounts were to be adjusted to reflect the goodwill valuation, no goodwill account being raised. Roger had paid in the capital sum but the other adjustments had not been made by the year-end, 30 June 19-0, when the books showed

Trial Balance at 30 June 19-0

	Dr £	Cr £
Gross profit (earned evenly over the year)		120,000
Land and buildings (cost)	50,000	
Equipment and vehicles (book value 1 July 19-9)	40,000	
Stock at end of year	12,000	
Administrative expenses (including Roger's salary to 31 March 19-0)	54,000	
Bank		5,000
Capital accounts (H £40,000, P £30,000, R £10,000)		80,000
Drawings (H £30,000, P £20,000, R £2,000)	52,000	
Debtors and creditors	38,000	41,000
	246,000	246,000

Depreciation is charged on the equipment and vehicles at 20% of book value per annum. At 1 April 19-0 the net current assets value in the book was £5,000.

Required:

Prepare the Profit and Loss Account for the year ended 30 June 19-0 and a Balance Sheet at that date.

(ACCA)

QUESTION 10

Dare, Chance and Venture have carried on a trading partnership for a number of years, making up the accounts to 31st March in each year.

The balance sheet as on 31st March, 19-9 showed the following position:

	£	£
Fixed Assets		
Goodwill		45,000
Freehold property, at cost		14,500
Fixtures and fittings, at written down value		16,000
		75,500
Current Assets		
Stock	8,010	
Sundry Debtors	4,100	
Balance at bank	5,730	
		17,840
		93,340
Less Current Liabilities		
Sundry creditors		9,640
		83,700
Representing		
Capital Accounts		
Dare	37,800	
Chance	11,500	
Venture	15,200	
		64,500
Loan Account - Dare		15,000
Current Accounts		
Dare	1,600	
Chance	900	
Venture	1,700	
		4,200
		83,700

It was decided that the business should be taken over with effect from 1st April 19-9 by Enterprise Ltd, a company formed by the partners for that purpose.

You are also given the following information:

1. the terms of the partnership specify:
   - (i) Interest is allowed on capital accounts at 8% per annum.
   - (ii) No interest is allowed or charged on current accounts.
   - (iii) The partners receive annual salaries of Dare £4,000, Chance £5,000 and Venture £3,000.
   - (iv) Dare, Chance and Venture share the profits in the ratio 6 : 5 : 4.

2. Dare's loan account which carries interest at 10% is not to be repaid at present but provision is to be made for repayment not later than 20-6.
3. Goodwill is to be revalued at £30,000 and the freehold property at £25,000 for the purposes of the takeover. All other assets and liabilities are to be taken over at book values.
4. Current accounts are to be cleared in cash.
5. The partnership profit for the year ended 31st march 19-9 before charging interest was £24,000, which has been reflected in the balance sheet.

You are required:

(a) to set out your proposals for the issue of shares, at par, in such numbers and classes as will retain the partners' rights in capital and profits as they would enjoy in the partnership, incorporating in your answer a statement comparing the distribution of profits for the year ended 31st March

19-9, after adjustment of asset values in the partnership with the distribution which would have taken place had the company been in existence for that year, and

(b) to show the initial balance sheet of the company after the acquisition of the partnership has been effected.

Ignore taxation.

(ICAEW)

SECTION II Chapter 1

QUESTION 1

During April 19-5, S of Eston consigned 60 crates of crockery, at a cost of £200 per crate, to his selling agent Z of Zedmouth.

S paid (by cheque) transport charges £106, insurance £42 and sundries £17. After receipt of the crates Z paid (by cheque) advertising charges, £63, sundry expenses £10, storage £30 and delivery charges to customers £24.

Z sold the whole consignment for £350 per crate and was entitled to a commission of 10%. He paid the net proceeds to S.

Required:

Open, post and balance the Goods on consignment, Consignment to Z and the Agent Z accounts, recording the above transactions in S's ledger.

QUESTION 2

The facts are precisely the same as in Question 1 (above).

Required:

Open, post and balance the Consignor S account recording the above transactions in Z's ledger.

QUESTION 3

The facts are precisely the same as in Question 1 (above), except that by 30 April 19-5 Z had sold 45 crates and had paid delivery charges of £18.

Required:

Calculate the cost of stock held by the consignee at 30 April 19-5.

QUESTION 4

The facts are precisely the same as in Question 3 (above).

Required:

Open, post and balance the appropriate accounts into the consignor's ledger recording the stated transactions to 30 April 19-5.

QUESTION 5

The facts are precisely the same as in Question 3 (above) except that whilst in transit to Z, 10 crates were stolen. The insurance policy covered loss by damage but not loss by theft. Sundry expenses paid by S had totalled £32 and storage charges paid by Z had amounted to £37.

Required:

Calculate:

(a) the cost of the stock loss; and
(b) the cost of stock held by the consignee at 30 April 19-5.

SECTION II Chapter 2

QUESTION 1

Young and Smart entered into a joint venture to buy and sell video games at Sunday markets, sharing profits and losses $\frac{2}{3}$rds and $\frac{1}{3}$rd respectively.

At the start of the venture, Young sent Smart a cheque for £2,500 to enable him to buy a selection of games from the importers.

They sold their entire stock by 28 February 19-5. Their joint venture transactions, which had been conducted entirely in cash, had been:

	Young £	Smart £
Purchases	–	2,100
Sales	2,700	2,880
Travelling expenses	450	330
Market dues	132	171
Sundry expenses	100	200

Settlement between the co-venturers then took place by cheque.

Required:

Open, post and balance:

(a) memorandum joint venture account;

(b) joint venture accounts in the separate ledgers of the co-venturers.

QUESTION 2

The facts are the same as in Question 1 (above) except that by 28 February 19-5 sales had been Young £3,211 and Smart £1,637 and stock was valued at £342 for Young and £105 for Smart.

Required:

Open, post and balance:

(a) memorandum joint venture account;

(b) joint venture accounts in the separate ledgers of the co-venturers.

QUESTION 3

Two unemployed secretaries, Jane and Sally, decided to start up in business as high class mobile caterers, providing an exclusive catering service at weddings, business conferences etc.

Jane's husband, Andrew, was enthusiastic about the idea and agreed to provide the finance out of his redundancy pay and to help run the business side of affairs.

As this was their first experience of running a business, they decided it would be unwise to enter into a formal partnership. Instead they considered it more appropriate to operate the business as a joint venture in which they all had an equal share in the profits and losses.

Andrew made himself responsible for the "office work", Jane undertook to organise each outside function and Sally cooked the food and transported it to the venues.

After one month they assembled the various items of receipts and expenditure as shown below:

	Andrew £	Jane £	Sally £
Travelling expenses	80	92	69
Telephone expenses	18	22	–
Sundry expenses	31	35	11

Andrew had also given Jane and Sally a cheque *each* for £2,500, and had paid for advertisements, £118 and printing of menus, £147.

Jane had bought crockery £200, silver table decorations and cutlery, £670 and tablecloths, £58. She had paid £120 for room hire, £619 for musical groups and mobile discos, £232 for entertainers, £37 for laundering and £274 for waitress hire.

At the end of the the month, as the result of losses, breakages etc., the crockery was thought to be worth £150, silverware £430 and tablecloths £40.

Sally had bought ingredients costing £630 (of which £41 worth were still unused at the end of the month) and had used electricity and gas estimated at £53 and £140, respectively. She was also entitled to an allowance of £74 for her services in cooking, setting the tables, serving the food and washing up.

Receipts from clients during the month totalled £4,365 and were received by Andrew.

Required:

Prepare, for the month ended 30 June 19-4:

(a) a memorandum joint venture account; and

(b) joint venture accounts from the viewpoint of each of the co-venturers.

QUESTION 4

Sun Ltd and Shine Ltd agree to enter into a joint trading venture sharing profits and losses in the ratio 3 : 2 respectively.

The bankers to the joint venture agree to provide overdraft facilities during each month and on the last day to transfer the balance to separate accounts of the partners in their profit sharing ratio. For this service the bank proposes to charge $1\frac{1}{2}$% interest on the amount transferred each month. Shine Ltd agrees with the bank to clear the amount charged to their account immediately it is transferred. Sun Ltd, however, arranges with the bank to accumulate the balance on their account paying interest of $1\frac{1}{2}$% each month on the balance outstanding on the last day before transfer from the joint venture account.

The following estimates have been made of the first four month's trading:

1. Sales of the first month are expected to be £30,000 with expected increases in each subsequent month of 10% over the previous month.
2. A selling commission is to be paid of $2\frac{1}{2}$% on all sales, payable one month in arrear.
3. Wages and overheads are expected to be £4,750 in the first month and increase by £200 in each succeeding month.
4. The partners expect to make an average gross profit of 25% on selling price before calculating sales commission.
5. Payments for goods are made in the month following that in which they are purchased and it is agreed to have sufficient stock at the end of each month to cover the next two months' sales.
6. Debtors are expected to take an average of two months' credit.

You are required to prepare:

(a) a statement showing the monthly bank position;

(b) a draft profit and loss account for the four month period;

(c) a statement for the directors of Sun Ltd showing the position so far as that company is concerned at the end of the period.

(ICAEW)

SECTION II Chapter 3

QUESTION 1

A retail business in Radham had a branch shop in Ceeton for which it maintained ledger accounts. The main shop supplied its branch with goods for resale.

The following balances related to the branch for the year ended 30 April 19-5.

	£
Stock of goods for resale, 1 May 19-4	12,600
Goods transferred from Radham	70,000
Goods returned to Radham	1,000
Goods returned to Ceeton from customers (at selling prices)	600
Cash sales	72,000
Credit sales	18,000
Stock of goods for resale, 30 April 19-5	7,100

Required:

Open, post and balance the following accounts in the Radham ledger on the assumption that all goods are supplied to the branch at cost:

Goods sent to Ceeton;

Ceeton branch stock.

QUESTION 2

The facts are precisely the same as in Question 1 above, except that Radham invoices goods to Ceeton at selling price which is cost price plus 20%.

Required:

Prepare the same accounts as in Question 1 above, using the memorandum column method for the branch stock account.

QUESTION 3

The facts are precisely the same as in Question 2 above.

Required:

Prepare the same accounts as in Question 1 above, together with a branch stock adjustment account to record the profit element.

QUESTION 4

The facts are precisely the same as in Question 2 above, except that Radham invoices goods to Ceeton at a transfer price which is cost plus 10%.

Required:

(a) Prepare the same accounts as in 2 above.

(b) State what the balancing figure in the memorandum column of the branch stock account represents.

QUESTION 5

The facts are precisely the same as in Question 4 above.

Required:

(a) Prepare the same accounts as in Question 3 above.

(b) State what the balancing figure in the branch stock account represents.

QUESTION 6

The balances on the current accounts of a head office and its branch were £21,630 before the transactions listed below were posted.

	£
Goods sent to branch by head office	57,240
Goods received from head office by branch	54,090
Remittances sent to head office by branch	78,700
Remittances received by head office from branch	73,030
Branch profit for the period	15,130

The differences in goods and remittances figures represent items in transit.

Required:

Open, post and balance the current accounts in the ledgers of head office and its branch.

QUESTION 7

A main shop in Toton has branch shops at Colwick and Ranby.

At the beginning of the period, the current account balances in the Toton ledger, which agreed with those in the branch ledgers, were Colwick £21,060 and Ranby £16,810.

The following transactions occurred during the period.

		£
At Toton		
	-goods sent to Colwick	40,510
	-goods sent to Ranby	29,600
At Colwick		
	-goods returned to Toton	470
	-goods sent to Ranby	1,400
	-remittances sent to Toton	55,200
	-profit for the period	6,070
At Ranby		
	-remittances sent to Toton	31,070
	-goods sent to Colwick	1,860
	-goods returned to Colwick	110
	-loss for the period	4,050

Required:

Open, post and balance the columnar current accounts in the main shop and branch ledgers.

QUESTION 8

A main shop in Lenton has a branch in Strelley. The business trades as Suburban Merchants Ltd.

The following transactions arose during year ended 31 December 19-5.

	£
At Lenton	
Sales	118,000
Transfers to Strelley (at transfer prices)	75,000
Stocks	
-on 1 January 19-5 (at cost)	56,700
-on 31 December 19-5 (at cost)	39,400
Purchases	118,100
At Strelley	
Sales	88,000
Transfers from Lenton (at transfer prices)	70,000
Stocks	
-on 1 January 19-5 (at transfer prices)	20,000
-on 31 December 19-5 (at transfer prices)	15,000

Transfer prices are cost plus 25%.

Required:

Prepare in columnar form a trading account for the year for

(a) Lenton (main shop);
(b) Strelley (branch);
(c) Suburban Merchants Ltd.

QUESTION 9

The facts are precisely the same as in Question 8 above, and the following additional information is available at 31 December 19- 5.

	£
Ordinary share capital issued (£1.00 shares)	100,000
Profit and loss account balance carried forward	50,300

	Lenton	Strelley
	£	£
Fixed assets (at written down values)		
-premises	47,000	36,200
-fixtures etc.	11,500	9,300
Curent assets (other than stocks)		
-debtors	1,100	300
-bank/cash	6,700	3,100
Current liabilities		
-creditors	15,600	6,300
At 31 December 19-5 there was cash in transit		600

Required:

Prepare in columnar form, a balance sheet as at 31 December 19-5 for

(a) Lenton (main shop);

(b) Strelley (branch);

(c) Suburban merchants Ltd.

QUESTION 10

Chambers and Potter decided to form a partnership and commenced trading on 1st July 19-4 as dealers in earthenware from a head office in Birmingham and a branch at Swansea. Separate records were maintained at Swansea. Chambers introduced £6,750 as his capital in the firm and Potter £10,125.

Goods sent from Birmingham to Swansea were charged at invoice cost plus 10%. Other than goods sent to Swansea, all sales by Birmingham were made at a uniform gross profit of $33\frac{1}{3}\%$ on selling price, whilst all sales by Swansea were made at a uniform gross profit to the branch of 25% on selling price.

The following transactions took place during the year ended 30th June 19-5:

1. Birmingham purchases totalled £97,600, returns were £4,110 and discount allowed by suppliers for prompt payment amounted to £2,006.
2. Birmingham sales including £36,300 invoiced to Swansea, were £108,300 and discounts allowed to outside customers amounted to £612.
3. Goods invoiced to Swansea for £4,400 in June 19-5 were not received or recorded at the branch until July 19-5.
4. In addition to goods sent from Birmingham, Swansea had also paid outside suppliers £10,175 for goods after having deducted cash discounts amounting to £325 and there were outstanding creditors on 30th June 19-5 of £2,000.
5. Swansea sales were £48,000, discounts allowed to customers £376, and breakages (at cost price to Swansea) £534.
6. Overhead expenses were: Birmingham £18,684 (including bank interest £3,600) and Swansea £5,365.

Stock at Swansea on 30th June 19-5 included stock invoiced by Birmingham at £7,700. Chambers was in charge at Birmingham and Potter at Swansea. Each partner was entitled to 10% of the net profit of his own branch after charging such percentage and the balance of profit was to be divided in the ratio of their capital in the firm.

You are required:

(a) to prepare trading and profit and loss accounts for the year ended 30 June 19-5, showing in columnar form the results of the partnership, the head office and the branch, and

(b) to comment briefly on the amount of capital employed in the firm and on the fairness as between the partners of the amounts of capital provided and in the manner in which the profits are divided.

(ICAEW)

QUESTION 11

Tor Ltd which trades in sporting equipment from its head office in Manchester decided to open a branch in Leeds at a capital outlay cost of £18,000. Separate records were maintained at Leeds.

Goods sent to Leeds by Manchester were invoiced at wholesale price to give the branch a uniform gross profit of $33\frac{1}{3}\%$ on selling price. Any purchases by the branch from outside suppliers were sold with a similar return. Manchester obtained the same margin but in addition received a quantity discount from its suppliers for all goods at 10% from wholesale price.

During the year ended 31st March 19-9:

1. Manchester purchases at wholesale prices totalled £116,000 and returns were £5,150.
2. Manchester sales were £137,800, including £39,700 invoiced to Leeds and discounts allowed to outside customers amounted to £1,482.
3. Leeds sales were £51,000, discount allowed to customers £848, and goods stolen amounted to £786 at cost price to Leeds.
4. In addition to goods received from Manchester, Leeds had also paid outside suppliers £6,350 for goods and there were outstanding creditors for purchases on 31st March 19-9 of £1,850.
5. Goods invoiced to Leeds for £4,900 in March 19-9 were not received or recorded at the branch until April 19-9.
6. Overhead expenses amounted to £16,627 at head office and £16,416 at the branch.

Stock at Manchester as on 31st March 19-8 had been valued at wholesale price less the quantity discount and amounted to £8,885. Stock at Leeds on 31st March 19-9 included stock invoiced by Manchester at £7,850.

The managers in charge of Manchester and Leeds were each entitled to a commission of 10% of the net profit of their particular branch after charging such commission.

The company are concerned with the viability of the Leeds branch and have indicated that if the capital involved was employed in another direction they could reasonably expect a return of 20%. However, the loss of turnover at Leeds would mean that the company would lose the quantity discount received from suppliers.

You are required:

(a) to prepare for the directors a detailed Profit and Loss Account for the year ended 31st March 19-9 showing in columnar form the results of the head office and branch, and

(b) to set out a statement showing the effect of closing the Leeds branch on the company's business, based cn the results of the year.

(ICAEW)

QUESTION 12

E Hartle Ltd, a company in Hyde, manufacturing and selling leather goods, set up a branch in Wigan in January 19-9 to sell goods (mostly made at Hyde) and for repairs to footwear and other items. Goods from Hyde are sent to Wigan at manufacturing cost plus 15%, 10% of which is for manufacturing profit and the other 5% to cover delivery charges. The branch keeps its own ledger accounts. Wages and salaries are paid from Hyde but are notified to Wigan for inclusion in the branch books.

At 31 December 19-9, the company's year-end, the Wigan trial balance showed:

	£	£
Sales of goods		47,200
Repair charges		33,600
Goods from Hyde	18,400	
Hyde current account		31,200
Goods and materials purchased from other suppliers	12,300	
Wages and salaries	23,900	
Other operating expenses	13,600	
Fixed assets	36,000	
Debtors and creditors	2,900	1,900
Bank balance	6,800	
	113,900	113,900

At 31 December 19-9 the balance in the Wigan current account in the Hyde books was £34,190. On investigation the difference between the current account balances was found to comprise:

- goods delivered by Hyde but not yet entered in the Wigan books, £690;
- £200 paid by a Wigan debtor to the Hyde office and not notified to Wigan;
- the branch wages and salaries for December which had been paid and entered in the Hyde books but not notified to Wigan. (This accounts for the balance of the difference).

Stocks at Wigan at 31 December 19-9 were valued at £4,600 for goods from Hyde and £500 for other goods and materials. The late consignment from Hyde (£690) was not included in the stock. The fixed assets at Wigan are to be written off on a straight line basis over 12 years.

Required:

(a) Show any journal entries which need to be made in the Wigan books before the profit is calculated.

(b) Prepare the Wigan profit and loss account for the year to 31 December 19-9.

(c) Show any journal entries which need to be made in the Hyde books.

(d) Briefly explain how, and to what extent, the Wigan profit calculation could be made more useful for management purposes.

(ACCA)

SECTION II Chapter 4

QUESTION 1

On 1 January 19-1 GS Ltd bought some plant from V Ltd on hire purchase.

Under the terms of the contract, an initial deposit of £30,000 was payable followed by four instalments of £35,000 payable annually on 31 December from 19-1 onwards. The cost of the plant for immediate payment would have been £130,000.

Interest is allocated to financial years on the sum of the digits method.

The financial years of both companies end on 31 December.

Required:

Answer the following questions.

(a) How much hire purchase interest was included in the hire purchase selling price?

(b) What amounts of interest would be allocated to each of the four years of the contract?

(c) Post the V Ltd. account in the GS Ltd. ledger for the year 19-1.

(d) Show the relevant extract from GS Ltd's balance sheet as at 31 December 19-1. Plant is depreciated on cost at 20% per annum.

(e) Show the relevant extract from V Ltd's balance sheet as at 31 December 19-1. This company also allocates interest receivable on hire purchase sales on the sum of the digits method. The manufacturing cost of the plant was £97,500.

QUESTION 2

A business commenced selling electrical appliances on hire purchase on 1 January 19-1. During that year, goods which had cost £60,000 were sold for £100,000. Deposits and instalments received amounted to £30,000.

Required:

Post the relevant ledger accounts using each of the methods:

(a) provision for unrealised profit;

(b) stock on hire.

QUESTION 3

The facts are the same as in Question 2, except that goods costing £6,000 which had been sold on hire purchase for £10,000 were repossessed after the buyer defaulted having paid sums amounting to £3,000.

After repossession it was estimated that renovations costing £400 would be needed before the goods could be resold for £2,500.

Required:

Post the relevant ledger accounts using each of the methods.

(a) provision for unrealised profit;

(b) stock on hire.

QUESTION 4

Included in the transactions of A. Presto Ltd during its financial year to 30 June 19-7 were the following:

(i) A machine (cash price £8,000) was bought from C.B.A. Ltd on hire purchase. The terms were a deposit of £800 on 1 October 19-6 (the date of purchase) and four half-yearly instalments of £2,052 each on 31 December 19-6, 30 June and 31 December 19-7 and 30 June 19-8.

(ii) A. Presto Ltd has been given sole manufacturing and selling rights for a patented product by F.E.D. Ltd. The agreement is that 50p will be paid to F.E.D. Ltd for each unit sold during the year (1 October to 30 September) subject to a minimum payment of £5,000 each year. These royalty payments are to be made at the end of each quarter and any shortfall below £5,000 for the year made up to £5,000 and included with the September payment. Such "shortfall" payments cannot be recovered later.

The quantities actually sold in 19-6 to 19-7 were:

October to December	1,000 units
January to March	1,200 units
April to June	1,800 units

A market for the product is gradually being established and it is expected that about 2,400 units will be sold in the next quarter.

(iii) A. Presto Ltd has agreed to act as selling agent for I.H.G. Ltd and will receive 5% commission on all goods sold. In May 19- 7 goods costing £4,000 are sent to A. Presto Ltd and expenses of £120 paid by that company on behalf of the principal. In June 19-7 half of the goods are sold for £3,600 cash and the amount due settled between the parties.

Required:

(a) Show all of the ledger accounts (except Cash account) required to record the above information relating to the year ended 30 June 19-7 including any transfers to the profit and loss account at the end of the year. Assume that all payments are made on due dates.

(b) Briefly justify your calculations of the amounts to be transferred to the profit and loss account in respect of (i) and (ii), indicating what alternative(s) might have been possible and any basic accounting principles involved.

(ACCA)

QUESTION 5

The draft final accounts of Venda Ltd disclosed a Stock figure of £532,641 on 31st March, 19-0.

During the course of the audit, the following matters were noted.

1. One stock sheet had been under-added by £900 and another over-added by £1,000.
2. A sheet total of £19,270 had been carried forward as £12,970.
3. Free samples supplied by manufacturers had been included at normal cost (£4,010).
4. Other items sent by manufacturers to Venda Ltd for inspection on a sale or return basis had been included at the amount payable (£3,600) if retained, but no decision regarding this had been made.
5. Goods sent by Venda Ltd to various retailers on a sale or return basis (cost £4,800) had been included at their selling price (£6,400).
6. Display equipment supplied to retailers (cost £8,100) on a leasing basis had been included in stock at its written down value (£5,700).
7. Some goods had been supplied to retailers on a credit sale agreement basis (£7,200) (cost); £9,900 (credit sale price)). Payments totalling £1,900 had been received in respect of these goods up to the year end. These goods had been included in stock at the amount still payable.
8. Other goods had been supplied to retailers on hire purchase terms. The total cost of these goods was £10,000; hire purchase selling price was £16,800 of which £4,200 has so far been received. None of these goods had been included in the stock figure.
9. Venda Ltd received goods, valued at £2,500 from suppliers six days before the financial year-end but the invoices did not arrive until April 19-0. These goods have been included in the stock figure.
10. Invoices amounting to £5,100 were received by Venda Ltd during the last week of March 19-0, but the goods to which they related were delayed as the result of a drivers' strike and did not arrive until the second week of April 19-0. They have not been included in the stock figures.
11. Some goods in the warehouse have been damaged but have been included in stock at the normal cost price of £2,200. After rectification, estimated at £600 they can be sold as new. Normal selling price is £4,000.
12. Venda Ltd sells some goods through agents. Unsold goods on consignment, amounting to £15,300 (cost) have not been included in stock on the grounds that they are held in stock by the Agent (consignee).
13. Details of another consignment are:-

	£
Cost (ex warehouse)	6,000
Insurance, freight etc incurred by consignor	1,200
Landing charges, customs duties, freight etc incurred by consignee	3,600
Consignee's selling expenses	1,500
	12,300

The consignment had been despatched in 20 packing cases. On the sea journey, two of these cases were washed overboard during a storm and lost. Twelve cases had been sold by 31st March, 19-0 and the remainder included in Stock at £3,690 ($\frac{6}{20}$ of £12,300).

Required:

Using such of the above information as is relevant, prepare a schedule of corrections to the stock figure in the following form.

ONLY the adjustments to stock are required in the schedule; corresponding adjustments to other figures are not required:

Stock Adjustment Schedule

Item No.	Stock		Reason for adjustment
	Increase £	Decrease £	

QUESTION 6

During 19-8, Spruce Ltd started selling two types of its paint sprayers on hire-purchase terms.

> Model A   Cost price £200:   Deposit £60:   8 quarterly instalments of £30
>
> Model B   Cost price £300:   Deposit £80:   8 quarterly instalments of £50.

A hire-purchase stock account is debited with the cost of goods sold on hire purchase and credited with the deposits and instalments due. At the year end the cost of stock out on hire-purchase is calculated by reference to the amount of the instalments not yet due as a proportion of the total hire-purchase price. During 19-8, 10 model A and 12 model B sprayers were sold and all of the instalments (a total of 12 for A and 16 for B) were paid on the due dates. The balance sheet figure for stock out on hire-purchase at 31 December 19-8 was £3,860.

A customer who had paid the deposit for a model B sprayer in 19-8 paid the first instalment on the due date in 19-9 but then defaulted and, after following the appropriate procedure, the unit was repossessed. It was brought into a separate used stock account at a value of £100. Otherwise all further instalments for the 19-8 sales which were due in 19-9 were received, except for two in respect of model A sprayers which were outstanding on 31 December 19-9 but were expected to be collected soon afterwards.

Further sales in 19-9 were 12 model A and 20 model B sprayers. The number of instalments due during 19-9 in respect of these sales were 20 for A and 32 for B. These were all paid on the due dates.

Required:

(a) Prepare ledger accounts to record the 19-9 transactions, including the closing entries and balances carried forward.

(b) What alternative policy for recognising the profit on hire-purchase sales might have been adopted, and why, if the experience of hire-purchase trading had been materially different from the above?

(ACCA)

QUESTION 7

Brown commenced trading on 1st July 19-8 dealing in home office units. He restricts his business to two models, one being standard which he purchases for £100 and the other de luxe which he purchases for £140.

His cash selling price is based on a uniform gross profit of $33\frac{1}{3}\%$ on selling price. He sells some units on hire purchase with the same deposit of £42 for either model followed by 24 monthly instalments of £6 for the standard model and £9 for the de luxe. He also leases units on five year agreements with quarterly payments of £12 and £15 respectively.

The following draft accounts were produced by Brown for the year ended 30th June 19-9:

Profit and Loss Account

	£	£
Sales		21,060
Lease rentals		
- standard	504	
- de luxe	840	
		1,344
Closing stock, at cost		9,560
		31,964
Less		
Purchases	22,400	
Wages		
- staff	3,140	
- self	4,200	
Overhead expenses	496	
		30,236
Net profit for year		1,728

685

Balance Sheet

	£
Stock on hand	9,560
Hire purchase debtors	
- standard	2,160
- de luxe	4,104
Balance at bank	1,800
	17,624
Less Creditors	896
	16,728
Representing:	
Opening capital account	15,000
Profit and loss account	1,728
	16,728

He also gives the following information:

1. Units supplied by Brown during the year were:

	Standard Model	De luxe Model
Cash Sales	46	22
Hire Purchase sales	18	24
Lease	22	32

2. Units on lease have been included in stock on hand as on 30th June 19-9. At the end of the leasing period they will have no scrap value.

You are required to:

(a) redraft the accounts in accordance with recognised accounting principles, and

(b) set out the reasons for the changes you have made.

ICAEW

SECTION II Chapter 5

QUESTION 1

QR PLC entered into a five year non-cancellable finance lease on a machine from 1 January 19-5 at an annual rental of £30,000 payable in advance. The machine could have been bought outright on 1 January 19-5 for £120,000.

Required:

(a) Calculate the total finance charge over the life of the lease.

(b) State how QR would show this transaction (including notes) in a balance sheet prepared on 1 January 19-5, assuming that the first rental payment included a finance charge allocation of £12,000.

(c) Calculate the fractions to be used in allocating the finance charge to accounting years over the life of the lease using the sum of digits method.

(d) Calculate the finance charges allocated to accounting years on the basis of your answer to (c) above.

(e) Show extracts from QR's balance sheet (including notes) as at 31 December 19-5, relating to the leasing arrangements. QR normally charges depreciation on machinery at 10% per annum on cost.

(f) Recalculate the fractions to be used in allocating the finance charges to accounting years over the life of the lease, using the sum of digits method, if the lease rentals were payable annually from 31 December 19-5.

(g) Calculate the finance charges allocated to financial years on the basis of your answer to (f) above.

QUESTION 2

ST (Leasing) PLC is the lessor of equipment which had an initial fair value of £140,000. The equipment was leased on a five year non-cancellable lease at an annual rent of £40,000, payable in advance from 1 January 19-5.

Required:

(a) Calculate the total gross earnings over the life of the lease.

(b) State how ST would show this transaction (including notes) in a balance sheet prepared on 1 January 19-5, assuming that the first rental payment included a gross earnings allocation of £24,000.

(c) Calculate the fractions to be used in allocating the gross earnings to accounting years over the life of the lease using the sum of digits method.

(d) Calculate the gross earnings allocated to accounting years on the basis of your answer to (c) above.

(e) Show extracts from ST's balance sheet (including notes) as at 31 December 19-5, relating to the leasing arrangements.

SECTION II Chapter 6

QUESTION 1

During 19-5, Barwell PLC was engaged on constructing a river bridge for the Rutcoln County Council at an agreed price of £460,000.

At the beginning of 19-5 plant allotted to the contract was valued at £85,000. During the year materials were issued totalling £193,200, wages were £41,100, payments to sub-contractors, £26,200, overheads £58,900 and sundry expenses £7,300.

At 31 December 19-5, relevant balances were:

	£
Plant	60,500
Materials	25,700
Work certified by civil engineers	300,000
Work not certified (at cost)	59,200
Profit for year recognised	26,100
Work certified (at cost)	266,300
Profit for year suspended	7,600

Required:

Prepare the bridge construction contract account in Barwell PLC's ledger, under each of the following methods.

(a) engineers' certificates;

(b) work-in-progress.

QUESTION 2

The facts are precisely the same as in Question 1 above, but the following further information is available.

	£
Progress payments received	200,000
Retentions	20,000
Progress payments invoiced	80,000

Required:

Prepare, on the basis of the engineers' certificates method, each of the following accounts in Barwell PLC's ledger.

(a) Rutcoln County Council;
(b) Engineers' certificates;
(c) Retentions.

QUESTION 3

The facts and answers are as in Questions 1 and 2 above and the further estimated costs to the completion of the contract are £74,500, the outcome of which can be reasonably forseen.

Required:

On the basis of SSAP 9 (Stocks and Work-in-progress):

(a) calculate the amount of profit which should be recognised on the contract in 19-5;
(b) show the compilation of the work-in-progress figure for inclusion in the balance sheet at 31 December 19-5.

QUESTION 4

Carter Engineering Ltd undertakes a variety of manufacturing and construction work. At the end of its financial year to 30 June 19-9, decisions are needed on how to deal with the following items when closing off the accounts:

(a) A contract for A Ltd was commenced in February 19-9 and should be completed by July 19-0. The contract price is £335,000, and the original estimate of total costs, £245,000. Work in progress to date is valued at £68,000.
(b) A contract for B Ltd was commenced in February 19-8 and should be completed by August 19-9. The contract price is £480,000, and work in progress to date is valued at £340,000. It is estimated that a further £60,000 costs will be incurred before completion.
(c) The raw materials stock includes some items costing £12,000 which were bought for processing and assembly against a special order. Since buying these items the cost price has fallen to £10,000.
(d) A customer, D ltd, ordered a special-purpose machine at an agreed price of £60,000. The manufacture was completed in October 19-8 at a cost of £46,800. However, because D ltd was then experiencing exceptional cash flow problems, it was agreed that the sale should be on hire purchase terms with an initial deposit of £6,000 and four half-yearly instalments of £15,000 each. By June 19-9 the deposit and one instalment had been paid.
(e) E Ltd had ordered some equipment to be designed and constructed at an agreed price of £18,000. This has recently been completed at a cost of £16,800 higher than expected, due to unforeseen problems. It has now been discovered that the design does not meet certain statutory regulations, and conversion at an estimated extra cost of £4,200 will be required. E Ltd has accepted partial responsibility and agreed to meet half of the extra cost.

Required:

For each of the above items, say what figure you would include in stock (or work in progress) at the end of the year, and give a short explanation of the principle(s) or reasoning behind your answer. If appropriate, indicate any assumptions or qualifications where additional information may be required.

(ACCA)

QUESTION 5

AB Limited, building contractors, commenced to trade on 1st January 19-6.

From the information given below you are required to prepare for management purposes:

(a) detailed trading and profit and loss account for the year ended 31st December 19-6;
(b) statement showing how the profit or loss on uncompleted contracts was calculated, giving reasons for the basis you have used;
(c) balance sheet at at 31st December 19-6;
(d) a note to the balance sheet setting out in detail how the value of work-in-progress has been calculated to comply with the relevant Statement of Standard Accounting Practice No. 9.

1. The summarised trial balance at 31st December 19-6 was

	£	£
Ordinary share capital: 320,000 shares of £0.25 each		80,000
Plant and machinery at cost	40,000	
Vehicles, at cost	25,000	
Furniture and fixtures, at cost	7,000	
Sales, including progress payments invoiced		526,000
Debtors	53,000	
Creditors		34,000
Balance at Bank	7,000	
Contract costs:		
Wages	230,000	
Materials	107,000	
Plant hire	8,000	
Direct expenses	19,000	
Plant running expenses	39,000	
Administration expenses		
Salaries	58,000	
Office and administration	21,000	
Auditors' remuneration	2,000	
Directors' remuneration	20,000	
Bank charges	4,000	
	640,000	640,000

2. At 31st December 19-6 there were three contracts, Nos. 13, 17 and 21, uncompleted. All other contracts had been completed before the year end at a profit and none had any retentions outstanding.
3. The details of uncompleted contracts at 31st December 19-6 were as follows:

	Contract Number		
	13	17	21
	£	£	£
Cost	29,700	31,200	15,300
Value of work certified	37,000	26,000	16,000
Less - retentions	3,700	2,600	1,600
Sales value to date	33,300	23,400	14,400
Progress payments invoiced at 31st December 19-6	30,000	19,200	12,000
Progress payments received, at 31st December 19-6	25,000	16,000	10,000
Estimate of final cost	32,000	36,000	50,000
Sales value	40,000	29,000	60,000

4. The value of materials and stores not allocated to a particular contract at 31st December 19-6 was £5,000.
5. Plant and machinery and vehicles are to be depreciated by 25% and furniture and fixtures by 10%.
6. Taxation is to be ignored.

(ICMA)

QUESTION 6

Jack and Gerry, who are both building contractors, decided to purchase a 6 acre piece of land for £108,000 and develop this as a separate equal partnership.

The partnership is to provide the roads and main services but the actual building of the properties is to be subcontracted to the individual partners' own businesses at agreed fixed prices.

Phase 1 will cover 2 acres of the site and Jack's firm contracts to build 6 executive style houses on 1 acre at a cost of £22,000 each and Gerry's firm contracts to build 8 bungalows on the other acre at a cost of

£18,000 each.

On 1st April 19-9 the partnership purchased plant and machinery for the site development at a cost of £40,000. This will be used on the site for three years, after which it will have a residual value of £4,000. Depreciation is to be charged by the straight line method.

During the year ended 31st march 19-0, expenditure on the site was as follows:

	£	£
Wages and national insurance		19,716
Materials		12,482
Plant and machinery running cost		1,702
Payments to Jack		
completed houses	110,000	
progress payment on house	5,000	
		115,000
Payments to Gerry		
completed bungalows	108,000	
progress payments on 2 bungalows	8,000	
		116,000

Stock of materials on the site on 31st March 19-0, amounted to £2,520.

Partnership costs on the site in the year are attributed as to two-thirds for the overall site development and one-third to the properties in Phase 1 in particular. A provision is required in Phase 1 account for final road surfacing estimated at £60 for each executive house and £45 for each bungalow. There are no other outstanding costs of the overall site development which will affect Phase 1. Work in progress is to be valued at cost.

By 31st March 19-0 all completed houses and bungalows had been sold for £35,000 each, and £32,000 each respectively. Profit is taken on each property as it is sold.

You are required to prepare for the year ended 31st March 19-0:

(a) partnership site development account;
(b) Phase 1 profit and loss account, and
(c) a statement comparing the profitability of each type of property built on the site.

(ICAEW)

SECTION II Chapter 7

QUESTION 1

Greylands PLC whose accounting year ends on 31 December invested some surplus liquid funds in marketable securities.

Required:

In respect of each of the following occurrences

(a) post and balance for the year concerned, the investment account in Greylands PLC's ledger, assuming that the appropriate amount of interest is received on the due date(s);
(b) as a separate calculation, justify the figure of investment income for the year.

Brokerage etc. charges and taxation should be ignored.

(i) Initial investment on 1 August 19-4 in £300,000 (nominal) 12% Broxton Borough Council Loan Stock at 96 c.i. Interest is payable half-yearly on 30 June and 31 December.
(ii) The facts are as in (i). The holding was sold on 1 October 19-5 at 99 c.i.
(iii) The facts are as in (i). The holding was sold on 1 December 19-5 at 87 xi.
(iv) The facts are as in (i). A further £100,000 (nominal) was acquired on 1 December 19-4 at 94 xi.

(v)   The facts are as in (i). A further £100,000 (nominal) was acquired on 1 November 19-4 at 97 ci.

(vi) The facts are as in (v). £350,000 (nominal) was sold on 1 September 19-5 at 94 ci. The company applies the FIFO method of calculating cost of disposals.

(vii) The facts are as in (vi), except that the company employs the averaging method of calculating cost of disposals.

(viii) On 27 February 19-4 Greylands PLC acquired 100,000 ordinary shares of £1.00 per share in Fastfoodz PLC at a cost of £173,000. Fastfoodz PLC paid the final dividend on the 19-3 profits of 6% on 25 May 19-4.

On 25 August 19-4 Fastfoodz declared a 1 for 5 bonus issue.

(ix) The facts are as in (viii). On 9 November 19-4, Fastfoodz PLC declared a 1 for 4 rights issue at £1.20 per share. Greylands PLC took up 20,000 shares and sold the remaining rights for £1.40 per share on 11 November 19-4.

SECTION II Chapter 8

QUESTION 1

Radford Cycles PLC had accepted bills of exchange totalling £43,764 during year ended 31 March 19-5. Of these, the drawers had discounted £35,431 with their various banks for discounts totalling £878.

By 31 March 19-5 the company had met, on maturity, bills totalling £39,720.

Required:

State to what extent, if any, the above matters would directly appear in the balance sheet of Radford Cycles PLC at 31 March 19-5.

QUESTION 2

Radford Cycles PLC had drawn bills of exchange totalling £253,080 during year ended 31 March 19-5. Of these, the company had discounted £194,610 with their bank at a discount of £4,270.

By 31 March 19-5, bills totalling £201,434 (including discounted bills, £176,302) had been met on maturity.

Required:

State to what extent, if any, the above matters would directly appear in the company's balance sheet at 3 March 19-5.

SECTION II Chapter 9

QUESTION 1

N.G Neers Ltd acquired the right to make a specialised machine component from its patentee I.N. Ventor.

The agreement contained the following principal terms:

(a) payment of a royalty of £25 per 100 components manufactured;

(b) a minimum payment of £600 per year;

(c) a right to recoup shortworkings up to the end of year 2 after which the right will lapse.

During the first three years of the agreement, the following numbers of components were made.

Year	No.
1	1,000
2	3,000
3	5,000

The accounting years of both parties end on 31 December. Settlement takes place on 31 January following each year end.

Required:

Prepare a schedule of workings for these transactions to enable the company's accounts to be prepared for each of the three years.

QUESTION 2

The facts are as in Question 1 above.

Required:

(a) Open, post and balance the appropriate accounts in the books of N.G. Neers Ltd for each of the three years.

(b) Show an extract from the company's balance sheet as at the end of year 1.

Taxation implications should be ignored.

QUESTION 3

The facts are the same as in Question 1 above, except that the agreement allows short-workings to be recouped up to the end of year 3 (after which the right is to lapse) and the output for year 3 was 3,000 components.

Required:

Prepare a schedule of workings for these transactions to enable the patentee's accounts to be prepared for each of the three years.

QUESTION 4

The facts are as in Question 3 above.

Required:

(a) Open, post and balance the appropriate accounts in the books of I.N. Ventor for each of the three years.

(b) Show an extract from his balance sheet as at the end of year 2.

Taxation implications should be ignored.

QUESTION 5

Bacon Ltd owns a patent for a new method of manufacturing potato crisps.

On 31 March 19-1, Bacon granted a licence to Plain Ltd to manufacture and sell crisps using the new process. The terms of the licence were that:

(a) Plain would pay Bacon a royalty of £1.00 per carton of crisps sold, with a minimum royalty of £15,000 p.a.

(b) If royalties in any one year should be less than the minimum, the shortfall could be recouped out of royalties in excess of the minimum for the 2 years immediately following.

On the same day, Plain Ltd granted a sub licence to Salted Ltd for the same purpose. The royalty payable to Plain by Salted was £1.50 for each carton of crisps manufactured by Salted, with a minimum annual royalty of £6,000 p.a. A similar shortworkings clause existed as that between Bacon and Plain.

You are given the following information.

	Sales by Plain Ltd units	Sales by Salted Ltd units	Stock held by Salted Ltd units at 31 March
to 31 March 19-2	9,000	2,400	630
to 31 March 19-3	12,400	5,600	140
to 31 March 19-4	11,400	3,900	800

All payments due were made on 31 March each year.

Required:

Open, post and balance the appropriate accounts in the books of Plain Ltd for each of the years ended 31st March 19-2, 19-3, and 19-4.

Ignore Taxation.

SECTION II Chapter 11

QUESTION 1

The final accounts of a holding company, Major PLC, and its wholly owned foreign subsidiary, OS Pty, were

Summarised balance sheets
as at 31 March 19-6

	Major PLC £000	Major PLC £000	OS Pty $000	OS Pty $000
Tangible fixed assets		520		380
Investment in OS Pty		40		
Stock	150		50	
Net monetary assets	130		40	
		280		90
		840		470
Share capital		700		288
Reserves				
– pre-acquisition			72	
– post-acquisition			110	
		140		182
		840		470

Summarised profit and loss accounts
for year ended 31 March 19-6

	Major PLC £000	Major PLC £000	OS Pty $000	OS Pty $000
Profit before tax		190		154
Taxation		(60)		(44)
Profit after tax		130		110
Proposed dividends		(50)		—
Retained profit		80		110

Required:

Major had acquired its holding on 1 April 19-5.

Exchange rates were:

	$ = £1
1 April 19-5	12
31 March 19-6	10
Average for the year	11

Required:

Translate the OS Pty. profit and loss account and balance sheet into £s sterling using the closing rate/net investment method.

QUESTION 2

The facts are exactly the same as in Question 1.

Required:

(a) Prepare, for the Major Group, the consolidated profit and loss account for year ended 31 March 19-6 and consolidated balance sheet at that date.

(b) Show the composition of group reserves at 31 March 19-6.

QUESTION 3

The trial balance of the Farwest branch of Local PLC at 30 September 19-6 was:

	Dr $	Cr $
Tangible fixed assets (at cost)	286,000	
Provision for depreciation		114,000
Sales		1,440,000
Stock at 1 October 19-5	520,000	
Expenses	132,000	
Debtors	270,000	
Goods from head office	1,212,000	
Creditors		210,000
Head Office current account		736,000
Bank and cash	80,000	
	2,500,000	2,500,000

Stock at 30 September 19-6   600,000

Fixed assets had been acquired as follows:

	Cost $	Accumulated depreciation $	Exchange rate
	68,000	51,000	17
	128,000	48,000	16
	90,000	15,000	15
Total per trial balance	286,000	114,000	

Exchange rates were:

	$ = £1
1 October 19-5	13
30 September 19-6	10
Average for the year	12

In the head office ledger, balances at 30 September 19-6 included

	£
Goods to branch	98,000
Farwest current account	49,000

Required:

Translate the Farwest branch trial balance at 30 September 19-6 into £s sterling using the temporal method.

QUESTION 4

The facts are exactly the same as in Question 3.

Required:

Prepare in £s sterling the Farwest trading and profit and loss account for the year ended 30 September 19-6 and a balance sheet at that date.

QUESTION 5

There are two commonly used methods of converting the results of overseas operations into sterling. They are termed 'historical rate' and 'closing rate' (sometimes called 'current rate').

You are required:

(a) to describe briefly the two methods;

(b) based on the information set out below and using the historic cost method, to:

(i) prepare a branch profit and loss account in sterling for the year ended 30th June 19-1;

(ii) prepare the branch account in the head office books bringing down the balance at 30th June, 19-1;

(iii) show the assets and liabilities represented by such balance.

Workings should be shown and conversions taken to the nearest £1.

1. GH Limited, a company in England manufacturing consumer goods, has an overseas branch in Holland.

2. The products are sent in bulk to the branch and invoiced at cost plus freight. Packing materials are purchased locally by the branch.

3. The branch keeps a complete set of books in the local currency.

4. The branch trial balance sent to the head office was as follows:

	Guilders	Guilders
Furniture and fixtures, at cost	37,400	
Bulk products from head office		67,200
Purchases:		
Bulk products	67,200	
Packing	48,000	
Sales		244,800
Wages	19,200	
General expenses	20,545	
Balance at bank	43,000	
Stock at 1st July, 19-0:		
Bulk products	26,220	
Packing	7,125	
Local agent, balance due from him	28,160	
Head office account:		
Balance at 1st July 19-0		22,610
Remittances:		
31st December, 19-0	27,930	
30th June 19-1	30,000	
Creditors		6,200
Depreciation at 1st July, 19-0		13,970
	354,780	354,780

5. The following exchange rates are relevant:

	Guilders to £1
1st July 19-0	4.75
31st December 19-0	4.90
30th June 19-1	5.00
Average for year	4.80

6. The sterling value in the head office books of the fixtures and fittings is £6,800.

7. The agent is entitled to a commission of $12\frac{1}{2}\%$ on the net profits of the branch before charging any such commission or any profit or loss on exchange.

8. Stocks at the branch at 30th June, 19-1 were:

	Guilders
Bulk products	9,320
Packing material	8,240

9. Depreciation of 6,050 guilders on fixtures and fittings has to be charged for the year.

(ICMA)

QUESTION 6

The results of a subsidiary for the year ended 31st August 19-1 are shown below.

	19-1 K's 000	19-0 K's 000
BALANCE SHEET		
Issued ordinary share capital	20,500	20,500
Reserves	20,700	17,400
Debentures	10,000	5,000
Current liabilities	15,000	3,000
	66,200	45,900
Fixed assets (net)	38,700	22,400
Stock	17,543	19,389
Cash and bank balances	9,957	4,111
	66,200	45,900
PROFIT AND LOSS ACCOUNT		
Trading profit	6,432	4,271
Taxation	2,789	1,164
Profit after taxation	3,643	3,107
Dividend paid to parent	343	300
Retained	3,300	2,807

Further information is provided below.

		Exchange rate £1 = K
1.	The shares were acquired by the investor company several years ago	5K
2.	Fixed assets were acquired as follows:	
	10,000,000K in 19-8/-9	5K
	16,000,000K in 19-9/-0	4K
	12,000,000K in 19-0/-1	4K
	9,000,000K in 19-0/-1	3K
3.	Depreciation is charged at the rate of 10% pa on cost including a charge for the whole year during the year of purchase.	
4.	Dividend was paid during 19-0/-1	3K
5.	K5 million of debentures were raised in past years	5K
6.	K5 million of debentures raised in 19-0/1	3K
7.	Average rate during the year	3.5K
8.	Rate at 31st August 19-1	3K

You are required to:

(a) explain the terms translation, temporal method, closing rate method, net investment concept; and

(b) translate the profit and loss account for the year ended 31st August 19-1 and balance sheet at this date of the subsidiary using:

(i) the temporal method, and

(ii) the closing rate method.

(ICAEW)

SECTION III Chapter 1

QUESTION 1

Miall PLC has an authorised capital of £4,000,000 ordinary shares of £1.00 per share, of which £2,500,000 have been issued and are fully paid.

The directors have resolved to issue a further 1,000,000 shares at £1.50 per share payable as follows:

		Per share £
On		
	application	0.25
	allotment (including premium)	0.75
	1st call	0.20
	final call	0.30
		1.50

Applications were received for 1,600,000 shares of which 100,000 were rejected and the money repaid to the applicants. The rest were allotted on a 2 for 3 basis and the surplus money was carried forward on account to allotment.

The calls were duly made. The holder of 10,000 shares paid the final call money with that for the first call. A holder of 30,000 shares failed to pay either call. These shares were subsequently declared forfeit but were later reissued to another person on payment of £0.80 per share.

Required:

(a) Open, post and balance the relevant accounts (except Bank) in Miall PLC's ledger to record the above transactions.

(b) Show an extract from the balance sheet of Miall PLC at the end of each of the following stages:

  (i) 1st call;

  (ii) forfeiture;

  (iii) reissue of forfeited shares.

QUESTION 2

Forster PLC purchased 300,000 of the 1,800,000 of its own ordinary shares of £1.00 per share, which had originally been issued at £1.30 per share, for £1.40 per share.

The company issued 100,000 5% preference shares of £1.00 per share at a price of £1.20 per share, to provide partial financing for the purchase. Before the new issue share premium account had a balance of £80,000. There are adequate distributable profits.

Required:

(a) Calculate the amount of:

  (i) share premium (if any) which can be utilised for meeting the premium payable on purchase of the company's own shares;

  (ii) transfer (if any) to capital redemption reserve.

(b) State what difference it would make to your calculations in (a) if, before the new issue, share premium account had a balance of £30,000.

QUESTION 3

The facts are the same as in Question 2 above except that the company is a private company, Forster Ltd, and distributable profits are £230,000.

Required:

Calculate:

(a) permissible capital payment;

(b) transfer (if any) to capital redemption reserve.

QUESTION 4

The facts are the same as in Question 3 above except that distributable profits are £60,000.

Required:
Calculate:
(a) permissible capital payment;
(b) transfer (if any) to capital redemption reserve.

QUESTION 5

Redoubt PLC had, a number of years ago, issued 600,000 12% redeemable debentures, on which interest is payable half yearly on 30 June and 31 December.

Under the terms of issue they were to be redeemed by equal annual drawings over a 12 years' period.

On 1 January 19-5, the balances on debenture redemption reserve and on 12% redeemable debentures were £500,000 and £100,000 respectively.

A further redemption was effected in 19-5 at 97xi and the final redemption in 19-6 at par xi.

Required:

Open, post and balance the appropriate accounts to record the above transactions for each of the years 19-5 and 19-6.

QUESTION 6

Citadel PLC had, some years ago, issued £400,000 12% redeemable debentures. Under the terms of the Trust Deed, the debentures could be redeemed or bought back on the open market at any time. A sinking fund had been established for this purpose.

On 1 January 19-5 the balance on debenture redemption fund was £152,400, and on debenture redemption fund investments, £112,800.

The following transactions occurred during 19-5:

			£
Jan	14	Sinking fund investments bought	38,100
May	16	Sinking fund investment income received	8,700
June	30	Debenture interest paid for half year	24,000
Sept	15	Sinking fund investments sold (cost £57,000)	61,200
	30	£60,000 debentures bought back on open market at 97 ci and cancelled	58,200
Oc	16	Sinking fund investment income received	5,100
Nov	21	Sinking fund investments sold (cost £43,200)	40,000
	30	£40,000 debentures redeemed at 96 ci and cancelled	38,400
Dec	31	Debenture interest paid	18,000
	31	Annual appropriation	32,000

Required:
Open, post and balance the appropriate accounts to record the above transactions.

QUESTION 7

The facts are the same as in Question 6 except that the debentures bought back on 30 September were not cancelled but held pending future reissue.

Required:
Open, post and balance the appropriate accounts to record the above transactions.

QUESTION 8

Expanding Ltd has an authorised capital of £2 million. Already in issue are 500,000 7% Cumulative Preference share of £1 and 1,000,000 ordinary shares of 75p each. It published a prospectus in connection with issuing the remainder of its authorised capital, as ordinary shares at a price of £1.25.

25p per share was payable on application (due by the 1st October 19-1), the balance of the nominal value upon allotment and the final balance on or before 31st December 19-1.

£3 million was received with properly completed application forms and all applications were scaled down pro rata with the excess money being applied first towards the amount due on allotment and any further excess being returned.

By 31st December 19-1 all amounts due had been received.

You are required to:

present the journal entries (including cash) recording all aspects detailed above in connection with the share issue; and

SECTION III Chapter 2

QUESTION 1

The balances in the books of two companies at 31 December 19-4 included the following:

	Gamma PLC	Delta PLC
	£000	£000
Net assets	6,000	4,300
Share capital	5,000	4,000
Share premium account	200	100
Capital redemption reserve	70	30
Realised		
- profits	700	600
- losses	420	330
Unrealised		
- profits	600	300
- losses	150	400

Required:

(a) Calculate the distributable profits of each company at 31 December 19-4;

(b) State what differences (if any) it would make to your calculations if either of these companies was a private company.

SECTION III Chapter 3

QUESTION 1

On 31 December 19-5, the following balances were extracted from the ledger of Faraday PLC.

	Dr.	Cr.
	£	£
Value added tax		29,000
Provisions for corporation tax		
-current		94,000
-future		-
Advance corporation tax		
-payable		-
-recoverable	39,000	
Deferred taxation		27,000

The following matters have not yet been dealt with in the accounts:

(i) VAT output tax £137,000, input tax £92,000, payments to Customs and Excise £64,000.

(ii) Transfer to deferred taxation £11,000.

(iii) The balance on provision for corporation tax (current) comprises estimated corporation tax £121,000 less ACT recoverable £27,000. The newly agreed assessment figure of £130,000 is now to be substituted for the estimate.

(iv) Corporation tax of £136,000 is to be provided on profits for the year 19-5. Profits before tax were £500,000.

(v) ACT of £30,000 is payable on the final dividend proposed at 31 December 19-5.

NB. The balance of ACT recoverable (£39,000) included in the above list relates to the interim dividend paid in July 19-5 and the final 19-4 dividend paid in May 19-5.

Required:

Prepare extracts from the profit and loss account for the year ended 31 December 19-5 and from the balance sheet as at 31 December 19-5, incorporating the effects of the above matters.

QUESTION 2

On 1 January 19-5 Leen Ltd had a credit balance on Income Tax account of £4,800. Basic rate of income tax is 30%.

The following transactions arose during the year 19-5.

			£
Jan	12	Paid income tax due for December 19-4 quarter	1,800
Feb	3	Paid royalties (net) for second half year 19-4	7,000
April	13	Paid income tax due for March 19-5 quarter	
May	17	Received investment income interest (net)	4,900
June	30	Paid debenture interest (net)	8,400
July	14	Paid income tax due for June 19-5 quarter	
Aug	2	Paid royalties (net) for first half-year 19-5	5,600
Sept	5	Received investment income interest (net)	6,300
Dec	31	Paid debenture interest (net)	8,400
	31	Provided royalties (net) for second half year 19-5	4,200

Required:

(a) Open, post and balance the appropriate accounts to record the above transactions.

(b) Prepare the relevant profit and loss account and balance sheet extracts after (a) has been completed.

QUESTION 3

During 19-5 Leen Ltd also received dividends on investments and paid dividends as follows. In each case the amount listed is the net. Basic rate of income tax is 30%.

			£
June	5	Paid final dividend proposed at end of 19-4	14,000
July	13	Paid ACT for June 19-5 quarter	
Aug	2	Received dividends on investments	2,100
Sept	24	Paid interim dividend for first half year 19-5	7,000
Oct	14	Paid ACT for September 19-5 quarter	
Nov	9	Received dividends on investments	2,800
Dec	31	Proposed final dividend for 19-5	21,000

Required:

(a) Open, post and balance the appropriate accounts to record the above transactions.

(b) Prepare the relevant profit and loss account and balance sheet extracts after (a) has been completed.

SECTION III Chapter 4

QUESTION 1

After all the year end adjustments had been posted, the trial balance of Canterbury PLC included the following balances at 31 March 19-6.

	Dr £	Cr £
Administrative expenses	83,600	
Sales		3,191,600
Distribution costs	190,300	
Bank overdraft interest	12,000	
Extraordinary loss	78,800	
Cost of sales	2,503,200	
Royalties received (gross)		15,000
Proposed dividends	63,000	
Corporation tax - current year charge	92,700	
(including tax benefit (£22,000) on extraordinary loss)		

Required:

Prepare the profit and loss account of Canterbury PLC for year ended 31 march 19-6 using Format 1.

QUESTION 2

The facts are the same as in Question 1. Total costs comprise:

	£
Cost of Sales	2,503,200
Distribution costs	190,300
Administrative expenses	83,600
	2,777,100

representing:

	£
Increase in stocks of finished goods and work-in- progress	(381,300)
Own work capitalised	(30,600)
Depreciation	174,600
Raw materials and consumables used	2,680,500
Staff costs	291,700
Other operating charges	42,200
	2,777,100

Required:

Prepare the profit and loss account of Canterbury PLC for year ended 31 March 19-6 using Format 2.

QUESTION 3

The facts are the same as in Questions 1 and 2 and these further balances were included:

	Dr. £	Cr. £
Debtors currently due		
-trade	215,100	
-other	17,200	
Cash at bank and in hand	21,600	
Advance corporation tax (on proposed dividends) recoverable	27,000	
Creditors currently due		
-trade		373,500
-proposed dividends		63,000
-mainstream corporation		58,400
-ACT payable (on proposed dividends)		27,000
Vehicles	85,100	
Finished goods stock	219,300	
Plant and machinery	432,700	
Work-in-progress	322,400	
Land and buildings	211,000	
Raw materials stock	260,500	
Called up share capital		800,000
Share premium		46,000
Creditors not currently due		
-maintstream corporation tax (less income tax recoverable, £4,500)		64,200
Profit and loss account		362,700
Capital redemption reserve		17,100

Required:

Prepare the balance sheet of Canterbury PLC as at 31 march 19-6 using Format 1.

QUESTION 4

XY Public Limited Company is a mail order business selling its goods through agents.

From the information given below **you are required**:

to prepare a profit and loss account for the year ended 31st March, 19-3 and a balance sheet as at that date, in accordance with the requirements of the Companies Act 1948 to 1981, subsequently consolidated into the Companies Act 1985, together with the notes required. In a separate statement of accounting policies, give three examples of such policies which are being followed.

Comparative figures and the directors' report are not required. All workings are to be shown.

The following is a list of balances extracted from the accounting records as at 31st March 19-3, the financial year-end.

	£000
Ordinary share capital, allotted, issued and fully paid	45,000
Cost of goods sold	242,550
Bank overdraft	10,832
Salaries and wages	25,560
Profit and loss account balance, 1st April, 19-2	4,050
Audit fees	34

Interest on bank overdraft	855
Provision for doubtful debts	34
Prepaid expenses	288
Trade creditors	37,980
General reserve	22,500
Interim dividend, paid November, 19-2	2,520
Advance corporation tax recoverable on interim dividend	1,080
Stock of goods for resale	55,407
Other administrative, selling and delivery expenses	18,473
Directors' total emoluments	322
Bad debts written off	1,003
Value added tax - credit balance	1,845
Corporation tax account - debit balance	36
Deferred tax	10,350
Sales, exclusive of value added tax	337,500
Agents' commission	24,345
Hire of equipment	207
Debtors	78,300
Accrued expenses	225
Unclaimed dividends	2
Proceeds of the disposal of equipment and vehicles	57
Purchases of equipment and vehicles during the year	292
Fixed assets, written down values at 1st April, 19-2	19,103

Other relevant information:

1. The authorised share capital consists of 300,000,000 ordinary shares of £0.25 per share.
2. Account must be taken of the following outstanding items:

   (a) Agents' commission £855,000

   (b) Audit fees £22,000

3. The provision for doubtful debts is to be increased to £54,000.
4. Appropriations are to be made for:

   (a) a final dividend of 1.89p per share proposed for payment in June 19-3;

   (b) the creation of a stock replacement reserve by transfer of £135,000.

5. A provision of £90,000 is to be made for obsolete stock.
6. Corporation tax is to be taken at 50% and advance corporation tax at a rate of 3/7ths of distribution, if required.
7. Corporation tax, at the rate of 50% has been estimated to be £12,600,000 based on the year's profit. £112,000 is to be transferred to the deferred tax account representing the excess of capital allowances over depreciation charges. The company provides for all timing differences, on the liability method, except for those which are not expected to reverse in the future. Tax paid in January 19-3 (based on the 19-1/-2 profits) was £7,936,000, which was £36,000 more than originally estimated. No final dividend had been paid in respect of 19-1/-2.
8. Salaries and wages are to be apportioned between the administrative and distributive functions on the basis of 3:7. The amount shown in the list of balances includes:

   Social security costs of £4,065,000

   Contributions to works and staff pension fund of £3,375,000.

9. The average number of persons employed during the year was 4,531, including 11 directors. The directors' total emoluments of £322,000 include fees of £14,500 and compensation of £41,000 paid to a director who resigned during the year. The total amount is to be charged as £265,000 to administrative expenses and £57,000 to distributive expenses.

   Two non-executive directors each received £4,500. The chief executive received £34,000; the merchandise and the catalogue directors each received £27,500; the chairman £16,000; the distribution and the operations directors £25,000 each, and the computer, personnel and finance directors each received £20,000.

10. Other administrative, selling and delivery expenses include £7,184,000 of administrative costs.

11. The charge for bad debts is unusually high due to the substantial increase in the agency recruitment programme in the previous year and the effect on collection methods during the changeover from manual to computer operation. These two items account for £900,000.

12. The hire of equipment relates to the company's computer facility.

13. The equipment and vehicles disposed of were all used in the distribution of the company's goods. They had a written-down value of £90,000 and originally cost £158,000.

An analysis of the fixed assets at 1st April 19-2 revealed:

	Freehold property	Equipment and vehicles
	£	£
Cost or valuation	17,797,000	5,738,000
Accumulative depreciation	1,822,000	2,610,000

The amounts to be charged for the year as depreciation are:

Freehold property   £203,000   -   of which £72,000 is to be charged to administrative expenses

Equipment and vehicles   £540,000   -   of which £180,000 is to be charged to administrative expenses.

This is based on a rate of 2% per annum on cost or valuation for buildings included in freehold properties and at rates between 5% and 25% per annum on cost, appropriate to their expected lives, for equipment and vehicles.

14. Stocks, which include goods held on approval by agents, have been valued at the lower of purchase price and estimated net relisable value.

15. The capital commitments at 31st March were contracts for new equipment amounting to £990,000. The directors have also authorised a further £902,000 of capital expenditure. These are not provided for in the above transactions.

16. The company is producing its accounts for the year ended 31st March 19-3 using the 1985 Companies Act formats.

SECTION III Chapter 5

QUESTION 1

The summarised profit and loss account of Denham PLC (for internal circulation) for year ended 30th June 19-5 was:

Denman PLC Trading and profit and loss account for year ended 30 June 19-5

	£	£
Sales		6,549
less		
Cost of sales		4,825
Gross profit		1,724
less		
Wages and salaries	409	
Interest paid	110	
Depreciation	387	
Other expenses	131	
		1,037
Profit before tax		687
less		
Corporation tax		172
Profit after tax		515
less		
Dividends paid and proposed		84
Retained profit for year		431

Required:

Prepare a value added statement for the year, treating depreciation as an appropriation of value added.

QUESTION 2

The facts are the same as in 1.

Required:

Prepare a value added statement for the year, treating depreciation as an input value.

SECTION III Chapter 6

QUESTION 1

Jones and Roberts, who were in partnership, and Bertam Ltd agreed to amalgamate with effect from 1 June 19-6.

A new company Jorotam PLC was incorporated for this purpose and had issued 70,000 ordinary shares of £1.00 per share at par and £40,000 6% debentures at par, in each case for cash, by 31 May 19-6.

At close of business on 31 May 19-6, the separate balance sheets of the partnership and of the old company, were as shown below:

Balance Sheets as at 31 May 19-6

Jones & Roberts			Bertam Ltd	
£	£		£	£
		Fixed assets (at written down values)		
		Freehold property	40,000	
54,700		Equipment	62,800	
16,400		Vehicles	26,300	
	71,100			129,100
		Current assets		
26,000		Stock	36,600	
37,800		Debtors	28,900	
700		Bank and cash	21,800	
64,500			87,300	
		less		
		Current liabilities		
21,300		Creditors	43,300	
-		Proposed dividends	5,800	
12,500		Bank overdraft	-	
33,800			49,100	
	30,700	Net current assets		38,200
	101,800	Net assets employed		167,300
		Financed by		
		Capital accounts		
51,000		Jones		
17,000		Roberts		
	68,000			
		Current accounts		
12,000		Jones		
1,800		Roberts		
	13,800			
	20,000	Loan from Jones		

	Share capital		
	Ordinary shares of £1.00 per share		88,000
	Reserves		
	Profit and loss	20,400	
	General reserve	1,800	
			22,200
	Shareholders' funds		110,200
	7% Debentures		57,100
101,800			167,300

It was agreed that Jorotam PLC would acquire all the assets, except bank and cash, of the partnership and assume responsibility for the creditors (but not for the loan and the overdraft) at the following values.

	£
Goodwill	14,300
Equipment	51,500
Vehicles	15,900
Stock	26,000
Debtors	35,200
Creditors	21,300

The purchase consideration (£121,600) was discharged by a payment of £33,600 and by the issue of 80,000 ordinary shares of £1.00 per share in Jorotam PLC at a premium of 10%, of which 60,000 were taken by Jones and 20,000 by Roberts.

The partners discharged the overdraft liability and repaid the loan from Jones.

Partnership profits and losses are shared in capital account proportions.

Required:

Post and balance the following accounts on dissolution of the partnership.

> Bank and cash
> Realisation
> Jorotam PLC
> Shares in Jorotam PLC
> Capital accounts.

QUESTION 2

The facts are exactly the same as in Question 1 but this further information is available.

Bertam Ltd retained the balance on bank and cash, paid the proposed dividends and redeemed the 7% debentures at book value. All other assets and liabilities were taken over by Jorotam PLC at the following values. Liquidation expenses totalled £1,600.

	£
Freehold property	54,600
Equipment	59,700
Vehicles	25,200
Stock	34,300
Debtors	27,800
Creditors	43,300

The purchase consideration was discharged by a payment of £43,000 and by the issue of 120,000 ordinary shares of £1.00 per share in Jorotam PLC at a premium of £0.10 per share.

Required:

Post and balance the following accounts on the liquidation of Bertam Ltd.

> Bank and cash
> Realisation
> Jorotam PLC
> Shares in Jorotam PLC
> Sundry shareholders.

QUESTION 3

The facts are exactly the same as in Question 2.

Required:

Post and balance the following accounts to record the amalgamation in the books of Jorotam PLC.

> Business acquisition
> Jones and Roberts
> Liquidators of Bertam PLC
> Bank and cash
> Ordinary share capital.

QUESTION 4

The facts are exactly the same as in Question 3.

Required:

Prepare for internal use, the balance sheet of Jorotam PLC immediately after the amalgamation has taken place on 1 June 19-6.

QUESTION 5

AB Limited and CD Limited, two private companies, decided to amalgamate their businesses into a new holding company, EF Limited, which was incorporated on the 1st November, 19-1, with an authorised capital of £4,000,000 in ordinary shares of £0.25 each. The new company plans to commence operations on 1st January, 19-2.

From the information given below, and assuming that all share transactions are completed by 30th June, 19-2, you are required to:

(a) project the balance sheet of EF Limited at 30th June, 19-2;
(b) project the profit and loss account of EF Limited for the six months ending 30th June 19-2;
(c) show the computation of the number of shares to be issued to the former shareholders of AB Limited and CD Limited.

Workings must be shown.

1. EF Limited will acquire the whole of the ordinary share capital of AB Limited and CD Limited by issuing its own shares fully paid.
2. The number of shares to be issued is to be calculated by multiplying the future annual maintainable profits available to the ordinary shareholders in each of the two companies by agreed 'price earnings ratios'. The following information is relevant:

	AB Limited	CD Limited
	£	£
Ordinary share capital in £1 shares, issued and fully paid	1,000,000	400,000
8% Cumulative preference shares of £1 each	-	100,000
10% Debentures 19-6 to 19-1	200,000	-
Future annual maintainable pre tax profit before deduction of preference dividends and debenture interest	230,000	110,000
Price/earnings ratio	10 times	8 times

3. Shares in the holding company are to be issued to shareholders in the subsidiary companies at a premium of £0.05 per share and thereafter these shares will be marketed on the stock exchange.

4. It is expected that the group profits of the new company in 19-2 will be at least £450,000 but that additional working capital will be required to facilitate expansion. Accordingly, it is planned to make a further issue of 1,500,000 ordinary shares to the public for cash at a premium of £0.075 per share on 1st May 19-2. These new shares will not rank for the interim dividend to be paid on the 30th June 19-2.

5. Out of the proceeds of the rights issue, EF Limited will advance £250,000 to AB Limited and £200,000 to CD Limited on 1st May, 19-2, for working capital. These advances will carry interest at 15% per annum to be paid monthly.

6. Preliminary expenses are estimated at £8,000 and administration expenses for the half year ended 30th June 19-2, at £16,000 but this expenditure will be covered by temporary overdraft facilities. It is estimated that the bank interest cost will be £1,600 in the six months.

7. A provision for £7,500 should be made for directors' fees for the half year.

8. On 30th June, 19-2, it is planned to pay interim dividends as follows:

	Per share £
AB Limited	0.050
CD Limited	0.044
EF Limited	0.010

Corporation tax is to be taken at 50% and advance corporation tax is to be ignored.

(ICMA)

QUESTION 6

Bloom, Dedalus and Boylan are partners in a mercantile business, sharing profits 2:2:1, after allowing for interest on capital, 10% per annum, and annual salaries of £5,000 to Bloom, £4,000 to Dedalus, and £3,000 to Boylan. They close their books on 31 March 19-1, and on 1 April 19-1 transfer the business to a new company, Ulysses Limited, in return for shares and/or debentures therein. The three old partners then become the only directors of Ulysses Limited.

The final Balance Sheet of the partnership is shown below.

Bloom, Dedalus & Boylan
Balance Sheet
31 March 19-1

	£	£		Cost or Valuation £	Depreciation £	£
Equity of Partners			**Fixed Assets**			
Capital Accounts			Freehold Land	160,000	-	160,000
Bloom	250,000		Freehold Buildings	300,000	60,000	240,000
Dedalus	150,000		Motor Vehicles	100,000	55,000	45,000
Boylan	100,000		Equipment	60,000	21,000	39,000
		500,000		620,000	136,000	484,000
Current Accounts			**Current Assets**			
Bloom	60,000		Stock		250,000	
Dedalus	36,000		Debtors		150,000	
Boylan	24,000		Cash Balance		3,000	
		120,000	Prepayments		5,000	
		620,000				408,000
Partner's Loan						
Bloom (15% pa)		100,000				

709

Current Liabilities						
Bank Overdraft	50,000					
Creditors	110,000					
Accruals	12,000					
		172,000				
		892,000				892,000

The loan from Bloom is secured by a mortgage on the firm's freehold property.

The following assets are to be revalued on transfer to Ulysses Limited:

Freehold Land, at market value, £220,000;

Freehold Buildings, on the basis of current replacement cost as new, £380,000;

Motor Vehicles and Equipment, at current second-hand values, respectively £50,000 and £36,000; and

Stock, at current replacement cost, £267,500, less an allowance for obsolescent and damaged stock, £8,000.

A provision for bad and doubtful debts, equal to 5% of Debtors, is to be raised.

Goodwill is to be valued at £60,000, and amortised by equal instalments over five years commencing from 1 April 19-1.

The company's pre-tax profits for the year ending 31 March 19-2 are forecast as £150,000, *before* charging any directors' emoluments, debenture interest, or goodwill amortisation.

Corporation tax is to be taken as 40% on profits up to £80,000 and 52% on *total* profits of higher amount, subject to an allowance of 8% of any amount by which profits fall short of £200,000. (Goodwill amortisation is *not* deductible in computing corporation tax).

Income tax basic rate 30%, up to £11,250 taxable income per individual.

You are required:

(a) to compute the capital employed (after depreciation) of Ulysses Limited as at 1 April 19-1;

(b) to draw up a scheme for financing the capital employed as computed in (a) above, fair to all the partners, and involving the issue by Ulysses Limited of a mixtures of preference shares, ordinary shares and debentures, or some of these; and

(c) to compute the forecast equity earnings of the company for its first year, after allowing for suitable directors' emoluments and debenture interest. (Ignore the taxation problems peculiar to close companies).

(ACCA)

SECTION III Chapter 7

QUESTION 1

The financial position of Jinxt PLC was as follows:

Balance Sheet
as at 31 October 19-6

	£	£
Fixed assets (at written down values)		
Freehold property	90,600	
Equipment	89,800	
Vehicles	55,100	
		235,500
Current assets		
Stock	79,100	
Debtors	50,200	
Bank and cash	14,600	
	143,900	

710

Less

Current liabilities

Creditors	40,300	
Net current assets		103,600
Net assets employed		339,100

Financed by:

Share capital	Authorised	Called up and fully paid
	£	£
8% preference shares of £1.00 per share	200,000	50,000
Ordinary shares of £1.00 per share	500,000	500,000
	700,000	550,000
Reserves		
Profit and loss account (debit balance)		(210,900)
		339,100

The preference dividends were two years in arrear.

As the direct result of the succession of trading losses, a reorganisation scheme was drawn up and approved to become effective from 1 November 19-6, the main terms of which are listed below:

1. The ordinary shares are to be written down to £0.40 per share and then to be converted into new ordinary shares of £1.00 per share, fully paid.
2. The preference shareholders are to receive 30,000 new ordinary shares of £1.00 per share, fully paid at par, in exchange for their preference shares.
3. The preference shareholders have also agreed to waive the rights to the dividend arrears and to accept in lieu, 5,000 new ordinary shares of £1.00 per share fully paid, in full settlement.
4. In part satisfaction of the sums due to them, the creditors have agreed to accept 30,000 new ordinary shares of £1.00 per share, fully paid, at par.
5. The debit balance on profit and loss account is to be written off.
6. Assets are to be revalued as follows:

	£
Freehold property	101,800
Equipment	62,300
Vehicles	40,700
Stock	52,100
Debtors	45,500

Required:

Open, post and balance the capital reduction and share capital accounts to record the reorganisation arrangements.

QUESTION 2

The facts are exactly the same as in Question 1.

Required:

Prepare the balance sheet of Jinxt PLC on 1 November 19-6 immediately after the reorganisation has been effected.

SECTION III Chapter 8

QUESTION 1

The following data relates to Unsatiable Appetites Ltd for the two years ended 31st December 19-0

	19-9	19-0
	£	£
Trading profit before tax	67,220	103,580
Taxation (Marginal rate 52%)	27,630	35,760
Profit after taxation	39,590	67,820
Dividends		
Preference paid 31st December	(5,400)	(5,400)
Ordinary		
paid 14th September	(19,250)	(14,000)
proposed	(9,625)	(16,000)
Retained	5,315	32,420

At 1st January, 19-9 the issued share capital consisted of 160,000 ordinary shares of 50p each and 100,000 5.4% cumulative preference shares of £1 each.

On 1st April 19-9 a bonus issue was made on the basis of one new ordinary share for every four held.

On 1st October 19-9 options were granted to the senior executives to subscribe for a total of 100,000 ordinary shares at the current market price of 75p each. Thes options were exercisable on the 1st December 19-0, 19-1, or 19-2.

An investment of £100 $2\frac{1}{2}$% consolidated stock would have given a gross yield of:

16% on 1st January 19-9, 15% on 1st December 19-9,
14% on 1st January 19-0, 13% on 1st December 19-0.

On 1st January 19-0 a previously announced rights issue of ordinary shares was taken up by all eligible shareholders. The basis was one for four at 60p per share and the market price on the last day of dealing, cum rights, was 70p.

On 1st July 19-0 the company issued £300,000 of a 15% convertible debenture. The terms of conversion were one ordinary share for each £1 of the debenture exercisable on the 31st December of any year up to and including 19-5. Interest was payable each year on 30th June and 31st December.

On 1st December 19-0, 20,400 ordinary shares were issued on the exercise of the executives share options.

You are required to:

(a) explain the purpose of presenting the earnings per share statistics in the annual accounts and
(b) calculate the earnings per share figures that will be disclosed in the published accounts for the year ended 31st December 19-0, (the published explanatory note is not required but clear working notes are expected).

(ICAEW)

QUESTION 2

Part of a listed company's Consolidated Profit and Loss Account is shown below.

Chasewater Public Limited Company
Consolidated Profit and Loss Account (extract)
for the year ended 30 June 19-1

	£	£
Group Net Profit Before Taxation		500,000
Taxation		270,000
Group Net Profit After Taxation		230,000
Minority Interests in subsidiaries		20,000
Attributable to Shareholders in Chasewater PLC		210,000
Extraordinary Items (after taxation)		11,000
Net Profit for year		221,000
Dividends (net)		
Preference	25,000	
Ordinary	100,000	
		125,000
Retained Earnings for Year		96,000

Notes

(i) Issued share capital (fully paid), 1 July 19-0:
250,000 10% Cumulative Preference Shares of £1 each, and 4,000,000 Ordinary Shares of 25p each.

(ii) Loan Capital, 1 July 19-0:
£500,000 7% Convertible Debentures (convertible into 200 Ordinary Shares per £100 Debenture, with proportionate increases for subsequent bonus issues, and for the bonus element in subsequent rights issues).

(iii) Changes during the year ended 30 June 19-1:

1 October 19-0	Rights issue of Ordinary Shares (ranking for dividend 19-0 to 19-1): 1 for 4 at £0.90 per share; market price before issue, £1.00
1 January 19-1	Conversion of £100,000 of 7% Convertible Debentures
1 March 19-1	Bonus issue of Ordinary Shares, 1 for 3.

(iv) Basic Earnings Per Share for the year ended 30 June 19-0 were 4.0p

(v) Corporation tax, 52%; income tax basic rate, 30%.

You are required:

(a) to compute the company's Basic Earnings Per Share for the current year, and its comparative BEPS for the previous year; and

(b) to compute the company's Fully Diluted Earnings Per Share for the current year only, and to state, with reasons, whether it ought to be published.

(ACCA)

QUESTION 3

Explain what is meant by:-

(i) basic earnings per share; and
(ii) fully diluted earnings per share,

as outlined in Statement of Standard Accounting Practice No. 3 (Revised).

From the information below, relating to A p.l.c., calculate the basic and fully diluted earnings per share for the year ended 31st December, 19-1. Where necessary, assume a corporation tax rate of 50%.

A p.l.c.
Summary Profit and Loss Account
for the year ended 31st December, 19-1

	£	£
Profit before tax and extraordinary items		700
Corporation tax on the profit for the year		260
Profit after taxation		440
Extraordinary items less tax		30
Profit after extraordinary items		410
Dividends		
- interim paid	80	
- final proposed	150	230
Retained profit		180

On 1st January, 19-1 the company had in issue 1,000,000 ordinary shares of £1 each and £400,000 of 10% convertible loan stock. During February, 19-1, the holders of £100,000 value of convertible loan stock exercised their option to convert into ordinary shares. The terms of the conversion were two ordinary shares for every £5 nominal value of convertible loan stock.

(ICMA)

SECTION III Chapter 9

QUESTION 1

At the end of year 4, a business had the following figures for equipment. Depreciation, for both historical and current cost purposes is calculated at 20% on a straight line basis, assuming no residual value.

Year of acquisition	Historical cost	Current cost Index	
	£		
1	70,000	140	mid-year
2	70,000	160	mid-year
3	50,000	170	mid-year
4	20,000	180	mid-year
4		200	end of year

Required:

Calculate the current cost depreciation adjustment for year 4.

QUESTION 2

The facts are exactly the same as in Question 1.

Required:

Calculate the revaluation surplus to be transferred to current cost reserve at the end of year 4.

QUESTION 3

The facts are exactly the same as in Question 1.

Required:

Calculate the net book value of equipment for inclusion in the current cost balance sheet at the end of year 4.

QUESTION 4

At the end of the company's year in March, year 5, the following historical cost figures were available.

	£
Opening stock	262,700
Purchases for year	854,900
Closing stock	231,200

An average of two months' sales is held in stock.

For current cost purposes a single index is used for stocks.

714

Mid-month:	Year			Index
	4	January		416.0
		February		418.2
		March		419.2
	5	January		442.6
		February		443.8
		March		445.2
	6	April		446.6
Average for	5			430.4

Required:

Calculate the current cost of sales adjustment for year 5.

QUESTION 5

The facts are exactly the same as in Question 4.

Required:

Calculate the revaluation surplus transferred to current cost reserve at the end of year 5.

QUESTION 6

The facts are exactly the same as in Question 4.

Required:

Calculate the closing stock figure included in the current cost balance sheet at the end of year 5.

QUESTION 7

The facts are exactly the same as in Question 4, except that an average of three months' sales is held in stock.

Required:

State the conversion ratios which would be used to arrive at current cost opening and closing stock at the end of year 5.

QUESTION 8

A company's monetary working capital at the end of year 5 was composed of:

	Opening £	Closing £
Debtors	922,600	1,075,400
Creditors	541,800	603,100

The average age of these items is two months.

The index numbers given in Question 4 above apply also to monetary working capital items.

Required:

Calculate the current cost monetary working capital adjustment for year 5.

QUESTION 9

The facts are exactly the same as in Question 8, except that,

	Opening £	Closing £
Debtors	1,075,400	922,600
Creditors	603,100	541,800

Required:

Calculate the current cost monetary working capital adjustment for year 5.

QUESTION 10

The facts are exactly the same as in Question 8, except that,

	Opening £	Closing £
Debtors	603,100	541,800
Creditors	1,075,400	922,600

Required:

Calculate the current cost monetary working capital adjustment for year 5.

QUESTION 11

The current cost balance sheet of a company contained the following figures.

	£000
Current assets	
Bank and cash (not included in MWC)	310
Current liabilities	
Hire purchase creditors	150
Taxation	260
Proposed dividends	300
Bank overdraft (not included in MWC)	140
Net assets employed	2,650
Shareholders' funds	1,950
Long term loans	
Debentures	430
Deferred liabilities	
Deferred taxation	270

Required:

Calculate the current cost gearing proportion.

QUESTION 12

The facts are exactly the same as in Question 11 and the current cost adjustments were:

	£000
Depreciation	930
Fixed asset disposals	100
Cost of sales	970
Monetary working capital	450

716

Required:

Calculate the current cost gearing adjustment.

QUESTION 13

The current assets and current liabilities of a high class retail company at the beginning and end of the year to 31st December 19-0 are summarised below.

	Opening £000	Opening £000	Closing £000	Closing £000
Current assets				
Stock	54		75	
Debtors	40		50	
Cash	21		15	
		115		140
Less Current liabilities				
Trade creditors	50		60	
Bank overdraft	30		50	
		80		110
Net current assets		35		30

The bank overdraft is considered a permanent source of finance. Stock at the end of each year represents purchases made equally during the preceding three monhs. Debtors represent sales in the preceding two months.

The monthly index of stock prices and the general price index was:

		Stock Price Index	General Price Index
19-9	October	115	162
	November	117	164
	December	118	167
19-0	January	120	170
	February	124	174
	March	126	178
	April	129	175
	May	132	176
	June	132	177
	July	134	179
	August	134	180
	September	135	181
	October	138	182
	November	140	184
	December	141	186
	Average for year	132	177

You are required to:

(a) explain the purpose of the monetary working capital adjustment;

(b) calculate the monetary working capital adjustment in accordance with SSAP 16 by reference to the data given above (work to the nearest £000), and

(c) explain briefly why some authorities do not consider that a monetary working capital adjustment is necessary.

(ICAEW)

SECTION IV Chapter 1

QUESTION 1

The balance sheets of Norton's business as at the end of 19-5 and 19-6 are as shown below:

Norton
Summarised Balance Sheets as at 31 December

	19-5			19-6	
£	£			£	£
	45,000	Fixed assets (at written down values)			32,000
		Current assets			
20,000		Stock		35,000	
25,000		Debtors		40,000	
4,000		Bank balance		-	
49,000				75,000	
		less			
		Current liabilities			
20,000		Creditors		26,000	
-		Bank overdraft		10,000	
20,000				36,000	
	29,000	**Working capital**			39,000
	74,000	Net assets employed			71,000
		Financed by:			
	59,000	Capital			56,000
	15,000	10% Loan			15,000
	74,000				71,000

Other information:

	19-5	19-6
	£	£
Opening stock	20,000	20,000
Sales	100,000	80,000
Cost of sales	60,000	55,000
Gross profit	40,000	25,000
Net profit	12,000	7,000
Purchases	60,000	70,000

Required:

1. Calculate the following ratios for 19-5 and 19-6.
    Gross profit/sales
    Net profit/sales
    Net operating profit/sales
    Net operating profit/net assets employed
    Sales/net assets employed
    Cost of sales/average stock
    Debtor collection (in months)
    Creditor payment (in months)
    Current assets/current liabilities
    Quick assets/current liabilities
    Total debt/total assets
    Total debt/capital
    Capital/total assets

2. Comment briefly on profitability, solvency and liquidity of the business in 19-6.

QUESTION 2

The capital employed by two companies was financed as follows:

	Dorking PLC		Wilton PLC	
	£	£	£	£
Ordinary £1.00 shares	5,000		11,000	
8% Preference £1.00 shares	2,000		-	
		7,000		11,000
Reserves		2,000		3,000
Shareholders' funds		9,000		14,000
Loan capital				
10% debentures	6,000		5,000	
11% debenture stock	4,000		-	
9% convertible loan stock	1,500		2,000	
Other loans	500		-	
		12,000		7,000
		21,000		21,000

Required:

Calculate the gearing of each company and state whether it is high or low.

QUESTION 3

The summarised accounts of a trading business are

Guthrie
Trading and profit and loss account
for year ended 31 December

19-5			19-6	
£	£		£	£
	160,000	Sales		185,000
	117,000	*less* Cost of Sales		136,200
	43,000	Gross profit		48,800
	20,600	*less* Expenses		28,100
	22,400	Net profit		20,700

Guthrie
Balance Sheet as at 31 December

19-5			19-6	
£	£		£	£
	104,000	Fixed assets (at written down values)		168,000
		Current assets		
21,600		Stock	32,800	
5,300		Debtors	6,900	
7,400		Bank and cash	3,100	
34,300			42,800	

		less		
		Current liabilities		
13,100		Creditors	20,200	
	21,200	**Working capital**		22,600
	125,200	**Net assets employed**		190,600
70,000		Capital	120,000	
37,200		Retained profit	42,600	
	107,200			162,600
	18,000	Long term loans		28,000
	125,200			190,600

Stock on 1 January 19-5 was £18,000

The average figures of performance for that type and size of business (obtained from trade association sources) were

Gross profit/sales	27.2%
Net profit/sales	17.0%
Net profit/net assets employed	20.0%
Stock turnover	4.8 times
Current ratio	1.9:1

Required:

(a) Calculate for Guthrie's business ratios, corresponding with the above average figures, for each of the years 19-5 and 19-6.

(b) Compare and comment on

  (i) the ratios for 19-6 with those for 19-5, and

  (ii) the ratios for Guthrie's business with those of an average business given above.

QUESTION 4

You have been asked by your employer to analyse the financial position of your company and to compare it with the overall position of similar sized businesses in the same industry.

Figures have been obtained from trade association souces and you have drawn up the following table

	Industry average	This company
Gross profit/sales	27.1%	28.6%
Net profit (before tax)/sales	12.2%	11.3%
Net profit (before tax)/Total Assets	14.7%	18.1%
Debtor collection period	42 days	28 days
Creditor payment period	25 days	31 days
Sales/Total Assets	1.2	1.6

Required:

(a) Comment on the company's performance as disclosed by the above data.

(b) Suggest possible reasons for the difference between the company's figures and those of the average for the industry.

QUESTION 5

The balance sheets of Stubton Ltd, for internal circulation, at 30 September 19-5 and 19-6, disclosed:

Stubton Ltd
Balance Sheets as at 30 September

19-5				**19-6**			
Cost	Deprec'n	Net		Cost	Deprec'n	Net	
£	£	£		£	£	£	
			Fixed assets				
70,000	10,000	60,000	Land and buildings	80,000	12,000	68,000	
142,000	38,000	104,000	Plant and equipment	167,000	51,000	116,000	
36,000	27,000	9,000	Vehicles	41,000	28,000	13,000	
248,000	75,000	173,000		288,000	91,000	197,000	
			Current assets				
	53,600		Stock		74,100		
	24,800		Debtors		19,700		
	10,200		Bank balance		-		
	700		Cash		400		
	89,300				94,200		
			less				
			Current liabilities				
36,900			Creditors	44,300			
15,400			Corporation tax	14,700			
11,800			Proposed dividends	13,500			
-			Bank overdraft	15,600			
	64,100				88,100		
		25,200				6,100	
		198,200				203,100	
			Financed by:				
			Ordinary shares of				
		150,000	£1.00 per share			170,000	
		10,200	Profit and loss			13,100	
		160,200	Shareholders' funds			183,100	
		38,000	Long term loans			20,000	
		198,200				203,100	

During 19-5 and 19-6, sales totalled £243,600 and £278,700 and gross profit was £62,500 and £70,400, respectively. There were no cash sales. Opening stock for 19-5 was £46,400.

At 30 September 19-4, profit and loss account balance was £10,000.

In each year, the company had declared dividends (including interim dividends) of 10%. The shares were valued at £1.70 and £1.80 per share on 30 September 19-5 and 19-6 respectively.

Required:

Calculate, for each of the two years

(i) ratios suitable for measuring the solvency, liquidity and profitability of Stubton Ltd.;

(ii) dividend yield, earnings yield and price/earnings ratio.

[Note: There were no extraordinary items].

QUESTION 6

The shareholders' funds employed in M Limited at the end of the year, consist of:

	£000
1,000,000 Ordinary shares of £0.25 each, fully paid	250
Retained profits	146
Total	<u>396</u>

Apart from current liabilities there are no other sources of finance.

The information given below relates to the actual results of M Limited given in the financial statements for the year of 365 days.

Net current assets to fixed assets	0.32:1
Current assets to current liabilities	1.65:1
Sales to fixed assets	2.75:1
Cost of sales to sales	0.60:1
Net profit to sales	12.5%
Number of days sales outstanding	61
Number of days stock held (based on cost of sales)	32.75

You are required to:

(a)

    (i)   prepare the operating account for the year and the balance sheet as at the end of the year;

    (ii) extract from the statements you have prepared, two further important ratios;

(b) assume that this is the first time that M Limited has calculated any financial ratios and state the advice you would give to the directors to enable them to use this approach most effectively.

(ICMA)

QUESTION 7

The annual accounts of LM Limited, a company selling both at home and overseas, discloses the following figures at the 31st December:

	19-9	19-0
	£	£
Sales for year	3,700,000	4,400,000
Trade debtors, at year end	680,000	1,085,000
	days	days
Rate of collection	67	90

You are required to:

(a) suggest reasons for the deteriorating rate of debt collection;

(b) indicate the measures the company should take to improve the collection of debts and cash flow and set out the control and accounting information you would require for this purpose.

(ICMA)

QUESTION 8

Below is the (simplified) published Profit and Loss Account of a company. From it you are required:

(a) to compute NINE *useful* accounting ratios, for the current *and* previous years; and

(b) to attempt an appraisal of the changes in the company's efficiency and profitability, as between the two years.

Enterprise PLC
Profit and Loss Account for the year ended 30 une 19-1

£000	£000		£000	£000
800		Turnover		1,000
110		Net Trading Profit		150
		after charging:		
	40	Directors' Emoluments	45	
	8	Auditors' Fees and Expenses	10	
	25	Depreciation	30	
30		Income from Listed Investments (gross)		25
140				175
(27)		Interest on 15% Debentures (gross)		(27)
113		Net Profit Before Taxation		148
		Taxation:		
	(35)	Corporation Tax - Current Year	(50)	
	(15)	Transfer to Deferred Taxation	(20)	
	(10)	Tax Credits on Investment Income	(8)	
	(60)		(78)	
	5	Overprovision in Previous Year	6	
(55)				(72)
58		Net Profit Before Extraordinary Items		76
9		Extraordinary Items (after taxation)		(14)
67		Net Profit for Year		62
		Dividends (Net):		
	(12)	Paid - 12% Preference	(12)	
	(15)	Paid - Ordinary	(20)	
	(20)	Proposed - Ordinary	(20)	
(47)				(52)
20		Retained Earnings for Year		10

(ACCA)

SECTION IV Chapter 2

QUESTION 1

The owner of a small business, Smith's Stores, is very concerned that his bank account is overdrawn at the end of 19-6 despite the fact that he made a profit during the year. He has asked you to explain the position to him and has brought along a copy of his latest balance sheet, as shown below:

Smith's Stores
Balance Sheets as at 31 December

	19-5				19-6	
Cost £	Deprec'n £	Net £		Cost £	Deprec'n £	Net £
			Fixed assets			
3,000	1,800	1,200	Premises	3,000	1,950	1,050
1,500	500	1,000	Fixtures/fittings	4,100	650	3,450
4,500	2,300	2,200		7,100	2,600	4,500
			Current assets			
	3,440		Stock		5,650	
	1,170		Debtors		2,660	
	3,200		Bank		–	
	140		Cash		250	
	7,950				8,560	
			less			
			Current liabilities			
2,150			Creditors	1,860		
–			Bank overdraft	2,000		
	2,150				3,860	
		5,800	**Working capital**			4,700
		8,000	**Net assets employed**			9,200
			Financed by:			
		7,300	Capital - opening balance			8,000
		3,400	Net profit for year			4,300
		10,700				12,300
		(2,700)	Drawings			(3,100)
		8,000	**Capital - closing**			9,200

Required:

Prepare a statement of source and application of funds for 19-6 in any format other than that illustrated in SSAP 10.

QUESTION 2

The facts are the same as in Question 1.

Required:

Prepare a statement of source and application of funds in the SSAP 10 format.

QUESTION 3

The balance sheets of Stubton Ltd, for internal circulation, at 30 September 19-5 and 19-6, disclosed:

Stubton Ltd
Balance Sheets as at 30 September

	19-5				19-6	
Cost £	Deprec'n £	Net £		Cost £	Deprec'n £	Net £
			Fixed assets			
70,000	10,000	60,000	Land and buildings	80,000	12,000	68,000
142,000	38,000	104,000	Plant and equipment	167,000	51,000	116,000
36,000	27,000	9,000	Vehicles	41,000	28,000	13,000
248,000	75,000	173,000		288,000	91,000	197,000

		Current assets			
53,600		Stock			74,100
24,800		Debtors			19,700
10,200		Bank balance			-
700		Cash			400
89,300					94,200
		less			
		Current liabilities			
36,900		Creditors	44,300		
15,400		Corporation tax	14,700		
11,800		Proposed dividends	13,500		
-		Bank overdraft	15,600		
64,100				88,100	
	25,200				6,100
	198,200				203,100
		Financed by:			
		Ordinary shares of			
	150,000	£1.00 per share			170,000
	10,200	Profit and loss			13,100
	160,200	Shareholders' funds			183,100
	38,000	Long term loans			20,000
	198,200				203,100

Notes:

1. Plant which had originally cost £29,600 and on which £11,200 depreciation had been provided, was sold for £23,700 in 19-6.
2. A vehicle which had originally cost £9,700 and on which depreciation of £5,100 had been provided, was sold for £3,900 in 19-6.
3. The additional shares in 19-6 were issued for cash.

Required:

Prepare a statement of source and application of funds for Stubton Ltd. for year ended 30 September 19-6, in any format other than that illustrated in SSAP 10.

QUESTION 4

The facts are the same as in Question 3.

Required:

Prepare a statement of source and application of funds , in the format illustrated in SSAP 10.

QUESTION 5

Assume that it is now 31st December, 19-9 and that the directors of J Limited are reviewing their company's financial position for the next two years.

From the information given below you are required to:

(a) prepare a forecast balance sheet for 31st December, 19-1;
(b) give your comments on any matters to which you feel the directors should give their attention.

Advance corporation tax should be ignored and workings should be shown.

J Limited
Balance sheet as at 31st December 19-9

	£000	£000
Issued share capital:		
5.6% Redeembale preference shares		1,000
Ordinary shares of £0.25 each, fully paid		4,500
Revenue reserves		8,600
10% Convertible unsecured loan stock 20-8 to 20-0		4,800
6% Mortgage debenture stock 19-8 to 19-2		5,000
Corporation tax, due 1st January 19-1		2,500
Current liabilities:		
Bank overdraft	1,345	
Corporation tax, due 1st January, 19-0	2,200	
Creditors and accrued charges	9,856	
Proposed dividends	1,327	
		14,728
		41,128

	Cost £000	Depr'n to date £000	£000
Fixed assets:			
Freehold land	1,060	–	1,060
Buildings	4,960	1,200	3,760
Plant and equipment	11,400	6,750	4,650
Vehicles	1,950	870	1,080
	19,370	8,820	10,550
Trade investments, at cost			650
Current assets			
Stocks			11,828
Debtors			15,700
Short-term deposits			2,400
			41,128

Forecast statement of source and applcation of funds:

	Year ending 31st December	
	19-0 £000	19-1 £000
Sources of funds:		
Profit before tax	4,230	5,260
Depreciation charged against profits:		
Buildings	120	144
Plant	1,063	970
Vehicles	460	550
Transfer from capital grants	(55)	(84)
Proceeds of fixed assets sold	170	330
Capital grants	380	270
	6,368	7,440

Disposition of funds:

Dividends paid	2,111	2,302
Tax paid	2,165	2,500
Purchase of fixed assets	3,193	3,883
Repayment of preference shares	1,050	–
Trade investments	160	–
	8,679	8,685

Decrease in funds available for use as working capital	2,311	1,245

Change in working capital:

Increase in stocks	2,470		4,080	
Increase in debtors	3,560		3,770	
Increase in creditors	(3,080)		(3,650)	
		2,950		4,200
Increase in bank overdraft		5,261		5,445

Further information is given as follows:

1. The preference shares are due to be redeemed immediately following the payment of their final half year dividend on 30th June 19-0.
2. December 19-0 is the final date for the holders of the 10% Convertible unsecured loan stock to exercise their option to convert into ordinary shares. All are expected to exercise this option, at the conversion rate of one ordinary share for two pounds nominal value of loan stock. They will receive their interest for the year (£480,000) and then rank for ordinary dividends in respect of the year ended 31st December 19-1.
3. The trade investment consists of 1.3 million shares in T Limited who have just announced a rights issue of two shares for every thirteen held at a price of £0.80 per share. The directors intend to take up the offer on behalf of J Limited.

	Year ending 31st December	
	19-0	19-1
	£000	£000
4. Proposed capital expenditure:		
Freehold land	220	–
Buildings	870	548
Plant and equipment	1,736	2,450
Vehicles	367	885
5. Proposed disposals:		
Plant and equipment, at cost	530	460
Plant and equipment, depreciation to date of sale	450	400
Vehicles at cost	–	580
Vehicles, depreciation to date of sale	–	490
6. Provision for corporation tax	2,000	2,600
Forecast interim dividend (payable October)	756	938
Forecast final dividend (payable March)	1,364	1,658

7. The corporation tax to be paid on 1st January, 19-0 will actually be £2,165,000, the original provision has not yet been adjusted.

(ICMA)

QUESTION 6

The forecast Balance Sheet of Shalstone Agricultural Products Ltd as at 30th June 19-7 is:

	Cost £	Dep'n £	Net £
Fixed Assets			
Land and buildings	200,000	–	200,000
Plant and machinery	160,000	90,000	70,000
Vehicles	15,000	7,000	8,000
Office equipment	2,000	800	1,200
	377,000	97,800	279,200
Current assets			
Stocks			
Raw materials	30,00		
Work-in-Progress	14,000		
Finished goods	26,000		
		70,000	
Debtors and prepayments		30,000	
Bank		14,000	
Cash		2,600	
		116,600	
Less **Current Liabilities**			
Creditors and accruals	27,000		
Proposed dividends	18,000		
Corporation Tax (on 19-5/-6 profits)	28,000		
		73,000	
Working capital			43,600
Net assets employed			322,800
Financed by:			
Share capital authorised, issued and fully paid			
200,000 Ordinary shares of £1 per share			200,000
Reserves			
Share Premium account		5,000	
Plant Replacement Reserve		20,000	
Appropriation Account		25,800	
			50,800
Shareholders' Funds			250,800
Deferred liabilities			
Corporation Tax (on 19-6/-7 profits)			32,000
Long term liabilities			
10% Debentures 19-5/19-1			40,000
			322,800

N.B. Advance Corporation Tax (ACT) payable and recoverable has been ignored.

The forecast Statement of Sources and Application of Funds for the year to 30 June 19-8 is:

	£	£
Sources of funds		
Profit for the year before tax	54,200	
Adjustments for items not involving movements of funds		
Depreciation	12,600	
Profit on sale of motor vehicle	(400)	
Total funds generated from operations		66,400
Funds from other sources		
Issue of 6% Debentures 19-5/19-3	47,700	
Sales of fixed assets - motor vehicle	1,000	
		48,700
		115,100
Application of funds		
Dividends paid	18,000	
Tax paid	28,000	
Purchase of fixed asssets - motor vehicle	5,800	
Redemption of 10% Debentures 19-5/-1	40,400	
		92,200
		22,900
Movements in Working Capital		
Increase/(decrease) in stock		
Raw materials	10,100	
Work-in-progress	2,600	
Finished goods	3,700	
Debtors and prepayments	4,200	
(Increase)/decrease in creditors (other than for		
dividends and tax) and accruals	(3,100)	
Increase/(decrease) in net liquid funds		
Bank	4,700	
Cash	700	
		22,900

Notes:

1. The charge for depreciation for the year is categorised:

	£
Plant and machinery	9,500
Vehicles (see also Notes 3. and 4. below)	2,900
Office machinery	200
	12,600

2. The amount shown for 6% Debentures 19-5/19-3 (£47,700) represents the issue of £50,000 of such debentures at £96 per cent. The issue cost, £300, and discount are to be debited to Share Premium account.

3. The amount shown for sale of motor vehicle (£1,000) is the agreed price at which a lorry is to be sold in August 19-7. The lorry originally cost £3,400 and depreciation on it to 30th June 19-7 is £2,600. Depreciation from this date to date of sale was £200 and has been included in the amount of depreciation of motor vehicles (£2,900) in Note 1. above.

4. The amount shown for purchase of motor vehicle (£5,800) is the cost of the new replacement vehicle. Depreciation on this vehicle from August 19-7 to June 19-8 has been included in the amount for derpeciation of motor vehicles (£2,900) in Note 1. above.

5. The 10% Debentures 19-5/19-1 are to be redeemed during the year at an expected price of £101 per cent. The premium on redemption is to be debited to Share Premium Account.
6. For year ended 30th June 19-8, the following forecast figures are also available.

	£
Corporation Tax (on 19-7/-8 profits)	26,000
Ordinary share dividends (to be declared at year end)	20,000
Transfer to Plant Replacement Reserve	5,000

Required:

Using the information given, prepare the forecast Balance sheet for this company as at 30th June 19-8.

QUESTION 7

From the following information **you are required** to prepare for your management, source and application of funds statements complying with Statement of Standard Accounting Practice No. 10 in respect of:

(a) year six only, and
(b) years six to nine inclusive.

Side by side presentation should be adopted. Advance corporation tax is to be ignored.

	Actual Year 5		Estimated Year 6		Year 7		Forecast Year 8		Year 9	
	£000	£000	£000	£000	£000	£000	£000	£000	£000	£000
Freehold property, at cost or valuation		1,234		1,234		1,560		1,560		1,300
Equipment, at cost	586		586		716		716		460	
Depreciation to date	(226)		(316)		(416)		(491)		(352)	
		360		270		300		225		108
		1,594		1,504		1,860		1,785		1,408
Quoted investments, at cost		–		392		621		–		–
Current assets:										
Stocks	875		975		1,254		1,390		1,280	
Debtors	1,588		1,872		2,170		2,483		1,965	
Cash	187		315		–		–		–	
		2,650		3,162		3,424		3,873		3,245
		4,244		5,058		5,905		5,658		4,653
Current liabilities:										
Creditors	925		1,418		1,502		1,270		995	
Proposed dividends	100		160		160		100		50	
Current tax	165		355		12		–		–	
Bank overdraft	–		–		810		813		490	
		(1,190)		(1,933)		(2,484)		(2,183)		(1,535)
		3,054		3,125		3,421		3,475		3,118
Ordinary share capital		1,500		2,000		2,000		2,000		2,500
Share premium		–		500		500		500		–
Reserves		554		625		921		975		618
9% Convertible loan stock		1,000								
		3,054		3,125		3,421		3,475		3,118

	Act'l Year 5 £000	Est'd Year 6 £000	F'cast Year 7 £000	Year 8 £000	Year 9 £000
Sales	9,593	11,170	12,257	11,890	8,958
Trading profit (loss) before tax	406	626	(123)	154	(282)
Depreciation charge for the year	120	90	100	75	36
Income from investments (gross)			48		
Profit on sale of investments			257		
Profit on sale of freehold property					30
Loss on sale of equipment					(55)
Taxation for the year	165	355	12		
Interim dividends payable during the year	50	40	40		

The equipment to be sold in year nine originally cost £256,000 in year five.

(ICMA)

QUESTION 8

You are required to prepare for B Limited a source and application of funds statement for 19-9, complying with Statement of Standard Accounting Practice No. 10 from the information given in schedule B issued with this paper.

Schedule B:

Information relating to B Limited:

	19-6 £000	19-7 £000	19-8 £000	19-9 £000
Sales	75,000	82,000	90,000	95,000
Depreciation	4,800	4,800	4,800	8,500
Rent of premises	3,000	3,000	3,000	–
Hire of plant	–	2,500	2,500	2,500
Research and development	–	60	100	170
Interest on loan stock	2,000	2,000	2,000	–
Premium on repayment of loan stock	–	–	–	3,000
Profit on sale of plant	–	–	–	(2,400)
Other costs	55,200	57,640	63,600	67,830
Total	65,000	70,000	76,000	79,600
Profit before tax	10,000	12,000	14,000	15,400
Taxation	5,000	6,500	7,000	7,500
Profit after tax	5,000	5,500	7,000	7,900
Dividends	3,500	3,500	3,500	4,500
Retained earnings	1,500	2,000	3,500	3,400
Ordinary share capital	40,000	40,000	40,000	55,000
Share premium	5,000	5,000	5,000	15,000
Reserves	2,200	4,200	7,700	6,100
10% unsecured loan stock	20,000	20,000	20,000	–
	67,200	69,200	72,700	76,100

Assets Employed				
Leasehold premises at cost	–	–	–	25,000
Depreciation	–	–	–	(2,500)
Plant and machinery at cost	48,000	48,000	48,000	60,000
Depreciation	(9,600)	(14,400)	(19,200)	(18,800)
Total fixed assets	38,400	33,600	28,800	63,700
Research and development	–	240	340	520
Current assets:				
Stock	15,600	18,200	20,000	22,000
Debtors	13,200	15,700	18,100	20,000
Cash in hand	16,000	22,060	26,960	–
Total	44,800	55,960	65,060	42,000
Current Liabilities:				
Trade creditors	10,000	12,000	14,000	20,000
Current tax	4,000	6,600	5,500	5,800
Proposed dividends	2,000	2,000	2,000	2,500
Bank overdraft	–	–	–	1,820
Total	16,000	20,600	21,500	30,120
Net current assets	28,800	35,360	43,560	11,880
Net assets employed	67,200	69,200	72,700	76,100

You are advised that:

(i) During 19-9 and prior to the rights issue, the company made a bonus issue of one new share for every eight shares already held.

(ii) At the beginning of 19-9, plant and machinery which had originally cost £16,000 and had a book value of £9,600 was sold and replaced with more modern equipment.

(ICMA)

QUESTION 9

(iii) From the following comparative Balance sheets and other information supplied, **you are required** to produce a Statement of Source and Application of Funds for the year ended 30 June 19-0, in a form suggested by SSAP 10, and showing taxes, and dividends, PAID as applications.

Progressive PLC
Balance Sheets, 30 June 19-9 and 19-0

	30 June 19-9		30 June 19-0	
	£000	£000	£000	£000
Net Assets				
Fixed Assets				
Cost		620		1,200
Depreciation		(180)		(400)
		440		800
Goodwill (cost *less* amortisation)		25		21
		465		821
Long-Term investments – Listed				
Cost		50		20
Current Assets				
Stocks	190		280	
Debtors	210		250	
Bank Balnces	15		–	
	415		530	

Current Liabilities				
Bank Overdraft	–		(38)	
Creditors	(150)		(175)	
Proposed Dividends (net)	(30)		(40)	
ACT on Proposed Dividend	(13)		(17)	
	(193)		(270)	
Net Current Assets		222		260
		737		1,101
Financed by				
Ordinary share Capital(£1 shares)		300		400
Reserves				
Share Premium Account	20		50	
Fixed Assets Revaluation Reserve	–		175	
Retained Earnings	34		60	
		54		285
		354		685
12% Debentures	300		300	
Discount unamortised	(12)		(9)	
		288		291
Deferred Taxation		50		71
Mainstream Corporation Tax				
- Current Year		45		54
		737		1,101

Notes

(i) Figures from Progressive PLC's Profit and Loss Account for the year ended 30th June 19-0:

	£000
Corporation Tax based on Current year's Profits	95
Transfer to Deferred Taxation Account	25
Tax Credits on Dividends Received	6
	126
Adjustment of Previous Year's Charge	(7)
	119

(Mainstream corporation tax payable 31 March after year-end)

Extraordinary Items (all after 52% corporation tax)(*Dr*)	24
Dividends (net): Ordinary	
- paid	20
- proposed	40
	60

(ii) Year ended 30 June 19-0:

Additions to fixed assets, at cost	430
Disposals of fixed assets (not revalued):	
depreciation accrued, to date	80
proceeds of sale	35
Revaluation of fixed assets: gross adjustment	250
Revaluation of fixed assets: depreciation adjustment	(75)

(no deferred taxation adjustment)

(iii) Long-term investments - listed: proceeds of sale   70

(iv) Corporation tax, 52%; income tax (basic rate), 30%

(v) All computations to the nearest £1,000

(ACCA)

SECTION V Chapter 1

QUESTION 1

The summarised balance sheets of E PLC and F PLC at 30 June 19-5 were:

	E PLC £000	E PLC £000	F PLC £000	F PLC £000
Ordinary shares of £1.00 per share		600		100
Reserves				
-profit and loss	230		60	
-general	70		-	
		300		60
		900		160
Tangible fixed assets		370		120
Investment in F PLC (80,000 shares)		250		
Net current assets		280		40
		900		160

When E acquired its holding, F's profit and loss and general reserve balances were £80,000 and £60,000 respectively.

Required:

Prepare the consolidated balance sheet of the E Group as at 30 June 19-5.

QUESTION 2

The facts are exactly the same as in Question 1, except that E's Investment in F cost £140,000 and E's net current assets were £390,000.

Required:

Prepare the consolidated balance sheet of the E Group as at 30 June 19-5.

QUESTION 3

The summarised balance sheets of G PLC and H PLC at 31 July 19-5 were:

	E PLC £000	E PLC £000	F PLC £000	F PLC £000
Ordinary shares of £1.00 per share		800		250
Reserves - profit and loss		125		90
Shareholders' funds		925		340
Long term loans		-		130
		925		470
Tangible fixed assets		145		370
Trade investments - loans		250		-
Investments in H PLC (250,000 shares)		180		-
Current assets				
Stock	270		190	
Debtors	200		50	
Bank and cash	70		35	
	540		275	

Current liabilities						
Creditors		<u>190</u>		<u>175</u>		
			350		100	
			<u><u>925</u></u>		<u><u>470</u></u>	

G had acquired its holding when H's profit and loss account had a credit balance of £25,000. Since that date, G has made a long term loan of £110,000 to H and, as a separate arrangement, has supplied H with trading stock (at cost) amounting to £150,000 for which H has not yet paid.

Required:

Prepare the consolidated balance sheet of the G Group as at 31 July 19-5.

QUESTION 4

The facts are exactly the same as in Question 3, except that the goods supplied to H for £150,000 had cost G £120,000 and H still had one third of these goods in stock at 31 July 19-5.

Required:

Specify the items in your answer to Question 3 which would be affected by these circumstances and the amounts by which they would alter.

QUESTION 5

The facts are exactly the same as in Question 4, except that, additionally, during the year G had also supplied H with plant which H retained as a fixed asset. The plant had cost G £210,000 but the transfer price was £270,000. H depreciates plant over a 10 year life using the sraight line method and assuming no residual value.

Required:

(a) Specify the items in the consolidated balance sheet which would be affected by these circumstances and the amounts by which they would alter.

(b) Prepare the consolidated balance sheet of the G Group as at 31 July 19-5, incorporating the above matters.

QUESTION 6

The facts are exactly the same as in Question 3, except that, subsequent to its acquisition, H declared and paid a dividend of £12,000 from pre-acquisition profits.

Required:

Rewrite the balance sheet of G PLC given in Question 3, incorporating the above matters. Ignore the taxation implications.

QUESTION 7

The facts are exactly the same as in Question 3, except that H subsequently declared a dividend of 20% out of post-acquisition profits. G's policy is not to take credit for investment income until it is actually received.

Required:

(a) State the effects of H's dividend declaration on the balance sheet of:
   (i)   G PLC;
   (ii) H PLC;
   (iii) G Group.

(b) State the effects on your answer to Question 7(a), of H's actual payment of the dividend, on the balance sheet of:

  (i) G PLC;

  (ii) H PLC;

  (iii) G Group.

QUESTION 8

The facts are exactly the same as in Question 7, except that G holds only 200,000 ordinary shares in H and G has also proposed a dividend of 12%.

Required:

Prepare the consolidated balance sheet of the G Group after the dividends have been proposed. Ignore the taxation implications.

QUESTION 9

The summarised balance sheets of three companies at 31 March 19-6 were:

	J PLC	K PLC	L PLC
	£000	£000	£000
Tangible fixed assets	852	687	504
Investment in subsidiary companies			
- J in K (640,000 shares)	461	-	-
- K in L (360,000 shares)	-	206	-
Net current assets	305	227	146
	1,618	1,120	650
Ordinary shares of £1.00 per share	1,000	800	600
Reserves			
- profit and loss	418	220	50
- other	200	100	-
	1,618	1,120	650

At the date of the acquisition by J of its holding, K's profit and loss account had a credit balance of £120,000 and other reserves £40,000. L's profit and loss account had a debit balance of £60,000 when K acquired its holding on the same day.

Required:

Prepare separate consolidated balance sheets of the J Group as at 31 March 19-6, using

 (a) the direct method, and

 (b) the indirect method

of consolidation.

QUESTION 10

M PLC had acquired 80% of the ordinary share capital of P PLC during 19-3. For the year ended 30 September 19-5, their individual summarised profit and loss accounts disclosed:

	M PLC £000	P PLC £000
Profit before tax (from trading activities)	723	426
Corporation tax	(305)	(126)
Profit after tax	418	300
Proposed dividends	(180)	(80)
Retained profit		
- for year	238	220
- brought forward	204	116
- carried forward	442	336

Retained profit brought forward by P included pre-acquisition profit, £56,000.

Required:

Prepare the consolidated profit and loss account for the M Group for year ended 30 September 19-5.

QUESTION 11

The facts are exactly the same as in Question 10, except that P also had 200,000 10% preference shares of £1.00 per share in issue (of which 20,000 had been acquired by M in 19-2) and on which the dividend had been paid.

Required:

Prepare the consolidated profit and loss account for the M Group for year ended 30 September 19-5.

QUESTION 12

The turnover and directors' emoluments of Q PLC and its subsidiaries R PLC and S PLC for year ended 30 June 19-6, are as shown below.

Sales to:	Sales by			
	Total £000	Q PLC £000	R PLC £000	S PLC £000
Q	261	-	89	172
R	484	64	-	420
S	274	210	64	-
External customers	10,567	6,652	2,720	1,195
	11,586	6,926	2,873	1,787

Directors' emoluments

Paid to:	Paid by			
	Total £000	Q PLC £000	R PLC £000	S PLC £000
Lambert	21	17	2	2
Marriott	19	15	2	2
Norton (Chairman)	38	38	-	-
Ortzen	45	33	7	5
Palin	8	-	8	-
Redoubt	6	-	-	6
	137	103	19	15

Required:

State the amounts which would appear in the consolidated profit and loss account of the Q Group for:

(a) turnover, and

(b) directors' emoluments

so far as information is available.

QUESTION 13

The facts are exactly the same as in Question 10, except that M PLC had also acquired 40% of the £200,000 equity share capital of T PLC during 19-3, when that company's reserves stood at £160,000, at a cost of £173,000.

For the year ended 30 September 19-5, data relating to T included:

	£000
Retained profit at 1 October 19-4	230
Profit before tax	300
Corporation tax	120
Extraordinary gain (net of tax)	90
Proposed dividends	20

Required:

(a) Prepare the consolidated profit and loss account of the M Group for the year ended 30 September 19-5.

(b) Prepare extracts from the M Group consolidated balance sheet as at 30 September 19-5, showing how the relevant data for T PLC would be incorporated. Ignore the taxation aspects.

QUESTION 14

The summarised consolidated accounts of the Y Group were as shown below:

Y Group
Consolidated profit and loss account
for year ended 31 December 19-6

	£000
Profit before depreciation	718
Depreciation	(211)
Profit before tax	507
Corporation tax	(126)
Profit after tax	381
Minority and outside interests	(78)
	303
Extraordinary loss	(161)
Profit for year attributable to Y PLC shareholders	142
Dividends proposed	(58)
Retained profit	
- for year	84
- brought forward	120
- carried forward	204

Y Group
Consolidated balance sheet
as at 31 December

19-5 £000		19-6 £000
-	Goodwill	44
711	Tangible fixed assets(at written down values)	1,291
711		1,335
	Current assets	
260	Stock	366
198	Debtors	289
187	Bank and cash	218
645		873
	Current liabilities	
213	Creditors	307
40	Proposed dividends	58
85	Taxation	126
338		491
307	Net current assets	382
1,018	Net assets employed	1,717
680	Ordinary shares of £1.00 per share	880
	Reserves	
120	- profit and loss	204
18	- other	18
818		1,102
-	Minority and outside interests	311
200	12% debentures	304
1,018		1,717

N.B. For simplicity, ACT has been ignored.

During 19-6, Y had acquired a controlling interest in X PLC, thus:

Net assets acquired	£000	Consideration	£000
- goodwill	44	- issue of	
- tangible fixed assets	403	-ordinary shares	200
- stock	81	-12% debentures	104
- debtors	60		
- creditors	(51)		
- minority interests	(233)		
	304		304

Required:

Prepare the group statement of source and application of funds for year ended 31 December 19-6, on each of the following bases:

(a) individual assets and liabilities of Y and X are merged, and

(b) net assets of X are shown as a single application.

QUESTION 15

On 1st January, 19-0, JK Limited acquired 55% of the ordinary share capital of L Limited at a price of 50 pence per share and 25% of the ordinary share capital of X Limited at a price of 55 pence per share. On 1st July, 19-0, it acquired a further 25% of the ordinary share capital of L Limited at 60 pence per share.

From the information given below you are required to prepare:
  (a)   a consolidated balance sheet for JK Limited as at 31st December, 19-0;
  (b)   a statement showing make up of retained profits in the consolidated balance sheet.

Workings must be shown.

  1. The balance sheets at 31st December, 19-0 were as follows:

	JK Ltd £	L Ltd £	X Ltd £
Share capital, issued and fully paid,			
Ordinary shares of 25p pence each	300,000	150,000	160,000
Capital reserve	126,000	40,000	12,000
Retained profits	113,000	52,000	72,000
Loan from L Limited	50,000		
Taxation	90,000	58,000	39,000
Creditors	52,800	39,000	45,700
Proposed dividend	45,000	27,000	28,000
L Limited, current account	2,400		
	779,200	366,000	356,700
Plant and machinery, at cost	310,000	162,000	296,400
less: depreciation	136,000	50,000	129,600
	174,000	112,000	166,800
Investments:			
Shares in subsidiary company	255,000		
Shares in associated company	88,000		
Loan to JK Limited		50,000	
Stocks and work-in-progress	122,000	96,000	95,200
Debtors	90,000	67,000	80,600
Bank	21,600	37,000	14,100
Dividends receivable	28,600		
JK Limited, current account		4,000	
	779,200	366,000	356,700

  2. Capital and reserves in L Limited amounted to £210,000 at 1st January, 19-0 and £234,500 at 1st July 19-0 (after provision for taxation).
  3. The summarised profit and loss accounts for the year ended 31st December, 19-0 were as follows:

	JK Ltd £	L Ltd £	X Ltd £
Profit	134,000	114,000	70,000
Dividends receivable	28,600	-	-
	162,600	114,000	70,000
Taxation	81,000	55,000	32,000
	81,600	59,000	38,000
Dividends payable, 1st March, 19-1	45,000	27,000	28,000
Retained profit for year	36,600	32,000	10,000

  4. Cash of £1,600 remitted by L Limited to JK Limited on 29th December, 19-0 was not received by the latter until 2nd January, 19-1.
  5. Advance corporation tax is to be ignored.

(ICMA)   741

QUESTION 16

X Limited holds shares in other companies as follows:

A Limited	150,000 ordinary shares of £1 each, acquired 1st July, 19-9
B Limited	80,000 ordinary shares of £1 each, acquired 1st April, 19-0
C Limited	30,000 ordinary shares of £1 each, acquired 1st January, 19-0

From the information given below you are required to prepare a consolidated profit and loss account for the year ended 31st December, 19-0. This account should show the make-up by company of the retained profit for the year ended 31st December, 19-0.

Workings should be shown.

1. The profit and loss accounts of the companies for the year ended 31st December, 19-0 are set out below:

	X Ltd £	A Ltd £	B Ltd £	C Ltd £
Trading profits	126,000	72,000	84,000	40,000
Dividends receivable	58,500	2,400	–	6,000
	184,500	74,400	84,000	46,000
Corporation tax	54,000	30,000	37,200	22,000
	130,500	44,400	46,800	24,000
Dividends proposed	90,000	30,000	36,000	12,000
	40,500	14,400	10,800	12,000
Balance brought forward	252,750	108,000	73,500	27,000
Balance carried forward	293,250	122,400	84,300	39,000

2. The issued share capital of the various companies, which has been unchanged since 1st January, 19-9 is as follows:

A Limited	200,000 ordinary shares of £1 each
B Limited	100,000 ordinary shares of £1 each
C Limited	120,000 ordinary shares of £1 each

3. Trading profits are deemed to accrue evenly throughout the year.
4. X Limited received a dividend of £4,200 from a trade investment during the year.
5. In September 19-0 X Limited sold a machine, which had cost £21,000 to B Limited for £25,000.
6. A 'group election' for tax purposes in respect of distributions was in force at all relevant times.
7. In the year ended 31st December, 19-9, A Limited made a profit of £60,000 of which taxation absorbed £27,000 and dividends £16,000.

(ICMA)

QUESTION 17

Below are the published Balance Sheets (summarised) of Wimsey Ltd, its subsidiary Bunter Ltd, and its associated company Vane Ltd, as at 31 December 19-0.

	Wimsey Ltd £	Bunter Ltd £	Vane Ltd £
Assets			
Freehold Land - cost or valuation	150,000	50,000	100,000
Freehold Buildings - cost or valuation	300,000	120,000	200,000
Freehold Buildings - depreciation	(50,000)	(20,000)	(40,000)
Plant - cost or valuation	500,000	180,000	300,000
Plant - depreciation	(200,000)	(90,000)	(140,000)
	700,000	240,000	420,000
Shares in Subsidiary (cost)	180,000	-	

Shares in Associated Company (cost)	120,000	-	-
Stocks	300,000	110,000	220,000
Debtors	150,000	50,000	120,000
Amount owed by Subsidiary	5,000	-	-
Bank and Cash Balances	25,000	-	40,000
	1,480,000	400,000	800,000

	£	£	£
Equity and Liabilities			
Share Capital - 12% Cumulative Preference (£1 shares)	100,000	-	-
Share Capital - ordinary (25p shares)	600,000	150,000	200,000
Share Premium Account	80,000	-	50,000
Fixed Assets Revaluation Reserve	-	-	100,000
Retained Earnings	100,000	61,000	85,000
	880,000	211,000	435,000
12% Debentures	300,000	100,000	200,000
Deferred Taxation	34,286	17,286	31,429
Corporation Tax - Current Year (*less* ACT)	40,000	12,000	25,000
Bank Overdraft	-	10,000	-
Creditors	140,000	34,000	80,000
Amount owing to Holding Company	-	5,000	-
Proposed Dividend (net)	60,000	7,500	20,000
ACT on Proposed Dividend	25,714	3,214	8,571
	1,480,000	400,000	800,000

Notes

(i) Wimsey Ltd acquired 480,000 ordinary shares in Bunter Ltd, by issuance of 400,000 of its own ordinary shares at an imputed price of 45p per share. At that time Bunter Ltd had reserves totalling £30,000.

(ii) Wimsey Ltd purchased 320,000 ordinary shares in Vane Ltd for cash, at a time when the latter company had retained earnings totalling £20,000, and no outstanding dividends. Vane Ltd has not issued any shares since then, but has subsequently revalued its fixed assets.

(iii) ACT (3/7ths in all cases) on proposed dividends has been offset against Deferred Taxation. Rate of corporation tax, 52%.

(iv)

	Wimsey Ltd	Bunter Ltd	Vane Ltd
	£	£	£
Deferred taxation	60,000	23,500	40,000
Amount due to holding company	—	2,000	—
ACT on proposed dividend	Nil	Nil	Nil

£25,000 of Wimsey Ltd's stock had been purchased from Bunter Ltd; cost to latter, £20,000. Cash remitted by Bunter Ltd, £3,000, was not received by Wimsey Ltd until January and had not been recorded in Wimsey Ltd's books prior to the year end.

You are required:

(a) to prepare a Consolidated Balance Sheet in vertical form as at 31 December 19-0; and

(b) to explain your treatment of the inter-company stock profit, and to describe ONE alternative treatment.

All figures are to be calculated to the nearest pound.

(ACCA)

QUESTION 18

Recently there has been discussion of the "equity" method of accounting for an investor company's equity interest in the shares of another company. One of the contentious points is whether this method should be used in the preparation of group accounts only, or also for the accounting records of the investor company.

M Ltd bought 75,000 shares out of the issued 100,000 shares of £1 in P Ltd on 1st January 19-0 for £3 per share payable in cash. At this date the share capital and reserves of P Ltd totalled £225,000 after including the assets at a fair value. During the year to 31st December 19-0 the profit after all charges and tax was £60,000 and a dividend of £30,000 was paid before the year end.

M Ltd bought 200,000 shares out of the issued share capital of 800,000 shares of £1 of R Ltd on 1st April 19-0 for £300,000 payable in cash. On 25th April 19-0, the sales director of M Ltd was appointed a director of R Ltd. He attended and participated at the subsequent meetings of the board. R Ltd had profits after tax for the year ended 31st December 19-0 of £250,000 and a first and final dividend of £100,000 was paid in respect of these profits on 30th December 19-0.

You are required to:

(a) present the journal entries to show how these transactions would be dealt with if they were included in the accounts of M Ltd using

    (i) the traditional cost method, and

    (ii) the equity method and

(b) compare (using appropriate figures from the data provided) these two methods in relation to the adjustments required in the subsequent preparation of consolidated accounts in respect of

    (i) a subsidiary company, and

    (ii) an associated company.

(ICAEW)

QUESTION 19

Below are the Profit and Loss Accounts of Plantagenet Limited, and of its subsidiary Tudor Limited, for the year ended 31 December 19-0.

Plantagenet Limited
Profit and Loss Account
for the year ended 31 December 19-0

	£	£	£
Turnover			5,000,000
Net Trading Profit			350,000
after charging			
Auditor's Remuneration		20,000	
Depreciation -			
Freehold Buildings	20,000		
Plant and Fixtures	100,000		
Motor Vehicles	30,000		
		150,000	
Dividends Received (gross) -			
From Subsidiary		51,429	
From Associated Company		85,714	
			137,143
Net Profit Before Interest			487,143
Interest Payable -			
On 12% Debentures (gross)		120,000	
Add: Amortisation of Discount			
on 12% Debentures		10,000	

		130,000
		357,143

Net Profit Before Taxation		
Taxation -		
Corporation Tax based on Current year's Profits	150,000	
Transfer from Deferred Taxation	(35,000)	
Tax Credits on Dividends Received	41,143	
Corporation Tax Overprovided in Previous Year	(5,000)	
		151,143
Net Profit Before Extraordinary Items		206,000
Extraordinary Items (after taxation)		(72,000)
Net Profit For Year		134,000
Dividends (net) -		
7% Preference - paid	17,500	
Ordinary - paid	25,000	
Ordinary - proposed	75,000	
		117,500
Retained Earnings For Year		16,500

Tudor Limited
Profit and Loss Account
for the year ended 31 December 19-0

	£	£	£
Turnover			2,000,000
Net Profit Before Interest			150,000
after charging			
Auditors' Remuneration		10,000	
Depreciation -			
Freehold Buildings	8,000		
Plant and Fixtures	50,000		
Motor Vehicles	18,000		
		76,000	
Interest (gross) -			
Receivable, on 12% Debentures in Holding Company		12,000	
Add: Amortisation of Discount on 12%			
Debentures in Holding Company		1,000	
		13,000	
Less: Payable, on Bank Overdraft		11,000	
			2,000
Net Profit Before Taxation			152,000
Taxation -			
Corporation Tax based on Current Year's Profits		60,000	
Transfer to Deferred Taxation		20,000	
Corporation Tax Overprovided in Previous Year		(3,000)	
			77,000
Net Profit Before Extraordinary items			75,000
Extraordinary items (after taxation)			24,000
Net Profit For Year			99,000
Dividends (net) -			
Ordinary - paid		25,000	
Ordinary - proposed		25,000	
			50,000
Retained Earnings For Year			49,000

Notes

(i) Plantagenet Limited owned 80% of the ordinary shares in Tudor Limited.

(ii) Inter-company sales (from Tudor to Plantagenet) in 19-0 were £250,000, of which £60,000 remained in stock at 31 December 19-0. These goods had cost Tudor £45,000. Corresponding figures of inter-company stocks at 31 December 19-9 were respectively £40,000, and £30,000.

(iii) Plantagenet Limited owned 40% of the ordinary shares of Stewart Limited, and had a seat on that company's board. Stewart's latest accounts, for the year ended 30 September 19-0, showed pre-tax profits £500,000, taxation £240,000, and extraordinary items (after taxation) £12,000 *Dr.*

(iv) 10% of Plantagenet's debentures were held by Tudor throughout the year 19-0.

(v) Inter-company stock profits are to be apportioned *pro rata* between majority and minority shareholders in Tudor, and appropriate deferred taxation adjustments are to be made in respect of them.

(vi) Goodwill arising on consolidation (as at the acquisition of Tudor by Plantagenet, 1 January 19-9), £30,000 is being amortised by the straight line method over five years.

(vii) Corporation tax 52%; income tax basic rate, 30%.

You are required:

(a) to prepare a Consolidated Profit and Loss Account of the group, in a form which enables a separate parent company Profit and Loss Account to be dispensed with; and

(b) to analyse the group retained earnings for the year ended 31 December 19-0 between the three companies concerned (as required by SSAP 1: Accounting for the results of associated companies), showing your workings throughout.

(ACCA)

QUESTION 20

On 31st December 19-0 the balance sheet of Hand Ltd showed an issued share capital of 100,000 ordinary shares of £1 each, fully paid, and a balance on revenue reserve of £72,000.

On that date the following transactions had taken place:

1. Hand Ltd purchased 80,000 ordinary shares of 50p each in Fingers Ltd for £96,000. Fingers Ltd had an issued share capital of 100,000 ordinary shares of 50p each, fully paid, and a balance on revenue reserve of £62,000. Some years ago Fingers Ltd had purchased as an investment 12,500 ordinary shares in Hand Ltd.

2. Hand Ltd purchased 40,000 ordinary shares of £1 each in Thumb Ltd for £25,000. Thumb Ltd had an issued share capital of 50,000 ordinary shares of £1 each, fully paid, and 50,000 10% cumulative preference shares of £1 each, fully paid, and a debit balance on revenue reserve of £20,000. The preference dividend was in arrear for 19-9 and 19-0, and no provision had been made in the accounts of Thumb Ltd.

3. Hand Ltd purchased 75,000 ordinary shares of £1 each in Digit Ltd for £100. Digit Ltd had an issued share capital of 100,000 ordinary shares of £1 each, fully paid, and a debit balance on revenue reserve of £120,000.

You are required to show how the above items would be reflected in the consolidated balance sheet of Hand Ltd on 31st December 19-0, and to provide detailed schedules showing the make up of the relevant figures.

(ICAEW)

QUESTION 21

The issued capitals in ordinary shares of £1 each of Amalgam Ltd, Drill Ltd and Probe Ltd were £400,000, £250,000 and £200,000 respectively. Drill Ltd also had issued 150,000 8% preference shares of £1 each. All the companies made up their accounts to 30th September in each year.

The following figures were extracted from the companies' records for the year ended 30th September 19-1:

	Amalgam Ltd	Drill Ltd	Probe Ltd
	£	£	£
Revenue reserves as on 30th September 19-0	29,690	42,000	64,000
Stocks on hand as on 30th September 19-0	90,270	167,230	96,540
Sales	1,151,250	938,000	756,000
Purchases	710,970	499,620	308,200
Overhead expenses	142,900	87,200	75,000
Distribution expenses	27,600	54,800	81,000
Interim deividends paid 1st April 19-1			
on ordinary shares	48,000	25,000	20,000
on preference shares		6,000	

You also obtain the following information:

1. On 1st May 19-1, Amalgam Ltd purchased 200,000 ordinary shares and 100,000 preference shares in Drill Ltd.
2. On 1st June 19-1 Amalgam Ltd purchased 150,000 ordinary shares in Probe Ltd.
3. The profits of Drill Ltd and Probe Ltd are deemed to accrue evenly throughout the year.
4. Amalgam Ltd buys goods for resale from Drill Ltd at a price which yields a profit to Drill Ltd of 33 $\frac{1}{3}$% on selling price. Amalgam Ltd also sells goods to Probe Ltd at price which yields a profit to Amalgam Ltd of 25% on selling price. In the stocks on hand as on 30th September 19-1, Amalgam Ltd held stocks purchased from Drill Ltd for £36,000 and Probe Ltd held stocks purchased from Amalgam Ltd for £28,000.
5. Stocks on hand as on 30th September 19-1 were: Amalgam Ltd £110,490; Drill Ltd £120,850; and Probe Ltd £84,740.
6. Provision for corporation tax based on the profits for the year at 52% is to be made as to: Amalgam Ltd £150,000; Drill Ltd £130,000; and Probe Ltd £145,000.
7. Amalgam Ltd proposes to pay a final dividend on ordinary shares of 33p; Drill Ltd a half-year's dividend on the preference shares and a final dividend on ordinary shares of 30p; and Probe Ltd a final dividend on ordinary shares of 40p.

You are required to prepare a consolidated profit and loss account of Amalgam Ltd and its subsidiary companies for the year ended 30th September 19-1, together with your consolidation schedules.

Ignore advance corporation tax.

(ICAEW)

QUESTION 22

Public consideration has recently been given to the composition of a group for the purpose of presenting the group accounts of a commercial organisation.

Consider the following data relating to the year ended 31st August 19-1 of Octopus Ltd and Uncertain Ltd.

	Octopus Ltd	Uncertain Ltd
Balance Sheet		
	£000	£000
Issued ordinary share capital	2,000	1,000
Reserves	3,450	2,000
Debentures	2,000	1,500
Current liabilities	4,550	2,500
	12,000	7,000
Fixed assets (net)	6,500	4,000
Investment in Uncertain Ltd at cost	2,000	-
Current assets	3,500	3,000
	12,000	7,000

Profit and loss account

Trading profit before tax	1,100	500
Dividend from Uncertain Ltd, including tax credit	130	-
Taxation	(630)	(200)
Profit after tax	600	300
Dividends paid	(300)	(200)
Retained	300	100

Octopus Ltd acquired 50% of the ordinary share capital of Uncertain Ltd on 1st September 19-0 for £2,000,000 when its reserves were £1,900,000 and sold this holding on 3rd September 19-1 for £2,050,000.

You are required to:

(a) prepare the 'group' profit and loss account and balance sheet on three bases:
   (i) when Uncertain is treated as a subsidiary,
   (ii) when Uncertain is treated as an associated company,
   (iii) when uncertain is treated as an investment;

(b) calculate relevant financial ratios from the financial data produced by these three bases; and

(c) comment on the validity of these three alternative bases.

(ICAEW)

Section VII

Appendices

I   Companies Acts 1985 and 1989 disclosure requirements

II Annual Report and Accounts 1989 –
    BPP HOLDINGS PLC

Appendix 1
Companies Acts 1985 and 1989

A. Disclosure Requirements
B. Summary of Main Requirements regarding Group Accounts

A. Disclosure Requirements

GENERAL.

1.0 On 11th March 1985, the Companies Act received the Royal Assent. It is an exceedingly lengthy statute comprising twenty seven parts which together contain seven hundred and forty seven separate sections. These are then followed by twenty five schedules.

1.1 This Act, along with three others - the Business Names Act 1985, the Companies Consolidation (Consequential Provisions) Act 1985 and the Company Securities (Insider Dealing) Act 1985 - consolidates the legislation contained in earlier Acts and statutory instruments etc. made under those Acts.

1.2 The earlier Acts referred to in 1.1. were repealed from the date the 1985 Act came into force on 1st July 1985. They are the Companies Acts 1948, 1967, 1976, 1980, 1981 and the Companies (Beneficial Interests) Act 1983.

1.3 This appendix is concerned only with the accounting disclosure provisions of this Act, as modified by the Companies Act 1989.

COMPANIES ACT 1985 PART VII AND SCHEDULE 4.

2.0 Included in this part are provisions dealing with, inter alia

format of accounts,
content of accounts,
notes to the accounts,
directors' report,
group accounts,
publication of accounts,
accounting exemptions,

each of which will be dealt with separately in the following sub- sections.

2.1 The accounts of certain types of companies, namely

banking, shipping and insurance companies (and their holding companies in each case), which
are classed as special category companies

are not dealt with in this Appendix.

2.2 One feature of the Act is that certain matters, hitherto required by a Statement of Standard Accounting Practice, are now mandatory by Statute.

2.3 An example of this is to be found in Part II Section A of Schedule 4, whereby the accounting principles to be applied in determining the amounts to be included in a company's accounts are stated as being:

presumption of going concern basis;
application of consistent accounting policies;
exercise of prudence concept;
application of accruals basis;
separate determination of each asset or liability (that is, 'setting-off' is not allowed).

Departures from the above principles are, however, allowed if the directors have special reasons for so doing but particulars of, reasons for and effect(s) of the departure must be given in notes to the accounts. (The first four items in the above list were part of the subject-matter of SSAP 2).

2.4 In connection with the prudence concept in 2.3, the Act states that only profits realised at balance sheet date are to be included in the profit and loss account. 'Realised' in this context means treated as realised by generally accepted accounting principles, and thus allows the (SSAP 9) practice of taking credit for profit during the life of long-term contracts, to be continued.

2.5 As an innovation in UK company law, the Act gives rules for the calculation of amounts for certain other assets and liabilities. In particular, items are permitted to be included according either to historical cost accounting rules or to alternative rules, thereby allowing, inter alia, current cost accounting based figures to be used.

2.6 The true and fair view principle is an overriding one to the extent that the requirements of the Companies Acts should not be complied with if adherence would result in a breach of this principle. However, particulars of, reasons for and effect(s) of such departures must be stated in notes to the accounts.

2.7 Except where otherwise stated, the rules and provisions of the Act apply equally to the accounts of individual companies and of groups.

FORMAT OF ACCOUNTS.

3.0 Schedule 4 Part 1 contains alternative formats for company balance sheets and profit and loss accounts. Companies are free to select the format which they prefer; once chosen, however, the format should be followed consistently in subsequent years unless there are valid reasons, which must be disclosed in the accounts, for not so doing.

3.1 Two alternative layouts are permitted for the balance sheet, one vertical, the other horizontal. These are shown as Formats 1 and 2, respectively.

3.2 In the case of profit and loss accounts, four alternatives are available, labelled Formats 1 to 4, respectively. Formats 1 and 2 are in vertical format and 3 and 4 in horizontal format. Formats 2 and 4 are suitable for manufacturing companies and 1 and 3 for trading companies.

3.3 Every balance sheet and every profit and loss account must show the items under the headings and sub-headings according to the chosen format unless, either the amounts are immaterial, or combination of items would facilitate assessment of the state of affairs or of profit or loss of a company.

3.4 Combination of items can, however, apply only to those items labelled in the format with Arabic numerals; main headings and main sections labelled (respectively) with capital letters and Roman numerals must never be combined. (The letters and numerals included in the formats are for identification purposes only and need not be shown in the actual published accounts).

BALANCE SHEET - FORMAT 1 (vertical layout).

3.5

A. Called up share capital not paid
B. Fixed assets

   I   Intangible assets

      1. Development costs
      2. Concessions, patents, licences, trade marks and similar rights and assets
      3. Goodwill
      4. Payments on account

   II Tangible assets

      1. Land and buildings
      2. Plant and machinery
      3. Fixtures, fittings, tools and equipment
      4. Payments on account and assets in course of construction

   III Investments

      1. Shares in group undertakings
      2. Loans to group undertakings
      3. Participating interests (excluding group undertakings)
      4. Loans to undertakings in which the company has a participating interest
      5. Other investments other than loans
      6. Other loans
      7. Own shares

C. Current assets

   I   Stocks

      1. Raw materials and consumables
      2. Work in progress
      3. Finished goods and goods for resale
      4. Payments on account

    II   Debtors

        1. Trade debtors

        2. Amounts owed by group undertakings

        3. Amounts owed by undertakings in which the company has a participating interest

        4. Other debtors

        5. Called up share capital not paid

        6. Prepayments and accrued income

    III   Investments

        1. Shares in group undertakings

        2. Own shares

        3. Other investments

    IV   Cash at bank and in hand

D.   Prepayments and accrued income

E.   Creditors: amounts falling due within one year

    1. Debenture loans

    2. Bank loans and overdrafts

    3. Payments received on account

    4. Trade creditors

    5. Bills of exchange payable

    6. Amounts owed to group undertakings

    7. Amounts owed to undertakings in which the company has a participating interest

    8. Other creditors including taxation and social security

    9. Accruals and deferred income

F.   Net current assets (liabilities)

G.   Total assets less current liabilities.

H.   Creditors: amounts falling due after more than one year

    1. Debenture loans

    2. Bank loans and overdrafts

    3. Payments received on account

    4. Trade creditors

    5. Bills of exchange payable

    6. Amounts owed to group undertakings

    7. Amounts owed to undertakings in which the company has a participating interest

    8. Other creditors including taxation and social security

    9. Accruals and deferred income

I.   Provisions for liabilities and charges

    1. Pensions and similar obligations

    2. Taxation, including deferred taxation

    3. Other provisions

J.   Accruals and deferred income

K.   Capital and reserves

    I   Called up share capital

    II   Share premium account

    III   Revaluation reserve.

    IV   Other reserves

        1. Capital redemption reserve

        2. Reserve for own shares

3. Reserves provided for by the articles of association

4. Other reserves

V Profit and loss account

BALANCE SHEET - FORMAT 2 (horizontal layout).

3.6

ASSETS

A. Called up share capital not paid

B. Fixed assets

   I Intangible assets

      1. Development costs

      2. Concessions, patents, licences, trade marks and similar rights and assets

      3. Goodwill

      4. Payments on account

   II Tangible assets

      1. Land and buildings

      2. Plant and machinery

      3. Fixtures, fittings, tools and equipment

      4. Payments on account and assets in course of construction

   III Investments

      1. Shares in group undertakings

      2. Loans to group undertakings

      3. Participating interests (excluding group undertakings)

      4. Loans to undertakings in which the company has a participating interest

      5. Other investments other than loans

      6. Other loans

      7. Own shares

C. Current assets

   I Stocks

      1. Raw materials and consumables

      2. Work in progress

      3. Finished goods and goods for resale

      4. Payments on account

   II Debtors

      1. Trade debtors

      2. Amounts owed by group undertakings

      3. Amounts owed by undertakings in which the company has a participating interest

      4. Other debtors

      5. Called up share capital not paid

LIABILITIES

A. Capital and reserves

   I Called up share capital

   II Share premium account

   III Revaluation reserve

   IV Other reserves

      1. Capital redemption reserve

      2. Reserve for own shares

      3. Reserves provided for by the articles of association

      4. Other reserves

   V Profit and loss account

B. Provisions for liabilities and charges

      1. Pensions and similar obligations

      2. Taxation including deferred taxation

      3. Other provisions

C. Creditors

      1. Debenture loans

      2. Bank loans and overdrafts

      3. Payments received on account

      4. Trade creditors

      5. Bills of exchange payable

      6. Amount owed to group undertakings

      7. Amounts owed to undertakings in which the company has a participating interest

      8. Other creditors including taxation and social security

      9. Accruals and deferred income

D. Accruals and deferred income

6. Prepayments and accrued
income

   III Investments

      1. Shares in group undertakings

      2. Own shares

      3. Other investments

   IV Cash at bank and in hand

D. Prepayments and accrued income

PROFIT AND LOSS ACCOUNT - FORMAT 1 (vertical layout).

3.7

1. Turnover
2. Cost of sales
3. Gross profit or loss
4. Distribution costs
5. Administrative expenses
6. Other operating income
7. Income from shares in group undertakings
8. Income from participating interests (including group undertakings)
9. Income from other fixed asset investments
10. Other interest receivable and similar income
11. Amounts written off investments
12. Interest payable and similar charges
13. Tax on profit or loss on ordinary activities
14. Profit or loss on ordinary activities after taxation
15. Extraordinary income
16. Extraordinary charges
17. Extraordinary profit or loss
18. Tax on extraordinary profit or loss
19. Other taxes not shown under the above items
20. Profit or loss for the financial year

PROFIT AND LOSS ACCOUNT - FORMAT 2 (vertical layout).

3.8

1. Turnover
2. Change in stocks of finished goods and in work in progress
3. Own work capitalised
4. Other operating income
5. (a) Raw materials and consumables
   (b) Other external charges
6. Staff costs:

   (a) wages and salaries
   (b) social security costs
   (c) other pension costs

7. (a) Depreciation and other amounts written off tangible and intangible fixed assets
   (b) Exceptional amounts written off current assets
8. Other operating charges
9. Income from shares in group undertakings
10. Income from participating interests (including group undertakings)
11. Income from other fixed asset investments
12. Other interest receivable and similar income
13. Amounts written off investments
14. Interest payable and similar charges

15. Tax on profit or loss on ordinary activities
16. Profit or loss on ordinary activities after taxation.
17. Extraordinary income
18. Extraordinary charges
19. Extraordinary profit or loss
20. Tax on extraordinary profit or loss
21. Other taxes not shown under the above item
22. Profit or loss for the financial year.

PROFIT AND LOSS ACCOUNT - FORMAT 3 (horizontal layout).

3.9

A. Charges

1. Cost of sales
2. Distribution costs
3. Administrative expenses
4. Amounts written off investments
5. Interest payable and similar charges
6. Tax on profit or loss on ordinary activities
7. Profit or loss on ordinary activities after taxation
8. Extraordinary charges
9. Tax on extraordinary profit or loss
10. Other taxes not shown under the above items
11. Profit or loss for the financial year

B. Income

1. Turnover
2. Other operating income
3. Income from shares in group undertakings
4. Income from participating interests (excluding group undertakings)
5. Income from other fixed asset investments
6. Other interest receivable and similar income
7. Profit or loss on ordinary activities
8. Extraordinary income
9. Profit or loss for the financial year

PROFIT AND LOSS ACCOUNT - FORMAT 4 (horizontal layout).

3.10

A. Charges

1. Reduction in stocks of finished goods
2. (a) Raw materials and consumables
   (b) Other external charges
3. Staff costs:
   (a) wages and salaries
   (b) social security costs
   (c) other pension costs
4. (a) Depreciation and other amounts written off tangible and intangible fixed assets
   (b) Exceptional amounts written off current assets
5. Other operating charges
6. Amounts written off investments
7. Interest payable and similar charges
8. Tax on profit or loss on ordinary activities
9. Profit or loss on ordinary activities after taxation

B. Income

1. Turnover
2. Increase in stocks of finished goods and in work in progress
3. Own work capitalised
4. Other operating income
5. Income from shares in group undertakings
6. Income from participating interests (excluding group undertakings)
7. Income from other fixed asset investments
8. Other interest receivable and similar income
9. Profit or loss on ordinary activities after taxation
10. Extraordinary income
11. Profit or loss for the financial year

10. Extraordinary charges
11. Tax on extraordinary profit or loss
12. Other taxes not shown under the above items
13. Profit or loss for the financial year

3.11   It is apparent from an examination of the profit and loss account formats in 3.7 to 3.10 (above) that, contrary to expectation, three important items are missing, namely:

(a) profit before tax
(b) dividends paid and proposed
(c) transfers to reserves.

In fact these three items are required to be disclosed but the authority for their disclosure is contained within the narrative section of the general rules in Schedule 4 Part 1 Section A.

3.12   Other matters dealt with by these general rules are

(a) the permission to include in a company's balance sheet and profit and loss account, those items not included in set formats as assets, except that the following items must not appear in the balance sheet as assets

   (i) preliminary expenses,
   (ii) expenses of, and commission on, any issue of shares and debentures,
   (iii) research costs.

(b) the permission to include in a company's balance sheet and profit and loss account, those items prescribed by the set formats but in greater than legally required detail.

(c) the requirement to include, for all items, corresponding figures for the immediately preceding financial year, adjusted if necessary to the same basis as the current year figures.

CONTENTS OF ACCOUNTS

3.13   Amplification for the items in the various formats is to be found in notes in Schedule 4. The more important ones are:

Balance Sheet
Called up share capital not paid

   May be shown either at A or at C II 5.

Concessions, patents, licences etc. (B I 2)

   Include only if
   (a) the assets were acquired for valuable consideration and have not been included in goodwill; or,
   (b) the assets were created by the company.

Goodwill (B I 3)

   Include only to the extent that it has been acquired for valuable consideration.

Own shares (B III 7; C III 3)

   Separate disclosure required of nominal value.

Debtors (C II 1 to 6)

   For each item, separate disclosure is required of amount due after more than one year.

Prepayments and accrued income

   May be shown either at C II 6. or at D.

Payments received on account (E 3 and H 3 (Format 1); C 3 (Format 2))

   Include only to the extent that they have not been shown as deductions from stock.

Debenture loans (E 1 and H 1 (Format 1); C 1 (Format 2))

> Separate disclosure required of convertible loans.

Other creditors including taxation and social security (E 8 and H 8. (Format 1); C 8 (Format 2))

> Separate disclosure required of creditors for taxation and social security.

Accruals and deferred income (E 9 and H 9 and J (Format 1); C 9 and D (Format2))

> In Format 1, may be shown at either E9 and H9 (as appropriate) or at J. In Format 2, may be shown at either C9 or at D.

Net current assets/liabilities (F (Format 1))

> Must take into account prepayments and accrued income at C II 6 or at D.

Called up share capital (K 1 (Format 1); A 1 (Format 2))

> Separate disclosure required of allotted share capital and amount of called up share capital.

Creditors (C 1 to 9 (Format 2))

> For each item, separate and aggregate amounts are required for creditors, falling due within one year and after more than one year.

3.14 Profit and Loss Account

Cost of sales (2. (Format 1); A 1 (Format 3). Distribution expenses (4. (Format 1); A 2 (Format 2)). Administrative expenses (5. (Format 1); A 3. (Format 2))

> Amounts appearing under these headings are after depreciation or diminution in value have been accounted for.

Income from other fixed asset investments (9. (Format 1); 11. (format 2); B 5. (Format 3); 12. (Format 4)). Other interests receivable and similar income (10. (Format 1); 12. (Format 2); B 6. (Format3); B 8. (Format 4).

> Separate disclosure required of income and interest derived from group companies.

Interest payable and similar charges (12. (Format 1); 14. (Format 2); A 5. (Format 3); A 7. (Format 4))

> Separate disclosure required of amount payable to group companies.

Depreciation and other amounts written off tangible and intangible fixed assets. (7 a. (Format 2); A 4 a. (Format 4))

> When accounts are prepared under Format 1 or Format 3, the amount concerned must be disclosed in a note to the profit and loss account.

NOTES TO THE ACCOUNTS

4.0 Part III of Schedule 4 of the 1985 Act is the main source of disclosures required to be given in notes to the accounts in respect of various matters not otherwise included in the accounts, together with Schedule 5 Part V and VI and Schedule 6 Parts I and II. The principal disclosures are itemised in the following subsections. These requirements have been modified in some particulars by the Companies Act 1989.

BALANCE SHEET NOTES.

4.1

Share capital

> Amount Authorised.
> For each class of share allotted:
> - number allotted
> - aggregate nominal value
> - amount of called up share capital paid

Redeemable shares

Earliest and latest permissible redemption dates. Whether redemption is mandatory or at company's option. Whether (and if so, what) premium is payable on redemption.

Shares allotted during current financial year

Reasons for allotment. Class(es) of shares allotted.
For each class allotted:

- number
- aggregate nominal value
- consideration received

Contingent right to allotment of shares

For the shares concerned:

- number
- description
- amount
- period during which right is exercisable
- price payable for the allotment

Debentures issued during current financial year

Reasons for issue. Class(es) of debenture issued.
For each class:

- amount issued
- consideration received

Convertible debentures

Amount of loan

Redeemed debentures

Particulars of company's power to reissue

Nominee and/or trustee holding of company's debentures

Nominal amount. Book value.

Fixed assets (Intangible assets, tangible assets and investments)

For each fixed asset heading in the balance sheet, or its notes where items are combined:

- cost or revaluation at the beginning and end of the financial year
- accumulated depreciation at the beginning and end of the financial year

Movements during the year, to show:

- revaluations
- additions
- disposals
- transfers to and from the category

Movements of accumulated depreciation during the year, to show effects on provisions of:

- charge for year
- disposals
- other movements

For fixed assets (other than listed investments) shown at a valuation (including a current cost valuation

- years and amounts of the valuations
- for fixed assets valued during the financial year

    - names or qualifications of the valuers
    - bases of valuation

For land and buildings, distinguish

- freehold
- long leasehold
- short leasehold

Development costs capitalised

Reasons for capitalisation. Period of write off

Goodwill (other than that arising on consolidation) shown as an asset

Period of write-off. Reasons for choosing that period

Investments (fixed and current)

Nominal value of own shares held. Listed investments analysed into

(a) listed on a recognised Stock Exchange, and

(b) other listed investments

Market value of listed investments if different from book value (NB. Not now required for unlisted investments). Stock Exchange value of listed investments if less than market value. Where at the end of its financial year, the company holds in another body corporate

(a) more than 10% of the nominal value of the issued shares of any class of equity share capital; or

(b) more than 10% of the allotted share capital; or

(c) share capital having a total book value exceeding 10% of its own assets

it must disclose

- name of the body corporate
- country of incorporation if outside Great Britain; or
- country of registration, if incorporated in Great Britain, if body corporate is registered in a different country from the company concerned.

Where at the end of its financial year, the company holds in another body corporate more than 20% of the allotted share capital, it must disclose the following additional information

- aggregate capital and reserves of that body corporate at the end of its most recent financial year
- the profit (or loss) of that body corporate.

Exemption from providing the foregoing information applies if,

- the company, itself being the wholly owned subsidiary of another body corporate incorporated in Great Britain, is exempt from preparing group accounts; or
- the company prepares group accounts which include those of the subsidiary; or
- the investment of the company in the shares of the subsidiary are included in the company's accounts, or in a note thereto, on the equity basis; or
- the body corporate is not required to delivery a copy of its balance sheet to the Registrar and does not otherwise publish that balance sheet in Great Britain or elsewhere and less than 50% of the nominal value of the allotted share capital of that body corporate is held by the company.

Reserves and provisions for liabilities and charges

For each reserve or provision heading in the balance sheet, or its notes where items are combined, if any amount is transferred

- to or from a reserve; or
- to any provision for liabilities and charges; or
- from any provision for liabilities and charges otherwise than for the purpose for which the provision was established

disclose

- opening and closing balances for the financial year
- sums transferred to and from reserves and provisions during that year
- source and application of transfers

- particulars of each provision included in "other provisions"
- treatment for taxation purposes of sums debited or credited to revaluation reserve

Provisions for taxation

Amount of any provision for taxation other than deferred taxation

Indebtedness

For each item of creditors in the balance sheet, or its notes where items are combined, disclose
- aggregate amounts included which are payable or repayable other than by instalments and fall due in more than five years after the financial year end
- aggregate amounts included which are payable or repayable by instalments, some or all of which fall due in more than five years after the financial year end
- aggregate amounts of instalments falling due in more than five years after the financial year end
- terms of payment or repayment and rate of interest payable for each debt, except that a general indication is sufficient if, in the opinion of the directors, an excessively long statement would result
- aggregate amount of secured liabilities
- an indication of the nature of the securities given

Where fixed cumulative dividends on the company's shares are in arrear, state
- amount of arrears
- period(s) for which dividends are in arrear, by class

Aggregate amount of proposed dividend

Guarantees and financial commitments

Particulars of any charge on the company's assets to secure the liabilities of any other person, showing, where practicable, the amount secured. Contingent liabilities
- amount or estimated amount
- legal nature
- whether, and if so, what security provided

Future capital expenditure
- aggregate or estimated amount contracted but not so far provided
- aggregate or estimated amount authorised but not so far contracted

Pension commitments

(a) included under any balance sheet provision, and
(b) for which no provision has been made
(c) separate particulars of commitments relating entirely or partly to pensions payable to past directors

Any other financial commitments, relevant to assessing the company's state of affairs, not provided for. Any commitments undertaken on behalf of, or for the benefit of the company's holding company or fellow subsidiary

Loans for acquisition of own shares

Aggregate amount, under any balance sheet heading of outstanding loans granted under Companies Act 1985 S 153(4)(a) (provision of money) or S 153 (4)(b) (making of loans) for an employees share scheme or under S 155 (provision of financial assistance by a private company).

Stocks

The difference, where any stocks bought or manufactured have been included in the balance sheet at amounts determined by one of the methods
- FIFO or
- LIFO or
- Weighted average or

- any other suitable method

and the amount differs materially from the relevant alternative amount, being, in the opinion of the directors, the most appropriate of

- the most recent actual purchase price, or
- the most recent actual production cost, or
- replacement cost

Debtors

For each item - the amount receivable after more than one year

Transactions with directors and connected persons

Particulars of non-exempt transactions, arrangements or agreements (loans, quasi-loans, securities and guarantees, credit transactions) and of any other transaction or arrangement in which a director or connected person had a direct or indirect material interest

- the principal terms of the transaction etc.
- statement that the transaction etc was made or subsisted during the year
- the name of the person for whom it was made (including the name of the director where a connected person is involved)
- the name of the director with the material interest and the nature of that interest

Where a loan or an agreement or an arrangement etc. of a loan is involved

- the maximum amount of liability during the period
- the borrower's liability for principal and interest at the start and end of the period
- amount of any overdue interest
- amount of any sum provided against the borrower's failure to repay the loan or its interest

Where a guarantee or security or an arrangement of either of these is involved

- the company's liability at the start and end of the accounting period
- the maximum amount of liability for which the company may become liable
- any amount paid or liability incurred in fulfilling the guarantee or discharging the security

Other non-exempt transactions - the value of the transaction, arrangement or agreement.

Exempt transactions etc. for which disclosure need not be made include

- transactions etc. between one company and another in which a director of one company is interested solely by virtue of his directorship
- directors' service contracts
- transactions etc. not entered into or subsisting during the accounting period
- credit transactions, guarantees and securities for credit transactions, assignments of or agreements to enter into credit transactions where the net amount for any director or connected person has been less than £5,000 throughout the period
- where a majority of other directors deem the transaction etc. to be immaterial
- transactions in which the director has an interest where the net amount for any director or connected person has been less than £1,000 throughout the period, or was less than the lower of £5,000 and 1% of the company's net assets

Transactions with officers

Particulars of loans, quasi-loans, credit transactions and of any guarantees, securities, assignments, arrangements and agreements in connection with these

- a statement of the transactions etc.
- the total amount outstanding at the end of the period for each type of transaction
- the number of officers for whom each type of transaction was made

PROFIT AND LOSS ACCOUNT NOTES

4.2

Interest on (or any similar charge)

> Bank loans, overdrafts and other loans
>
> - repayable, otherwise than by instalments, in full within 5 years
> - repayable, by instalments, in full within 5 years.
>
> Loans of any other kind. Interest on or charges on loans to the company from group companies are excluded from disclosure

Redemption of share capital and of loans

> Amounts set aside (separately for shares and loans)

Investment income

> From listed investments

Rents received

> Rents from land (net of outgoings, ground rents, rates, etc), if forming a material part of the company's revenue

Plant and machinery hire

> Amount charged against revenue

Auditors' remuneration

> Amount of fees and expenses

Depreciation

> Charge for the year (when profit and loss account Format 1 and Format 3 is used)

Taxation

> Basis of calculation of UK corporation tax and income tax. Particulars of special circumstances affecting the liability in respect of taxation of
>
> - profits; or
> - income; or
> - capital gains
>
> for
>
> - current financial year; and
> - succeeding financial years
>
> Amount of the charge for UK corporation tax. Amount of the charge for UK corporation tax before double taxation relief, if such is the case. Amount of the charge for UK income tax. Amount of the charge for taxation imposed outside the UK on profits, income and (so far as charged to revenue) capital gains. Each of the foregoing charges must be split between the items
>
> - tax on profit or loss on ordinary activities; and
> - tax on extraordinary profit and loss

Turnover

> Analysis of amount by
>
> - different class of business; and
> - geographically bounded areas
>
> except that
>
>> immaterial amounts may be aggregated with material classes or areas, and this information may be withheld, if the directors hold the opinion that disclosure would damage the best interests of the company and the fact of non-disclosure is stated

Pre-tax profit or loss

Analysis of amount by different class of business, the class boundaries to be identical with those used for the analysis of turnover

Staff

Average number of persons employed during the financial year. Average number of persons employed within each employee category. In respect of the average number of persons employed during the financial year

- amount of wages and salaries paid or payable in respect of the financial year
- social security costs incurred by the company
- other pension costs incurred

Preceding year items

Effect on the profit and loss account of items included in respect of any preceding year

Extraordinary items

Particulars of any extraordinary income or charge(s) arising in the financial year

Exceptional items

Effect on the profit and loss account of items within the ordinary activities of the company which, on account of size or incidence, are exceptional

Directors' emoluments

Emoluments (fees, salaries, bonuses, commissions, payments for accepting office, taxable allowances and perquisites, and pension scheme contributions) in aggregate. Payments to third parties for making available the services of a person as a director. Directors' or past directors' pensions, including monetary value of non-cash benefits, in aggregate. Compensation paid to directors or past directors for loss of office, including monetary value of non-cash benefits, in aggregate. Analysis of each of the above three aggregates between sums receivable by directors in respect of

- services as directors (or past directors)
- other offices

Where aggregate emoluments exceed £60,000 exclusive of pension scheme contributions and of emoluments of directors whose duties were discharged wholly or mainly outside the UK

- total emoluments of chairman (or chairmen, if more than one during the year)
- total emoluments of highest paid director(s) if more than those of the chairman
- the numbers of directors whose emoluments fall within bands of £5,000
- the number of directors who have waived their rights to receive emoluments and the total amount waived

Higher paid employees' emoluments

This requirement has now been abolished.

GENERAL REQUIREMENTS NOTES

4.3

Accounting policies

Statement of accounting policies adopted in determining amounts included in the balance sheet and in the profit and loss account (including policies in respect of depreciation and diminution in the value of assets)

Foreign currency translation

Basis of translation, in respect of any items originally denominated in foreign currencies, and accounted for in either the balance sheet or in the profit and loss account

Corresponding amounts

For every item stated in a note to the accounts, the corresponding amount of the immediately preceding financial year. Where the corresponding amount is not comparable, it should be adjusted and there should be disclosure of

- particulars
- reasons

Combination of amounts

Where amounts are combined in the balance sheet and profit and loss account formats, where permitted, (see subsections 3.3 and 3.4 above), individual amounts of combined items must be disclosed if material in amount

Capitalised interest

Interest incurred on capital borrowed to finance the production of any asset and included in the production cost of the asset

Assets included at other than historical cost

Where assets are included in the balance sheet under alternative accounting rules, ie at a valuation or at current cost,

- items concerned (individually)
- basis of valuation
- comparable historical cost and cumulative depreciation
- differences between valuation and historical cost amounts

(the last two disclosures are inapplicable to stocks)

DIRECTORS' REPORT

4.4

Principal, activities

Nature and significant changes during the financial year

Review

A fair review of the development of the business of the company and its subsidiaries during the financial year and their position at the end of it

Post balance sheet events

Particulars of important events, affecting the company, which occurred since the end of that financial year

Future developments

An indication of likely such developments in the business of the company and its subsidiaries

Research and development

An indication of the activities of the company and its subsidiaries

Fixed assets

Significant changes during the year

Land and buildings

Difference between market value and balance sheet value, if significant

Dividends

Amounts recommended

Reserves

Amounts transferred

Charitable and political contributions

Details, if in excess of £200

Directors' interests in shares in, and debentures of, the company

In lieu of a statement in the Directors' Report, there may now be given in notes to the accounts

- number and nominal value of shares and/or debentures
  - at the beginning of the financial year (or date at which appointment became effective)
  - at the end of the financial year
- statement that no such interests exist, if such is the case

Shares of the company bought by the company during the financial year

Number and nominal value of shares purchased. Aggregate consideration paid. Reasons for the purchase. Percentage of called-up capital represented by shares so purchased

Shares of the company otherwise acquired by the company during the financial year, or charged

In respect of shares acquired eg by forfeiture or surrender or made subject to a lien

- number and nominal value of shares
  - acquired by the company
  - acquired by another person
  - charged
- maximum number and nominal value of shares so acquired or charged, held by the company or other person at any time during the year
- number and nominal value of shares so acquired or charged, disposed of or cancelled at any time during the year
- percentage of called-up share capital represented by shares so acquired or charged in each of the above circumstances

In respect of shares so charged - amount of charge. In respect of share disposals (above) for money or money's worth - amount or value of consideration

Directors

Names of all directors during the year

The following matters, previously required to be disclosed in the Directors' Report, have already been included in either 4.1 or 4.2 as requiring disclosure in notes to the accounts:

Analysis of turnover by class of business
Analysis of pre-tax profit or loss by class of business
Particulars of shares issued during the financial year
Particulars of debentures issued during the financial year
Average number of staff and total remuneration during the financial year.

The following matters are no longer required to be disclosed at all

Particulars of exports
Corresponding amounts of preceding financial year

PUBLICATION OF ACCOUNTS

5.0 The Act lays down rules for publication of accounts. Publication arises when the company issues, circulates or otherwise makes available for public inspection in a manner calculated to invite any members, or class or members, of the public generally to read it.

5.1 Publication may give rise to

full accounts, or
modified accounts, or
abridged accounts

FULL ACCOUNTS

5.2 Full accounts are those which are prepared under the Companies Acts and which comply with all the disclosure requirements. They are laid before the company in general meeting.

ABBREVIATED ACCOUNTS

5.3   Small and medium sized companies (see 6.2 and 6.4) are allowed to file abbreviated accounts with the Registrar. As the description implies, less information is contained in abbreviated accounts. Abbreviation in the case of small companies is even more drastic. In all instances where abbreviated accounts are filed, full accounts must have been laid before the company in general meeting.

ABRIDGED ACCOUNTS

5.4   Abridged accounts are usually published in the business sections of newspapers. They are condensed versions of the full accounts. Accompanying abridged accounts must be a statement that

- the accounts are not full accounts
- full accounts have been delivered to the Registrar (or not)
- that the auditor has reported on the full accounts (or not) and that the audit report was qualified (or not)

ACCOUNTING EXEMPTIONS

6.0   The Act allows certain disclosure exemptions for private companies which are classed as medium sized and small sized.

MEDIUM SIZED COMPANIES

6.1   To be accorded this status, the company must, for the current and preceding year, satisfy at least two of the following criteria:

(i)   Turnover for the year not to exceed £8 m
(ii)   Balance sheet totals [A to D (Format 1); ASSETS (Format 2)] not to exceed £3.9 m.
(iii)   .Average number of persons employed by the company during the year not to exceed 250 per week.

After achieving medium sized company status, a company which fails to satisy the criteria in a single financial year, is able to retain that status provided that it then falls within the criteria in the year after that.

6.2   Modified accounts for a medium sized company include a profit and loss account in which the gross profit or loss is a single item comprising:

> Format 1 – items 1, 2, 3 and 6
> Format 2 – items 1 to 5
> Format 3 – items A1, B1 and B2
> Format 4 – items A1, A2, B1 and B4

There is no need to give the particulars of turnover, that is, the analyses by classes of business and by geographical areas.

SMALL-SIZED COMPANIES

6.3   To be accorded this status, the company must, for the current and preceding year, satisfy at least two of the following criteria.

(i)   Turnover for the year not to exceed £2 m.
(ii)   Balance sheet total [A to D (Format 1); ASSETS (Format 2)] not to exceed £0.975 m.
(iii)   Average number of persons employed by the company during the financial year not to exceed 50 per week.

After achieving small sized company status, a company which fails to satisfy the criteria in a single financial year is able to retain that status provided that it then falls within the criteria in the year after that.

6.4   Modified accounts for a small sized company comprise a modified balance sheet only, showing only those items to which a letter or Roman number is assigned in the formats

Information to be given in notes is limited to particulars of

- accounting policies
- share capital
- allotments of shares and debentures
- creditors due for repayment in more than five years
- security given for creditors due
- basis of translation of foreign currency into sterling
- corresponding figures for the previous year

The company's profit and loss account and directors' report is not required to be delivered to the Registrar.

B. Summary of Main Requirements regarding Group Accounts

GENERAL.

1.0 Publication of group accounts by a holding company first became a statutory requirement with the enactment of the Companies Act 1948. Subsequent Acts have modified the original requirements. These have now all been incorporated into the Companies Act 1985, as modified by the Companies Act 1989.

1.1 Under the law, a subsidiary undertaking is one of which another body corporate (termed a holding company) either is a member of it and controls the composition of its board of directors or holds or controls (for example, by agreement or contract) a majority of voting rights. This definition is extended to include any company which is in a subsidiary relationship to a holding company's subsidiary company. Such a company is referred to as a sub-subsidiary. The Companies Act 1989 has extended this further to include all undertakings, for example, partnerships, joint ventures etc., which the parent controls but does not own.

PUBLICATION OF GROUP ACCOUNTS

2.0 A holding company must lay group accounts, along with its own accounts, before the company in general meeting.

2.1 Exemption from the obligation to lay group accounts applies only if the holding company is itself at its financial year end the wholly owned subsidiary of another body incorporated within the European Community or, if the holding company's directors hold the opinion that

(a) inclusion is of no real value due to the insignificant amounts involved or the holding is exclusively for resale and has not previously been consolidated; or

(b) inclusion is impractical, or would involve disproportionate delay or expense; or

(c) the result would be misleading or harmful to the business; or

(d) dissimilarity of the business conducted by the holding company and subsidiary company, incompatible with the obligation to give a true and fair view.

(e) the group is small or medium sized and does not include a public company. The criteria stated in Part A of this appendix at para 6.1 apply. If the figures are <u>before</u> making consolidation adjustments, the turnover and asset limits are increased by 20%.

Secretary of State approval is required for c. and d.

2.2 When the holding company resorts to the exemption provisions it must annex a statement to its balance sheet, showing

(a) the reasons for exclusion;

(b) the net aggregate of the subsidiaries' revenue profits less losses so far as they relate to the holding company, but not included in its accounts, for

  (i) their financial years coinciding with or ending during that of the holding company, and

  (ii) the financial years since they became subsidiaries;

(c) the same information as for (b) (i) (ii) to the extent to which they are included in the holding company's accounts;

(d) any auditors' report qualifications on the subsidiaries accounts for the current year and any note or saving in those accounts calling attention to a matter which would otherwise have been referred to in such qualification, so far as the matter concerned is both material from the point of view of the members and is not covered by the company's own accounts, or a statement to the effect that this information is unobtainable, if such is the case.

On the application by, or with the consent of, the company's directors, the Secretary of State may direct that requirements a. to d. above shall either not apply at all or only to a limited extent.

2.3 The requirement stated in 2.2 (b) and (c) is inapplicable if the holding company is itself a wholly-owned subsidiary of another body incorporated in Great Britain if annexed to the balance sheet there is a statement to the effect that in the directors' opinion the aggregate value of the assets of the company consisting of shares in, or amounts owing from, the company's subsidiaries is the same as or more than the aggregate of the amounts at which those assets are stated(or included in) the balance sheet.

2.4   A statement must be annexed to the balance sheet of a holding company, whether or not it submits group accounts, stating, in relation to any subsidiaries whose financial years are not coterminous with its own

(a) reasons why the holding companies directors do not consider coterminous accounting years to be necessary;

(b) dates on which the subsidiaries' immediate past accounting years, ending before that of the holding company, ended or, where different ending dates are involved, the earliest and latest of those dates.

2.5   There is a general requirement that the financial years of a subsidiary company must coincide with that of the holding company. Statutory power is available to the Secretary of State to direct that the financial years do so coincide. The holding company's directors, however, have the discretion to reject the general requirement if, in their opinion, there are good reasons for so doing. Where the directors rely on this dispensation, that statement referred to in 2.4 (above) must be submitted.

FORM OF GROUP ACCOUNTS

3.0   Under normal circumstances group accounts should take the form of consolidated accounts, that is, accounts dealing with the affairs of the holding company and its subsidiaries as though they are a single entity. By this device, the accounts of different, individual companies are regarded as relating to a single company. This all-embracing "company", called a group, is an expedient means of accounting for these interlocking companies, but is in reality a legal fiction in that the group is not in itself a legally constituted body corporate with a separate existence.

3.1   Consolidated accounts for a group comprise

(a) a consolidated balance sheet showing the state of affairs, as of a single entity, of the holding company and its subsidiaries, and

(b) a consolidated profit and loss account showing the profit or loss, as of a single entity, of the holding company and its subsidiaries.

3.2   Employment of other forms of group accounts is at the discretion of the holding company's directors, if they hold the opinion that the purpose of presenting the same or equivalent information about the state of affairs and profit or loss of the company, or of presenting it that it may be readily appreciated by the company's members, could better be served by an alternative means.

3.3   Allowable alternative formats include

(a) sets of consolidated accounts dealing with the holding company and different groups of subsidiaries;

(b) separate accounts for each subsidiary;

(c) statements expanding information about the subsidiaries in the holding company's own accounts;

(d) any combination of (a), (b) and (c)

3.4   Information and figures appearing in the consolidated balance sheet and consolidated profit and loss account are aggregated from the separate balance sheets and profit and loss accounts of the companies involved but the holding company's directors are empowered to make adjustments (for example, to achieve uniformity of accounting policies).

3.5   Non-corporate joint ventures should be consolidated on an item-by-item, proportional consolidation, basis.

MAIN DISCLOSURE REQUIREMENTS OF THE COMPANIES ACT 1985 RELATING TO HOLDING COMPANIES AND SUBSIDIARY COMPANIES.

4.0 Statutory requirements regarding disclosure of figures and information in the accounts of all UK companies are contained in the Companies Act 1985, as modified by the Companies Act 1989. The main requirements are summarised earlier in this Appendix.

4.1 Accounts for groups of companies are prepared in accordance with the above noted provisions; in addition to these, however, certain special provisions apply to the accounts of holding and subsidiary companies.

4.2 The main legislation is contained in Sections 228 to 234, in Schedule 4 Part IV and in Schedule 5 Parts I to IV of the 1985 Act. These provisions, which have the effect of modifying and supplementing the general provisions, are summarised below.

4.3 In the holding company's balance sheet there must be separately disclosed:

as assets

 – shares in subsidiary companies
 – amounts owing (on loan or otherwise arising) from subsidiary companies

as liabilities

 – aggregate amount of indebtedness (on loan or otherwise arising) to subsidiary companies

4.4 As a note on the holding company's balance sheet or in a statement or report annexed to it, there must be disclosed, in respect of shares in and debentures of the company held by its subsidiary companies or their nominees,

 (a) the number
 (b) the description
 (c) the amount

Disclosure need not however be made if the subsidiary is concerned as personal representative or as a trustee and neither the company nor any subsidiary is beneficially interested under the trust except by way of security for the purposes of a transaction entered into by it in the ordinary course of business.

4.5 Where one company, which may or may not itself be a holding company, is a subsidiary of another company, there must be separately disclosed in its balance sheet, in respect of all bodies corporate of which it is a subsidiary or fellow subsidiary

as assets

 - aggregate amount of indebtedness to it distinguishing between
 (a) indebtedness in respect of debentures and otherwise; and
 (b) aggregate amount of assets consisting of shares in fellow subsidiaries

as liabilities

 - aggregate amount of indebtedness to all bodies corporate of which it is a subsidiary.

4.6 Disclosures required
 (a) when subsidiaries are not dealt with in group accounts; and
 (b) when the financial year end of a subsidiary is not coterminous with that of its holding company
have already been itemised in 2.2 and 2.4 (above) respectively.

4.7 Every holding company which has subsidiaries at the end of its financial year, must state in its accounts or, in a statement annexed to, or in a note on, those accounts in respect of each subsidiary company:
 (a) the name
 (b) the country of incorporation, if different from that of the holding company (for this purpose Scotland is regarded as a separate country)
 (c) the identity of the class and the proportion held of the nominal value of the shares of that class, distinguishing between nominee, holding company and (other) subsidiary company holdings.

4.8   Exemption from disclosure under 4.7 may be obtained if, in the opinion of the directors of the holding company

(a) disclosure would be harmful to the business interests of that company or any of its subsidiary companies, if

    (i) it is either incorporated outside the UK or, that not being the case, carries on business outside the UK; and

    (ii) the Secretary of State sanctions the non-disclosure

(b) the number of subsidiary companies is such that the particulars supplied would be excessively long; in this instance, disclosure is limited to the requisite details of those subsidiaries principally affecting the profit or loss, or the assets, of the holding company and its subsidiaries with a statement to that effect. The omitted details must, however, be included in the company's Annual Return.

4.9   Subsidiary companies must state in their accounts, or in a statement annexed to, or in a note on, those accounts the name of the body corporate regarded as the ultimate holding company together with its country of incorporation, if known. Exemption from such disclosure is available on the same grounds as noted in 4.8 (a) (i) and (a) (ii).

4.10   In the accounts of the holding company, the general disclosure provisions regarding investments and fixed asset valuation in relation to fixed assets consisting of interests in subsidiary companies, are inapplicable.

4.11   Where a holding company prepares group accounts but omits any subsidiary companies from the consolidation, disclosures regarding the excluded subsidiary companies is identical with that dealt with in 2.2, 4.3 and 4.4. (above).

GROUP ACCOUNTS NOTES

4.12
Holding company's profit or loss for the financial year

    Statement of

- amount included in the group profit and loss account
- reliance on S 228(7) CA 1985 which, when the group profit and loss account is framed as a consolidated profit and loss account and complies with the requirements of the CA 1985, allows a holding company not to publish its own profit and loss account

Group companies' balance sheet at the end of the financial year

    Separate disclosure by way of either

(a) subdivision of relevant items within the balance sheet, or

(b) notes to the accounts

of aggregate amounts attributable to dealings with, or interests in

- any holding company or fellow subsidiary of the company
- subsidiary of the company

Shares in and debentures of the holding company held by its subsidiaries

    Note stating

- number
- description
- amount

Group accounts not prepared as consolidated accounts

    The same information and disclosures as for consolidated accounts

Subsidiaries of the holding company not included in the consolidated accounts

    Disclosures required regarding the holding company's profit or loss for the financial year (see above) and the group companies' balance sheet at the end of the financial year (see above) to be as though the subsidiary companies results had been consolidated. Where the exclusion arises because either

(a) the holding company does not prepare group accounts, or

(b) the holding company prepares group accounts but excludes one (or more) subsidiaries

the following requirements apply in the case of the excluded subsidiaries

- reasons for exclusion (or for not preparing group accounts)
- statement of qualifications contained in the auditors' reports on their accounts for the financial years ending with or during the financial year of the company and any note which would otherwise have been referred to in such qualification, so far as it is
  - material
  - not covered by the company's own accounts

Aggregate amount of the total investment of the holding company in the shares of subsidiaries to be stated on the equity basis of valuation, or, where the company is the wholly owned subsidiary of a UK incorporated company

a statement that, in the opinion of the directors of the company, the aggregate value of the assets of the company, consisting of shares in, or amounts owing from, the company's subsidiaries is not less than the aggregate of the amounts at which those assets are stated or included in the company's balance sheet

Statement that any information regarding excluded subsidiaries is not available, if such is the case

Subsidiaries whose financial years are non-coterminous with that of the holding comapny

Reason for non-alignment of financial year ends. Dates on which subsidiaries' financial years ended before that of the company or the earliest and latest of those dates.

Appendix 2

Annual Report and Accounts 1989
B P P Holdings PLC

(Reproduced by permission of the Board of Directors)

DIRECTORS' REPORT

The directors submit their report and the audited financial statements for the year ended 31 December 1989.

Results and dividends

The group's trading profit for the year, after taxation and minority interests, amounted to £2,013,000.

The directors recommend a final ordinary dividend of 3.25 pence per share, amounting to £640,000 making a total of 5.25 pence per share (after adjusting for the one-for-one bonus issue on 15 September 1989) and £1,034,000 for the year, which leaves a profit of £979,000 to be retained.

The final dividend will be payable on 18 May 1990 to shareholders on the register on 20 April 1990.

Principal activities and business review

The group is engaged in education, training and related publishing. Past and future developments in the business of the group and the position of group companies at the end of the accounting period are dealt with in the Chairman's statement on page 3.

Future developments

The group intends to continue to develop its range of activities. Further acquisitions in related areas of business are also being sought.

Fixed assets

The changes in fixed assets during the year are summarised in the notes to the accounts. The most significant were in connection with the acquisition of two freehold properties for approximately £3,100,000, the acquisition of Language School Holdings NV which brought tangible assets valued at £2,955,000 into the group and the revaluation of the group's Shepherds Bush headquarters on 1 December 1989. The group's headquarters were professionally valued by Jaggard Baker at £6,900,000, an increase of £2,197,000 on cost. The basis of valuation was open market value for existing use.

Disabled employees

The group gives every consideration to applications for employment from disabled persons where the requirements of the job may be adequately covered by a handicapped or disabled person.

Employee involvement

Employees are encouraged to present their suggestions and views on the group's performance and senior employees are encouraged directly to participate in the success of the business through the company's share option scheme.

Share capital

On 17 March 1989 49,500 ordinary shares were issued when options granted under the BPP Share Option scheme were exercised.

On 14 July 1989 4,494,445 ordinary shares were issued in connection with the acquisition of Language School Holdings NV, Markus Verbeek en Co BV and to provide additional working capital for the group.

DIRECTORS' REPORT

On 15 September 1989 9,844,975 ordinary shares were issued fully paid as a one-for-one bonus issue to shareholders.

Details of these transactions and options outstanding at 31 December 1989 are shown in Note 19 to the accounts.

Close company status

The company is not a close company within the meaning of the Income and Corporation Taxes Act 1988.

Directors

Mr W E Nuttall was appointed a director on 13 July 1989 on the acquisition by the company of Language School Holdings NV. Mr W E Nuttall, a chartered accountant, is the chief executive officer of Language School Holdings NV.

Mr A D Brierley, the group's only non-executive director, resigned from the Board on 13 July 1989. Mr A D Brierley was a co-founder of the company. He resigned from the Board to pursue other business interests, although he remains as a non-executive director of a subsidiary company.

In accordance with the articles of association, Mr W E Nuttall retires and offers himself for re-election. He has a service contract with a subsidiary company which expires on 13 July 1994.

Mr J H Ruston retires by rotation and, being eligible, offers himself for re-election. He has a service contract with a subsidiary company which expires on 30 June 1994.

Given below are details of the interests in the shares of the company at 31 December 1988 or subsequent date of appointment and 31 December 1989 of those people who were directors of the company on 31 December 1989.

	Description of interest	Ordinary shares of 10p each		Options	
		1989	*1988	1989	*1988
R R Price	Beneficial	1,177,540	1,200,540	120,000	–
C C L Prior	Beneficial	940,000	960,000	120,000	–
	Non-beneficial	146,000	150,000	–	–
J A Cooper	Beneficial	289,398	291,898	60,000	–
J M D Cooper	Beneficial	202,000	201,000	170,000	110,000
B Coyle	Beneficial	50,000	50,000	110,000	90,000
W E Nuttall	Beneficial	–	–	60,000	–
J H Ruston	Beneficial	256,694	308,030	60,000	–

* Adjusted for one-for-one bonus issue on 15 September 1989

	Number of ordinary shares of 10p each	Price per share
Options are exercisable between:		
March 1989 and March 1996	40,000	80.0p
March 1990 and March 1997	40,000	127.5p
August 1991 and August 1998	80,000	160.5p
September 1992 and September 1999	540,000	216.0p

There have been no movements in the above interests since the year end.

Other than disclosed in Note 23 to the accounts, none of the directors held any interest, either during, or at the end of the financial year, in any material contract or arrangement with the company or any subsidiary company.

DIRECTORS' REPORT

Substantial shareholdings

On 19 March 1990 the following companies held shares representing over 5% of the company's share capital.

	Number of ordinary shares of 10p each	% of share capital
Legal & General Investment Management Limited	1,481,552	7.5
Prudential Portfolio Managers Limited	1,892,684	9.6
Sun Alliance Investment Management Limited	1,104,100	5.6

Apart from the directors' holdings above, no other notification of any interest in 5% or more of the share capital has been received.

Auditors

Arthur Young merged their practice with Ernst & Whinney on 1 September 1989 and now practise in the name of Ernst & Young. Accordingly, they have signed their audit report in their new name. Ernst & Young have expressed their willingness to continue in office as auditors and a resolution proposing their re-appointment will be put to members at the Annual General Meeting.

By Order of the Board
B COYLE
22 March 1990

AUDITORS' REPORT

TO THE MEMBERS OF BPP HOLDINGS plc

We have audited the financial statements on pages 9 to 28 in accordance with Auditing Standards.

In our opinion the financial statements give a true and fair view of the state of affairs of the company and the group at 31 December 1989 and of the profit and source and application of funds of the group for the year then ended and have been properly prepared in accordance with the Companies Act 1985.

ERNST & YOUNG
Chartered Accountants
London
22 March 1990

GROUP PROFIT AND LOSS ACCOUNT
FOR THE YEAR ENDED 31 DECEMBER 1989

	Note	1989 £'000	1988 £'000
Turnover	2	21,085	10,230
Cost of sales		(11,098)	(5,600)
		9,987	4,630
Distribution and administrative expenses		(7,087)	(2,981)
Operating profit	3	2,900	1,649
Other income	4	425	53
Interest payable	5	(95)	–
Profit on ordinary activities before taxation	8	3,230	1,702
Tax on profit on ordinary activities	9	(1,176)	(619)
Profit after taxation		2,054	1,083
Minority shareholders' interest		(41)	29
Profit attributable to members of the holding company	10	2,013	1,112
Dividends	11	(1,034)	(437)
Retained profit	20	979	675
Earnings per share	12	13.5p	10.8p *

A statement regarding the movement on reserves is given in Note 20 to the financial statements on page 24.

* Adjusted for one-for-one bonus issue on 15 September 1989.

GROUP BALANCE SHEET
AT 31 DECEMBER 1989

	Note	1989 £'000	1989 £'000	1988 £'000	1988 £'000
Fixed assets					
Tangible assets	13		13,119		3,860
Investments	14		944		–
			14,063		3,860
Current assets					
Stocks		957		502	
Debtors	16	6,593		2,785	
Cash at bank and in hand		4,055		985	
		11,605		4,272	
Creditors: amounts falling due within one year	17	10,908		3,805	
Net current assets			697		467
Total assets less current liabilities			14,760		4,327
Creditors: amounts falling due after more than one year	17		1,623		–
Provision for liabilities and charges					
Deferred taxation	18		78		–
			13,059		4,327
Minority interests			398		–
			12,661		4,327
Capital and reserves					
Called up share capital	19		1,969		530
Revaluation reserve	20		2,197		–
Share premium account	20		–		781
Other reserves	20		–		42
Capital reserves	20		6,043		1,642
Profit and loss account	20		2,452		1,332
			12,661		4,327

R R Price

Directors

C C L Prior

22 March 1990

COMPANY BALANCE SHEET
AT 31 DECEMBER 1989

	Note	1989 £'000	1989 £'000	1988 £'000	1988 £'000
Fixed assets					
Tangible assets	13		9,131		3,136
Investments	14		29		–
Investments in subsidiary companies	15		17,180		5,572
			26,340		8,708
Current assets					
Stocks		432		260	
Debtors	16	3,843		1,512	
Cash at bank and in hand		2,588		1,052	
		6,863		2,824	
Creditors: amounts falling due within one year	17	4,611		2,564	
Net current assets			2,252		260
Total assets less current liabilities			28,592		8,968
Creditors: amounts falling due after more than one year	17		568		–
			28,024		8,968
Capital and reserves					
Called up share capital	19		1,969		530
Revaluation reserve	20		2,197		–
Share premium account	20		–		781
Other reserves	20		13,021		4,879
Capital reserves	20		9,319		1,642
Profit and loss account	20		1,518		1,136
			28,024		8,968

R R Price

Directors

C C L Prior

22 March 1990

GROUP STATEMENT OF SOURCE AND APPLICATION OF FUNDS FOR THE YEAR ENDED 31 DECEMBER 1989

	1989 £'000	£'000	1988 £'000	£'000
Sources of funds				
Profit on ordinary activities before taxation less minority interests		3,189		1,731
Items not involving the movement of funds				
Minority interest in retained profits for the year	79		(29)	
Depreciation	636		477	
Profit on disposal of fixed assets	(27)		(11)	
Exchange gains on fixed assets and retranslation of acquisition balances	(39)		–	
		649		437
Total generated from operations		3,838		2,168
Funds from other sources				
Loan received to provide a hedge against foreign equity investments	568		–	
Loan received for purchase of property	1,400		–	
Net proceeds of issue of shares for cash	8,105		806	
Issue of shares for acquisition of subsidiaries	8,372		–	
Sale of fixed assets	162		107	
Hire purchase obligations on acquisition of subsidiaries	31		–	
		18,638		913
		22,476		3,081
Application of funds				
Repayment of loan	1,529		–	
Repayment of property loan	1,400		–	
Purchase of fixed assets	4,790		763	
Purchase of investments	71		–	
Adjustment to goodwill on acquisition of subsidiaries re prior years	17		4	
Acquisition of subsidiaries	11,480		251	
Dividends paid	659		374	
Tax paid	715		461	
		20,661		1,853
Components of increase in working capital				
Stocks	335		128	
Debtors/creditors	120		133	
		455		261
Increase in cash resources		1,360		967
		22,476		3,081

The analysis of the acquisition of subsidiaries is given on page 13

GROUP STATEMENT OF SOURCE AND APPLICATION OF FUNDS FOR THE YEAR ENDED 31 DECEMBER 1989

Analysis of the acquisition of subsidiaries

	Net assets acquired £'000		Discharged by £'000
Fixed assets	2,955	Cash paid for acquisitions	9,882
Investments	781	Cash paid for acquisition costs	494
Stock	120	Further consideration payable	1,104
Debtors/creditors	(1,733)		
Cash resources	1,379		
Taxation	(551)		
Long term creditors	(2,553)		
Deferred taxation	(42)		
Goodwill on acquisition	11,443		
Minority interests	(319)		
	11,480		11,480

1. **Accounting policies**

    (a) *Accounting convention*

    The accounts are prepared under the historical cost convention, modified to include the revaluation of certain land and buildings.

    (b) *Basis of consolidation*

    The group accounts consolidate the accounts of BPP Holdings plc and all its subsidiaries made up to 31 December each year.

    The group profit and loss account includes the results of subsidiary companies acquired during the year from the date of acquisition.

    In accordance with the exemption allowed by S.228(7) of the Companies Act 1985 the company has not presented its own profit and loss account.

    (c) *Goodwill*

    The goodwill arising on the acquisition of subsidiary companies is written off directly against reserves.

    (d) *Stocks*

    Stocks, which principally consist of finished goods, are valued at the lower of printed cost, which includes delivery costs, and net realisable value. Origination costs of new titles are absorbed into the printed cost of the first edition.

    (e) *Capitalised interest*

    The gross interest on loans to finance the acquisition and development of freehold properties, in the period up to occupation, is included in the cost. Tax relief on this interest is reflected in the taxation charge for the year.

    (f) *Depreciation*

    Depreciation is provided on all tangible fixed assets other than freehold properties at rates calculated to write off the cost, less estimated residual value, of each asset evenly over its expected useful life.

    Depreciation is not provided on freehold properties as the directors consider that this departure from SSAP 12 is justified on the grounds that the properties' remaining useful lives are more than 50 years and that since it is the company's policy to maintain them to a high standard any depreciation would be insignificant.

    (i)   Depreciation on leasehold properties is provided on a straight line basis over the duration of the leases, or over 10 years if no lease period.

    (ii) Depreciation on fixtures is at 20% per annum on cost.

    (iii) Depreciation on equipment is at $33^1/3\%$ per annum on cost.

    (iv) Depreciation on motor vehicles is at 25% per annum on cost.

    (g) *Deferred taxation*

    Provision is made for deferred taxation using the liability method on all timing differences expected to give rise to taxation liabilities in the foreseeable future. No credit is taken for reversal of differences which will give rise to reduced taxation liabilities in future years unless such reversals can be predicted with reasonable certainty.

    (h) *Foreign currencies*

    On consolidation, assets and liabilities of overseas subsidiaries are translated into sterling at the rates of exchange ruling at the balance sheet date. Income and source and application of funds statements are translated at average rates of exchange for the period.

    Exchange differences arising on consolidation and on foreign currency borrowings arranged to finance or provide a hedge against overseas investments together with the exchange differences on the carrying amount of the related investments, are dealt with as movements on reserves.

    Any other exchange differences are dealt with in the profit and loss account.

(i) *Lease and hire purchase commitments*

Rentals paid under operating leases are charged to income on a straight line basis over the term of the lease.

Assets obtained under hire purchase agreements are capitalised in the balance sheet and are depreciated over their useful lives.

The interest element of the rental obligations is charged to the profit and loss account over the period of the lease and represents a constant proportion of the balance of capital repayments outstanding.

2. Turnover

Turnover represents the invoiced amount of goods and services provided and is stated net of value added tax. Amounts invoiced at the year end but unearned are treated as deferred revenue.

	Consolidated turnover	
	1989	1988
Geographical analysis	£'000	£'000
United Kingdom [1]	14,957	9,512
Germany	1,030	–
Rest of Europe	2,988	–
Japan	1,185	–
Rest of world	925	718
	21,085	10,230

[1] Includes sales of 'English in England' in the United Kingdom to overseas customers

3. Operating profit

Profit is stated after charging/(crediting) the following items

	1989	1988
	£'000	£'000
Distribution expenses	316	249
Depreciation	622	477
Depreciation of assets under hire purchase agreements	14	–
Directors' emoluments	492	303
Operating lease rentals (see also Note 22)	345	246
Auditors' remuneration	121	40
Rental income	(17)	(44)

4. Other income

	1989	1988
	£'000	£'000
Income from listed investments	3	–
Interest receivable	422	53
	425	53

NOTES TO THE ACCOUNTS
AT 31 DECEMBER 1989

5. Interest payable	1989	1988
	£'000	£'000
Bank loans and overdrafts wholly repayable within five years	29	–
Other loans	60	–
Finance charges payable under hire purchase contracts	6	–
	95	–

Interest paid in the year of £28,000 on loans to finance the acquisition and development of freehold properties, in the period up to occupation, has been capitalised as part of the cost of the asset.

6. Emoluments of directors and senior employees	1989	1988
	£'000	£'000
Directors' emoluments (including pension contributions)	492	303

The emoluments, excluding pension contributions of the chairman and highest paid director, were:

	1989	1988
Chairman	82	52
Highest paid director	78	53

Emoluments, excluding pension contributions of other directors and those senior employees of the group earning in excess of £30,000, were within the following categories:

	Directors		Employees	
	1989	1988	1989	1988
£5,001 – £10,000	–	1	–	–
£15,001 – £20,000	1	–	–	–
£30,001 – £35,000	–	–	20	2
£35,001 – £40,000	–	–	8	1
£40,001 – £45,000	–	2	1	1
£45,001 – £50,000	–	–	2	–
£50,001 – £55,000	–	2	1	–
£55,001 – £60,000	3	–	–	–
£65,001 – £70,000	1	–	–	–
£70,001 – £75,000	1	–	–	–

7. Employees		
Average number of employees	1989	1988
Professional	480	187
Administrative	205	85
	685	272

	1989	1988
Remuneration	£'000	£'000
Wages and salaries	8,039	3,454
Social security costs	959	328
Other pension costs	11	7
	9,009	3,789

NOTES TO THE ACCOUNTS
AT 31 DECEMBER 1989

Other pension costs are payments to pension schemes on behalf of certain employees whose service contracts state that their employment is pensionable. Other than for these employees the group does not operate a pension scheme and therefore the provisions of SSAP 24 do not apply.

8. Profit on ordinary activities before taxation

The profit before taxation includes the results of Language School Holding NV and Markus Verbeek en Co BV from the date of acquisition. The effect on group profit before taxation of the results of Language School Holdings NV and Markus Verbeek en Co BV from 14 July 1989, the date of their acquisition, to 31 December 1989 is as follows:

	£'000
Language School Holdings NV	645
Markus Verbeek en Co BV	174
	819

9. Tax on profit on ordinary activities

	1989 £'000	1988 £'000
Based on profit for the year		
Corporation tax (@ 35%)	953	661
Deferred taxation	36	–
	989	661
Overseas taxation	171	–
	1,160	661
Taxation under/(over) provided in previous years	16	(42)
	1,176	619

10. Profit attributable to members of the holding company

Of the profit attributable to members of the holding company for the year, £1,289,000 (1988 – £1,048,000) has been dealt with in the accounts of the company.

11. Dividends

	1989 £'000	1988 £'000
Ordinary		
Interim paid 2.0p (1988 – 1.7p)	394	172
Final proposed 3.25p (1988 – 2.5p)	640	265
	1,034	437

The interim dividend for 1989 and the interim and final dividends for 1988 have been adjusted to reflect the one-for-one bonus issue made on 15 September 1989.

12. Earnings per share

The calculation of earnings per share is based on earnings of £2,013,000 (1988 – £1,112,000) and 14,891,952 ordinary shares (1988 – 10,285,312) being the weighted average number of shares in issue during the year.

The earnings per share on a fully diluted basis is not materially different.

13. Tangible fixed assets

GROUP	Land and buildings Freehold £'000	Short leasehold £'000	Fixtures £'000	Equipment £'000	Motor vehicles £'000	Total £'000
Cost or valuation						
At 1 January 1989	2,494	617	560	529	643	4,843
New subsidiaries	1,935	802	1,123	195	247	4,302
Exchange adjustments	35	14	47	6	9	111
Additions	3,724	90	291	275	410	4,790
Transfers	41	(41)	–	–	–	–
Disposals	–	–	(1)	(2)	(299)	(302)
Revaluation surplus	2,197	–	–	–	–	2,197
At 31 December 1989	10,426	1,482	2,020	1,003	1,010	15,941
Depreciation						
At 1 January 1989	–	100	300	323	260	983
New subsidiaries	–	561	632	73	81	1,347
Exchange adjustments	–	3	14	3	3	23
Charge for the year	–	66	172	208	190	636
Disposals	–	–	–	(1)	(166)	(167)
At 31 December 1989	–	730	1,118	606	368	2,822
Net book value						
At 31 December 1989	10,426	752	902	397	642	13,119
At 1 January 1989	2,494	517	260	206	383	3,860

Freehold land and buildings include £215,000 (1988 – £87,000) of interest capitalised in respect of loans to finance the acquisition and development of freehold properties to the date of occupation. Of the £215,000 capitalised, £100,000 relates to interest capitalised by Language School Holdings NV prior to acquisition by the group.

COMPANY	Land and buildings Freehold £'000	Short leasehold £'000	Fixtures £'000	Equipment £'000	Motor vehicles £'000	Total £'000
Cost or valuation						
At 1 January 1989	2,494	56	317	336	472	3,675
Additions	3,627	4	153	134	279	4,197
Transfers	41	(41)	–	–	–	–
Disposals	–	–	–	–	(230)	(230)
Revaluation surplus	2,197	–	–	–	–	2,197
At 31 December 1989	8,359	19	470	470	521	9,839
Depreciation						
At 1 January 1989	–	1	128	213	197	539
Charge for year	–	–	77	98	120	295
Disposals	–	–	–	–	(126)	(126)
At 31 December 1989	–	1	205	311	191	708
Net book value						
At 31 December 1989	8,359	18	265	159	330	9,131
At 1 January 1989	2,494	55	189	123	275	3,136

NOTES TO THE ACCOUNTS
AT 31 DECEMBER 1989

Freehold land and buildings include £115,000 (1988 – £87,000) of interest capitalised in respect of loans to finance the acquisition and development of freehold properties to the date of occupation.

Certain of the group's freehold properties were professionally valued by Jaggard Baker at 1 December 1989. The basis of valuation was open market value for existing use. If the land and buildings were sold at their valuation, tax liabilities of £800,000 would arise. The historical cost of freehold properties included at valuation is as follows:

	Group £'000	Company £'000
At 31 December 1989	4,703	4,703

Included in motor vehicles are the following amounts relating to assets acquired under hire purchase agreements.

	Hire purchase £'000
GROUP	
Cost	
At 1 January 1989	–
New subsidiaries	82
Additions	25
At 31 December 1989	107
Depreciation	
At 1 January 1989	–
New subsidiaries	14
Charge for the year	14
At 31 December 1989	28
Net book value	
At 31 December 1989	79

14. Investments

	1989 £'000
GROUP	
Cost	
At 1 January 1989	–
Acquisitions of subsidiaries	781
Exchange adjustments	92
Additions	71
At 31 December 1989	944

Investments comprise the following:

	£'000
Investments listed on a stock exchange	835
Fixed term deposits	109
	944

The market value of investments, which are listed on a recognised stock exchange at 31 December 1989, was £837,000.

	1989 £'000
COMPANY	
Cost	
At 1 January 1989	–
Additions	29
At 31 December 1989	29

The market value of investments, which are all listed on a recognised stock exchange at 31 December 1989, was £31,000.

15. Investments in subsidiary companies

	£'000
Cost	
At 1 January 1989	5,931
Cost of acquisitions	10,317
Deferred consideration payable for subsidiaries under terms of acquisition agreements	1,104
Exchange adjustments	187
At 31 December 1989	17,539
Amounts provided	
At 1 January 1989 and 31 December 1989	359
Net book value	
At 31 December 1989	17,180
At 1 January 1989	5,572

On 14 July 1989 the company acquired the whole of the issued share capital of Language School Holdings NV for £8,976,000 (including costs of acquisition). Further consideration of £675,000 is payable on 1 July 1990 under the terms of the acquisition agreement based on the adjusted profit of the Language School Holdings group to 31 December 1989.

Under the terms of the acquisition agreement deferred consideration up to a maximum of £9,225,000, payable in cash or shares at the option of BPP Holdings plc, may be payable based on the adjusted profit of the Language School Holdings group for the year to 31 December 1990.

On 14 July 1989 the company acquired 67.7% of the issued share capital of Markus Verbeek en Co BV for £1,341,000 (including costs of acquisition). Further consideration of Dfl600,000 (approximately £191,000) is payable on 1 May 1990 under the terms of the acquisition agreement based on the adjusted profit of Markus Verbeek en Co BV to 31 December 1989.

The company has entered into put and call options with the vendors of the company in respect of the balance of Markus Verbeek en Co BV's issued share capital, which are exercisable in January of each year from 1995 to 1999 inclusive. The maximum amount payable, based on operating profits for the three years prior to the exercise of the option and the net assets on the last day of the three year period, upon the exercise of either option is Dfl15,000,000 (approximately £4,800,000) which may be satisfied by a combination of cash and shares at BPP Holdings plc's option.

Deferred consideration of £238,000 is payable under the terms of the acquisition agreement for Mander Portman Woodward Limited. Further deferred consideration up to a maximum of £17,000 in cash may be payable. The amount and timing for payment of this consideration is dependent upon the company's turnover and upon its colleges being registered as schools by the Department of Education and Science.

NOTES TO THE ACCOUNTS
AT 31 DECEMBER 1989

Subsidiary companies

The group's principal trading subsidiaries are:

	Percentage of issued share capital held directly or indirectly by BPP Holdings plc	Country of registration or incorporation
Specialist publications		
Blackstone Press Ltd	77.5	England
D P Publications Ltd	100	England
Professional and vocational training		
Cadmus Ltd	51	England
CPE Courses Ltd	100	England
Mantech Training Ltd	100	England
Markus Verbeek en Co BV	67.7	The Netherlands
Academic Education		
Mander Portman Woodward Ltd	100	England
Language Training		
Executive Language Services KK	100	Japan
Linguarama Ltd	100	England
Linguarama Belgium SPRL	100	Belgium
Linguarama France SARL	100	France
Linguarama Iberica SA	100	Spain
Linguarama Italia Srl	100	Italy
Linguarama Nederland BV	50	The Netherlands
Linguarama Sprachen Institute GmbH	100	Germany
Linguarama Suomi OY	100	Finland

For all companies the country of registration or incorporation is also the principal country of operation.

16. Debtors

	Group		Company	
	1989 £'000	1988 £'000	1989 £'000	1988 £'000
Trade debtors	5,547	2,386	1,494	990
ACT recoverable	213	133	213	133
Other taxes	14	14	–	–
Subsidiary companies	–	–	1,973	270
Other debtors	324	64	41	21
Prepayments	495	188	122	98
	6,593	2,785	3,843	1,512
Amounts included above falling due in over one year				
Subsidiary companies	–	–	1,529	–
ACT recoverable	213	66	213	66
	213	66	1,742	66

17. Creditors

	Group		Company	
	1989 £'000	1988 £'000	**1989** £'000	1988 £'000
Amounts falling due within one year				
Bank overdrafts	331	–	–	–
Trade creditors	809	574	177	440
Subsidiary companies	–	–	1,065	763
Corporation tax	1,818	762	668	385
Other taxes and social security costs	826	317	158	99
Proposed dividend	640	265	640	265
Other creditors	1,914	282	1,232	166
Deferred revenue	3,477	1,216	351	302
Accruals	1,065	389	320	144
Obligations under hire purchase agreements (Note 22)	28	–	–	–
	10,908	**3,805**	**4,611**	**2,564**
Amounts falling due in over one year				
Bank loans	1,592	–	568	–
Obligations under hire purchase agreements (Note 22)	31	–	–	–
	1,623	**–**	**568**	**–**

Included in bank loans are:

A mortgage loan of £1,024,000 which is secured on one of the group's freehold properties. This loan bears interest at 2% over LIBOR (London Inter Bank Offer Rate) and is repayable over the next 24 years. Since the year end this loan has been repaid without any penalties.

A loan of Dfl1,750,000 (£568,000) which is secured by an equivalent sterling deposit. The loan, which was arranged to provide a hedge against foreign currency equity investments, bears interest fixed annually at $1/2$% over AIBOR (Amsterdam Inter Bank Offer Rate) and is repayable in $4^{1}/2$ years.

	Group		Company	
	1989 £'000	1988 £'000	**1989** £'000	1988 £'000
Borrowings				
Bank overdrafts	331	–	–	–
Bank loans (secured)	1,592	–	568	–
	1,923	**–**	**568**	**–**
Total borrowings are repayable as follows				
In five years or more	1,024	–	–	–
Between two and five years	568	–	568	–
Between one and two years	–	–	–	–
	1,592	**–**	**568**	**–**
Within one year	331	–	–	–
	1,923	**–**	**568**	**–**

NOTES TO THE ACCOUNTS
AT 31 DECEMBER 1989

18. Deferred taxation

Deferred taxation provided in the accounts and the amounts not provided are as follows:

	Provision		Not provided	
	1989 £'000	1988 £'000	1989 £'000	1988 £'000
GROUP				
Capital allowances in advance of depreciation	18	–	21	13
Other differences in recognising revenue and expense items in other periods for tax purposes	60	–	6	7
	78	–	27	20
Taxation on valuation surplus	–	–	800	–
	78	–	827	20
COMPANY				
Capital allowances in advance of depreciation	–	–	2	–
Other differences in recognising revenue and expense items in other periods for tax purposes	–	–	6	7
			8	7
Taxation on valuation surplus	–	–	800	–
	–	–	808	7

19. Called up share capital

	Authorised number of 10p shares '000	Allotted and fully paid	
		Number of 10p shares '000	Nominal value £'000
At 1 January 1989	6,000	5,301	530
Increase in authorised share capital	21,600	–	–
Issued during year	–	4,544	455
One-for-one bonus issue	–	9,845	984
At 31 December 1989	27,600	19,690	1,969

The authorised share capital of the company was increased on two occasions during the financial year:

On 10 July 1989 the authorised share capital was increased from £600,000 to £1,380,000 by the creation of 7,800,000 new ordinary shares.

On 15 September 1989 the authorised share capital was increased from £1,380,000 to £2,760,000 by the creation of 13,800,000 new ordinary shares.

The following issues of shares were made during the financial year:

On 17 March 1989 49,500 ordinary shares were issued and allotted at 160 pence per share in accordance with the terms of the company's share option scheme.

On 14 July 1989 4,494,445 ordinary shares were issued pursuant to a placing at 375 pence per share (subject to clawback under an open offer to shareholders) for the acquisition of Language School Holdings NV, a 67.7% interest in Markus Verbeek en Co BV and to raise additional working capital for the group; 2,292,234 shares were consideration shares for Language School Holdings NV and 2,202,211 shares were for cash.

On 15 September 1989 9,844,975 ordinary shares were issued by way of one-for-one bonus issue to shareholders on the Register on 29 August 1989.

At 31 December 1989 options existed under the terms of the company's share option scheme as follows:

	Number of ordinary shares of 10p each	Price per share
Exercisable between:		
March 1989 and March 1996	42,000	80.0p
March 1990 and March 1997	50,000	127.5p
August 1991 and August 1998	163,000	160.5p
September 1992 and September 1999	826,000	216.0p
	1,081,000	

20. Reserves

	Capital reserves £'000	Share premium £'000	Other reserves £'000	Revaluation reserve £'000	P & L account £'000
GROUP					
At 1 January 1989	1,642	781	42	–	1,332
Issue of 49,500 shares under share option scheme	–	74	–	–	–
Issue of 2,202,211 shares for cash	–	8,038	–	–	–
Issue of 2,292,234 shares as consideration	–	–	8,367	–	–
Costs of above issues	–	(232)	(225)	–	–
Issue of 9,844,975 shares as a one-for-one bonus	–	(984)	–	–	–
Goodwill on acquisition of subsidiaries	–	–	(11,460)	–	–
Exchange adjustments	–	–	–	–	141
Transfer (approved by court)	7,677	(7,677)	–	–	–
Revaluation surplus	–	–	–	2,197	–
Utilisation of special reserves to write off goodwill on consolidation	(3,276)	–	3,276	–	–
Retained profit for the year	–	–	–	–	979
	6,043	–	–	2,197	2,452

Exchange adjustments comprise gains on consolidation of £201,000 less a loss on foreign currency borrowings of £60,000.

NOTES TO THE ACCOUNTS
AT 31 DECEMBER 1989

	Capital reserves £'000	Share premium £'000	Other reserves £'000	Reval- uation reserve £'000	P & L account £'000
COMPANY					
At 1 January 1989	1,642	781	4,879	–	1,136
Issue of 49,500 shares under share option scheme	–	74	–	–	–
Issue of 2,202,211 shares for cash	–	8,038	–	–	–
Issue of 2,292,234 shares as consideration	–	–	8,367	–	–
Costs of above issues	–	(232)	(225)	–	–
Issue of 9,844,975 shares as a one-for-one bonus	–	(984)	–	–	–
Exchange adjustments	–	–	–	–	127
Transfer (approved by court)	7,677	(7,677)	–	–	–
Revaluation surplus	–	–	–	2,197	–
Retained profit for the year	–	–	–	–	255
	9,319	–	13,021	2,197	1,518

Exchange adjustments comprise a gain arising on the retranslation of the equity investment in Markus Verbeek en Co BV partially offset by related foreign currency borrowings.

21. Effect of acquisitions during the year

(a) *Goodwill written off*

	£'000
Acquisition of Language School Holdings NV (including £675,000 of deferred consideration)	10,205
Acquisition of Markus Verbeek en Co BV (including £191,000 of deferred consideration)	1,000
Deferred consideration for Mander Portman Woodward Ltd	238
Fair value adjustment in connection with the acquisition of Blackstone Press Ltd	17
	11,460

As explained in Note 15, the final consideration in respect of these acquisitions has not yet been determined. As a result, additional goodwill may arise in future years.

NOTES TO THE ACCOUNTS
AT 31 DECEMBER 1989

(b) *Fair value of acquisitions*

Language School Holdings NV

	£'000	Unaudited consolidated accounts as at date of acquisition and fair value to the group £'000
Consideration		
Issue of 2,292,234 shares at 375 pence as a vendor placing		8,596
Additional consideration		675
		9,271
Acquisition costs		420
		9,691
Net assets acquired		
Tangible fixed assets		2,955
Stocks	120	
Debtors	2,537	
Cash	1,312	
Taxation	(436)	
Other creditors	(4,351)	
Net current liabilities		(818)
Creditors over one year		(2,553)
		(416)
Deferred taxation		(42)
Total net liabilities		(458)
Minority interests		(56)
Total net liabilities attributable to group		(514)
Goodwill on consolidation written off to reserves		10,205

There were no significant fair value or other accounting adjustments.

NOTES TO THE ACCOUNTS
AT 31 DECEMBER 1989

Markus Verbeek en Co BV

		Unaudited accounts as at date of acquisition and fair value to the group
	£'000	£'000
Consideration		
Initial consideration		1,286
Additional consideration		191
		1,477
Acquisition costs		74
		1,551
Net assets acquired		
Investments		781
Debtors	187	
Cash	67	
Taxation	(115)	
Other creditors	(106)	
Net current assets		33
Total net assets acquired		814
Minority interests		(263)
Total net assets attributable to group		551
Goodwill on consolidation written off to reserves		1,000

There were no fair value or other accounting adjustments.

22. Obligations under leases and hire purchase agreements

Rentals payable by the group during 1990 under operating leases will be as follows:

	Leasehold property
	£'000
Leases expiring within one year	63
Leases expiring within two to five years	330
Leases expiring in more than five years time	534
	927

Amounts payable under hire purchase agreements are as follows:

	£'000
Amounts payable	
Within one year	35
Within two to five years	39
	74
Less finance charges allocated to future periods	15
	59
Shown as	
Current obligations	28
Non current obligations	31
	59

23. Director's interest in a contract

Mr J Ruston has an interest in a freehold property relating to a lease granted to a subsidiary company on which the total annual rent payable is £48,000. The Board of Directors considers this to be a fair market rent.

24. Capital commitments

Amounts authorised by the directors but not contracted for were £800,000 (1988 – nil) for the group and £760,000 (1988 – nil) for the company.

NOTICE OF ANNUAL GENERAL MEETING

NOTICE IS HEREBY GIVEN that the Annual General Meeting of the members of BPP Holdings plc will be held on 15 May 1990 at 5 pm at BPP House, Aldine Place, 142/144 Uxbridge Road, London, W12 8AA for the following purposes:

AS ORDINARY BUSINESS

1. To receive, approve and adopt the Accounts for the year ended 31 December 1989 together with the reports of the directors and auditors.

2. To declare a final dividend.

3. To re-elect Mr J H Ruston, a director, retiring by rotation in accordance with Article 84 of the Articles of Association of the Company and, being eligible, offering himself for re-election.

4. To re-elect Mr W E Nuttall, a director, retiring pursuant to Article 90 of the Articles of Association of the Company and, being eligible, offering himself for re-election.

5. To re-appoint Ernst & Young as auditors and to authorise the directors to fix their remuneration.

AS SPECIAL BUSINESS

To consider and, if thought fit, to pass the following Resolution, being that numbered 6 as a Special Resolution:

6. THAT in substitution for any existing authority for the purposes of Section 95 of the Companies Act 1985 the Directors be and are hereby given power to allot equity securities (within the meaning of Section 94 of the said Act) for cash pursuant to their general authority for the purposes of Section 80 of the said Act as if sub-section (1) of Section 89 of the said Act did not apply to any such allotment provided that this power shall be limited to the allotment of equity securities up to an aggregate nominal amount of £49,224.80 and shall expire (unless previously revoked varied or extended) on the earlier of the conclusion of the Annual General Meeting of the Company to be held in 1991 and 30 June 1991 save that the Company may before such expiry make an offer or agreement which would or might require equity securities to be allotted after such expiry and accordingly the Directors may allot equity securities pursuant to such an offer or agreement as if such authority had not expired.

BPP House
Aldine Place
142/144 Uxbridge Road
London
W12 8AA

By Order of the Board

B COYLE
Secretary
22 March 1990

NOTES

1. A member entitled to attend and vote is entitled to appoint one or more proxies to attend and vote instead of him. A proxy need not be a member of the Company. A form of proxy is enclosed with this notice for use in connection with the business set out above. Completed forms of proxy must reach the Company's Registrars, Ravensbourne Registration Services Limited, 34 Beckenham Road, Beckenham Kent BR3 4TU not later than 48 hours before the time appointed for holding the meeting.

2. All service contracts between the Company or any subsidiary and the Company's directors will be available for inspection 15 minutes prior to and during the Annual General Meeting and at the registered office of the Company during the period of the notice.

3. The Board of Directors of the Company recommend each of Mr J H Ruston and Mr W E Nuttall for appointment to the Board.

NOTICE OF ANNUAL GENERAL MEETING

EXPLANATORY NOTE

Special business

Resolution 6 above will, if passed, confer a new authority on your Directors to deal with the issue of shares for cash otherwise than to existing Shareholders on a proportional basis. The Stock Exchange does not require Shareholders to give their consent to each specific issue by the Company of shares for cash made otherwise than to existing Shareholders on a proportional basis, provided the Company obtains Shareholders' authority under Section 95 of the Companies Act 1985 to disapply the provisions of Section 89(1) of such Act. The effect of the Resolution will be to disapply such sub-section and enable the Directors to issue shares for cash up to an aggregate nominal amount not exceeding £49,224.80, being equal to 2.5% of the Company's current issued share capital, without first offering them to existing Shareholders. This authority will expire on 30 June 1991 or, if earlier, on the date of the Company's next Annual General Meeting. Although there is no present intention of issuing any shares (other than pursuant to the Company's Share Option Scheme) your Directors consider it desirable to maintain the flexibility afforded by these provisions. It is envisaged that the renewal of such provision will continue to be sought on an annual basis.

Directors' recommendation

The Directors are of the opinion that the Resolution referred to in this note is in the best interests of the Company and its Shareholders and the Board accordingly recommends that you vote in favour of the Resolution. Each Director proposes to so vote his own beneficial holdings, totalling 2,915,632 Ordinary Shares representing 14.8 per cent of the present issued share capital of the Company. In addition the Trustees of the non-beneficial holding of a Director intend to vote in favour of the Resolution in respect of the holding of 146,000 Ordinary Shares, representing 0.7 per cent of the present issued share capital of the Company.

FIVE YEAR FINANCIAL REVIEW

	1985 £'000	1986 £'000	1987 £'000	1988 £'000	1989 £'000
Turnover	2,164	2,796	5,995	10,230	21,085
Operating profit	397	545	924	1,649	2,900
Interest (net) and investment income	8	80	137	53	330
	405	625	1,061	1,702	3,230
Less non-recurring directors' emoluments	250	–	–	–	–
Profit on ordinary activities before tax	155	625	1,061	1,702	3,230
Taxation	65	244	371	619	1,176
Profit after tax	90	381	690	1,083	2,054
Minority interest	–	–	–	29	(41)
Profit for the year	90	381	690	1,112	2,013
Dividends	–	168	314	437	1,034
Added to reserves	90	213	376	675	979
Earnings per share* (pence)	(1) 6.10	6.90	8.65	10.80	13.50
Dividends per share* (pence)	–	2.80	3.30	4.20	5.25

*   Adjusted for the one-for-one bonus in 1989
(1)   Adjusted for notional tax rate of 35% and excluding non-recurring directors emoluments

	1985 £'000	1986 £'000	1987 £'000	1988 £'000	1989 £'000
Share capital and reserves	301	1,211	3,132	4,327	12,661
Minority interests	–	–	–	–	398
Borrowings (over one year)	–	–	–	–	1,623
	301	1,211	3,132	4,327	14,682
Tangible assets	167	216	3,670	3,860	13,119
Investments	–	–	–	–	944
Cash	68	1,222	(42)	985	4,055
Stocks, debtors less creditors (including deferred tax)	66	(227)	(496)	(518)	(3,436)
	301	1,211	3,132	4,327	14,682

Index
Advanced Accounting Practice 2.9

References are to Section, Chapter, Paragraph

A.
Accounting Standards Board III.4.3.11.
Accounting Standards Committee
    Discussion papers III.4.3.10.
    Exposure Drafts (EDs) III.4.3.10.
    Statements of Intent (SOIs) III.4.3.10.
    Statements of Recommended Practice (SORPs) III.4.3.10.
    Statements of Standard Accounting Practice (SSAPs) III.4.3.0.
    (individual SSAPs are listed under their respective headings)
Absorptions III.6.2.3.
Acquisition of controlling interest III.6.2.4.
Acquisitions and mergers V.2.1.0.
    SSAP 23 V.2.4.0.
Added value (see Value added)
Amalgamations III.6.2.1.
Annual Report and Accounts – DAKS Simpson Group PLC Appx II
Associated companies (see Groups)

B
Bills of Exchange II.8.1.0.
    Bills Payable II.8.2.3.
    Bills Receivable II.8.2.3.
    Discounting II.8.2.4.
Branches II.3.3.0.
    Branch accounts maintained by head office II.3.4.0.
    Transfers of goods at cost II.3.4.2.
    Transfers of goods at selling price II.3.4.3.
        Adjustment account method II.3.4.5.
        Memorandum column method II.3.4.4.
    Transfers of goods at cost plus a predetermined percentage II.3.4.6.
        Adjustment account method II.3.4.8.
        Memorandum column method II.3.4.7.
    Branch accounts maintained in branch ledgers II.3.5.0.
        Current accounts with head office II.3.5.3.
        Inter-branch current accounts II.3.5.5.
        Effect of transfer pricing on head office branch and total
        business results II.3.5.7.
        Items in transit II.3.5.9.
        Remittances II.3.5.8.
    Profit and loss account II.3.4.9.
Business combinations III.6.1.0.

C
Cash flow analysis IV.2.5.0.
Capital reconstruction III.7.2.5. III.7.3.4.
Capital redemption reserve (see Shares)

Capital reorganisation III.7.2.0. III.7.3.1.
Companies Acts 1985 and 1989 Appx I
    Main disclosure requirements Appx I
Clubs and societies I.4.1.0.
Combination of business III.6.1.0.
    Consignments II.1.1.0.
    Consignee's accounts II.1.3.25.
    Consignor's accounts II.1.3.4.
    Bills of exchange II.1.3.24.
    Foreign currency II.1.4.2.
    Stock losses II.1.3.15.
    Stock valuation II.1.3.13.
Consolidated accounts (see Group Accounts)
Containers II.10.1.0.
Contracts (long term) II.6.1.0.
    Amounts recoverable II.6.6.7
    Architects'/engineers' certificates method II.6.3.1.
    Costs incurred II.6.6.9 II.6.6.10
    Work in progress method II.6.3.8.
    Payments on account II.6.6.7
    Interim profit II.6.4.0. II.6.4.6.
    SSAP 9 II.6.4.6.
    SSAP 9 (Revised) II.6.6.0
    Valuation of work in progress II.6.5.0.
Convertible loan stock II.1.3.5.
Credit sales (see Hire purchase and)
Current cost accounting (CCA)
    Adjustments III.9.4.5.
        Cost of sales (COSA) III.9.5.14.
        Depreciation III.9.5.1.
        Gearing proportion III.9.5.40.
        Gearing III.9.5.36.
        Monetary working capital (MWCA) III.9.5.24.
    Advantages III.9.3.0.
    Defects of historical cost system III.9.2.0.
    Preparation and presentation of current cost accounts III.9.6.0.
    SSAP 16 III.9.4.0.
Current Purchasing Power (CPP) III.9.9.0.
    Monetary items III.9.9.5.
    Non-Monetary items III.9.9.5.

D

    Debentures III.1.3.0.
    Convertible loan stock III.1.3.5.
    Issue III.1.3.0.
    Redemption III.1.5.0.
        Redemption reserve III.1.5.5.
        Purchase in open market III.1.5.19.
        Sinking Fund III.1.5.8.
Distributable profits III.2.1.0.
    Realised losses III.2.2.1.
    Realised profits III.2.2.3.
    Unrealised profits III.2.2.4.
    Unrealised losses III.2.2.2.
    Public limited companies III.2.3.2.

E

Earnings per share III.8.1.0.

    Definition III.8.1.4.

    Fully diluted III.8.3.0.

        convertible securities III.8.3.7.

        options or warrants to subscribe III.8.3.16.

        separate class of equity share III.8.3.5.

    Issues

        for cash at full market pice III.8.2.1.

        for the discharge of a liability III.8.2.4.

        in exchange for the acquisition of an asset III.8.2.3.

        part of a capitalisation scheme (bonus issue) III.8.2.5.

        to secure a controlling interest in a subsidiary company III.8.2.8.

        rights issues III.8.2.10.

    Net basis III.8.1.6.

    Nil basis III.8.1.5.

    Negative EPS III.8.1.8.

    Scope and coverage III.8.1.3.

    Two or more classes of equity share III.8.1.11.

    SSAP 3 III.4.3.17.

F

Financial Reporting Council III.4.3.11.

Financial statement analysis and interpretation IV.1.1.0.

    Analytical methods IV.1.2.0.

    Balance sheet ratios IV.1.3.3.

    Classification of ratios by type IV.1.4.0.

    Efficiency and profitability IV.1.4.3.

    Long term solvency and stability IV.1.4.1.

    Other ratios IV.1.3.7.

    Potential and actual growth IV.1.4.4.

    Profit and loss account ratios IV.1.3.2.

    Profit and loss account to balance sheet ratios IV.1.3.6.

    Ratios in common use IV.1.3.0.

    Short term solvency and liquidity IV.1.4.2.

    Trading account ratios IV.1.3.1.

    Trading account to balance sheet ratios IV.1.3.5.

    Trading account to profit and loss account ratios IV.1.3.4.

    Validity of ratio analysis IV.1.5.0.

    (see also Cash flow analysis, Funds Flow analysis)

Foreign currency transactions II.11.1.0.

Foreign currency translation II.11.1.1.

    Basic closing rate method II.11.3.0.

    Basic temporal method II.11.2.0.

    Closing rate/net investment method II.11.4.12.

    Cover concept II.11.4.16.

    Equity investment financed by foreign currency loans II.11.4.16.

    Foreign branches II.11.5.0.

    Net investment concept II.11.4.10.

    Preparation of consolidated financial statements II.11.4.7.

    Preparation of individual company statements II.11.4.2.

    SSAP 20 II.11.4.0.

Funds flow analysis IV.2.2.0.

G

Goodwill V.1.9.0

    SSAP 22 V.1.9.2

Groups of companies

Acquisitions and Mergers IV.2.1.0.
    SSAP 23 IV.2.4.0.
Acquisition of control by degrees IV.1.4.59.
      interest in subsidiary during year IV.1.5.9.
      preference shares in subsidiaries IV.1.4.68.
Associated companies IV.1.6.0.
    SSAP 1 IV.1.6.1.
Balance sheets IV.1.4.0. IV.1.8.8.
      full holding acquired IV.1.4.2.
          at date of acquisition IV.1.4.13
      partial holding acquired IV.1.4.15
          at date of acquisition IV.1.4.18.
          subsequent to acquisition IV.1.4.20.
Changes in proportion of minority interests IV.1.4.65
Consolidated of sub-subsidiaries IV.1.4.78
          mixed groups IV.1.4.89.
Constraints IV.1.2.0.
    Legal IV.1.2.1.
    SSAP IV.1.2.2.
    Stock Exchange IV.1.2.4.
    Other IV.1.2.5.
Directors' remuneration IV.1.5.15.
Disclosure requirements (Companies Acts) Appx I
Dividends received from preacquisition profits IV.1.4.47.
Dividends received from post-acquisition profits IV.1.4.52.
Extraordinary items IV.1.5.18.
General background IV.1.1.0.
Group election for ACT purposes IV.1.5.19.
Holding and subsidiary companies IV.1.1.3.
Inter company dividends IV.1.4.46.
Inter company transactions IV.1.4.24.
Inter group indebtedness IV.1.4.27.
Intra group unrealised profit IV.1.4.30.
Mergers (see Acquisitions and)
Merger relief IV.2.2.0.
Mixed groups IV.1.4.89
Outside holding of preference shares IV.1.5.5.
Preparation and presentation of group financial
    accounts and statements IV.1.3.0.
Profit and loss accounts IV.1.5.0. IV.1.8.2.
    Proforma IV.1.5.20
    Publishing dispensation IV.1.5.12
SSAP 1 IV.1.6.1
SSAP 14 IV.1.3.3
SSAP 10 IV.1.7.1
SSAP 22 IV.1.9.2
SSAP 23 IV.2.4.0
Statements of source and application of funds IV.1.7.0.
    Format IV.1.7.1.
Turnover IV.1.5.13
Unrealised profit IV.1.4.41
    trading stocks IV.1.4.34.
    fixed assets IV.1.4.37

H

Hire purchase and credit sales II.4.1.0.

Goods bought on hire purchase II.4.3.0.
Goods sold on hire purchase II.4.4.0.
    large items II.4.4.3.
    small items II.4.4.11.
    Stock on hire II.4.4.16
Provision for unrealised profit II.4.4.25.
Repossessions II.4.4.35.
Hire purchase interest II.4.3.8.
    actuarial method II.4.3.10
    sum of the digits method II.4.3.12
SSAP 21 II.4.2.6.

I

Incomplete records I.1.1.0.
Investments II.7.1.0.
    Cum div./int. purchases II.7.2.3; II.7.3.2.
        Sales II.7.3.9.
    Ex div./Int. purchases II.7.2.9; II.7.3.6.
        Sales II.7.3.12
    Profit and loss on investments II.7.3.15
    Partial disposal of holding II.7.3.18
    Bonus issues II.7.5.0.
    Rights issues II.7.4.0.
    Valuation for balance sheet II.7.6.0.

J

Joint ventures II.2.1.0.
    Accounts of co-venturers II.2.3.0.
    Memorandum joint venture account II.2.3.8.

L

Leases II.5.1.0.
Accounting treatment of leasing and hire
       purchase transactions II.5.3.0.
    accounting by lessees II.5.3.16
       by lessors II.5.3.6.
    Actuarial methods II.5.5.0.
    Difference between leasing and
       hire purchase transactions II.5.2.0.
    Final accounts disclosures
       by lessees II.5.3.20
       by lessors II.5.3.15
    Inclusion of capitalised leases and leasing
       obligations in the balance sheet II.5.3.28.
    Finance charges II.5.5.0.
    Gross earnings II.5.5.0.
    Interest on borrowed funds – II.5.5.16.
       Net investment II.5.5.2.
    Net cash investment II.5.5.2.
    Profit after tax II.5.5.15.
    Regional development grants II.5.3.25.
    Sale and leaseback transactions II.5.3.21.
    SSAP 21 II.5.3.3.
    Taxation implications II.5.5.15.
Limited companies
    Constraints III.4.2.0.
    Preparation of final accounts III.4.4.0.
    SSAPs (see SSAPs)
    Companies Acts 1985 and 1989 (see Companies Acts 1985 and 1989) Appx I
Long term contracts (see Contracts)

M

Mergers (Acquisitions and) V.2.1.0.
Merger relief V.2.2.0.

P

Partnership I.3.1.0.
    Formation I.3.2.0.
    Changes in constitution I.3.3.0.
        Revaluations I.3.3.1.
        Goodwill I.3.3.5.
    Dissolution I.3.4.0.
        Conversion into limited company I.3.4.1.
        Termination and dissolution I.3.4.13.
        Insolvency of partner(s) I.3.4.22.
    Piecemeal realisations and distributions I.3.4.26.
        Surplus capital method I.3.4.32.
        Assumed loss method I.3.4.35.
Pension costs III.4.3.103.

R

Ratio analysis (see Financial Statement analysis) IV.1.1.0.
Reconstructions (see also Capital reconstructions) III.7.4.0.
Reorganisations (see also Capital reorganisations) III.7.4.0.
Returnable containers (see Containers)
Royalties II.9.1.0.
    Royalties Payable II.9.3.0.
        Shortworkings recoverable II.9.3.1.
        Shortworkings irrecoverable II.9.3.4.
    Royalties Receivable II.9.4.0.
        Shortworkings allowable II.9.4.1.

S

Shares
    Issues III.1.2.0.
        Bonus (Scrip) III.1.2.19.
        Premium III.1.2.3.
        Payable in instalments III.1.2.6.
        Rights III.1.2.25.
    Forfeiture III.1.2.14.
        Reissue III.1.2.15.
    Redemption and purchase of own shares III.1.4.0.
        Premium paid III.1.4.9.
    Share premium account III.1.2.3.
    Transfers to Capital Redemption Reserve III.1.4.5.1.
    Private limited companies III.1.4.20
        Permissible capital payment III.1.4.21.
Societies (see Clubs and)
Sole traders I.2.1.0.
Statement of Intent (SOIs) III.4.3.11.
Statements of Recommended practice (SORPs) III.4.3.11
Statements of Source and Application of Funds III.4.5.0; IV.2.1.1.
    Nature IV.2.2.0.
    Construction IV.2.3.0.
    Disclosure IV.2.4.0.
    Format IV.2.4.5.
        Group consolidated accounts V.1.7.1.
    Individual company accounts IV.2.4.6.
    SSAP 10 III.4.3.56; IV.2.2.2.
Statements of Standard Accounting Practice (SSAPs)
    General III.4.3.0.
    Nature III.4.3.5.
    Application and enforcement III.4.3.8.

SSAPs III.4.3.12
1   Accounting for the results of associated companies V.1.6.1
2   Disclosure of accounting policies III.4.3.13.
3   Earnings per share III.4.3.17 III.8.1.0.
4   Accounting treatment of government grants III.4.3.28.
5   Accounting for value added tax III.4.3.30.
6   Extraordinary items and prior year adjustments III.4.3.32.
8   Treatment of taxation under the imputation system III.4.3.42.
9   Stocks and work-in-progress III.4.3.48 II.6.4.6
9   Stocks and long-term contracts II.6.6.0.
10   Statements of source and application of funds III.4.3.56
12   Accounting for depreciation III.4.3.59
13   Accounting for research and development III.4.3.65
14   Group accounts V.1.3.3
15   Accounting for deferred tax III.4.3.71
16   Current cost accounting III.9.4.0
17   Accounting for post balance sheet events III.4.3.84
18   Accounting for contingencies III.4.3.91.
19   Accounting for investment properties III.4.3.97.
20   Foreign currency translation II.11.4.0.
21   Accounting for leases and hire purchase contracts II.4.2.6 II.5.3.3.
22   Accounting for goodwill V.1.9.2.
23   Accounting for acquisitions and mergers V.2.4.0
24   Accounting for pension costs III.4.3.103.

T
Taxation in accounts III.3.1.0.
    Advance corporation and the imputation system III.3.4.15.
    Corporation tax III.3.4.0.
        Pre Finance Act 1965 companies III.3.4.7.
        Post Finance Act 1965 companies III.3.4.11.
    Income tax (businesses) III.3.3.0.
    Value added tax III.3.2.0.
    Deferred taxation III.3.5.0.
        Timing differences III.3.5.2.
        Stock appreciation relief III.3.5.10
        Fixed asset revaluation surpluses III.3.5.14.
        Fixed assset sale surpluses III.3.5.17.
        Methods
            Deferral III.3.5.20.
            Liability III.3.5.26.
    Income tax (PAYE) III.3.6.1.
    National insurance contributions III.3.6.4.
    Vehicle excise licences III.3.6.8.

V
Value added statements III.5.1.0.
    Content and format III.5.3.0.
    Contentious items III.5.3.6.
    Depreciation III.5.3.3.
    Extraordinary items III.5.3.7.
    Format
        Simple circumstances III.5.3.5.
        Complicated circumstances III.5.3.13.
    Investment income III.5.3.8.
    PAYE and national insurance contributions III.5.3.10.
    Share of profits and losses of associated companies III.5.3.9.
    Users III.5.1.4.
    Users III.5.1.5.
    Value added concept III.5.2.0.